Economies and Polities in the Aztec Realm

Studies on Culture and Society

Volume 1. Gary H. Gossen, ed.
Symbol and Meaning Beyond the Closed Community: Essays in Mesoamerican Ideas

Volume 2. J. Jorge Klor de Alva, H. B. Nicholson, and Eloise Quiñones Keber, eds.
The Work of Bernardo de Sahagún: Pioneer Ethnographer of Sixteenth-Century Aztec Mexico

Volume 3. Victoria R. Bricker and Gary H. Gossen, eds.
Ethnographic Encounters in Southern Mesoamerica: Essays in Honor of Evon Zartman Vogt, Jr.

Volume 4. John Gledhill
Casi Nada: A Study of Agrarian Reform in the Homeland of Cardenismo

Volume 5. Brenda Rosenbaum
With Our Heads Bowed: The Dynamics of Gender in a Maya Community

Volume 6. Mary G. Hodge and Michael E. Smith, eds.
Economies and Polities in the Aztec Realm

Economies and Polities

in the Aztec Realm

Edited by

Mary G. Hodge and Michael E. Smith

Studies on Culture and Society
Volume 6

Institute for Mesoamerican Studies

The University at Albany
State University of New York
Albany, New York

Distributed by
University of Texas Press

For submission of manuscripts address the publisher:
Institute for Mesoamerican Studies
The University at Albany
State University of New York
Albany, New York 12222

For copies address the distributor:

University of Texas Press
Post Office Box 7819
Austin, Texas 78713-7819

Library of Congress Cataloging in Publication Data

Economies and polities in the Aztec realm / edited by Mary G. Hodge
 and Michael E. Smith.
  p. cm. — (Studies on culture and society ; v. 6)
 Includes bibliographical references and index.
 ISBN 0-942041-15-1 (pbk.) : $32.00
  1. Aztecs—Economic conditions. 2. Aztecs—Politics and
government. 3. Indians of Mexico—Economic conditions. 4. Indians
of Mexico—Politics and government. I. Hodge, Mary G. II. Smith,
Michael Ernest, 1953–   . III. Series.
F1219.76.E36E385 1994
330.972'.018—dc20   92-76222
                                                          CIP

Contents

Preface vii

1. An Introduction to Late Postclassic Economies and Polities 1
   Michael E. Smith and Mary G. Hodge

2. Polities Composing the Aztec Empire's Core 43
   Mary G. Hodge

3. The Archaeological Signature of Local Level Polities in Tepetlaoztoc .. 73
   Barbara J. Williams

4. Cloth in the Political Economy of the Aztec State 89
   Frederic Hicks

5. The Lip Plugs of Xaltocan: Function and Meaning in Aztec
   Archaeology 113
   Elizabeth M. Brumfiel, Tamara Salcedo, and David K. Schafer

6. Stylistic and Spatial Variability in Early Aztec Ceramics:
   Insights into Pre-Imperial Exchange Systems 133
   Leah D. Minc, Mary G. Hodge, and M. James Blackman

7. The Organization of Provincial Craft Production and the Aztec
   City-State of Otumba 175
   Deborah L. Nichols

8. Plebeians and Patricians: Contrasting Patterns of Production and
   Distribution in the Aztec Figurine and Lapidary Industries 195
   Cynthia Otis Charlton

9. Economic Heterogeneity and State Expansion: The Northeastern
   Basin of Mexico during the Late Postclassic Period 221
   Thomas H. Charlton

10. Late Postclassic Salt Production and Consumption in the
    Basin of Mexico: Some Insights from Nexquipayac 257
    Jeffrey R. Parsons

11. Economic Alternatives under Imperial Rule: The Eastern
    Aztec Empire 291
    Frances F. Berdan

12. Economies and Polities in Aztec-Period Morelos: Ethnohistoric
    Overview 313
    Michael E. Smith

13. Rural Economy in Late Postclassic Morelos: An Archaeological
    Study 349
    Michael E. Smith and Cynthia Heath-Smith

14. Huaxyacac: Aztec Military Base on the Imperial Frontier 377
    Manlio Barbosa-Cano

15. After The Conquest: Quauhtinchan and the Mexica Province
    of Tepeacac 405
    José Luis de Rojas

16. The Impact of the Xochiyaoyotl in Southwestern Puebla 433
    Patricia Plunket and Gabriela Uruñuela

17. Late Postclassic Imperial Expansion and Economic Exchange
    within the Tarascan Domain 447
    Helen Perlstein Pollard and Thomas A. Vogel

Contributors 471

Index 473

Preface

The past decade has been a busy time for studies of Aztec economic and political organization. In particular, the archaeological study of Aztec sites has accelerated tremendously. The organizers of a symposium on Late Postclassic (Aztec) archaeology at the 1981 meetings of the Society for American Archaeology had a hard time finding enough papers to fill the session, whereas our symposium on "Aztec Archaeology: Trade, Production, and Economic Issues" at the 1991 International Congress of Americanists easily filled a whole day and threatened to spill over to a second day. The growth of research is not entirely archaeological, however. Ethnohistoric research on topics of Aztec economics and politics has a long and distinguished history, and the past decade has brought great progress as scholars have focused more of their attention on local areas throughout Central Mexico.

The chapters of this book present new data and new approaches that contrast with the standard view of the Aztec economy as portrayed in the works of Sahagún, Durán, Zorita, and the other Spanish chroniclers. Perhaps the key finding of the book is the existence of a diversity of local economic and political conditions throughout the area we call the Aztec realm. Local and regional economies flourished beneath the veneer of the Aztec empire that was previously thought to be more monolithic and centralized than the new evidence suggests. These chapters all make significant contributions to this theme, and we are pleased to help disseminate the exciting new research results presented in this volume.

Economies and Polities in the Aztec Realm is a direct outgrowth of the symposium we jointly organized for the 1991 International Congress of Americanists, held at Tulane University in New Orleans. Our primary reason for holding the symposium was to present the results of the great acceleration of archaeological research (both fieldwork and analytical studies) addressing economic issues. We invited mostly archaeologists, plus several ethnohistorians working on economic topics. We scheduled periods for discussion throughout the day rather than have the usual formal discussants at the end of the entire symposium. The discussion periods were filled with lively debates and exchange of information, and they helped make the symposium a success for both the presenters and the audience. Most of the chapters in this book originated as papers presented at the symposium. Two participants were not able to contribute their papers to the volume (Susan Evans and Dorothy Hosler). José Luis de

Rojas was unable to attend the Congress but did send a paper. Three additional chapters were solicited especially for the book, one from another session at the Congress (Barbara Williams, chap. 3), and two independent papers (Elizabeth Brumfiel et al., chap. 5, and Michael Smith, chap. 12).

We would like to thank all of the participants in the original symposium (including the audience) for an informative and intellectually vigorous session, and we thank the Organizing Committee of the International Congress of Americanists for facilitating a well-attended and stimulating meeting. Two reviewers provided helpful comments and suggestions on the book. We thank the authors for their timely schedules of writing and revision, and the editorial staff of the Institute for Mesoamerican Studies for their help in getting the book edited and produced without delay. Editing, design, and production were carried out by Cynthia Heath-Smith. We also thank Ellen Cesarski, James Wessman, and the staff of the University at Albany. Graphics Department for help during the production process.

Note on Orthographic Conventions

Scholars routinely encounter varied spellings for Nahuatl place and proper names as a result of the efforts of Spanish scribes to transcribe words that contained unfamiliar sounds and of the variations in spelling that characterized sixteenth century Spanish. In this volume proper names and place names correspond to the rules of Nahuatl language construction as closely as possible rather than to Spanish colonial or modern usage (e.g., Nahuatl terms do not have accents). We use spellings from the *Codex Mendoza* as a standard for Nahuatl names (following the editorial practice described by Frances Berdan and Patricia Anawalt in the *Codex Mendoza* [1992:v.4:1-3]). In some cases, Spanish colonial and/or modern renderings of names appear in parentheses following the Nahuatl version. Modern names are used in a few cases, however, where the modern name for an archaeological site predominates in published literature (for example, Otumba and Cholula). In these cases Spanish colonial and/or Nahuatl names appear in parentheses following the modern archaeological site name.

1

An Introduction to Late Postclassic Economies and Polities

Michael E. Smith and Mary G. Hodge

The purpose of this book is to present a cross-section of current research on Aztec economics and politics. A new model of Aztec society is emerging that integrates the complementary data of archaeology and ethnohistory. A major finding of recent research is that beneath a veneer of imperial organization existed a wide variety of local and regional economic and political institutions that in many ways were more important to the people of Central Mexico than was the Aztec empire. The new approach emphasizes diversity—the diversity of local and regional economic networks and political units that influenced life in the Aztec realm. This view contrasts with previous approaches to Aztec economics and politics, in which scholars often began with ethnohistoric accounts of the Aztec empire and its capital, and then used these to interpret local archaeological and ethnohistorical information. Most researchers in both ethnohistory and archaeology now begin with specific communities and areas from which they build models of economic and political organization upon a secure, empirical base of local and regional data. It has become clear that the Aztec empire was but one institution affecting life in the Aztec realm and that diverse local and regional patterns probably had greater overall social significance than did the imperial institutions.

This new view of Aztec society is due in large part to a recent acceleration of research on Aztec polities and economies that has significance beyond the domain of Aztec studies. Although the rich corpus of ethnohistoric sources has long provided a detailed, almost "ethnographic," picture of Aztec society and institutions (e.g., Berdan 1982; Clendinnen 1991; Zantwijk 1985), comparisons with earlier Mesoamerican societies that are known primarily from the archaeological record have been difficult. For example, one cannot make direct comparisons between cases of craft production documented by artifactual remains like waste materials of obsidian tool manufacture (e.g., Spence 1985) and cases documented by prose descriptions of the activities of artisans and marketplaces (e.g., Sahagún 1950-1982, books 8, 9). Ethnohistoric models of Aztec economic institutions, such as the *pochteca* trade, have been applied widely to earlier Mesoamerican societies known only from archaeological remains, with little consideration of what *pochteca* trade, marketplace exchange, or other ethnohistorically-documented practices would look like in terms of material culture. With the results of new archaeological research on the Aztec economy, we now have the kind of data that permit more appropriate and useful comparisons between the Aztecs and other state-level societies of Prehispanic Mesoamerica.

This increased comparability among Mesoamerican economies has an important benefit beyond the general stimulation of comparative studies. We can use Aztec archaeology as a "test case" to examine the archaeological expressions of institutions known from ethnohistory. Such a procedure will permit a more rigorous and sophisticated archaeological evaluation of economic models and lead to advances in the study of non-Aztec societies.

Another area of significance for the new research in Aztec economics lies in the comparative study of early states and empires in general. We are in a better position than ever before to evaluate theoretical models of economic and political organization as they apply to the Aztec case and to use Aztec data to refine and extend our understanding of the nature and organization of agrarian economies in general. In addition to many of the articles in this book, recent examples of this comparative approach include Blanton (1994), Blanton et al. (1993), Brumfiel (1987a), Hodge (1984), Smith and Berdan (1992), and Stark (1990).

THE CONTEXT OF ECONOMIES AND POLITIES IN THE AZTEC REALM

This collection of papers forms a major sample of current archaeological and ethnohistorical research on Aztec economies and polities. The term "Aztec," in the book title and this essay, has a broad connotation. Chronologically, we include both the Early Aztec (A.D. 1150-1350) and Late Aztec (A.D. 1350-1520+) archaeological phases (see below), thereby covering both the pre-imperial period and the better known time of the Aztec or Triple Alliance empire. Spatially, we interpret the phrase "Aztec realm" to include the traditional core area in the Basin of Mexico (fig. 1.1), the outer provinces of the Aztec empire, and surrounding neutral areas and enemy states, such as Tlaxcalla and the Tarascan empire. This broad spatial definition is necessary to provide an adequate political and economic context for Late Postclassic Central Mexican societies (fig. 1.2). The expanding Aztec and Tarascan empires affected nearly all areas of northern Mesoamerica to some degree, and a wide perspective is required to understand the nature of ancient empires and their expansion. Political scientist Michael Doyle identifies four factors that together account for imperial expansion and dynamics:

> the metropolitan regime, its capacities and interests [the polities of the Basin of Mexico], the peripheral political society, its interests and weaknesses [the Aztec provinces], the transnational system and its needs [processes of interaction between the core area and the provinces], and the international context and the incentives it creates [the larger macroregional setting, including enemy states]. (Doyle 1986:46)

Our focus on the "Aztec realm" is designed to take into account these four factors.

The phrase "economies and polities" in the book title is significant. Much traditional scholarship on the Aztecs has been framed in terms of one basic economic system ("*the* Aztec economy") and one political institution ("*the* Aztec empire"). This is a natural consequence of the past heavy reliance upon the normative and generalized accounts of the early Spanish chroniclers (e.g., Conrad and Demarest 1984; Davies 1973, 1987; Hassig 1985; Soustelle 1961; Vaillant 1962). One of the important findings of the research described in this book is that a multiplicity of distinct "economies" existed in the Aztec realm, a pattern in accord with the already recognized diversity of Central Mexican polities (e.g., Gibson 1964; Hodge 1984). In this context, the concept of interaction assumes an important role in the chapters that follow. The authors are concerned with interactions among different regional economies, among regional polities, among functional and hierarchical divisions of economies and polities, and between economic and political phenomena in general. This last issue is a topic of debate within the context of Aztec studies and in the field of early state dynamics in general. The chapters of this book make important contributions towards the clarification of this issue.

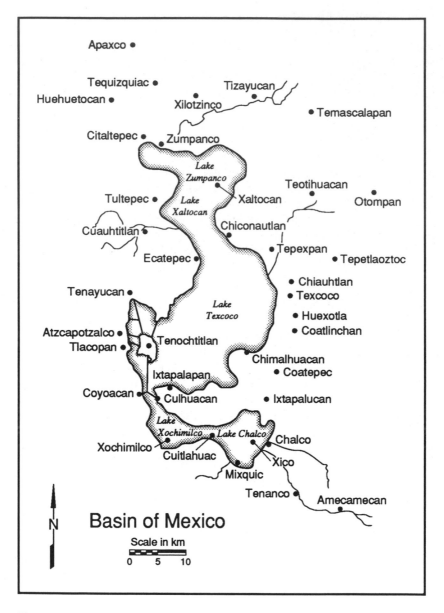

Fig. 1.1.   The Basin of Mexico. The map shows places discussed in the book.

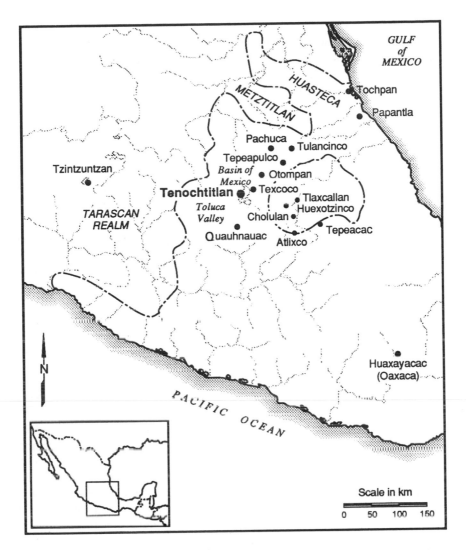

Fig. 1.2.   The Aztec realm. The map shows places discussed in the book. Map by R. Richard Rogers.

Chronological Framework

Scholars working on the Aztec civilization have two independent chronological records, archaeological and native historical. Although some scholars dismiss the historical accuracy and validity of the Aztec native histories on principle (e.g., Gillespie 1989), we follow Nicholson's (1971) and Davies' (1973, 1980, 1987) historiographic approach. Text criticism and comparison suggest that much of the native historical tradition does indeed preserve reliable chronological information and that the accuracy and reliability of these sources declines with age. From the Toltec period until the Spanish Conquest, the major events in the native historical record for Central Mexico may be summarized as follows: First, Nahuatl-speaking immigrants moved into Central Mexico from the north (Smith 1984). This migration initiated a period of town foundation, dynasty establishment, and city-state growth in the twelfth through fourteenth centuries (Calnek 1978). Out of this volatile period of "peer polity interaction" (Renfrew 1986), two states emerged as major powers in the Basin of Mexico—the Acolhua and the Tepaneca (Davies 1980). After much conflict, the Tepaneca polity developed into a small empire that dominated the Basin of Mexico in the early fifteenth century. In 1428 the Mexica, Acolhua, and a group of Tepaneca from Tlacopan defeated the Tepaneca empire and joined to form the Triple Alliance or Aztec empire. The growth of the Aztec empire in the next 90 years is well documented (e.g., Hassig 1988); when the Spaniards arrived in 1519, the empire was still strong and expanding its frontiers.

The archaeological record for Postclassic Central Mexico typically is divided into three periods: Early, Middle and Late Postclassic (fig. 1.3). The Early Postclassic or Toltec period corresponds to the major occupation of Tula and the ethnohistorically attested, but archaeologically invisible, Toltec empire. The Middle Postclassic period covers the period of town foundation and city-state growth. The Late Postclassic period, beginning around A.D. 1350, covers the periods of Tepaneca domination and the formation and expansion of the Aztec empire, plus an undetermined span of time after the Spanish Conquest.

The most significant problem in correlating the native historical and archaeological chronologies is the long length of the archaeological periods currently defined for the Basin of Mexico. This problem has been reduced somewhat in western Morelos by the derivation of a more refined archaeological sequence (fig. 1.3; see Smith and Doershuk 1991), a procedure that needs to be repeated in other areas. Many archaeologists make comparisons of Middle and Late Postclassic archaeological findings and use these to contrast pre-imperial and imperial organization in the Basin of Mexico (e.g., Brumfiel 1980). This correlation is only valid, however, in the rough sense that it compares the early city-state period with the Tepaneca and Aztec imperial periods combined.

To investigate the changes brought about by the formation and expansion of the Aztec empire specifically, the Late Postclassic period must be subdivided into shorter phases. Beyond Central Mexico proper, many Postclassic archaeological sequences are quite rough, making comparisons difficult. Pollard's chronological work in Central Michoacan (Pollard and Vogel, chap. 17, and personal communication) is an important advance, and we hope that chrono-

Date, A.D.	Period	Basin of Mexico	Western Morelos	Southwest Puebla	Central Michoacan
1500	Late Postclassic	Late Aztec	Late Cuauhnahuac	Martir	Tarlacuri (Tarascan)
1400			Early Cuauhnahuac		
1300	Middle Postclassic	Early Aztec	Temazcalli	Tecama	Early Milpillas
1200			Tlancingo		
1100	Early Postclassic	Mazapan	Aquiahuac	Palacio	
1000			Huautli		

Fig. 1.3.   Chronology of Central Mexico. The chart shows Postclassic ceramic phases for various areas of Central Mexico.

logical refinement can be extended to other areas as well. Moreover, recent data from the Basin of Mexico suggest that local chronologies will emerge as Basin of Mexico sequences are refined on the basis of radiocarbon dates from systematic excavations (Parsons et al. 1993).

Aztec Economies and Polities

The sections of this chapter that follow review the current state of knowledge on Aztec economic and political patterns and note some of the contributions the articles in this book make to an emerging view of Aztec economics. The over-riding theme, common to all of these papers, is diversity—the existence of spatial, functional, and interactional variations in economic phenomena. Earlier simplistic or monolithic models of the Aztec economy are giving way to an appreciation of the existence of multiple economies and multiple polities. We discuss these new developments under three general headings: Cities, Towns, and Villages; Social and Political Hierarchies; and Economic Patterns.

CITIES, TOWNS, AND VILLAGES

Tenochtitlan

Images of Aztec society, economy, and polity have been derived for many years from descriptions of Tenochtitlan, the imperial capital. Central attributes of Tenochtitlan as a settlement were: (1) a quadriform urban layout created by causeways running into grand avenues that divided the city into four quarters (Calnek 1976), (2) a central plaza-temple-palace complex (Aveni et al. 1988; Broda et al. 1987; Matos 1988), and (3) the existence of *chinampa* garden areas around the outskirts of the urban settlement (Calnek 1976). Within the four great quarters of the city were residential divisions or *tlaxillacalli,* each with its own temple and civic officials. Domestic architecture outside the palace complexes consisted of both walled compounds composed of a number of separate dwellings occupied by extended families and separate individual houses (Calnek 1976:298-300; Rojas 1986:29-55).

In functional terms Tenochtitlan was the focus of imperial political decision making by A.D. 1500. Economic activities centered at Tenochtitlan included imperial tribute collection (Gibson 1971) and marketplace trade (Tenochtitlan's rulers controlled the central marketplace of the Basin of Mexico at neighboring Tlatelolco). Tenochtitlan was the center for *pochteca* trade as well (Sahagún 1950-1982, book 9). As the largest settlement in the Basin (150,000 to 250,000 residents and an area of 12-15 km), Tenochtitlan's impact on the surrounding communities is undeniable, though its effect on specific regions and communities was variable. Understanding these variations is contributing to a more textured image of the economy of the Aztec empire's core zone and that of greater highland Mexico.

Recent research challenges the normative descriptions of greater Aztec society as derived from documents produced in Tenochtitlan. Current understanding of the capital leads us to regard this city as atypical, rather than representative of Postclassic communities. Social strata and political offices, previously used to typify Postclassic society as a whole, have been taken from descriptions of the capital (e.g., Durán 1967; Sahagún 1950-1982), but analyses of the social dynamics of the capital now identify change over time from a less specialized and more dynamic system to a more specialized and more rigid system of social and political roles (Brumfiel 1983; Rounds 1979). The variety and specialization of economic and political offices reported in Tenochtitlan ca. A.D. 1500 was not duplicated in most communities outside the capital, and recent research has revealed that there was variability in institutions among Aztec cities (e.g., Hodge 1984; Offner 1983; Schroeder 1991). Similarly, recent archaeological research has expanded the documentary record and challenges long-standing assumptions developed from a more limited archaeological record. The results of new archaeological research indicate variability complementary to that already apparent in textual studies, as individual communities are studied in detail and compared to the capital (e.g., Arroyo 1990; Brumfiel 1991b; Charlton et al. 1991). Excavations at the Templo Mayor (Boone 1987; Broda et al. 1987; Matos 1988) and other research (Townsend 1992; Umberger 1987; Zantwijk 1985) reveal that Tenochtitlan incorporated much from other cities while redefining traditional relationships.

Other Cities and Towns

The new understanding that Tenochtitlan was not at all typical of Aztec urban centers gives greater importance to the study of other cities and towns. Most were considerably smaller than the imperial capital, which was a true primate city within Central Mexico. The Acolhua capital Texcoco was the second-largest city in the Basin of Mexico with a population on the order of 30,000, and a number of other cities had populations between 10,000 and 20,000 (Sanders et al. 1979:154; Smith et al. 1994; see Hodge, chap. 2). Most Aztec urban settlements, however, were smaller civic-religious centers that are more appropriately labelled towns. These were the capitals of city-states, and indeed the key defining feature of an Aztec towns was the palace of the ruler (Schroeder 1991). In addition to the royal family, other related nobles resided in town. A second key architectural trait was the temple-pyramid of the town's patron deity.

These administrative and religious functions of Aztec towns are generally agreed upon (see Smith 1989), but the economic functions of the city-state capitals continue to be a subject of debate. Sanders and Webster (1988) argue from theoretical grounds that most Mesoamerican urban centers, including the Aztec city-state capitals, fit Richard Fox's (1977) "regal-ritual center" model in which towns serve as administrative and religious centers but do not have a significant economic role. Intensive surface collections at Huexotla (Brumfiel 1980) and Coatlan Viejo in Morelos (Mason 1980) failed to locate evidence of specialized craft production, thus supporting Sanders and Webster's model. However, Marcus

(1983) suggests that there was greater diversity among Mesoamerican cities, and more recent excavations and surface collections at the Otumba town center have uncovered strong evidence for a variety of intensive and probably specialized craft industries (Charlton and Nichols 1990; Charlton et al. 1991; Otis Charlton 1993; see Nichols, chap. 7, and Otis Charlton, chap. 8). In addition, Charlton (chap. 9) shows that Tepeapulco also had intensive obsidian production, probably carried out by specialists, and preliminary results of fieldwork at Yauhtepec point at a variety of urban craft industries (Smith and Heath-Smith 1994).

These data suggest that Aztec urban centers outside of Tenochtitlan may exhibit more variation in their economic roles than Sanders and Webster's model admits (see also Blanton 1994). The recognition of this variability points to an urgent need for more archaeological research at Aztec town sites. Unfortunately, most Aztec towns lie buried today under modern cities and towns, and the sample of sites available for archaeological analysis is quite small (Parsons 1990). Only a few of the larger Aztec cities (apart from Tenochtitlan) have sufficient ethnohistoric documentation to analyze urban structure and functions (e.g., Hicks 1982; Hodge 1984). Given the prevalence of modern settlement on top of Aztec sites in the Basin of Mexico, the analysis of urban sites may be more profitably pursued in nearby areas like Morelos, Puebla, or the Toluca Valley, although to date little fieldwork has been done. Recent fieldwork at Yauhtepec in Morelos is reported by Smith et al. (1994) and Smith and Heath-Smith (1994).

Settlement Patterns

The long-term Basin of Mexico Archaeological Survey Project established dramatically the extent of settlement in the Basin of Mexico and the large size of the Late Postclassic population (Parsons 1971; Parsons, Brumfiel, Parsons, and Wilson 1982; Sanders 1965; Sanders et al. 1979). These regional surveys provided information on rural populations and the economic base of the Postclassic polities that can be integrated into a regional perspective on Postclassic economy. Regional surveys in Morelos (O'Mack 1991; Sterpone 1988), Puebla (Plunket and Uruñuela, chap. 16), and other areas (Stark 1990) are also producing expanded regional perspectives on populations and settlements.

Early Aztec occupation in the Basin of Mexico tended to cluster around the lakeshore in nucleated settlements. Many of the towns were new settlements without Early Postclassic occupation, a situation compatible with ethnohistoric descriptions of the arrival of immigrant groups and the founding of towns and polities. The transition to the Late Aztec phase was marked by a continuity in settlement location and a considerable increase in the number and size of sites. Late Aztec settlement patterns reveal a dense yet dispersed population in the Basin of Mexico (Sanders et al. 1979:153-176). As discussed above, Tenochtitlan was the only truly large urban center, and most of the populace lived in rural areas or in the small city-state capitals. Regional population densities (as determined from archaeological data) were quite high, and recent settlement research by Evans (1985, 1990), Williams (chap. 3), and Sterpone (1988) suggests that population dispersal was related to the labor requirements of intensive agriculture, particularly terracing and infield cultivation (see Netting [1968, 1989] for ethnographic and theoretical analyses of this phenomenon).

SOCIAL AND POLITICAL HIERARCHIES

City-States

The city-state was the fundamental political and territorial building-block of Postclassic society. It was called *altepetl* in Nahuatl, a term that incorporates the concept of "water-hill" or the fundamental necessities for a community (Kartunnen 1983:9). The sixteenth century Spanish translations of *altepetl,* *"pueblo"* and *"rey,"* reveal both the political and geographic elements of the concept (Molina 1970).

City-states were governed by a single ruler, *tlatoani,* or in a few cases several rulers, *tlatoque.* Rulers were assisted by administrators from the elite class (Carrasco 1977; Hicks 1986; Hodge 1984). The city-state rulers also conducted or were figureheads for rituals central to city-state political and religious functions (Chimalpahin 1965; Paso y Troncoso 1905-1906:v.6).

City-states were geographical units focused on a central community or urban center. Dependent towns, villages, and hamlets surrounded the central settlement. The regional surveys of the Basin indicate wide variation in the sizes and populations of city-state centers, ranging from 1,000 to 50,000 inhabitants (Hodge, chap. 2; Smith et al. 1994). Tendencies toward nucleated settlement in the central portions of the Basin and more dispersed settlement in the southeastern part of the Basin also have been revealed by the regional surveys (Parsons 1971; Parsons, Brumfiel, Parsons, and Wilson 1982; Sanders et al. 1979). Variation in size and complexity of city-states is emerging from recent ethnohistorical studies (Hodge 1984; Schroeder 1991), and archaeological studies of individual city-state centers are allowing us to define distinct regional economic functions among these settlements. In the past, there has been some dissonance between documentary accounts of these polities and archaeological data, but new research projects are attempting to combine the two lines of evidence more effectively in order to address questions about the Postclassic economy (Hodge, chap. 2; Minc, Hodge, and Blackman, chap. 6; Nichols, chap. 7; Otis Charlton, chap. 8; Charlton, chap. 9).

City-state centers were economic central places. Documentary sources report a hierarchy of markets that met at different intervals in the city-state centers throughout the Basin of Mexico (Hassig 1982) and Morelos (Smith, chap. 12). Some of these markets specialized in particular classes of products, and we assume that the larger, more frequent markets offered more products and greater variety than smaller, less frequent markets (Blanton et al. 1993; Blanton 1994). Archaeological study of city-state economic systems is providing more detailed perspectives on the interaction of markets in greater Central Mexico (Brumfiel 1983; 1991a; Charlton and Nichols 1990; Charlton et al. 1991; Hodge and Minc 1990). In this volume, the emergence of market systems in the Basin is examined and several papers focus on the articulation of city-state economic systems with each other and with the imperial capital (e.g., Charlton, chap. 9; Hodge, chap. 2; Minc et al., chap. 6).

Confederations

Political confederations of city-states are known from documentary sources, which associate these long-standing alliances with ethnic groups whose ancestors settled in the Basin of Mexico in the A.D. 900s-1100s (*Anales de Cuauhtitlan* 1938; Durán 1967:v.1:10; Gibson 1964; Smith 1984). The political confederations in the Basin (Tenochca, Tepaneca, Acolhua, Culhua, Xochimilca, Cuitlahuaca, Mixquica) were initially distinct geographic units. At first independent, they later formed the administrative units of the Aztec empire's center. Outside the Basin, other confederations formed power blocs controlling the Puebla area, Tlaxcalla, and Morelos.

The confederations of earlier Postclassic times are portrayed in the chronicles as having more flexible boundaries and structures than those of later times. More inter-confederation conflict is noted among these early confederations, at least within the Basin of Mexico. Early Postclassic confederation boundaries are evident from open areas between settlement groups (Parsons, Brumfiel, Parsons, and Wilson 1982) and as boundaries among market exchange systems involving decorated ceramics (Minc et al., chap. 2). How these confederations articulate with ethnic identities is the focus of current archaeological study (Brumfiel, Salcedo, and Schafer, chap. 5). Such a question is important for understanding the social dynamics of the Late Postclassic period. Most city-states and confederations may be regarded as multiethnic, in that each was occupied by a dominant language group and some subordinate ones; nevertheless, each is designated a particular identity in the historical chronicles. Archaeological research, with its possibilities for great time depth, can evaluate the textual claims by investigating whether emblems such as city-state deities or distinctive costumes were adopted in later times, perhaps as a mechanisms for self-definition under the pressures of imperialization, or whether, as the chronicles relate, such identities represented long-standing ethnic and social traditions.

The Triple Alliance Empire

The formation and early development of the Triple Alliance or Aztec empire followed patterns of expansion and control already prevalent in the Postclassic Basin of Mexico. Nearby city-states were conquered and forced to pay tribute, and local rulers were generally left in power. Within the Basin, the Triple Alliance rulers (particularly the Mexica) employed a number of political and economic strategies designed to consolidate their power and control, and to stimulate economic growth. Administrative positions and hierarchies were manipulated where necessary to assure the political dominance of the Mexica dynasty, and social links were cemented with subordinate city-state dynasties through marriage alliances, gift-giving, and other means (Brumfiel 1983, 1987b; Hodge 1984; Hicks 1992; Berdan et al. 1994). As a result, city-states continued to be units of political significance, while local economies were interfered with in selective ways. The actual extent of imperial economic meddling and its political economic significance remain topics of debate, however.

As the Aztec empire expanded beyond the Basin of Mexico, its patterns of indirect rule, or hegemonic control (see Doyle 1986; Hassig 1985), became more pronounced since the degree of political interference in distant provinces was far lower than in the Basin (Stark 1990). The impact of Aztec expansion on provincial populations can be discussed in terms of four categories. First, the most obvious effect was the economic impact of imperial tribute demands. Although scholars have long discussed this effect, the central quantitative question—how heavy was the economic burden on the household or community level?—has remained unanswered. The current studies of Hicks (chap. 4) and Smith (chap. 12) are making headway on this question, but the issue is far from settled. A second economic impact of Aztec expansion was the stimulation of trade and exchange throughout the empire, described by Berdan (chap. 11). A third category of impact concerned the status of local nobles and dynasties under the empire. In some cases the empire interfered directly in local politics, a situation best known from the Tepeacac-Quauhtinchan area (Olivera 1978; Rojas, chap. 15). In other cases, Aztec expansion and hegemonic control strengthened local elites, who thus had the opportunity to augment their own levels of exploitation of commoners through increased tribute demands and other means (Brumfiel 1991a:230; Smith 1986).

Unfortunately, there are substantive and methodological problems that render analyses of these issues difficult. The Aztec empire did not have a strong material impact in provincial areas, largely because of the way it was organized (Smith and Berdan 1992). Furthermore, even when socioeconomic changes can be shown to have been concurrent with Aztec conquest of an area, it is difficult to assess the relative importance of Aztec imperialism versus independent local development as determinants of the observed changes (Smith and Berdan 1992; Smith and Heath-Smith, chap. 13).

A fourth major impact of Aztec expansion concerns the military activities of the empire and their local implications. In many parts of the empire, imperial expansion brought about regional peace and stability (see Barbosa-Cano, chap. 14; Rojas, chap. 15), but in 1519 there remained several active enemy frontiers where military activity was still important. In these areas frequent battles and skirmishes were significant factors in local social dynamics.

Major Aztec Enemies: Tlaxcalla and the Tarascan Empire

The two most powerful and important unconquered enemy states were Tlaxcalla and the Tarascan empire. The Aztecs confronted these states both directly, through active wars, and indirectly through the creation of networks of client states along the enemy frontiers (Berdan et al. 1994; see Berdan, chap. 11). Some scholars suggest the Aztecs were strong enough to have conquered these enemies had they wished (e.g., Hassig 1988), but most agree these states were serious threats that the Aztecs simply were not able to eliminate (e.g., Berdan et al. 1994; Davies 1987; Gorenstein 1985; Isaac 1983). In support of this notion, Plunket and Uruñuela (chap. 16) show that the well-known battles between the Aztecs and Tlaxcallans caused regional destruction and displacement of settlement in southwestern Puebla (see also Rojas, chap. 15).

The polities of the Tlaxcalla area—Huexotzinco, Cholula, and others in addition to Tlaxcalla proper—shared a common linguistic and cultural background with the peoples of the Basin of Mexico. By the time the Aztec empire began to expand out of the Basin, they had become strong states able to resist conquest successfully. The Aztecs encircled the area, established client states along key borders, and began a process of gradual conquest through siege (external trade was cut off) and attrition (via periodic wars and battles). The Tlaxcalla area retained its independence until the arrival of Cortés, but the Aztecs appear to have had the upper hand and were advancing in their gradual submission of these states. The articles by Berdan (chap. 11), Rojas (chap. 15) and Plunket and Uruñuela (chap. 17) deal with aspects of Aztec-Tlaxcallan relations.

The Tarascan empire presents another picture altogether. Centered in the productive Patzcuaro Basin of Michoacan, the Tarascans had an expanding hegemonic empire that came close to rivaling the Aztec empire in size and wealth, and equalled it in military strength (Gorenstein 1985; Pollard 1982). The single most costly defeat of the Aztec army prior to 1519 was inflicted by the Tarascans in 1478 when Axayacatl's Mexica army lost a reported 20,000 troops (Durán 1967:v.2:281-285). After that battle, the two enemies established a long north-south frontier buffer zone guarded by fortresses, garrisons, and armed local towns along both sides (Berdan et al. 1994; Gorenstein 1985).

Knowledge of both Tlaxcalla and the Tarascan empire is important for the economic and political analysis of the Aztec realm for two reasons. First, they interacted with the Aztecs, both peacefully through trade and violently through wars. These frontiers were active military zones into which the Aztecs and their enemies channelled resources and labor. Thus the military confrontations were significant components of both the Aztec and Tarascan imperial economies. These enemy states are also important because they present parallel cases of Late Postclassic political and economic evolution. The Tlaxcallans were culturally very similar to the Aztecs, while the Tarascans were unrelated ethnically. Nevertheless, all three areas were characterized by rapid political evolution, imperialistic expansion, high population levels, intensive agriculture, pronounced social stratification, and active exchange systems (Pollard and Vogel chap. 17; Rojas, chap. 15). Any comprehensive account of Aztec economies and polities must include discussion of their powerful and influential enemies.

Social Stratification

Traditionally imperial societies are defined as those in which one ethnically or politically defined stratum dominates another with force and with economic structures (Adams 1979; Eisenstadt 1963). In Aztec studies, however, the principle of indirect rule practiced by the Triple Alliance empire and the bias of documentary sources toward descriptions of conquests and military actions may have perhaps deflected interest in the social impact of the empire on areas outside the Basin. More recently, it has become clear that the interests of provincial elites were woven into the fabric of the empire. Common interests of the elites were integrated through marriage alliances, exchange of luxury goods, cultural/religious codes, and period consumption rituals (Smith 1986:74-75). This wider perspective about Postclassic society as a social system has much potential for further clarification of the dynamics of greater highland Mexico during this period. Archaeological investigations combined with textual data offer to provide new insights on the societies and economies of provincial centers within the empire (e.g., McVicker and Urquizo 1991).

Within the Basin of Mexico, new perspectives are also emerging on the structure of Postclassic social organization. The normative view is that society consisted of the two discrete social classes described in the chronicles: nobility and commoners. Noble status was conferred through birth into the noble class. Groups of these elite were organized by noble houses, called *tecpan* or *tecalli*. The head of the noble house was called *teuctli* ('lord') and his children *pilli* (Hicks 1986). Commoners were distinguished by the term *macehualli* ('subject'). Recent textual analyses of the terms and their usage in chronicles referring to the precolonial period, in vocabularies and dictionaries, and in early colonial documents, suggest much texture and variation within these two great divisions (e.g., Carrasco 1976b, 1977; Carrasco and Broda 1976; Carrasco and Monjarás-Ruiz 1976, 1978; Cline 1990, 1993; Hicks 1986; Schroeder 1991). Hicks (1986:46) makes the important observation that "commoners varied in the degree of their subjection." They might be obligated only to provide occasional tribute or labor to a noble house or ruler, or they might have more specific and long-lasting requirements to particular nobles to whom they provided daily or weekly domestic service, cultivated fields, or gave craft goods that they produced.

Archaeological research focused on the identification of material components of class stratification in Precolumbian times has provided much new data. Within rural society it appears there was a gradation in material wealth, with only modest differences between the elites and commoners in access to goods (Evans 1988,1993; Smith 1992; Smith and Heath-Smith, chap. 13). Differences may have been manifested in visual terms (for example, more elaborate housing for more elite individuals, variation in clothing and personal accessories), or in activities (such as hosting feasts or participation in decision-making), some of which are more directly evident in the material record than others (Brumfiel 1987b; Evans 1988, 1991; Smith 1987; see Brumfiel et al., chap. 5).

ECONOMICS

Demography

Late Postclassic population densities were very high in Central Mexico, and they were achieved fairly rapidly in a massive episode of population growth during Middle to Late Postclassic times. Both of these observations have important consequences for economic and political organization and change in the Aztec realm. High regional population densities are reported by the Basin of Mexico survey projects. The overall average population density for the Late Aztec phase as measured from archaeological settlement patterns was well over 100 persons per km^2, but regional levels varied from around 50 persons per km^2 in some areas to over 400 in others (Hodge, chap. 2; Sanders et al. 1979:217).

In a detailed historical demographic study of the Aztec period, Sanders extrapolates from early colonial census data to estimate the total Basin of Mexico population at 1.16 million, with an overall density of around 160 persons/km^2 (1970:430). Whitmore's (1992) recent simulation model of colonial population loss produces slightly higher figures for the Aztec population in 1519: 1.59

inhabitants, with a density of 220 persons/km^2. High densities are confirmed in detailed analyses of documentary data from individual areas (e.g., Offner 1984; Whitmore 1992; Williams 1989; see also Williams, chap. 3), and Hodge's data (chap. 2) show that the pattern of regional variation in density is replicated on a smaller scale as well. Smith's historical demographic reconstruction for Morelos (chap. 12) indicates that high population densities were not limited to the Basin of Mexico, and this appears to have been a common situation throughout the central highlands (Sanders 1970).

Archaeological surveys show that the high population densities of Late Aztec times had a relatively short history. The archaeological estimates for total Basin of Mexico population jump from 175,000 people in the Early Aztec phase to nearly 1,000,000 in Late Aztec times (Sanders et al. 1979:184). This growth works out to an average annual increase of about 0.7%, a very high rate for a preindustrial population (Cowgill 1975). Although questions might be raised about the methods of site measurement or population estimation, there can be little doubt that the final centuries of the Prehispanic epoch witnessed an explosion of population in the Basin of Mexico. A similar pattern of rapid Middle to Late Postclassic demographic growth characterized western Morelos as well (Smith chap. 12), again suggesting that the demographic patterns observed in the Basin of Mexico were not unique in Postclassic Central Mexico.

The causes of the Late Postclassic population surge are difficult to determine. Migration into the Basin of Mexico is unlikely as a major cause for the increase since rapid growth also was taking place in potential donor areas such as Morelos. The problem needs to be considered on a wider scale than just the Basin of Mexico, and we offer several suggestions here. First, the Middle Postclassic period was a time of colonization and expansion as new Nahuatl speaking populations settled and spread throughout highland Central Mexico. Economically this was probably a time of abundant land with a shortage of labor, the kind of setting that favors larger families, leading to increasing population growth (Polgar 1975; White 1973). The Late Postclassic surge therefore would be the end result of economic and demographic changes initiated in the Middle Postclassic period.

Second, political competition among city-states during Middle Postclassic times may have helped to generate population growth. Brumfiel (1983) argues that the rulers of Middle Postclassic polities competed with one another for commoner clients. It was in the interests of these rulers to have large numbers of people in their polities to permit greater agricultural production and to field larger armies. Comparative data suggest that this situation could have stimulated not only immigration but also natural population increase (Cowgill 1979; Eberhard 1977:49; Polgar 1975). Third, the resulting agricultural intensification during the Late Postclassic period, once the initial growth began, would have in turn favored higher populations. These factors need to be investigated using finer chronologies in order to understand better the origin and timing of Late Postclassic population growth.

In contrast to its causes, the consequences of the Late Postclassic demographic surge have received greater attention. William Sanders, whose survey research first documented the pattern, argues that population growth led to a condition of population pressure, which he sees as generating processes of cultural evolution in Central Mexico (Sanders and Price 1968; Sanders et al. 1979:369-385). Much of his reasoning is deductive in nature and draws on theorists like Boserup (1965) to postulate population pressure as a cause of not only agricultural change, but also more general economic and political changes. The theoretical and empirical conclusions of Sanders and other population pressure theorists have been challenged by a number of authors, however (e.g., Blanton 1983, Brumfiel 1983; Cowgill 1975).

In our view, population growth in Postclassic Central Mexico was a significant force, but its consequences more directly influenced agricultural and labor changes than general processes of political centralization or cultural evolution (see Netting [1989, 1990] for theoretical discussions of this issue). Parson's interpretation of intensified salt production (chap. 10) fits this model. The following sections deal with three sectors where the results of population growth were significant: diet and subsistence, agricultural methods, and labor patterns.

Diet and Subsistence

Major sources of animal protein, such as deer, were probably overhunted in Central Mexico from the Classic period at least, and Sanders et al. (1979:281-287) estimate that by the Late Aztec period, hunting contributed less than 0.1% to the average diet (p. 286). Deer bones are quite rare at Aztec sites in comparison to rabbit, dog, and turkey (Cynthia Heath-Smith, personal communication). Wild plants were important secondary sources of food (Sanders et al. 1979:87-91; Amie Limón, personal communication), but their overall contribution to the diet was modest. Like other Mesoamerican cultures, the Aztecs derived the bulk of their calories and nutrients from agricultural products, particularlyl maize, beans, chile, tomato, and amaranth (Ortiz de Montellano 1990).

As discussed in the following section, Aztec agricultural practices were quite intensive in terms of labor input and caloric output (see Turner and Doolittle 1978). The massive population surge discussed above has been cited as the primary cause of this intensification although other factors may have been important as well. In spite of (or perhaps because of) the high level of effort that went into farming, Cook and Borah (1979:159-164) suggest that Aztec commoners suffered from chronic undernutrition (see also Williams 1989). They base this conclusion on a combination of quantitative dietary and energetic reconstructions, ethnohistoric descriptions to the effect that peasants had a poor diet, and a very high estimate of the Aztec population. Social class differences in diet were pronounced (Cook and Borah 1979:139-159; Ivanhoe 1978), with the nobility having greater access to meat and other desired items. Unfortunately, the relative lack of Aztec skeletal remains prevents the osteo-logical testing of the hypothesis of commoner undernutrition, which is disputed by Ortiz de Montellano (1990:72-119). Aztec diet and nutritional status are crucial economic issues, and more bioarchaeological research is urgently needed. The small number of Aztec skeletal samples, due to a paucity of excavated burials, is a major obstacle to this line of investigation.

Agricultural Methods

From William Sanders's initial survey work in the Teotihuacan Valley, through the entire Basin of Mexico Archaeological Survey Project, intensive agriculture and land use have been important topics of study. As a result, agricultural ter-races and irrigation systems have been identified throughout the Basin. The system of *chinampa* agriculture has long been recognized in the southern Basin of Mexico (Armillas 1971), and archaeological investigations of these systems continue as new techniques are developed for reconstructing environmental features and for analyzing botanical data (Parsons, Brumfiel, Parsons, Popper, and Taft 1982; Avila 1991). Irrigation was widespread in Aztec times (Palerm 1973; Doolittle 1990), as were systems of stone terracing (Sanders et al. 1979) and semi-terracing using maguey (Evans 1990). Although use of irrigation, terracing, and *chinampas* began in the Early Aztec period or earlier, all evidence indicates that their major period of expansion came in Late Aztec times. This expansion represented a significant level of agricultural intensifi-cation, probably brought about by a number of factors, including population pressure, an increase in urban food needs, and perhaps greater tribute demands by the growing Aztec nobility. Ethnohistoric and archaeological data indicate that intensive agriculture in the form of irrigation and terracing was also widespread in Morelos (Maldonado 1990; Price and Smith 1992; Smith and Price 1994; Smith, chap. 12) and other areas (Whitmore and Turner 1992), confirming Sanders's (1956) prescient observation that the entire area of Central Mexico (the "central Mexican symbiotic region") was characterized by intensive agriculture at the time of the Spanish Conquest.

Some forms of intensive agriculture were probably carried out under the direction and control of the state, while other forms were organized on a local or even household level. A number of authors have argued from documentary data that irrigation and water control in the Basin of Mexico lakes were under state control (e.g., Palerm 1973; Sanders et al. 1979). The regularity of orienta-tion in some *chinampa* zones is interpreted as evidence for state organized projects dating from the 1430s and later (Parsons, Brumfiel, Parsons, Popper, and Taft 1982; Parsons 1991). At the same time, other forms of intensive culti-vation were organized on a more local level, for example maguey-based semi-terracing (Evans 1990), intensive infield cultivation (Williams, chap. 3), and stone terrace agriculture (Smith and Price 1994; Smith and Heath-Smith, chap. 13). It is likely that large, state-organized building projects, along with other forms of intensification, created a system of feedback: greater intensifica-tion produced more food, which in turn permitted a larger population of nonfood producers as well as farmers, which created still greater demand and more intensification. As suggested above, more secure chronological control will help to define the sequence more precisely.

Land and Labor

There is a large literature on Aztec land tenure and labor patterns (see Berdan [1982], Carrasco [1976a, 1976b], Cline [1990], and Hicks [1986]). Earlier simplistic arguments over issues such as the existence of "private property" have been replaced by a more sophisticated understanding of the complexities of land and labor in Central Mexico, based upon new data from administrative documents in several regions. As summarized in Hicks' (1986) excellent review, it appears that, at least in the Basin of Mexico and Morelos, all land was under the control of either a noble or a state institution. Even *calpulli* lands, previously thought to have been outside the direct jurisdiction of nobles or the state, were in fact subject to noble estates (Carrasco 1976a, 1976b; Cline 1993; Hicks 1986).

The distinction made in some documentary sources between two catego-ries of commoners—*macehual,* or "free commoner," and *mayeque,* serf-like dependant laborer—is now known to be a misleading oversimplification (Hicks 1986). The rights and obligations of commoners varied considerably, and it is difficult to distinguish discrete categories valid for more than a very small, local area. This finding (see also Carrasco 1976a, 1976b) casts doubt on some recent archaeological interpretations that associate dispersed Aztec settlement with landless *mayeque* tenants and nucleated settlement with corporate *macehual* commoners organized into *calpulli* (e.g., Parsons, Brumfiel, Parsons, and Wilson 1982; Brumfiel 1991b). The new approach to labor moves our analyti-cal framework from questions of classifying or categorizing groups of people to questions of the relationship of communities and regions to one another. Archaeological studies can now compare the emic categories derived from ethnohistoric documents to etic behavioral data derived from archaeological study, and ongoing research will help to clarify the status of Postclassic rural populations (Avila 1991; Evans 1993; Kellogg 1993; Parsons 1990; see Smith and Heath-Smith chap. 13; Williams, chap. 3).

The population surge of the Late Postclassic period probably had signifi-cant effects on patterns of land tenure and labor organization, although diachronic data are scarce. An increasing labor supply would have affected the relation-ships between nobles and their commoner retainers, whose services were an important source of support for nobles (Hicks 1986). Netting (1990) suggests that agricultural intensification that results from population growth strength ns smallholdings as farmers invest more labor in their own intensively cultivated plots. The implications of such changes, if they occurred, are difficult to relate to our knowledge of Aztec tenure patterns. Population growth and agricultural intensification also led to deforestation, soil erosion, and other harmful envi-ronmental consequences (Cook 1949; Denevan 1992; O'Hara et al. 1993), but empirical evidence is scanty because of a neglect of archaeo-environmental research in Central Mexico.

Craft Production

We have already touched upon one of the current issues of Aztec craft produc-tion—were Aztec towns centers of craft specialization? This is but one aspect of the more general issue that Costin (1991) calls the *concentration of produc-tion,* referring to the spatial distribution of production activities. Charlton et al. (1991), Nichols (chap. 7), and Otis Charlton (chap. 8) address this issue by contrasting the nucleated with the dispersed model of craft production. They present strong evidence that, on a regional scale, craft activities were nucleated at the Otumba and Tepeapulco town sites; in contrast, there is little evidence for urban craft specialists at Huexotla, Xico, or Coatlan Viejo. Again, the Aztec economy was regionally and functionally diverse, making it difficult to gener-alize from a single site or area. When the spatial scale is magnified, however, production within the Otumba town site takes on a dispersed pattern with pro-duction loci distributed throughout the settlement, generally outside of the urban core zone (Nichols, chap. 7).

One of the major unresolved questions regarding production concentration (on a regional scale) is the extent of utilitarian craft production in Tenochtitlan. Direct data on this topic are scarce, leading to a wide variety of models in the literature. Hassig (1985:127-137) argues that most Aztec craft specialists lived in the imperial capital, with hinterland areas devoted almost exclusively to agri-culture. Brumfiel (1987a), on the other hand, suggests that only attached luxury specialists lived in Tenochtitlan, with utilitarian artisans scattered in rural areas outside of the capital. These contrasting interpretations appear to derive more from theoretical presuppositions than from data, a situation difficult to remedy without additional archaeological or ethnohistoric information from Tenochtitlan. At present, evidence from hinterland zones tends to support Brumfiel's thesis that significant utilitarian craft production was conducted outside of Tenochtitlan (e.g., Blanton 1994; Brumfiel 1987a; Charlton, chap. 9; Nichols, chap. 7; Otis Charlton, chap. 8). This interpretation is also supported by recent ceramic characterization work that reveals Aztec III Black-on-Orange ceramics to have been manufactured in at least four separate production areas (Hodge et al. 1992, 1993).

Another important issue in the analysis of craft production is what Costin (1991) calls *context*—the attached versus independent status of the artisans (see also Brumfiel and Earle 1987). Brumfiel (1987a) was the first to apply this concept specifically to the Aztec economy. In her model, artisans producing luxury items for consumption by the elite (e.g., metal workers, lapidaries, and featherworkers) were full-time specialists who worked either directly for elite patrons (the *attached* model) or for elite customers in the markets; producers of utilitarian items were part-time specialists dispersed in rural areas (the *independent* model). Although the data from Otumba and Tepeapulco show that utilitarian production was not exclusively a rural phenomenon, the luxury/attached versus utilitarian/independent distinction remains important. Otis Charlton's article on figurine and lapidary production at Otumba (chap. 8) is one of the few explicit archaeological studies of this topic (see also Otis Charlton 1993).

The production of cloth in Aztec society does not fit into either the attached or independent models, however, and must be considered a third model according to Hicks (chap. 4). The widespread domestic production of cloth by Aztec women is commonly noted (e.g., Berdan 1987a; Brumfiel 1991a; Smith and Hirth 1988), but Hicks goes further and argues that it was in fact an economically efficient way to organize the production of large numbers of textiles given the nature of the technology and labor requirements. Ethnographic data on maguey fiber spinning (Parsons and Parsons 1990:312-314) support Hick's model, but the Otumba data suggest that maguey cloth production may have been spatially concentrated, unlike the dispersed nature of cotton cloth production (Nichols, chap. 7; Charlton et al. 1991).

The scale of craft production activities is another important current issue. Previously, Mesoamericanists were quick to use the term "workshop" whenever they encountered evidence of a production locale. John Clark's (1986) critique of the traditional model of the Classic period Teotihuacan obsidian industry called this practice into question and led to more careful consideration of just what archaeologists mean by the term workshop and how production areas are to be identified and modelled (e.g., Parry 1990; Charlton et al. 1991). Peacock (1982:8-11) provides an archaeologically useful classification of levels of craft production intensity. *Household production,* the lowest level, refers to low-level domestic production for household use. Smith and Heath-Smith (chap. 13) argue that chert tool manufacture and perhaps other undetermined activities that used basalt polishing stones, bronze awls, and bronze chisels, may fit this category. *Household industry* refers to part-time producers working in a domestic setting, producing goods for both domestic consumption and exchange beyond the household. This term covers Brumfiel's (1987a) interpretation of Aztec utilitarian craft production, and examples include the production of textiles and paper at sites in Morelos (Smith and Heath-Smith, chap. 13), perhaps the basalt, lapidary, and maguey fiber industries at Otumba, and obsidian tool production at Aztec-period Teotihuacan (Spence 1985). *Individual workshops* are facilities that are normally separated from residences where production is carried out more intensively by full-time, or nearly full-time, artisans. Smith and Heath-Smith (chap. 13) find no evidence for this level of production in rural Morelos, but at Otumba, the obsidian core-blade workshops and perhaps figurine or lapidary production would fit this category (Otis Charlton 1993; chap. 9). Parsons's (chap. 10) description of Late Aztec salt production is another example of a workshop industry.

The chapters in this book show that major advances are being made in the study of Aztec craft production, but some serious problems remain. First, we still have little information on the production of the most abundant artifact class, pottery. Although petrographic studies (Goodfellow 1990), chemical characterization (Hodge et al. 1992, 1993), and regional stylistic studies (Hodge 1992; Hodge and Minc 1990) are providing important information, we still have little idea of exactly where ceramics were manufactured within communities, or how the industry was organized. Second, archaeological research has furnished much information on Aztec utilitarian industries, while nearly all of our information on luxury crafts comes from ethnohistorical documents. This situation makes comparisons and comprehensive analyses difficult. Otis Charlton's (chap. 8) excavation and analysis of a lapidary workshop area is a significant contribution toward improving the situation, but more studies of luxury craft industries are needed.

Trade and Exchange

For a long time studies of Aztec trade were dominated by ethnohistoric descriptions of *pochteca,* tribute, and markets (e.g., Berdan 1975). As archaeologists began to devote more attention to Aztec sites, quantification of imported ceramics and obsidian expanded the analysis of Aztec trade (Brumfiel 1980; Smith 1990; Hodge and Minc 1990). Current archaeological research on Aztec exchange, represented here by Minc, Hodge, and Blackman (chap. 6), Charlton (chap. 9), Parsons (chap. 10), Smith and Heath-Smith (chap. 13), and Pollard and Vogel (chap. 17) has produced some surprising findings that require a re-evaluation of prior models.

One result of current studies is the discovery of a high volume of exchange in utilitarian products, with Aztec ceramics traded more extensively than many archaeologists had predicted from cost-distance calculations (e.g., Sanders and Santley 1983). Imported ceramics constituted over eight percent of the average nonelite household ceramic inventory in Morelos (Smith and Heath-Smith, chap. 13), and characterization studies indicate a high volume of ceramic exchange in the Basin of Mexico as well (Hodge et al. 1992, 1993). A second finding, closely related to the first, is that exotic goods, whether decorated ceramics, obsidian, metal items, or jade beads, were obtained by commoner as well as elite households (Evans 1988; Smith 1992). Smith and Heath-Smith's data (chap. 13) show that although elite residential contexts had greater frequencies of some imports compared with nonelite residences, no foreign goods were associated exclusively with elite houses. Fancy, imported decorated ceramics were present in all houses and therefore cannot be considered an "elite good" as many archaeologists typically suggest. Hirth (1994) sees this pattern as a hallmark of the widespread use of market networks, a finding that has ample confirmation in Aztec ethnohistoric sources describing the prevalence of marketplace trade (e.g., Blanton 1994; Smith, chap. 12).

One of the more interesting discoveries of current research on Aztec trade is that a good deal of exchange activity at all levels bypassed the official channels of the state. Much of the long-distance trade was apparently carried out independently of the Aztec empire (Berdan 1988; Smith, chap. 12; Parsons, chap. 10), a situation paralleled in Pollard and Vogel's (chap. 17) data from Michoacan where the obsidian trade was apparently not controlled by the Tarascan empire. Similarly, recent ceramic studies employing neutron activation analysis indicate that the overall similarity among Late Aztec Black-on-Orange ceramics, which have long been a marker for Aztec presence (e.g., Smith 1990), is a stylistic similarity only. Compositional analyses show that several discrete regions within the Basin of Mexico or near it produced vessels of this style (Neff et al. 1991; Hodge et al. 1992, 1993). The implication again is that ceramic exchange was carried out independently of strong state control. Once more our findings support a model of a high degree of diversity among Aztec exchange mechanisms, a point also stressed by Berdan (1985, 1988; see also chap. 11).

CURRENT ISSUES AND DEBATES

In this section we review current issues and debates on Aztec economics and politics under three broad headings: (1) factors influencing the *formation* of large-scale economic systems, (2) analyses of the *relationships* between economic and political systems, and (3) identification of the *scale* of different Postclassic exchange, production, and consumption systems

Causes for the Formation of Complex Economic Systems

Analyses of the structures and dynamics of highland economies in the Postclassic period cannot ignore the fundamental question of the identification of the specific factors that contributed to the emergence of these systems. The categories of evidence that archaeologists have traditionally examined to explain the initial emergence of complex societies are important for understanding the evolution of secondary state systems in the Postclassic period as well. For studies of the Postclassic period, however, our research also emphasizes these factors' influences on the structures and dynamics of mature states and empires. Research on Postclassic economies thus provides insights into the operation of economic systems rather than emphasizing origins per se.

Understanding the opportunities and constraints offered by the material and productive base of Postclassic societies remains fundamental to archaeological studies. The combined influences of ecological factors and human potential (specifically environmental potential, population size, and agricultural carrying capacity) continue to be investigated.

The ecological diversity characteristic of highland Mesoamerica has been cited as an important influence on the structure of economy and society in this area (Sanders 1956; Sanders and Price 1968), and related factors such as transportation costs and distance also figure in current analyses of the highland Postclassic regional economy (Bell et al. 1988; Blanton 1994; Drennan 1984; Hassig 1985; Sanders and Santley 1983; Santley 1986; Sluyter 1993). The agricultural potential offered within different areas is another influence on the complex societies of Central Mexico that continues to see work (Sanders et al. 1979; Smith, chap. 12; Williams, chap. 3).

Still under discussion are the relative importance of agricultural potential and population size in the emergence of large-scale political systems. Whether population growth was a stimulus or a response to Precolumbian socioeconomic complexity remains an issue, though debated most hotly in regard to the emergence of primary states in the Late Formative-Early Classic periods. William Sanders and associates have assigned population growth a central role in the emergence of economically complex systems in the Basin of Mexico and elsewhere (Sanders and Price 1968; Sanders et al. 1979), but their population pressure models have been criticized by others (e.g., Blanton 1983, 1990; Brumfiel 1983; Feinman and Nicholas 1990). In Netting's (1990) model, which we discuss briefly above, population pressure leads to agricultural intensification and changes in household labor and tenure, but not to political centralization or class stratification. Smith and Price (1994) find support for this model in their analysis of agricultural terracing in Morelos.

The data on Postclassic societies present special opportunities for archaeologists to investigate the ways in which societies and political economies use ecological and human potential. Tension, struggle, and competition among polities, ethnic groups, and social units are described in ethnohistoric sources, and they are given important roles as motivators for conquests, taxation and other forms of economic expansion. Archaeologists have recently begun to develop methods for identifying class, status, ethnicity, and comparative wealth in the archaeological record (Brumfiel 1987b; Smith 1987; Brumfiel et al., chap. 5). This new socio-economic archaeology of the Aztecs, much of it outlined in this book, promises to link systematically the material attributes of Postclassic societies with cultural dynamics.

The Relationship Between Economic and Political Systems

A number of perspectives have emerged regarding the loci of decision making that structured the Late Postclassic economic systems. On the basis of settlement patterns, architectural remains, and other archaeological data, scholars agree that the Aztec state was less centralized as a society and as an economy than was Classic period Teotihuacan (Blanton 1976; Blanton et al. 1993; Calnek 1976). The origins of this "weaker state" economic system with its strong market system (Blanton et al. 1993) are not clear. To what extent was it initiated through "top-down" decision making on the part of imperial rulers, and to what extent did it emerge because of "bottom-up" processes such as supply and demand, competition, and other market dynamics. Additional empirical evidence will help scholars identify those aspects of the economy that were strongly state-controlled and those that were more independent.

Current research focuses on the identification of archaeologically recoverable materials that can serve as measures of political control and which denote supply and demand pressure in production and exchange of goods. For example, Brumfiel (1987b) has identified decorated ceramics as more sensitive indicators of interpolity feasting in the Early Aztec period than in Late Aztec times. The mapping of concentrations of ceramic types and design motifs across the Basin of Mexico has disclosed that political affiliations predict a community's access to decorated serving vessels more than does its proximity to major markets (Hodge 1992; Hodge and Minc 1990). Blanton (1994) discusses locational and ethnohistoric evidence for the manipulation of market locations and specializations by Aztec imperial rulers to benefit their cities at the expense of subordinate state elites. Brumfiel et al. (chap. 5) discuss how material symbols such as obsidian lip plugs were used to claim certain rights to land and tribute, and to create ideologies of solidarity and dominance.

In summary, the questions of when, where, and how economic systems were influenced by political systems still require further investigation. Information about specific Postclassic production specializations or material exchange systems that developed in response to top-down initiatives or to bottom-up pressures is required to fully characterize the economies of Postclassic Mesoamerica. Archaeological research designs for evaluating and identifying factors such as increasing commercialization, the extent of political control over market systems, and the manipulation of material culture in the political process are helping to address such questions.

The Scale of Postclassic Economic Systems

Economic systems in complex agrarian states like those of Late Postclassic Central Mexico operate at a variety of spatial scales, from the household to the macro-regional. The most visible scale in the ethnohistoric record is the *imperial scale,* including tribute from the provinces and the trade of the *pochteca.* Unfortunately this scale of economic activity has proven difficult to analyze archaeologically because of the indirect or hegemonic nature of Aztec imperialism (Smith and Berdan 1992). Nevertheless, this is a crucial level for understanding Aztec economics throughout the Central Highlands. There is evidence of deliberately selective policies on the part of the Aztec empire in its dealings with politically subject areas outside and within the Basin of Mexico, and the nature of imperial actions was determined by an overall economic strategy (Berdan et al. 1994; Berdan, chap. 11).

The *economic region,* corresponding to the area of one or more city-states, has been the dominant scale of economic analysis by archaeologists. Studies of agricultural systems, regional demography and settlement patterns, market trade, and craft production are all dependent upon a regional framework. Many of the debates over issues like the role of population pressure or the degree of political autonomy of the market system take place at this level. More recently, the focus on *community* and *household levels* has opened up the study of local and family-level economics for Aztec Central Mexico (see Evans 1993; Kellogg 1993; Smith 1993).

Many of the important questions concerning economic scale involve inter-relationships among processes or institutions at different spatial scales. For example, how did imperial tribute affect subject households? or, how did local agricultural intensification relate to imperial expansion? It is often difficult to disentangle the relative importance of forces at different scales, and observed changes in an area sometimes cannot be partitioned between macro- and micro-level forces. An example of such equifinality is provided by Smith and Heath-Smith's (chap. 13) research in western Morelos (see also Smith and Berdan 1992). Major economic changes within the Late Postclassic period in this area include increased agricultural and textile production coupled with lowered standards of living; these could be due to either a regional economic crisis, or to the indirect effects of Aztec conquest of the area, or to a combination of the two forces. Brumfiel et al. (chap. 5) argue that changes in the frequency of obsidian lip plugs in Middle to Late Postclassic Xaltocan reflect the decreasing utility of idealogies of ethnicity under conditions of imperial dominance.

One issue of economic scales that has been widely addressed involves rural-urban differences and interactions. The question of utilitarian craft production has been debated in this context. As discussed above, there was considerable variability in the scale and context of Aztec craft industries, with at least some production in rural areas, in city-state capitals, and in Tenochtitlan itself.

Yet another important issue for understanding the scale of Postclassic Mesoamerican economies is the degree of centralization of these systems. The imperial tribute lists present an image of a rather well defined economic organization that covered much of Central Mexico. Studies of individual products and their movement, however, indicate that certain categories of goods, including both luxury and subsistence items, moved through exchange networks outside the tribute system and even bypassed the more administered market system of the Basin of Mexico (see, for example, Berdan 1987b on trade in luxury goods; Berdan 1988 on independent merchants; Spence 1985 on obsidian processing and trade; and Smith 1990 on ceramic and obsidian trade outside of the Basin). Such studies suggest that "gray markets" that operated outside the official economy can be identified and incorporated into analyses of Postclassic Central Mexico's economy. Knowledge about the operation of informal economies within the imperial or regional state systems, compared with the more normative view of the Aztec economy presented by textual sources, are creating a more dynamic model of the Postclassic economy, one developed systematically from archaeological data and one which incorporates the official and informal economies as well as the center and the periphery.

Finally, the extent to which economic activities and patterns at Tenochtitlan typified Aztec Central Mexico is another question of scale. We have considerable documentary evidence on the economy of the Aztec capital (Rojas 1986), and in the past, scholars tended to overgeneralize from these data. One of the more important results of the recent archaeological fieldwork reported in this book is the demonstration that provincial and hinterland areas had economic profiles quite different from the imperial metropolis.

CONCLUSION: IMPERIAL AND LOCAL ECONOMIES

The research reported in this book reveals that beneath a highly visible imperial veneer lay a foundation of local polities and estates, small urban centers, rural villages, and hamlets, all integrated into local economies. These settlements and polities existed prior to incorporation into the Aztec, Tarascan, or other major states, and many continued to be significant units even under Spanish rule in the Colonial period. The subimperial polities and economies represent enduring structures that supported the imperial political and social orders, and for the population of the Aztec realm, they held more importance than did the distant empires and imperial capitals.

A recognition of the durability and persistence of local economic and political structures within and bordering on the Aztec empire is one of the major advances of the research described in the chapters to follow. Another significant discovery is the high level of variability that existed in economic and political patterns. This variability is found regionally and socially, in both the horizontal and vertical dimensions of social complexity (see McGuire 1983). Horizontally, Late Postclassic economies and polities were characterized by variation in levels and types of land tenure, farming systems, merchants and markets, craft specialization, patterns of urbanization, and other dimensions of heterogeneity. In the vertical dimension, inequality pervaded Late Postclassic society but with great variation in its degree and organization. In sum, the economies and polities of Late Postclassic Central Mesoamerica present modern scholars with a complex social mosaic whose patterns of organization are being brought to light by current archaeological and ethnohistorical research. The remaining chapters in this book describe much of this work, and collectively we feel they signal a major advance in our understanding of the Aztec realm.

ACKNOWLEDGMENTS

We would like to thank the authors of the other chapters and members of the audience at the symposium "Aztec Archaeology: Trade, Production, and Economic Issues" held during the 47th International Congress of Americanists in New Orleans, July 7-11, 1991, for comments on many of the ideas and topics covered in this paper. Frances Berdan, Elizabeth Brumfiel, Cynthia Heath-Smith, Frederic Hicks, Patricia Plunket, and Helen Pollard provided helpful comments and suggestions on an earlier draft.

REFERENCES CITED

Adams, Robert McC.
   1979 Late Prehispanic Empires of the New World. In *Power and Propaganda: A Symposium on Ancient Empires,* edited by Mogens Trolle Larsen, pp. 59-73. Akademish Forlag, Copenhagen.

Anales de Cuauhtitlan

1938   *Der geschichte der Konigreiche von Colhuacan und Mexiko.* Text mit uberzetzung von Walter Lehmann. Quellenwerke zur alten Geschicthe Amerikas aufgeziechnet in den Sprachen der Eingeborenen No. 1. Kohlhammer, Stuttgart.

Armillas, Pedro

1971   Gardens on Swamps. *Science* 174:653-661.

Arroyo, Salvador Guillerm

1990   El templo a Ehecatl en Tlatelolco. Paper presented at Seminario Alfonso Caso, "La época final del México antiguo, siglos XII a XVI," Museo Nacional de Antropología y Instituto Nacional de Antropología e Historia, Mexico City, July 23-27, 1990.

Aveni, Anthony F., Edward E. Calnek, and Horst Hartung

1988   Myth, Environment, and the Orientation of the Templo Mayor of Tenochtitlan. *American Antiquity* 53:287-309.

Avila, Raúl

1991   *Las chinampas de Ixtapalapa, D.F.* Instituto Nacional de Antropología e Historia, Mexico City.

Bell, Thomas L., Richard L. Church, and Larry Gorenflo

1988   Late Horizon Regional Efficiency in the Northeastern Basin of Mexico: A Location-Allocation Perspective. *Journal of Anthropological Archaeology* 7: 163-202.

Berdan, Frances F.

1975   *Trade, Tribute and Market in the Aztec Empire.* PhD Dissertation, Department of Anthropology, University of Texas. University Microfilms, Ann Arbor.

1982   *The Aztecs of Central Mexico: An Imperial Society.* Holt, Rinehart, and Winston, New York.

1985   Markets in the Economy of Aztec Mexico. In *Markets and Marketing,* edited by Stuart Plattner, pp. 339-367. University Press of America, Lanham, Maryland.

1987a   Cotton in Aztec Mexico: Production, Distribution, and Uses. *Mexican Studies/Estudios Mexicanos* 3:235-262.

1987b   The Economics of Aztec Luxury Trade and Tribute. In *The Aztec Templo Mayor,* edited by Elizabeth H. Boone, pp. 161-183. Dumbarton Oaks, Washington, D.C.

1988   Principles of Regional and Long-Distance Trade in the Aztec Empire. In *Smoke and Mist: Mesoamerican Studies in Memory of Thelma D. Sullivan,* edited by J. Kathryn Josserand and Karen Dakin, pp. 639-656. British Archaeological Reports, International Series Vol. 402. British Archaeological Reports, Oxford.

Berdan, Frances F., Richard E. Blanton, Elizabeth H. Boone, Mary G. Hodge, Michael E. Smith, and Emily Umberger

1994   *Aztec Imperial Strategies.* Dumbarton Oaks, Washington, D.C. In press.

Blanton, Richard E.

1976 The Role of Symbiosis in Adaptation and Sociocultural Change in the Valley of Mexico. In *The Valley of Mexico,* edited by Eric R. Wolf, pp. 181-201. University of New Mexico Press, Albuquerque.

1983 Advances in the Study of Cultural Evolution in Prehispanic Highland Mesoamerica. *Advances in World Archaeology* 2:245-288.

1990 Theory and Practice in Mesoamerican Archaeology: A Comparison of Two Modes of Scientific Inquiry. In *Debating Oaxaca Archaeology,* edited by Joyce Marcus, pp. 1-16. Anthropological Papers No. 84. Museum of Anthropology, University of Michigan, Ann Arbor.

1994 The Aztec Market System and the Growth of Empire. In *Aztec Imperial Strategies,* by Frances F. Berdan, Richard E. Blanton, Elizabeth H. Boone, Mary G. Hodge, Michael E. Smith, and Emily Umberger. Dumbarton Oaks, Washington, D.C. In press.

Blanton, Richard E., Stephen A. Kowalewski, Gary M. Feinman, and Laura M. Finsten

1993 *Ancient Mesoamerica: A Comparison of Change in Three Regions.* 2nd ed. Cambridge University Press, New York.

Boone, Elizabeth H. (editor)

1987 *The Aztec Templo Mayor.* Dumbarton Oaks, Washington, D.C.

Boserup, Esther

1965 *The Conditions of Agricultural Growth: The Economics of Agrarian Change Under Population Pressure.* Aldinc, Chicago.

Broda, Johanna, Davíd Carrasco, and Eduardo Matos Moctezuma

1987 *The Great Temple of Tenochtitlan: Center and Periphery in the Aztec World.* University of California Press, Berkeley.

Brumfiel, Elizabeth M.

1980 Specialization, Market Exchange, and the Aztec State: A View from Huexotla. *Current Anthropology* 21:459-478.

1983 Aztec State Making: Ecology, Structure, and the Origin of the State. *American Anthropologist* 85:261-284.

1987a Elite and Utilitarian Crafts in the Aztec State. In *Specialization, Exchange, and Complex Societies,* edited by Elizabeth M. Brumfiel and Timothy K. Earle, pp. 102-118. Cambridge University Press, New York.

1987b Consumption and Politics at Aztec Huexotla. *American Anthropologist* 89: 676-86.

1991a Weaving and Cooking: Women's Production in Aztec Mexico. In *Engendering Archaeology: Women and Prehistory,* edited by Joan M. Gero and Margaret W. Conkey, pp. 224-251. Basil Blackwell, Oxford.

1991b Agricultural Development and Class Stratification in the Southern Valley of Mexico. In *Land and Politics in the Valley of Mexico,* edited by Herbert R. Harvey, pp. 43-62. University of New Mexico Press, Albuquerque.

Brumfiel, Elizabeth M., and Timothy K. Earle
1987 Specialization, Exchange, and Complex Societies: An Introduction. In *Specialization, Exchange, and Complex Societies,* edited by Elizabeth M. Brumfiel and Timothy K. Earle, pp. 1-9. Cambridge University Press, New York.

Calnek, Edward E.
1976 The Internal Structure of Tenochtitlan. In *The Valley of Mexico: Studies in Prehispanic Ecology and Society,* edited by Eric R. Wolf, pp. 287-302. University of New Mexico Press, Albuquerque.

1978 The City-State in the Basin of Mexico: Late Pre-Hispanic Period. In *Urbanization in the Americas from Its Beginnings to the Present,* edited by Richard P. Schaedei, Jorge E. Hardoy, and Norma S. Kinzer, pp. 463-470. Mouton, The Hague.

Carrasco, Pedro
1976a Estratificación social indígena en Morelos durante el siglo XVI. In *Estratificación social en la Mesoamérica prehispánica,* edited by Pedro Carrasco and Johanna Broda, pp. 102-117. Instituto Nacional de Antropología e Historia, Mexico City.

1976b The Joint Family in Ancient Mexico: The Case of Molotla. In *Essays on Mexican Kinship,* edited by Hugo Nutini, Pedro Carrasco, and James M. Taggert, pp. 45-64. University of Pittsburgh Press, Pittsburgh.

1977 Los señores de Xochimilco en 1548. *Tlalocan* 7:229-65.

Carrasco, Pedro, and Johanna Broda (editors)
1976 *Estratificación social en la Mesoamérica prehispánica.* Instituto Nacional de Antropología e Historia, Mexico City.

Carrasco, Pedro, and Jesús Monjarás-Ruiz (editors)
1976 *Colección de documentos sobre Coyoacan, Vol. 1 (visita del Oider Gómez de Santillán al pueblo de Coyoacan y su sujeto Tacubaya en el año de 1553).* Instituto Nacional de Antropología e Historia, Mexico City.

1978 *Colección de documentos sobre Coyoacan, Vol. 2 (Autos referentes al cacicazgo de Coyoacan que proceden del AGN).* Instituto Nacional de Antropología e Historia, Mexico City.

Charlton, Thomas H., and Deborah L. Nichols (editors)
1990 *Los procesos del desarrollo de los estados tempranos: El caso del estado Azteca de Otumba.* 4 vols. Report submitted to the Instituto Nacional de Antropología e Historia. Publications in Anthropology No. 4. University of Iowa, Iowa City

Charlton, Thomas H., Deborah L. Nichols, and Cynthia Otis Charlton
1991 Aztec Craft Production and Specialization: Archaeological Evidence From the City-State of Otumba, Mexico. *World Archaeology* 23:98-114.

Chimalpahin Quauhtlehuanitzin, Diego Francisco de San Antón Muñón
1965 *Relaciones originales de Chalco Amequemecan escritas por Don Francisco de San Antón Muñón Chimalpahin Quauhtlehuaniztin.* Translated by Sylvia Rendón. Fondo de Cultura Económica, Mexico City.

Clark, John E.
1986 From Mountains to Molehills: A Critical Review of Teotihuacan's Obsidian Industry. In *Economic Aspects of Prehispanic Highland Mexico,* edited by Barry L. Isaac, pp. 23-74. Research in Economic Anthropology, Supplement No. 2. JAI Press, Greenwich.

Clendinnen, Inga
1991 *Aztecs: An Interpretation.* Cambridge University Press, New York.

Cline, S. L.
1990 *Colonial Culhuacan, 1580-1600: A Social History of an Aztec Town.* University of New Mexico Press, Albuquerque.
1993 (editor and translator) *The Book of Tributes: Early Sixteenth-Century Nahuatl Censuses from Morelos.* U.C.L.A. Latin American Center, Los Angeles.

Conrad, Geoffrey W., and Arthur A. Demarest
1984 *Religion and Empire: The Dynamics of Aztec and Inca Expansion.* Cambridge University Press, New York.

Cook, Sherburne F.
1949 *Soil Erosion and Population in Central Mexico.* Ibero-Americana No. 34. University of California Press, Berkeley.

Cook, Sherburne F., and Woodrow Borah
1979 Indian Food Production and Consumption in Central Mexico Before and After the Conquest (1500-1650). In *Essays in Population History: Mexico and California,* Vol. 3, pp. 129-176. University of California Press, Berkeley.

Costin, Cathy L.
1991 Craft Specialization: Issues in Defining, Documenting, and Explaining the Organization of Production. *Archaeological Method and Theory* 3:1-56. University of Arizona Press, Tucson.

Cowgill, George L.
1975 On Causes and Consequences of Ancient and Modern Population Changes. *American Anthropologist* 77:505-525.
1979 Teotihuacan, Internal Militaristic Competition, and the Fall of the Classic Maya. In *Maya Archaeology and Ethnohistory,* edited by Norman Hammond and Gordon R. Willey, pp. 51-62. University of Texas Press, Austin.

Davies, Nigel
1973 *The Aztecs: A History.* University of Oklahoma, Norman.
1980 *The Toltec Heritage: From the Fall of Tula to the Rise of Tenochtitlan.* University of Oklahoma Press, Norman.
1987 *The Aztec Empire: The Toltec Resurgence.* University of Oklahoma Press, Norman.

Denevan, William M.
1992 The Pristine Myth: The Landscape of the Americas in 1492. *Annals of the Association of American Geographers* 82:369-385.

Doolittle, William E.

1990   *Canal Irrigation in Prehistoric Mexico: The Sequence of Technological Change.* University of Texas Press, Austin.

Doyle, Michael W.

1986   *Empires.* Cornell University Press, Ithaca.

Drennan, Robert D.

1984   Long-Distance Transport Costs in Pre-Hispanic Mesoamerica. *American Anthropologist* 86:105-112.

Durán, Fray Diego

1967   *Historia de las Indias de Nueva España e Islas de la Tierra Firme.* Edited by Angel María Garibay K. 2 vols. Editorial Porrúa, Mexico City.

Eberhard, Wolfram

1977   *A History of China.* 4th ed. University of California Press, Berkeley.

Eisenstadt, Shmuel N.

1963   *The Political Systems of Empires.* The Free Press, New York.

Evans, Susan T.

1985   The Cerro Gordo Site: A Rural Settlement of the Aztec Period in the Basin of Mexico. *Journal of Field Archaeology* 12:1-18.

1988   *Excavations at Cihuatecpan, an Aztec Village in the Teotihuacan Valley.* Vanderbilt University Publications in Anthropology No. 36. Vanderbilt University, Nashville.

1990   The Productivity of Maguey Terrace Agriculture in Central Mexico During the Aztec Period. *Latin American Antiquity* 1:117-132.

1991   Architecture and Authority in an Aztec Village: Form and Function of the Tecpan. In *Land and Politics in the Valley of Mexico: A Two-Thousand Year Perspective,* edited by Herbert R. Harvey, pp. 63-92. University of New Mexico Press, Albuqerque.

1993   Aztec Household Organization and Village Administration. In *Prehispanic Domestic Units in Western Mesoamerica: Studies of the Household, Compound, and Residence,* edited by Robert S. Santley and Kenneth G. Hirth, pp. 173-189. CRC Press, Boca Raton.

Feinman, Gary, and Linda Nicholas

1990   The Monte Albán State: A Diachronic Perspective on an Ancient Core and its Periphery. In *Core/Periphery Relations in Precapitalist Worlds,* edited by Christopher Chase-Dunn and Thomas D. Hall, pp. 240-276. Westview Press, Boulder.

Fox, Richard G.

1977   *Urban Anthropology: Cities in Their Cultural Settings.* Prentice Hall, Englewood Cliffs.

Gibson, Charles

1964   *The Aztecs Under Spanish Rule: A History of the Indians of the Valley of Mexico, 1519-1810.* Stanford University Press, Stanford.

1971 Structure of the Aztec Empire. In *Archaeology of Northern Mesoamerica,* pt. 1, edited by Gordon F. Ekholm and Ignacio Bernal, pp. 376-94. Handbook of Middle American Indians, vol. 10, Robert Wauchope, general editor. University of Texas Press, Austin.

Gillespie, Susan D.

1989 *The Aztec Kings: The Constitution of Rulership in Mexica History.* University of Arizona Press, Tucson.

Goodfellow, Susan T.

1990 *Late Postclassic Period Economic Systems in Western Morelos, Mexico: A Study of Ceramic Production, Distribution and Exchange.* PhD dissertation, Department of Anthropology, University of Pittsburgh. University Microfilms, Ann Arbor.

Gorenstein, Shirley

1985 *Acambaro: Frontier Settlement on the Tarascan-Aztec Border.* Vanderbilt University Publications in Anthropology No. 32. Vanderbilt University, Nashville.

Hassig, Ross

1982 Periodic Markets in Precolumbian Mexico. *American Antiquity* 47:46-51.

1985 *Trade, Tribute, and Transportation: The Sixteenth Century Political Economy of the Valley of Mexico.* University of Oklahoma Press, Norman.

1988 *Aztec Warfare: Imperial Expansion and Political Control.* University of Oklahoma Press, Norman.

Hicks, Frederic

1982 Tetzcoco in the Early 16th Century: The State, the City and the Calpolli. *American Ethnologist* 9:230-249.

1986 Prehispanic Background of Colonial Political and Economic Organization in Central Mexico. In *Ethnohistory,* edited by Ronald Spores, pp. 35-54. Supplement to the Handbook of Middle American Indians, vol. 4, Victoria Bricker, general editor. University of Texas Press, Austin.

1992 Subject States and Tribute Provinces: The Aztec Empire in the Northern Valley of Mexico. *Ancient Mesoamerica* 3:1-10.

Hirth, Kenneth G.

1994 *Ancient Urbanization at Xochicalco, Morelos.* Manuscript on file at the Department of Anthropology, Pennsylvania State University.

Hodge, Mary G.

1984 *Aztec City-States.* Memoirs No. 18. Museum of Anthropology, University of Michigan, Ann Arbor.

1992 The Geographical Structure of Aztec Imperial-period Market Systems. *National Geographic Society Research and Exploration* 8:428-445.

Hodge, Mary G., and Leah D. Minc

1990 The Spatial Patterning of Aztec Ceramics: Implications for Prehispanic Exchange Systems in the Valley of Mexico. *Journal of Field Archaeology* 17: 415-437.

Hodge, Mary G., Hector Neff, James M. Blackman, and Leah D. Minc
   1992   A Compositional Perspective on Ceramic Production in the Aztec Empire. In *Chemical Characterization of Ceramic Pastes in Archaeology*, edited by Hector Neff, pp. 203-220. Prehistory Press, Madison.
   1993   Black-on-Orange Ceramic Production in the Aztec Empire's Heartland. *Latin American Antiquity* 4:130-157.

Isaac, Barry L.
   1983   Aztec Warfare: Goals and Battlefield Comportment. *Ethnology* 22:121-131.

Ivanhoe, Francis
   1978   Diet and Demography in Texcoco on the Eve of the Spanish Conquest: A Semiquantitative Reconstruction from Selected Ethnohistorical Texts. *Revista Mexicana de Estudios Antropológicos* 34:137-146.

Karttunen, Frances
   1983   *An Analytical Dictionary of Nahuatl.* University of Texas Press, Austin.

Kellogg, Susan
   1993   The Social Organization of Households Among the Tenochca Mexica Before and After the Conquest. In *Prehispanic Domestic Units in Western Mesoamerica: Studies of the Household, Compound, and Residence,* edited by Robert S. Santley and Kenneth G. Hirth, pp. 207-224. CRC Press, Boca Raton.

Maldonado Jiménez, Druzo
   1990   *Cuauhnahuac y Huaxtepec: Tlalhuicas y Xochimilcas en el Morelos prehispánico.* Centro Regional de Investigaciones Multidisciplinarias, Universidad Nacional Autónoma de México, Cuernavaca.

Marcus, Joyce
   1983   On the Nature of The Mesoamerican City. In *Prehistoric Settlement Patterns: Essays in Honor of Gordon R. Willey,* edited by Evon Z. Vogt and Richard Leventhal, pp. 195-242. University of New Mexico Press, Albuquerque.

Mason, Roger D.
   1980   *Economic and Social Organization of an Aztec Provincial Center: Archaeological Research at Coatlan Viejo, Morelos, Mexico.* PhD dissertation, Department of Anthropology, University of Texas. University Microfilms, Ann Arbor.

Matos Moctezuma, Eduardo
   1988   *The Great Temple of the Aztecs.* Thames and Hudson, New York.

McGuire, Randall
   1983   Breaking Down Cultural Complexity: Inequality and Heterogeneity. *Advances in Archaeological Method and Theory* 6:91-142. Academic Press, New York.

McVicker, Donald, and Laurene Urquizo
   1991   Report on the Aztec Presence at Tlacotepec. Unpublished manuscript.

Molina, Fray Alonso de
   1970   *Vocabulario en lengua Castellana y Mexicana y Mexicana y Castellana.* Editorial Porrúa, Mexico City.

Neff, Hector, Michael Glascock, Donald McVicker, and Laurene Urquizo
  1991 Aztec Colonial Presence at Tlacotepec in the Valley of Toluca, Mexico. Unpublished Final Report on Neutron Activation Analysis. Missouri University Research Reactor, University of Missouri, Columbia.

Netting, Robert McC.
  1968 *Hill Farmers of Nigeria: Cultural Ecology of the Jos Plateau.* University of Washington Press, Seattle.

  1989 Smallholders, Householders, Freeholders: Why the Family Farm Works Well Worldwide. In *The Household Economy: Reconsidering the Domestic Mode of Production,* edited by Richard R. Wilk, pp. 221-244. Westview Press, Boulder.

  1990 Population, Permanent Agriculture, and Polities: Unpacking the Evolutionary Portmanteau. In *The Evolution of Political Systems: Socio-Politics in Small Scale Societies,* edited by Steadman Upham, pp. 21-61. Cambridge University Press, New York.

Nicholson, H. B.
  1971 Pre-Hispanic Central Mexican Historiography. In *Investigaciones contemporáneas sobre la historia de México,* pp. 38-81. El Colegio de México and University of Texas Press, Mexico City and Austin.

Offner, Jerome A.
  1983 *Law and Politics in Aztec Texcoco.* Cambridge University Press, New York.
  1984 Household Organization in the Texcocan Heartland. In *Explorations in Ethnohistory: Indians of Central Mexico in the Sixteenth Century,* edited by Herbert R. Harvey and Hanns J. Prem, pp. 127-146. University of New Mexico Press, Albuquerque.

O'Hara, Sara L., F. Alayne Street-Perrott, and Timothy Burt
  1993 Accelerated Soil Erosion Around a Mexican Highland Lake Caused by Prehispanic Agriculture. *Nature* 362:48-51.

Olivera, Mercedes
  1978 *Pillis y macehuales: Las formaciones sociales y los modos de producción de Tecali del siglo XII al XVI.* Centro de Investigaciones y Estudios Superiores en Antropología Social, Mexico City.

O'Mack, Scott H.
  1991 *The Tetlama Lienzo Project: Final Report.* Unpublished report to the National Geographic Society.

Ortiz de Montellano, Bernard R.
  1990 *Aztec Medicine, Health, and Nutrition.* Rutgers University Press, New Brunswick.

Otis Charlton, Cynthia
  1993 Obsidian as Jewelry: Lapidary Production in Aztec Otumba, Mexico. *Ancient Mesoamerica* 4:231-243.

Otis Charlton, Cynthia, Thomas H. Charlton, and Deborah L. Nichols
   1993   Aztec Household-Based Craft Production: Archaeological Evidence from the
   City-state of Otumba, Mexico. In *Prehispanic Domestic Units in Western
   Mesoamerica: Studies of the Household, Compound, and Residence,* edited by
   Robert S. Santley and Kenneth G. Hirth, pp. 147-171. CRC Press, Boca Raton.

Palerm, Angel (editor)
   1973   *Obras hidraúlicas prehispánicas en el sistema lacustre del Valle de México.*
   Instituto Nacional de Antropología e Historia, Mexico City.

Parry, William J.
   1990   Analysis of Chipped Stone Artifacts from Otumba (TA-80) and Neighboring
   Rural Sites in the Eastern Teotihuacan Valley of Mexico. In *Early State Formation Processes: The Aztec City-State of Otumba, Mexico, Part 1, Preliminary Report
   on Recent Research in the Otumba City-State,* edited by Thomas H. Charlton and
   Deborah L. Nichols, pp. 73-88. Report No. 3. Mesoamerican Research Colloquium,
   Department of Anthropology, University of Iowa, Iowa City.

Parsons, Jeffrey R.
   1971   *Prehistoric Settlement Patterns in the Texcoco Region, Mexico.* Memoirs No.
   3. Museum of Anthropology, University of Michigan, Ann Arbor.
   1990   Arqueología regional en la Cuenca de México: Una estrategía para la
   investigación futura. *Anales de Antropología* 27:159-257.
   1991   Political Implications of Prehispanic Chinampa Agriculture in the Valley of
   Mexico. In *Land and Politics in the Valley of Mexico: A Two-Thousand Year
   Perspective,* edited by Herbert R. Harvey, pp. 17-42. University of New Mexico
   Press, Albuquerque.

Parsons, Jeffrey R., Elizabeth M. Brumfiel, Mary H. Parsons, and David J. Wilson
   1982   *Prehispanic Settlement Patterns in the Southern Valley of Mexico: The Chalco-
   Xochimilco Region.* Memoirs No. 14. Museum of Anthropology, University of
   Michigan, Ann Arbor.

Parsons, Jeffrey R., Elizabeth M. Brumfiel, Mary H. Parsons, Virginia Popper, and
Mary Taft
   1982   *Late Prehispanic Chinampa Agriculture on Lake Chalco-Xochimilco: Preliminary Report.* Report submitted to the Instituto Nacional de Antropología e
   Historia.

Parsons, Jeffrey R., and Mary H. Parsons
   1990   *Maguey Utilization in Highland Central Mexico: An Archaeological Ethnography.* Anthropological Papers No. 82. Museum of Anthropology, University of
   Michigan, Ann Arbor.

Parsons, Jeffrey R., Elizabeth M. Brumfiel, and Mary G. Hodge
   1993   Are Aztec I Ceramics Epiclassic? The Implications of Early Radiocarbon Dates
   from Three Aztec I Deposits in the Basin of Mexico. Paper presented at the symposium, "Rethinking the Epiclassic in Central Mexico," 13th International Congress
   of Anthropological and Ethnological Sciences, Mexico City, July 29-Aug. 5, 1993.

Paso y Troncoso, Francisco del (editor)
1905-1906   *Papeles de Nueva España.* Segunda Serie, Geografía y Estadística. 7 vols. Sucesores de Rivadeneyra, Madrid.

Peacock, D. P. S.
1982   *Pottery in the Roman World: An Ethnoarchaeological Approach.* Longman, New York.

Polgar, Steven
1975   Population, Evolution, and Theoretical Paradigms. In *Population, Ecology, and Social Evolution,* edited by Steven Polgar, pp. 1-26. Mouton, The Hague.

Pollard, Helen Perlstein
1982   Ecological Variation and Economic Exchange in the Tarascan State. *American Ethnologist* 9:250-268.

Price, T. Jeffrey, and Michael E. Smith
1992   Agricultural Terraces. In *Archaeological Research at Aztec-Period Rural Sites in Morelos, Mexico, Volume 1: Excavations and Architecture,* by Michael E. Smith, pp. 267-292. Monographs in Latin American Archaeology No. 4. University of Pittsburgh, Pittsburgh.

Renfrew, Colin
1986   Introduction: Peer Polity Interaction and Socio-political Change. In *Peer Polity Interaction and Socio-Political Change,* edited by Colin Renfrew and John F. Cherry, pp. 1-18. Cambridge University Press, New York.

Rojas, José Luis de
1986   *México Tenochtitlan: Economía e sociedad en el siglo XVI.* Fondo de Cultura Económica, Mexico City.

Rounds, J.
1979   Lineage, Class, and Power in Aztec History. *American Ethnologist* 6:73-86.

Sahagún, Fray Bernardino de
1950-1982   *Florentine Codex: General History of the Things of New Spain.* Translated and edited by Arthur J. O. Anderson and Charles E. Dibble. 12 books. School of American Research and the University of Utah Press, Santa Fe and Salt Lake City.

Sanders, William T.
1956   The Central Mexican Symbiotic Region: A Study in Pre-historic Settlement Patterns. In *Prehistoric Settlement Patterns in the New World,* edited by Gordon R. Willey, pp. 115-127. Viking Fund Publications in Anthropology No. 23. Wenner-Gren Foundation for Anthropological Research, New York.

1965   *The Cultural Ecology of the Teotihuacan Valley.* Unpublished report, Department of Anthropology, Pennsylvania State University, University Park.

1970   The Population of the Teotihuacan Valley, the Basin of Mexico, and the Central Mexican Symbiotic Region in the 16th Century. In *The Teotihuacan Valley Project, Final Report,* by William T. Sanders, Anton Kovar, Thomas Charlton and Richard Diehl, pp. 385-452. Occasional Papers in Anthropology No. 3. Department of Anthropology, Pennsylvania State University, University Park.

Sanders, William T., Jeffrey R. Parsons, and Robert S. Santley
  1979   *The Basin of Mexico: Ecological Processes in the Evolution of a Civilization.* Academic Press, New York.
Sanders, William T., and Barbara J. Price
  1968   *Mesoamerica: The Evolution of a Civilization.* Random House, New York.
Sanders, William T., and Robert S. Santley
  1983   A Tale of Three Cities: Energetics and Urbanization in Pre-Hispanic Central Mexico. In *Prehistoric Settlement Patterns: Essays in Honor of Gordon R. Willey,* edited by Evon Z. Vogt and Richard Leventhal, pp. 243-291. University of New Mexico Press, Albuquerque.
Sanders, William T., and David Webster
  1988   The Mesoamerican Urban Tradition. *American Anthropologist* 90:521-546.
Santley, Robert S.
  1986   Prehispanic Roadways, Transport Network Geometry, and Aztec Politico-Economic Organization in the Basin of Mexico. In *Economic Aspects of Prehispanic Highland Mexico,* edited by Barry L. Isaac, pp. 223-44. Research in Economic Anthropology, Supplement No. 2. JAI Press, Greenwich.
Schroeder, Susan
  1991   *Chimalpahin and the Kingdoms of Chalco.* The University of Arizona Press, Tucson.
Sluyter, Andrew
  1993   Long-Distance Staple Transport in Western Mesoamerica: Insight Through Quantitative Modeling. *Ancient Mesoamerica* 4:193-199.
Smith, Michael E.
  1984   The Aztlan Migrations of the Nahuatl Chronicles: Myth or History? *Ethnohistory* 31:153-186.
  1986   The Role of Social Stratification in the Aztec Empire: A View from the Provinces. *American Anthropologist* 88:70-91.
  1987   Household Possessions and Wealth in Agrarian States: Implications for Archaeology. *Journal of Anthropological Archaeology* 6:297-335.
  1989   Cities, Towns, and Urbanism: Comment on Sanders and Webster. *American Anthropologist* 91:454-461.
  1990   Long-Distance Trade Under the Aztec Empire: The Archaeological Evidence. *Ancient Mesoamerica* 1:153-169.
  1992   *Archaeological Research at Aztec-Period Rural Sites in Morelos, Mexico. Volume 1, Excavations and Architecture.* Memoirs in Latin American Archaeology No. 4. Department of Anthropology, University of Pittsburgh, Pittsburgh.
  1993   Houses and the Settlement Hierarchy in Late Postclassic Morelos: A Comparison of Archaeology and Ethnohistory. In *Prehispanic Domestic Units in Western Mesoamerica: Studies of the Household, Compound, and Residence,* edited by Robert S. Santley and Kenneth G. Hirth, pp. 191-206. CRC Press, Boca Raton.

Smith, Michael E., and Frances F. Berdan
1992   Archaeology and the Aztec Empire. *World Archaeology* 23:353-367.
Smith, Michael E., and John F. Doershuk
1991   Late Postclassic Chronology in Western Morelos, Mexico. *Latin American Antiquity* 2:291-310.
Smith, Michael E., and Cynthia Heath-Smith
1994   Excavations of Aztec-Period Houses at Yautepec, Morelos, Mexico. Paper presented at the 1994 Annual Meeting, Society for American Archaeology, Anaheim.
Smith, Michael E., and Kenneth G. Hirth
1988   The Development of Prehispanic Cotton-Spinning Technology in Western Morelos, Mexico. *Journal of Field Archaeology* 15:349-358.
Smith, Michael E., and T. Jeffrey Price
1994   Aztec-Period Agricultural Terraces in Morelos, Mexico: Evidence for Household-Level Agricultural Intensification. *Journal of Field Archaeology* 21. In press.
Smith, Michael E., Cynthia Heath-Smith, Ronald Kohler, Joan Odess, Sharon Spanogle, and Timothy Sullivan
1994   The Size of the Aztec City of Yautepec: Urban Survey in Central Mexico. *Ancient Mesoamerica* 5.1-11.
Soustelle, Jacques
1961   *Daily Life of the Aztecs on the Eve of the Spanish Conquest.* Stanford University Press, Stanford.
Spence, Michael W.
1985   Specialized Production in Rural Aztec Society: Obsidian Workshops of the Teotihuacan Valley. In *Contributions to the Archaeology and Ethnohistory of Greater Mesoamerica,* edited by William J. Folan, pp. 76-125. Southern Illinois University Press, Carbondale.
Stark, Barbara J.
1990   The Gulf Coast and the Central Highlands of Mexico: Alternative Models for Interaction. *Research in Economic Anthropology* 12:243-285.
Sterpone, Osvaldo
1988   Late Postclassic Settlement Patterns in Northwestern Morelos. Paper presented at the 1988 Annual Meeting, American Anthropological Association, Phoenix.
Townsend, Richard F.
1992   *The Aztecs.* Thames and Hudson, New York.
Turner, B. L., II, and William E. Doolittle
1978   The Concept and Measure of Agricultural Intensity. *Professional Geographer* 30:297-301.
Umberger, Emily
1987   Antiques, Revivals, and References to the Past in Aztec Art. *Res* 13:62-105.

Vaillant, George C.

    1962   *Aztecs of Mexico: Origin, Rise and Fall of the Aztec Nation.* Revised by
    Suzannah B. Vaillant. Doubleday, Garden City, New York.

White, Benjamin

    1973   Demand for Labor and Population Growth in Colonial Java. *Human Ecology*
    1:217-236.

Whitmore, Thomas M.

    1992   *Disease and Death in Early Colonial Mexico: Simulating Amerindian
    Depopulation.* Westview Press, Boulder.

Whitmore, Thomas M., and B. L. Turner, II

    1992   Landscapes of Cultivation in Mesoamerica on the Eve of the Conquest.
    Annals of the Association of American Geographers 82:402-425.

Williams, Barbara J.

    1989   Contact Period Rural Overpopulation in the Basin of Mexico: Carrying-
    Capacity Models Tested with Documentary Data. *American Antiquity* 54:715-732.

Zantwijk, Rudolf van

    1985   *The Aztec Arrangement: The Social History of Pre-Spanish Mexico.* Uni-
    versity of Oklahoma Press, Norman.

2

Polities Composing the
Aztec Empire's Core

Mary G. Hodge

Information about intra-polity political organization is essential for a detailed understanding of the Aztec empire's infrastructure and operation. In this paper I explore methods for combining evidence from documents with archaeological settlement data in order to acquire detailed and consistent information about Aztec political geography. I then use the information on local political organization derived from documents and archaeological surveys to examine the relationship between the political power of city-states[1] (as indicated by their ranking in the regional political hierarchy) and their total populations, urban populations, urban-rural population distribution, territory size, and internal political structures. Comparing basic aspects of city-state polities provides information about the extent to which the parts of the Aztec empire are microcosms of the regional organization, and in what ways they differ from the imperial capital and from each other.

For this study I selected 15 city-states located in the eastern and southern parts of the Basin of Mexico. Archaeological settlement data from these polities have been fully published (Parsons 1971; Parsons et al. 1982; Parsons et al. 1983), and documentary records are available (for example, Alva Ixtlilxochitl 1975-1977; Chimalpahin 1965, 1960; Paso y Troncoso 1905-1906). Additionally, this area is the focus of a project that is comparing the boundaries of ceramic exchange zones with political territories (Hodge and Minc 1990, 1991; Minc et al., chap. 6).

DATA AND METHODS FOR IDENTIFYING
AZTEC POLITICAL BOUNDARIES

To expand knowledge of Postclassic Mesoamerican societies we must increase our integration of textual and archaeological data (see also, Marcus 1984; Berdan, chap. 11; Smith and Heath-Smith, chap. 13; Williams, chap. 3). Documents most often emphasize the politically dominant Aztec settlements but omit data on the settlements and territories that supported these centers. The uneven coverage of sub-imperial political units by documentary sources makes comparisons based solely on data from texts difficult. In contrast, archaeological settlement data derived from regional surveys provide information on communities of all sizes. However, these archaeological data are limited if used alone for comparing local polities, because Late Postclassic city-state boundaries are seldom discernible in the archaeological data. The density of Late Aztec[2] (A.D. 1350-1520) settlements in the Basin of Mexico is so great that, unlike earlier periods, unoccupied areas that could be interpreted as buffer zones between polities do not exist (Alden 1975; Gorenflo and Gale 1990; Sanders et al. 1979). In addition, few man-made markers survive to help archaeologists define polity boundaries, and the uneven topography of the Basin renders many standard techniques for analyses of settlement patterns ineffective (Evans and Gould 1982).

Ethnohistoric Data on Aztec Political Geography

I began this investigation with a direct historical approach: I collected information on Aztec political territories and their boundaries from historical chronicles, codices, maps painted in the indigenous tradition, and early colonial period administrative documents. Such documents list communities that were dependencies of a political center in prehispanic times, lists of communities conquered by particular political centers, or both. They also may contain pictorial depictions of prehispanic polity territories and lists of topographic or man-made boundary markers. Useful documents from the early Colonial period include lists of cabeceras' dependencies, maps and lists of town boundaries prepared by Nahua scribes for colonial legal proceedings, and community censuses and corresponding maps. The Relaciones Geográficas of 1579-1580, and the maps accompanying them, are another rich source of information on Aztec polities (for descriptions of such documents, see Cline 1973-1975).

The documents most appropriate for defining Aztec political territories are chronicles that refer to prehispanic times and that list the names of communities subordinate to particular city-states, and communities or geographic features that demarcated city-state boundaries (see Alva Ixtlilxochitl 1975-1977; Anales de Cuauhtitlan 1938:149, 296, 1945; Chimalpahin 1965; Durán 1967; Códice Kingsborough 1912; Mapa Quinatzin 1920).[3] Early colonial municipal documents, censuses, and the 1580 *Relaciones Geográficas* often contain names of small communities that go unmentioned in texts that refer to prehispanic events (for example, Acuña 1984-1987; Anderson et al. 1976; Carrasco and Monjarás-Ruiz 1976; Lemoine Villicaña 1961; Paso y Troncoso 1905-1906; Williams and Harvey 1988).

Because civil boundaries most closely approximated precolumbian political boundaries early in the Colonial period, my study emphasizes information from documents predating A.D. 1600. When using later documents, I considered whether the *congregaciones* of Aztec communities in the 1590s affected areas included in the study (Gibson 1964:286). Like Gerhard, I find data from parochial reports less useful for identifying Aztec period territories because colonial civil boundaries were often different from those of ecclesiastical territories (Gerhard 1970:31).[4]

Nahuatl place-names are yet another source of information. Modern names can indicate the locations of Aztec communities, since in many cases the prehispanic place-names have been retained, with the addition of saints' names to the Nahuatl names and occasional changes in orthography. Many place-names appear on contemporary maps, and the archaeological survey reports include modern and/or historic names of communities, hills, and rivers near Late Aztec sites (Blanton 1972; Parsons 1971; Parsons et al. 1982).

Archaeological Data on City-State Polities

Based on regional archaeological surveys the Late Aztec population in the Basin of Mexico was approximately one million (Sanders et al. 1979:12-14, 33-40). These surveys group Late Aztec settlements into categories according to size, density of artifact scatters, and complexity of architectural remains.[5] The survey data disclose that at least one-half of the Basin's million residents lived in nucleated centers and that the rest resided in a "suburban" periphery (Sanders et al. 1979:162).

Late Aztec urban centers around the lake bed were spaced ca. 20 km apart. The largest, Tenochtitlan, had an estimated population of 250,000. Approximately 25,000 people resided in Texcoco, the empire's second-ranking political center. Another dozen city-state centers in the Basin contained 20,000-40,000 residents, and the same number had populations of 10,000-20,000. As many as sixteen centers had resident populations of 10,000 or fewer (Hicks 1982; Hodge 1984, 1994; Parsons 1971, 1974; Parsons et al. 1982; Parsons et al. 1983; Sanders et al. 1979:154).

The archaeological survey results reveal a bias in the documentary records. Settlements of 500 or fewer people (Small Hamlets, Hamlets, and Small Villages) are almost always omitted from documentary accounts, but the surveys demonstrate that they constituted 90 percent of Late Aztec residential settlements. In contrast, the communities mentioned most frequently in documents (Regional Centers, Local Centers, and Large Villages) represent only 3 percent of settlements identified by the surveys (Sanders et al. 1979:166).

The archaeological surveys found Late Aztec sites distributed almost continuously across the Basin's land areas, interspersed among the lakes and hills (Parsons 1974; Sanders et al. 1979:165-166). Subsequent studies note the difficulties of using the Late Aztec settlement pattern data for spatial analyses that assume a regular patterning of settlements and populations (e.g., Gorenflo and Gale 1990). The difficulties in defining Aztec period political units using archaeological data by themselves may have contributed to past neglect of comparative analyses of sub-imperial political units.

Methods for Delimiting Aztec Political Territories

To define prehispanic territories of city-states in the Basin of Mexico, my first step was to use ethnohistoric sources to compile as many names and locations as possible of dependencies within each of the city-states included in this study. Charles Gibson's study of early colonial *cabeceras* and their subordinate communities, and his discussion of continuities and discontinuities in political jurisdictions from Aztec to colonial times, provided a starting point for mapping Late Postclassic city-state territories (Gibson 1964:map 3, 32-57, 435-447). A systematic search of published chronicles, codices, *Relaciones Geográficas,* early colonial administrative documents, and recent studies of these sources produced additional information on the communities that were political dependencies of specific centers. I recorded the names of dependent communities and their locations, information about changes in their political affiliations and any evidence of abandonment, relocation, or consolidation of communities in prehispanic or in colonial times. Manuscripts and maps in Mexico's Archivo General de la Nación provided data on areas minimally described in published documents (Colín 1966).

My second step in delineating Aztec city-state political boundaries was to locate settlements on the earliest maps available as well as on later ones. Useful for this project were the Santa Cruz map of ca. 1550 on which appear Nahuatl place glyphs and Spanish glosses (Linné 1948); the *Relaciones Geográficas* maps (Acuña 1984-1987, vol. 6; Paso y Troncoso 1905-1906); maps prepared by Nahua scribes for colonial legal actions; and colonial administrative maps containing Nahuatl place names. Modern maps such as the *Cartas Topográficas* 1:50,000 series (Instituto Nacional de Estadística, Geografía e Informática, Mexico) include many names of communities, rivers, and hills that have been retained since the 1500s.[6]

Third, after the communities listed as political dependencies of specific centers had been located on indigenous, colonial, or modern topographic maps,

I transferred this information to the archaeological settlement maps (Blanton 1972; Parsons 1971; Parsons et al. 1982; Parsons et al. 1983:map 8; Sanders et al. 1979:map 18). This was done by comparing the locations of documented political dependencies of Aztec urban centers on historical and modern maps to the spatial distributions of archaeological sites near these centers.

Among the 15 city-states mapped here, the number of archaeological sites in each polity, that could be identified by continuity in the name of the site, the name of a community contiguous with the site, or by named landmarks such as hills or rivers, varied from 10 percent to 90 percent. This range accurately reflects the vast differences in content, specificity, and even existence of documentary reports concerning sub-imperial political units. The lower percentages characterize city-state territories that contain many archaeological sites too small to have been named in documents.

Since many of the smallest sites identified by the archaeological surveys were not named as dependencies of city-state centers in any of the documents consulted, the fourth step in this study was to approximate each city-state territory from information about boundary markers. Natural features such as hills or rivers, or man-made markers such as hilltop pyramids, constituted some polity boundaries. When no documentation on boundary markers was found, boundaries were placed hypothetically at rivers, hills, or roads, since texts report that such features often marked Aztec territorial boundaries (e.g., *Anales de Cuauhtitlan* 1938:149, 296; Motolinía 1950:88). In some cases, less populated areas (possible buffer zones) located between polity centers were designated as hypothetical boundaries.

Finally, once each city-state's geographical boundaries had been approximated, the remaining archaeological sites were assigned to the polity within whose boundaries they were located.[7] Below, I illustrate this method's use by outlining the process of defining one city-state territory, Coatepec.

Locating Aztec Political Territories: An Example

The polity of Coatepec was located east of the Ixtapalapa peninsula in the piedmont below the Sierra de Nevada at ca. 2300 m in altitude. Its central settlement, Coatepec (Tx-A-99), contained 1250-2500 people in both Early and Late Aztec times (Parsons 1971:141).[8]

Chronicles referring to Late Aztec times do not list Coatepec's dependencies, but its 1579 *Relación Geográfica* names five *cabeceras* or head towns in Coatepec's *partido* or territory. Besides Coatepec itself, the *cabeceras* were Santa Ana Tetitlan, San Francisco Aquauhtla, San Miguel Tepetlapa, and Santiago Quatlapanca. *Estancias* (small subordinate communities) of the five cabeceras are also named in the *Relación Geográfica*. The estancias directly subordinate to Coatepec were San Martín Tlaylotlacan, San Juan Tlachichco, San Sebastián

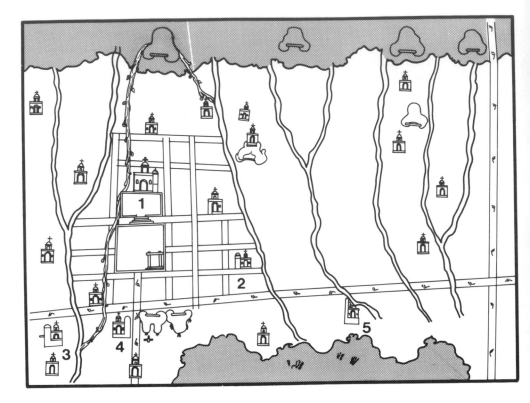

Fig. 2.1.   Coatepec and its *sujetos* from the *Relación Geográfica* map of 1579. East is at the top. The political center of Coatepec *(1)* is depicted along with Coatepec's dependencies Santa Ana Tetitlan *(2)*, San Miguel Tepetlapa *(3)*, Santiago Quatlapanca *(4)*, and San Francisco Aquauhtla *(5)*. The north-south road from Texcoco to Chalco and the east-west road from Mexico to Veracruz delimit Coatepec's territory, as do the mountains to the east. After Paso y Troncoso 1905-1906:*mapa de Coatepec*; see also Acuña 1984-1987, vol.6; traced with Spanish notations removed to accentuate locations of landmarks and communities.

Xocoatlauhco, Santa María Magdalena Ameyalco, and Santa Catalina Ancapa (Acuña 1984-1987:v.6:123-155; Paso y Troncoso 1905-1906:39-65).

Three colonial period maps helped to delineate Coatepec's territory. The Santa Cruz map depicts Coatepec's location and place-glyph (Linné 1948), and Coatepec's five *cabeceras* appear on a map accompanying the 1579 *Relación Geográfica* (fig. 2.1). Coatepec proper and one of its nearby estancias, Santa María Ameyalco, appear on a map dating to 1574 (fig. 2.2) that was painted for a legal proceeding between the community of Coatepec and individuals who claimed an *estancia* within the district (AGN, Tierras, v.1526, exp.1, f.435; *Catálogo de Ilustraciones:*3:no. 1088). The locations of four *estancias* named in the *Relación Geográfica* can be determined from glosses on the 1574 map.

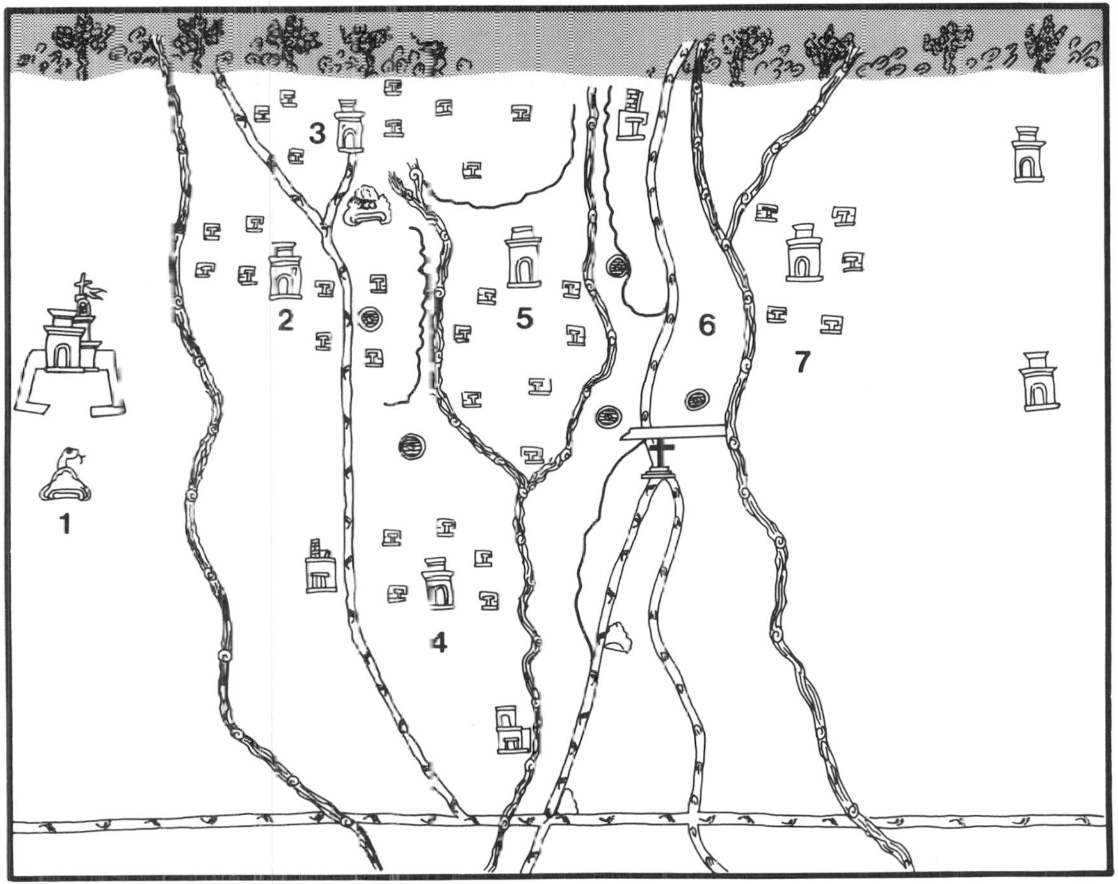

Fig. 2.2. Coatepec and some of its *sujetos*, from a map prepared for litigations in 1574. East is at the top. This map depicts Coatepec proper (*1*); Santa María Ameyalco, an *estancia* directly under Coatepec (*2*); San Andrés Chiauhtla (*3*) and Santo Tomás Texcaltitlan (*4*), both *estancias* of Aquauhtla; and San Mateo Oztotlitic, an *estancia* of Tetitlan (*5*), plus rivers, hills, roads, springs, and mountains. The road from Mexico to Veracruz (*6*) delimits Coatepec's territory from that of Ixtapalucan and its *sujetos* (*7*). Redrawn by R. Richard Rogers after AGN, Tierras, v.1526, exp.1, f.435, with Spanish text removed to accentuate landmarks and locations of communities.

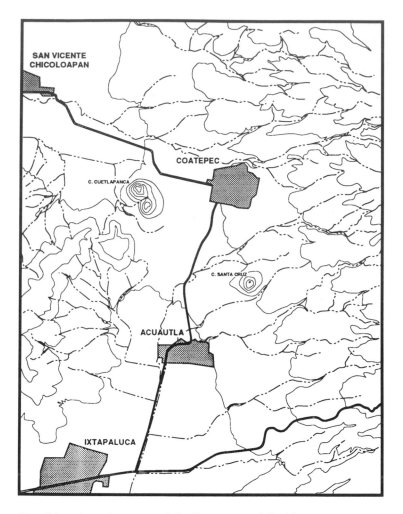

Fig. 2.3.   A modern map of the Coatepec area. Prehispanic names appearing on this map include Cerro Cuetlapanca to the west and the settlement of Acuautla to the south. After *Instituto Nacional de Estadística Geografía e Informática, Cartas Topograficas 1:50,000*:map E14B31, Chalco.

This map also locates Santa María, the *estancia* directly administered by Coatepec. Other *estancias* on the map include San Andrés Chiautla and Santo Tomás Texcaltitlan, dependencies of the *cabecera* of Aquauhtla, and San Mateo Oztotlitic, a *sujeto* of Tetitlan.[9]

The locations of Coatepec's dependencies provide a basis for identifying the extent of Coatepec's territory. The modern topographic map shows Acuautla

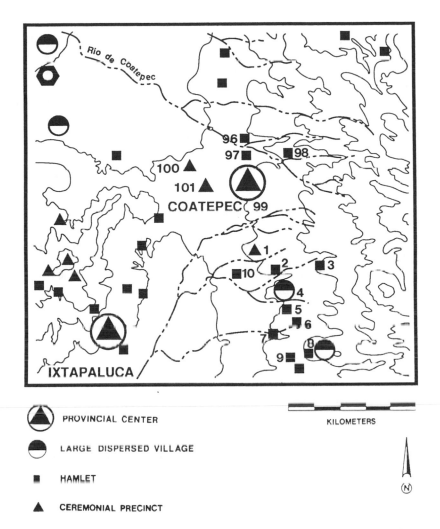

Fig. 2.4.   Archaeological sites in the Coatepec area. After Sanders et al. (1979: map 18); for other versions, see Parsons (1971) and Blanton (1972).

(Aquauhtla) to the south (fig. 2.3). The hill west of Coatepec, Cerro Cuetlapanca, most likely corresponds to the general location of Quatlapanca, one of the *cabeceras* named on the *Relación Geográfica* list and map. Cerro Cuetlapanca and another hill near it are described in the *Relación Geográfica* as places of worship (Acuña 1984-1987:v.6:137) and were recorded by the archaeological surveys (Parsons 1971:141) as ceremonial centers (Tx-A-100 and Tx-A-101; see fig. 2.4). Gibson (1964:map 3) located another dependency, Xocotlahco (Xocoatlauhco), to the north.

A comparison of the information from prose descriptions and early maps to the archaeological settlement maps indicates that several of Coatepec's subordinate communities can be correlated with Late Aztec sites with some confidence (fig. 2.4). Coatepec is Tx-A-99, and the ceremonial hill sites located close to it are Tx-A-100 and Tx-A-101. Sites located to its south, in the area of modern Acuautla, can also be assigned to Coatepec's archaeological territory (Ixtapalapa Survey sites 1 through 10, in Blanton 1972). Ix-Az-2 is a hilltop ceremonial center that probably corresponds to the hill glyphs appearing to the south of Coatepec on the colonial maps. Based on Charles Gibson's mapping of the Coatepec dependency Xocotlahco to the north (1964:map 3), sites Tx-A-96, -97, and -98 are also assigned to Coatepec's territory.

Boundary markers per se are not described in the text of the *Relación Geográfica,* but Coatepec's boundaries are indicated on the colonial period maps. The *Relación Geográfica* map shows the road from Mexico to Veracruz as the southern boundary and a river as the northern boundary. The western boundary is a road both on the AGN map (*Catálogo de Ilustraciones*:v.3:no.1088) and on the Santa Cruz map (Linné 1948).[10] Mountains form the eastern limit of Coatepec's territory on all maps.

This method of locating boundaries and identifying communities within a political territory shows that Coatepec was a small polity, approximately 46 km^2. The archaeological site categories within Coatepec's territory include 1 Local Center; 2 Large Villages, 13 Hamlets, and 3 Ceremonial Centers. The sum of the individual population estimates for each of these sites (Parsons et al. 1983) yields a Late Aztec population for Coatepec of 3210. This is the population upon which a local official would have been able to draw for tribute in the form of goods and labor.[11] I argue below that when compared to other imperial period political units, Coatepec's size is congruent with its status as a city-state reduced in political status during imperial times to an administered territory (see note 8 and Acuña 1984-1987:v.6:141-145).

COMPARISON OF CITY-STATE TERRITORIES

Identification of the political affiliations of archaeological sites in the eastern and southern Basin of Mexico provides quantified, uniformly-collected data for comparing selected attributes of city-state polities. The archaeological definitions of city-states derived here produced quantified estimates of population, territory size, and internal settlement composition, in contrast to figures obtained from documentary accounts, which seldom encompass all prehistoric sites and are almost never available in comparable form for all polities.

The archaeological definitions of city-states are used here to assess two questions concerning the impact of the Aztec regional political hierarchy upon lower level centers. The first question deals with the correlation of rank to polities' size. Tenochtitlan's and Texcoco's large urban populations suggest, for example, that urban centers of the highest political rank had the largest populations. But can we assume that city-states in the middle ranks in the political hierarchy contained urban centers with correspondingly mid-size populations? And did city-states with the least populated urban centers rank at the bottom of the political ladder? How were urban populations supported? Were urban centers with the largest populations supported by large rural territories and populations or did they, like Tenochtitlan, possess limited local resources and derive income from outside their immediate territories?

Second, did the ranking of city-states in the political hierarchy of the Basin of Mexico during the Late Aztec period correlate with specific attributes of these polities' internal organizations? It is evident from both texts and archaeological surveys that political relations between city-states were hierarchically organized in Late Aztec times (Blanton 1976b; Sanders et al. 1979). Whether well developed hierarchies also characterized the internal settlement patterns and administrative systems of city-states remains to be demonstrated. Documents report several levels of administrators present in the more populous (and more documented) city-state capitals, though less frequently in the rural areas of these city-states (Hodge 1984). Whether larger territory size or greater population of an Aztec political unit predicts a settlement hierarchy, isomorphic with a political hierarchy through which several levels of administrators operated, is addressed here by means of archaeological data. Though studies of complex societies suggest hierarchy formation might have occurred (see Berry et al. 1976; Blanton 1976a), an alternative organizational response to complexity is that of a "primate" system (Blanton 1976a) in which "... one or two very large settlements dominate the [site] distribution" (Hodder and Orton 1976:70-71). Since documents report efforts of imperial rulers to bypass or even to reduce hierarchies in some dependent city-states, it seemed reasonable to explore exactly what kind of organization characterized sub-imperial political units in Late Aztec times.

The Aztec Regional Political Hierarchy

The political hierarchy of the Basin of Mexico in ca. A.D. 1500 can be reconstructed from documentary accounts (Hodge 1994; Smith 1979). Tenochtitlan, the imperial capital, is the sole polity in the highest level, level 1. Texcoco, a regional state capital and member of the Triple Alliance, occupies level 2. Texcoco was the highest-ranking polity in the study area. Level 3 city-states were governed by *tlatoque,* hereditary rulers directly subordinate to the rulers

Table 2.1   Political ranks in the Basin of Mexico, ca. A.D. 1500

Rank	Category	Definition
1	Imperial Capital	(Tenochtitlan)
2	Regional State Capital	Founding member of Triple Alliance empire
3	City-State Center	Tlatoani subordinate to the ruler of a regional state capital
4	Dependent City-State	Tlatoani subordinate to the ruler of a level 3 city-state
5	Administered City-State	Tlatoani removed; polity governed by Triple Alliance administrator

of Texcoco or Tenochtitlan. Next in political rank were city-states whose rulers were subordinate to level 3 city-state rulers (level 4), followed by city-states governed by administrators appointed by Tenochtitlan or Texcoco (level 5). The definitions of these ranks are summarized in table 2.1.

The Size of Subordinate Centers

Estimated populations and territory sizes appear in table 2.2 for each of 15 city-states in the eastern and southern parts of the Basin of Mexico. These population figures were derived, as described above, by adding together the survey population estimates for all of the sites assigned to a particular polity (from Blanton 1972; Parsons 1971; Parsons et al. 1982; Parsons et al. 1983). The territory sizes were obtained by calculating the number of square kilometers in the area covered by sites assigned to each city-state urban center, i.e., the extent of the spread of dependent sites around a center (see figure 2.5. For a list of archaeological sites in each polity, see Hodge and Minc 1991:table 1.3).[12]

Much variation is present among the 15 city-states. Comparison of the data on 15 polities indicates that some of the factors considered here correlate positively with a city-state's political rank, but others do not. The total population size of city-states generally displays a positive association with their position in the regional political hierarchy (fig. 2.6). The city-state with the highest rank, Texcoco, has the largest total population. City-states at level 3 in the political hierarchy were characterized by a wide range of population sizes, which overlap with those in level 4, suggesting that differences between these two levels were not great. Historical chronicles in fact indicate that the level 4 polities in

Table 2.2 Area and population of Aztec polities

Polity	Area (sq. km)	Population Total	Urban	%	Rural	%
Level 2						
Texcoco	117	40,430	25,000	62	15,430	38
Level 3						
Chimalhuacan	37	12,560	12,000	96	560	4
Cuitlahuac	68	9,480	4,500	47	4,980	53
Culhuacan/ Mexicaltzinco [a] }	20	4,830	3,250 1,100	90	480	10
Huexotla	37	23,405	15,000	65	8,405	35
Ixtapalapan	20	5,358	2,800	52	2,558	48
Mixquic	16	2,740	2,250	82	490	18
Tepetlaoztoc	93	22,265	13,500	60	8,765	40
Tlalmanalco/ Chalco [b] }	228	21,570	4,000 12,500	76	4,340 730	24
Xochimilco	164	14,245	10,700	75	3,545	25
Level 4						
Amecamecan	55	10,515	10,000	95	515	5
Tenanco	143	6,500	150	2	6,350	98
Level 5						
Coatepec	46	3,210	2,500	78	710	22
Ixtapaluean	27	2,026	1,630	80	396	20

Sources: Data in this table are from Parsons (1971), Blanton (1972), and Parsons et al. (1983).

Note: Two city-states in the study area (fig. 2.5) are omitted from these comparisons. Chiauhtlan, unusual because no central settlement could be identified by the archaeological surveys, had a territory of 18 km² and a total population estimated at 1,790. Coatlinchan's urban center contained 5,500 to 11,000 people, but since most of the territory fell outside the regional survey boundaries, its total population could not be estimated using the methods employed in this study.

[a] The adjacent territories of Culhuacan and Mexicaltzinco cannot be distinguished from one another on the basis of data available for this study; hence their rural and total populations are combined.

[b] Since Chalco was governed from Tlalmanalco after the Triple Alliance conquered the Chalco region (see note 14), Chalco is combined here with Tlalmanalco.

this study performed the same functions prior to the imperial period (approximately A.D. 1430-1521) as those which ended up at level 3 in the political hierarchy. The level 4 city-states included in this study were located in the Chalco region and were demoted when a provincial administrative structure was con-

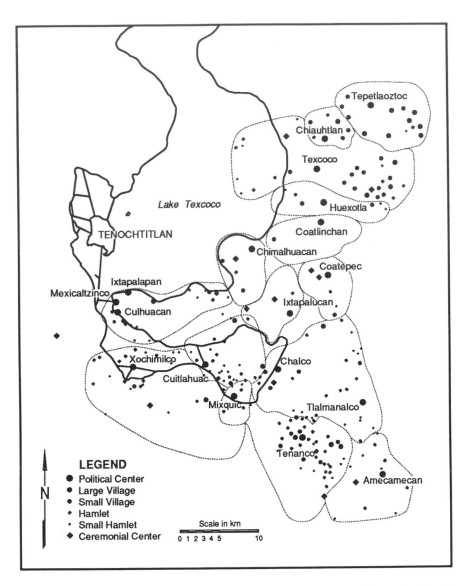

Fig. 2.5. Map of city-state territories, ca. A.D. 1500. This map is derived from ethnohistoric and archaeological data. Points represent the 221 sites included in a study of ceramic collections from regional surveys (see Minc et al., chap. 6). The scale required for this map does not permit display of all Late Aztec sites, especially in the southern Basin where small sites are closely spaced; for maps that include all sites, see Parsons (1971:map 14); Blanton (1972:fig. 50); Parsons et al. (1982:maps 27, 28); Parsons et al. (1983:map 9).

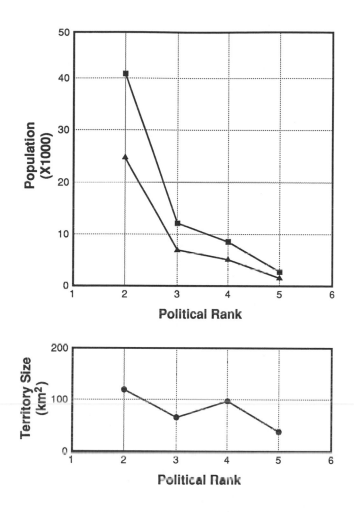

- ■ Mean total population of city-states compared to rank in the political hierarchy. Higher political rank correlates with higher population.

- ▲ Mean urban center population of Aztec city-states compared to rank in the regional political hierarchy. High urban center population correlates with high political rank.

- ● Mean territory size of city-states compared to political rank. Larger territory size does not correlate with higher political status.

Fig. 2.6. Graphs of city-state territory size and population levels by political rank. Data from table 2.2.

structed in this area after its conquest by Tenochtitlan and Texcoco (e.g., Chimalpahin 1965). Polities governed by administrators (level 5) were less populous than polities governed by hereditary rulers (levels 3-4) in every case but one. Comparing the total population mean in each rank emphasizes the strong relationship between political rank and population size (fig. 2.6).

Urban center population likewise correlates positively with a city-state's position in the political hierarchy (fig. 2.6). Information from documents helps to account for this: documentary sources report that some urban centers collected tribute from communities located in other city-states, in addition to those located directly inside their local territories. For example, documents representing the larger Acolhua centers included in this study (Texcoco, Tepetlaoztoc, Chimalhuacan, and perhaps Huexotla) report that the elites and institutions in these cities were supplied with goods by communities in other city-states (Acuña 1984-1987:v.6:164, 249; Alva Ixtlilxochitl 1975-1977; *Códice Kingsborough* 1912; *Mapa Quinatzin* 1920). Such supplementary tribute would have permitted a larger number of non-agriculturalists to reside in these centers than local resources alone might support.[13]

The data collected here show that unlike population size, territory size is not a reliable indicator of a city-state's political rank (fig. 2.6). Tlalmanalco, at political level 3 had the largest estimated territory (ca. 228 km^2), followed by Xochimilco also at level 3 (with a territory of ca. 164 km^2), and Tenanco at level 4 (143 km^2). Texcoco, politically the most important city-state in the study area, follows, with an area estimated at 117 km^2. Of the higher ranking Acolhua confederation city-states, Tepetlaoztoc had a fairly large territory (93 km^2), but the second-largest Acolhua urban center, Huexotla, had a surprisingly small territory (37 km^2). As stated above, since we know from documents that Texcoco and other major Acolhua centers controlled labor in communities outside their home city-state territories, these figures verify that access to labor rather than land was the basis of political power in the Late Postclassic Basin of Mexico.

Another finding is that populous urban centers do not necessarily predict large rural populations (table 2.2). The city-state with the most populous urban center, Texcoco, has a 62% urban to 38% rural population distribution. Similarly, Huexotla (the second largest center) housed 64% of its total polity population in its urban zone (Brumfiel 1976; Parsons 1971:139). In contrast, the regional surveys of the southern part of the Basin encountered many small rural settlements of less than 50 people, indicating a large, dispersed rural population (Parsons et al. 1982). This is true of Cuitlahuac, for instance, which was located on an island and surrounded by chinampa agricultural sites. Cuitlahuac had an urban-rural population distribution of 47% to 53%. Another extreme example, Tenanco, had no nucleated urban center at all; instead it appears to have had administrative centers that lacked large resident populations (e.g., site Ch-Az-131; Parsons et al. 1982). Other city-states mapped here, however, display a very nucleated settlement pattern. Of Chimalhuacan's total population, 95% lived in its urban center, and 96% of \'s populace lived in its urban center. No clear patterns emerge that characterize urban-rural population distribution among these 15 city-states, and further investigation of land-use and political factors beyond the scope of this study will be necessary to clarify patterns of population distribution in Aztec polities.

Internal Structures of Aztec City-States

By observing the categories of site sizes within individual city-states some insights are gained into the internal operation of these polities. Out of nearly five hundred (492) sites located within the 15 polities in this study, only 17 sites were classified by the archaeological surveys as Large Villages, compared with 46 Small Villages, 115 Hamlets, and 250 Small Hamlets. The Large Village settlement category is defined by the presence of pronounced ceremonial-civic architecture, suggesting administrative functions at such sites. The pronounced absence of settlements in the Chalco-Xochimilco survey region that represent intermediate levels in the site-size classification (Nucleated Large Villages and Dispersed Large Villages; see Parsons et al. 1982) supports the suggestion that administrative activities were conducted principally at city-state urban centers. An absence of elaborate internal settlement hierarchies in the other city-states studied here suggests that most internal administrative and political functions were performed in these city-states' urban centers. The pronounced nucleation of population in some city-state urban centers (e.g., Amecamecan, Chimalhuacan) further supports this conclusion. The internal structures of the city-states examined in this study thus do not display well-developed, many-level hierarchies that can be observed using extant archaeological data, in contrast to the regional picture in which a hierarchy of Late Aztec settlement sizes is clearly present Basin of Mexico as a whole (Blanton 1976b, 1994).

The short distances between urban centers and their hinterland communities give additional support to the argument that many activities within individual city-state units were centrally-conducted. Even though the city-states show diversity in territory shape and size (see note 7), the average distance from urban center to farthest dependent community within these local territories was only 7.1 km (ranging from 2.0 km to 14.5 km). Even considering changes in elevation over which people had to travel, most rural communities were within a few hours walking distance from their political centers. Thus, the majority of a city-state's populace could readily have attended political functions, participated in rituals, worked at the *tlatoani's* palace, delivered tribute, and conducted economic exchanges at the city-state center. Given these relatively short distances there would have been little necessity within individual city-states for additional administrative centers.

Some qualifications must be appended to these findings before closing this discussion. First, the evidence for centralized, rather primate internal organizations in most city-states does not mean that there was no administration in communities outside the city-state centers. Documents report that there were administrators below the level of *tlatoani* in city-states, who organized activities in divisions of the urban centers and in communities outside the urban centers (*Anales de Cuauhtitlan* 1938; Carrasco and Monjarás-Ruiz 1976; Hodge 1984). If village administration was conducted at community leaders' houses (as excavated by Evans [1991]), the regional surveys would not have detected this level of administration because it did not leave remains of civic-ceremonial architecture readily detectable by survey. Nonetheless, the absence of elaborate facilities for administration in the majority of villages argues for centralized use of political resources.

A second qualification is that results based on 15 city-states should not be generalized without empirical study of the internal organization of city-states in other regions of the Basin. Further study may reveal region-specific reasons for the suppression of internal hierarchies in the eastern and southern parts of the Basin, and all-inclusive conclusions must be deferred until a larger number of Late Aztec polities can be compared. Second, the data gathered here pertain to the Basin of Mexico at roughly A.D. 1350-1520, the time when the Aztec empire was at a developed stage. To investigate the emergence and development of this system requires study of Early Aztec polities. Although there is some continuity from the Early Aztec period (A.D. 1150-1350) to Late Aztec times, such as the many cases in which Late Aztec city-state territories expanded around Early Aztec centers, the findings here should not be extended back to Early Aztec times without further research.[14]

DISCUSSION AND CONCLUSIONS

In this paper I have explored methods for combining evidence from documents with archaeological settlement data in order to acquire detailed and consistent information about Aztec political geography, to gain insight into the Late Aztec period regional political structure in the Basin of Mexico, and to obtain data on the internal structures of local political units within the Aztec empire's core zone. First, I defined city-state political units using both archaeological settlement data and ethnohistoric reports of political boundaries and community affiliations. Next, I used these definitions to examine the relationships between polities' positions in the political hierarchy and their total populations, urban populations, urban-rural population distributions, territory sizes, and internal settlement hierarchies.

Comparisons of these attributes across 15 polities showed that some but not all intra-polity measures of size correlate with regional political rank.

Comparisons of the political geography of 15 city-states showed that political rank correlates positively with a city-state's total population. The politically higher ranking Late Aztec city-states contained the most populous urban centers as well as the most populous territories. In contrast, territory size of a city-state is not a reliable predictor of political rank. It appears that the political rank of an urban center was related to factors other than the size of its surrounding territory in imperial times, such as its ability to collect tribute and acquire labor from dependent communities in other city-states, e.g., its population of tribute-payers. Likewise, the patterning of urban-rural population distributions varied. No particular pattern correlated with high or low political rank among the 15 polities compared. The concentration (or lack of concentration) of population in urban centers may be related to non-political factors such as land use traditions as much as to political concerns (see Williams, chap. 3).

The relative absence of secondary civic-ceremonial centers (Large Villages) identified by archaeological surveys in the 15 city-states compared here suggests centralization of political and religious functions at city-state urban centers, irrespective of population distribution. Documentary reports that administrators and elites resided in the city-state urban centers support this conclusion (see Hodge 1984). In the city-states examined here, presence of an internal site size hierarchy did not correlate with political rank.

Earlier in this paper I posed questions regarding the form of internal political and settlement structure characteristic of city-states and to what degree internal city-state organization was comparable to the hierarchically-organized regional system. The archaeological settlement and territory data collected here indicate that Aztec city-states in the eastern and southern parts of the Basin of Mexico generally were characterized by a primate form of settlement and, by inference, that political activity was conducted primarily in the city-state urban centers. The archaeological settlement data for 15 polities parallel documentary evidence that city-state political functions and officials were concentrated in city-state capitals (Hodge 1984, 1994). Elsewhere I have examined political motives for suppression of internal city-state hierarchies by the Aztec empire's rulers and for construction of a regional political hierarchy (Hodge 1984, 1994; see Blanton 1994 for related changes in the economic system). The broad organizational hierarchy of the Aztec empire's core zone (composed of many centers at levels 3 and 4) provided the benefits of hierarchy without the cost of creating and maintaining many levels of administrators and administrative centers (Hodge 1994). Likewise, use of existing city-state internal hierarchies, consisting of a principal political center where most political activities were carried out and which administered a territory of limited size with few subsidiary administrative centers, permitted control of large populations using few new administrative structures.

The data collected here support the generalizations that the Aztec imperial period political structure rested to a large extent on the pre-existing organizations of city-states and their subordinate communities, and that new imperial administrative structures more often concerned the imperial tribute system (see Berdan et al. 1994). In sum, although the regional Late Aztec organizational pattern was a hierarchically-organized central-place system, the internal structures of the 15 city-states suggest that political functions were concentrated at city-state urban centers.

This study demonstrates that combining textual and archaeological data on Aztec political geography can produce new perspectives on the infrastructure of the Aztec empire.[15] The analyses of documentary accounts described here produce details that allow Aztec political boundaries to be approximated and archaeological sites to be associated with specific city-state political units. By dividing regional archaeological settlement data into city-state territories, systematic comparison of Aztec imperial period political units can produce new perspectives for interpreting the political structure of the Aztec empire's core zone.

ACKNOWLEDGMENTS

I would like to thank Frances Berdan, Elizabeth Brumfiel, Richard Diehl, Janine Gasco, Cynthia Heath-Smith, Joyce Marcus, Michael Smith, and Barbara Williams for providing comments on various drafts of this paper. Editorial back-up was provided by Craig Leach and Paula Garcia, Research Assistants at the University of Houston Clear Lake. Thanks go to artist R. Richard Rogers, who prepared figures 2.1-2.4. Archival research for this paper was supported by the University of Houston Clear Lake Faculty Research and Support Fund, and I am grateful to the staff of the Archivo General de la Nación, Mexico, for permission to study maps and documents in the Archivo.

NOTES

1.   The geographic scale of this study is that of the basic political unit larger than the individual community in the Basin of Mexico during Aztec times: the city-state (Bray 1972; Hodge 1984). A city-state was called *altepetl* in Nahuatl, a term including the concepts "water" and "hill", or the necessities for a community's existence (Karttunen 1983). City-states were political units governed by an hereditary ruler, or *tlatoani*. They were territorial units consisting of an urban center and its dependent settlements (see Smith and Hodge, chap. 1; Hicks 1986; Licate 1980).

2. The Late Aztec period, also called Late Horizon (Sanders et al. 1979), dates from approximately A.D. 1350 to 1520. Archaeologists distinguish this period from the Early Aztec or Second Intermediate Phase III (Sanders et al. 1979) period, A.D. 1150-1350, on the basis of a change in pottery styles (Vaillant 1938). Ethnohistoric studies, however, can distinguish a pre-Imperial period, extending from the initial foundation of Postclassic settlements in the Basin of Mexico, from an Aztec Imperial period, dating from formation of the Triple Alliance Empire in A.D. 1428-1430 to the Spanish Conquest in A.D. 1521 (see Sanders et al. 1979; Vaillant 1938). As noted in Smith and Hodge (chap. 1) archaeologists must refine chronologies for material culture in the Basin of Mexico in order to securely distinguish pre-imperial and imperial period activities.

3. Lists of places conquered by particular centers and/or lists of their political dependencies sometimes conflict. Since such lists often were generated in different locations, there is always a possibility that chroniclers of specific communities exaggerated their polity's extent or importance. Lists of dependencies may conflict also because documents refer to different times and circumstances. In the case of conflicting reports, the researcher must judge from the number of independent sources represented and the possible biases of the writers, which source to use for evidence or whether to omit conflicting evidence. Another category of document regarded as problematic for study of prehispanic territories is the "primordial titles" or *titulos primordiales* documents. Written to defend Indian communities in Spanish courts, most extant copies date to the late seventeenth century or later (Lockhart 1982:370-372). Careful textual analysis and comparison with other sources are necessary to determine whether to extend the information on town property in these documents back to Aztec times.

4. The geographic scale of some documentary sources limits their usefulness for mapping city state political territories. Aztec imperial tribute lists (Barlow 1949; *Codex Mendoza* 1992; Scholes and Adams 1957) are not appropriate for this study because these tax districts had different boundaries from political units in the Basin of Mexico. In addition, data in intra-community censuses on the locations of fields and houses are too detailed in scale for use here. The data derived here should complement studies encompassing larger geographic scales (Berdan, chap. 11; Berdan et al 1994; Smith, chap. 12) as well as studies of the internal organization of individual communities (e.g., Williams and Harvey 1988; Williams 1989; Williams, chap. 3).

5. The regional survey site categories for the Late Aztec period include: Supra-regional centers (with monumental public architecture and 25,000+ residents); Provincial centers (with distinct elite architecture, well-defined public architecture, and 1000-10,000 residents); Large and Small Nucleated Villages (concentrated populations of 500-1000+ and 100-500, respectively, but minimal public architecture); Large and Small Dispersed Villages (with populations of 500-1000 and 100-500, respectively, and light surface remains); Hamlets (20-100 people; no public architecture); Small Hamlets (20 or fewer residents), and Isolated Ceremonial Centers (no permanent occupants) (Parsons 1971:21-25; Sanders et al. 1979:55).

6. The repetitive nature of Nahuatl place-names presents occasional problems in differentiating and locating communities with the same name. Often such communities can be located if the source describing them includes the general region in which the community is located. Communities that have a Nahuatl name in common can some-

times be distinguished in colonial texts because they have different saints' names attached to their Nahuatl names.

7.   Mapping 15 Aztec territories using the direct historical approach revealed several different categories of settlement systems in the area studied. One typical city-state settlement system encompasses an identifiable geographic unit such as a valley (see also the discussion of the territory of Amecamecan in Hodge 1984:33-40). A second category is a vertical strip running from lake shore to piedmont (see also Carrasco 1980). The three polities composing the central portion of the Acolhua state (Texcoco, Huexotla, Coatlinchan) exhibit this form. Others flank a hillside (Tepetlaoztoc, Ixtapalucan, and Chimalhuacan, for example). Most difficult to delineate were city-state territories located around and in lakes Chalco and Xochimilco. The closely-packed, small sites in the lakes and lakeshore zone do not form discrete clusters, nor are they well documented. To discover the divisions between polity territories there, archival records of early colonial land disputes were consulted. When even these sources failed to describe the affiliations of settlements, archaeological sites were assigned to political territories hypothetically through the use of established geographic measures of approximating boundaries, such as equidistance between centers (Hodder and Orton 1976:59-60). Since not all archaeological sites could be connected directly through documentary references with prehispanic or colonial political centers, the boundaries developed by this method are tentative rather than precise reconstructions and may be altered by new documentary or archaeological evidence. Here they serve as models developed for comparing polities.

8.   Coatepec's existence as a polity has some time depth, since chronicles state that Coatepec was part of Xolotl's political sphere after the collapse of Tollan (Tula) (Offner 1983:25) and that Coatepec had a ruler contemporary with Quinatzin of Texcoco in the mid-1300s (Alva Ixtlilxochitl 1975-1977:v.1:310; Offner 1983:34). Based on documentary reports and archaeological survey data, it appears that Coatepec served as a buffer state between the Chalca confederation to the south and the Acolhua confederation to the north (Parsons 1971; Parsons et al. 1982; Paso y Troncoso 1905-1906). By imperial times (after A.D. 1430 and before 1521), Coatepec had become part of the Acolhua regional state, and Coatepec's hereditary ruler was replaced by administrators appointed by the Triple Alliance rulers Motecuhzoma and Nezahualcoyotl (Alva Ixtlilxochitl 1975-1977:v.2:89-90; Gibson 1964:43; Paso y Troncoso 1905-1906:51-53).

9.   It should be noted that a map prepared for a court case might be biased and therefore not a reliable source. But since the communities depicted on the 1574 map of Coatepec appear to have been placed on it for purposes of demonstrating the location of lands and were not part of the legal dispute, one can assume there would have been no reason for the painter to have intentionally distorted the location of *cabeceras, estancias,* roads, or other details on this map that were not directly relevant to the lands under dispute.

10.   The road glossed *"el camino de Tezcuco para Chalco"* that runs through the settlement on the *Relación Geográfica* map appears to be a different road, likely the one that today goes from Coatepec to Acuautla and on to Ixtapaluca. Alternatively its placement may be a result of the overall distortion of this map's western border; note that the distance from Coatepec to the lakeshore is distorted on the *Relación Geográfica* map (Acuña 1984-1987:v.6:*Pintura de Coatepec*).

11. The archaeological estimate of Coatepec's population is based on the sum of the populations of all the sites assigned to the city-state's territory. Estimating the populations of Aztec sites, such as Coatepec, that are nearly covered by modern urban centers presents special problems (Parsons 1971:22-28; Parsons et al. 1982:61-71, 237-240; Sanders et al. 1979:34-40, 54-55, 60-65). For this reason, many sites' populations are expressed in potential minimums and maximums in the survey reports (Blanton 1972; Parsons 1971; Parsons et al. 1982). In this study the maximum population estimates are used (Parsons et al. 1983); readers interested in the full range of potential urban versus rural population distributions should consult the original survey reports for both minimum and maximum urban population estimates.

The total population figure derived from the sum of archaeological sites in Coatepec's territory differs wildly from the Late Prehispanic population figure of more than 10,000 reported in the *Relación Geográfica* (Acuña 1984-1987:v.6:137). It is possible that the informants for this document exaggerated, or that they were referring to Coatepec's later Colonial period territory, which extended beyond its Aztec period boundaries (Gerhard 1972:76-78).

The archaeological population estimate for Coatepec obtained here—3210 people— is 18% lower than an estimate of 3947 based on a combination of population counts of sixteenth century tax districts and twentieth century judicial districts' populations (Sanders 1970:414). The Basin of Mexico Survey reports, however, estimate that erosion and other destructive elements have resulted in a ca. 20% loss of sites observed by archaeological survey (Parsons et al. 1982:70; Sanders et al. 1979:38, 51). This additional 20% would give Coatepec a maximum population based on archaeological and ethnohistoric data of 3850, close to but still slightly lower than the earlier document-based estimate of 3947 (Sanders 1970:414). The document-based estimate (Sanders 1970) may also differ from the one derived here for the Late Aztec period political territory because the sixteenth century tax district for Coatepec had larger boundaries (see Gerhard 1972). The method of combining archaeological sites and Aztec period boundary data presented here should replicate Late Aztec political territories more closely in many areas than colonial tax documentation. Also, because they follow epidemics and subsequent episodes of depopulation, population figures from colonial documents may require adjustment to more accurately reflect Late Aztec levels (Sanders 1970; see Smith, chap. 13).

12. Since no attempt was made to assign all geographic space to city-states, the total size of the territories of the city-states included here does not equal the size of the archaeological survey zones. These figures also differ because some political territories estimated here include some unsurveyed areas, particularly within the Texcoco zone where unsurveyed strips are interspersed between surveyed areas (Parsons 1971).

13. Study of the carrying capacity of each city-state territory—an endeavor outside the scope of this essay—would be the next logical step to establishing further which city-state centers could have subsisted on local resources and which could not.

14. Estimation of Early Aztec polity boundaries involves additional attention to historical events since documents contain evidence of some changes in political boundaries prior to the Late Aztec period (e.g., Chimalpahin 1965:173-174; Gibson 1964:14-15; Parsons et al. 1982:81). Documents report cases of discontinuity in Early Aztec city-state boundaries due to fission or defection of communities from one city-state or

confederation to another. Since these incidents seem exceptional enough to have been noted in documentary accounts, it seems likely that significant changes in community affiliations from Early Aztec to Late Aztec times can be identified from textual sources. Among the city-states studied here no examples were encountered of communities changing affiliations in the Late Aztec period, though the confederation boundaries changed during Early Aztec times when entire city-states changed confederation alliance as a result of conquests or other military actions (see Parsons et al. 1982:75-92). The most dramatic change in the study area's political boundaries concerns Chalco Atenco, a city-state center during the Early Aztec period, whose elites abandoned Chalco Atenco and fled to Tlalmanalco during the years after A.D. 1430 and up to A.D. 1465 when the Triple Alliance sought to defeat the Chalca city-states (in the area studied here, Tlalmanalco, Amecamecan, Tenanco, and Chalco Atenco; see Chimalpahin 1965; Schroeder 1991).

In other areas of the Basin, it should be noted, study of Late Aztec city-states as discrete geographic entities using the methods described here is more problematic than in the area included in this study. For example, in the Teotihuacan area, dependencies of city-states were geographically so intermixed by the Acolhua state that study of city-states as distinct geographic units there is more complicated (Evans 1980; Gibson 1964:46).

15. The use of ethnohistoric data to assign archaeological sites to the political units to which they belonged produces information that can be extended to investigations of economic activities in the Aztec empire's core zone. The approximations of political territories derived using the methods described here are being employed for comparing polity boundaries to geographic concentrations of ceramics in order to investigate spatial relationships between exchange systems, production practices, and political units (Hodge and Minc 1990; Hodge et al. 1992; Minc et al., chap. 6). Factors not included in these comparisons (for example, the presence of resident artisans, traders, or markets in individual city-state centers), which may be measured by future and ongoing archaeological research, will also likely prove important for developing a comprehensive view of the Late Aztec regional system.

REFERENCES CITED

Acuña, René (editor)
  1984-1987 *Relaciones Geográficas del siglo XVI: México.* 9 vols. Universidad Nacional Autónoma de México, Mexico City.
Alden, John
  1975 A Reconstruction of Toltec Period Political Units in the Valley of Mexico. In *Transformations: Mathematical Approaches to Culture Change,* edited by Colin Renfrew and Kenneth L. Cooke, pp. 169-200. Academic Press, New York.
Alva Ixtlilxochitl, Fernando de
  1975-1977 *Obras históricas.* Edited by Edmundo O'Gorman. 2 vols. Universidad Nacional Autónoma de México, Mexico City.

Anales de Cuauhtitlan

1938 *Die Geschichte der Königreiche von Colhuacan und Mexiko.* Translated by Walter Lehmann. Quellenwerke zur alten Geschichte Amerikas aufgezeichnet in den Sprachen der Eingeborenen, 1. Kohlhammer, Stuttgart (reprinted 1974).

Anderson, Arthur J.O., Frances F. Berdan, and James Lockhart

1976 *Beyond the Codices: The Nahua View of Colonial Mexico.* University of California Press, Berkeley.

Barlow, Robert H.

1949 *The Extent of the Empire of the Culhua Mexica.* Ibero-Americana No. 28. University of California Press, Berkeley.

Berdan, Frances F., Richard E. Blanton, Elizabeth H. Boone, Mary G. Hodge, Michael E. Smith, and Emily Umberger

1994 *Aztec Imperial Strategies.* Dumbarton Oaks, Washington, D.C. In press.

Berry, Brian J. L., Edgar C. Conkling, and D. Michael Ray

1976 *The Geography of Economic Systems.* Prentice Hall, Englewood Cliffs.

Blanton, Richard E.

1972 *Prehispanic Settlement Patterns of the Ixtapalapa Region, Mexico.* Occasional Papers No. 6, Department of Anthropology, Pennsylvania State University. University Park.

1976a Anthropological Studies of Cities. *Annual Review of Anthropology* 5:249-264.

1976b The Role of Symbiosis and Adaptation and Sociocultural Change in the Valley of Mexico. In *The Valley of Mexico,* edited by Eric R. Wolf, pp. 181-202. University of New Mexico Press, Albuquerque.

1994 The Aztec Market System and the Growth of Empire. In *Aztec Imperial Strategies,* by Frances F. Berdan, Richard E. Blanton, Elizabeth H. Boone, Mary G. Hodge, Michael E. Smith, and Emily Umberger. Dumbarton Oaks, Washington, D.C. In press.

Bray, Warwick

1972 The City-State in Central Mexico at the Time of the Spanish Conquest. *Journal of Latin American Studies* 4:161-185.

Brumfiel, Elizabeth M.

1976 *Specialization and Exchange at the Late Postclassic (Aztec) Community of Huexotla, Mexico.* Ph.D. dissertation, Department of Anthropology, University of Michigan. University Microfilms, Ann Arbor.

Carrasco, Pedro

1980 La aplicabilidad a Mesoamérica del modelo Andino de verticalidad. *Revista de la Universidad Complutense, Madrid* 28:247-243.

Carrasco, Pedro, and Jesús Monjarás-Ruiz (editors)

1976 *Colección de documentos sobre Coyoacan.* Vol. 1. Visita del Oidor Gómez De Santillán al Pueblo de Coyoacan y su Sujeto Tacubaya en el Año 1553. Instituto Nacional de Antropología e Historia, Mexico City.

Catálogo de ilustraciones
1979   *Catálogo de ilustraciones.* Vol. 3. Centro de Información Gráfica del Archivo General de la Nación, Mexico City.

Chimalpahin Quauhtlehuanitzin, Don Francisco de San Antón Muñón
1960   *Das Geschichtswerke des Domingo de Muñon Chimalpahin Quauhtlehuanitzin.* Quellenkritische Studien zur frühindianisches Geschichte Mexikos. Beiträge zur mittelamerikanischen Völkerkunde 5. Hamburgishen Museums für Völkerkunde und Vorgeschichte, Hamburg.

1965   *Relaciones originales de Chalco Amequemecan escritas por Don Francisco de San Antón Muñón Chimalpahin Cuauhtlehuanitzin.* Edited and translated by Sylvia Rendón. Fondo de Cultura Económica, Mexico City.

Cline, Howard F. (editor)
1973-1975   *Guide to Ethnohistorical Sources.* Handbook of Middle American Indians, vols. 12-15. Robert Wauchope, general editor. University of Texas Press, Austin.

Codex Mendoza
1992   *The Codex Mendoza.* Edited by Frances F. Berdan and Patricia Reiff Anawalt. 4 vols. University of California Press, Berkeley and Los Angeles.

Códice Kingsborough
1912   *Códice Kingsborough. Memorial de los indios de Tepetlaoztoc.* Edited by Francisco del Paso y Troncoso. Hauser y Menet, Madrid.

Colín, Mario
1966   *Indice de documentos relativos a las pueblos del Estado de México, AGN.* Ramo de Tierras. Archivo General de la Nación, Mexico City.

Durán, Fray Diego
1967   *Historia de las Indias de Nueva España e Islas de la Tierra Firme.* Edited by Angel María Garibay K. 2 vols. Editorial Porrúa, Mexico City.

Evans, Susan T.
1980   *A Settlement System Analysis of the Teotihuacan Region, Mexico, A.D. 1350-1520.* Ph.D. dissertation, Department of Anthropology, Pennsylvania State University. University Microfilms, Ann Arbor.

1991   Architecture and Authority in an Aztec Village: Form and Function of the Tecpan. In: *Land and Politics in the Valley of Mexico: A Two-Thousand Year Perspective,* edited by H.R. Harvey, pp. 63-92. University of New Mexico Press, Albuquerque.

Evans, Susan T., and Peter Gould
1982   Settlement Models in Archaeology. *Journal of Anthropological Archaeology* 1:275-304.

Gerhard, Peter
1970   A Method for Reconstructing Precolumbian Political Boundaries in Central Mexico. *Journal de la Société de Américanistes* n.s. 59:27-41.

1972   *Guide to the Historical Geography of New Spain.* Cambridge University Press, Cambridge.

Gibson, Charles
1964 *The Aztecs Under Spanish Rule: A History of the Indians of the Valley of Mexico, 1519-1810.* Stanford University Press, Stanford.

Gorenflo, L. J., and Nathan Gale
1990 Mapping Regional Settlement in Information Space. *Journal of Anthropological Archaeology* 9:240-274.

Hicks, Frederic
1982 Tetzcoco in the Early 16th Century: The State, the City, and the Calpolli. *American Ethnologist* 9:230-249.

1986 Prehispanic Background of Colonial Political and Economic Organization in Central Mexico. In *Ethnohistory,* edited by Ronald Spores, pp. 35-54. Supplement to the Handbook of Middle American Indians, vol. 4, Victoria Bricker, general editor. University of Texas Press, Austin.

Hodder, Ian, and Clive Orton
1976 *Spatial Analysis in Archaeology.* Cambridge University Press, Cambridge.

Hodge, Mary G.
1984 *Aztec City-States.* Memoirs No. 18. Museum of Anthropology, University of Michigan. Ann Arbor.

1994 Political Organization of the Central Provinces. In *Aztec Imperial Strategies,* by Frances F. Berdan, Richard E. Blanton, Elizabeth H. Boone, Mary G. Hodge, Michael E. Smith, and Emily Umberger. Dumbarton Oaks, Washington, D.C. In press.

Hodge, Mary G., and Leah D. Minc
1990 The Spatial Patterning of Aztec Ceramics: Implications for Prehispanic Exchange Systems in the Valley of Mexico. *Journal of Field Archaeology* 17:415-437.

1991 *Aztec-Period Ceramic Distribution and Exchange Systems.* Final Report to the National Science Foundation for Grant #BNS-8704177.

Hodge, Mary G., Hector Neff, M. James Blackman, and Leah D. Minc
1992 Ceramic Production in the Aztec Empire: A Compositional Perspective. In: *Chemical Characterization of Ceramic Pastes in Archaeology,* edited by Hector Neff, pp. 203-220. Prehistory Press, Madison.

Karttunen, Frances
1983 *An Analytical Dictionary of Nahuatl.* University of Texas Press, Austin.

Lemoine Villicaña, Ernesto (editor)
1961 Visita, congregación y mapa de Amecameca de 1599. *Boletín del Archivo General de la Nación* (Mexico City) Segunda Serie 2:5-46.

Licate, Jack A.
1980 The Forms of Aztec Territorial Organization. *Geoscience and Man* 21:27-45.

Linné, Sigvald
1948 *El valle y la ciudad de México en 1550.* Publication No. 9, n.s. The Ethnographical Museum of Sweden, Stockholm.

Lockhart, James

1982   Views of Corporate Self and History in Some Valley of Mexico Towns: Late Seventeenth and Eighteenth Centuries. In *The Inca and Aztec States, 1400-1800,* edited by George A. Collier, Renato A. Rosaldo, and John D. Wirth, pp. 367-393. Academic Press, New York.

Mapa Quinatzin

1920   Mapa Quinatzin. In: *Sources and Authenticity of the History of the Ancient Mexicans,* edited by Paul Radin, pp. 38-41. University of California Publications in American Archaeology and Ethnology 17(1):1-150.

Marcus, Joyce

1984   Mesoamerican Territorial Boundaries: Reconstructions from Archaeology and Hieroglyphic Writing. *Archaeological Review from Cambridge* 3:48-62.

Motolinía, Toribio de Benavente

1950   *Motolinía's History of the Indians of New Spain.* Translated and edited by Frances Borgia Steck. Academy of American Franciscan Society, Washington, D.C.

Offner, Jerome

1983   *Law and Politics in Aztec Texcoco.* Cambridge University Press, Cambridge.

Parsons, Jeffery R.

1971   *Prehispanic Settlement Patterns of the Texcoco Region, Mexico.* Memoirs No. 3. Museum of Anthropology, University of Michigan, Ann Arbor.

1974   The Development of a Prehistoric Complex Society: A Regional Perspective from the Valley of Mexico. *Journal of Field Archaeology* 1:81-108.

Parsons, Jeffrey R., Elizabeth M. Brumfiel, Mary H. Parsons, and David J. Wilson

1982   *Prehispanic Settlement Patterns in the Southern Valley of Mexico: The Chalco-Xochimilco Regions.* Memoirs No. 14. Museum of Anthropology, University of Michigan, Ann Arbor.

Parsons, Jeffrey R., Keith W. Kintigh, and Susan A. Gregg

1983   *Archaeological Settlement Pattern Data from the Chalco, Xochimilco, Ixtapalapa, Texcoco and Zumpango Regions, Mexico.* Research Reports in Archaeology, Contribution No. 9. Technical Reports No. 14. Museum of Anthropology, University of Michigan, Ann Arbor.

Paso y Troncoso, Francisco del (editor)

1905-1906   *Papeles de Nueva España.* Segunda serie, Geografía y Estadística. Vol. 6. Sucesores de Rivadeneyra, Madrid.

Sanders, William T.

1970   The Population of the Teotihuacan Valley, the Basin of Mexico, and the Central Mexican Symbiotic Region in the 16th Century. In *The Teotihuacan Valley Project, Final Report,* by William T. Sanders, Anton Kovar, Thomas Charlton, and Richard Diehl, pp. 385-452. Occasional Papers in Anthropology No. 3. Department of Anthropology, Pennsylvania State University, University Park.

Sanders, William T., Jeffrey R. Parsons, and Robert S. Santley

 1979 *The Basin of Mexico: Ecological Processes in the Evolution of a Civilization.* Academic Press, New York.

Scholes, France V., and Eleanor B. Adams

 1957 *Información sobre los tributos que los indios pagaban a Moctezuma, año de 1554.* Documentos para la historia de México colonial, vol. 4. José Porrúa, Mexico City.

Schroeder, Susan

 1991 *Chimalpahin and the Kingdoms of Chalco.* University of Arizona Press, Tucson.

Smith, Michael E.

 1979 The Aztec Marketing System and Settlement Patterns in The Valley of Mexico: A Central Place Analysis. *American Antiquity* 52:37-54.

 1987 Archaeology and the Aztec Economy: The Social Scientific Use of Archaeological Data. *Social Science History* 11:238-259.

Vaillant, George

 1938 A Correlation of Archaeological and Historical Sequences in the Valley of Mexico. *American Anthropologist* 40:535-573.

Williams, Barbara

 1989 Contact Period Rural Overpopulation in the Basin of Mexico: Carrying Capacity Models Tested with Documentary Data. *American Antiquity* 54:715-732.

Williams, Barbara J., and H. R. Harvey

 1988 Content, Provenience, and Significance of the *Codex Vergara* and the *Códice de Santa María Asunción. American Antiquity* 53:337-351.

3

The Archaeological Signature of Local Level Polities in Tepetlaoztoc

Barbara J. Williams

During the Late Aztec period the rural landscape in the Basin of Mexico was populated by largely agricultural, peasant *(macehualtin)* communities, many of which did not survive the population crash that followed soon after contact with the Spaniards and the adverse effects of colonial rule. Because historical continuity of peasant settlement was disrupted in the aftermath of the Spanish Conquest, understanding the character of the indigenous landscape relies heavily upon interpretation of archaeological materials. Whether the archaeological record adequately reflects rural settlement organization and the population size that existed during the contact period is an important question. The most direct method for addressing this issue is to analyze archaeological findings in conjunction with ethnohistorical sources, but meaningful assessment demands high resolution data sets, both written and archaeological. Such data exist for Tepetlaoztoc, a village on the lower piedmont of Acolhuacan in the eastern Basin of Mexico.

In this paper I use the ethnohistorical record on population and land-holdings to predict the distribution of surface archaeological remains, which is then compared to surveyed occupational debris. The results provide a measure of archaeological preservation and a better understanding of the archaeological expression of local level polities in the contact-period rural countryside.

THE DATA

In the late 1960s Jeffrey Parsons directed an archaeological surface survey of the Texcoco Region. He found it difficult to determine archaeologically discrete settlement sites for the Late Aztec period in Northern Acolhuacan, and concluded that much of the area was occupied by a dispersed rural population. This was particularly true of Aztec Tepetlaoztoc, one of the important *señoríos* and a primary regional center of Acolhuacan (see Smith and Hodge, chap. 1, fig. 1.1). The site (Tx-A-24) encompasses 450 ha with an estimated Late Aztec population of 6750 to 13,500 (Parsons 1971:161). Here, as in northern Acolhuacan in general, occupational remains indicated that population was spread "somewhat more continuously and evenly in the form of intermittent occupational clusters within broad settlement bands on the Lower Piedmont" (Parsons 1971:220).

Complementing the surface archaeological record for a portion of Aztec Tepetlaoztoc, as defined by Parsons, are population and cadastral records by household and locality contained in the *Códice de Santa María Asunción* (Biblioteca Nacional de México, Ms. 1497bis). The data in the Asunción codex reveal great spatial complexity of rural settlement within a relatively small area of approximately 230 ha of agricultural land. While specific to only one of several wards (sing. *tlaxilacalli*) in Tepetlaoztoc, the records reveal a sub-*tlaxilacalli* settlement pattern and territorial organization probably typical of Acolhuacan in general.

Drawn ca. 1540-1544 in the style of prehispanic records, the codex depicts households and their landholdings residing in 11 named sub-divisions of what in the codex is called the "tlaxilacalli" of Santa María Asunción. Records for another settlement located within the *tlaxilacalli* are found in the *Codex Vergara* (Bibliothèque Nacionale de Paris, Ms. Mex. 37-39), a document similar to the Asunción codex in format and content. Data for this community are included in the present analysis, bringing the total to 12 localities, ranging in size from 6 to 82 households.

The codex provides three sets of information for each locality. Locality records begin with a household population census. A second section, glossed *milcocoli,* lists household landholdings showing perimeter measurements and the soil type of each field (fig. 3.1a). In a third section, glossed *tlahuelmatli,* the landholdings of each household are drawn again, but here, instead of perimeter measures, the area of each field is recorded, again with soil type (fig. 3.1b). A detailed description of the codex content is found in Harvey and Williams (1988).

Because the Asunción codex contains cadastral registers, it is amenable to direct statistical analyses at the individual, household, locality, and *tlaxilacalli* levels. A transformation of the data is required, however, to reconstruct the spatial organization of the communities to compare with the archaeological record.

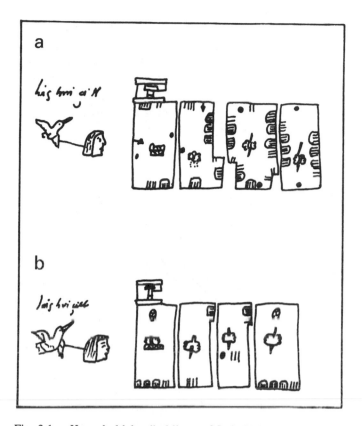

Fig. 3.1.   Household landholdings of Luis Huiçitl, *Códice de Santa María Asunción*. *a,* landholdings depicted in the *milcocoli* convention with field perimeters and soil types (f.9r). *b,* landholdings depicted in the *tlahuelmatli* convention with field areas and soil types (f.18v).

MAPPING THE TLAXILACALLI SUB-DIVISIONS

The external boundaries of the *tlaxilacalli* of Santa María Asunción are recorded in text on several folios of the codex. Many of the boundary toponyms are extant and correspond to those of the Barrio of Asunción in modern Tepetlaoztoc. The location of the sub-*tlaxilacalli* communities, therefore, is constrained within a known geographic area (fig. 3.2; Williams 1991). On the other hand, only a few place names and toponyms relating to the specific location of the sub-divisions have survived and indirect evidence must be used to reconstruct some locations.

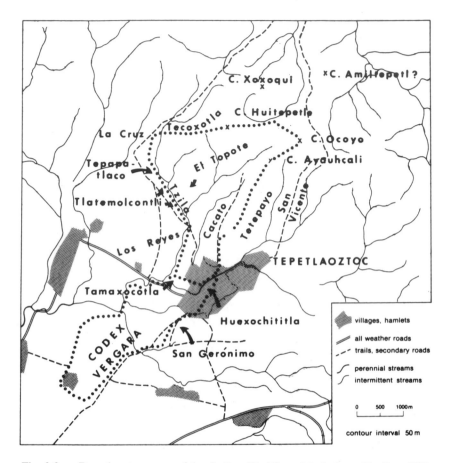

Fig. 3.2.   Boundary toponyms of the *tlaxilacalli* of Santa María Asunción (from Williams 1991:192). Dotted lines mark the land area recorded in the *Codex Vergara* (south) and in the *Códice de Santa María Asunción* (north). The latter is enlarged in figure 3.3.

Transformation of the cadastral registers into a *tlaxilacalli* settlement map requires an important assumption, that is, that households censused in a specific, named locality also had their landholdings in the same locality. Contemporary land tenure patterns in rural communities suggest that this assumption might be invalid, because fragmentation and dispersal of milpas (fields) commonly occurs among peasant landholdings due to inheritance and purchase. The record also shows nobility in prehispanic times to have had fragmented properties located in all parts of the Basin and beyond. Absentee ownership or usufruct, however, in practice may have been uncommon within *macehualtin* jurisdictions because of usufruct rules such as those described by Zorita (1963:107-108). Further, if household landholdings were located in a *paraje* (named tract of land) other than that of the residential site, then the *paraje* name probably would have been recorded following the indigenous convention as seen, for example, in the *Humboldt Fragment 8* (Seler 1904) or the *Oztoticpac Lands Map* (Harvey 1991). With perhaps one exception, *paraje* names do not appear in the Asunción codex. Several texts in the codex imply that the named sub-divisions encompassed both the household residences and their landholdings: "Here end the lands of the Huiznahuac people" (f. 31v) and "Here end the lands that belong to us the people of Tlancomolco" (f. 39v). Also, soil types of the agricultural fields show some patterning by locality, supporting the assumption that *tlaxilacalli* sub-divisions were spatial entities and that the households and their landholdings were located in the same policy.

Location of the *tlaxilacalli* head town, Cuauhtepuztitla, is unambiguous because some barrio residents still recall the place name (now Cuauhtepoztla) and the *paraje* boundaries. In this *paraje,* overlying a prehispanic structure (Tlatel 398), are the ruins of what informants say was once the principal barrio church. For the other, dependent settlements, only two place names have survived: modern el Topote, equated with Topotitla, a hamlet censused in the *Codex Vergara* but whose place glyph shows it to pertain spatially to Cuauhtepuztitla, and modern Cuixtla, perhaps a corruption of Cuitlahuac. In the absence of other surviving community place names, the territorial extent of each community was reconstructed by aggregating the amount of household agricultural land shown in the *tlahuelmatli* registers and converting Indian measures *(tlalquahuitl)* into hectares.[1] These areas then were plotted on an aerial photograph, taking into account codex soil types and soils today, physical features, field patterns, and the few fragmentary locational references noted in the codex texts. For example, the texts state that Tlancomolco bounds Topoian/ Topotitla (extant). Tlantozcac lies on Cerro Ayaucali (extant). And, going up and over the hill called Tzautepetl (extant), to the Cuevas (extant), across the barranca, one comes to Zapotlan. The least certain locations are found in the southern part of the ward (Chiauhtenco, Chiauhtlan, Tlaltecahuacan, Antecontla, and Conzotlan).

Internal territorial boundaries were drawn so as to encompass the amount of agricultural land recorded for each settlement. Limitations of scale (approximately 1:13,500) precluded mapping to an accuracy within one or two hectares per community. Allowance for nonagricultural land was not made in plotting settlement territories because the codex lacks explicit data on such land and because nonagricultural land would have been probably on the order of only one to two hectares per community, below the resolution of the air photo. As reconstructed, the territorial limits of the 12 settlements encompass nearly all land which has vestiges of agricultural activity or is currently under cultivation in the Barrio of Asunción.

ARCHAEOLOGICAL PRESERVATION RATE OF DOMESTIC STRUCTURES

The lands of the *tlaxilacalli* of Santa María Asunción fall within the southeastern sector of Aztec Tepetlaoztoc. On the published site map (Parsons 1971:100), enlarged here with reconstructed settlement perimeters superimposed (fig. 3.3), small dots denote occupational debris and large dots are numbered mounds. All but two mounds were identified by Parsons as domestic structures. Occupational debris occurs within all but three *tlaxilacalli* sub-divisions, but preservation of domestic structures has been very poor, at least on the surface. For example, Cuauhtepuztitla had 64 contact-period houses represented by only 4 domestic mounds today; Tlantozcac had 11 houses represented by vestiges of only 2 mounds; Tlanchiuhca, 17 houses represented by 4 mounds; none of the houses in 8 communities appeared in the surface survey (23 in Tlancomolco; 6 in Topotitla; 5 in Cuitlahuac; 8 in Conzotlan; 5 in Tlaltecahuacan; 7 in Chiauhtla; 14 in Antecontla; 7 in Chiauhtenco). Overall, of the 169 houses in the *tlaxilacalli* (based on the *tlahuelmatli* listing), vestiges of only .06 % are identifiable on the surface.

Several factors account for the poor preservation of Aztec period domestic structures. Harvey (1986:108) has shown that in the epidemic of 1545-1548, population in Santa María Asunción declined by 71 percent. The decline in every community was greater than 50 percent. The smaller communities effectively disappeared: Tlanchiuhca and Conzotlan, suffered 81 percent mortality; Tlantozcac, 84 percent mortality; up to 97 percent mortality in Cuitlahuac. Depopulation because of epidemics and out-migration, as Indians fled the cruelties of the *encomenderos*, would have caused abandonment of erosion control in the barrancas and on the terraces, leading to upper slope erosion of soil and archaeological materials and concurrent sedimentation and burial of material on the lower slopes. Also, early introduction of livestock in Tepetlaoztoc by both Spaniards and Indians very likely accelerated the processes of erosion, sedimentation, and site destruction. Unlike other zones in the Basin, modern settlement

Fig. 3.3. Southeastern portion of Aztec Tepetlaoztoc site map. The map shows reconstructed settlement sub-divisions within the *tlaxilacalli* of Santa María Asunción. Large dots are mounds; small dots, occupational debris. Contour lines are impressionistic (after Parsons 1971:100). Hachures delimit community boundaries. Occupational debris is more scattered than predicted by area in house gardens in communities marked "M" and less scattered than predicted in those marked "L." Numbers following placenames indicate percent of agricultural land in house gardens: 1=Cuauhtepuztitla, 66%; 2=Antecontla, 59%; 3=Chiauhtenco, 36%; 4=Chiauhtlan, 38%; 5=Tlaltecahuacan, 26%; 6=Conzotlan, 66%; 7=Cuitlahuac, 33%; 8=Tlancolmolco,38%; 9=Topotitla, 27%; 10=Zapotlan, 18%; 11=Tlanchiuhca, 37%; 12=Tlantozcac, 45%.

is juxtaposed to a lesser degree over contact-period occupation sites. Nevertheless, lack of surface material remains on the gentle slopes in the southern part of the ward (Chiauhtenco, Chiauhtlan, Antecontla) may be ascribed both to sedimentation and to continuous occupation in sections of this zone. Also, further site destruction near Tlancomolco has occurred recently due to government efforts to reforest and to reclaim *tepetate,* an indurated subsoil exposed to the surface by erosion.

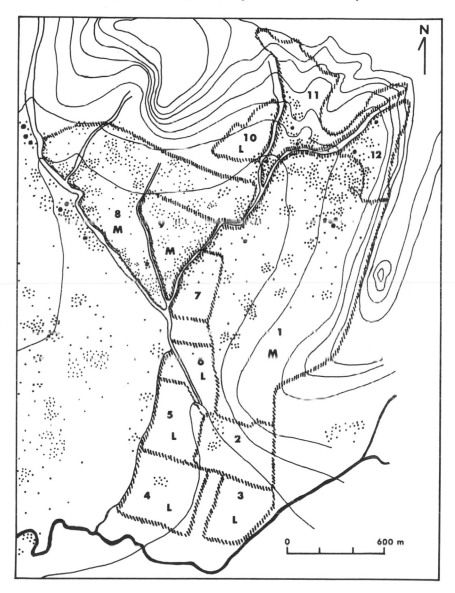

HORTICULTURAL STRATEGIES, SETTLEMENT STRUCTURE, AND ARCHAEOLOGICAL REMAINS

The poorly-preserved domestic architectural remains thus reveal little about the size and structure of sub-*tlaxilacalli* settlement of Santa María Asunción. Fortunately the drawings of *milcocoli* fields in the codex permitted me to predict where domestic structures might have been located and to interpret the surface scatter.

Many *milcocoli* fields, usually the first listed for a household, are depicted with a house glyph, either a flat-roofed house *(calli)* or a thatched-roof house *(xacalli)*. A field shown with either of these glyphs probably is a house garden, a *calmil* (pl. *calmilli*). Because most, but not all, landholding household heads have a house garden indicated (15 are without in the *milcocoli* record), the *calli* or *xacalli* glyph probably reads "Here is the *calmil* of household x", rather than "Here begin the lands of household x." If the latter alternative were the correct reading, then all landholding heads would have had such a glyph. Furthermore, subordinate landholding families within the household usually do not have a field with house glyph separate from that of the head's, but a few do. Again, the drawing of the house glyph on a specific field must have indicated something special about the land parcel.

The indigenous, two-fold classification of fields recorded in the codex, those with house glyphs and those without, reflects the dual system of agriculture that prevailed in drier parts of the piedmont in Acolhuacan, many aspects of which are still observable today. House gardens, one of the two elements in the system, are typically found adjacent to residences. House gardens are managed intensively and are planted with many species of herbs, fruit trees, ornamentals, and vegetables, as well as corn. In contrast to the house garden, where residential horticulture predominates, households also plant milpas—fields intercropped in corn and/or beans and squash, and pulque magueys—away from the residences. Milpas are managed less intensively, receive fewer amendments, and have less labor input than house gardens (see also Evans 1990:125). Because the distance to the milpas did not exceed approximately thirty minutes walking time, the milpas in the *tlaxilacalli* fit the category of "infields" as defined by Killion (1990).

A number of inferences about settlement structure in the local level polities may be made because the codex depicts two different horticultural strategies— residential horticulture in house gardens and milpa horticulture on infields. The data suggest that soil type conditioned the location of house gardens and, therefore, the location of residential sites. In three-quarters of the communities (8 of 12), most *calmilli* parcels were located on fertile soil, including irrigated or *de humedad* (permanently moist) alluvium, clayey, yellow, and sandy soils (table 3.1). The adjacent residential structures as well would have been sited on the

Table 3.1   Soil fertility of house gardens (calmilli) in Santa María Asunción

Locality	Most Fertile Soil[a]			Least Fertile Soil[b]		
	No. of Calmilli	Total Area	Avg. Area	No. of Calmilli	Total Area	Avg. Area
Tlancomolco	23	13.28	.5772	--	--	--
Antecontla	14	6.67	.4764	--	--	--
Chiautenco	7	3.97	.5674	--	--	--
Chiauhtlan[c]	8	4.13	.5161	--	--	--
Conzotlan	8	4.54	.5673	--	--	--
Topotitla	6	3.39	.5647	--	--	--
Tlantozcac	9	5.34	.5932	2	.87	.4343
Cuitlahuac	4	2.34	.5856	1	.22	.2237
Cuauhtepuztit	38	12.60	.3317	26	8.23	.3163
Tlaltecahuaca	3	1.86	.6214	2	.85	.4243
Zapotlan	1	.26	.2600	1	.97	.9693
Tlanchiuhca	6	4.47	.7451	11	5.72	.5195
Total	127	62.85	.4949	43	16.86	.3921

Note: Data are derived from the *tlahuelmatli* record. All areas are expressed in hectares.

[a] Includes irrigated alluvium, yellow, clay, and sandy soils.

[b] Includes hill slope, *tepetates,* and stony soil.

[c] Data derived from *milcocoli* record; the tlahuelmatli record shows 7 calmilli in 5.92 ha.

most productive land available, rather than on the least productive. Cases in which house gardens were located on poor soils, such as *tepetates* or stony soil, may be explained by examining individual household landholdings. In most instances, all lands of these households were of poor quality. For example, in Tlanchiuhca no better land was available to eight out of the 11 households whose *calmilli* were on poor land. No better land was available to 18 out of 26 households (70 percent) in Cuauhtepuztitla, and none to the households in Zapotlan. Given a choice, therefore, houses and house gardens were located on the better lands. Only a total of five households in Tlaltecahuacan, Tlantozcac, and Cuitlahuac are exceptions to the general pattern. Archaeologically, then, residential structures should be expected on the better rather than poorer soils.

The presence of house gardens resulted in semi-dispersed settlement pattern in residential districts instead of wall-to-wall housing. Assuming a natural tendency toward compact settlement (Drennan 1988:285) but constrained by the practice of residential horticulture on good soils, the degree of residential dispersal was affected by house garden size. For the *tlaxilacalli* as a whole, the average size of all house gardens shown in the *tlahuelmatli* record is .48 ha (N=169; *milcocoli* data: N=156, average=.44 ha), but the range between localities is notable, from a low of .3 ha for Cuauhtepuztitla to a high of .9 ha for

Chiauhtlan (table 3.2). These data support Susan T. Evans's (1990) use of an average of .5 ha/house garden in her analysis of maguey terrace agriculture, with the caveat that significant differences, up to three-fold, might be expected between communities. Interestingly, households in the most populous community, Cuauhtepuztitla, had the smallest house gardens and, incidently, the least amount of land per household. Inferring from house garden size, the spacing of residences in Cuauhtepuztitla would have been less dispersed than in other communities. In an archaeological context, increasing density of occupational debris would indicate a decrease in house garden size and a concomitant increase in residential density.

Table 3.2   Average area of house gardens (calmilli) in Santa María Asunción

Locality	Total Calmilli Area (ha)	No. of Calmilli	Avg. Area per Calmil
Cuauhtepuztitla	20.83	64	.33
Antecontla	6.67	14	.48
Cuitlahuac	2.57	5	.51
Tlaltecahuacan	2.71	5	.54
Topotitla	3.39	6	.55
Tlantozcac	6.21	11	.56
Chiauhtenco	3.97	7	.57
Conzotlan	4.54	8	.57
Tlancomolco	13.28	23	.58
Tlanchiuhca	10.19	17	.60
Zapotlan	1.23	2	.61
Chiauhtlan	5.92	7	.85
All localities	81.51	169	.48

The pattern of residential density within a community territory can be predicted not only by the size of house gardens but also by the percentage of total agricultural land in house gardens. A low percentage of land in house gardens suggests a pattern of a residential core area surrounded by infields, whereas a high percentage of total agricultural land in house gardens implies a reduction in area of infields and an even distribution of houses throughout the community territory. The data show substantial variation between communities (table 3.3) and that both patterns obtained. For example, the community of Conzotlan had dispersed settlement throughout its territory because 66 percent of its agricultural land was in house gardens, whereas Zapotlan had a residential core surrounded by milpas: only 18 percent of the land was in house gardens.

Table 3.3   Percent of agricultural land in house gardens
(calmilli), Santa María Asunción

Locality	Total Land	Calmilli Land	
		Area	Percent
Conzotlan	6.92	4.54	66
Antecontla	11.32	6.67	59
Tlantozcac	13.77	6.21	45
Chiautlan	15.76	5.92	38
Tlancomolco	34.51	13.28	38
Tlanchiuhca	27.51	10.19	37
Chiauhtenco	10.99	3.97	36
Cuitlahuac	7.74	2.57	33
Cuauhtepuztitla	72.51	20.83	29
Topotitla	12.10	3.39	27
Tlaltecahuacan	10.36	2.71	26
Zapotlan	6.91	1.23	18
All localities	230.40	81.51	36

Ethnographic analogy for the Basin suggests that the *calmilli* were reposi-tories, at least ultimately, of household refuse. Thus, the percentage of total agricultural land in *calmilli* would be a simplistic predictor of the expected areal extent of occupational debris. The data presented in table 3.3 suggest that occupational debris would be encountered over roughly one-quarter to two-thirds of the territories of each *tlaxilacalli* sub-division. Visual inspection of the site map, where percentages of agricultural land in house gardens are indicated by locality (fig. 3.3), suggests that in some localities—Tlancomolco, Cuauhtepuztitla, Topotitla—occupational debris is more widely scattered than predicted by the area of house gardens ("M" on the map) and is nil or less than expected in others ("L" on the map). Interestingly, the spatial distribution of occupational debris correlates reasonably well with the percentage of area in *calmilli* in two of the three distant hamlets on the steep slopes of the hills to the north. Here, also, a larger number of domestic structures are preserved.

Accounting for the obviously uneven pattern in preservation of the archaeo-logical materials requires high resolution data on both land use history and the effects of physical environmental processes. Both types of data are lacking for the area at present. Speculating from distributions shown on the *tlaxilacalli* map, preservation is poor on lower slopes where sedimentation, continuous habi-tation, and cultivation have occurred over the past four-and-one-half centuries. Poor preservation would result in underestimates of the population for that zone. On footslopes, where cultivation was abandoned and stock raising was intensive, occupational debris has been scattered and overestimates of population would result for this zone. On the distant, steeper slopes where fewer cattle and sheep grazed, preservation is best, in spite of high soil erosion rates, which had already exposed the *tepetate* substrate by the 1540s.

Finally, the map seems to contradict a logical presumption that vestiges of larger rural communities are more apt to remain than those of smaller ones. For example, Tlanchiuhca, fifth in size, and Tlantozcac, sixth in size, had better preservation than Antecontla, fourth in size.

SUMMARY AND CONCLUSIONS

The *tlaxilacalli* of Santa María Asunción was a sub-section of the *altepetl* (city-state) of Tepetlaoztoc and, in turn, it was sub-divided into many political-territorial units of varying population size and land area. Considered on a regional scale, most of these local level polities were extremely small. The Asunción codex data suggest that the settlement pattern within the sub-divisions in part resulted from the practice of horticulture adjacent to residences on *calmilli* parcels averaging .5 ha in size, which forced spacing of domestic structures, a practice and resulting pattern that survived in the countryside until recently.

Comparison between the pictorial and archaeological survey data suggests an extremely poor archaeological preservation rate for domestic household structures in Tepetlaoztoc. Occupational scatter does not adequately reflect the presence of households known to have resided in the *tlaxilacalli* twenty years after Spanish contact. The codex substantiates the conclusion of Parsons and others that settlement in Tepetlaoztoc was dispersed in a broad band with intermittent occupation clusters.

In explaining this dispersed settlement pattern, William Sanders, Jeffrey Parsons, and Robert Santley note,

> We have long been puzzled and frustrated by this kind of occupa-
> tion [dispersed Aztec period occupation] as it so perversely defies
> our standard practices of site definition. We are now wondering if
> the main reason for our methodological and conceptual problems
> might be the fact that such occupation does not represent communi-
> ties at all, but rather reflects some very different kind of sociological
> category. (Sanders et al. 1979:54)

They suggest occupation by a social category of tenants *(mayeques* or *tlalmaitl),* renters or workers on elite estates.

In contrast to the search for a sociologically based model to account for dispersed settlement, Robert Drennan sees land use as a primary causal factor (1988:288-290). He concludes that dispersed settlement results when large numbers of households are involved in intensive agriculture and concentrate much labor on individual small plots of land.

The Asunción codex data substantiate not only the role of intensive agriculture in settlement dispersal; they also confirm that dispersed communities composed of scattered households pertained to local level polities and constituted the lowest rung of the organization hierarchy above individual households or household compounds. The spatial distribution of house mounds and occupation debris is explained by the percentage of the total community agricultural land in house gardens. Where most of the agricultural land of a community was in house gardens, residential structures would have been spaced more evenly over the landscape, accounting for Parsons finding occupation in "broad settlement bands" (1971:220). In communities where a substantial portion of the land was in infields, residential structures would appear more clustered, Parsons's "intermittent occupational clusters" (1971:220).

The conjunctive interpretation of archaeological and ethnohistorical data leads to the conclusion that dispersed settlement in a broad band with intermittent occupation clusters reflects the presence of households residing in local level polities whose subsistence strategies combined residential and milpa horticulture. Rather than well-defined, spatially isolatable sites, the archaeological signature is a nearly continuous distribution of surface pottery, of variable density from light to light-to-moderate sherd concentrations, and little if any ceremonial-civic architecture. Many of these small communities disappeared by the mid-sixteenth century, and most of the others later were abandoned as well. The melding of archaeological and documentary data assures that these *macehualtin* settlements, and perhaps others like them, will not go unrecognized as important components of the contact-period indigenous landscape.

ACKNOWLEDGMENTS

I wish to thank Jeffrey Parsons for graciously providing access to field materials from the Texcoco survey during the early stages of research on Tepetlaoztoc and for permission to use the Aztec Tepetlaoztoc site map. Also I wish to thank Michael Smith for helpful comments and suggestions on the original manuscript. The University of Wisconsin Centers provided research support enabling manuscript completion.

NOTES

1.   One *tlalquahuitl* 'land rod' equals 2.5 m; 1600 square *tlalquahuitl* equal one ha (Harvey and Williams 1988:500).

REFERENCES CITED

Drennan, Robert D.
  1988   Household Location and Compact versus Dispersed Settlement in Prehispanic Mesoamerica. In *Household and Community in the Mesoamerican Past,* edited by Richard R. Wilk and Wendy Ashmore, pp. 273-293. University of New Mexico Press, Albuquerque.

Evans, Susan T.
  1990   The Productivity of Maguey Terrace Agriculture in Central Mexico During the Aztec Period. *Latin American Antiquity* 1:117-132.

Harvey, H. R.
  1986   The Population of Tepetlaoztoc in the Sixteenth Century. *Mexicon* 8:107-111.
  1991   The Oztoticpac Lands Map: A Reexamination. In *Land and Politics in the Valley of Mexico: A Two-Thousand-Year Perspective,* edited by H. R. Harvey, pp. 163-185. University of New Mexico Press, Albuquerque.

Killion, Thomas W.
  1990   Cultivation Intensity and Residential Site Structure: An Ethnoarchaeological Examination of Peasant Agriculture in the Sierra de los Tuxtlas, Veracruz, Mexico. *Latin American Antiquity* 1:191-215.

Parsons, Jeffrey R.
  1971   *Prehistoric Settlement Patterns in the Texcoco Region, Mexico.* Memoirs No. 3. Museum of Anthropology, University of Michigan, Ann Arbor.

Sanders, William T., Jeffrey R. Parsons, and Robert S. Santley
  1979   *The Basin of Mexico: Ecological Processes in the Evolution of a Civilization.* Academic Press, New York.

Seler, Eduard
  1904   The Mexican Picture Writings of Alexander von Humboldt. In *Mexican and Central American Antiquities, Calendar Systems, and History,* edited by Charles P. Powditch, pp. 127-229. Bureau of American Ethnology Bulletin 28. Smithsonian Institution, Washington, D.C.

Williams, Barbara J.
  1991   The Lands and Political Organization of a Rural Tlaxilacalli in Tepetlaoztoc, c A.D. 1540. In *Land and Politics in the Valley of Mexico: A Two-Thousand-Year Perspective,* edited by H. R. Harvey, pp. 187-208. University of New Mexico Press, Albuquerque.

Williams, Barbara J., and H. R. Harvey
  1988 Content, Provenience, and Significance of the *Codex Vergara* and the *Códice de Santa Maria Asunción*. *American Antiquity* 53:337-351.
Zorita, Alonso de
  1963 *Life and Labor in Ancient Mexico: The Brief and Summary Relation of the Lords of New Spain*. Translated by Benjamin Keen. Rutgers University Press, New Brunswick.

4

Cloth in the Political Economy
of the Aztec State

Frederic Hicks

Once cloth becomes incorporated into the culture of a reasonably complex society, the potential uses for it soon become virtually inexhaustible and the demand for it nearly insatiable. Aztec Mexico was no exception. Cloth was used for clothing: for men, a loin cloth *(maxtlatl)* and cape *(tilmahtli)*, and for women a wrap-around skirt *(cueitl)* and a huipil *(huipilli,* a pullover upper garment). It was also used for carrying cloths, bedding, food covers, bags, swaddling clothes, awnings and decorative hangings, battle armor, adornment for images of the gods, and finally as shrouds for the dead (Anawalt 1981; Berdan 1987:239; *Codex Mendoza* 1992:esp f 43r-45r, f 52r, f 57r, f 58r, f 61r).

Furthermore, since cloth can be elaborated with many kinds of decoration, one can vary one's attire, devise special patterns of garment decoration for different purposes or occasions, or special decorations for cloth armor, and even for carrying cloths or tortilla covers, all of which results in a desire for still more cloth.

The demand for cloth thus was very high, and for that reason, cloth in one form or another came to have two additional functions: it served as a medium of marketplace exchange and, when appropriately decorated, as elite valuables or wealth items whose transfer and display were important in the pattern of high-level gift exchange. Needless to say, so useful a commodity was commonly demanded as tribute on the local, state, and imperial levels. These functions might suggest a steady flow of cloth up the social hierarchy, yet it seems that everyone in Aztec society, down to the lowliest peasant, normally had the full range of basic cloth garments plus cloth for other household uses. The technology of cloth production nevertheless remained very simple. The yarn was spun on a simple hand spindle, and weaving was limited to the backstrap loom. Consequently, it took a long time to produce a piece of cloth.

This combination of high demand, simple technology, and long production time presents a number of problems. Because it was time-consuming to produce, cloth should have been scarce and valuable, yet it was in widespread use among all levels of society. It was used by everyone as a medium of exchange, yet it was also an elite valuable. How did the ancient Mexican economy accommodate such apparently contradictory features? And given that it did, what does that tell us about the nature of that economy?

THE TECHNOLOGY OF CLOTH PRODUCTION

There are a number of accounts of cloth production at the time of the Spanish conquest (e.g., Sahagún 1950-1982:bk.8:47; Suárez de Peralta 1878; Torquemada 1975:v.2:488; for good summaries, see Berdan [1987] and Mastache de Escobar [1971]). In addition, cloth is still being made in parts of Mexico and Guatemala using many of the same techniques that were used in pre-Spanish times, and ethnographic accounts of these are very helpful for understanding pre-Spanish production methods.

Cloth was woven of either cotton or one or another kind of agave fiber (in Highland Mexico, maguey). Cotton was the more highly esteemed material, but it took equally long to make cloth from either fiber. Mesoamerican cotton *(ichcatl)* was all of a single species, and while most of it was white, there was a variety that had yellowish or tan fibers (Berdan 1987:236-237). Cotton does not grow in the altiplano, so the cloth maker there had to obtain it either in trade or through redistribution.

Both of these fibers had to be prepared prior to spinning. Maguey fibers had to be laboriously processed—roasted, fermented, beaten, scraped, washed, and treated with maize water—before they could be spun and woven, and most of this work was done by men (Anawalt 1981:12; Bernard and Salinas 1989:322-330; Medina and Quezada 1975:79-86; Nolasco 1963:170-172; Parsons and Parsons 1990:145ff). Cotton had to be ginned, cleaned, beaten and combed, and probably all of this work was done by women.

One presumes that ginning was done by the cotton grower, although I have no actual evidence; the seeds make up more than half the weight of a cotton boll, so it would make sense to remove them before carrying the cotton to the highlands. But the cloth maker still had to remove some debris from the cotton and comb the fibers. Then the cotton was laid out on mats on the house floor and beaten to thin it, so the fibers could be more easily separated. It was then spun, using a spindle *(malacatl)* made of wood with a ceramic whorl. For short-staple fibers such as cotton, a small bowl *(caxitl,* or more explicitly *tzahualcaxitl)* was used to support the spindle as it was twirled. Medium and long-staple fibers, such as maguey, can often be spun with a drop-spindle technique, and sometimes cotton can too, but the bowl gives more control (Cordry and Cordry 1941:107-108; Sahagún 1950-1982:bk.8:49; Smith and Hirth 1988:349). Drop spinning can often be done while walking about and doing other things, but spinning with the bowl requires the spinner to remain stationary. Jeffrey R. Parsons and Mary H. Parsons (1990:181) describe a technique for spinning especially fine thread from maguey fiber, which requires holding the spindle in one hand while twirling it with the other, and this also keeps the spinner stationary. A piece of lime *(tizatl)* was rubbed on the spindle or the bowl, apparently to make it spin better (Mastache de Escobar 1971:28). In some parts of southern Mexico today, the cotton warp threads are soaked or boiled in a solution of maize and water to strengthen them or make them easier to handle (Cordry and Cordry 1941:111; Jopling 1977:222).

The spun thread was measured out on a warping frame *(tzatzaztli),* and then transferred to the loom. The backstrap loom puts a limit on the width that can be woven: about two-thirds to seven-eighths of a vara, or about 22 to 30 in. (Borah and Cook 1958:27; Suárez de Peralta 1878:30). Some pattern and color variation is possible, but such a loom makes tapestry or other weft-faced decorative methods difficult. Thus Mesoamerica did not develop the weaving art to the degree that the ancient Peruvians did through the use of additional loom types (Anawalt 1981:11-12J; Schneider 1987:422-425).

Dyes were made from a wide variety of plant and animal materials. The cloth maker dyed her own yarns but did not make the dyes. Sahagún (1950-1982:bk.11:239-245) lists many of the sources of dyes, and Alba Guadalupe Mastache de Escobar (1971:18-24) provides an excellent overview based on many sources, archaeological as well as ethnographic and ethnohistorical. In general, the process of dye making involved crushing the leaves or other color yielding part (such as the insect which produced red cochineal) and boiling it in a pot to extract the pigment. This then settled as a residue which could be formed into cakes. Few of the major dye sources grew in the Central Mexican plateau, but in cake form they could be transported efficiently, and a weaver could get them on the market or from her lord. A mordant or fixative was used to make the dye permanent; a double sulfate of aluminum and potassium *(tlalxocotl,* Span. *piedra alumbre)* was especially popular (Clavijero 1971:249; Sahagún 1950-1982:bk.11:243).

Other decorative techniques involved variations in weaving. These included damask, brocade, figure gauze, double cloth, warp-and-weft face stripes, and others (Anawalt 1981:12; Mastache de Escobar 1971:43-49). There were also embroidery using a thread composed of finely-spun fur from the underbelly of the rabbit *(tochomitl);* the attachment of feathers (not to be confused with the specialized featherwork of the *amanteca*); and the use of strands of something called "indigenous wild silk," which took on especially brilliant colors when dyed (Anawalt 1981:12).

A woman ordinarily wove not just undifferentiated cloth but a specific garment or other cloth object. For larger cloth items, such as the *mantas* (*cuachtli,* sometimes called *"toldillos"* in early Spanish documents) so often mentioned as media of exchange or tribute items, Early Colonial sources suggest that the basic unit was a *zotl,* which was the cloth that came off a backstrap loom; in Spanish it was usually called a *"pierna."* A *manta* used in exchange consisted usually of four *zotl* joined together (although in Morelos there was also a *tequicuachtli,* or "tribute *manta,"* of only one *zotl* and in Tepeaca, Puebla, a *patolcuachtli* of three relatively small *zotl*). The dimensions of a *zotl* varied, but they seem generally to have been from four to five varas long and three-fourths of a vara wide (Hinz et al. 1983, passim; *Libro de tasaciones* 1952:179, 230-231, 303, 340; Paso y Troncoso 1905:v.5:28, v.6:233-234). If a vara was 36 in. (Borah and Cook 1958:27), then each *pierna* must have contained about three and one-third varas or yards squared. When weaving specific garments, however, the full width capacity of the loom was not always used.

THE RATE OF PRODUCTION

I have found in the sources on pre-Spanish Mexico almost no data on the rate at which cloth could be produced and very little information from which we might deduce the rate. But we do have some information based on observations of modern spinners or weavers using pre-Spanish implements, and in most cases, these will have to do.

Some data tell us the time needed for specific operations or groups of operations, and this information is presented in table 4.1. I have omitted such operations as dyeing, which simply involve letting the yarn sit in the dye for a day or so, during which time other work can be done. These figures give us some idea of the amount of work involved, but they do not tell us much about the rate of production. If we were to add up these operations, it would appear to take between seven and nine days to make a square yard of plain cloth; and if a *zotl* is 3 1/3 yd.^{2}, it would seem to take about 26 or 27 days to make one *zotl* out of unprocessed cotton.

But of course not all these processes were carried out sequentially by a single person. Particularly instructive are the data on the production of *ayates,*

Table 4.1   Time required for specific textile operations

Operation	Garment	Time	Place	Source
Beating cotton	--	4 hours	Mexico, 16th cent.	A
Preparing maguey fiber for spinning	ayate, 1 m	3 days	Mezquital Valley	B
Spinning maguey fiber	ayate, 1 m	2 days	Mezquital Valley	B
Spinning cotton[a]	4 lbs.	4 days	Panajachel	C
Warping loom	huipil	1.5 days	Panajachel	C
Weaving complex patterns of various colors	huipil	10.5 days	Panajachel	C
Weaving with decorative stripes	half of a 2-panel huipil, 17x60 in.	25 hours	San Sebastián Huehuetenango	D
Weaving	huipil	5-7 days	Yalálag	E
Weaving	skirt	5-8 days	Yalálag	E
Weaving	sash for shirt	3 days	Yalálag	E

Sources. (A) Juárez de Peralta (1076); (B) Medina and Quezada (1975:83); (C) Tax (1953:153); (D) Sperlich and Sperlich (1980:85-86); (E) Jopling (1977:228-229).

[a] The actual operation was twisting the fibers, but Sperlich and Sperlich (1980:11) indicate this takes the same amount of time as spinning.

the all-purpose cloths of maguey fiber, about 1 m², made in the Mezquital Valley, Hidalgo. Here too, if one adds up the time required for each operation (table 4.1), it would appear to require seven days to make a single *ayate,* but Nolasco (1963:172) and Medina and Quezada (1975:83) report that a person can turn out five to six *ayates* a week, working at a normal pace, or 10 per week if working intensively (Bernard and Salinas [1989:326] say she could make 12 per week). Most *ayates* made in the Mezquital Valley today are rather loosely woven; it takes considerably more time to make fabrics of high quality, and more time still if they are decorated. I would estimate that a household can produce five or six yd.² a week of coarse maguey fiber cloth, or about four per week of more tightly woven cotton cloth, and three per week of really fine cloth (extrapolating from the data of Tax, Jopling, and the Sperlichs given in table 4.1). If a *zotl* is 3 1/3 yd.², the household should be able to produce a little more than one *zotl* per week, some of it average and some of it fine quality, out of unprocessed cotton or maguey fiber. This illustrates the advantage of the domestic mode of production, typical of peasant households, in which all household members help out. Many garments require less than a full *zotl* of cloth, but the loom has to be warped anew for each one, so the time saved is not proportional to the size of the garment.

THE SOCIAL ORGANIZATION OF PRODUCTION

Cloth making, like food production, was carried on as part of the domestic economy. It was a task of women, just as farming was a task of men.[1] Women had many other tasks, but almost always, it was cloth making that was used to symbolize proper femininity. At their bathing ceremonies shortly after birth, girls were provided with "women's equipment" *(cihuatlatquitl)*, which consisted of spinning and weaving materials, and cloth making figures prominently in descriptions of the training of girls (e.g., *Codex Mendoza* 1992:f.58-60; Motolinía 1941:41; Zorita 1941:109-110). When the gods created the first woman, they commanded her to weave, just as they commanded the first man to cultivate the soil (Carrasco 1976:244). The early sources frequently equate cloth making with farming, and with good reason: cloth was like food; everyone had to have an adequate supply, yet it also figured in the high level gift economy, which frequently involved both gifts of fine cloth and lavish banquets featuring elaborately prepared dishes (Sahagún 1950-1982:bk.8:39; Smith 1986:75-76). Women produced cloth as tribute to their lords, just as the men of their households produced food.

One of the main characteristics of the domestic mode of production is that it makes use of the available labor time of all possible members of the household (Netting 1990:39-41). As Sheldon Annis (1987:34-38) puts it, it "is built on the principle of optimizing inputs rather than maximizing outputs." It makes use of all sorts of spare labor time, skills, and knowledge that would go unused in a different productive setting. Thus children can be put to work cleaning the cotton, the husband can help put yarn on a warping frame (and of course he builds the frame, loom, and other equipment), older female children can spin, all at the same time that the woman is weaving. In the agricultural slack season, men might also lend a hand. Of course, all members of the household perform other tasks as well: numerous little chores associated with agriculture, food preparation, and housekeeping; and weaving or spinning can be put aside temporarily to take care of these tasks, and resumed whenever a few spare minutes are available. Because cloth could be traded for virtually anything offered on the market, a household would have an incentive to use as many of those spare minutes as possible in cloth production, and output would in fact be maximized per household if not per person. It is virtually impossible to distinguish between producers and nonproducers in this mode of production; almost everybody is a producer to some extent. The main reason why ethnographers have obtained so little data on how long it takes to make cloth is that a woman intersperses her cloth making with so many other activities that she finds it hard to say how many hours she spends in one or another operation. It is much easier to see how much cloth a household can produce in a week or longer period of time, and that is really the more relevant figure in this kind of production setting.

To be sure, recognized craft or service specialists may have operated in a similar way. What little we know suggests that they too worked in their homes, probably helped by family members, much as the women worked at cloth making. But as a general rule in Mesoamerica, most specialists, who were male, worked at their specialty only part-time, and relied on their subsistence plots for their day-to-day livelihood. They could be mobilized for rotational labor service or special draft labor *(coatequitl)* when their specialty was needed; otherwise they produced for the market or tended their fields (Hicks 1984; T. Rojas 1979). But any given specialty was practiced in only a minority of households; most men were farmers, and when they performed rotational labor service or special draft labor, it was to cultivate land or perform other manual labor. Only a small fraction of the cloth that was actually produced could have been produced if it had been a task of specialists. Cloth making was as much a full-time activity of women as farming was of men, unlike the professional activities of specialists.

Women provided the clothing and other cloth for the household's own needs as well as the cloth used as a medium of exchange, traded in the market place, and given as tribute. Normally they worked at home. They might serve in the house of a local or regional lord grinding corn and hauling water (AGI Justicia 164/2:f.26v-28r; Hinz et al. 1983), but when they spun and wove the lord's cotton, or otherwise wove cloth to give him, they did it in their own homes. There were no special workshops, in the European sense, but as Motolinía (1971:148) notes, nobles might have many women in their households who devoted much time to spinning and weaving. Bernal Díaz (1968:276) states that in the house of Motecuhzoma, the daughters of the lords wove beautiful cloth for him, and that many other women, who lived "like nuns" in a house near the Temple of Huitzilopochtli, were recruited to weave for him. These may have been the women who, according to Motolinía (1941:61), entered temple service and spent their days weaving. Lesser nobles might have in their households poor relations or unrelated women from other regions (sometimes purchased slaves) who wove. Significantly, both Sahagún (1950-1982:bk.6:210, 216) and Durán (1967:v.1:26) say that when a girl was to be dedicated to the *calmecac* for special training, she was told to expect to sweep, clean, and prepare food, but apparently not to weave; weaving was something done at home.[2]

Archaeological surveys confirm that most cloth was produced in the home. In Late Postclassic Huexotla, Otumba, and small communities in Morelos, spindle whorls were found evenly distributed throughout the inhabited area, as would be expected if spinning were done in virtually every household, and never in large dense concentrations as would be expected with full-time specialization (Brumfiel 1987:107; Charlton et al. 1991; Smith 1989; Smith and Heath-Smith, chap. 13). The one exception involves the large whorls associated with maguey fiber spinning, whose distribution was concentrated in only a few parts of Otumba (Nichols, chap. 7).

The evidence seems to indicate that finely decorated cloth as well as plain cloth was produced in every peasant household. Sahagún (1950-1982:bk.10:51) describes the skilled weaver of designs in a chapter on the common women, and in 1553 a *mayordomo* of Metztitlan was able to mobilize all the women of a village to make some very fine lace bedding for the *oidor* Lic. Santillán (AGI México 205:f.2r-2v). The evident skill of these women should not be surprising: in indigenous villages of Guatemala and Mexico today, some extremely fine decorated fabrics are produced, probably the equal of those produced for nobles in pre-Spanish times. These fabrics are made by all of the women of the villages involved, who learn it at their mothers' side from an early age (Annis 1987; Jopling 1977). To be sure, some of the finest cloth was produced in noble houses, but only because these households were served by many women, most of whom were commoners (Carrasco 1976:226).

SURPLUS PRODUCTION

William T. Sanders and David Webster (1988; see also Sanders and Santley 1983) have attributed the system of part-time specialization to the inefficiency of Mesoamerican technology, transportation, and agriculture. The procedure used by Sanders and Santley is to calculate the rate of productivity of craftsmen of various kinds and the rate at which their products would have been consumed; from these figures they calculate how many consumer families a craftsman could supply if he worked full-time. They cite figures indicating that a family of five would require the grain equivalent of 1000 kg of maize a year, so a specialist would have to receive that much from all of his clients combined. If, for example, a potter could supply 66 families,[3] he would have to receive 1000/66 = 15.5 kg of grain, or the equivalent value in items that could be exchanged for food, from each household, plus something in addition for the person-days spent in travel from the point of production to the marketplace. Sanders and his collaborators had no figures on the rate of production and consumption of cloth, but Sanders and Webster (1988:542) remarked that "our impression is that a craftsperson who practiced weaving, a very time-consuming activity, could supply so few families that effective specialization would be impossible." Let us see.

The women of a household had to produce enough to clothe the family and supply its other cloth needs, to meet tribute demands, and hopefully, to have a little left over to exchange on the market. We have looked at how much cloth could have been produced; now we must ask, how much did the family consume?

Unfortunately, but not unexpectedly, I have absolutely no information on family consumption of cloth. However, we know what a family used as clothing, and we can guess at their additional needs for carrying cloths, food covering cloths, bedding, infant wrappings, etc. Also, until a few decades ago, most peasant men in central and southern Mexico wore clothing made of cotton *"manta,"* which may have resembled the pre-Spanish product in its durability. Data from Ocotepec, Morelos (Basauri 1940:v.3:163) and Chamula, Chiapas (Pozas 1959:95) indicate that a set of cotton work clothing had to be replaced twice a year, while in Chan Kom, Yucatán, a man used three sets of work clothing a year (Redfield and Villa Rojas 1934:41). Let us assume that each person in pre-Spanish Mexico needed two new sets of clothing each year. A household of seven persons (the average for Tepetenchic [see below]), evenly divided between the sexes (this is a model, not real life), would have needed 14 of each basic garment: loincloth, cape, huipil and skirt. To this let us add seven plain carrying cloths, each about a yard squared, plus five additional square yards for miscellaneous purposes, a total of 12 square yards. Let us further assume that these are all made of plain cloth. The early sources do not tell us the size of these garments, but Patricia Anawalt of the Fowler Museum of Cultural History at UCLA has kindly provided me with dimensions based on dressing museum mannequins. A loincloth would be about 6 in. wide and 140 in. long (0.6 yd.^{2}). Anawalt (1990:300) has estimated the dimensions of an imperial cape worn by King Nezahualpilli of Texcoco as 1.4 m by 1.0 m, but an ordinary commoner's cape would have been smaller, say 1.2 m by 1.0 m (1.4 yd.^{2}). A skirt was made of two loom widths of 18 to 19 in., each about 36 to 38 in. long (1 yd.^{2}, total), and the huipil was usually made of three panels, each about 2 yd. long, the panels probably about 11 in. wide (cf. Cordry and Cordry 1941:112), for a total of 2 yds.^{2}). In San Sebastián Huehuetenango today, huipiles are of two panels, each about 17 in. by 60 in. (Sperlich and Sperlich 1980:85), but those worn in pre-Spanish Central Mexico were probably longer. In terms of cloth area, 14 of each garment would total 70.42 yd.^{2} We have previously calculated that a woman could make about 5 yd.^{2} of plain cloth in a week, starting from scratch, but actual garments would take longer, even if undecorated, because each panel of a garment would require a new warping of the loom, a task which required about one day for an average garment (table 4.1), so let us reduce that to 4 yd.^{2} per week. Thus a household could make all of its clothing in 17.5 weeks, plus 2.5 weeks to make the 12 yd.^{2} of miscellaneous cloth, for a grand total of 20 weeks. If these figures are anywhere near accurate, they would lead to the conclusion that if she didn't have any tribute obligations, a cloth maker could supply only one and a half households in addition to her own.

But she did have tribute obligations. The *Libro de tasaciones* (1952:230-231, 303, 349) gives some indications of the tribute assessments in cloth per household in the Early Colonial period (between one and two *piernas* per mar-

ried tributary per year), but our best quantitative data on the tribute requirements in cloth for a household come from the house-by-house censuses taken
around 1540 of several communities of the Marquesado in Morelos. The complete censuses of two of the communities, Molotlan and Tepetenchic, both probably dependencies of Yauhtepec, have been published (Hinz et al. 1983). I have
not had time to analyze all 244 households in these two communities, but let us
take one *calpulli,* that of Tlocalpan in Tepetenchic, which seems pretty typical.
Tlocalpan consisted of 19 households, with an average of 5.8 persons per household (this figure is somewhat low; the average for Tepetenchic as a whole is
7.0, and for Molotlan 8.3 [Hinz et al. 1983:v.1:xxix]). In these 19 households
there were a total of 109 persons, of whom 41 (37%) were women aged 12 and
above, a percentage almost exactly that for all of Molotlan and Tepetenchic.
Their total cloth tribute, given to the Marqués, was 58 *cuauhnahuacayotl (mantas de Cuernavaca)* of four *zotl* each; 73 *tequicuachtli* ("tribute cloth"), apparently composed of just one *zotl;* 76 *nemapopohualoni (paño de manos* according
to Molina; Hinz et al. [1983:passim] gloss it as *"Servietten"),* which are smaller
cloths, probably comparable to the *ayates* of modern Hidalgo or the all-purpose
cloths called *tzut* or *servilletas* in San Antonio, Guatemala; six *cuauhyo tomahuac*
(Hinz et al. [1983] call these *feste dicke Decken* or firm thick cloths); three
tlamach huipilli (fine *huipiles*); and three *tlamachcueitl* (fine skirts), for a total
of 219 items. Assuming four *zotl* per *cuauhnahuacayotl,* one *zotl* per *tequicuachtli*
and *cuauhyo tomahuac,* and one-third *zotl* per *nemapopohualoni,* we have 336
zotl of plain cloth. Assuming 2 yds.^{2} per *huipil* and 1 yd.^{2} per *cueitl,* we get 9
yd.^{2} of decorated cloth. It comes to 17.7 *zotl* of plain cloth per household per
year, or 8.2 *zotl* per adult woman per year, plus about 0.5 yd.^{2} of decorated cloth
per household per year. Using the rate of 5 yd.^{2} (1.5 *zotl*) per household per
week, the task could probably have been accomplished in a little under 12 weeks
for the plain cloth, and probably another 1.5 weeks for the decorated.

What these censuses record is tribute to Hernán Cortés, the Marqués del
Valle, 20 years after the Spanish conquest, and they are not entirely representative of the pre-Spanish situation in two ways: First, the Indians complained
frequently and persuasively that Cortés's tribute demands, in labor time, were
excessive (e.g., Riley 1973:36, 43; Villanueva 1985:23; Zavala 1984:19-20, 44,
107). Second, they show a disproportionately high ratio of plain to decorated
cloth, which reflects the increasing use of plain cloth as a medium of exchange
after the Spanish conquest, due to a shortage of coined money as the Spanish
expanded the market sector of the economy (Borah and Cook 1958:24 and
passim; Villanueva 1985; Zavala 1984:56-60), while at the same time there was
a diminishing need for finely decorated textiles in the native style due to the
decline of the native gift economy and the increasing use of plain tailored garments by native men. We do not know what ratio of decorated to undecorated
cloth would have been demanded in tribute in pre-Spanish times, but perhaps

the well-known tribute rolls, the *Codex Mendoza* and *Matrícula de Tributos,* can guide us. By my count of the *Codex Mendoza* (1992) rolls, Tenochtitlan received in any given tribute period 32,400 loads of plain cloth and 39,600 of decorated cloth garments, but on average the plain cloth *mantas* were larger, so a more accurate measure would probably yield a somewhat higher volume of plain than of decorated cloth. I would feel comfortable with a guess that about 35% of the cloth received was decorated to some degree. However, only about 5% of that given to the Marqués in Morelos was decorated. If in pre-Spanish times 35% of the tribute cloth was decorated and 65% was plain, and it takes twice as long on the average to make decorated cloth as to make plain, those 13.5 weeks would have been sufficient to produce only 16.2 *zotl* instead of 19.

So far, we have our household devoting about 20 weeks to supply its own cloth needs, and 13 or 14 weeks to meet tribute demands. That leaves another 18 weeks or so in which it might have produced perhaps 27 *zotl* of plain cloth, or 6.75 *cuachtli,* such as could have been used as a medium of exchange on the market. What could a person get for 6.75 *cuachtli?*

We know remarkably little about exchange values in pre-Spanish times. We know something of the value of slaves (8 to 40 *mantas*), feathers (a bunch of 20 for 20 *mantas*), a square *braza* of land (one *manta de Cuernavaca*), and a large *canoa* of water for a fiesta (one *manta*) (AGI Justicia 124/5:f.95v; Carrasco 1970:375; Sahagún 1950-1982:bk.9:46, 48; Zavala 1984:59), but not that of ordinary consumer goods, despite the valiant efforts of José Luis de Rojas (1986:263-269) to squeeze such information out of very inadequate sources. One exchange value may be of interest, however. According to Sahagún (1950-1982:bk.9:48), *mantas* were worth either 100, 80, or 65 cacao beans each, depending on their quality. Cacao was among the items sometimes given by householders as tribute to their local lords in pre-Spanish times (e.g., Hicks 1978:135), and cacao does not grow in the Mexican highlands, so it could only have been obtained on the market. We do not really know how much cacao a household was assessed in pre-Spanish times. In 1540, the 19 households of the small barrio of Tlocalpan, Tepetenchic, Morelos, gave a total of 1,460 cacaos to Cortés; most households gave between 20 and 60, but many gave none, and a few gave more than 100 (Hinz et al. 1983:v.2:57-76). But colonial data are not reliable indicators because the Spanish quickly introduced a market-based, monetized economy, and tribute was to be paid partly in money. Yet cacao continued to serve as a medium of exchange for several decades after the Spanish conquest (Gibson 1964:348-349, 358; Tiryakian 1979). The Spanish also gained control of the trade in cacao, which was exported to Europe as well as consumed locally. Thus colonial tribute assessments in cacao may not have been what they had been before.

There is one datum that should be addressed, however. Starting with Jacques Soustelle (1962:76), several people have cited Motolinía to the effect that 20 *mantas* represented the cost of living for a year in Tenochtitlan (Berdan 1982:44; Durand-Forest 1971:116; J. L. Rojas 1986:269). This is not an accurate interpretation. What Motolinía (1971:367) said was that some gamblers, out of necessity, "in order to have something with which to gamble, sold themselves and made themselves slaves; the most common price was twenty *mantas* ..." and further that women of bad repute, in order to have something with which to dress themselves well, also sold themselves into slavery. In either case, says Motolinía, "first they made use of their price [*gozaban de su precio*], then they entered into service; and seldom did the year pass before the price was used up." Motolinía implies that these 20 *mantas* were not used for subsistence, but for pleasures such as gambling, drink, and adornment. He gives no reason to assume that the future slave had necessarily abandoned his or her normal means of subsistence.

I would guess that exchange values for products in pre-Spanish times might have been roughly equivalent to the time required to make the product. If this is so, a surplus of six or so *cuachtli* should have enabled a household to meet its needs for such things as pottery, sandals, cutting implements, rope, mats, charcoal, pitch pine, medicinal herbs, dyestuffs, and the like on the market, as well as to acquire cacao if required for tribute payments.[4] It also suggests that specialists, and very likely some nonspecialist households as well, could have met at least some of their tribute demands in cloth by exchanging their products or services for cloth on the market; indeed, Brumfiel (1991:234) presents archaeological data suggesting that they did so.

CLOTH AS A MEDIUM OF EXCHANGE

In addition to its direct, practical uses, cloth or cloth garments also functioned as a medium of exchange and as wealth objects or what George Dalton (1977) terms "primitive valuables." The latter were used to form and maintain interpersonal relations of various kinds and involved primarily (but not exclusively) decorated cloth garments. The former were used to facilitate marketplace exchange and involved primarily (but probably not exclusively) plain cloth. Let us turn first to the use of cloth as a medium of exchange.

The primary advantage of having a standardized medium of exchange is that it minimizes search costs; that is, finding someone who has what one wants and wants what one has. This means that it greatly facilitates marketplace exchange. What makes a commodity suitable as a medium of exchange is high liquidity relative to carrying costs. That is, it is so much in demand that it is readily acceptable in exchange for a wide range of other goods, and it is easy to keep without spoilage or other loss (Melitz 1974:56-59). Cloth meets both these conditions.

Much of the marketplace exchange in pre-Spanish Mexico was conducted by direct barter (Berdan 1982:43; Durán 1967:v.1:178-179; Las Casas 1958:236; Paso y Troncoso 1905:v.6:265); possibly the majority of it was. To paraphrase Motolinía (1971:374), everything was money, although in some regions one thing was more commonly used than another. In Central Mexico, cloth and cacao beans were most commonly used. Although cloth may receive more mention overall (Calnek 1978:110), it is cacao that is mentioned in accounts of actual marketplace trade. Cacao beans made a more easily divisible currency than cloth, and Las Casas (1958:236) notes that they were used to buy cheap things and to equalize the value of an object traded for something of higher value.

Cloth was what Dalton (and other economists) have called "commodity money" because as a commodity it had uses other than as money. It has sometimes been suggested that plain cloth or *cuachtli* was used only as a medium of exchange and was made for no other purpose, but on theoretical grounds, if no other, that seems to me unlikely.[5] Considering that the vast majority in ancient Mexico used the market only as "target marketers" and not as the primary source of their daily necessities, and given the low degree of monetization of the Aztec economy (Carrasco 1978; Hicks 1987; Kurtz 1974), there should have been relatively little demand for something whose only use was as money. If on the other hand there had been a high degree of monetization of the Aztec economy and a high volume of marketplace exchange, then cloth would have been unsuitable as a medium of exchange because of its bulk and because its costs of production in labor time were too high. When the monetized sector of the economy is relatively small, the best medium of exchange is something that also has other uses. Taking it out of circulation to use is equivalent to profit-taking (H. Schneider 1974:168).[6]

Just what was traded for cloth in Aztec times? The sources list many items that were available in the marketplace at Tlatelolco (Cervantes de Salazar 1971:327-330; Cortés 1963:72-73; Díaz del Castillo 1968:v.1:278-279; Motolinía 1971:372-374; Sahagún 1950-1982:bk.8:67-69) as well as in the smaller periodic markets. Much of what the average peasant householder needed from the market was probably worth less than a *zotl* of cloth and would have been obtained by barter or with cacao beans; it would have been the more expensive goods and services that were traded for cloth.

What about land? It is not inconceivable that some house plots or a few square meters of crop land could have been exchanged by the residents, with a few pieces of cloth thrown in to sweeten the offer or make up the difference in what would otherwise have been an unequal exchange. But I know of no unambiguous pre-Spanish examples.[7] Edward E. Calnek (1975:53-54, 1978:110), citing a document of the 1530s in which the price of a large landholding was given in *mantas de Cuernavaca*, takes this, along with some sales of urban house lots, as evidence for a pre-Spanish real estate market. In the document in question (AGI

Justicia 124/5), which is a dispute that began in 1527 over three large landhold-ings in the Ecatepec region, witnesses were asked if they agreed that "las tierras y labranzas sobredichas comunmente todas tres valen dos mil castellanos de oro de minas si hubiese de vender," and that there are people who would give that and more. Because witnesses were unfamiliar with Spanish money, they were encouraged to give its value in *mantas de Cuernavaca*. Their answers, as I interpret them, indicate that any land sales at all were rare, that when they did occur only very small quantities were involved, and that they were unaccus-tomed to expressing large values in terms of *mantas*.[8] As Pedro Carrasco (1978:25, 1983:71) has pointed out, large landholdings were provided to nobles by virtue of the nobility of their lineage and in order that they could carry out their political duties. This was a common way to finance the state in a great many pre-industrial or pre-mercantile states (Brumfiel and Earle 1987; Claessen 1978; Wolf 1966:50-51, 1982:79-82), and Aztec Mexico was in no way unusual in this respect; but it is incompatible with a free market in large landholdings.

Cloth figured very prominently as a tribute item on the local, state, and imperial levels and so tended to flow up the social and political hierarchy (Smith, chap. 12). Nobles were its principal possessors, so to the extent that it served as a medium of exchange, nobles would have been able to make the most use of it.

CLOTH AS A WEALTH ITEM

Media of exchange are impersonal; one *cuachtli* is as good as another, assuming it is in reasonably good condition. They are used in impersonal marketplace trans-actions. Wealth items are personal; they are unusual, exotic, attractive, made to be cherished and admired. And as one cherishes and admires them, one recalls from whom they came. Thus they are eminently suitable as gifts, and the point of gift-giving is to build personal relationships and alliances, particularly relations of dependency or patron-client ties. The basic point is that the recipient of a gift is morally obligated to the one who gave it, so the more one can give, the more powerful one becomes (Gregory 1982). The role of the gift economy in Aztec Mexico has been well documented by Elizabeth M. Brumfiel (1987:111ff; see also Hicks 1991).

Cloth garments, tightly woven of fine cotton yarn dyed in diverse colors, sometimes with rabbit fur embroidery or with feathers attached, played a major role in the high-level gift exchange economy, as innumerable sources attest (e.g., Durán 1967:v.2:227-228, 295-298; Motolinía 1971:339, 348; Sahagún 1950-1982:bk.8:52-53, 65, 76; bk.9:5-7; for a summary see Brumfiel 1987:111). I have argued that these too were made by peasant women as part of their domestic duties, as required in tribute to their local or regional lord, or in some cases to the empire. To be sure, most of the cloth woven by women attached to the households of major lords or kings was probably fine decorated cloth rather than plain cloth, but it is unlikely that these women alone could have produced enough to meet the demand (which was, as we have noted, much higher in pre-Spanish times than after the Spanish conquest).

The long production time and consequent scarcity of cloth may have limited its usefulness as a medium of marketplace exchange; however, these factors would have enhanced its usefulness as an elite valuable. Although most of the fine textiles used in high level gift exchange were probably produced by peasant women working in their own homes and on their own time, they would rarely have had time, after producing for tribute and household needs, to produce such textiles for their own family to use as comparable gifts. Even if they did, it would not enable them to enhance their status, because when a lord lavished gifts of fine textiles on his peers or subordinates, it simply confirmed or reinforced status that was also indicated by kinship ties, landholdings, official position, etc. And just to be on the safe side (because there were doubtless ways, legal or otherwise, for a commoner to come into the possession of quantities of fine textiles), there were also sumptuary laws (Alvarado Tezozomoc 1975:353, Durán 1967.v.2.211-212).[9]

CONCLUSIONS

Because textiles took so long to produce, cloth making would have been uneconomical as a recognized craft specialty, on the order of such specialties as sandal making, wood working, pottery making or floral decorating, unless it were to be exclusively an elite valuable. As it was, a specialist could have supplied too few households to have made it worthwhile, and the amount of cloth in the society would have been far less if only specialists produced it. As a household task, the equivalent for a woman to farming for men, cloth making was put on the same level as basic food production. Enough was produced to supply the household and to provide a surplus for tribute or exchange.

The simplicity of the cloth-making technology made this feasible; the looms, spindles, and other equipment could easily be made in any household. Had cloth making developed as a specialty, rather than as a household task, the technology might well have evolved to become more efficient, capable of greater output. As Esther N. Goody (1982:6) notes, it is when different stages of production are made by different specialists that bottlenecks in the process become evident, and steps are taken to speed up the slower ones. When all stages are carried out by the same people under the conditions of peasant production previously described, such bottlenecks are unimportant: one simply spends less time at one activity and more at another. Because cloth making was a domestic task, more cloth was produced than there would have been otherwise, but the further development of cloth-making technology, such as might have increased the rate of production, was hindered.

That cloth was both one of the main commodities that functioned as a medium of marketplace exchange and a common item of tribute implies that the nobles, who received so much cloth, were among the major patrons of the markets. This should not be surprising; the rich ought to be able to buy more than the poor. But it reminds us that the markets of ancient Mexico may have had more in common with upscale department stores than with the peasant markets of Middle America today.

The quantity of cloth available for use as a medium of exchange must have been limited since cloth also served as an elite valuable in high-level gift exchange. The same women who produced the *cuachtli* that were used as a medium of exchange also produced the fine, decorated cloth that was used as an elite valuable. The more of the latter they were required to produce, the less time they had to produce the former. Of course, it was the domestic mode of cloth production, with its relative inefficiency, that kept cloth scarce enough to be useful as an elite valuable, yet widely enough available for everyone to use.

NOTES

1.   Although women were the primary cloth makers, the preparation of maguey fibers prior to spinning was usually done by men (Medina and Quezada 1975:82). The censuses of the Marquesado in Morelos record that the *tlacochteuctli* of the barrio of Tepepan, in Tepetenchic (Yauhtepec), had a slave named Icaconic whose duties included spinning the *tlacochteuctli's* cotton. Hinz et al. (1983:v.2:45) use the masculine pronoun in translating the census entry on this person, but Nahuatl is a pretty genderless language, and I can find nothing in the corresponding Nahuatl text that I recognize as indicating Icaconic's gender.

2.   José Luis de Rojas (1986:160) cites Charles Gibson (1964:337, 562 in the English edition) to the effect that there were specialized weavers, and that some were male. Gibson's only reference for this seems to be AGN Indios 3:41r, which I have not seen, although Torquemada (1975:v.2:488), in a section on *"oficiales,"* includes *"texedores,"* using the masculine noun ending (we assume Torquemada carefully proofread his galleys). That large quantities of textiles were sold in the market does not by itself indicate that weaving was a specialized occupation; food, after all, was also sold in large quantities.

3. I am not prepared to endorse the specific figures on production time used by Sanders and his collaborators, but even if the figures should be wrong, the model is still useful.

4. Sahagún (1950-1982:bk.6:chap. 23) records an oration given to a newly-married noble woman by her husband's kin in which they gave her five *mantas*, from her husband, with which she could trade on the market for chile, salt, torches, and firewood. This gives us a hint of what sort of things a household would expect to get from the market, but it does not tell us how long they were expected to last. It seems a little odd that the husband should give *mantas* to the wife instead of vice-versa, but this was a noble household, and he probably got them in tribute from his peasants.

5. While it seems unlikely that *cuachtli* were used only for exchange, it is not wholly impossible. Many of the *"mantas grandes"* depicted in the *Codex Mendoza* are described as made of *"tela torcida"* (*Codex Mendoza* 1992:f.19v, f.22v, f.24r, f.27v, f.37v). The meaning of this is not clear, but it implies that these were made of a special kind of fabric, possibly heavy, not easily convertible into garments. I suspect this is the kind of native cloth the Spanish sometimes called *"toldillo,"* a word I have been unable to find (with an appropriate meaning) in any of the major Spanish historical dictionaries (Alonso, Corominas), but it suggests sailcloth or canvas because *"toldo"* (tent) originally entered Spanish from the Germanic in a nautical context.

6. Normally, people will select the best specimens for use and pass on the others; Harold K. Schneider (1974:165) sees this as a manifestation of "Gresham's Law." This practice probably accounts for the frequent observation (e.g., J. L. Rojas 1987:77) that the cacao beans that circulated as currency were inferior to those consumed by nobles.

7. Occasionally, as Carrasco (1978:28) has noted in connection with a document on Tula, a Nahuatl passage may be loosely translated into a European language in a way that implies sale or purchase, or one may confuse the giving of gifts following a land transfer as if one were payment for the other.

8. One witness, named Juan, is recorded as having said, "que un poço de tierra que se vende por necesidad vale muchas mantas y que podía valer tanto número de tierras y casas y maceguales que le parece que vale mucho, y que eso sabe de esta pregunta" (AGI Justicia 124/5:f.93v-93r). Another, named Martín, "no sabe numerar lo que se puede valer por oro, porque por muy poca tierra que entre ellos se suele vender vale muchas mantas, y comunmente una braza de tierra una manta de cuernavaca, y que por esta causa las dichas tierras valen tanto que este testigo no sabe numerarla" (AGI Justicia 124/5:f.95v). Only a certain Alonso was willing to generalize that "cuando se vende algun pedazo de tierra por cada veinte brazas, sin maceguales, se suele vender y comprar en una carga de mantas de cuernavaca," but he insisted that the lands in question would not normally be sold (AGI Justicia 124/5:f.100r).

9. The passage in Durán and Alvarado Tezozomoc commonly cited for sumptuary laws refers to a decree issued by Motecuhzoma I in the mid-fifteenth century, which may or may not have remained in force up to the Spanish conquest, and a good part of the decree actually refers to insignia of rank or office.

REFERENCES CITED

AGI Justicia 124/5
Gil González de Benavides y el gobernador y principales de Xaltocan, con los del pueblo de Tlatelolco, sobre ciertas estancias (1536). *Archivo General de Indias* (Seville), Sección Justicia, Leg. 124, No. 5.

AGI Justicia 164/2
El gobernador y principales del pueblo de Tepexpan con los indios de la estancia de Temascalapa sobre quererse substraer de su cabecera (1564). *Archivo General de Indias* (Seville), Sección Justicia, Leg. 164, No. 2.

AGI México 205
Información de testigos tomadas en el pueblo de Meztitlan por el señor Diego Ramírez, visitador, contra el Lic. de Santillán (1553). *Archivo General de Indias* (Seville), Sección México, Leg. 205, Ramo 1, No. 6.

Alvarado Tezozomoc, Fernando de
1975   *Crónica mexicana.* Commentary by Manuel Orozco y Berra. Editorial Porrúa, Mexico City.

Anawalt, Patricia Rieff
1981   *Indian Clothing Before Cortés: Mesoamerican Costumes from the Codices.* University of Oklahoma Press, Norman.
1990   The Emperor's Cloak: Aztec Pomp, Toltec Circumstances. *American Antiquity* 55:291-307.

Annis, Sheldon
1987   *God and Production in a Guatemalan Town.* University of Texas Press, Austin.

Basauri, Carlos
1940   *La población indígena de México.* 3 vols. Secretaría de Educación Pública, Mexico City.

Berdan, Frances F.
1982   *The Aztecs of Central Mexico: An Imperial Society.* Holt, Rinehart and Winston, New York.
1987   Cotton in Aztec Mexico: Production, Distribution and Uses. *Mexican Studies/Estudios Mexicanos* 3:235-262.

Bernard, H. Russell, and Jesús Salinas Pedraza
1989   *Native Ethnography: A Mexican Indian Describes His Culture.* Sage Publications, Newbury Park, California.

Borah, Woodrow, and Sherburne F. Cook
1958   *Price Trends of some Basic Commodities in Central Mexico, 1531-1570.* Ibero-Americana No. 40. University of California Press, Berkeley.

Brumfiel, Elizabeth M.
1987   Elite and Utilitarian Crafts in the Aztec State. In *Specialization, Exchange, and Complex Societies,* edited by Elizabeth M. Brumfiel and Timothy K. Earle, pp. 102-118. Cambridge University Press, Cambridge.

1991 Weaving and Cooking: Women's Production in Aztec Mexico. In *Engendering Archaeology*, edited by Joan M. Gero and Margaret W. Conkey, pp. 224-251. Basil Blackwell, Oxford.

Brumfiel, Elizabeth M., and Timothy K. Earle
1987 Specialization, Exchange, and Complex Societies: An Introduction. In *Specialization, Exchange, and Complex Societies*, edited by Elizabeth M. Brumfiel and Timothy K. Earle, pp. 1-9. Cambridge University Press, Cambridge.

Calnek, Edward E.
1975 Organización de los sistemas de abastacimiento urbano de alimentos: el caso de Tenochtitlán. In *Las ciudades de América Latina y sus áreas de influencia a través de la historia*, edited by Jorge E. Hardoy and Richard P. Schaedel, pp. 41-60. Ediciones SIAP, Buenos Aires.

1978 El sistema de mercado en Tenochtitlan. In *Economía política e ideología en el México prehispánico*, edited by Pedro Carrasco and Johanna Broda, pp. 97-114. Editorial Nueva Imagen, Mexico City.

Carrasco, Pedro
1970 Las clases sociales en el México antiguo. *Verhandlungen des XXXVIII Internationalenkongresses* 2:371-376. Klaus Renner, Munich.

1976 La sociedad mexicana antes de la conquista. In *Historia general de México*, coordinated by Daniel Cosío Villegas, vol. 1, pp. 167-288. El Colegio de México, Mexico City.

1978 La economía del México prehispánico. In *Economía política e ideología en el México prehispánico*, edited by Pedro Carrasco and Johanna Broda, pp. 15-76. Editorial Nueva Imagen, Mexico City.

Cervantes de Salazar, Francisco
1971 *Crónica de la Nueva España*. Ediciones Atlas, Biblioteca de Autores Españoles, Madrid.

Charlton, Thomas H., Deborah L. Nichols, and Cynthia Otis Charlton
1991 Aztec Craft Production and Specialization: Archaeological Evidence from the City-State of Otumba, Mexico. *World Archaeology* 23:98-114.

Claessen, Henri J. M.
1978 The Early State: A Structural Approach. In *The Early State*, edited by Henri J. M. Claessen and Peter Skalnik, pp. 533-596. Mouton, The Hague.

Clavijero, Francisco Javier
1971 *Historia antigua de México*. Edited by Mariano Cuevas. Editorial Porrúa, Mexico City.

Codex Mendoza
1992 *The Codex Mendoza*. Edited by Frances F. Berdan and Patricia Reiff Anawalt. 4 vols. University of California Press, Berkeley.

Cordry, Donald Bush, and Dorothy M. Cordry
1941 *Costumes and Weaving of the Zoque Indians of Chiapas, Mexico*. Southwest Museum Papers No. 15. Southwest Museum, Los Angeles.

Cortés, Hernán
    1963   *Cartas y documentos.* Editorial Porrúa, Mexico City.
Dalton, George
    1977   Aboriginal Economies in Stateless Societies. In *Exchange Systems in Prehistory,* edited by Timothy K. Earle and Jonathan E. Ericson, pp. 191-212. Academic Press, New York.
Díaz del Castillo, Bernal
    1968   *Historia verdadera de la conquista de la Nueva España,* vol. 1. Editorial Porrúa, Mexico City.
Durán, Fray Diego
    1967   *Historia de las Indias de la Nueva España e Islas de la Tierra Firme.* Edited by Angel María Garibay K. 2 vols. Editorial Porrúa, Mexico City.
Durand-Forest, Jacqueline de
    1971   Cambios económicos y moneda entre los aztecas. *Estudios de Cultura Náhuatl* 9:105-124.
Gibson, Charles
    1964   *The Aztecs Under Spanish Rule: A History of the Indians of the Valley of Mexico, 1519-1810.* Stanford University Press, Stanford.
Goody, Esther N.
    1982   Introduction. In *From Craft to Industry: The Ethnography of Proto-Industrial Cloth Production,* edited by Esther N. Goody, pp. 1-37. Cambridge University Press, Cambridge.
Gregory, C. A.
    1982   *Gifts and Commodities.* Academic Press, London.
Hicks, Frederic
    1978   Los calpixque de Nezahualcoyotl. *Estudios de Cultura Náhuatl* 13:129-152.
    1984   Rotational Labor and Urban Development in Prehispanic Tetzcoco. In *Explorations in Ethnohistory: Indians of Central Mexico in the Sixteenth Century,* edited by H. R. Harvey and Hanns J. Prem, pp. 147-174. University of New Mexico Press, Albuquerque.
    1987   First Steps Toward a Market-Integrated Economy in Aztec Mexico. In *Early State Dynamics,* edited by Henri J. M. Claessen and Pieter van de Velde, pp. 91-107. E. J. Brill, Leiden.
    1991   Gift and Tribute: Relations of Dependency in Aztec Mexico. In *Early State Economics,* edited by Henri J. M. Claessen and Pieter van de Velde, pp. 197-212. Transaction Publishers, New Brunswick.
Hinz, Eike, Claudine Hartau, and Marie-Luise Heimann-Koenen
    1983   *Aztekischer Zensus: Zur indianischen Wirtschaft und Gesellschaft im Marquesado um 1540.* Band 1: Molotla; Band 2: Tepetenchic. Verlag für Ethnologie, Hannover.
Jopling, Carol F.
    1977   Yalálag Weaving: Its Aesthetic, Technological and Economic Nexus. In *Material Culture: Styles, Organization, and Dynamics of Technology,* edited by Heather Lechtman and Robert S. Merrill, pp. 211-236. West Publishing Co., St. Paul.

Kurtz, Donald V.
1974 Peripheral and Transitional Markets: The Aztec Case. *American Ethnologist* 1:687-705.

Las Casas, Fray Bartolomé de
1958 *Apologética historia sumaria.* Biblioteca de Autores Españoles, vol. 105. Ediciones Atlas, Madrid.

Libro de tasaciones
1952 *El libro de las tasaciones de pueblos de la Nueva España, siglo XVI.* Archivo General de la Nación, Mexico City.

Mastache de Escobar, Alba Guadalupe
1971 *Técnicas prehispánicas del tejido.* Série Investigaciones No. 20. Instituto Nacional de Antropología e Historia, Mexico City.

Medina, Andrés, and Naomi Quezada
1975 *Panorama de las artesanías otomíes del Valle del Mezquital.* Universidad Nacional Autónoma de México, Instituto de Investigaciones Antropológicas, Mexico City.

Melitz, Jacques
1974 *Primitive and Modern Money: An Interdisciplinary Approach.* Addison-Wesley Publishing Co., Redding, Massachusetts.

Motolinía, Fray Toribio de Benavente
1941 *Historia de los indios de la Nueva España.* Editorial Salvador Chávez Hayhoe, Mexico City.

1971 *Memoriales, o libro de las cosas de la Nueva España y de los naturales de ella.* Edited by Edmundo O'Gorman. Universidad Nacional Autónoma de México, Instituto de Investigaciones Históricas, Mexico City.

Netting, Robert McC.
1990 Population, Permanent Agriculture, and Polities: Unpacking the Evolutionary Portmanteau. In *The Evolution of Political Systems,* edited by Steadman Upham, pp. 21-61. Cambridge University Press, Cambridge.

Nolasco Armas, Margarita
1963 Los Otomíes: Análisis de un grupo marginal. *Anales del Instituto Nacional de Antropología e Historia* 15:153-185.

Parsons, Jeffrey R., and Mary H. Parsons
1990 *Maguey Utilization in Highland Central Mexico.* Anthropological Papers No. 82. Museum of Anthropology, University of Michigan, Ann Arbor.

Paso y Troncoso, Francisco del (editor)
1905 *Papeles de Nueva España,* 2a. Serie, Geografía y estadística, vols. 5, 6. Sucesores de Rivadeneyra, Madrid.

Pozas, Ricardo
1959 *Chamula: Un pueblo indio de los altos de Chiapas.* Memoriales No. 8. Instituto Nacional Indigenista, Mexico City.

Redfield, Robert, and Alfonso Villa Rojas
1934 *Chan Kom, A Maya Village.* University of Chicago Press, Chicago.

Riley, C. Micheal
1973   *Fernando Cortés and the Marquesado in Morelos, 1522-1547.* University of New Mexico Press, Albuquerque.

Rojas Rabiela, Teresa
1979   La organización del trabajo para las obras públicas: el coatéquitl y las cuadrillas de trabajadores. In *El trabajo y los trabajadores en la historia de México,* edited by E. C. Frost, M. C. Meyer, and J. Zoraida Vazques, pp. 41-66. El Colegio de México and University of Arizona Press, Mexico City.

Rojas, José Luis de
1986   *México Tenochtitlan: Economía y Sociedad en el Siglo XIV.* El Colegio de Michoacán y Fondo de Cultura Económica, Mexico City.
1987   La moneda indígena en México, *Revista Española de Antropología Americana* 17:75-88.

Sahagún, Fray Bernardino de
1950-1982   *Florentine Codex: General History of the Things of New Spain.* Translated and edited by Arthur J. O. Anderson and Charles E. Dibble. 12 books. School of American Research and the University of Utah Press, Santa Fe and Salt Lake City.

Sanders, William T., and Robert S. Santley
1983   A Tale of Three Cities: Energetics and Urbanization in Pre-Hispanic Central Mexico. In *Prehistoric Settlement Patterns: Essays in Honor of Gordon R. Willey,* edited by Evon Z. Vogt and Richard M. Leventhal, pp. 243-291. University of New Mexico Press, Albuquerque.

Sanders, William T., and David Webster
1988   The Mesoamerican Urban Tradition. *American Anthropologist* 90:521-546.

Schneider, Harold K.
1974   *Economic Man: The Anthropology of Economics.* Free Press, New York.

Schneider, Jane
1987   The Anthropology of Cloth. *Annual Review of Anthropology* 16:409-448. Annual Reviews, Inc., Palo Alto.

Smith, Michael E.
1986   The Role of Social Stratification in the Aztec Empire: A View from the Provinces. *American Anthropologist* 88:70-91.
1989   Morelos Peasants and the Aztec Empire. Paper presented at the conference, "Morelos in a Global Economy," Cocoyoc, Morelos, Mexico.

Smith, Michael E., and Kenneth G. Hirth
1988   The Development of Prehispanic Cotton-Spinning Technology in Western Morelos, Mexico. *Journal of Field Archaeology* 15:349-358.

Soustelle, Jacques
1962   *The Daily Life of the Aztecs on the Eve of the Spanish Conquest.* Macmillan, New York.

Sperlich, Norbert, and Elizabeth Katz Sperlich
1980   *Guatemalan Backstrap Weaving.* University of Oklahoma Press, Norman.

Suárez de Peralta, Joan

1878 *Noticias históricas de la Nueva España.* Edited by Justo Zaragoza. Imprenta de Manuel G. Hernández, Madrid.

Tax, Sol

1953 *Penny Capitalism: A Guatemalan Indian Economy.* University of Chicago Press, Chicago (Reprint 1963).

Tiryakian, Josefina Cintrón

1979 The Indian Labor Policy of Charles V. In *El trabajo y los trabajadores en la historia de México,* edited by E. C. Frost, M. C. Meyer, and J. Zoraida Vazques, pp. 9-41. El Colegio de México and University of Arizona Press, Mexico City.

Torquemada, Fray Juan de

1975 *Monarquía Indiana.* 3 vols. Editorial Porrúa, Mexico City.

Villanueva, Margaret A.

1985 From Calpixqui to Corregidor: Appropriation of Women's Cotton Textile Production in Early Colonial Mexico. *Latin American Perspectives* 12:17-40.

Wolf, Eric R.

1966 *Peasants.* Prentice-Hall, Englewood Cliffs.

1982 *Europe and the People without History.* University of California Press, Berkeley.

Zavala, Silvio

1984 *Tributos y servicios personales de indios para Hernán Cortés y su familia (Extractos de documentos del siglo XVI).* Archivo General de la Nación, Mexico City.

Zorita, Alonso de

1941 Breve y sumaria relación de los señores y maneras y diferencias que había de ellos en la Nueva España ... In *Relaciones de Texcoco y de la Nueva España,* edited by J. García Icazbalceta, pp. 65-205. Salvador Chávez Hayhoe, Mexico City.

5

The Lip Plugs of Xaltocan

Function and Meaning in Aztec Archaeology

Elizabeth M. Brumfiel, Tamara Salcedo, and David K. Schafer

To account for changing consumption patterns, formal economists examine changes in the relative costs of goods and the purchasing power of consumers. Economists rarely inquire as to how consumption patterns might be altered by changes in product desirability. Archaeologists, however, conventionally treat consumption patterns (as observed in frequencies of discarded artifacts) as evidence for changes in consumer preference, and they constantly ask what these changes in preference indicate about altered cultural circumstances. How archaeologists should infer cultural patterns from consumption patterns is currently the subject of vigorous debate. Older, "middle range theory" approaches, based upon cross-cultural generalizations about artifact form and function (Binford 1962, 1977, 1982), have been challenged by newer approaches emphasizing culturally specific artifact meanings (Hodder 1986).

Binford argues for the feasibility and necessity of "middle range research." Postulating that material culture and behavior are united by constant relationships of functional interdependence, Binford seeks to define properties in the archaeological record that are universal and invariant indicators of sociocultural behavioral systems. Changes in material indicators can then be explained as reflecting changes in behavioral systems. Explaining behavioral systems is the archaeologist's ultimate goal.

Hodder argues that artifact frequencies reflect the goal-oriented behavior of culturally conditioned individuals. In artifact manufacture and use, function and meaning are inextricably tied, particularly for artifacts serving social and ideological ends: "we cannot discuss the social functions of tombs without also discussing what they meant" (Hodder 1986:33). Since meaning is determined by historically and culturally unique social contexts, generalizing about function cross-culturally is impossible. The study of behavior and material culture in one society provides little insight into their relationship in another.

Can function be defined without attention to culturally specific meaning? Do cross-cultural studies provide useful insights for archaeologists investigating particular changes in artifact frequencies? These questions are explored with reference to the distribution of rod-shaped obsidian lip plugs in archaeological and ethnohistoric contexts from the Postclassic Basin of Mexico. We argue that functionalist explanations of consumption patterns can explain most of the distributional data concerning lip plugs but that an understanding of culturally-specific meanings attributed to the artifacts by their users is also useful.

XALTOCAN'S LIP PLUGS AS ETHNIC MARKERS

Xaltocan is a low island in an ancient lake bed in the northern Basin of Mexico (fig. 5.1). In 1987, a program of intensive systematic surface collection was carried out at Xaltocan. Artifacts from a total of 1003 7m x 7m squares were collected from 44.7 ha of site occupation, constituting an 11 percent sample. A 23.3 ha area in the center of town could not be sampled because of modern settlement. The collections included large quantities of decorated and undecorated ceramics, stone tools and waste flakes, ceramic figurines and spindle whorls, fragments of daub and plaster, and a total of 51 narrow, ground obsidian, rod-shaped artifacts which we suggest were lip plugs symbolizing Xaltocan's ethnic identity (fig. 5.2).

The finished artifacts are 4-5 mm wide at their tops and 28 mm long. Examination of 48 partially finished examples enabled us to reconstruct the process of manufacture. An obsidian blade was heavily retouched along its lateral edges below the striking platform until a narrow Tau-shaped outline was achieved. All edges of the blade were then ground smooth. In some cases, grinding proceeded until the entire length of the blade was ground to an even cylinder and all traces of the original surface were obscured. In other cases, grinding appears to have ended once the lateral edges were smoothed, leaving shiny, unground surfaces along the top and bottom of the blade. These artifacts do not seem to have required much time to produce; experimental attempts at their production suggest that they could be turned out in less than an hour (John E. Clark, personal communication 1989). Forty-seven examples of these artifacts occurred

Fig. 5.1.   The Basin of Mexico during the Late Postclassic period.
This map shows the locations of Xaltocan and other major settlements
of the time.

in 40 of the systematic collection units (the other four examples were collected from structures). They were found in all areas of the site; although a
particularly dense concentration of these artifacts was found in the northwest
corner of the site, no sector of the site was entirely free of them (fig. 5.3).
For several reasons, we believe that these artifacts are markers of Xaltocan's
ethnic identity.

First, these artifacts look like items of personal adornment. They are small,
lightweight, and fragile. They could easily have been worn as lip plugs, passing
through a hole in the lower lip. The grinding that occurs on their edges is extensive and even, as if it were carried out to achieve a smoothed surface. We doubt

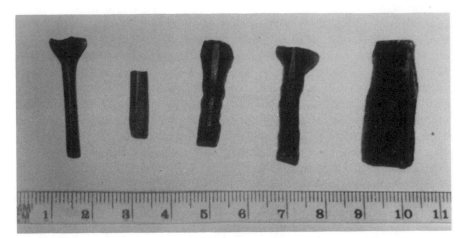

Fig. 5.2.   Partially finished lip plugs from Xaltocan. This series of blades illustrates stages in the manufacture of rod-shaped lip plugs. The blade on the far right bears heavy retouch along its lateral edges below the striking platform. Other blades show successive stages of grinding until the finished lip plug (far left) is achieved.

that the grinding is wear from using these artifacts as drills. As we shall see, similar objects, used as lip plugs, appear in native pictorial documents.

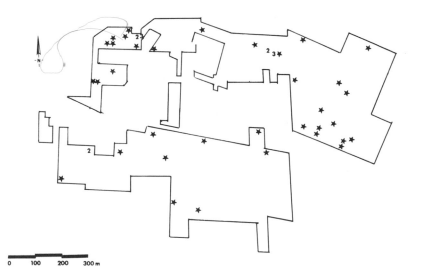

Fig. 5.3.   The distribution of lip plugs within the survey area at Xaltocan.

Second, as items of personal adornment, these artifacts are probably not markers of high status. Cross-cultural studies of status markers leads us to believe that such artifacts are characterized by difficult production processes that limit their availability to those who control skilled specialists (Clark and Parry 1990; Earle 1987; Peregrine 1991). The ease with which these artifacts were produced argues against their use as status markers. This argument is supported by lip plug distribution at Xaltocan. Decorated pottery is a good index of elite status and household wealth in Postclassic Central Mexico (Brumfiel 1987:681; Smith 1994). But at Xaltocan, lip plugs are not associated with unusual concentrations of decorated pottery; the proportion of decorated pottery in surface collections containing lip plugs is not much higher than the proportion of decorated pottery in surface collections without them (table 5.1).

Table 5.1 Decorated pottery in units with and without lip plugs

Context	Decorated Rims		Total Rims
	No.	Percent	
Middle Postclassic Collection Units			
Units with lip plugs	301	34.8	866
Units without lip plugs	1,012	31.8	5,659
Late Postclassic Collection Units			
Units with lip plugs	157	28.0	560
Units without lip plugs	1,407	24.6	5,727

Third, these artifacts conform to established functionalist expectations of what ethnic markers should look like. Ethnographic studies of ethnicity suggest that items of personal adornment frequently serve as symbols of ethnic affiliation (Despres 1975:194; Hoetink 1975:22; Spicer 1971:798; Wobst 1977:330-335). According to Wobst (1977:329), ethnic group markers tend to occur in contrasting sets, with the markers of each ethnic group having paradigmatic relationships with the markers of the other groups. The lip plugs of Xaltocan may have been elements in a region-wide system of facial jewelry where each item of jewelry defined a particular ethnic group, differing from the jewelry of other ethnic groups in shape, raw material, and the part of the face adorned. For example, Chimalpahin (1965:76) reports that at Yacapixtlan, Morelos, "All went about with worked metal ornaments in their noses in honor of the devil [their patron deity, Tezcatlipoca]."

Fourth, ethnohistorical documents from Central Mexico suggest that ethnicity was an important principle of social organization in late prehispanic Mexico (Zantwijk 1973, 1985). During the Middle and Late Postclassic periods (A.D. 1150-1520), the basic political unit was the multiethnic city-state

(Chimalpahin [1965:63-77, 139-50] describes the multiethnic composition of Amecamecan; Alva Ixtlilxochitl [1975-1977:v.2:32, 34] does the same for Texcoco). Each ethnic group constituted a ward or *calpulli* which was the basic land-holding, tribute-paying unit within the city-state (Carrasco 1971:363-368). Commoner groups legitimated their rights to land and ruling lineages legitimated their rights to labor and tribute by preserving their particular ethnic histories and ethnic identities (Brumfiel 1994). Cross-cultural studies of ethnicity indicate that ethnic identity is strongest when it legitimates access to important resources (Barth 1969). Given the important role of ethnicity in the Basin of Mexico political economy, we might expect ethnic groups to elaborate symbols of their identity.

Fifth, ethnohistoric evidence links obsidian lip plugs to a particular ethnic group, the Otomi, and additional evidence establishes the importance of the Otomi in Xaltocan. The *Florentine Codex* records the connection between obsidian lip plugs and Otomi identity: "The lip plugs of the [Otomi] rulers were green stone lip plugs, or sea shell lip plugs, or gold lip plugs ... The lip plugs of all the [other Otomi] people were of rock crystal, obsidian or smoky stone." (Sahagún 1950-1982:bk.10:177-178). The native historian Alva Ixtlilxochitl (1975-1977:v.1:423, v.2:299) states that Xaltocan was first settled and ruled by people of Otomi ancestry, although the community's population came to include many other ethnic groups (Nazareo 1940:123-124).

The spatial distribution of rod-shaped lip plugs may support their interpretation as markers of Otomi identity, but the picture is somewhat complex. On the local level, as we have seen, the lip plugs are scattered across the site, and this does not conform to the model of community organization suggested by ethnohistoric sources, i.e., localized wards of ethnically distinct *calpulli* groups. Instead, the scattered distribution of lip plugs suggests one of three possibilities: either the entire population of Xaltocan was Otomi; or the members of the Otomi *calpulli* groups did not co-reside in localized wards; or ethnic identity was somewhat smeared at Xaltocan, with many residents choosing to identify with the ethnic group of the community's ruling lineage.

The first possibility is flatly contradicted by Nazareo (1940:123-124) who insists that Xaltocan was a multiethnic community. The second possibility is somewhat more likely. *Calpulli* groups have been considered as coresidential units primarily because of the Spanish habit of equating *calpulli* with barrio, and by the coincidence of *calpulli* names with barrio names in historical or contemporary communities (Carrasco 1971:363-364). And yet, it is possible that the localized character of the *calpulli* was established with reference to the location of the sanctuary of its patron deity rather than with reference to the residence of its members. The third possibility seems even more likely. Community members might come to identify the ruling lineage and its patron deity as protectors and benefactors of the entire community. Smith (1984) points to the acquired identification of residents with their town, citing Chimalpahin's statement (1965:66), "[I]t was the custom that when a person moved from his town and went to settle in another already established town, such a person would assume as his own name that of the town to which he had moved." The distribution of lip plugs at Xaltocan may indicate that, despite the historically diverse ethnic composition of Central Mexican communities, ethnicity served as a unifying ideology at the community level.

On the regional level, rod-shaped obsidian lip plugs are unique to Xaltocan within the Basin of Mexico. This is consistent with Alva Ixtlilxochitl's (1975-1977:v.2:36) statement that Xaltocan was the capital of the Otomi. In addition, four almost identical lip plugs displayed at the Field Museum in Chicago come from areas of presumed Otomi occupation outside the Basin of Mexico. The museum catalog states that these lip plugs were collected from Calixtlahuaca and Tlacotepec in the Toluca Valley. The Toluca Valley contained Otomi speakers at the time of European contact, and Carrasco (1950:241-255) suggests that the neighboring Mazahua area was the point of origin for Otomi speakers in the Basin of Mexico. On the other hand, the Otomi site of Otumba (in Nahuatl, Otonpan, "place of the Otomi") in the northeastern Basin of Mexico has yielded obsidian lip plugs quite unlike those from Xaltocan. Otumba's lip plugs are button-shaped rather than rod-shaped (Otis Charlton 1990). This suggests that, if obsidian lip plugs did serve as Otomi ethnic markers, they assumed at least two regional forms.

The evidence from sixteenth-century pictorial manuscripts is also complex. Lip plugs are sometimes present and sometimes absent when Otomi figures are depicted. For example, a rod-shaped lip plug adorns the image of the Otomi patron deity Otonteuctli in the *Codex Magliabecchiano* (1983:v.1:f. 38) illustration of the festival Xocotl huetzi (fig. 5.4). Rod-shaped lip plugs are also worn by Otomi dancers in the festival of Xocotl huetzi depicted in the *Codex Borbonicus* (1974) (fig. 5.5). Rod-shaped lip plugs are worn by the Otomi residents of Teocalhueyacan who offer shelter to the Spanish conquistadors in Book 12 of the *Florentine Codex* (Sahagún 1950-1982:bk.12:chap.26) (fig. 5.6). And a lip plug is worn by the honorary "Otomi" warrior depicted in the *Codex Mendoza* (1992:f.64r) (fig. 5.7), although this appears to be a much more complex affair than the rod-shaped lip plugs recovered archaeologically. On the other hand, in four cases, Otomi figures appear without lip plugs. These occur in the place glyph for Otumba in the *Codex Mendoza* (1992:f.3v) (fig. 5.8); the illustration of Otonteuctli in Sahagún's *Primeros Memoriales* (Paso y Troncoso 1905-1907:v.6:fig. 8) (fig. 5.9); the illustration of Chiconcuauh and subsequent early Otomi rulers of Xaltocan in the *Codex Xolotl* (1951:pl. 1) (fig. 5.10), and the *Florentine Codex* illustrations that accompany Sahagún's (1950-1982:bk.10:chap. 29) statement that the Otomi wore obsidian lip plugs (fig. 5.11)!

Fig. 5.4.   The Otomi patron deity Otonteuctli. This god, wearing a rod-shaped lip plug, appears in the festival of Xocotl huetzi (*Codex Magliabecchiano* 1983:v.1:f. 38).

Why is the pictorial evidence so inconsistent? In part, it may be a faithful mirror of a complex reality. If, as indicated in the archaeological record, the Otumba Otomi did not use rod-shaped lip plugs as ethnic markers, then it is entirely appropriate that such lip plugs not be present in the place glyph for Otumba and in the depiction of Otonteuctli drawn by the Tepeapulco informants used by Sahagún in preparing the *Primeros Memoriales* (Tepeapulco and Otumba probably shared symbolic conventions since they lie together at the northeast edge of the Basin of Mexico and are connected by a major trade route; Xaltocan is 35 km west of Otumba and is not connected to it by any major route). In addition, some of the complexities of the pictorial evidence may be due to the intent of Aztec artists who failed to depict lip plugs in order to comment upon the character of the Otomi people and the legitimacy of the Aztec state. In order to consider this possibility, we must depart from a cross-cultural, functionalist analysis of ethnic symbolism and explore the meanings that facial jewelry had for the people of late prehispanic Central Mexico. Alfredo López Austin's (1988) discussion of Aztec conceptions of the human head provides a useful point of departure.

Fig. 5.5.   Otomi dancers. The dancers, wearing rod-shaped lip plugs,
celebrate the festival of Xocotl huetzi (*Codex Borbonicus* 1974).

Fig. 5.6. Otomi residents of Teo-calhueyacan. Here, the Otomi of Teocalhueyacan offer shelter to the Spanish conquistadores (Sahagún 1950-1982:bk.12:chap. 26).

Fig. 5.7. An honorary "Otomi" warrior. The warrior, wearing an elaborate lip plug, seizes a captive (*Codex Mendoza* 1992:f.64r).

Fig. 5.8. The Otumba place glyph (*Codex Mendoza* 1992:f.3v).

Fig. 5.9. The Otomi patron deity Otonteuctli. Here, Otonteuctli appears without a lip plug (Paso y Troncoso 1905-1907:v.6:fig. 8).

Fig. 5.10. The Otomi ruler Chiconcuauh. Chiconcuauh, the middle of the three figures on the right, appears without a lip plug (*Codex Xolotl* 1951:pl. 1).

Fig. 5.11. An Otomi hunter. The hunter appears without a lip plug (Sahagún 1950-1982:bk.10:chap. 29).

ETHNIC JEWELRY AND THE AZTEC HEAD

According to López Austin (1988:170-172), the Aztecs considered the head to have several outstanding attributes. First, it was the locus of four of the five senses, and as such, it was the center of the human powers of reason. López Austin (1988:195) states that the ancient Nahuas attributed to the sense organs not only the powers of perception but also the powers of reasoning, judgement, and understanding based on experience. Perception leads to experience, and experience to understanding and good judgement, according to the Aztecs. To educate people is "to make people acquire the power of perception" (López Austin 1988:195). An "exceedingly wise" person is one who "possesses ears and eyes to the highest degree" (López Austin 1988:195). The head was also the part of the body which revealed social position. The head and face reflected experience and education that an individual had acquired as a member of society and hence that individual's position within society.

All this suggests that, from the Aztec point of view, facial jewelry would have been a highly appropriate means of demarcating ethnicity. Facial jewelry adorns the sense organs: the ears, nose, and mouth. Facial jewelry that is ethnic-specific particularizes the sense organs; it converts them from universally human ears, noses, and mouths to specifically Otomi or Matlatzinca or Tlahuica ears, noses, and mouths. In doing so, it calls attention to the cultural construction of human perception and the culturally-specific nature of human experience. Given Aztec conceptions of perception, experience, and education, it is hard to think of a more appropriate way of symbolizing the enculturated individual than through ethnic-specific facial jewelry.

Why then is facial jewelry sometimes omitted when Otomi individuals appear in sixteenth-century pictorial documents? The omission may have been intentional, allowing the Aztecs to communicate their view of the Otomi.

ETHNICITY AND THE AZTEC STATE

Cross-cultural studies suggest that ethnic identity has two faces: ethnic affiliation and ethnic attribution (Comaroff 1987; see also Jenkins 1986:177). Ethnic affiliation refers to individuals' assertions of their own ethnic group membership; ethnic attribution refers to the attributes ascribed to ethnic groups by nonmembers. Ethnic affiliation is an in-group phenomenon; attribution is the work of outsiders. The Aztec state appears to have used ethnic attribution as an ideological stratagem for maintaining state power.

The Aztec state maintained an official policy of tolerance toward ethnic diversity (Zantwijk 1985), but this coexisted with widespread, derogatory ethnic stereotypes. Sahagún's Mexica informants, for example, characterized the Otomi as gaudy dressers, lazy, improvident, shiftless and untrained blockheads; the Matlatzinca were great witches who blew evil upon their victims; the Huasteca were drunkards, and the Tlahuica were cowards (Sahagún 1950-1982:bk.10:chap. 29). These ethnic stereotypes may have been actively promoted by the cultural policies of the Aztec state. State-sponsored ritual performances provided opportunities for the state to define categorical distinctions between ethnic groups. It seems likely that the ethnic images presented in state-sponsored performances were an important source for the stereotypes enunciated by Sahagún's informants.

At the festival of Xocotl huezti, for example, warriors dressed as Otomi danced publicly with the captives they had taken prior to offering them for sacrifice (Sahagún 1950-1982:bk.2:chap. 29). Although the manner of their dance is not recorded, this occasion provided a good opportunity for the state to comment upon the meaning of Otomi-ness. The Aztec image of the Otomi was also communicated by the dress and behavior of the elite Aztec soldiers admitted to the ranks of honorary "Otomi" warriors. "Otomi" warriors wore their hair in the defined Otomi fashion (shaved in front, long in back). They wore special jewelry (white gastropod shell necklaces and lip plugs formed like the broad leaf of a water plant [see Sahagún 1950-1982:bk.2:chap. 27]). Such warriors were valued for their capacity for violence, but they were not considered qualified to govern: "The rulership they entrusted to no one who was a wicked but brave warrior, one furious in battle ... those who only come paying the tribute of death, ... called *quaquachictin,* Otomi, *tlaotonxinti*" (Sahagún 1950-1982:bk.6:110). The image of "Otomi" warriors as too brutal to hold political power was a commentary on the ethnic Otomi's capacity for self-government.

The Aztec state, then, may well have promoted an image of the Otomi as lacking in the experience, education, reason, judgement, and wisdom that would qualify them for self-rule. What better way to illustrate this than by depicting the Otomi face stripped of jewelry, i.e., lacking any cultural elaboration of their powers of perception? We can suggest, then, that the Otomi in Book 10 of the *Florentine Codex* were depicted without facial jewelry as a way of underscoring the untutored character of their ethnic group. In a similar vein, the depiction of the Otomi (and all other ethnic groups) without conventional facial jewelry in the *Codex Xolotl* could have been a way of communicating the proto-cultural, primeval character of the world of the Chichimec migrations.

CULTURAL POLITICS AND CHANGES IN LIP PLUG CONSUMPTION AT XALTOCAN

The cross-cultural studies of ethnicity and the state suggest that states act opportunistically, in some cases suppressing ethnic identity to weaken local resistance to outside rule while in other cases promoting ethnic identity to undermine the solidarity of subordinate classes (Patterson 1987). State policies toward ethnicity are an important determinant of the coherence of different ethnic groups within the state, whether they will mobilize to pursue group goals or whether they will disappear as their members seek alternative identities (Comaroff 1987). The treatment of group leaders is particularly important in determining the intensity and persistence of ethnic identity (Brass 1985).

The ethnic policies of the Aztec state were complex. As mentioned above, a policy of official tolerance of ethnic diversity coexisted with widespread, derogatory ethnic stereotypes. At the same time, the Aztecs attempted to absorb local elites into the Aztec power structure. At Xaltocan, for example, members of the local ruling lineage consistently took wives from the Mexica ruling lineage (Nazareo 1940:124-125). Given the cognatic character of Aztec kinship structure (Carrasco 1984; Kellogg 1988), the intermarriage of Mexica and Xaltocan elites would have produced offspring able to claim privileges in either the local or regional hierarchy. Local elites also participated in ritual activities at the Aztec capitals, where they were rewarded with generous gifts of imperial wealth (Anunciación 1940:261; Durán 1967:v.2:172, 279, 297-298, 311, 325, 346, 415, 483). Smith (1986) argues that the Aztecs, in interacting with local elites, built upon shared class interests. We might predict that this strategy would

Table 5.2   Lip plug frequencies at Xaltocan

Category	Middle Postclassic	Late Postclassic
Number of lip plugs	14	6
Number of rim sherds	6,562	6,287
Lip plug frequency per 100 rim sherds	0.21	0.10

undermine the distinctive ethnic identities of local rulers and devalue the ethnic affiliation of their subjects.

The devaluation of Otomi ethnic identity under Aztec rule may have lowered lip plug frequency (i.e., consumption) at Xaltocan. Twenty of the 51 lip plugs from Xaltocan occur in collections that can be securely dated on the basis of their ceramics (table 5.2). Fourteen occur in collections that contain predominantly (i.e., >70%) Early-and-Middle Postclassic pottery, from the period A.D. 800-1350 when Xaltocan was an autonomous center of regional importance in the northern Basin of Mexico. Six occur in collections with predominantly (i.e.,>70%) Late Postclassic pottery, from the period A.D. 1350-1521 when Xaltocan was subject to first Tepaneca and later Aztec rule. Although these numbers are small, they are suggestive. They indicate that when Xaltocan's rulers were absorbed into a regional elite, the value of Otomi identity declined. This, in turn, lowered the consumer preference for and consumption of the rod-shaped lip plugs that asserted Otomi identity.

CONCLUSIONS: THE FUNCTION AND MEANING OF ETHNIC SYMBOLS

This interpretation of the narrow, rod-shaped, obsidian artifacts from Xaltocan has relied extensively upon generalizations drawn from cross-cultural studies. These generalizations have been used to generate a series of expectations concerning the differences between status markers and ethnic markers, the differences between symbols of ethnic affiliation and ethnic attribution, and the situations in which these identities would be salient. We modified these expectations, however, as we encountered evidence that contradicted them. For example, we anticipated that ethnic identity would demarcate the resource-holding groups of Central Mexican society, the *calpulli* groups, but contradictory contextual evidence (i.e., the scatter of lip plugs across Xaltocan) suggested that Xaltocan's lip plugs expressed ethnicity at the community level (the identification of community members with the ethnic origins of their ruler). Thus, the use of generalizations based upon cross-cultural studies did not rule out the identification of culturally-specific, unique patterns of behavior and belief. On the contrary, the use of generalizations threw such patterns into sharp relief, making them more apparent.

This discussion has also relied upon ethnohistoric documents that provide some insight into the meaning of ethnicity and facial jewelry in late prehispanic Central Mexico. These documents suggested that ethnicity was an important category in native social thought, that ethnicity coincided with the control of resources, and that ethnicity was sometimes symbolized by facial jewelry. These suggestions coincided well with our cross-culturally derived expectations and lent support to our assertion that the rod-shaped artifacts from Xaltocan served as ethnic symbols. In addition, ethnohistoric information on native concepts of the face suggested how facial jewelry could have been used by social actors to comment upon the claims and capabilities of particular social groups. This information enabled us to resolve the seeming contradiction between the archaeological evidence of Otomi facial jewelry and the ethnohistoric documents that sometimes depict the Otomi without facial jewelry.

In a sense, the "functional" approach, involving the application of cross-cultural generalizations, helped to establish the "meaning" of the artifacts being studied. Knowing how and why people have alluded to concepts of shared cultural inheritance in situations outside the Basin of Mexico enabled us to establish expectations as to how and why such allusions were made in the late prehispanic era. Thus, the non-Basin of Mexico cases served as an important source of our "historical imagination," that is, our ability to make inferences about the "meaning content" of the past (Hodder 1986:94-95).

What are the implications of this discussion for the study of archaeologically preserved consumption patterns? First, it is useful to phrase questions about consumption in terms of a cross-culturally based theoretical understanding of human society and material culture. Our examination of lip plugs at Xaltocan suggests that there are principles of social structure and social negotiation that are invoked repeatedly by actors in historically unrelated contexts and to deny the existence of these principles in the analysis of consumption patterns is to forgo a much needed analytical aid. On the other hand, the applicability of these theory-based propositions must be validated for each individual case through an examination of the relevant archaeological contexts. We should expect that each case will yield some unique and surprising results because, as Hodder (1986:148) observes, in the complex web of variables that actors take into account when determining their behavior, "other things" are never "equal."

ACKNOWLEDGMENTS

The systematic surface collection of Xaltocan was supported by a grant from the H. John Heinz III Charitable Trust. John Clark, George Cowgill, Mary Hodge, Thomas Patterson, and Michael Smith supplied valuable comments and criticisms on earlier drafts of this paper. Maggie LaNoue produced the drawings from native manuscripts that illustrate this chapter. For all these forms of assistance, we are grateful.

REFERENCES CITED

Alva Ixtlilxochitl, Fernando de
  1975-1977 *Obras históricas.* Edited by Edmundo O'Gorman. 2 vols. Universidad Nacional Autónoma de México, Mexico City.
Anunciación, Fray Domingo de la
  1940 Parecer de fray Domingo de la Anunciación, sobre el modo que tenían de tributar los indios ... (20 de septiembre de 1554). In *Epistolario de Nueva España,* vol. 7, edited by Francisco del Paso y Troncoso, pp. 259-266. Antigua Librería Robredo, Mexico City.
Barth, Frederik
  1969 Introduction. In *Ethnic Groups and Boundaries,* edited by Frederik Barth, pp. 9-38. Little, Brown, Boston.
Binford, Lewis R.
  1962 Archaeology as Anthropology. *American Antiquity* 28:217-225.
  1977 General Introduction. In *For Theory Building in Archaeology,* edited by Lewis R. Binford, pp. 1-10. Academic Press, New York.
  1982 Objectivity—Explanation—Archaeology 1981. In *Theory and Explanation in*

Archaeology, edited by Colin Renfrew, Michael J. Rowlands, and Barbara A. Segraves, pp. 125-146. Academic Press, New York.

Brass, Paul R.

1985   Ethnic Groups and the State. In *Ethnic Groups and the State,* edited by Paul R. Brass, pp. 1-56. Barnes and Nobel Imports, Savage, Maryland.

Brumfiel, Elizabeth M.

1987   Consumption and Politics at Aztec Huexotla. *American Anthropologist* 89: 676-686.

1994   Ethnic Groups and Political Development in Ancient Mexico. In *Factional Competition and Political Development in the New World,* edited by Elizabeth M. Brumfiel and John W. Fox, pp. 89-102. Cambridge University Press, Cambridge.

Carrasco, Pedro

1950   *Los Otomíes: cultura e historia prehispánica de los pueblos Mesoaméricanos de habla Otomiana.* Instituto de Historia, primera serie, 15. Universidad Nacional Autónoma de México, Mexico City.

1971   Social Organization of Ancient Mexico. In *Archaeology of Northern Mesoamerica,* pt. 1, edited by Gordon F. Ekholm and Ignacio Bernal, pp. 349-375. Handbook of Middle American Indians, vol. 10, Robert Wauchope, general editor. University of Texas Press, Austin.

1974   Sucesión y alianzas matrimoniales en la dinastía Teotihuacana. *Estudios de Cultura Náhuatl* 11:235-241.

1984   Royal Marriages in Ancient Mexico. In *Explorations in Ethnohistory,* edited by H. R. Harvey, and Hanns J. Prem, pp. 41-81. University of New Mexico Press, Albuquerque.

Chimalpahin Quauhtlehuanitzin, Domingo Francisco de San Antón Muñón

1965   *Relaciones originales de Chalco Amaquemecan,* translated by Sylvia Rendón. Fondo de Cultura Económica, Mexico City.

Clark, John E., and William J. Parry

1990   Craft Specialization and Cultural Complexity. *Research in Economic Anthropology* 12:289-346.

Codex Borbonicus

1974   *Codex Borbonicus.* Codices Selecti, Vol. 44. Akademische Druck-u. Verlagsanstalt, Graz, Austria.

Codex Magliabecchiano

1983   *Codex Magliabecchiano.* 2 vols. Translation and commentary by Elizabeth H. Boone and Zelia Nuttall. University of California Press, Berkeley.

Codex Mendoza

1992   *The Codex Mendoza.* Edited by Frances F. Berdan and Patricia Reiff Anawalt. 4 vols. University of California Press, Berkeley.

Codex Xolotl

1951   *Codex Xolotl.* Edited by Charles E. Dibble. Universidad Nacional de México and the University of Utah, Mexico City and Salt Lake City.

Comaroff, John L.
1987 Of Totemism and Ethnicity: Consciousness, Practice and the Signs of Inequality. *Ethnos* 52:301-323.

Despres, Leo A.
1975 Towards a Theory of Ethnic Phenomena. In *Ethnicity and Resource Competition in Plural Societies,* edited by Leo A. Despres, pp.187-207. Mouton, The Hague.

Durán, Fray Diego
1967 *Historia de las Indias de Nueva España e Islas de la Tierra Firme.* Edited by Angel María Garibay K. 2 vols. Editorial Porrúa, Mexico City.

Earle, Timothy K.
1987 Specialization and the Production of Wealth: Hawaiian Chiefdoms and the Inka Empire. In *Specialization, Exchange, and Complex Societies,* edited by Elizabeth M. Brumfiel and Timothy K. Earle, pp. 64-75. Cambridge University Press, Cambridge.

Hodder, Ian
1986 *Reading the Past.* Cambridge University Press, Cambridge.

Hoetink, Harmannus
1975 Resource Competition, Monopoly, and Socioracial Diversity. In *Ethnicity and Resource Competition in Plural Societies,* edited by Leo A. Despres, pp. 9-25. Mouton, The Hague.

Jenkins, Richard
1986 Social Anthropological Models of Inter-ethnic Relations. In *Theories of Race and Ethnic Relations,* edited by John Rex and David Mason, pp. 170-186. Cambridge University Press, Cambridge.

Kellogg, Susan
1988 Cognatic Kinship and Religion: Women in Aztec Society. In *Smoke and Mist: Mesoamerican Studies in Memory of Thelma D. Sullivan,* edited by J. Kathryn Josserand and Karen Dakin, pp. 665-681. International Series No. 402. British Archaeological Reports, Oxford.

López Austin, Alfredo
1988 *The Human Body and Ideology: Concepts of the Ancient Nahuas.* Translated by Thelma Ortiz de Montellano and Bernardo Ortiz de Montellano. 2 vols. University of Utah Press, Salt Lake City.

Nazareo de Xaltocan, Don Pablo
1940 Carta al Rey Don Felipe II. In *Epistolario de Nueva España,* edited by Francisco del Paso y Troncoso, vol. 10, pp.109-129. Antigua Librería Robredo, Mexico City.

Otis Charlton, Cynthia
1990 Operation 11, Field 169, Mound 41, Lapidary Workshop. In *Early State Formation Processes: The Aztec City-State of Otumba, Mexico, Part 1, Preliminary Report on Recent Research in the Otumba City-State,* edited by Thomas H. Charlton and Deborah L. Nichols, pp. 177-199. Research Report No. 3.

Mesoamerican Research Colloquium, Department of Anthropology, University of Iowa, Iowa City.

Patterson, Thomas C.

1987 Tribes, Chiefdoms, and Kingdoms in the Inca Empire. In *Power Relations and State Formation,* edited by Thomas C. Patterson and Christine W. Gailey, pp. 117-127. American Anthropological Association, Washington, D.C.

Paso y Troncoso, Francisco del

1905-1907 *Fray Bernardino de Sahagún: Historia de las cosas de Nueva España.* 6 vols. Hauser y Menet, Madrid.

Peregrine, Peter N.

1991 Power and the Division of Labor: A Critical Review. Paper presented at the 90th annual meeting of the American Anthropological Association, Chicago.

Sahagún, Fray Bernardino de

1950-1982 *Florentine Codex: General History of the Things of New Spain.* Translated and edited by Arthur J. O. Anderson and Charles E. Dibble. 12 books. School of American Research and the University of Utah Press, Santa Fe and Salt Lake City.

Smith, Michael E.

1984 The Aztlan Migrations of the Nahuatl Chronicles: Myth or History? *Ethnohistory* 31:153-186.

1986 The Role of Social Stratification in the Aztec Empire: A View from the Provinces. *American Anthropologist* 88:70-91.

1994 Social Complexity in the Aztec Countryside. In *Archaeological Views from the Countryside: Village Communities in Early Complex Societies,* edited by Glenn Schwartz and Steven Falconer, pp. 143-159. Smithsonian Institution Press, Washington, D.C.

Spicer, Edward H.

1971 Persistent Cultural Systems. *Science* 174:795-800.

Wobst, H. Martin

1977 Stylistic Behavior and Information Exchange. In *For the Director: Research Essays in Honor of James B. Griffin,* edited by Charles E. Cleland, pp. 317-342. Anthropological Papers No. 61. Museum of Anthropology, University of Michigan, Ann Arbor.

Zantwijk, Rudolph van

1973 Politics and Ethnicity in a Prehispanic Mexican State Between the 13th and 15th Centuries. *Plural Societies* 4(2):23-52.

1985 *The Aztec Arrangement: The Social History of Pre-Spanish Mexico.* University of Oklahoma Press, Norman.

6

Stylistic and Spatial Variability in Early Aztec Ceramics

Insights into Pre-Imperial Exchange Systems

Leah D. Minc, Mary G. Hodge, and M. James Blackman

Aztec markets constitute one of the better documented aspects of the prehispanic economy, yet the development of the market system and the degree to which the formation of the Aztec empire fostered that development remain points of active debate. A clear prerequisite for understanding the imperial Aztec market system is baseline data on commodity exchange systems for the period immediately preceding the rise of the Aztec empire. This study attempts to fill that current gap by examining the structure of exchange systems through which one class of utilitarian goods, decorated ceramics, was circulated in the pre-imperial or Early Aztec period.

AZTEC MARKETS AND MARKET-INTEGRATED ECONOMY

The Aztec market system on the eve of the Spanish conquest has been characterized as a complex interlocking system consisting of a hierarchy of periodic market centers serviced by both local producers and itinerant merchants that provided a high degree of economic integration for regional and community-level specialization in production (Berdan 1975, 1985; Durán 1971; Gibson 1964; Hicks 1987; Smith 1979; cf. Evans 1980; Kurtz 1974). The degree of economic integration achieved by the Aztec market network suggests that the imperial system was verging on a "market-integrated" economy (Hicks 1987). Frederic Hicks (1987) suggests that a truly market-integrated economy has four requirements: (1) a series of full-time specialists of many kinds, who do not produce their own food staples; (2) a corresponding body of producers who supply food staples and other necessities; (3) a market network to bring these complementary elements together effectively and continuously; and (4) a state power to maintain order and stability in the productive spheres as well as in the market, by ensuring access to the market, adjudicating disputes, etc. Under such a market-integrated economy, a substantial proportion of the populace depended on the market for the satisfaction of their daily subsistence needs.

The origins of the Aztec market system and of the imperial market-integrated economy remain problematical. Richard Blanton (1994) argues that the foundations of a regional market network were established in the pre-imperial or Early Aztec period, although the system was unevenly and incompletely developed at that time. Based on the number and spatial organization of primary and secondary centers or central places that serviced the local hinterland during that period, Blanton concludes that even at this early time a commercial principle (visible as competition among centers for consumers) was operating as a major determinant of central-place development in some portions of the Basin. The extremely regular spacing of the Early Aztec regional centers suggests that centrality to local hinterlands was a major factor in determining the locations and spacing of centers; however, the interstitial spaces of the settlement lattices were not completely filled in, indicating that the region's system of central places was not yet fully developed.

Blanton (1994) suggests that "The fact that a commercial principle appears to best predict the locations of secondary centers ... strongly implies that the major force in determining the settlement system we observe was commerce, and that a market principle (the 'transport principle') appears to have been operative in determining the locations of secondary centers." The transport principle (or K=4 system) locates lower-level centers between two higher-level centers, minimizing transport costs by minimizing the number of roads that must be constructed between centers. This system seems to be most efficient for servicing agglomerated settlements with bulk goods and is the most common pattern of central place networks (Smith 1974:174-175).

The use of central place theory to infer that market principles were the dominant forces generating a hierarchy of settlements rests on several behavioral assumptions, the primary ones of which are that market exchange is integrated and part of a single region-wide system and that consumers have a choice as to which market they will patronize such that there is competition for retailers (Smith 1974:168-169). Given this competition, markets will be situated to maximize access to consumers. In particular, both the K=4 and the alternative K=3 (or 'market principle') locations assume that rural market participants are free to choose market destinations (Blanton 1994).

The existence of a single, region-wide market system for the Early Aztec period can be questioned, however. The pre-imperial period in the Basin of Mexico is described in the ethnohistoric documents as a time of extreme political decentralization and instability, characterized by almost continual conflict between small, independent polities. The settlement patterns for the Early Aztec period support the documents on this point. The distribution of sites during the Early Aztec period consists of "a series of local centers, each dominating a small part of the Basin and each separated from its neighboring polities by a frontier of contested, not well-inhabited borderland" (Blanton et al. 1981:152).

The apparent political insularity of polities would make it unlikely that the subject population was able to exercise a great deal of choice in which market they patronized or that they could travel safely to the market center of a hostile polity. Thus, the regular spacing of the Early Aztec centers may well reflect, not competition for free-ranging market-goers, but rather attempts to maximize distance and minimize conflict between potentially hostile polities. Such hostilities would also explain the underdevelopment of secondary centers in the contested buffer zones between polities. In fact, Blanton (1994) concludes his analysis with the cautionary statement that the existence of a regional market network "seems to be a highly counter-intuitive conclusion to draw, since from the historical accounts of the period we learn primarily about political struggles, battles between ethnic groups, and rulers, not markets, regional centrality, or the advantages of locations at the interstices of regional central-place lattices."

In keeping with the political milieu of the Early Aztec period, several authors (Hassig 1985:71-73, Hicks 1987; Smith 1979) have suggested that prior to imperial consolidation market exchange was not organized in a regional network, but in a "solar" market system. Hicks (1987:93), for example, argues that: "The Early States [preceding the Triple Alliance] would appear to have had a 'solar' central place pattern with regard to both tribute and market activities ... By this I mean that tribute in goods and services were brought to the royal palace in the city by commoners in the city's immediate hinterland, and the people patronized only the marketplace of their own city". Hicks suggests that one of the means by which imperial power was consolidated involved the breakdown of this "solar" marketing system to reduce local autonomy and bring about a regional economy (1987:94-95).

As a system of central places, a solar market system consists of a localized, low-level market hierarchy (usually involving an administrative center serviced by several small rural market places) that is poorly articulated with other low-level hierarchies in the same region (Smith 1974:176). Causal factors of solar market systems include local autonomy in the political sphere, extensive efforts by the ruling class to control markets and regulate prices, the suppression of direct trade between communities, and poor transport facility (Kaplan 1965; Nash 1966; Smith 1974, 1976). Solar market systems frequently develop in a colonial context and are associated with the fragmentation of a regional economy into a number of local economies, each tending to become self-sufficient and independent of the others, with only the administrative centers linked through elite-controlled trade. In some developing countries, however, poorly articulated local systems have developed around the administrative capitals of independent kingdoms (Smith 1974:177), and proponents of the solar market model suggest that this was the case for Early Aztec polities.

The two marketing systems contrasted above, the regionally integrated market network and the solar market system, generate distinctive spatial patterns of commodity flow and distribution that should be visible in the archaeological record. As noted above, the existence of a regional network of central places governed by the marketing principle presupposes that consumers have a choice as to which market they will patronize and that both suppliers and consumers maximize their freedom to choose optimal marketing destinations. As a result, market territories are overlapping areas, defined only loosely by the process of shifting consumer and supplier habits (Blanton et al. 1981:234). Further, such market systems require a relatively unbounded space for efficient operation; regions with market integration will be resistant to restrictions on movement that might be imposed by administrative institutions. These characteristics suggest several key aspects of spatial patterning generated by a regionally integrated market system: (1) the structure is characterized by a series of fluid, overlapping market territories; and (2) the network is spatially unbounded by political or administrative boundaries (i.e., political boundaries should be permeable to commodity flow).

In contrast, solar market systems result in poor rural terms of trade in that rural market participants are unable to exercise choice in market destinations (Smith 1974:176-177). The enforced dependence on the primary market/administrative center for goods and services and the inward flow of tributary goods toward the administrative center suggest that exchange interactions are spatially limited to the sphere of political control. At the regional level, poor articulation between solar market systems results in discontinuous, bounded market territories. Linkages between solar market systems occur only as elite-controlled trade between administrative centers, marked by the exchange of foreign commodities only between primary central places. Thus, the spatial patterns of commodity flow under a solar market system should be characterized by (1) bounded, discontinuous market territories that are coterminous with political administrative units; and (2) political boundaries that are relatively impermeable with respect to commodity flow such that the presence of foreign goods is largely restricted to administrative centers.

In this paper, we examine the spatial patterning of pre-imperial market systems by monitoring the movement of one class of utilitarian goods, decorated ceramics, relative to the territorial boundaries of the independent polities of the Early Aztec period. We explicitly assume, based on documentary accounts, that since ceramics were exchanged at market places in the 1500s, that market exchange was the primary means of distributing ceramics in Early Aztec times as well. We first delineate political territories for the Early Aztec period within the southern and eastern portions of the Basin of Mexico. We then examine spatial patterns of commodity flow utilizing regional archaeological ceramic collections generated by the Texcoco, Ixtapalapa, Chalco, and Xochimilco surveys (Blanton 1972; Parsons 1971; Parsons, Brumfiel, Parsons, and Wilson 1982; Sanders et al. 1979). To achieve a truly comprehensive understanding of ceramic exchange in Aztec times, similar studies must be carried out for all regions of the Basin of Mexico. This investigation should therefore be regarded as a pilot study based on a portion of the Basin of Mexico for which data are most accessible.

EARLY AZTEC POLITICAL BOUNDARIES IN THE EASTERN AND SOUTHERN BASIN OF MEXICO

During the Early Aztec period, the Basin of Mexico was divided among a number of independent, competing, and often conflicting polities that can best be described as city-states (Bray 1972; Hodge 1984). Each city-state contained a central settlement that was the locus of political administration, elite residence, ritual, and market activities for the rural population of the city-state territory. Documents report that groups of city-states formed alliances or confederations for purposes of mutual defense or military campaigns (Alva Ixtlilxochitl 1975-1977; *Anales de Cuauhtitlan* 1938, 1945; Chimalpahin 1950, 1965; Durán 1967).

The eastern and southern portions of the Basin that form our study area contained at least 14 city-states during the Early Aztec period (fig. 6.1). The territorial boundaries for these city-states have been identified utilizing the methodology described by Hodge (chap. 2) for the Late Aztec period, but applied here to archaeological sites and polities of the Early Aztec period.

In the south-central section of the Basin of Mexico, the major Early Aztec political centers were Culhuacan and Xochimilco. Among the original migrants into the Basin, the Culhua of Culhuacan are reputed to have originally controlled a large territory encompassing much of the southern lake bed during the

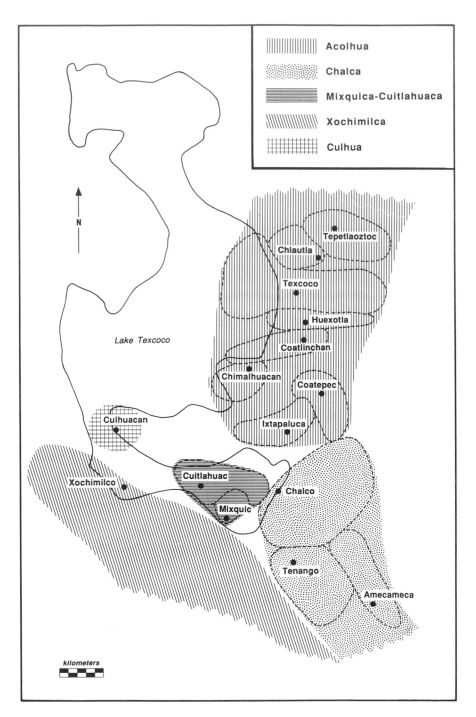

Fig. 6.1.　Early Aztec city-state and confederation political territories.

period of Toltec hegemony (Davies 1980:23; Zimmermann 1960:29).[1] Culhuacan continued to be an influential center in the Early Aztec period, but it is difficult to reconstruct Culhua political territory for this period. Charles Gibson (1964:11) suggests that by the mid-1300s the principal Culhua communities included, in addition to Culhuacan, only the nearby centers of Ixtapalapa, Mexicaltzinco, and Huitzilopocho, indicating that Culhua domain had contracted considerably to a core area surrounding Culhuacan. Since both documentary and archaeological data on Culhuacan's territorial extent are limited for the Early Aztec period, Culhua territory is conservatively estimated for this study to have been a small area on the western end of the Ixtapalapa peninsula. South of Culhuacan, Xochimilco and the Xochimilca confederation controlled a large territory throughout Early Aztec times, much of which extended south of our study area (Parsons, Brumfiel, Parsons, and Wilson 1982:76-78). Xochimilco unfortunately remains an unknown figure in our archaeological study since very few collections exist from its territory; as a result, we are forced to exclude this polity from our analyses.

The major political entities occupying the southeastern corner of the Basin were the city-states of the Chalco confederation. Of these, Chalco, Tenango, and Amecameca fall within our study area (Chimalpahin 1965; Schroeder 1991). Two small states, Mixquic and Cuitlahuac, were sandwiched between the stronger forces of the Chalca, Xochimilca, and Culhua polities. These small states often shared the same fate in the expansionist campaigns of their neighbors (*Anales de Cuauhtitlan* 1945:61-62; Gibson 1964:12), and are claimed in documentary accounts as dependencies of the larger political confederations (Alva Ixtlilxochitl 1975-1977:v.1:310, 329; *Anales de Cuauhtitlan* 1945:23; Durán 1967:v.1:22; Parsons, Brumfiel, Parsons, and Wilson 1982:78-79).

To the north, spread along the piedmont east of Lake Texcoco, were the Acolhua polities. The principal Early Aztec Acolhua city-state centers within our study include Huexotla, Coatlinchan, Texcoco, Chiautla, and Tepetlaoztoc (Alva Ixtlilxochitl 1975-1977; Offner 1983; Parsons 1971). South of these, the Acolhua city-states of Chimalhuacan, Coatepec, and Ixtapaluca occupied a buffer zone with the Chalca confederation farther south. Although some sources report that this area fell under Chalca confederation control in the mid-fourteenth century along with the entire Ixtapalapa peninsula (*Anales de Cuauhtitlan* 1945:29; Parsons, Brumfiel, Parsons, and Wilson 1982:81), in imperial times, these border polities were clearly part of the Acolhua state. The sparse population and lack of extended suburban areas in this zone are archaeological confirmation of this area's role as a border zone (Parsons 1971:229-230).

The combined documentary accounts and the archaeological settlement data for the Early Aztec period suggest that city-state territories were relatively stable, discrete entities throughout this period, while confederation boundaries shifted more radically with the winds of political expansion or defeat. Accordingly, we have examined both scales of political control—city-state and confederation—as units against which to compare the geographic distribution of ceramic types.

EARLY AZTEC BLACK-ON-ORANGE CERAMICS

To monitor economic interaction within and among these Early Aztec political units, we have focused on the exchange of decorated ceramics, a commodity that is highly visible in the archaeological record and for which chronological sequences are well established. In particular, we examine Black-on-Orange (hereafter Black/Orange) ceramics, the predominant decorated ceramic type for the Aztec period. Our analysis of ceramic exchange first involves identifying stylistically distinct ceramic variants; instrumental neutron activation (INA) analyses of paste composition are subsequently used to verify that these visually distinct stylistic variants were produced in different places using different sources of clays. The spatial distributions and concentrations of the stylistic variants are then mapped using the Basin of Mexico survey collections. From distribution maps of Early Aztec ceramics originating from different production sources, we can then define the scale and location of Early Aztec ceramic exchange networks and examine their spatial distribution relative to the political boundaries as reconstructed for that period.

Early Aztec Black/Orange ceramics are traditionally divided into two types: Aztec I or Culhuacan Black/Orange and Aztec II or Tenayuca Black/Orange. Aztec I (Culhuacan) and Aztec II (Tenayuca) Black/Orange ceramics were initially considered to represent sequential phases of occupation in the Basin (Griffin and Espejo 1947, 1950; Vaillant 1938), with Culhuacan being earlier than and replaced by Tenayuca. During the course of Basin-wide surveys, however, it was demonstrated that the occupations represented by Aztec I and Aztec II ceramics differ more in space than in time (Whalen and Parsons 1982:437-438). Aztec I or Culhuacan Black/Orange ceramics predominate in the southern Basin around Lakes Chalco and Xochimilco, while Aztec II or Tenayuca Black/Orange ceramics are found largely to the north, in the Texcoco region (Parsons, Brumfiel, Parsons, and Wilson 1982:345-351). Although Tenayuca Black/Orange also occurs in the southern Basin, this type is relatively low in frequency and almost always co-occurs with Aztec I Black/Orange ceramics in surface collections; thus, there does not appear to be a distinct phase of Aztec II Black/Orange ceramics in the south. The converse holds for the northern Basin, where Tenayuca Black/Orange is the dominant type. Within the Basin as a whole, the present view is that these Early Aztec types are largely, if not wholly, contemporaneous (Whalen and Parsons 1982:437-438).[2]

Originally defined at the type site of Culhuacan, the term "Culhuacan" Black/Orange has subsequently been applied to all apparently early Black/Orange ceramics in the southern Basin. In our analysis of the regional survey collections, however, we have found that the southern Basin contains several distinct Early Aztec Black/Orange types, that are quite different from "classic" Culhuacan as first defined at that type site (cf. Griffin and Espejo 1947). Two new Black/Orange types have been defined in the south (Minc 1991), which we have provisionally named Chalco Black/Orange and Mixquic Black/Orange after two major sites in the southern lake basin where they are found in abundance. The term Culhuacan Black/Orange has been reserved for the material originally defined at that type site (table 6.1).

Table 6.1   Early Aztec Black/Orange ceramic terminology

Vaillant (1938)	Griffin and Espejo (1947, 1950)	This study
		Chalco
Aztec I	Culhuacan	Mixquic
		Culhuacan
Aztec II	Tenayuca	Calligraphic Tenayuca
		Geometric Tenayuca

On Chalco Black/Orange, the painted decoration consists of a panel of repetitive, linear designs running around the interior vessel wall (fig. 6.2). The characteristic motif in this panel is the "undulating comb", formed by either a wavy or zig-zag line which alternates with sets of short vertical lines. One of the more distinctive members of the Chalco type is a vessel form we refer to as Chalco Chunky after its rather hefty proportions. These vessels appear to have had stamped bases, and the wear indicates that they were used as grater bowls or *molcajetes*. The Chalco undulating comb motif also occurs on the interiors of simple, rounded bowls and miniature dishes with tripod supports, and on the exterior of upright-rim bowls.

Mixquic Black/Orange also bears a panel of decoration on the vessel wall, but the motifs are quite distinct (fig. 6.3). Instead of the continuous comb motif, the panel is subdivided by sets of diagonal wavy lines interset with concentric loops or chevrons. Vessel form is also highly distinctive, especially with respect to modifications of the rim. Mixquic decoration occurs on dishes with a unique bolstered rim (termed Mixquic Bolstered) and on rounded bowls or dishes with a groove around the exterior of the rim just below the lip (Mixquic Grooved). A third vessel shape is that of upright or shouldered bowls (Mixquic Shouldered), also with a groove just below the lip, which bear the panel of decoration around the upper exterior vessel wall.[3]

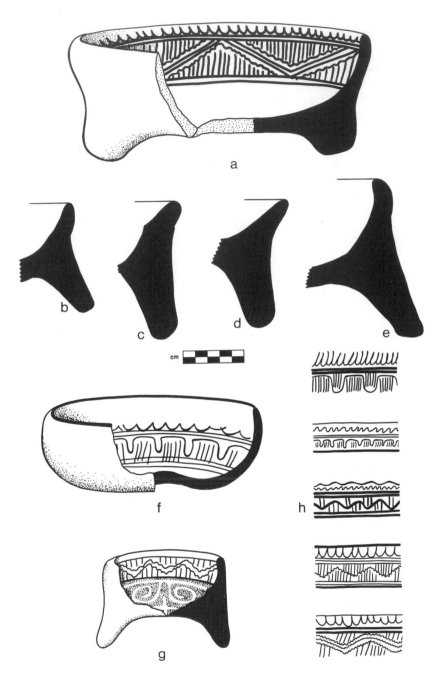

Fig. 6.2.　Chalco Black/Orange: Chalco Chunky grater bowl *(a-e)*, bowl with dimple base *(f)*, miniature grater bowl *(g)*, and variations on the Chalco undulating comb motif *(h)*. Profile *c* shows extreme wear from grinding commonly seen on grater bowls.(Examples *a* and *f-h* redrawn from Séjourné 1983:figs. 79-82.)

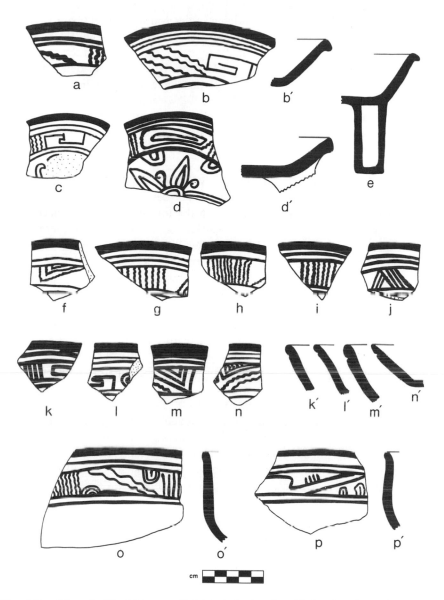

Fig. 6.3. Mixquic Black/Orange: Bolstered-rim bowls with interior decoration *(a-j)*, grooved-rim dishes with interior decoration *(k-n)*, and shouldered or upright-rim bowls with exterior decoration *(o, p)*. (Profile *e* redrawn from Séjourné 1983:fig. 69.)

Both the Chalco and the Mixquic Black/Orange types differ markedly from "classic" Culhuacan (fig. 6.4) as originally defined at that type site (Brenner 1931; Griffin and Espejo 1947, 1950; Peterson 1957). Culhuacan Black/Orange also utilizes a panel of decoration on the interior vessel wall, but the motifs are distinct from those of both Chalco and Mixquic Black/Orange. Best known of these motifs are the floral and so-called glyph-like motifs, including the *caracol* or spiral motif, and representations of serpent jaws and reptile eyes. In addition, the base is painted, often with complex curvilinear or zoomorphic designs. The primary vessel form is the tripod-support dish, but Culhuacan motifs are also found as interior decoration on simple, rounded bowls and on the exterior of upright-rim bowls.

We have also examined decorative variation within the more northern Tenayuca Black/Orange ceramics. Previous analyses of Tenayuca Black/Orange focused on the grasslike *zacate* element at the top of the panel of decoration that runs around the interior vessel wall (Franco 1945, 1947; Noguera 1930, 1935; Parsons 1966:161-162). These analyses identified possible chronological variation in whether the *zacate* are free or bounded between parallel lines, with the free *zacate* believed to be earlier than the bounded form.[4] In this study, we have focused instead on the panel of decoration below the *zacate* element and have examined the painted motifs which occur in this zone.

In Tenayuca Black/Orange dishes, plates, and *molcajetes* (grater bowls), two basic design categories are apparent in this panel: the Geometric and the Calligraphic (Hodge 1991). As suggested by its name, the Geometric approach uses a repetitive pattern of a given stylized geometric motif or motifs to create a panel of decoration which runs around the interior vessel wall (fig. 6.5). The motifs are highlighted using a "false negative" technique, in which the motif is outlined in black and the background around it then darkened with a fine-line filler, leaving the motif highlighted in orange (Griffin and Espejo 1950). Two of the more common motifs are the feather-and-scroll and the stepped-fret or *xicalcoliuhqui* (Enciso 1953; Franco 1945, 1947, 1957: 22-25; Hodge 1991). Geometric motifs occur with both the free and bounded *zacate* rim elements.

In contrast to the Geometric approach, Calligraphic decoration (Brenner 1931:29-32; Gamio 1913:7; Griffin and Espejo 1950:34; King 1981:93; Séjourné 1970:158) fills the wall panel with a series of vertical squiggles, circles, half-circles, and loops that resemble a hand-writing exercise (fig. 6.6). Most vessel walls are completely covered with this decoration although the calligraphic elements may be interrupted by curves, oblique lines, or undulating lines. In our sample, Calligraphic decoration appears only in association with free *zacate.*

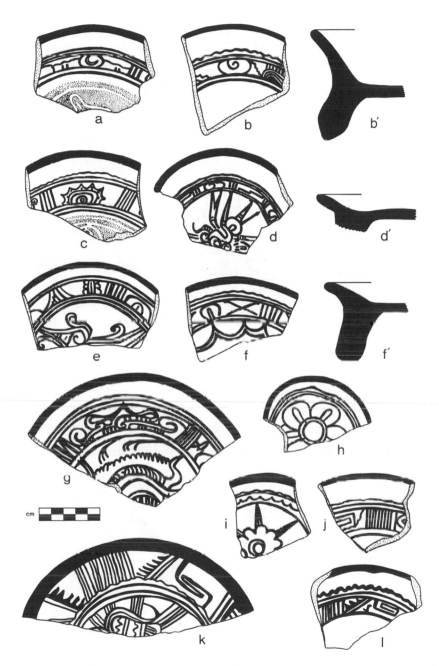

Fig. 6.4. Culhuacan Black/Orange: Dishes with interior decoration. Characteristic motifs include 'glyphic' elements such as spirals *(a, b, d)* and the *ojo estelar (c, e, f)*, the serpent jaw *(g)*, floral designs *(h, i)*, and the geometric *xicalcoliuhqui (j-l)*.

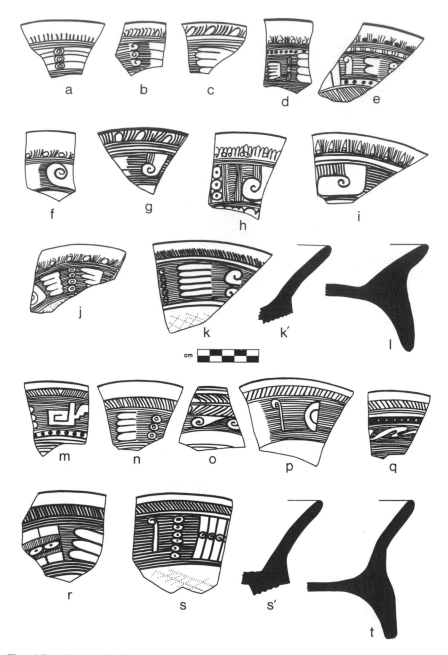

Fig. 6.5.   Geometric Tenayuca Black/Orange: Plates, dishes, and *molcajetes* with free *zacate (a-k)* and bounded *zacate (m-s)*. Common geometric motifs include the feather or wing motif *(c, d, e, j, k, n, r)*, the scroll *(f-i)*, and the *xicalcoliuhqui (m)*. (Dish and *molcajete* profiles *l* and *t* redrawn from Parsons 1971:fig. 76.)

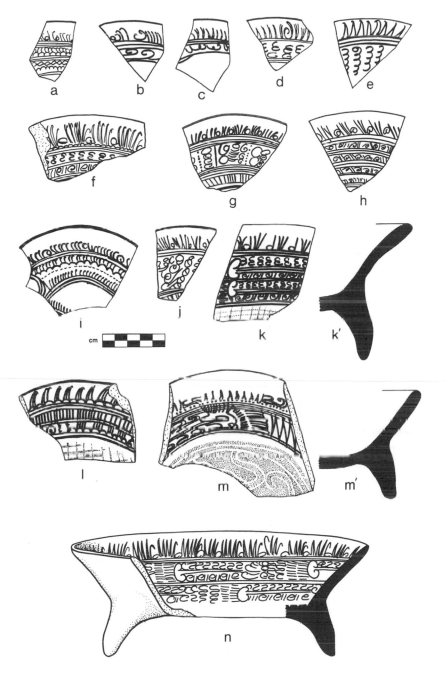

Fig. 6.6.   Calligraphic Tenayuca Black/Orange: Plates, dishes, and *molcajetes*. Influence from the Culhuacan style is evident in the serpent jaw motifs and stamped base present on *m*. (Vessel *n* redrawn from Séjourné 1970:fig. 110.)

NEUTRON ACTIVATION ANALYSIS OF EARLY AZTEC CERAMICS

Trace-element analyses of ceramic paste composition were utilized to corroborate the visual distinctions between the Early Aztec Black/Orange ceramic variants and to confirm that these stylistic differences represent different manufacturing and clay sources. Clay sources carry a signature of trace elements characteristic of the specific parent material from which the clay was derived. Examination of the trace-element composition of ceramics can therefore identify ceramics produced from the same clay source, or conversely, identify several production sources for a single ceramic type (e.g. Arnold et al. 1991; Bishop and Neff 1989; Harbottle 1976).[5]

A sample of 60 sherds was selected for INA analysis of trace elements. Our sample consisted of examples of the five types defined above and included Chalco Black/Orange (N=11), Mixquic Black/Orange (N=10), Culhuacan Black/Orange (N=13), Geometric Tenayuca (N=15), and Calligraphic Tenayuca (N=11) (table 6.2). In selecting the specific sherds for analysis, we attempted to sample each type from throughout its geographic range within our study area. The sample sizes are admittedly quite small; however, this study was designed in part as a pilot project to determine whether trace-element analysis would provide interpretable results in the Basin of Mexico, an area of complex geologic and volcanic history.

The INA analysis was conducted by James Blackman at the Smithsonian Institution's Conservation Analytical Laboratory. The pulverized sherd samples were irradiated for six hours in polyethylene capsules at a neutron flux of 7.7 x 10-13th n/cm^2/sec; gamma spectra for each sample were then counted after a 6-day and again after a 30-day decay. The resulting spectra were analyzed for the concentrations of 20 elements (Ce, Co, Cr, Cs, Eu, Fe, Hf, K, La, Lu, Na, Rb, Sc, Sm, Sr, Ta, Tb, Th, Yb, and Zn), utilizing two replicates of coal fly ash (NBS-SRM-1633) as the standard reference material. These trace elements constitute their standard suite of the more precise, intermediate and long half-life elements used in the analysis of ceramic material.

Principal components analysis (table 6.3) was employed to identify the primary dimensions of variability inherent in the chemical composition of these ceramic samples and to explore the extent to which these dimensions corresponded to our stylistic variants. Clay groups were initially defined based on similarities among ceramic samples along the primary principal component axes (fig. 6.7a). The integrity of these clay groups was then assessed using the Mahalanobis D^2 statistic[6] to determine the multivariate probability of group membership for each sherd (see table 6.2). Canonical variates analysis based on all 20 elements was subsequently utilized to illustrate the degree of separation between groups (fig. 6.7b) and to assign previously unclassified sherds to the most likely clay group. (For a more complete discussion of group identification procedures, see Glascock 1992).

These analyses point to the existence of three compositionally distinct clay groups within our sample of Early Aztec Black/Orange ceramics. The separation between these groups, and their relationship to our stylistic groups, is illustrated in figure 6.7. Overall, these clay groups correspond well to our typological units.

The first clay group consists of members of the Chalco and Mixquic types, indicating that these two types are extremely similar in their trace elements and share a similar region of origin. The second clay group includes all examples of Tenayuca Geometric Black/Orange as a distinct cluster, but it also includes two extreme outliers of Chalco Black/Orange (AZP001 and AZP002), both of which were recovered from the Texcoco survey region. The third clay group contains all examples of Calligraphic Tenayuca and Culhuacan Black/Orange, suggesting a common origin for these two types as well. Trace-element analysis thus identifies two distinctive groups within Tenayuca Black/Orange, corresponding to the Calligraphic and Geometric styles. There is no apparent separation, however, between the different motifs within the Geometric style, and within the Geometric sample, there is no discernible difference between examples of bounded and free *zacate*.

The compositional groups identified through trace-element analysis represent regional differences in volcanic ash deposits and in the clays derived from those deposits. These groupings therefore indicate three regional production zones (as opposed to site-specific production sources) for the manufacture of Early Aztec Black/Orange ceramics. Based on the concentrated spatial distributions of the Early Aztec ceramic styles, the geographical locations of the production zones generating these styles can be roughly identified.

As demonstrated below, Chalco and Mixquic Black/Orange are concentrated primarily in the southern Basin area from Lake Chalco up to Amecameca; it is therefore likely that the first cluster represents compositional differences characteristic of clays in the southeastern portion of the Basin. The upland portions of this area form a distinct hydrological unit that drains into Lake Chalco. Conversely, Culhuacan Black/Orange has long been associated with the environs of its type site Culhuacan and several authors have suggested that Culhuacan was the production source for this type based on its abundance there (Brenner 1931; Gamio 1913; Griffin and Espejo 1947). The trace-element analyses indicate that Calligraphic ceramics in our sample share a common source with Culhuacan, based on similarities in composition. One Calligraphic sherd included in our analysis (AZP045) appears to have been a kiln waster, in that it shows a paint blotch on the interior decorated surface and spalling on the exterior. This waster was recovered near the site of Culhuacan and supports the interpretation that Calligraphic Black/Orange was produced at or near that site.

Table 6.2 Early Aztec Black/Orange sherds included in the INA analyses

INAA ID No.	Ceramic Type	Provenience	Clay Group	Probability of Group Membership[a]		
				CH	TX	CUL
AZP001[b]	Chalco Chunky	TX-A-40	TX	.019	.458	.008
AZP002[b]	Chalco Chunky	TX-A-87	TX	.016	.726	.021
AZP003	Chalco Chunky	CH-AZ-164	CH	.256	.002	.000
AZP004	Chalco Chunky	CH-AZ-111	CH	.394	.002	.002
AZP005	Chalco Chunky	CH-AZ-103	CH	.302	.006	.002
AZP006	Chalco Chunky	CH-AZ-29	CH	.595	.003	.000
AZP007	Chalco Bowl	CH-AZ-76	CH	.464	.000	.000
AZP008	probably Chalco	CH-AZ-172	CH	.548	.001	.000
AZP068	Chalco Chunky	CH-AZ-172	CH	.600	.012	.021
AZP069	Chalco Chunky	CH-AZ-172	CH	.583	.002	.001
AZP070	Chalco Chunky	IX-A-11	CH	.550	.004	.000
AZP011	Mixquic Bolstered	CH-AZ-190	CH	.422	.002	.007
AZP012	Mixquic Bolstered	CH-AZ-195	CH	.513	.036	.018
AZP013	Mixquic Bolstered	CH-AZ-192	CH	.573	.002	.000
AZP014	Mixquic Bolstered	CH-AZ-249	CH	.592	.025	.015
AZP015	Mixquic Bolstered	CH-AZ-252	CH	.434	.015	.001
AZP016	Mixquic Grooved	CH-AZ-195B	CH	.578	.001	.000
AZP017	Mixquic Grooved	CH-AZ-190	CH	.905	.003	.001
AZP018	Mixquic Grooved	CH-AZ-192	CH	.201	.112	.021
AZP019	Mixquic Shouldered	CH-AZ-195B	CH	.434	.001	.000
AZP020	Mixquic Shouldered	CH-AZ-249	CH	.522	.003	.001
AZP021	Geometric Tenayuca	IX-A-26	TX	.002	.687	.040
AZP022	Geometric Tenayuca	IX-A-26	TX	.006	.569	.018
AZP023	Geometric Tenayuca	IX-A-26	TX	.005	.292	.115
AZP024	Geometric Tenayuca	CH-AZ-6	TX	.033	.205	.005
AZP025	Geometric Tenayuca	TX-A-87	TX	.001	.400	.003
AZP026	Geometric Tenayuca	IX-A-26	TX	.065	.279	.011
AZP027	Geometric Tenayuca	TX-A-87	TX	.000	.486	.004
AZP028	Geometric Tenayuca	TX-A-40	TX	.001	.823	.021
AZP029	Geometric Tenayuca	TX-A-87	TX	.002	.541	.014
AZP030	Geometric Tenayuca	TX-A-87	TX	.006	.750	.031
AZP031	Geometric Tenayuca	TX-A-87	TX	.000	.443	.002
AZP032	Geometric Tenayuca	TX-A-16	TX	.005	.599	.047
AZP033	Geometric Tenayuca	TX-A-40	TX	.001	.730	.005
AZP034	Geometric Tenayuca	TX-A-109	TX	.003	.796	.030
AZP035	Geometric Tenayuca	TX-A-87	TX	.001	.485	.003

(continued)

Table 6.2 (continued)

INAA ID No.	Ceramic Type	Provenience	Clay Group	Probability of Group Membership[a]		
				CH	TX	CUL
AZP009	Culhuacanoid	CH-AZ-263	CUL	.065	.010	.111
AZP056	Culhuacan	Culhuacan	CUL	.004	.001	.691
AZP057	Culhuacan	Culhuacan	CUL	.025	.004	.992
AZP058	Culhuacan	Culhuacan	CUL	.023	.001	.689
AZP059	Culhuacan	Culhuacan	CUL	.077	.009	.544
AZP060	Culhuacan	Culhuacan	CUL	.007	.046	.413
AZP061	Culhuacan	Culhuacan	CUL	.035	.003	.591
AZP062	Culhuacan	Culhuacan	CUL	.005	.001	.761
AZP063	Culhuacan	Culhuacan	CUL	.005	.001	.433
AZP064	Culhuacan	Culhuacan	CUL	.063	.016	.573
AZP065	Culhuacan	Culhuacan	CUL	.053	.004	.796
AZP066	Culhuacan	Culhuacan	CUL	.012	.004	.471
AZP067	Culhuacan	Culhuacan	CUL	.004	.001	.603
AZP036	Calligraphic Tenayuca	TX-A-87	CUL	.004	.015	.498
AZP037	Calligraphic Tenayuca	TX-A-87	CUL	.034	.008	.872
AZP038	Calligraphic Tenayuca	CH-AZ-111	CUL	.002	.048	.455
AZP039	Calligraphic Tenayuca	XO-AZ-69	CUL	.002	.005	.409
AZP040	Calligraphic Tenayuca	XO-AZ-69	CUL	.015	.001	.385
AZP041	Calligraphic Tenayuca	XO-AZ-71	CUL	.028	.001	.694
AZP045	Calligraphic Tenayuca	Culhuacan	CUL	.010	.000	.313
AZP046 [b]	Calligraphic Tenayuca	Culhuacan	CUL	.000	.000	.007
AZP047	Calligraphic Tenayuca	Culhuacan	CUL	.006	.000	.405
AZP048	Calligraphic Tenayuca	Culhuacan	CUL	.194	.008	.359
AZP049	Calligraphic Tenayuca	Culhuacan	CUL	.003	.001	.422

[a] Probabilities of group membership are based on the first three principal components defined in table 6.3.

[b] Non-core members; not included in calculation of within-group covariance matrix nor in calculation of canonical variates.

Table 6.3 Principal components analysis of Early Aztec Black/Orange ceramics

Statistic	Component				
	1	2	3	4	5
Eigenvalues	6.33	3.92	2.14	1.42	1.07
% Variance Explained	31.66	19.62	10.68	7.11	5.37
Cumulative % Variance	31.66	51.28	61.96	69.07	74.44
Element	*Component Loadings*				
Ce	**0.763**	0.174	0.089	-0.142	-0.364
Co	0.316	**-0.626**	0.198	-0.345	-0.435
Cr	-0.166	**-0.875**	0.051	-0.150	0.182
Cs	0.368	**0.596**	0.447	0.239	-0.019
Eu	**0.727**	0.024	**0.521**	-0.174	0.085
Fe	0.519	**-0.534**	0.014	-0.082	-0.300
Hf	**0.694**	-0.483	-0.040	0.341	0.071
K	0.084	**0.613**	0.340	0.237	-0.263
La	**0.902**	0.204	0.141	-0.076	0.117
Lu	**0.581**	0.274	-0.175	0.091	0.381
Na	-0.491	-0.026	0.401	0.419	-0.194
Rb	0.446	0.303	**-0.490**	0.290	-0.285
Sc	0.428	**-0.777**	0.311	0.091	0.218
Sm	**0.807**	0.341	0.150	-0.152	0.101
Sr	**-0.573**	-0.175	0.380	-0.293	0.021
Ta	**0.542**	-0.439	-0.302	0.352	-0.106
Tb	0.505	0.204	-0.204	**-0.503**	-0.252
Th	**0.640**	-0.472	-0.206	0.343	-0.009
Yb	**0.562**	0.260	-0.371	-0.312	0.335
Zn	0.417	-0.003	**0.686**	0.105	0.155

Note: High positive and negative associations are indicated in bold type.

We therefore associate this second clay group with the western end of the Ixtapalapa peninsula and the drainage basin of Lake Xochimilco.

Finally, the origin of the third cluster, consisting of Geometric Tenayuca, can be attributed to the Acolhua province within the Texcoco survey region, an area of known Tenayuca Black/Orange dominance (Hodge and Minc 1990, 1991; Parsons, Brumfiel, Parsons, and Wilson 1982:345-351; Whalen and Parsons 1982:437-438). A comparison of the trace-element concentrations characteristic of this ceramic group to a modern source of pottery clay collected from a barrio of Texcoco (Branstetter-Hardesty 1978:192) confirms this regional provenience (Hector Neff, personal communication). Separated from the southern Basin by the Ixtapalapa peninsula, the Texcoco survey region forms a third, distinct hydrological unit, which drains into Lake Texcoco.

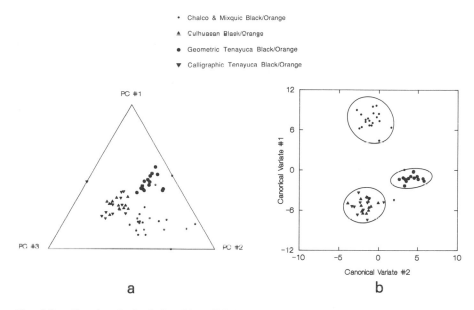

Fig. 6.7. Geochemical relationships of Early Aztec Black/Orange ceramic types based on trace-element concentrations. Separation of types as plotted on *(a)* the first three principal component axes and *(b)* the primary canonical variates indicates three distinct production zones for these types. Ellipses represent 95% confidence intervals for group membership.

Tenayuca Black/Orange ceramics also occur in unknown quantities in the Tepaneca-controlled area west of Lake Texcoco, outside our study area. Both the Calligraphic and Geometric types are reported from the type site of Tenayuca (Noguera 1935), although Calligraphic sherds predominate in the illustrated material. It is unfortunate that western examples of Tenayuca Black/Orange were not systematically included in this trace-element analysis of clay sources. Recent analyses (Hodge et al. 1992), however, indicate that a western Basin of Mexico source was also producing both Geometric and Calligraphic Tenayuca ceramics. However, of the Tenayuca ceramic samples included in our sample, only one (AZP046) appears as an outlier, falling far to the left of the Calligraphic Tenayuca cluster (fig. 6.7a). This sample has a low probability of inclusion in the Culhuacan clay group, but even lower probabilities of membership in either the Chalco or Texcoco clay group. Although such an outlier might be indicative of another production source, none of our samples from the eastern and southern portions of the Basin could be reassigned to the western Basin source (Hector Neff, personal communication). It therefore appears that although additional sources were producing Tenayuca ceramics, they were not supplying the sites included in this study—at least not in quantity. As a result, we can tentatively assume that the bulk of Geometric and Calligraphic Black/Orange in our study area originated from the two sources identified above, i.e., the environs of Texcoco and Culhuacan, respectively.

In summary, trace-element analysis of Early Aztec Black/Orange ceramics indicates that the different styles defined within this type represent several production sources. Three distinct groups of ceramics have been identified that reflect regional differences in clay composition and stylistic tradition. Two distinct southern regions of Early Aztec Black/Orange production are identified, corresponding to the eastern (Lake Chalco) and western (Lake Xochimilco) drainages. The southeast was the source area for the production of Chalco and Mixquic Black/Orange, while the southwestern or Culhuacan-Ixtapalapa area produced Culhuacan and Calligraphic Black/Orange. The third region identified represents a northern or Texcocan area or source that produced Geometric Tenayuca.

Because of our small sample sizes, the specific findings of the INA analyses need to be verified in the future with a larger number of samples from each of the ceramic types we defined. Larger sample sizes might also permit a greater refinement in the identification of production sources at a subregional scale. Based on these preliminary results, however, it appears that the visually distinct Early Aztec Black/Orange types represent different production zones. As a result, the distributions of these different types should reflect the spatial extent and organization of the exchange systems or market networks through which these ceramics were distributed from their source.

MONITORING PRE-IMPERIAL MARKET SYSTEMS

It is stated above that under a regionally integrated market system, we would expect market zones and the commodities distributed through those markets to create a series of fluid, overlapping territories that were spatially unconstrained by political or administrative boundaries. In contrast, a solar market system would be expected to form spatially discrete zones of commodity distribution whose boundaries were coterminous with those of the local, autonomous (city-state) administrative unit.

The comprehensive spatial coverage of the Basin of Mexico surveys has allowed us to map the distributions of the visually distinct Early Aztec Black/ Orange types and to test their distributions against the expectations of the regionally integrated and solar market models. Based on their distributions in the survey collections from the Texcoco, Ixtapalapa, and Chalco-Xochimilco survey areas, we have been able to gauge both the territorial extent of type distribution as well as the relationship of the revealed market territories to political boundaries for the Early Aztec period.

Spatial Organization of Market Zones

The degree of overlap in the market zones through which these types were distributed is revealed in the regional spatial patterning of type distributions. Within the southern Basin, the Aztec I Black/Orange types reveal distinctly different and relatively discrete spatial distributions when mapped on a presence/absence basis (fig. 6.8). Chalco Black/Orange is found in an area extending from the site of Chalco on the lakeshore, up the piedmont to Amecameca, and with an apparent concentration in the Tenango sub-valley. Isolated examples of this type have been found in the Texcoco region as well; however, the two paste samples of apparent Chalco Black/Orange from the Texcoco region do not appear to have originated from the Chalco clay source. It is noteworthy that although a few vessels apparently found their way north into Acolhua territory, there was apparently no trade to the west, since no Chalco Black/Orange vessels were recovered by the Basin of Mexico surveys further west than Xico.[7]

In contrast, Mixquic Black/Orange is narrowly restricted to the basin of Lake Chalco, within a triangle defined by the sites of Mixquic, Cuitlahuac, and Chalco. This type was found in abundance in excavations at the site of Mixquic (Séjourné 1983:155-161, figs. 66-71) and at Ch-Az-195 (Parsons, Brumfiel, Parsons, Popper, and Taft 1982), a small hamlet in Lake Chalco; only very small quantities were recovered at the site of Chalco (O'Neill 1962:93-95).

Culhuacan Black/Orange, although concentrated around its type site, extends eastward with a secondary concentration around the site of Cuitlahuac. This distribution is somewhat misleading, however, since some (but not all) of the Culhuacan Black/Orange sherds found in the environs of Cuitlahuac appear to be local imitations of Culhuacan in that only a subset of Culhuacan motifs are represented in these vessels. Most notably, the most diagnostic motifs, the so-called "glyph-like" elements, are conspicuously absent. However, it is apparent from the close similarity among the two areas' decorated ceramics that there was a fair degree of interaction between the Culhua and the Cuitlahuaca.

Unlike the spatial patterns of the Aztec I Black/Orange variants, the distributions of Geometric and Calligraphic ceramics are fairly widespread. Geometric Tenayuca is broadly distributed along the eastern side of Lake Texcoco; Calligraphic largely overlaps this distribution but extends both further south into the Chalco area and farther west along the Ixtapalapa peninsula. The widespread occurrence of these two types may partially reflect multiple production sources, as noted above. However, when type distributions are mapped as densities[8] (rather than on a presence/absence basis), concentrations of these styles are revealed that correspond spatially to the two production sources (fig. 6.9).

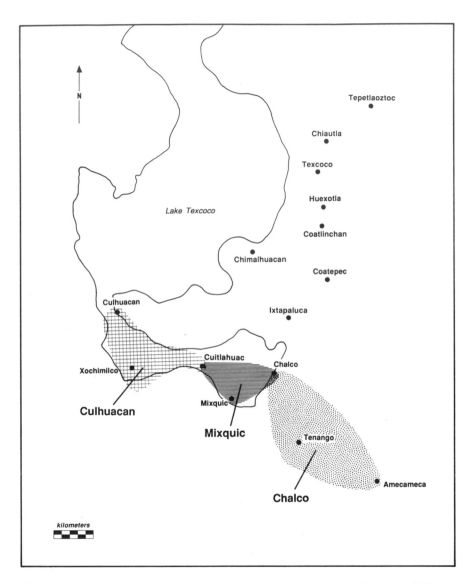

Fig. 6.8.   Spatial distributions of Aztec I Black/Orange ceramics: distributions of Chalco, Mixquic, and Culhuacan Black/Orange types mapped on a presence/absence basis.

Geometric Black/Orange is primarily concentrated within the northern Texcoco survey region; occurrences outside this zone are fairly low density. Calligraphic Tenayuca shows a marked concentration closely confined to one area of its presumed manufacture, i.e. the environs of Culhuacan at the western tip of the

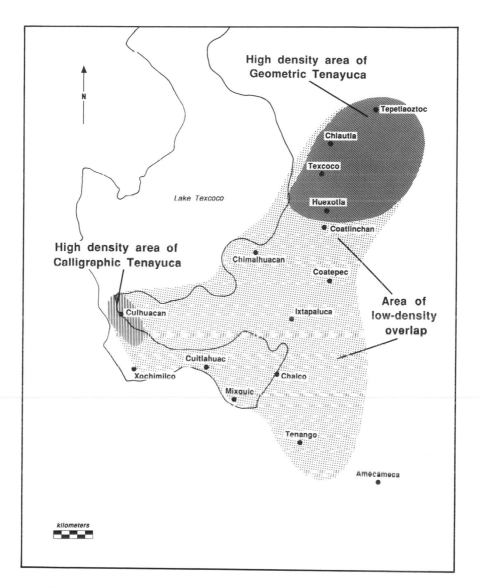

Fig. 6.9. Spatial distributions of Aztec II Black/Orange ceramics: concentrations of Geometric Tenayuca and Calligraphic Tenayuca Black/Orange types mapped from density of sherds recovered per ha of surface area collected in regional surveys. (Low density areas average less than 5 sherds/ha of a given type; high density areas range up to 200 sherds/ha.)

Ixtapalapa peninsula; lower density occurrences are found throughout the Texcoco and Chalco regions as well.

A quantitative measure of discreteness, that of a matrix of Jaccard's coefficients of association (table 6.4), was employed to determine the degree to which any two of these Early Aztec Black/Orange types co-occur in sites in the eastern and southern portions of the Basin of Mexico. This measure represents the proportion of sites containing both types out of a total of sites containing either or both types. All but two pairs of types show extremely low degrees of association. Culhuacan and Mixquic Black/Orange co-occur in roughly 25% of the sites that contain either of these types. Co-occurrences of these two types are concentrated near the site of Cuitlahuac. Similarly, Calligraphic and Geometric Tenayuca also co-occur one quarter of the time. Co-occurrences of these types are found throughout the study area and numerically support the apparent overlap in the market territories of the two Tenayuca types.

Several key patterns emerge from the distributions of these ceramic types. First, the Chalco, Mixquic, and Culhuacan Black/Orange types display localized and relatively discrete geographic territories within the southern Basin. The one point of overlap among these Aztec I Black/Orange type distributions occurs where Culhuacan Black/Orange (or a local imitation of that type) extends into the market territory of Mixquic Black/Orange. In contrast, the Calligraphic and Geometric types apparently circulated through spatially more extensive market networks. The market territories of these two types overlapped to a considerable extent while permeating the territories of the southern Basin types as well, although to a much lesser extent.

Table 6.4   Jaccard coefficients for the co-occurrence of Black/Orange types in surface collections

Types	Chalco	Mixquic	Culhuacan	Calligraphic	Geometric
Chalco	1.000				
Mixquic	.036 (2/55)	1.000			
Culhuacan[a]	.038 (2/53)	.263 (5/19)	1.000		
Calligraphic	.164 (10/61)	.026 (1/39)	.118 (4/34)	1.000	
Geometric	.126 (13/102)	.050 (4/80)	.079 (6/76)	.256 (20/78)	1.000

Note: Numbers in parentheses indicate the number of sites that contained both types out of the total number of sites that contained either type.

[a] Includes true Culhuacan Black/Orange only; does not include 'Culhuacanoid' material.

Political Boundary Permeability

The mapped concentrations of the Early Aztec Black/Orange ceramic types also reveal the degree to which market exchange was or was not constrained by political boundaries. A cursory comparison of Early Aztec political territories (fig. 6.1) to the ceramic type distributions (figs. 6.8 and 6.9) is sufficient to show that the market territories through which these ceramics circulated spatially exceed the boundaries of the local city-state polities. Within the southern Basin area, however, the spatially restricted market territories of the Chalco, Mixquic, and Culhuacan Black/Orange types do conform well to boundaries between confederations of allied city-states in that area. The distribution of Chalco Black/Orange falls almost entirely within the territory of the Chalca confederation, while Mixquic Black/Orange is distributed almost exclusively within the territory controlled by the Mixquica and Cuitlahuaca. The primary concentration of Culhuacan Black/Orange falls within the political territory of the Culhua confederation; the eastward extension of this type falls within territory formerly controlled by Culhuacan.

To the north, the conformity of market territories with political boundaries is not so clear. Although Geometric Tenayuca occurs in its greatest density within the ethnohistorically described borders of the Acolhua confederation, this type is also found in low frequencies south of that confederation border, particularly in the northernmost sites of the adjacent Chalco survey region (fig. 6.9). Here, our political boundaries based on ethnohistoric sources (fig. 6.1) do not parallel the marketing sphere evident from ceramic distributions since these sites appear to fall firmly within the market zone of the Acolhua, not the Chalca confederation. Only Calligraphic Tenayuca appears to have been distributed without regard to political boundaries. Overall, the relative conformity between market territories and confederation territories suggests political boundaries between confederations placed a major constraint on exchange.

The degree to which confederation political boundaries were permeable to trade can be assessed from both the volume of importation (the percentage of foreign types in the ceramic assemblage of a political confederation [table 6.5]) and from the volume of exportation (the percentage of a type occurring in its home territory versus that of a foreign polity [table 6.6]). Although these import/export measures should be used cautiously (given regional differences in site visibility and surface collection size[9]), the data at hand suggest that the boundaries of the political confederations were not uniformly permeable. Three of the confederations (the Acolhua, the Chalca, and the Mixquica-Cuitlahuaca), have similar levels of importation (19-23%) of foreign ceramics and fairly low export rates (3-13%) for ceramic types produced in their own territories. In contrast, the Culhua had fairly low levels of foreign goods (9%). The low importation rate for the Culhuacan polity is consistent with its apparent role as an

Table 6.5   Early Aztec Black/Orange ceramic imports by confederation

Confederation	% Foreign[a]	Black/Orange type, % of foreign					
		Chalco	Mixquic	Culhua.	Geometric	Calligr.	Other[b]
Acolhua	19	18	0	0	--	82	0
Chalca	21	--	4	13	48	24	11
Mixquica/ Cuitlahuaca	23	1	--	87	6	5	1
Culhua	9	0	0	--	100	--	0

[a] Total Early Aztec Black/Orange assemblage sizes by confederation are as follows: Acolhua (N=769), Chalca (N=201), Mixquica/Cuitlahuaca (N=304), and Culhua (N=75).
[b] Includes indeterminate non-local types (e.g., indeterminate Aztec II Black/Orange).

Table 6.6   Exportation rates for Early Aztec Black/Orange ceramics

Ceramic Type	By number of sites[a]			By total number of sherds[b]		
	% Local	% Foreign	# Sites	% Local	% Foreign	# Sherds
Chalco	78	22	46	87	13	121
Mixquic	85	15	13	97	3	106
Culhuacan	27	73	11	47	53	47
Culhuacanoid[c]	28	72	18	26	74	91
Geometric[d]	66	34	74	94	6	597
Calligraphic	21	79	29	18	82	163

[a] Total type occurances equal the total number of sites at which each type was recorded as present based on survey collections.
[b] Total type count equals the total number of sherds of each type recovered in survey collections.
[c] Includes both Culhuacan and related Culhuacanoid material.
[d] Includes all sherds with geometric motifs, whether Aztec II, Variant A with free zacate rim design or Variant B with bounded *zacate* rim decoration (see Hodge and Minc 1991).

exporter of decorated ceramics (table 6.6), in the form of both Culhuacan Black/Orange (53% of which was recovered in foreign territory) and Calligraphic Tenayuca (of which 82% comes from foreign territory).

In all cases, foreign ceramics are found in sites of all sizes and levels of sociopolitical significance and constitute roughly the same proportion of the ceramic assemblage for each class. Overall, foreign ceramic types account for 20% of the ceramics recovered in hamlets, 17% of those found in villages, and 22% of the assemblages of local (city-state) centers. Thus, foreign ceramics were clearly not restricted in their distribution to larger sites or political centers.

CONCLUSIONS AND DISCUSSION

The spatial distributions of the Early Aztec Black/Orange types do not provide support for the existence of a Basin-wide, integrative market system during the Early Aztec period. Nor do the data conform well to the expectations generated by the alternative model, that of a series of discrete solar market systems. Instead, the data suggest the existence of a number of subregional market systems of varied size and with varying degrees of interaction or articulation between neighboring systems.

Three regional production sources for Early Aztec Black/Orange ceramics were identified through INA analysis of trace elements and have been associated with distinct hydrologic units within the eastern and southern portions of the Basin of Mexico:

1. a southeastern (Lake Chalco drainage basin) source that produced Chalco and Mixquic Black/Orange. Although these types cannot be separated on the basis of their trace elements, they are stylistically distinctive and have virtually discrete areas of distribution. The market territories for Chalco and Mixquic types conform closely to the political territories of the Chalca and Mixquica-Cuitlahuaca confederations, respectively. These types co-occur in only two out of 55 sites, Xico and Chalco, the two largest sites on the confederation border. Chalco Black/Orange is exported in modest quantities north to Acolhua territory, but Mixquic Black/Orange appears to have been almost exclusively for local consumption. Imports into the Chalca and Mixquica-Cuitlahuaca provinces constitute 21% and 23% of the ceramic assemblages, respectively. Foreign ceramics in the Chalca area include primarily Calligraphic and Geometric Tenayuca; the Mixquica-Cuitlahuaca received predominantly Culhuacan Black/Orange.

2. a southwestern (Lake Xochimilco drainage basin) source that produced Culhuacan and Calligraphic Tenayuca. Although stylistically distinct, these types cannot be separated on the basis of their trace elements and both may well originate from the site of Culhuacan. Both of these types occur in greatest abundance within the political territory of the Culhua, but both appear to have been widely exported. Their distributions are somewhat different, however. Culhuacan Black/Orange is exported within the southern lake bed (to the Mixquica-Cuitlahuaca), while Calligraphic Tenayuca is found through-

out our study area. Imports into the Culhuacan polity are correspondingly low; all imports consist of Geometric Tenayuca originating in the north.

3. a northeastern (Eastern Lake Texcoco drainage basin) source that produced Geometric Tenayuca. Numerically the most prevalent Early Aztec Black/Orange type overall, this type is widely distributed throughout our study area. However, Geometric Tenayuca is clearly concentrated in the north-east corner of the study region, with the vast majority of this type (94%) found within the territory of the Acolhua confederation. Imports into the Acolhua region constituted 21% of the Early Aztec Black/Orange ceramics, and consist primarily of Calligraphic Tenayuca with much smaller quantities of Chalco Black/Orange.

At the regional level, the restricted spatial distributions of Black/Orange types within the southern Basin suggest the existence of discrete market territories that were fairly sharply bounded—a pattern consistent with a series of nonoverlapping solar market systems. However, the boundaries of these subregional market networks were not coterminous with the boundaries of the Early Aztec city-state territories as predicted for a solar market system. Instead, the boundaries of the larger political confederations or alliances of city-state polities appear to have been the primary restriction on market exchange, as indicated by the spatial conformity between ceramic distributions and reconstructed political confederation territories.

Further north, the spatial distributions of the Tenayuca variants are less well defined, a pattern consistent with a series of more fluid, overlapping market territories. Geometric Tenayuca appears much more widespread in its distribution than any of the southern Basin types; percentage-wise, however, most of this type falls within the political boundaries of the Acolhua confederation, again suggesting that the boundaries of that confederation limited consumer movements and/or market exchange. Only Calligraphic Tenayuca, which occurs in greatest density near its production source, is widely distributed and is distributed irrespective of political boundaries.

In all cases, confederation boundaries were somewhat permeable to market exchange, although not uniformly so, indicating a level of articulation not anticipated by the solar market model. Moreover, this articulation was not restricted to elite contact between administrative centers, as proposed by the solar market model. Rather, trade contacts apparently involved all levels of society since sites of all sizes and types had access to nonlocal or imported ceramics in about the same proportion.

In sum, ceramic exchange in the Early Aztec or pre-imperial period appears to have been organized through subregional market systems centered on the major political confederations of city-state polities. The picture that emerges is one in which consumers patronized primarily the markets within their own political confederation and were able to choose optimal marketing destinations within that territory. Consumer movements and exchange contacts across confederation borders were more limited, but not entirely restricted. Although limited in number, exchanges of foreign products apparently involved consumers of all socioeconomic levels and were not confined to an elite-controlled trade between administrative centers.

The exception to this general conformity between political and economic territories is Culhuacan. Unlike the other confederations that appear to have produced ceramics primarily for local consumption, the two ceramic types produced in the Culhuacan/Ixtapalapa region (Culhuacan and Calligraphic Tenayuca) were more widely distributed across political boundaries (table 6.6). The foreign popularity of ceramics produced in the Culhuacan-Ixtapalapa area is somewhat puzzling and constitutes one of the major questions raised by our study.

A partial answer to the question of Culhuacan's popularity may lie in the prestige and status attributed to that community as a center of Toltec heritage and artisanry (Davies 1980:23-41). As the oldest and most civilized Postclassic polity in the Basin of Mexico, the Culhua offered the stamp of legitimacy to other ethnic groups. Long after Culhuacan's political strength had declined, intermarriages and alliances with Culhuacan were sought out by other less prestigious groups within the Basin. Occupying such an influential position, Culhuacan may have maintained broader economic ties, and its borders may have been more open to traders than was the case for other polities. Further, goods produced in Culhuacan may have carried a special significance as products of "Toltec" artisans. Thus, the widespread distribution of Culhuacan ceramics could reflect the special political and/or religious role for that community in the Early Aztec period.

An alternative explanation is that the spatial distribution of Culhuacan ceramic products accurately reflects changes in the political territories and alliances of Culhuacan through time. In this case, the problem is not that Culhuacan does not conform to the general congruence of political and economic territories, but that a static characterization of Early Aztec political territories cannot adequately represent the political dynamics of that period. Although we have presented the major political divisions, fluctuations in territorial boundaries occurred throughout the Early Aztec period (Parsons, Brumfiel, Parsons, and Wilson 1982:75-85). A more historical approach may also shed some light on a second and related question concerning the different spatial distributions of Culhuacan's ceramic products: Culhuacan Black/Orange (restricted to the southern lake bed) and Calligraphic Tenayuca (distributed predominantly into Acolhua territory).

Early in the post-Toltec era, Culhuacan controlled much of the southern lake bed region, although this territory was later reduced to the small territory we have delimited. In A.D. 1253 or 1254, however, Culhuacan lost its independent status when it was conquered by Coatlinchan, one of the primary Acolhua city-states, and brought into the Acolhua confederation. Davies (1980:30) notes that after Coatlinchan's usurpation of the Culhua throne, the city remained within the Acolhua orbit for several generations and that Acolhua influences in Culhuacan persisted even as late as 1370. Given this shift in Culhuacan's political affiliation from southern to northern connections, it is tempting to associate the lake bed distribution of Culhuacan Black/Orange with a somewhat earlier period marked by continued contacts with Culhuacan's area of former sovereignty and to link the northward spread of Calligraphic Tenayuca to more intensive interaction of Culhuacan with northern cities after A.D. 1253.[10] Thus, as political boundaries shifted, so too did exchange interactions.

If this is the case, the production of Calligraphic Tenayuca at Culhuacan may reflect an attempt on the part of the Culhua to redesign their ceramic product to meet the aesthetic demands of northern consumers. Calligraphic material recovered from Culhuacan utilizes stylistic attributes of Culhuacan Black/Orange, including the serpent jaw motif and an occasional stamped base (e.g., fig. 6.6, *m*), within the broader Tenayuca tradition defined by vessel form and the diagnostic *zacate* element. Previous researchers (Brenner 1931; Griffin and Espejo 1947; Peterson 1957) have viewed this stylistic overlap as indicating an evolutionary progression of Tenayuca out of Culhuacan. However, the stylistic overlap could equally well represent the borrowing of traits between neighboring traditions, i.e., between Culhuacan Black/Orange and Tenayuca Black/Orange, to produce a new product designed for new markets in the north. As ceramic chronologies become more refined within the Basin, we ultimately may be able to resolve these questions concerning the origin and spread of ceramic styles.

The approach developed here to monitor the exchange systems of Early Aztec decorated ceramics has provided us with a direct line of archaeological evidence for examining the organization of market exchange, one that has proved useful for testing models of market organization derived from documentary evidence and from the spatial analyses of central places.[11] Of the two economic models proposed for market exchange in the Early Aztec period (the solar market system and the integrated market network), neither satisfactorily explains the observed patterns of commodity distribution. Ceramic exchange in the pre-imperial period was neither so politically and spatially restricted as to fit the solar market system model, nor so politically and spatially unbounded as to conform with the regionally integrated market network model. Rather, based on our findings here, a case can be made for a middle ground in which exchange interactions, constrained by the major political divisions of the pre-imperial period, were organized through a series of sub-regional market systems that corresponded spatially to confederation territories of allied city-states.

ACKNOWLEDGMENTS

We would like to thank Jeffrey R. Parsons of the University of Michigan Museum of Anthropology for making ceramic collections from the Basin of Mexico available for this study and Richard E. Blanton for providing field notes, maps, and data from his Ixtapalapa survey. Funding for stylistic and spatial analyses of the ceramics was generously provided by grants from The National Science Foundation (#BNS-8704177), The Wenner-Gren Foundation for Anthropological Research, The National Geographic Society, The Texas Higher Education Coordinating Board's Advanced Research Program, and The Faculty Research and Support Committee of the University of Houston-Clear Lake.

Neutron activation analyses were conducted by James Blackman at the Smithsonian Institution's Conservation Analytical Laboratory and were supported by the generosity of the Smithsonian Institution. Preparation of samples was made possible through the cooperation of the School of Natural and Applied Sciences, University of Houston-Clear Lake. We are particularly thankful to Hector Neff (Research Reactor Facility, University of Missouri-Columbia) for his assistance in these analyses.

Earlier versions of this paper were read by Richard Blanton, Elizabeth Brumfiel, Frederic Hicks, Joyce Marcus, Jeffrey Parsons, and Michael Smith. Their comments, corrections, and insights were highly appreciated.

NOTES

1. Chimalpahin (1958:3,5) reports that in the seventh and ninth centuries the Culhua controlled a large territory encompassing the centers of Xochimilco, Cuitlahuac, Mixquic, Coyoacan, Malinalco, and Ocuilan. Durán (1967:v.1:22), however, indicates that the Xochimilca were the more powerful and included in their territory Culhuacan as well as Cuitlahuac and Mixquic. By the early 1200s, Culhuacan's power was definitely on the wane and other polities encroached on the Culhua realm. The Chalca laid claim to Cuitlahuac in ca. 1233 (*Anales de Cuauhtitlan* 1945:17-18), and in 1239-40 the Culhua had to fend off the threat of the Xochimilca (*Anales de Cuauhtitlan* 1945:22). In 1253, Culhuacan was conquered by the ruler of Coatlinchan and brought into the Acolhua confederation (Davies 1980:28).

2. The issue of the relative temporal placement of Aztec I and Aztec II Black/Orange ceramics has been reopened by Elizabeth Brumfiel's ongoing research at Xaltocan (Brumfiel 1991). Based on a series of C-14 dates from excavated midden deposits, Brumfiel (personal communication) suggests that at Xaltocan, Aztec I Black/

Orange ceramics clearly predate Aztec II ceramics, although there is quite a long period where the two overlap.

Similarly, in the analyses of excavated materials from Culhuacan presented by Séjourné (1970:figs. 80-81A), the stratigraphy does not indicate a clear replacement of Aztec I by Aztec II materials, but rather a long period of coexistence. In commenting on the stylistic evolution of Aztec I into Aztec II proposed by Griffin and Espejo (1950:37), Séjourné (1970:55-56) concludes:

> La estratigrafía certifica ampliamente estas deducciones de tipo estilísticos, ya que ese grupo [Azteca II] emerge cuando el I está aún en plena fuerza, se multiplica a cada nivel hasta trastornar la proporción original: alcanza altas cifras mientras que el I reduce a lo mínimo sus vestigios. *La diferencia reside en que este no llega a desaparecer y que el II no goza por consiguiente nunca del aislamiento de su antecesor* (emphasis added).

Several recently released series of radiocarbon dates from the Basin of Mexico (Parsons, Brumfiel, and Hodge 1993) further substantiate a long period of overlap, if not complete synchrony, between Aztec I and Aztec II ceramics.

3.   Our Mixquic Black/Orange is similar to what O'Neill (1962) defines as an early variant of Culhuacan Black/Orange. In his excavations at Chalco, this type appears stratigraphically below (but mixed with) his Culhuacan Black/Orange (our Chalco Black/Orange), and so may be earlier. However, the distinct spatial distributions of these two types (as demonstrated in this paper) make it difficult to assess their contemporaneity, since they seldom co-occur. To the south of the Chalco-Mixquic region, excavations of an Early Aztec structure at Tetla, Morelos (Norr 1987a, 1987b) yielded both apparent Chalco Black/Orange ceramics and types very similar to Mixquic Black/Orange. This single component, Early Aztec occupation argues for some degree of temporal overlap in the Chalco and Mixquic types. Further, radiocarbon dates from the Tetla house (Norr 1987a:406-407) place both types firmly within the Early Aztec period for the Basin of Mexico.

4.   Parsons (1966) concluded that within Tenayuca Black/Orange, the free *zacate* element may represent a slightly earlier time period than the bounded *zacate*, as noted in the text. However, the multidimensional scaling seriation of decorated Aztec ceramics by Brumfiel (1976:66-86), based on the co-occurrence of types in surface collection units at Huexotla, found no temporal separation between free and bounded *zacate*.

5.   Ceramics are inherently variable due to two main factors: (1) natural chemical and mineralogic heterogeneity of raw materials, and (2) heterogeneity introduced by the potter during manufacture through such processes as the refinement of clays or the addition of aplastics as tempering agents (Rice 1987:406-411,418-419). We recognize that cultural factors may obscure natural variation in ceramic clays, confounding the identification of ceramic groups as well as the association of those groups with raw clay sources; for a discussion of this problem, see Neff et al. 1988, 1989; Elam et al. 1992.

In the Basin of Mexico, however, historic and ethnographic data indicate that potters minimally processed their clays prior to vessel fabrication, other than adding cattail fiber as a tempering material (Branstetter-Hardesty 1978:21-22, 59, 135-137; Sahagún 1950-1982:bk.11:257), a practice that apparently extends back at least to Late Classic times (Branstetter-Hardesty 1978:136). We therefore assume that the aplastic inclusions found in the Early Aztec ceramics represent naturally occurring aplastics in the raw clay and that these natural aplastics form part of the source's geochemical signature (Elam et al. 1992).

6. The D^2 statistic is calculated based on sample scores on the first three principal components. Probabilities of group membership are determined from the F-ratio for the multivariate distance D^2 between an individual point and the group centroid, following Sneath and Sokal (1973). Within-group distances are jack-knifed, that is, each sample was in turn removed from the calculation of the within-group covariance matrix and mean vector, prior to calculating the distance of that sample from the group centroid.

7. Chalco Polychrome is also strongly restricted in its distribution to the eastern end of the Chalco survey region (Parsons, Brumfiel, Parsons, and Wilson 1982:346). Its east-west distribution is essentially isomorphic with that of Chalco Black/Orange and further substantiates the existence of some barrier on exchange to the west of Chalco.

8. Ceramic type densities are calculated as the number of sherds of each type recovered per ha of surface area from collection areas designated during regional surveys:

$$\text{density per ha} = \frac{\text{sherd count(s)}}{\text{collection area (m}^2)} \times 10,000.$$

9. Regional differences in recovery create problems in mapping out the percentage of a type across survey region boundaries since in some areas a few sites with very large collections numerically dominate the count distributions. Thus, the Texcocan area may appear to be the major consumer of Calligraphic Tenayuca (presumably produced at Culhuacan/Ixtapalapa) because we have very large collections from the Texcoco area and fewer, much smaller collections from the Culhuacan area. Calculating assemblage composition percentages are thus more reliable indicators of foreign exchange.

10. This association between archaeological and historical phenomena should not be interpreted as the basis for applying a strict historical date to the development of Calligraphic Tenayuca (a practice that Smith [1987] has justifiably criticized), but as a possible indication of the relative chronology of the ceramic types in question. Although Whalen and Parsons (1982:437-438) concluded that Culhuacan and Tenayuca Black/Orange ceramics were contemporaneous throughout the Basin as a whole, minor or partial differences in their chronology may well exist (we are, after all, dealing with archaeological phases of 200 years duration). Further, Whalen and Parsons did not differentiate between the Calligraphic and Geometric styles of Tenayuca Black/Orange.

11. Although this study has shed some light on the organization of pre-imperial commodity exchange, the limitations of this study should be noted. We have examined the distribution of only one class of goods, decorated ceramics, and although this is a fairly ubiquitous utilitarian commodity, it may not be representative of exchange systems involving other classes of goods or even of other types of ceramics, such as the highly decorated and labor intensive polychromes. Further, since the current regional

chronology remains somewhat coarse-grained, and because we are limited at this time to a regional provenience for production sources for these ceramics, we anticipate that specific aspects of our results will be adjusted as both chronologies and paste characterizations for Aztec ceramics are refined.

REFERENCES CITED

Alva Ixtlilxochitl, Fernando de
  1975-1977   *Obras históricas*. Edited by Edmundo O'Gorman. 2 vols. Universidad Nacional Autónoma de México, Mexico City.
Anales de Cuauhtitlan
  1938   *Die Geschichte der Konigreiche von Culhuacan und Mexiko*. Translated by Walter Lehmann. Quellenwerke zur alten Geschichte Amerikas aufgezeichnet in den Sprachen der Eingeborenen, 1. Kohlhammer, Stuttgart (reprinted 1974).
  1945   *Códice Chimalpopoca: Anales de Cuauhtitlan y Leyenda de los Soles*. Translated and edited by Primo Feliciano Velázquez. Universidad Nacional Autónoma de México, Instituto de Investigaciones Históricas, Mexico City.
Arnold, Dean E., Hector Neff, and Ronald L. Bishop
  1991   Compositional Analysis and "Sources" of Pottery: An Ethno-archaeological Approach. *American Anthropologist* 93:70-90.
Berdan, Frances F.
  1975   *Trade, Tribute, and Market in the Aztec Empire*. Ph.D. dissertation, Department of Anthropology, University of Texas, Austin. University Microfilms, Ann Arbor.
  1985   Markets in the Economy of Aztec Mexico. In *Markets and Marketing*, edited by Stuart Plattner, pp. 339-367. University Press of America, New York.
Bishop, Ronald L., and Hector Neff
  1989   Compositional Data Analysis in Archaeology. In *Archaeological Chemistry IV*, edited by Ralph O. Allen, pp. 57-86. Advances in Chemistry Series 220, American Chemical Society, Washington, D.C.
Blanton, Richard E.
  1972   *Prehispanic Settlement Patterns of the Ixtapalapa Region, Mexico*. Occasional Papers in Anthropology No. 6, Department of Anthropology, Pennsylvania State University, University Park.
  1994   The Aztec Market System and the Growth of Empire. In *Aztec Imperial Strategies* by Frances F. Berdan, Richard E. Blanton, Elizabeth H. Boone, Mary G. Hodge, Michael E. Smith, and Emily Umberger. Dumbarton Oaks, Washington, D.C. In press.
Blanton, Richard E., Stephen A. Kowalewski, Gary Feinman, and Jill Appel
  1981   *Ancient Mesoamerica: A Comparison of Change in Three Regions*. Cambridge University Press, Cambridge.

Branstetter-Hardesty, Barbara
1978 *Ceramics of Cerro Portezuelo, Mexico: An Industry in Transition.* Ph.D. dissertation, Department of Anthropology, University of California, Los Angeles. University Microfilms, Ann Arbor.

Bray, Warwick
1972 The City-State in Central Mexico at the Time of the Spanish Conquest. *Journal of Latin American Studies* 4:161-185.

Brenner, Anita
1931 *The Influence of Technique on the Decorative Style in the Domestic Pottery of Culhuacan.* Columbia University Contributions to Anthropology 13. New York.

Brumfiel, Elizabeth M.
1976 *Specialization and Exchange at the Late Postclassic (Aztec) Community of Huexotla, Mexico.* Ph.D. dissertation, Department of Anthropology, University of Michigan. University Microfilms, Ann Arbor.

1991 *Postclassic Xaltocan: Archaeological Research in the Northern Valley of Mexico, 1990 Annual Report.* Unpublished Report. Albion College, Albion, Michigan.

Chimalpahin Quauhtlehuanitzin, Domingo Francisco de San Antón Muñon
1950 *Diferentes historias originales de los reynos de Culhuacan y México y de otras provincias.* Mitteilungen aus dem Museum für Völkerkunde in Hamburg 22.

1958 *Das Memorial Breve acerca de la Fundación de la Ciudad de Culhuacan und weitere ausgewählte Teile aus den "Diferentes Historias Originales ... "* Translated by Walter Lehmann and Gerdt Kutscher. Quellenwerke zur alten Geschichte Amerikas aufgezeichnet in den Sprachen der Eingebornen 7. Kohlhammer, Stuttgart.

1965 *Relaciones originales de Chalco Amequemecan escritas por Don Domingo Francisco de San Antón Muñon Chimalpahin Cuauhtlehuanitzin.* Translated by Sylvia Rendón. Fondo de Cultura Económica, Mexico City.

Davies, Nigel
1980 *The Toltec Heritage: From the Fall of Tula to the Rise of Tenochtitlan.* University of Oklahoma Press, Norman.

Durán, Fray Diego
1967 *Historia de las Indias de Nueva España e Islas de la Tierra Firme.* Edited by Angel María Garibay K. 2 vols. Editorial Porrúa, Mexico City.

1971 *Book of Gods and Rites and the Ancient Calendar.* Translated by Fernando Horcasitas and Doris Heyden. University of Oklahoma Press, Norman.

Elam, J. Michael, Christopher Carr, Michael D. Glascock, and Hector Neff
1992 Ultrasonic Disaggregation and INAA of Textural Fractions of Tucson Basin and Ohio Valley Pottery. In *Chemical Characterization of Ceramic Pastes in Archaeology,* edited by Hector Neff, pp. 93-111. Prehistory Press, Madison.

Enciso, Jorge
1953 *Design Motifs of Ancient Mexico.* Dover Publications, New York.

Evans, Susan T.
1980   Spatial Analysis of Basin of Mexico Settlement: Problems with the Use of the Central Place Model. *American Antiquity* 45:866-875.

Franco C., José L.
1945   Comentarios sobre tipología y filogenía de la decoración negra sobre color natural del barro en la cerámica "Azteca II." *Revista Mexicana de Estudios Antropológicos* 7:163-186.

1947   Algunos problemas relativos a la cerámica Azteca. *El México Antiguo* 7:162-208.

1957   Cenefas en la cerámica Azteca. In *Motivos Decorativos en la Cerámica Azteca,* by José Luis Franco C. and Frederick A. Peterson. Serie Científica 5. Museo Nacional de Antropología, Mexico City.

Gamio, Manuel
1913   *Arqueología del Valle de México.* Descripción general de las colecciones que se exhiben en esta exposición, año escolar de 1911-12. Anexo al informe del presidente de la Junta Directiva de la Escuela Internacional de Arqueología y Etnología América. Tipografía y litografía de Müller Hnos., Mexico City.

Gibson, Charles
1964   *The Aztecs Under Spanish Rule: A History of the Indians of the Valley of Mexico, 1519-1810.* Stanford University Press, Stanford.

Glascock, Michael D.
1992   Characterization of Archaeological Ceramics at MURR by Neutron Activation Analysis and Multivariate Statistics. In *Chemical Characterization of Ceramic Pastes in Archaeology,* edited by Hector Neff, pp. 11-26. Monographs in World Archaeology No. 7, Prehistory Press, Madison.

Griffin, James B., and Antonieta Espejo
1947   La alfarería correspondiente al ultimo período de ocupación Nahua del Valle de México: I. *Tlatelolco a Través de los Tiempos* 9:10-26.

1950   La alfarería correspondiente al ultimo período de ocupación Nahua del Valle de México: II. *Tlatelolco a Través de los Tiempos* 11:15-66.

Harbottle, Garman
1976   Activation Analysis in Archaeology. *Radiochemistry* 3. Chemical Society, London.

Hassig, Ross
1985   *Trade, Tribute, and Transportation: The Sixteenth-Century Political Economy of the Valley of Mexico.* University of Oklahoma Press, Norman.

Hicks, Frederic
1987   First Steps Toward a Market-Integrated Economy in Aztec Mexico. In *Early State Dynamics,* edited by Henri J. M. Claessen and Pieter van de Velde, pp. 91-107. E. J. Brill, New York.

Hodge, Mary G.
1984   *Aztec City-States.* Memoirs No. 18. Museum of Anthropology, University of Michigan, Ann Arbor.

1991 Appendix 3: Aztec II, III, and IV Black/Orange Type Descriptions. In *Aztec-Period Ceramic Distribution and Exchange Systems,* by Mary G. Hodge and Leah D. Minc, pp. 109-155. Final Report to the National Science Foundation for Grant #BNS-8704177.

Hodge, Mary G., and Leah D. Minc

1990 The Spatial Patterning of Aztec Ceramics: Implications for Pre-Hispanic Exchange Systems in the Valley of Mexico. *Journal of Field Archaeology* 17:415-437.

1991 *Aztec-Period Ceramic Distribution and Exchange Systems.* Final Report to the National Science Foundation for Grant #BNS-8704177.

Hodge, Mary G., Hector Neff, M. James Blackman, and Leah D. Minc

1992 A Compositional Perspective on Ceramic Production in the Aztec Empire. In *Chemical Characterization of Ceramic Pastes in Archaeology,* edited by Hector Neff, pp. 203-220. Prehistory Press, Madison.

Kaplan, David

1965 The Mexican Marketplace Then and Now. *Proceedings of the Annual Spring Meeting of the American Ethnological Society,* edited by June Helm, pp. 80-94. University of Washington Press, Seattle.

King, Heidi

1981 *Aztec Pottery Designs.* Unpublished Master's thesis, Graduate School of Arts and Sciences, Columbia University.

Kurtz, Donald V.

1974 Peripheral and Transitional Markets: The Aztec Case. *American Ethnologist* 1:685-705.

Minc, Leah D.

1991 Appendix 2: Aztec I Black/Orange Type Descriptions. In *Aztec-Period Ceramic Distribution and Exchange Systems,* by Mary G. Hodge and Leah D. Minc, pp. 69-108. Final Report to the National Science Foundation for Grant #BNS-8704177.

Nash, Manning

1966 *Primitive and Peasant Economic Systems.* Chandler Publishing, San Francisco.

Neff, Hector, Ronald L. Bishop, and Edward V. Sayre

1988 A Simulation Approach to the Problem of Tempering in Composition Studies of Archaeological Ceramics. *Journal of Archaeological Science* 15:159-172.

1989 More Observations on the Problem of Tempering in Compositional Studies of Archaeological Ceramics. *Journal of Archaeological Science* 16:57-69.

Noguera, Eduardo

1930 Decorative Aspects of Certain Types of Mexican Pottery. *Proceedings of the twenty-third International Congress of Americanists, held at New York, September 17-22, 1928,* pp. 85-92. Science Press, Lancaster, Pennsylvania.

1935 La cerámica de Tenayuca y las excavaciones estratigráficas. In *Tenayuca,* by Eduardo Noguera, pp. 141-201. Secretaría de Educación Pública, Departamento de Monumentos, Mexico City.

Norr, Lynette
1987a The Excavation of a Postclassic House at Tetla. In *Ancient Chalcatzingo*, edited by David C. Grove, pp. 400-408. University of Texas Press, Austin.
1987b Appendix 1: Postclassic Artifacts from Tetla. In *Ancient Chalcatzingo*, edited by David C. Grove, p. 525-546. University of Texas Press, Austin.

Offner, Jerome
1983 *Law and Politics in Aztec Texcoco.* Cambridge University Press, Cambridge.

O'Neill, George
1962 *Postclassic Ceramic Stratigraphy at Chalco in the Valley of Mexico.* Ph.D. dissertation, Faculty of Political Science, Columbia University. University Microfilms, Ann Arbor.

Parsons, Jeffrey R.
1966 *The Aztec Ceramic Sequence in the Teotihuacan Valley, Mexico.* Ph.D. dissertation, Department of Anthropology, The University of Michigan. University Microfilms, Ann Arbor.
1971 *Prehistoric Settlement Patterns in the Texcoco Region, Mexico.* Memoirs No. 3. Museum of Anthropology, University of Michigan, Ann Arbor.

Parsons, Jeffrey R., Elizabeth M. Brumfiel, and Mary G. Hodge
1993 Are Aztec I Ceramics Epiclassic? The Implications of Early Radiocarbon Dates from Three Aztec I Deposits in the Basin of Mexico. Paper presented at the 13th International Congress of Anthropological and Ethnological Sciences, Mexico City.

Parsons, Jeffrey R., Elizabeth M. Brumfiel, Mary H. Parsons, Virginia Popper, and Mary Taft
1982 *Late Prehispanic Chinampa Agriculture on Lake Chalco-Xochimilco, Mexico.* Preliminary Report to the National Science Foundation and the Instituto National de Antropología e Historia, Mexico City.

Parsons, Jeffrey R., Elizabeth M. Brumfiel, Mary H. Parsons, and David J. Wilson
1982 *Prehistoric Settlement Patterns in the Southern Valley of Mexico: the Chalco-Xochimilco Regions.* Memoirs No. 14. Museum of Anthropology, University of Michigan, Ann Arbor.

Parsons, Jeffrey R., Keith W. Kintigh, and Susan A. Gregg
1983 *Archaeological Settlement Pattern Data from the Chalco, Xochimilco, Ixtapalapa, Texcoco, and Zumpango Regions, Mexico.* Technical Reports No. 14. Museum of Anthropology, University of Michigan, Ann Arbor.

Peterson, Frederick A.
1957 El "motivo serpiente" en la cerámica de Culhuacán, in *Motivos decorativos en la cerámica Azteca,* by José Luis Franco C. and Frederick A. Peterson, pp. 37-48. Serie Científica No. 5. Museo Nacional de Antropología, Mexico City.

Rice, Prudence M.
1987 *Pottery Analysis: A Sourcebook.* University of Chicago Press, Chicago.

Sahagún, Fray Bernardino de
1950-1982 *Florentine Codex: General History of the Things of New Spain.* Trans-

lated and edited by Arthur J. O. Anderson and Charles E. Dibble. 12 books. School of American Research and the University of Utah Press, Santa Fe and Salt Lake City.

Sanders, William T., Jeffrey R. Parsons, and Robert S. Santley

1979   *The Basin of Mexico: Ecological Processes in the Evolution of a Civilization.* Academic Press, New York.

Schroeder, Susan

1991   *Chimalpahin and the Kingdoms of Chalco.* University of Arizona Press, Tucson.

Séjourné, Laurette

1970   *Arqueología del valle de México I: Culhuacan.* Instituto Nacional de Antropología e Historia, Mexico City.

1983   *Arqueología e historia del valle de México: de Xochimilco a Amecameca.* Siglo Ventiuno Editores, Mexico City.

Smith, Carol A.

1974   Economics of Marketing Systems: Models from Economic Geography. *Annual Review of Anthropology* 3:167-201.

1976   Exchange Systems and the Spatial Distribution of Elites: The Organization of Stratification in Agrarian Societies. In *Regional Analysis,* vol. 2, edited by Carol A. Smith, pp. 309-374. Academic Press, New York.

Smith, Michael E.

1979   The Aztec Marketing System and Settlement Pattern in the Valley of Mexico: A Central Place Analysis. *American Antiquity* 44:110-125.

1987   The Expansion of the Aztec Empire: A Case Study in the Correlation of Diachronic Archeological and Ethnohistorical data. *American Antiquity* 52:37-54.

Sneath, Peter H. A., and Robert R. Sokal

1973   *Numerical Taxonomy: The Principals and Practice of Numerical Classification.* W.H. Freeman, San Francisco.

Vaillant, George C.

1938   A Correlation of Archaeological and Historical Sequences in the Valley of Mexico. *American Anthropologist* 40:535-73.

Whalen, Michael E., and Jeffrey R. Parsons

1982   Appendix 1: Ceramic Markers used for Period Designations. In *Prehistoric Settlement Patterns in the Southern Valley of Mexico: the Chalco-Xochimilco Regions,* by Jeffrey R. Parsons, Elizabeth M. Brumfiel, Mary H. Parsons, and David J. Wilson, pp. 385-459. Memoirs No. 14. Museum of Anthropology, University of Michigan, Ann Arbor.

Zimmermann, Günter

1960   Memorial Breve. In *Das Geschichteswerk des Domingo de Muñon Chimalpahin Quauhtlehuanitzin.* Quellenkritische Studien zur frühindianischen Geschichte Mexikos, pp. 29-33. Beiträge zur mittelamerikanischen Völkerkunde 5. Hamburgishen Museums für Völkerkunde und Vorgeschichte, Hamburg.

7

The Organization of
Provincial Craft Production
and the Aztec City-State of Otumba

Deborah L. Nichols

On reaching the market place, escorted by the many Caciques whom
Montezuma had assigned to us, we were astounded at the great numbers of people and the quantities of merchandise, and at the
orderliness and good arrangements that prevailed, for we had never
seen such a thing before. (Díaz del Castillo 1963:232)

While ethnohistoric documents, like Bernal Díaz's eyewitness account of
the Tlatelolco marketplace, have formed the foundation for the study of
the Aztec economy, the potential of the archaeological record to offer a complementary perspective has only begun to be realized (Smith 1987:254; Smith and
Hodge, chap. 1). Archaeological data on the location of craft areas and "their
relationship to public structures, sources of raw materials (such as marketplaces)
and to one another" (Spence 1985:76) are especially relevant because even in a
preindustrial context the physical configuration of urban settlements was not
arbitrary and was significantly affected by the level of craft specialization (Costin
1991). This paper draws upon recent archaeological investigations in the Aztec
city-state of Otumba, located in the northeastern Basin of Mexico, to examine
models of the spatial organization of provincial craft production during the Late
Postclassic period (A.D. 1150-1519).

THE SPATIAL ORGANIZATION OF AZTEC CRAFT PRODUCTION

Following the breakup of the Toltec state ca. A.D. 1150, the basic political unit of the Basin of Mexico was the city-state, and the region was divided into about 15 such polities. After 1430 these city-states, along with approximately 35 new centers, were incorporated into the expanding domain of the Triple Alliance as semi-autonomous administrative units (Sanders et al. 1979). Each city-state consisted of rural dependencies organized around a city or town that housed the ruler's palace(s), major temples, craft specialists, and a marketplace (Berdan 1982; Bray 1972, 1977; Calnek 1978; Gibson 1964, 1971; Hodge 1984; Sanders et al. 1979). While the basic structure of the city-state is generally agreed upon, the organization of craft production as been variously described as nucleated or dispersed.

The Nucleated Pattern

As its name implies, the nucleated pattern presumes that specialists were concentrated in nucleated cities and towns for reasons of efficiency—i.e. economies of scale (Trigger 1972:578-579) or economic symbiosis (Sanders 1956). Centralization also made political control over specialists and exchange systems easier to enforce. Tenochtitlan-Tlatelolco best exemplifies this pattern of craft organization: by Late Aztec times (A.D. 1350-1519) it had become the largest center of specialized craft production and distribution in Mesoamerica and was occupied almost exclusively by nonagriculturalists (Calnek 1972).

Arturo Monzón's (1949) data suggested that specialists in a particular craft tended to reside together in Tenochtitlan as members of the same *calpulli* (or *tlaxilacalli*) or ward. Although much debate surrounds what the *calpulli* (pl. *calpultin*) represented, there is a general consensus that it formed a territorial division, a ward or a barrio, and an internally stratified land-holding group that served administrative, economic, military, and religious functions (Berdan 1982:18; Carrasco 1971:365-366). In the case of artisans who crafted luxury goods, the *calpulli* exhibited many of the same features as guilds (Sjoberg 1960:187-196), and some of these specialized *calpultin* were comprised of distinct ethnic groups who had immigrated relatively recently to the imperial cities (Berdan 1982:57, 1989:88).

The nucleated pattern of urban craft organization represented by Tenochtitlan has been a highly influential model. William T. Sanders et al. (1979) argue that the city-state capitals in the Basin of Mexico served as centers of craft production and distribution for their respective hinterlands in much the same manner, albeit greatly reduced, as Tenochtitlan and that the internal configuration of the provincial centers even mimicked that of Tenochtitlan. They suggest that Late

Aztec provincial centers consisted of dense nucleated cores (of 4,000 to 10,000 persons/km^2) where most nonfood producers, including craft specialists, resided. This area was surrounded by a second, less densely populated residential zone (1,000 to 4,000 persons/km^2) that gradually shifted to a more dispersed zone of rural occupation. "In some respects this physical configuration of smaller centers reproduces in miniature, and in much more simplified form, the settlement configuration of Greater Tenochtitlan" (Sanders et al. 1979:163).

Sanders (1965:67) suggests that in smaller centers the *barrio pequeño* (a lineage-size barrio), rather than the *calpulli,* formed the unit of craft specialization, but, like their counterparts in the imperial cities, the specialists in provincial centers were full-time; those in rural settlements were part-time. Sanders subsequently has modified his position, however, and now concludes that most specialists outside the imperial cities were part-time, practicing agriculture to meet most of their food needs and producing goods for exchange (Sanders and Webster 1988). Thus in the nucleated pattern, even though specialists might not have been full-time, they were concentrated within the nucleated core of provincial centers, and they resided in wards according to their specialty.

The Dispersed Pattern

In the second model, as discussed by Frederic Hicks (1982, 1984), specialists were scattered throughout the provincial center, and the center's physical configuration was dispersed, not nucleated. This pattern is thought to correlate with production in domestic settings, rather than workshops, and "geared more to local consumption than for commercial purposes" (Berdan 1989:94). While Hicks agrees that each provincial city contained a nucleated core centered on the palace, major temples, and related institutions, he argues that most of the settlement consisted of a large dispersed residential zone, which included specialists and non-specialists. Hicks views the nucleated form of Tenochtitlan as unique (except for Classic period Teotihuacan), which was not replicated even at Texcoco, the second largest city in the Basin: "I am sure, however, that if we could see the whole of Texcoco mapped as an archaeological site, we would be reminded much more of Tikal than Tenochtitlan" (Hicks 1984:167). Hicks draws the analogy to Tikal because of that city's dispersed settlement pattern and its lack of wards/barrios of craft specialists. Thus the correlation between craft specialization and wards reported for Texcoco might only apply to elite/luxury artisans—e.g., the goldsmiths and featherworkers described by Alva Ixtlilxochitl (1965:v.2:187).

In the dispersed pattern, specialists resided with nonspecialists and "were to be found in most barrios" (Hicks 1982:241). In Huexotzinco, for instance, specialists and nonspecialists commingled in the same wards, and even though some wards contained more specialists than others, "there was no localization of each occupation in a separate ward" (Carrasco 1971:365). Tribute payment and worship of patron deities, however, cut across wards and brought together specialists in a particular craft (Carrasco 1971:365; Hicks 1982, 1984).

This pattern, Hicks argues, reflected the nature of specialization. Most craft producers outside the imperial cities were part-time because of insufficient demand and unreliable surplus food production (Hicks 1987:99). The nonmonetarized nature of the Aztec economy and the system of rotational labor *(tequitl)* further inhibited the formation of highly nucleated cities. The dispersed model thus views the "pull" of agricultural production as stronger than the "push" of urbanization.

These two models of urban craft organization have been strongly influenced by the descriptions of the Aztec economy found in ethnohistoric documents from the imperial centers. These polarized idealizations may obscure some of the actual diversity in the structure of craft specialization. For further details about the pattern(s) of organization of craft production at provincial centers in the Basin, we need to turn to the archaeological record.

RECENT ARCHAEOLOGICAL INVESTIGATIONS AT PROVINCIAL CENTERS

Ethnohistoric records of the smaller provincial centers in the Basin of Mexico are often fragmentary, and colonial and modern settlements now cover most of the sites. Fortunately, a series of archaeological projects at the better-preserved Aztec sites have recovered information on provincial craft organization. Elizabeth M. Brumfiel's (1980, 1982, 1986, 1987a, 1987b) surface collections at Huexotla, Xico, and Xaltocan failed to find evidence of wards of craft specialists, although her investigations identified a few non-comestible craft workshops at Xaltocan (earlier extensive surveys at Huexotla and Xico have reported similar results [Parsons 1971; Parsons et al. 1982]). In his surface collections at the provincial city-state capital of Coatlan in Morelos, Roger Mason (1980) did not encounter any indications of craft wards, and Michael W. Spence (1981, 1985) described dispersed obsidian core-blade workshops at Aztec period Teotihuacan.

These findings have challenged the nucleated model of craft organization at provincial centers and their roles as loci of specialization and exchange (Smith and Hodge, chap. 1). On the other hand, surveys of the Otumba site, first by William G. Mather (1968) and later by Thomas H. Charlton (1981, 1988), reported large concentrations of debris from several crafts, including obsidian core-blades, ceramic figurines, maguey fibers, groundstone tools, and obsidian earspools, which implies that craft specialists were concentrated at this provincial center. Similar concentrations of manufacturing debris indicate that Tepeapulco, described by Charlton (chap. 9), also served as a center of utilitarian craft production.

Although questions have been raised about the adequacy of Brumfiel's sampling design for discovering evidence of craft specialization at Huexotla (Charlton 1980), the same reconnaissance methods and similar sampling designs identified workshop concentrations at Otumba and Xaltocan. This suggests that the differences are not just methodological. Thus, while neither the intensity of the reconnaissance coverage nor the sampling designs were appropriate for discovery-mode sampling of small, houschold-size concentrations, they were sufficient (ca. 2,500 m = the size of the sampling strata) to identify large concentrations of nonperishable manufacturing debris (Brumfiel 1976:154; Nichols et al. 1990).

THE OTUMBA CITY-STATE

Recent archaeological research in the Otumba city-state, designed to look at the role of craft specialization in the evolution of Late Postclassic political systems, involved a multi-stage methodology of surveys, systematic surface collections, and excavations (Charlton and Nichols 1990). Workshops as the loci of specialized production (i.e., production in excess of the needs of the producer's household) were identified on the basis of relatively dense concentrations of manufacturing tools and debris (Clark 1986; Clark and Parry 1990:297; Costin 1991:3-4). In addition to the investigations at Otumba, the city-state capital, systematic surface collections were also made at a series of rural sites (TA-36, TA-37, TA-39, TA-57, TA-59, SS-VI [a group of three small sites], TA-71, TA-86, and TA-236) that were tributary to Otumba. Although analyses of craft industries arc still in process, we have been able to delineate the broad outlines of the occupation and organization of craft production at Otumba (Charlton and Nichols 1990; Charlton et al. 1991; Otis Charlton et al. 1993).

The Otumba site encompasses 220 ha (fig. 7.1) and consists of two residential zones, including a nucleated core of about 40 ha that contains large mounds (at least one of which was probably a temple-pyramid) and other indications of elite occupation, such as painted plaster floors and walls and a higher proportion of decorated and foreign pottery (Charlton and Nichols 1992). A large dispersed residential zone makes up the rest of the site. Here most mounds have been reduced by erosion and plowing to concentrations of building rubble and domestic artifacts. Otumba's domain also included tributary settlements on the piedmont to the north, south, east and southwest and the Otumba obsidian source area (Charlton and Spence 1982:39-50).

Otumba and its tributaries receive only brief mention in Aztec documentary histories. According to these accounts, Otomi refugees who fled Xaltocan after its defeat by Azcapotzalco in 1395 were relocated at Otumba under the auspices of Techotlalatzin of Texcoco (Alva Ixtlilxochitl 1965:v.2:78; Offner 1979) and at least two major battles took place there in the early 1400s prior to Otumba's incorporation into the Triple Alliance (Alva Ixtlilxochitl 1965:v.1: 167-168, v.2:82-83; Davies 1973:57; Hassig 1988:136-139). Pottery found in excavated and surface contexts confirms a light Early Aztec occupation (A.D. 1150-1350) at Otumba and some of its tributaries. Preliminary analyses suggest that the occupation was heavier in the core zone at Otumba than elsewhere; however, there is little correlation between the locations of the Early and Late Aztec occupations (Charlton et al. 1991; Hirst and Mendoza 1990). The city-state grew substantially in Late Aztec times (A.D. 1350-1519), and evidence of this predominates at both the provincial center and rural sites. A definite elite presence in the nucleated core is also evident at this time (Charlton 1990b; Charlton and Nichols 1992). Occupation continued at Otumba until ca. A.D. 1620, although the Spanish shifted the center of the town onto the alluvial plain to the north.

Craft Production in the Otumba City-State

Noncomestible crafts produced in the Otumba city-state include cores, blades, and bifaces made of obsidian, obsidian earspools and ornaments of exotic stone, ground and chipped basalt tools, ceramic censers, figurines, molds, spindle whorls, and cotton and maguey fibers. Detailed discussions of the industries can be found in Biskowski (1990, 1991); Charlton (1990a); Charlton and Nichols (1990); Charlton et al. (1991); Nichols (1990); Otis Charlton (1990a, 1990b, 1990c, 1990d, 1993, chap. 8); Otis Charlton et al. (1993); and Parry (1990a, 1990b).

Except for one maguey fiber workshop and one lapidary workshop at TA-39, which lies so close to Otumba (less than 0.5 km) that it might have been an extension of the town, the only evidence of workshops at rural sites is in the production of bifaces and core-blades from Otumba obsidian (Evans 1988; Parry 1990a). Parry's analysis of a large (1.5 ha) biface workshop at TA-37 indicates that the level of biface production exceeded local consumption. Spindle whorls for spinning cotton and maguey fibers have also been recovered from rural households but not in concentrations indicative of workshops (Evans 1988; Nichols 1990).

In contrast to the rural sites, a number of different craft industries were concentrated in the city-state capital. Interestingly, they do not follow the same pattern of internal organization: some are dispersed, while others are aggregated in wards (fig. 7.1).

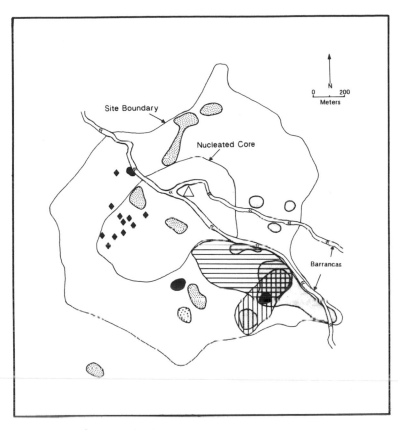

△ Central Pyramid

Core-blade Workshop (Pachuca Obsidian-Green)

Core-blade Workshop (Otumba Obsidian-Gray)

Lapidary Workshops

Groundstone Workshops

Figurine Workshops

Maguey Fiber Workshops

◆ Censer Molds

Fig. 7.1.   Schematic Map of Workshops at Otumba.

Dispersed Craft Production at Otumba. Although obsidian core-blade production was an important industry at Otumba, the core-blade workshops are scattered throughout the site rather than grouped into wards. The workshops occur in both the nucleated core and dispersed residential zone, and all but one of them used mostly obsidian from the Pachuca source area. They are the only workshops found in the core, which suggests the involvement of elites in the production/distribution of green Pachuca obsidian.

It is possible that these workshops, defined by concentrations of manufacturing debris (Parry 1990b), represent dumps rather than workshop loci (Clark 1986). Excavation of one of the core-blade concentrations in the nucleated core found the manufacturing debris in midden deposits intermixed with domestic refuse (Healan et al. 1990). Architectural remains—foundations of a house, an altar, a few postholes, and a badly disturbed fragment of a wall—were also uncovered, but deep plowing had so disturbed the stratigraphy that it was it difficult to determine the association between the architecture and manufacturing debris. Midden deposits with manufacturing debris overlaid what remained of the buildings' foundations; this might suggest that they are not contemporaneous, but the superimposition could also have been caused by plowing and erosion. The excavations revealed no evidence that the midden deposits had been deliberately transported or moved for use as construction fill, so it seems likely that the obsidian was worked in the area. The results of this excavation and the scattered distribution of the core-blade concentrations do not suggest a ward/barrio organization for these specialists.

Small concentrations of waste debris from the production of basalt tools also occur as isolates at Otumba and, like the core-blade concentrations, the basalt concentrations may be refuse dumps with the actual workshop loci located nearby (Biskowski 1990). Unlike the core-blade workshops, however, the basalt workshops are found only in the dispersed residential zone. All these concentrations lie in areas heavily disturbed by plowing, and no architectural associations were apparent from the surface. According to Biskowski (1990, 1991), most of the basalt grinding tools consumed at Otumba were produced in the town's workshops, which also exported tools to other settlements in the region. One basalt concentration adjoins a maguey-fiber workshop that used basalt scrapers. The basalt and obsidian core-blade workshops at Otumba not only supplied the town and rural settlements with everyday implements, but their products were also essential for other specialists, including lapidaries, who used slate tools to fashion earspools and labrets from exhausted obsidian cores (Otis Charlton 1993, chap. 8).

Nucleated Craft Production at Otumba. Unlike the core-blade and basalt workshops, the lapidary workshops cluster in the southeast section of the town and form their own ward; in fact, this part of the site is made up entirely of wards of craft specialists. (Isolated lapidary workshops also occur nearby to the north and east.) Otis Charlton's (1990a, 1990b, 1993) excavation of one lapidary concentration revealed traces of domestic activities, suggesting that this was a household industry, and she suspects that each lapidary workshop concentration might represent a single household. Few of the finished labrets and earspools made at Otumba have been found at the site (Parry 1990b). No doubt these highly valued items would not have been discarded casually; however, a significant part of Otumba's lapidary production might have been exported to other parts of the region and perhaps even carried by *pochteca* (professional merchants) based at Otumba to places outside the Basin of Mexico (Berdan 1975:147-148; Sahagún 1950-1982:bk.9).

A ward of figurine workshops lies just east of the lapidary workshops. There open-back figurine molds and figurines and ceramic artifacts such as clay balls, spindle whorls for spinning cotton, and possibly serpent handles for censers were produced (Otis Charlton 1990a, 1990b). Within the figurine workshop zone, the surface concentrations are not continuous, and Otis Charlton thinks that each one probably represents a group of households similar to those she excavated. The quantity of molds and manufacturing debris suggests that these specialists supplied figurines, and maybe molds, for the region.

A cluster of maguey fiber workshops forms a third ward of specialists. It lies to the south of the figurine ward (Nichols 1990). A small concentration of maguey whorls in the southwest part of the site (not illustrated) may represent an isolated workshop. These workshops processed maguey fibers, made spindle whorls, spun thread, and presumably wove cloth. Although none of these workshops was excavated, the manufacturing debris, which was interspersed with domestic refuse, suggests a household-based industry. A comparison of the number of spindle whorls recovered in intensive surface collections from the workshops and the number of spindle whorls in rural households indicates that some of the workshop production was for export. At least one maguey workshop at Otumba also made obsidian earspools and figurines.

While the maguey, figurine, and lapidary specialists each had their own wards, their manufacturing debris overlaps in the surface collections. "Households in the overlap zone may have participated in multiple occupations depending upon demand, or may have shifted the focus of their productive activities through time" (Charlton et al. 1991:105).

The remaining crafts produced at Otumba were apparently not made in workshops of their own. Molds for manufacturing two styles of ceramic censers, common items in Late Aztec domestic contexts, were found in low frequencies at the western edge of the nucleated core and in the adjoining section of the dispersed residential zone (Charlton 1990a). Since the surface collections contained no other kinds of debris from making censers these manufacturing areas have not been designated as workshops (Charlton et al. 1991;

Otis Charlton et al. 1993). Otis Charlton, however, found a concentration of censer rejects in the figurine workshop zone, indicating that those workshops produced a variety of mold-made ceramics. Charlton's on-going analysis of the Otumba pottery has identified a local pottery type that was made at Otumba; however, we have found no evidence of large-scale pottery manufacturing in the town. Small spindle whorls for spinning cotton are distributed throughout the site in low frequencies. The absence of concentrations of cotton whorls indicates that cotton spinning, and probably weaving, took place in most households. This agrees with chroniclers' accounts of the spinning and weaving of cotton cloth as activities performed by women in their households (Berdan 1988; Brumfiel 1991; Hicks, chap. 4).

DISCUSSION

Otumba exhibits many features of the nucleated model of urban craft production, but it also shows some characteristics of the dispersed pattern. Craft specialists concentrated at the urban center (and at the adjoining settlement, TA-39) and their proximity to each other facilitated a high degree of interdependence among industries, like obsidian core-blade production and lapidary working. The lapidary, figurine, and maguey specialists at the urban center were located in wards according to their specialty, suggesting a *calpulli* type of organization. As Hicks (chap. 4) notes, household-based industries are able to take advantage of the domestic mode of production and the labor of all household members. Why the basalt and core-blade workshops depart from the ward type of organization is not entirely clear, although the small number of specialists was probably one factor. According to Biskowski (1991), a few craftsmen could have supplied the entire Teotihuacan Valley with grinding tools, and the number of core-blade specialists was probably not large either (Clark 1986; Sanders and Santley 1983).

Except for two core-blade workshops, all the workshops occur in the dispersed residential zone and not in the nucleated core. Class membership appears to have been the primary criterion for residence in the core zone (Charlton and Nichols 1992) and thus most craft specialists, including the lapidaries, who are generally considered luxury artisans, lived and worked in the dispersed residential zone. The lack of direct association between workshops and elite residences and institutions suggests that most Otumba craft producers were independent specialists rather than attached ones "contractually bound to the patrons for whom they work" (Brumfiel and Earle 1987:5; Costin 1991:11-12), although ethnohistoric studies (e.g., Hicks 1987) indicate that Aztec elites manipulated the distribution and/or production of raw materials and finished goods in various other ways, such as through the tribute system (Otis Charlton et al. 1993).

The craft specialists at Otumba had a "commercial" orientation as well as a local one. Although our studies are not complete, preliminary estimates indicate that the workshops at the provincial center supplied other settlements in the region. Obsidian core-blades, lapidary ornaments, cotton and maguey textiles and bifaces from rural workshops were also probably exported outside the city-state through the market and tribute systems (Otis Charlton et al. 1993). However, this does not necessarily imply full-time specialization. Ethnographic and experimental data (e.g., Sanders and Santley 1983; Sanders and Webster 1988:542-543) suggest that obsidian core-blade production might be the best candidate for full-time specialization, but the absolute number of specialists involved in this industry would have been small (Clark 1986; Parry 1990a). Lapidary production may be another candidate because of the high value of the goods and the skill required to make them. Peacock (1982:17-23) argues that where workshops/manufacturing areas remain attached to residences—as the consistent association of manufacturing debris and domestic refuse indicates for Otumba—craft production is usually part-time and subsidiary to agricultural production even at the more specialized end of the spectrum of household industries dominated by men whose production is oriented to the market. Diversification, such as the mixed-production strategy employed by figurine, maguey, and lapidary specialists, would have been essential for most craft producers at Otumba and other provincial centers because of political and technological constraints on the economy.

Of the provincial centers so far examined in the Basin of Mexico, Otumba most closely fits the nucleated pattern of craft organization. The overall configuration of Otumba, however, appears to have been more dispersed than nucleated; buildings were not tightly clustered even in the core zone of the town, which supports Hicks' view of Late Postclassic urbanism. In contrast, Huexotla, which lacks the concentration of craft specialists found at Otumba, contains a nucleated core that is much larger in terms of its size and the scale of monumental architecture; the 300 ha core at Huexotla comprises 36 percent of the site area (Parsons 1971:137-138) while the core zone at Otumba makes up only 20 percent of the settlement. The fact that the organization of Aztec craft production does not conform to a single model should not be surprising, and elsewhere Charlton and I have offered some thoughts as to why (Charlton, chap. 9; Charlton et al. 1991; Nichols and Charlton 1988;).

The concentration of specialists and intensification of craft production at Otumba in Late Aztec times relates, in part, to its distance from Tenochtitlan and its location on the northeastern periphery of the Basin of Mexico where regional systems of production and distribution coexisted with the centralized tribute system dominated by Tenochtitlan. Population increase, which created a greater aggregate demand for craft goods, also facilitated the growth of craft specialization at Otumba. On the other hand, the marked increase in population probably could not have been sustained without ways of compensating for short-falls in staple food production in this marginal agricultural setting.

The intensification of exchange that accompanied the expansion of Late Postclassic macro-states would also have contributed to Otumba's development as a center of craft specialization and exchange since the settlement lies near an important transportation route connecting the Basin of Mexico with other parts of Mesoamerica and a group of *pochteca* was based in the town. The concentration of lapidary, figurine, and maguey fiber specialists at Otumba in sufficient numbers such that each had their own ward in the town was probably linked to the growth of inter-regional trade rather than being a reflection of an idealized city plan patterned after Tenochtitlan. Proximity to the Otumba obsidian source area (Sanders et al. 1979:179-180) was an additional factor, and several rural workshops along with one in the town specialized in this type of obsidian.

In contrast, Huexotla and Xico were situated in the core of the Basin, and by the Late Aztec period, craft production in this core area had become centered at Tenochtitlan. Huexotla is also only a short distance from Texcoco, the second-largest market center in the Basin (Hassig 1985:137), and Xico lies less than 5 km from the provincial center of Chalco. Xaltocan sits in an intermediary location on an island in Lake Zumpango-Xaltocan, and here Brumfiel encountered evidence of a few workshops, along with an emphasis on *chinampa* cultivation and exploitation of lacustrine resources. Historical and political factors also contributed to the diversity. The importance of Huexotla, Xaltocan, and Xico diminished considerably in Late Aztec times: with the growth of the Acolhua state and the Triple Alliance, nearby Texcoco overshadowed Huexotla; Xico, a regional capital in Early Postclassic times, declined in importance after it came under the control of Cuitlahuac; and Xaltocan apparently underwent a substantial reduction in size following its defeat by Azcapotzalco (Brumfiel 1987b, 1990).

Investigation of other Aztec cities and towns would reveal additional variability resulting from the interplay of ecological, demographic, economic, and political processes in Late Postclassic urbanization. In the case of Tenochtitlan this led to a remarkable degree of urbanism for a low-energy preindustrial civilization. Tenochtitlan's situation as the capital of the largest empire in prehispanic Mesoamerica makes it unwise to overgeneralize, however. Even provincial centers on the periphery of the Basin, like Otumba, that resembled Tenochtitlan as centers of craft production and distribution differed in other important respects. The dispersed configuration of many of them reflects limitations on the division of labor and their relatively brief urban histories. Despite an urban tradition of over 15 centuries, most Late Aztec cities became urban communities in the 100 years preceding the Spanish conquest.

ACKNOWLEDGMENTS

Current research of the Otumba city-state, carried out under a Permiso from the Instituto Nacional de Antropología e Historia, is supported by the National Science Foundation (BNS-871-9665: Thomas H. Charlton, principal investigator; BNS-871-8140: Deborah L. Nichols, principal investigator) and by the National Endowment for the Humanities (RO-21705-88: Thomas H. Charlton, principal investigator). Thomas H. Charlton also received support from the University of Iowa Faculty Development Assignment. Deborah L. Nichols received additional support from the Claire Garber Goodman Fund, the Dartmouth Class of 1962, and the Dartmouth Faculty Research Committee. The artifacts from the Otumba project are stored at the Teotihuacán Research Facility in San Juan Teotihuacán, Mexico, which is operated by Arizona State University. We gratefully acknowledge all support received and extend our appreciation to the people of the municipio and cabecera of Otumba—in particular, to the residents of the barrio of Tlamimilolopa and to the Presidencia Municipal of Otumba.

I would especially like to thank my colleagues, Martin Biskowski, Elizabeth Brumfiel, Thomas H. Charlton, Cynthia Otis Charlton, Mary Hodge, Jeffrey Parsons, William Parry, and Michael Smith, for sharing their ideas and their research with me.

REFERENCES CITED

Alva Ixtlilxochitl, Fernando de
1965 *Obras históricas.* Translated by Alfredo Chavero. 2 vols. Editora Nacional, Mexico City.
Berdan, Frances F.
1975 *Trade, Tribute, and Market in the Aztec Empire.* Ph.D. dissertation, Department of Anthropology, University of Texas, Austin. University Microfilms, Ann Arbor.
1982 *The Aztecs of Central Mexico: An Imperial Society.* Holt, Rinehart and Winston, New York.
1988 Cotton in Aztec Mexico. *Mexican Studies/Estudios Mexicanos* 3:235-262.
1989 Trade and Markets in Precapitalist States. In *Economic Anthropology,* edited by Stuart Plattner, pp. 78-107. Stanford University Press, Stanford.
Biskowski, Martin F.
1990 Ground Stone Tools at Otumba. Paper presented at the 55th Annual Meeting of the Society for American Archaeology, Las Vegas.
1991 *Spatial Distribution of Ground Stone Artifacts and Related Materials at Otumba.* Report submitted to the Instituto Nacional de Antropología e Historia, Mexico City.
Bray, Warwick
1972 The City-State in Central Mexico at the Time of the Spanish Conquest. *Journal of Latin American Studies* 4:161-185.

1977 Civilising the Aztecs. In *The Evolution of Social Systems,* edited by Jonathan Friedman and Michael J. Rowlands, pp. 373-398. University of Pittsburgh Press, Pittsburgh.

Brumfiel, Elizabeth M.

1976 *Specialization and Exchange at the Late Postclassic (Aztec) Community of Huexotla, Mexico.* Ph.D. dissertation, Department of Anthropology, University of Michigan, Ann Arbor. University Microfilms, Ann Arbor.

1980 Specialization, Market Exchange, and the Aztec State: A View from Huexotla. *Current Anthropology* 21:459-478.

1982 Intensive, Systematic Surface Collection at Ch-Az-92 (Xico). In *Late Prehispanic Chinampa Agriculture on Lake Chalco-Xochimilco, Mexico.* Report submitted to the National Science Foundation, edited by Jeffrey R. Parsons, Elizabeth M. Brumfiel, Mary H. Parsons, Virginia Popper, and Mary Taft, pp. 195-215. Manuscript on file at the Museum of Anthropology, University of Michigan, Ann Arbor.

1986 The Division of Labor at Xico: The Chipped Stone Industry. In *Economic Aspects of Prehistoric Highland Mexico,* edited by Barry L. Isaac, pp. 245-279. Research in Economic Anthropology Supplement No. 2. JAI Press, Greenwich.

1987a Elite and Utilitarian Crafts in the Aztec State. In *Specialization, Exchange, and Complex Societies,* edited by Elizabeth Brumfiel and Timothy K. Earle, pp. 102-118. Cambridge University Press, New York.

1987b *Aztec Xaltocan: Regional Articulation in the Late Postclassic Valley of Mexico.* Report submitted to the H. John Heinz III Charitable Trust. Manuscript on file at the Department of Anthropology and Sociology, Albion College, Albion, Michigan.

1990 Figurines and the Aztec State: The Case for and Against Ideological Dominance. Paper presented at the 91st Annual Meeting of the American Anthropological Association, New Orleans.

1991 Weaving and Cooking: Woman's Production in Aztec Mexico. In *Engendering Archaeology: Woman and Prehistory,* edited by Joan M. Gero and Margaret Conkey, pp. 224-254. Basil Blackwell, Cambridge.

Brumfiel, Elizabeth M., and Timothy K. Earle

1987 Specialization, Exchange, and Complex Societies: An Introduction. In *Specialization, Exchange, and Complex Societies,* edited by Elizabeth M. Brumfiel and Timothy K. Earle, pp. 1-9. Cambridge University Press, Cambridge.

Calnek, Edward E.

1972 Settlement Pattern and Chinampa Agriculture at Tenochtitlan. *American Antiquity* 37:104-115.

1978 The City-State in the Basin of Mexico: Late Prehispanic Period. In *Urbanization in the Americas from Its Beginnings to the Present,* edited by Richard P. Schaedal, Jorge E. Hardoy, and Nora Scott Kinzer, pp. 163-170. Mouton, The Hague.

Carrasco, Pedro

1971 Social Organization of Ancient Mexico. In *Archaeology of Northern Mesoamerica,* pt. 1, edited by Gordon Ekholm and Ignacio Bernal, pp. 349-375. Handbook of Middle American Indians, vol. 10, Robert Wauchope, general editor. University of Texas Press, Austin.

Charlton, Thomas H.

1980 Commentary on Specialization, Market Exchange, and the Aztec State: The View from Huexotla. *Current Anthropology* 21:468-469.

1981 Otumba: Archaeology and Ethnohistory. Paper presented at the 46th Annual Meeting of the Society for American Archaeology, San Diego.

1988 Otumba, México: reconocimientos de superficie del sitio de TA-80, Otumba: informe tecnico final. Report submitted to the Instituto Nacional de Antropología e Historia, Mexico City.

1990a Economics and Politics: The Case of Aztec Otumba. Paper presented at the 55th Annual Meeting of Society for American Archaeology, Las Vegas.

1990b Operations 9 and 10, Fields 33 and 34, The Nucleated Core of the Site. In *Early State Formation Processes: The Aztec City-State of Otumba, Mexico, Part 1, Preliminary Report on Recent Research in the Otumba City-State.* Report No. 3. Mesoamerican Research Colloquium, Department of Anthropology, University of Iowa, Iowa City.

Charlton, Thomas H., and Deborah L. Nichols

1992 Late Postclassic and Colonial Period Elites at Otumba, Mexico: The Archaeological Dimension. In *Mesoamerican Elites: An Archaeological Assessment,* edited by Diane Chase and Arlen Chase, pp. 242-258. University of Oklahoma Press, Norman.

Charlton, Thomas H., and Deborah L. Nichols (editors)

1990 *Early State Formation Processes: The Aztec City-State of Otumba, Mexico, Part 1, Preliminary Report on Recent Research in the Otumba City-State.* Report No. 3. Mesoamerican Research Colloquium, Department of Anthropology, University of Iowa, Iowa City.

Charlton, Thomas H., Deborah L. Nichols, and Cynthia Otis Charlton

1991 Aztec Craft Production and Specialization: Archaeological Evidence from the City-State of Otumba, Mexico. *World Archaeology* 23:98-114.

Charlton, Thomas H., and Michael W. Spence

1982 Obsidian Exploitation and Civilization in the Basin of Mexico. In *Mining and Mining Techniques in Ancient Mesoamerica,* edited by Phil C. Weigand and Gretchen Gwynne, pp. 7-86. Anthropology 4(1-2), State University of New York, Stony Brook.

Clark, John E.

1986 From Mountain to Molehill: A Critical Review of Teotihuacan's Obsidian Industry. In *Economic Aspects of Prehispanic Highland Mexico,* edited by Barry L. Isaac, pp. 23-74. Research in Economic Anthropology, Supplement No 2. JAI Press, Greenwich.

Clark, John E., and William J. Parry

1990 Craft Specialization and Cultural Complexity. *Research in Economic Anthropology* 12, edited by Barry L. Isaac, pp. 289-346. JAI Press, Greenwich.

Costin, Cathy
  1991   Craft Specialization: Issues in Defining, Documenting, and Explaining the Organization of Production. *Archaeological Method and Theory* 3:1-56. University of Arizona, Tuscon.

Davies, Nigel
  1973   *The Aztecs, a History.* University of Oklahoma Press, Norman.

Díaz del Castillo, Bernal
  1963   *The Conquest of New Spain.* Translated by J. M. Cohen. Penguin, London.

Evans, Susan T.
  1988   *Excavations at Cihuatecpan: An Aztec Village in the Teotihuacán Valley.* Vanderbilt University Publications in Anthropology No. 36. Vanderbilt University, Nashville.

Gibson, Charles
  1964   *The Aztecs under Spanish Rule: A History of the Indians of the Valley of Mexico, 1519-1810.* Stanford University Press, Stanford.

  1971   Structure of the Aztec Empire. In *Archaeology of Northern Mesoamerica,* pt. 1, edited by Gordon Ekholm and Ignacio Bernal, pp. 376-394. Handbook of Middle American Indians, vol. 10, Robert Wauchope, general editor. University of Texas Press, Austin.

Hassig, Ross
  1985   *Trade, Tribute, and Transportation: The Sixteenth Century Political Economy of the Valley of Mexico.* University of Oklahoma Press, Norman.

  1988   *Aztec Warfare: Imperial Expansion and Political Control.* University of Oklahoma Press, Norman.

Healan, Dan M., Thomas H. Charlton, and Deborah L. Nichols
  1990   Operations 2 and 3, Field 46, Obsidian Core-Blade Workshop. In *Early State Formation Processes: The Aztec City-State of Otumba, Mexico, Part 1, Preliminary Report on Recent Research in the Otumba City-State.* Report No. 3. Mesoamerican Research Colloquium, Department of Anthropology, University of Iowa, Iowa City.

Hicks, Frederic
  1982   Tetzcoco in the Early 16th Century: The State, the City, and the Calpolli. *American Ethnologist* 9:230-249.

  1984   Rotational Labor and Urban Development in Prehispanic Texcoco. In *Explorations in Ethnohistory: Indians of Central Mexico in the Sixteenth Century,* edited by H. R. Harvey and Hanns J. Prem, pp. 147-174. University of New Mexico Press, Albuquerque.

  1987   First Steps Toward a Market-Integrated Economy in Aztec Mexico. In *Early State Dynamics,* edited by Henri J. M. Claessen and Pieter Van de Velde, pp. 91-107. E. J. Brill, Leiden.

Hirst, K. Kris, and Marcela Mendoza
  1990   Ceramic Distribution. Paper presented at the 55th Annual Meeting of the Society for American Archaeology, Las Vegas.

Hodge, Mary G.
1984 *Aztec City-States*. Memoirs No. 18. Museum of Anthropology, University of Michigan, Ann Arbor.

Mason, Roger D.
1980 *Economic and Social Organization of an Aztec Provincial Center: Archaeological Research at Coatlan Viejo, Morelos, Mexico*. Ph.D. dissertation, Department of Anthropology, University of Texas, Austin. University Microfilms, Ann Arbor.

Mather, William G.
1968 *The Aztec State of Otumba, Mexico: An Ethno-Historical Settlement Pattern Study*. Unpublished Master's thesis, Department of Anthropology, Pennsylvania State University, University Park.

Monzón, Arturo
1949 *El calpulli en la organización social de los Tenochca*. Universidad Nacional Autónoma de México, Mexico City.

Nichols, Deborah L.
1990 Maguey Fiber Production in the Aztec City-State of Otumba, Mexico. Paper presented at the 55th Annual Meeting of the Society for American Archaeology, Las Vegas.

Nichols, Deborah L., and Thomas H. Charlton
1988 Processes of State Formation: Core versus Periphery in the Late Postclassic Basin of Mexico. Paper presented at the 53rd Annual Meeting of the Society for American Archaeology, Phoenix.

Nichols, Deborah L., Thomas H. Charlton, Cynthia Otis Charlton, and Evaristo Tenorio Coronel
1990 The Intensive Surveys and Surface Collections, 1988. In *Early State Formation Processes: The Aztec City-State of Otumba, Mexico, Part 1, Preliminary Report on Recent Research in the Otumba City-State*. Report No. 3. Mesoamerican Research Colloquium, Department of Anthropology, University of Iowa, Iowa City.

Offner, Jerome A.
1979 A Reassessment of the Extent and Structuring of the Empire of Techotlalatzin, Fourteenth-century Ruler of Texcoco. *Ethnohistory* 26:231-241.

Otis Charlton, Cynthia
1990a Figurine and Lapidary Production at Otumba: Craft Specialization in Domestic Contexts. Paper presented at the 55th Annual Meeting of the Society for American Archaeology, Las Vegas.

1990b Operation 11, Field 169, Mound 41, Lapidary Workshop. In *Early State Formation Processes: The Aztec City-State of Otumba, Mexico, Part 1, Preliminary Report on Recent Research in the Otumba City-State*. Report No. 3. Mesoamerican Research Colloquium, Department of Anthropology, University of Iowa, Iowa City.

1990c Operation 4, Field 39, Figurine Workshop Zone. In *Early State Formation Processes: The Aztec City-State of Otumba, Mexico, Part 1, Preliminary Report* on *Recent Research in the Otumba City-State*. Report No. 3. Mesoamerican Research Colloquium, Department of Anthropology, University of Iowa, Iowa City.

1990d Lapidary Materials from the Surface Collections. In *Early State Formation Processes: The Aztec City-State of Otumba, Mexico, Part 1, Preliminary Report on Recent Research in the Otumba City-State*. Report No. 3. Mesoamerican Research Colloquium, Department of Anthropology, University of Iowa, Iowa City.

1993   Obsidian as Jewelry: Lapidary Production in Aztec Otumba, Mexico. *Ancient Mesoamerica* 4:231-243.

Otis Charlton, Cynthia, Thomas H. Charlton, and Deborah L. Nichols
1993   Aztec Household-Based Craft Production: Archaeological Evidence from the City-State of Otumba, Mexico. In *Prehispanic Domestic Units in Western Mesoamerica: Studies of the Household, Compound, and Residence*, edited by Robert S. Santley and Kenneth G. Hirth, pp. 147-171. CRC Press, Boca Raton.

Parry, William J.
1990a Specialized Production and Consumption of Obsidian Tools in an Aztec City-State. Paper presented at the 55th Annual Meeting of the Society for American Archaeology, Las Vegas.

1990b Analysis of Chipped Stone Artifacts from Otumba (TA-80) and Neighboring Rural Sites in the Eastern Teotihuacan Valley of Mexico. In *Early State Formation Processes: The Aztec City-State of Otumba, Mexico, Part 1, Preliminary Report on Recent Research in the Otumba City-State*. Report No. 3. Mesoamerican Research Colloquium, Department of Anthropology, University of Iowa, Iowa City.

Parsons, Jeffrey R.
1971   *Prehistoric Settlement Patterns in the Texcoco Region, Mexico*. Memoirs No. 3. Museum of Anthropology, University of Michigan, Ann Arbor.

Parsons, Jeffrey R., Mary H. Parsons, and David J. Wilson
1982   *Prehispanic Settlement Patterns in the Southern Valley of Mexico: The Chalco-Xochimilco Region*. Memoirs No. 14. Museum of Anthropology, University of Michigan, Ann Arbor.

Peacock, D. P. S.
1982   *Pottery in the Roman World: An Ethnoarchaeological Approach*. Longman, London.

Sahagún, Fray Bernardino de
1950-1982   *Florentine Codex: General History of the Things of New Spain*. Translated and edited by Arthur J. O. Anderson and Charles E. Dibble. 12 books. School of American Research and the University of Utah Press, Santa Fe and Salt Lake City.

Sanders, William T.
1956   The Central Mexican Symbiotic Region. In *Prehistoric Settlement Patterns in the New World*, edited by Gordon R. Willey, pp. 115-127. Viking Fund Publications in Anthropology No 23. Wenner-Gren Foundation for Anthropological Research, New York.

1965   *Cultural Ecology of the Teotihuacan Valley.* Unpublished report to the Wenner Gren Foundation for Anthropological Research, New York. Manuscript on file at the Department of Sociology and Anthropology, Pennsylvania State University, University Park.

Sanders, William T., Jeffrey R. Parsons, and Robert S. Santley
1979   *The Basin of Mexico: Ecological Process in the Evolution of a Civilization.* Academic Press, New York.

Sanders, William T. and Robert S. Santley
1983   A Tale of Three Cities: Energetics and Urbanization in Pre-Hispanic Central Mexico. In *Prehistoric Settlement Patterns: Essays in Honor of Gordon R. Willey,* edited by Evon Z. Vogt and Richard M. Leventhal, pp. 243-291. University of New Mexico Press, Albuquerque.

Sanders, William T., and David Webster
1988   The Mesoamerican Urban Tradition. *American Anthropologist* 90:521-546.

Sjoberg, Gideon
1960   *The Preindustrial City.* The Free Press, New York.

Smith, Michael E.
1987   Archaeology and the Aztec Economy: The Social Scientific Use of Archaeological Data. *Social Science History* 11:237-259.

Spence, Michael W.
1981   On Aztec Specialization and Exchange. *Current Anthropology* 22:183-184.
1985   Specialized Production in Rural Aztec Society: Obsidian Workshops of the Teotihuacan Valley. In *Contributions to the Archaeology and Ethnohistory of Greater Mesoamerica,* edited by William J. Folan, pp. 76-125. Southern Illinois University Press, Carbondale.

Trigger, Bruce G.
1972   Determinants of Urban Growth in Pre-Industrial Societies. In *Man, Settlement and Urbanism,* edited by Peter J. Ucko, Ruth Tringham, and G. W. Dimbley, pp. 575-599. Schenkman, Cambridge.

8

Plebeians and Patricians

Contrasting Patterns of Production and Distribution in the Aztec Figurine and Lapidary Industries

Cynthia Otis Charlton

The Aztec city-state center of Otumba (Otompan) is located just to the south of the modern town of Otumba in the eastern reaches of the Teotihuacan Valley. By A.D. 1430 Otumba was one of some 15 city-states, semi-autonomous administrative units within the expanding domain of the Aztec Triple Alliance (Sanders et al. 1979:154). Prior to the Late Postclassic period the area of the future Otumba city-state and the eastern zone of the Teotihuacan Valley had only a light occupation. The Early Postclassic occupation appears here as a few scattered Mazapan mounds with some evidence for irrigation from seasonal drainages at the confluence of two barrancas, within what would later become the center of Otumba (Charlton 1978). The Middle Postclassic period is evidenced by Aztec II ceramics found in scattered concentrations in parts of the site, but not directly associated with the preceding Mazapan occupation. This Aztec settlement, also sparse, appears to be related to an expansion of the Acolhua state from the south and may represent a repopulation of this agriculturally marginal area.

After Xaltocan's collapse in A.D. 1395, escaping refugees were said to be relocated at Otumba by Techotlalatzin of Texcoco (Alva Ixtlilxochitl 1965:v.2:78; Gibson 1964:10; Offner 1979). At least two battles were fought here ca. A.D. 1415 and A.D. 1418 prior to the formation of the Aztec Triple Alliance. With the exception of Otumba's political role (Hassig 1988), there is scant *specific* information about Otumba in the documents. Fray Bernardino de Sahagún notes that *pochteca* traders were based here (1950-1982:v.9:48-49) and Toribio de Motolinía mentions that Otumba was the location of a market particularly known for its birds (1970:178). Hernán Cortés (1962:77) and Bernal Díaz del Castillo (1963:305) mention battles fought here in 1520. Otumba is also listed in the Early Colonial tribute lists in 1531 (Archivo General de Indias, Seville [AGI] Contaduría 785B f.99r).

Over the relatively short span of the Late Postclassic period, however, a wide variety of craft activities apparently developed at Otumba and had a broad impact on the local and regional economy of the area. Craft activities that can be demonstrated archaeologically include cotton spinning, maguey fiber production, obsidian biface and core-blade production, obsidian lapidary production, groundstone tool manufacture and manufacture of ceramic figurines, censers, spindle whorls (Charlton et al. 1991:fig. 2; Nichols, chap. 7), and a local Otumba Polished Tan pottery (Charlton 1992). All of these activities were apparently taking place in household contexts either as single units or as organized groups located in barrios or *calpultin*. Although our analyses are still at a preliminary stage, the broad extent of craft production at this one location outside the Triple Alliance centers is very apparent (Charlton and Nichols 1992; Charlton et al. 1991; Nichols, chap. 7; Otis Charlton et al. 1993). Craft production appears to have incorporated not only a wide variety of crafts but also various production strategies, each evidently unique to a particular craft.

I will focus here on the two most highly contrasting craft activities, obsidian lapidary jewelry production and ceramic figurine manufacture, as examples of two extremes on many levels of Otumba's production strategies. We have described these two industries as opposite ends of a spectrum referred to as *attached* or *independent* in terms of (on the simplest level) the control placed upon them, or at least the interest shown in them, by the ruling elite with respect to raw material acquisition as well as distribution of the final product. The interplay of plebeian and patrician, the worker and the elite, may be seen in this way from a different perspective which helps to add a further dimension to our understanding of the interaction of the levels of Aztec society. This method of analysis of production strategies has recently received much attention and requires some definitions of terminology as applied to the Otumba case.

HOUSEHOLD-BASED CRAFT PRODUCTION WORKSHOPS

In the relatively short span of time that Otumba existed as a city-state, about 130 years, a great deal of craft activity appears to have developed throughout the townsite, on at least a part-time basis. All activities appear to have been household-based. The relationship of the activity to the household, and the relationship of the household to other households and to the townsite organization in general, appears to have been craft specific. This makes the application of each of the various categories of craft specialization as organized by Sander van der Leeuw (1976), D.P.S. Peacock (1982), Timothy Earle (1981), Elizabeth Brumfiel and Timothy Earle (1987), and Cathy Costin (1986, 1991) somewhat difficult. Cotton spinning, for example, as evidenced by the presence of small spindle whorls, appears to have been carried out in virtually every household in Otumba without regard to location or status of the household in the community. Although this may be referred to as *household production,* low-level domestic production as defined by Peacock (1982:8), it may very well not have been solely for the use of that individual household (see Berdan 1980, 1987a, 1988; Hicks 1987, 1991; Hicks, chap. 4; see also Otis Charlton et al. 1993 for a more complete discussion). Some obsidian core-blade production and most ceramic censer manufacture seem to have involved separate households associated with the nucleated elite core of the site. Maguey fiber working, spindle whorl production, and figurine production involved households associated with each other within the more dispersed southeastern area of the townsite. These households were organized into barrios or *calpultin* with most households in each section apparently involved in the same type of production. Lapidary workshops were also present in this southeastern area of the site but appear to have involved fewer individual households. The remains of additional lapidary workshops may be located a short distance away from the main concentration. All the various types of craft specialization at Otumba, their locations and their relationships with each other, have been more thoroughly discussed elsewhere (Charlton and Nichols 1992; Charlton et al. 1991; Nichols, chap. 7; Otis Charlton et al. 1993).

Because Otumba contains so many craft activities in one site, it offers a good test case for the various theories of craft specialization and workshop organization in an Aztec context, based on direct evidence from both surface collections and excavated materials. Unlike cotton spinning, which appears to have been a general part-time activity of most households at Otumba, households involved in craft specialization exhibit two criteria for workshop production as articulated by John E. Clark: one, "demonstrating an 'unusually large concentration' of ... artifacts" and two, "demonstrating that the concentration represents manufacturing debris" (1986:30). In all cases of craft specialization at Otumba, these artifact concentrations appear in close association with households. Whether involving what we hypothesize to be full- or part-time occupations, the facilities where the actual craft work was carried out do not appear to have involved more than an additional use of a part of the regular house or houselot. The clustering of these household workshops in definable barrios or *calpultin* within Otumba would seem to place them generally in the categories of *workshop industries* as defined by van der Leeuw (1976:406 a, b, table 14) and *nucleated workshops* as defined by Peacock (1982:9). Something similar is referred to as *community specialization* by Costin, "autonomous individual or household-based production units, aggregated within a single community, producing for unrestricted regional consumption" (1991:8). Costin's definition of Community Specialists appears to be too constrictive in the Otumba case, however, since here there is an aggregation of specialized barrios within a single community, which may indicate some kind of managerial influence on the collective households. Furthermore, in the case of the lapidary workshops, the production is not necessarily for unrestricted regional consumption.

We have both surface and excavated materials for two of the most highly contrasting craft industries, obsidian lapidary jewelry production and ceramic figurine manufacture. Analyses of these materials are still ongoing but information available at this time permits some interpretations and evaluations of theories of craft production.

Lapidary Production

We have identified lapidary production at Otumba as an example of an *attached* activity producing high value products for tribute or trade. *Attached* specialists, as described by Earle (1981:230) and Brumfiel and Earle (1987:5), produce for elites, elite patrons, or a governing institution. "Attached specialists are contractually bound to the patrons for whom they work, and frequently, the patrons insure [sic] that all the specialists' basic needs are met" (Brumfiel and Earle 1987:5). This definition most securely applies to the specialists that were located at Tenochtitlan and Texcoco. Rulers intentionally congregated specialists producing luxury items within *calpulli* compounds in the cities (Alva Ixtlilxochitl 1965:v.1:317; Hicks 1987:241-243; Sahagún 1950-1982:v.9:83-97). There they would produce for the palace and the treasury, and to some extent for the market (Hicks 1982:241; Offner 1983:139). These specialists appear to have been supported to a large degree by the state, which probably determined the percentage of each type of production dedicated to each area (Hicks 1987:96-97). Lapidary workshop production at Otumba seems to meet most of these criteria except that, in all but one case, the workshops are not physically located near ceremonial or elite structures or residences as indicative of a degree of elite control or sponsorship (fig. 8.1). One workshop is located at the outer edge of the peninsula between two barrancas, an area which may have been restricted to civic-ceremonial activities.

Carla Sinopoli adds the concept of *centralized specialization* to the continuum as being somewhere between *independent* and *administered (attached)*, "with the political elite intervening primarily at the final stages of the production-distribution process" (1988:581). Her general definition for this central-

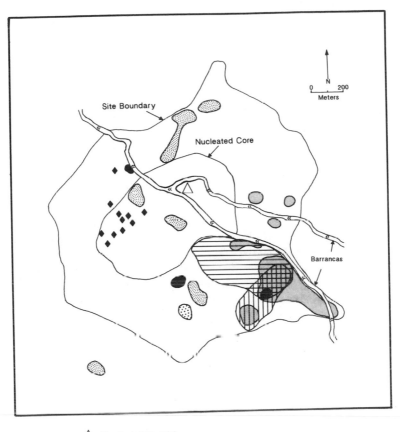

△ Central Pyramid

▦ Core blade Workshop (Pachuca Obsidian-Green)

▦ Core blade Workshop (Otumba Obsidian Gray)

◻ Lapidary Workshops

◼ Groundstone Workshops

▤ Figurine Workshops

▥ Maguey Fiber Workshops

◆ Censer Molds

Fig. 8.1. Otumba Site Map. This map shows the locations of the figurine-making barrio and lapidary workshops in relation to other workshop areas in Otumba. Adapted from Charlton et al. 1991:fig. 2.

ized type, however, seems to hinge on a high degree of supply and demand economics and refers most effectively to subsistence goods and essential household craft items, rather than to status items.

To the best of my knowledge, the Otumba workshops are the only Aztec obsidian lapidary workshops excavated to date. Francisco González Rul (1979:28) notes four perforator fragments from excavations at the Late Postclassic city of Tlatelolco, in a refuse dump near the market area in the city center. A few additional perforator fragments have been found during recent salvage excavations near the ceremonial area (Clemente Salazar A., personal communication 1993), but no workshops themselves have yet been located. Some earspool blanks have also been located in excavations at the site of Yautepec in Morelos (Michael E. Smith, personal communication 1993). In the context of Otumba we argue for attached specialization in the case of the lapidaries for several reasons. First, these workshops primarily produced earspools, lip plugs, and beads, of which the first two at least, were wealth items serving as symbols of class and ethnic status (Sahagún 1950-1982:v.10:177-178). "Sumptuary regulations were important in providing outward markers of status," however, "sumptuary regulations in both cities were far more concerned with public display than with possession of luxury goods" (Offner 1983:144; see also Anawalt 1980, 1981; Hicks 1991). This would seem to place lapidary production at the elite end of the elite-to-general demand continuum. Second, a high degree of skill and investment of time was required in the production of each object (Otis Charlton 1993). Although production took place in a household context, the high degree of skill necessary for lapidary production would presumably, by definition, involve only a few household members for most of the work. These members must have worked on a full-time basis in order to achieve any reasonable volume of production. Both the high value and production time needed as well as the limited number of workshops at Otumba would seem to argue for a certain amount of elite support, even if other uninvolved members of the household could still carry on other subsistence activities. This support would have involved both the provision of raw material and the distribution and consumption of at least some of the products. It is possible that the artisans were compensated with subsistence goods or with materials with which to trade in the market for subsistence goods, by the local elite as well as the merchants (cf. Carrasco 1977:234; see also discussion by Brumfiel 1987:106). In Otumba we believe support by patrons in the form of the local elite or the elite organized *pochteca* is indicated.

Although grey Otumba obsidian was readily available nearby, Pachuca obsidian was not. A two tiered system of Pachuca green obsidian exploitation and distribution has been postulated for the Late Aztec period by Thomas Charlton and Michael Spence (1982:72-73). Some obsidian would be paid in tribute directly to Tenochtitlan, and some would circulate in regional trade networks, bringing raw materials to the regional market at Otumba either through *pochteca* intraregional traders or through regional merchants of the type described by Frances Berdan (1988:649). These same traders would also have an interest/involvement in the distribution (as well as tribute) of finished lapidary materials to Texcoco and Tenochtitlan. This type of trade would occur along with trade in other goods such as the birds actually mentioned in the documents (Motolinía 1970:178), and presumably spun and probably woven cotton (Berdan 1980, 1987a, 1988; Hicks 1987, 1991; see also Hicks, chap. 4). We can document none of these other materials archaeologically.

Green Pachuca obsidian seems for the most part to have come into the lapidary workshops not directly, but in the form of exhausted prismatic blade cores, probably from core-blade workshops located, in many instances, in parts of Otumba generally associated with the elite. The exhausted obsidian cores, as well as some fashioned of chert in the lapidary workshops, were used as perforators, first to peck rough indentations on the sides of earspool blanks, then to ream this shatter area with the addition of an abrasive substance. After they had served their purpose as perforators, the upper sections of the tools made of green obsidian cores were flaked into blanks for earspools or lip plugs (fig. 8.2) while the drill end section often was flaked into sequin-like disks. Grey Otumba obsidian was more often used for

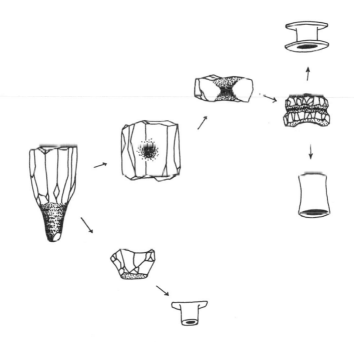

Fig. 8.2. Part of the lapidary production sequence. Shown are a green obsidian perforator made from an exhausted prismatic blade core, and earspools and a lip plug produced from used perforators. Adapted from Otis Charlton 1990a:fig. 2. Not to scale.

lip plugs. Prismatic blades were also made into disks, perforated disks, eccentrics, or very small lip plugs. Various bead shapes were made with various colored obsidians as well as chert. Some rock crystal was fashioned into lip plugs, and small obsidian and chert bifaces were also produced (see Otis Charlton 1991:fig. 2, for a more complete production sequence, and 1993 for a more complete production description; see also Mirambell 1968). Flat slate-like slabs of basalt were used as polishers and appear in areas where lapidary working seems to have taken place (Biskowski 1991).

Lapidary production differs from figurine production in that some of its products were considered important enough to be noted in documents. Sahagún not only mentions who wears the ornaments but also the occasions upon which they were worn (1950-1982:v.8:27-28, 47; v.10:177-178). The finished products were for display, symbols reflecting class and ethnic status in Aztec society (Brumfiel et al., chap. 5). Sahagún also describes those who performed lapidary work and the merchants who sold it (1950-1982:v.9:79-82; v.10:60-61, 85 [obsidian]). At Otumba the ornaments were probably produced for the personal use of the local elite of the Otumba city-state and to some extent for tribute, as well as for distribution through merchants in the local market and regional trade networks (see discussion by Berdan 1980). Hicks (1987:96), referring to the available documents, notes that artisans practicing the lapidary trade were collected in Tenochtitlan and Texcoco for the purpose of providing the quantities of these materials required by the rulers for their own use—as their gifts to other rulers as well as to their subordinate elites in other localities, as trade items, and as feast offerings or for monument dedication ceremonies (see also Hicks 1991). The quantities involved could very well have incorporated some of the output of these more distant Otumba workshops. "Numerically, the elite increased rapidly as the empire matured, and they required abundant supplies of exotic adornments for verification of their status through ostentatious display" (Berdan 1987b:163).

The finished earspools, lip plugs, and beads appear to have generally left the city-state. Fragments of the finished forms are extremely rare even in Otumba itself—currently there are fewer than 10 finished fragments found in the entire site. The time consuming job of the original working of the forms may have been done at a number of sites outside the Triple Alliance cities. "Concentration of luxury artisans in urban centers would suggest an emphasis in tribute on raw materials. Yet the emphasis was on manufactured or partially manufactured luxuries" (Berdan 1987b:178).

The archaeological and ethnohistorical data suggest that lapidary workers were full-time specialists with skills not easily acquired, in high demand to produce status items. At Otumba as in other larger centers they were concentrated in barrios or *calpultin,* though the small number of individual workshops may argue for a late beginning of this particular craft at Otumba. The locations of the workshops are not directly associated with elite residential areas or ceremonial zones (with the one possible exception previously noted), nor do the house remains of the excavated lapidary workshop exhibit more than the normal *macehualli* house structure and size found elsewhere in the valley (Charlton 1965, 1972; Evans 1988). The workshops were dependent on *pochteca* merchants for some raw materials such as emery for polishing, probably rock crystal, and some exotic obsidians, and on the core-blade workshops for green cores in a relationship we do not as yet fully understand. These merchants may have been necessary as well for the distribution of at least part of the workshop products. Although all aspects of these workshops do not fit exactly the definition of *attached* specialization as to physical workshop location, we feel by their concentration of debris and the intrinsic value of their product as well as its manufacturing difficulty, lapidary workshop production is nonetheless involved with, and dependent upon, patronage at Otumba and is therefore *attached* in this case.

Figurine Production

We place clay figurine production at Otumba in the category of an *independent* craft activity with what appears to be a low value product for distribution through the local/regional market system. The raw material, clay, was readily available in the Teotihuacan Valley, and the skills required for figurine manufacture are relatively easily learned. Beyond these basic contrasts with lapidary production, we have to deal with an almost total lack of written information. Aztec figurines were evidently so common as to be unnoticed or at least were not seen as worthy of mention by most chroniclers. They are absent from available documents with the possible exception of the writing of Fray Diego Durán who mentions "shrines or special niches where the idols were kept" (1971:452) and an occasional later mention when the Spaniards found them buried in the area of Christian altars. In ceremonial contexts, Esther Pasztory (1983) reports no figurines found in offerings at the Templo Mayor, though figurine fragments are found with fill materials (personal observation by the author 1993). Cook (1950) reports a figurine concentration as a possible workshop from materials salvaged by workmen near Tlatelolco, though the fact that the pieces illustrated are all well finished, apparently contain no duplicates, and no molds are mentioned may indicate a cache or offering rather than a workshop. Figurine offerings have been recovered from salvage excavations carried out in a Tlatelolco ceremonial area in 1992 (Margarita Carballal Staedler, María Flores Hernández and María del Carmen Lechuga García, personal communication 1993). They are not mentioned by Sahagún as being part of the production of potters, nor are they mentioned as being sold by merchants. That these "idols" were ubiquitous, whether crafted of wood, stone, or some other material, is evident from

Motolinía's comments written between 1536 and 1541 "... if a hundred years from now someone excavates in the patios of the temples of the ancient idols, he will always find idols, since the Indians had made so many of them. ... The foundations and walls of buildings are full of such idols, and many of them are in the patios" (1951:336). Because they are in fill, whether in the house interior, patio, or in the general vicinity, their actual use in these contexts is speculative (cf. Evans 1990). They are however, present in nearly every household, rural and urban, but to date are seldom found directly associated with burials.

The figurine workshops in Otumba appear to have been *calpulli*-based and to have clustered in the southeastern section of the city-state, outside the nucleated elite core area (fig. 8.1). The workshops produced a variety of ceramic goods, including serpent-handled censers, balls and marbles, wheeled toys, rattles, stamps, and spindle whorls (Otis Charlton 1990), as well as a local utilitarian ware we have defined as Otumba Polished Tan (Charlton 1992). As a group, the workshops involved large-scale spatially segregated production by specialists. This may fit the definition of *centralized production* as defined by Sinopoli. She notes however that this is "without imputing any *direct* involvement by the administrative apparatus of the state" (1988:581). The evidence of *calpulli* organization of the Otumba workshops suggests some management of output at that level, to meet demand and perhaps to discourage outside competition for their markets. A sort of internal 'quality control' may also "help elevate technique to the highest level and the industry will usually be characterised by a fairly standardised range of high-quality products" (Peacock 1982:9).

During the Late Postclassic period there were three major categories of anthropomorphic figurines commonly found in the general Basin of Mexico area: a hollow rattle figurine, a puppet figurine, and a solid flat figurine, referred to respectively as Types I, II, and III by Parsons (1972). These types were not necessarily produced at the same workshops. At Otumba only the Type III solid, flat variety was made. Type II puppet figures are relatively rare and may have been an earlier style. At the moment their location of manufacture is unknown. Types I and III recovered at Otumba differ in the type of mold used, in manufacturing technique, in surface treatment, in firing, and, most importantly, in paste. The hollow Type I figurines were made in a somewhat complicated process using a two-piece mold. They contain rattle balls, are usually burnished and red/orange slipped, and have a very fine paste (see Otis Charlton 1994). They are also fairly highly fired. The slip, paste, and firing has been compared to those attributes of Aztec orangeware. Carmen Cook (1950) notes that the hollow figurines she examined from near Tlatelolco appear to be similar in paste to Black-on-Orange "Lago de Texcoco" ceramics described by James B. Griffin and Antonieta Espejo (1947). Mary Hodge et al. (1992) have since determined at least four possible composition groups of some Late Postclassic Black-on-Orange ceramics through neutron activation analyses.

The Type III solid figurines from Otumba were made by a simple process of pressing clay into an open-back mold. These figurines may be carefully finished but are seldom burnished and almost never slipped. They have a fine textured paste, but it contains more and larger inclusions than the hollow figurine pastes. Bits of obsidian are often included as well. Type III figurines are also not as highly fired and often depend on painting after firing for color and detail. At Otumba, the Type III solid figurines were made in household-based workshops by artisans who could have produced them on a full-time basis. Unlike the lapidary workers, these artisans had skills that were relatively easy to acquire and produced items which required a substantial investment of time only if there were a high demand for the product. In addition, they had direct access to clay, the raw material. Given the ubiquitous nature of their products, there must have been a demand for them which could be met through the local, and perhaps regional, market system, by merchants or perhaps by the artisans themselves. Ethnographic analogy suggests that ceramic production in household contexts often involves many members of the household in various stages of production because of the relatively low levels of specialized skill necessary. Full-time production would not necessarily involve all members of the family at all times (Charlton and Otis Charlton 1993; Lackey 1982; Otis Charlton et al. 1971; Reiff Katz 1977; Sheehy 1993; Sinopoli 1991:34; Widmer and Sheehy 1990).

Workshop activity at Otumba appears to have involved an area of residences 10-12 ha in size (fig. 8.1). The size of the workshop zone, the number of artisans involved and estimates of output could be used to argue for either full- or part-time activity. Some indication of actual figurine function or how the figures were "consumed" would be useful (Patterson and Stocker 1990; Stocker 1991). The figures may have simply resided inactively in a niche or they could have been actively used in some rituals in which they were either intentionally or accidently broken. They could have had a limited lifespan, needing to be replaced on a regular calendrical feast or ritual cycle. Answers to such questions could help us determine the demand and quantities needed as well as the timing of demand peaks for the industry output. Sahagún (1950-1982) and Durán (1971), among others, attest to the large numbers of feasts and rituals in Aztec life, though figurines are not referred to specifically. Arnold's comment referring to utilitarian ceramic output, that "In order to meet a larger market demand, the potter will attempt to increase operational efficiency and may even begin to specialize in the production of a narrow range of goods" (1987:44) could apply to figurine manufacture as well. Variation in figurine forms by the Late Postclassic period fell within a narrow range. *Calpulli* organization as indicated by the barrio concentration of workshops and workshop debris, as well as production of the most easily produced figurine types, would seem to argue for a high demand and full-time production.

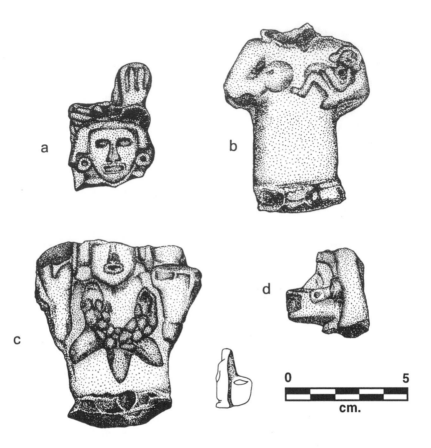

Fig. 8.3.   Aztec Type III solid figurines from Otumba. *(a)* Head-female (III-A), [2206]; *(b)* Torso-female (III-A-g), [OP-4 W4-N8 L.4]; *(c)* Centeocihuatl-Corn goddess (III-E), [OP-4 W4-N4 L.1 Grp.1]; *(d)* Human male with Ehecatl mouth mask (III-C-3), [OP-4 W4-N4 L.2].

Although analyses, and therefore figures, are incomplete, a large percentage of the types produced are of two general groups. Female fertility figures are the largest component, including females with and without a child, and corn-goddesses with an offering cup hand modeled on the back (fig. 8.3a-c). Ehecatl-Wind god figures are among the largest component of identifiable males (fig. 8.3d). This deity has been associated with one of the two *pochteca* orders (O'Mack 1991), possibly the one said to be resident at Otumba. The emphasis on these types may also support an assumption of cyclical ritual use. Further analyses however, will be needed to evaluate this proposal.

The Type I hollow figurines all depict fertility figures whether in female, monkey, bat, or deity form (Otis Charlton 1994). Their rattle function was probably involved in their ritual use. As mentioned previously, their manufacturing technique and their pastes differ from the Otumba workshop materials. Their apparent higher firing temperature may indicate somewhat more elaborate kilns similar to the types that may have been used for Black-on-Orange ceramic manufacture, probably centralized in or near the Triple Alliance cities (Hodge and Minc 1990; Hodge et al. 1992). It could also simply indicate access to a better fuel. The hollow figurines appear to have been distributed throughout the Basin of Mexico by way of the regional market system from the Triple Alliance centers, probably in much the same way as the ceramics themselves moved (Hodge and Minc 1990; Hodge et al. 1992; Minc et al., chap. 6). The hollow figurines were distributed at least as far as the Tepeapulco (Tepepulco) city-state to the east, in enough abundance so that most households whether urban or rural seem to have had some access to them. An earlier study indicated that the areas of the eastern Teotihuacan Valley where higher frequencies of these figurine fragments were found seemed to be those controlled by the *tlatoani* capital of Otumba. On the other hand, the areas with relatively few hollow figurine fragments seemed to be areas controlled by the *calpixqui* districts of Oxtotipac (Oztoticpac) and Cuauhtlacingo (Cuautlatzinco) (Otis Charlton 1994). This may point to a differing availability of this figurine type to the Otumba tributary rural population, or may indicate a differing pattern of use.

We have not yet determined whether the more easily produced solid figurines from the Otumba workshops, which appear widespread in this valley and for some distance to the east, were also distributed throughout the rest of the Basin of Mexico. As Berdan (1988:645) notes, "Regional and petty trading activities were entwined with the indigenous marketplace *(tianquiztli)*—a part of the everyday landscape which the great Colonial chroniclers and historians saw but rarely felt worthy of special detailed mention." Stylistically, Parsons's materials from other areas of the Basin of Mexico are very much the same as those from Otumba (Parsons 1972). Without trace element analyses of the pastes of the figurines from the two areas, however, we can only speculate. The relatively simple manufacturing technique of the solid figurines makes them a plausible product of any area where ceramic production took place. Beyond this rather vague suggestion which has yet to be tested, several other factors would seem to argue for region specific solid figurine manufacture and could also reflect aspects of the regionalism of Aztec figurine style.

Figurines from Rural Morelos. Michael E. Smith's 1986 Postclassic Morelos Archaeological Project dealt with Late Postclassic occupations at two locations, Capilco and Cuexcomate, in rural areas of western Morelos (Smith 1992, 1993; Smith et al. 1989; Smith and Heath-Smith, chap. 13). The peoples of Morelos had direct ties with the Basin of Mexico ethnically, politically, economically, and through religion. They were within another distinct geographical unit, however. This is reflected in subtle ways in the figurines.

There are four distinct figurine types:

1. Direct imports: finely made examples of Type I hollow rattle figurines appear here, apparently traded in directly from the Basin of Mexico. There is no visible difference in design or paste from the types of these materials seen at Otumba.

2. Direct copies: exact duplicates of Basin of Mexico hollow figurines, very well finished, but with a differing paste. According to Michael E. Smith (personal communication, 1991), this is the same paste used in the local common pottery of the area. Smith (1990:154) notes, however, that he has seen no "local imitation" Aztec III Black-on-Orange ceramics outside the Basin of Mexico. This paste is fine but somewhat more grainy than the exceptionally fine paste seen in rattle figurines from the Basin. These potters were either skilled enough to make their own molds from the "imported" Basin of Mexico hollow figurines or the molds were traded out of the Basin in small quantities as well.

   Some of the solid Type III figurines are also made of this fine local paste. Stylistically, however, they are identical to those of the Basin of Mexico and those made at Otumba. There are some minor variations in finishing such as indented backs, which are not common in the Late Postclassic Basin of Mexico types. Once again these figurines were either made in imported molds, or molds were made directly from imported figurines. Mold making from solid figurines is a relatively easy process, and this was probably what was done here.

3. Locally-made stylistic imitations: generally Mexica in style but very simplified forms and very poorly made (fig. 8.4a). There could be a number of explanations for this. These potters may have had no access to molds or Basin of Mexico samples, they may not have been skilled enough to create good molds themselves, or the general differences were not considered a problem by them or their consumers and could even have been a selling point. The clays used for these figures can be the local fine paste or can be a local paste which was not used for household pottery (Smith, personal communication 1991). This second paste has a very distinctive grainy texture

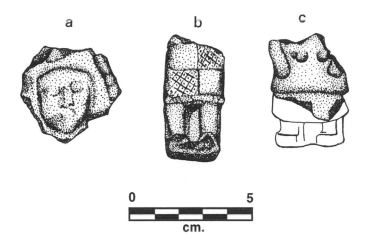

Fig. 8.4.   Morelos figurines. *(a)* Morelos version of female III-A-1 head, [206-242-03]; *(b)* Standing female wearing a shorter skirt with a different decorative design than most Basin of Mexico figures, [201-272-01A]; *(c)* Morelos-style plain female torso, [101-892-01B].

with large white inclusions and usually fires a very identifiable brick red. The potters also copied styles from other areas, as seen in some Huastec-style heads and a Mazapan-style head, all made with local pastes.

4. Local style with local paste. these are the same general figurine styles as those in the Basin of Mexico, but with definite "Morelos" stylistic variations. Skirts, which are always ankle-length in the Basin of Mexico, are knee-length here and have some different design patterns (fig. 8.4b). *Huipiles* are more visible as falling over the skirt at the waist. Many of the female figures are pear-shaped or bell-shaped, unlike the straight torso Basin of Mexico figures (fig. 8.4c).

The sample from Capilco and Cuexcomate would seem to indicate workshops functioning somewhere in the local region and utilizing at least two visually distinct local clays. The quality of the workmanship suggests either a minimum of two workshop areas or a deterioration in workshop technique over time (see also Smith and Heath-Smith, chap. 13, for suggestions regarding regional economic pressures during the Late Postclassic period). The variation would seem to suggest a number of small household workshops with relatively low production rates or part-time activity and without the overarching organizational control apparently working at Otumba and probably at other Basin of Mexico centers. It may also indicate production changes between Early and Late Cuauhnahuac periods as identified by Smith (1987) for the rural area. Continuing studies should shed some light on these alternatives, testing the stylistic and technological groupings.

Comparisons. During the Late Postclassic period, the extensive trade and market systems of the Aztec Triple Alliance centers seem to have had the effect of extending the market for the output of individual workshops or workshop areas, as may be seen in the wider geographic distribution of their styles. This, however, does not preclude the output being from local or regional workshops. In fact, increasing demand may have encouraged them. Recent trace element studies of Black-on-Orange ceramics might also help to provide information on production and distribution of figurines.

Mary Hodge notes in her study (with Leah Minc) of Basin of Mexico Aztec ceramics "… that Late Aztec ceramic *types* (emphasis mine) showed no statistically significant decrease with distance from a source area, indicating that they were dispersed through a regionally integrated market system" (1992:434), but that "some [Black-on-Orange] motifs are universally distributed but others concentrate in … [particular] … parts of the valley" (1992:440).

Late Postclassic Black-on-Orange ceramics from the site of Tlacotepec in the Toluca Valley to the west of the Basin of Mexico provide a particular case-study. A sample of these ceramics from the collection of the Field Museum of Natural History in Chicago was submitted for trace element analysis by Donald McVicker and Laurene Lambertino-Urquizo (1992; personal communication 1991 and 1992) and has demonstrated three such groups:

1. Basin of Mexico imported Black-on-Orange ceramics.
2. Visually similar Black-on-Orange designs, but made with local Toluca Valley paste.
3. Very sloppy local copies of Black-on-Orange designs done in a very grainy local paste.

This situation is similar to my interpretation of the rural Morelos figurines.

If figurines are seen as a utilitarian product, much like a utilitarian pottery, as a necessity that was "consumed" at certain events (Hicks 1991) and at certain of the calendrically-set religious feasts and rituals, then a demand needed to be met. In the case of the Type I hollow rattle figurines, consumption may have been low because they were produced elsewhere, were required for only one or a few specific rituals which did not occur often, or were not "consumed" in a single episode. It is also possible that their production/distribution was controlled in some way we do not yet understand (Otis Charlton 1994). What demand there was apparently was supplied by market trade. The solid Type III figurines, on the other hand, were in greater demand than trade alone from one source could supply, making their production at Otumba profitable enough for a barrio or *calpulli* to be dedicated to it. At rural sites in Morelos, at a somewhat greater distance from the Triple Alliance market centers, neither figurine type was imported in enough quantity, whether as a result of distance or lack of profit, making local production necessary or profitable. Type I figurines, whether imported or locally made are still a small percentage, again probably due to limitation for one reason or another as discussed above.

The Type III figurines in rural Morelos, however, show similarities to Tlacotepec ceramic adaptations in marketing strategy, from exact copies to similar but locally idiosyncratic varieties. This could indicate an isolated workshop and lack of competition or general lack of *calpulli*-organized stylistic design/ production control. However, from all appearances, the supply of figurines from the Basin of Mexico to rural sites in Morelos was inadequate. Demand was such that both hollow rattle and solid figurines were copied and/or independently produced locally.

At the moment, it appears there may have been either a single center producing hollow rattle figurines within the Basin of Mexico (Cook 1950; Otis Charlton 1994), or perhaps several centers (see Hodge 1992, Hodge and Minc 1990, and Hodge et al. 1992 regarding Black-on-Orange ceramic production centers), although this seems unlikely given the smaller numbers of these figurines found and the more complex technology involved. In contrast, the solid figurines were easier to copy and manufacture. There were undoubtedly centers other than Otumba in the greater Basin of Mexico where they were made, although none have been found to date. The overriding, *calpulli*-based figurine production system supported conformity in the Basin of Mexico molded figurines probably enforcing standards of design and production not found in rural Morelos. We hope trace element testing will help to indicate the extent to which the Otumba manufactured figurines were traded into the Triple Alliance cities as well as how far their trade extended away from production centers.

OTUMBA PRODUCTION IN SUM

Data from early documents point to a highly organized and regulated tribute/ trade market system for Late Postclassic Aztec society (Berdan 1988; Hicks 1992; López Austin 1986; Monjarás-Ruíz 1986; Rodriquez-Shadow 1990; Smith 1990). For the city-state of Otumba we have a few references that give glimpses of its political and economic roles. The *tlatoani* center of Otumba had a resident guild of *pochteca*, of the type restricted to trade within the state boundaries (Sahagún 1950-1982:v.9:49). There was a market located at Otumba said to have specialized in birds (Motolinía 1970:178). It was probably regional in nature, due to the importance of the city-state in the area, and most likely occurred on a five-day cycle for the same reason (Hassig 1982). That the area was also known for cloth production may be deduced from Otumba's 1531 tribute payment, which still included 14 *cargas de ropa toldillos* every 80 days (AGI, Seville, Contaduría 785B f.99r). The archaeology carried out to date in Otumba sheds some light on how the Aztec state and economy as presented in documentary sources is reflected in material terms.

The proximity of Otumba to the Aztec Triple Alliance centers and its physical organization of elite core and barrios or *calpultin* of various craft specialists, similar to that described by Hicks (1982) for its patron Texcoco, would seem to suggest an economic organization similar to that described by Brumfiel and Earle (1987:3) as a *political model*. This model of strong elite intervention in organizing specialization and exchange "enables rulers to become patrons of certain craft specialties and sponsors of long-distance trade" (Brumfiel and Earle 1987:3). In the case of Otumba, however, actual control over items of great prestige was limited. Of all the activities at Otumba, only some of the lapidary products and some of the cloth production might be considered prestige or wealth producing items. The degree of organization that is apparent at Otumba, however, would seem to preclude the *commercial development model* (Brumfiel and Earle 1987:1) or *bottom-up* forces for economic change seem by Smith and Heath-Smith (chap. 13) for western Morelos. The broader group of "utilitarian" products produced by Otumba, as opposed to "prestige" goods, plus the extent of organization, would seem to point to a more *adaptationist model* of development (Brumfiel and Earle 1987:2). Population pressure within the Basin of Mexico in the Late Postclassic period necessitated a greater production of all goods, including utilitarian ones. The Late Postclassic growth and development of Otumba provided both production and a market for an increasing population located some distance from the central Triple Alliance cities. Through Otumba, subsistence products were made available both from the more distant centers, and from local producers, to the rural and tributary population. Although located in a marginally productive agricultural area itself, Otumba could still act as a collection center for foodstuffs as well as a production center for some items of greater wealth for trade or tribute to the Triple Alliance centers, or into the local *pochteca* long-distance trade network. The organization apparent in the Otumba community layout provided management and control for this complicated process and would argue for a strong local contingent of regional and local professional merchants as well. In sum, our data suggest local development enhanced by a central rise in demand, but under local direction and organization.

We can see in some of the lapidary production at Otumba an item of visible wealth being produced outside the Triple Alliance cities and outside a physical location near the Otumba elites as well. Although the existence of this production was most likely stimulated by trade and exchange, it was also undoubtedly tied to a tribute burden and an amount of elite "exploitation" was involved. We can see in figurine production a utilitarian item produced for all households but possibly only in response to local and regional demand. Figurine production was also apparently centrally organized, but in a more managerial fashion. While we can see reflections of patricians and plebeians, they are interwoven in a complex web that their material remains are only just beginning to reveal.

ACKNOWLEDGMENTS

Research in the Otumba city-state was carried out under a permit from the Consejo de Arqueología of the Instituto Nacional de Antropología e Historia, Mexico, and was funded by the National Science Foundation (BNS 871 9665: Thomas H. Charlton, principal investigator; BNS-871-8140: Deborah L. Nichols, principal investigator), and by the National Endowment for the Humanities (RO-21705-88: Thomas H. Charlton, principal investigator). Thomas H. Charlton also received support from a University of Iowa Faculty Developmental Assignment. Deborah L. Nichols also received support from the Clair Garber Goodman Fund, the Dartmouth Class of 1962, and the Dartmouth Faculty Research Committee. Continuing analyses are being supported by the National Endowment for the Humanities (RO-22268-91: Thomas H. Charlton, principal investigator) and a University of Iowa Faculty Developmental Assignment.

We gratefully acknowledge the help of the people of Otumba and the barrio of Tlamimilolpa, and the Presidencia Municipal of Otumba, Mexico.

I would like to extend thanks for early help on figurine counts by Rani Sellers, Dartmouth College; spindle whorl analyses by Maura Benton, Dartmouth College, and Mary Jane and John McLaughlin, University of Iowa; groundstone studies by Martin F. Biskowski, University of California Los Angeles; and continuing obsidian analysis help by Vicente Aguirre, Otumba, William J. Parry, Hunter College, Timothy S. Hare, University of Iowa, and Rocío Vasquez Lom, Escuela Nacional de Antropología e Historia. Many thanks to Tom Charlton and Mike Smith for their patience and help.

REFERENCES CITED

Alva Ixtlilxochitl, Fernando de
1965 *Obras históricas.* Edited by Alfredo Chavero. 2 vols. Editoral Nacional, Mexico City.

Anawalt, Patricia Rieff
1980 Costumes and Control: Aztec Sumptuary Laws. *Archaeology* 33:33-43.
1981 *Indian Clothing Before Cortés: Mesoamerican Costumes from the Codices.* University of Oklahoma Press, Norman.

Arnold, Philip Justin, III
1987 *The Household Potters of Los Tuxtlas: An Ethnoarchaeological Study of Ceramic Production and Site Structure.* Unpublished Ph.D. dissertation, The University of New Mexico, Albuquerque.

Berdan, Francis F.
1980 Aztec Merchants and Markets: Local-Level Economic Activity in a Non-Industrial Empire. *Mexicon* 2(3):37-41.
1987a Cotton in Aztec Mexico: Production, Distribution and Uses. *Mexican Studies* 3:235-262.
1987b The Economics of Aztec Luxury Trade and Tribute. In *The Aztec Templo Mayor,* edited by Elizabeth Hill Boone, pp. 161-183. Dumbarton Oaks, Washington, D.C.
1988 Principles of Regional and Long-Distance Trade in the Aztec Empire. In *Smoke and Mist: Mesoamerican Studies in Memory of Thelma D. Sullivan,* edited by Henry B. Nicholson, Doris Heyden, Karen Dakin, and Nicholas A. Hopkins, pp. 639-656. BAR International Series 402(ii). British Archaeological Reports, Oxford.

Biskowski, Martin F.
1991 Distribuciones espaciales de los artefactos de piedra pulida y otros materiales relacionados en Otumba. In *Los procesos del desarrollo de los estados tempranos: el caso del estado Azteca de Otumba, parte 3, informe con resultados preliminares del análisis de los datos arqueológicos del estado Azteca de Otumba,* edited by Thomas H. Charlton, pp. 121-164. Research Report No. 5, Mesoamerican Research Colloquium, Department of Anthropology, University of Iowa, Iowa City.

Brumfiel, Elizabeth M.
1987 Elite and Utilitarian Crafts in the Aztec State. In *Specialization, Exchange, and Complex Societies,* edited by Elizabeth M. Brumfiel and Timothy K. Earle, pp. 102-118. Cambridge University Press, New York.

Brumfiel, Elizabeth M., and Timothy K. Earle
1987 Specialization, Exchange, and Complex Societies: An Introduction. In *Specialization, Exchange and Complex Societies,* edited by Elizabeth M. Brumfiel and Timothy K. Earle, pp. 1-9. Cambridge University Press, New York.

Carrasco, Pedro
1977 Los señores de Xochimilco en 1548. *Tlalocan* 7:229-265.

Charlton, Thomas H.

1965 *Archaeological Settlement Patterns: An Interpretation.* Ph.D. dissertation, Department of Anthropology, Tulane University. University Microfilms, Ann Arbor.

1972 *Post-Conquest Developments in the Teotihuacan Valley, Mexico. Part I: Excavations.* Report No. 5, Office of the State Archaeologist, University of Iowa, Iowa City.

1978 Investigaciones arqueológicas en el municipio de Otumba, temporada de 1978. 1a parte: resultos preliminares de los trabajos de campo, 1978. Report submitted to the Instituto Nacional de Antropología e Historia, Mexico City.

1992 Cerámica de las excavaciones. In *Los procesos de desarrollo de los estados tempranos: el caso del estado Azteca de Otumba, parte 5, informe con resultados preliminares del análisis de los datos arqueológicos del estado Azteca de Otumba,* edited by Thomas II. Charlton, pp. 85-98. Research Report No. 7, Mesoamerican Research Colloquium, Department of Anthropology, University of Iowa, Iowa City.

Charlton, Thomas H., and Deborah L. Nichols

1992 Late Post-Classic and Colonial Period Elites at Otumba, Mexico: The Archaeological Dimensions. In *Mesoamerican Elites: An Archaeological Assessment,* edited by Diane Chase and Arlen Chase, pp. 242-258. University of Oklahoma Press, Norman.

Charlton, Thomas H., Deborah L. Nichols, and Cynthia Otis Charlton

1991 Aztec Craft Production and Specialization. Archaeological Evidence from the City-State of Otumba, Mexico. *World Archaeology* 23:98 114.

Charlton, Thomas H., and Cynthia Otis Charlton

1993 Ethnoarchaeology: The Two Ceramic Traditions of San Sebastian. Paper presented at the 13th International Congress of Anthropological and Ethnological Sciences, Mexico City.

Charlton, Thomas H., and Michael W. Spence

1982 Obsidian Exploitation and Civilization in the Basin of Mexico. In *Mining and Mining Techniques in Ancient Mesoamerica,* edited by Phil C. Weigand and Gretchen Gwynne, pp. 7-86. Anthropology 4(1-2). State University of New York, Stony Brook.

Clark, John E.

1986 From Mountain to Molehill: A Critical Review of Teotihuacan's Obsidian Industry. In *Economic Aspects of Prehispanic Highland Mexico,* edited by Barry L. Isaac, pp. 23-74. Research in Economic Anthropology, Supplement 2. JAI Press, Greenwich.

Cook, Carmen

1950 Figurillas de barro de Santiago Tlatelolco. *Memorias de la Academía Mexicana de la Historia* 9(1):93-100.

Cortés, Hernán

1962 *Conquest: Dispatches of Cortés from the New World.* Translated by Irwin R. Blacker and H. M. Rosen. Grossett and Dunlap, New York.

Costin, Cathy Lynne

1986 *From Chiefdom to Empire State: Ceramic Economy Among the Prehispanic Wanka of Highland Peru.* Ph.D. dissertation, Departmant of Anthropology, University of California, Los Angeles. University Microfilms, Ann Arbor.

1991   Craft Specialization: Issues in Defining, Documenting, and Explaining the Organization of Production. In *Archaeological Method and Theory,* vol. 3, edited by Michael B. Schiffer, pp. 1-56. University of Arizona Press, Tucson.

Díaz del Castillo, Bernal

1963   *The Conquest of New Spain.* Translated by J. M. Cohen. Penguin Books, London.

Durán, Fray Diego

1971   *Book of the Gods and Rites and The Ancient Calendar.* Translated and edited by Fernando Horcasitas and Doris Heyden. University of Oklahoma Press, Norman.

Earle, Timothy K.

1981   Comment on "Evolution of Specialized Pottery Production: A Trial Model," by Prudence M. Rice. *Current Anthropology* 22:230-231.

Evans, Susan T.

1988   *Excavations at Cihuatecpan: An Aztec Village in the Teotihuacan Valley.* Vanderbilt University Publications in Anthropology No. 36. Vanderbilt University, Nashville.

1990   Household Ritual in Aztec Life. Paper presented at the 55th Annual Meeting of the Society for American Archaeology, Las Vegas.

Gibson, Charles

1964   *The Aztecs Under Spanish Rule: A History of the Indians of the Valley of Mexico, 1519-1810.* Stanford University Press, Stanford.

González Rul, Francisco

1979   *La lítica en Tlatelolco.* Instituto Nacional de Antropología e Historia, Mexico City.

Griffin, James B., and Antonieta Espejo

1947   La alfarería correspondiente al último período de ocupación nahua del Valle de México. *Memorias de la Academía Mexicana de la Historia* 6(2):131-147.

Hassig, Ross

1982   Periodic Markets in Precolumbian Mexico. *American Antiquity* 47:346-355.

1988   *Aztec Warfare:Imperial Expansion and Political Control.* University of Oklahoma Press, Norman.

Hicks, Frederic

1982   Tetzcoco in the Early 16th Century: The State, the City, and the *Calpolli. American Ethnologist* 9:230-249.

1987   First Steps Toward a Market-Integrated Economy in Aztec Mexico. In *Early State Dynamics,* edited by Henri J. M. Claessen and Pieter van de Velde, pp. 91-107. E. J. Brill, Leiden.

1991   Gift and Tribute: Relations of Dependency in Aztec Mexico. In *Early State Economics,* edited by Henri J. M. Claessen and Pieter van de Velde, pp. 199-213. Transaction, New Brunswick, New Jersey.

1992   Subject States and Tribute Provinces: The Aztec Empire in the Northern Valley of Mexico. *Ancient Mesoamerica* 3:1-10.

Hodge, Mary G.

1992   Aztec Market Systems. *National Geographic Research and Exploration* 8:428-445.

Hodge, Mary G., Hector Neff, M. James Blackman, and Leah D. Minc
   1992   A Compositional Perspective on Ceramic Production in the Aztec Empire. In *Chemical Characterization of Ceramic Pastes in Archaeology,* edited by Hector Neff, pp. 203-220. Prehistory Press, Madison.

Hodge, Mary G., and Leah D. Minc
   1990   The Spatial Patterning of Aztec Ceramics: Implications for Prehispanic Exchange Systems in the Valley of Mexico. *Journal of Field Archaeology* 17:415-437.

Lackey, Louana M.
   1982   *The Pottery of Acatlán: A Changing Mexican Tradition.* University of Oklahoma Press, Norman.

López Austin, Alfredo
   1986   Organización política en el altiplano central de México durante el posclásico. In *Mesoamérica y el centro de México,* edited by Jesús Monjarás-Ruiz, Rosa Brambila, and Emma Pérez-Rocha, pp. 196-234. Instituto Nacional de Antropología e Historia, Mexico City.

McVicker, Donald, and Laurene Lambertino-Urquizo
   1992   Fifteenth Century Aztec and Matlatzincan Encounters: Evidence from Tlacotepec, Valley of Toluca, Mexico. Paper presented at the College Art Association Annual Meeting, Chicago.

Mirambell, Lorena E.
   1968   *Técnicas lapidarias prehispánicas.* Serie Investigaciones 14, Instituto Nacional de Antropología e Historia, Mexico City.

Monjarás-Ruiz, Jesús
   1986   Algunos aspectos del surgimiento del aparato político tenochca. In *Mesoamérica y el centro de México,* edited by Jesús Monjarás-Ruiz, Rosa Brambila, and Emma Pérez-Rocha, pp. 371-380. Instituto Nacional de Antropología e Historia, Mexico City.

Motolinía, Fray Toribio de
   1951   *Motolinía's History of the Indians of New Spain.* Translated by Francis Borgia Steck. Academy of American Franciscan History, Washington, D.C.

   1970   *Memoriales e historia de los indios de la Nueva España.* Biblioteca de Autores Españoles, Madrid.

Offner, Jerome A.
   1979   A Reassessment of the Extent and Structuring of the Empire of Techotlalatzin, Fourteenth Century Ruler of Texcoco. *Ethnohistory* 26:231-242.

   1983   *Law and Politics in Aztec Texcoco.* Cambridge University Press, Cambridge.

O'Mack, Scott H.
   1991   Yacateuctli and Ehecatl-Quetzalcoatl: Earth-Divers in Aztec Central Mexico. *Ethnohistory* 38:1-33.

Otis Charlton, Cynthia
   1990   Figurine and Lapidary Production at Otumba: Craft Specialization in Domestic Contexts. Paper presented at the 55th Annual Meeting of the Society for American Archaeology, Las Vegas.

1991 Los procesos de desarrollo de los estados tempranos: el caso del estado Azteca de Otumba. Excavación de un taller de lapidaria. *Boletín del Consejo de Arqueología* 1990:74-78. Instituto National de Antropología e Historia, Mexico City.

1993 Obsidian as Jewelry: Lapidary Production in Aztec Otumba, Mexico. *Ancient Mesoamerica* 4:231-243.

1994 Hollow Rattle Figurines of the Otumba Area, Mexico. In *New World Figurine Project,* vol. 2. Research Press, Provo. In press.

Otis Charlton, Cynthia, Thomas H. Charlton, and Connie Miracchi
1971 An Ethnographic Study of Two Modern Pottery-Making Families of San Sebastian Xala, Mexico, 1971. Manuscript on file at the Department of Anthropology, University of Iowa, Iowa City.

Otis Charlton, Cynthia, Thomas H. Charlton, and Deborah L. Nichols
1993 Aztec Household-Based Craft Production: Archaeological Evidence from the City-State of Otumba, Mexico. In *Prehispanic Domestic Units in Western Mesoamerica: Studies of the Household, Compound, and Residence,* edited by Robert S. Santley and Kenneth G. Hirth, pp. 147-171. CRC Press, Boca Raton.

Parsons, Mary H.
1972 Aztec Figurines from the Teotihuacan Valley, Mexico. In *Miscellaneous Studies in Mexican Prehistory,* edited by Michael W. Spence, Jeffrey R. Parsons, and Mary H. Parsons, pp. 81-120. Anthropological Papers No. 45, Museum of Anthropology, University of Michigan, Ann Arbor.

Pasztory, Esther
1983 *Aztec Art.* Abrams, New York.

Patterson, Declan, and Terry Stocker
1990 One Interpretation of Mesoamerican Figurine Function. Unpublished manuscript on file, Foundation for Ancient Research, Provo, Utah.

Peacock, D. P. S.
1982 *Pottery in the Roman World: An Ethnoarchaeological Approach.* Longman, New York.

Reiff Katz, Roberta
1977 *The Potters and Pottery of Tonalá, Jalisco, Mexico: A Study in Aesthetic Anthropology.* Ph.D. dissertation, Department of Anthropology, Columbia University, New York. University Microfilms, Ann Arbor.

Rodríguez-Shadow, María
1990 *El estado Azteca.* Universidad Autónoma del Estado de México, Toluca.

Sahagún, Fray Bernardino de
1950-1982 *Florentine Codex: General History of the Things of New Spain.* Translated and edited by Arthur J. O. Anderson and Charles E. Dibble. 12 books. School of American Research and the University of Utah Press, Santa Fe and Salt Lake City.

Sanders, William T., Jeffrey R. Parsons, and Robert S. Santley
1979 *The Basin of Mexico: Ecological Process in the Evolution of a Civilization.* Academic Press, New York.

Sheehy, James

    1993   Etnoarqueología y la escala de producción de cerámica en Teotihuacan antiguo. Paper presented at the 13th International Congress of Anthropological and Ethnological Sciences, Mexico City.

Sinopoli, Carla M.

    1988   The Organization of Craft Production at Vijayanagara, South India. *American Anthropologist* 90:580-597.

    1991   *Approaches to Archaeological Ceramics.* Plenum Press, New York.

Smith, Michael E.

    1987   The Expansion of the Aztec Empire: A Case Study in the Correlation of Diachronic Archaeological and Ethnohistorical Data. *American Antiquity* 52:37-54.

    1990   Long-Distance Trade under the Aztec Empire: The Archaeological Evidence. *Ancient Mesoamerica* 1:153-169.

    1992   *Archaeological Research at Aztec-Period Rural Sites in Morelos, Mexico, Volume 1: Excavations and Architecture.* Memoirs in Latin American Archaeology No. 4. University of Pittsburgh, Pittsburgh.

    1993   Houses and Settlement Hierarchy in Late Postclassic Morelos: A Comparison of Archaeology and Ethnohistory. In *Prehispanic Domestic Units in Western Mesoamerica: Studies of the Household, Compound, and Residence,* edited by Robert S. Santley and Kenneth G. Hirth, pp. 191-206. CRC Press, Boca Raton.

Smith, Michael E., Patricia Aguirre, Cynthia Heath-Smith, Kathryn Hirst, Scott O'Mack, and Jeffrey Price

    1989   Architectural Patterns at Three Aztec-Period Sites in Morelos, Mexico. *Journal of Field Archaeology* 16:185-203.

Stocker, Terry

    1991   Discussion: Empire Formation, Figurine Function, and Figurine Distribution. In *The New World Figurine Project,* vol. 1, edited by Terry Stocker, pp. 145-165. Research Press, Provo.

van der Leeuw, Sander Ernst

    1976   *Studies in the Technology of Ancient Pottery.* 2 vols. Unpublished Ph.D. dissertation, Universiteit van Amsterdam, Amsterdam.

Widmer, Randolph J., and James J. Sheehy

    1990   Archaeological Implications of Architectural Changes in a Modern Potting Compound in Teotihuacan, Mexico. Paper presented at the 55th Annual Meetings of the Society for American Archaeology, Las Vegas.

9

Economic Heterogeneity and State Expansion

The Northeastern Basin of Mexico during the Late Postclassic Period

Thomas H. Charlton

Archaeological data from surveys and excavations within several regions of the northeast Basin of Mexico and immediately adjacent areas (fig. 9.1) provide the basis for an examination of the roles of ecology, locational history, demography, and political systems in economic heterogeneity and state expansion between A.D. 1350 and A.D. 1519. Although the northeast Basin of Mexico formed a secure part of the Acolhua domain in A.D. 1519 (Gibson 1956:2; Nicholson 1974:149), this situation had only existed since the decade following A.D. 1428. At that time, with the help of Tenochtitlan, Texcoco had recovered those portions of its domain lost to Tepaneca control during the late fourteenth and early fifteenth centuries (Gibson 1956:2; Hassig 1988:149; Nicholson 1974:150; Offner 1983:87-88).

The region is of particular importance because of the concentration there of four major obsidian sources used during the preconquest period (Charlton 1978a; Charlton et al. 1978; Charlton and Spence 1982). The topography of the area permits easy access to both nearby and distant regions of Mesoamerica for trade and resource exploitation (Charlton 1977a, 1978a) and conquest (Hassig 1988:163-165).

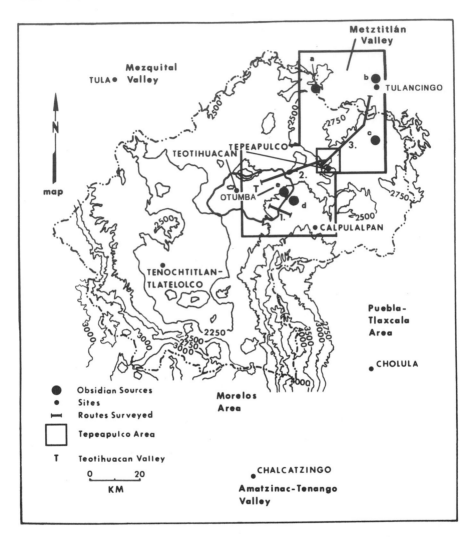

Fig. 9.1.   The Basin of Mexico. Major archaeological sites, subareas, routes, and obsidian source areas (*a,* Pachuca; *b,* Tulancingo; *c,* Tecocomulco; *d,* Malpais; *e,* Otumba) mentioned in the text are shown. Base map after Lorenzo 1968:54, fig. 1.

The presence of the city-states and centers of Tulancingo (Tulançinco), Tepeapulco (Tepepulco), and Otumba (Otompan), each with archaeological evidence of varying degrees of specialized nonagricultural craft production and trade, contradicts one economic model of the Late Postclassic economic system in the Basin of Mexico. That model, as proposed by Elizabeth Brumfiel (1976, 1980, 1983, 1986, 1987, 1991), consists of a simple dichotomy between a nonagricultural center (Tenochtitlan), and a Basin-wide agricultural hinterland. I propose, instead, that the Late Aztec economic system in the Basin of Mexico and areas surrounding it was characterized by substantial regionalism in both the production and the distribution of agricultural and nonagricultural products within an integrated economic system (Charlton 1969, 1971a, 1971b, 1977a, 1978a, 1981, 1987, 1990; Charlton et al. 1991; Nichols and Charlton 1988; Otis Charlton 1993; Otis Charlton et al. 1993).

Despite the early recognition of many aspects of the economic complexity of the Late Postclassic Basin of Mexico (Charlton 1971a, 1980, 1981; Mather 1968; Nichols and Charlton 1988), there has been some reticence to accept them as valid (e.g., Brumfiel 1980:475-477). Although this situation could derive from a conceptual lock as suggested by Stephen J. Gould (1986:10), it most probably results from the completion of only Stage I settlement pattern research in most areas (Charlton 1984; Sanders et al. 1979:12-30). Stage I settlement pattern research consists of efforts to locate the raw data and to assign them to culturally significant chronological periods, usually without the application of sampling procedures for site location or surface collections (Charlton 1984:198-202). The conclusions from Stage I research should be phrased as inferences to provide the basis for the formulation of hypotheses for future testing.

When regional economic complexity has been noted on the basis of Stage I research, it is open to criticism, particularly with reference to the potential biases present in collection methodology (Brumfiel 1980:475-477; Charlton 1984:202). It should be noted, however, that the restrictions on conclusions drawn from Stage I research may be mitigated by survey intensity. Survey intensity during Stage I research may play a role of equal, if not greater, importance than collection methodology in the identification of materials relevant to economic complexity (Nichols et al. 1990:15).

Stage II research, the testing of inferences and conclusions from Stage I research through excavations and surface collections made using sampling methodologies, has only been carried out in a few instances. Even in those cases there are restrictions evident. The non-random selection of a necessarily limited geographical area to be the focus of such a study means that the area selected cannot be used to reflect the economic composition of the Basin as a whole. The uncritical application to the entire Basin of the results derived from such datasets has effectively eliminated Basin-wide economic complexity. For example, Brumfiel— extrapolating from the results of research at a single city-state, Huexotla (Brumfiel 1976, 1980, 1983), and single sites, such as Xico (Brumfiel 1986, 1987) and Xaltocan (Brumfiel 1991)—postulates a Basin-wide economic system probably much less complex than that which existed (Charlton 1980; Nichols and Charlton 1988; Spence 1984).

If we blind people are to identify the beast with which we deal, we must place our localized and restricted observations (datasets) within the context of a regional approach. As an initial attempt, I examine the archaeological data from a major subregion of the Basin of Mexico and from a contiguous area to the northeast to evaluate the degree of heterogeneity of the Late Postclassic Basin of Mexico economy, and the relevant factors—ecological, locational-historical, demographic, and political-economic—involved in its development.

GEOGRAPHICAL SETTING

The Basin of Mexico, with the Tulancingo Valley (Metztitlan Valley) just outside its northeast border, forms part of the northern subregion of the Central Mexican Symbiotic Region (CMSR) as defined by William T. Sanders (1956:115-116, 1971:3-5). The northern subregion of the CMSR is situated entirely within the eastern section of the Mesa Central (West 1964a:46) and the Neovolcanic Axis Geological Province (Maldonado-Koerdell 1964:6). Described by Sanders as a "broad belt of elevated tableland" (1956:115), the northern subregion is internally complex and can be divided by topography into a number of hydrographic units that were the foci of Late Postclassic cultural development. The Basin of Mexico and the Tulancingo Valley are two such units.

The Basin of Mexico is an internally complex hydrographic and topographic unit (García 1968:14) containing major and minor lake and interior drainage systems along with some large expanses of open plains (Tamayo 1964:108-113; Sanders et al. 1979:81-89). The largest unit within the northern subregion of the CMSR, it extends through the west central section of the subregion and is demarcated by the southern escarpment, the Valley of Toluca to the west, the Mezquital Valley, to the northwest and north, the Tulancingo Valley to the northeast, and the Puebla-Tlaxcala Valley to the east and southeast (Tamayo 1964:108-113). The Tulancingo Valley, located between the northeast border of the Basin of Mexico and the eastern escarpment edge of the CMSR, falls within the upper drainage of the Metztitlan River, a tributary of the Panuco River (West 1964a:45).

The soils throughout the CMSR are volcanic in origin and often alluvially deposited in valleys and basins (West 1964b:371-372). Although variable in quantity and quality, they are generally fertile with soil depth and rainfall being the most relevant factors for crop yields (Sanders 1971:4-5). Rainfall is highly variable and dependent upon local topography. The northeast Basin of Mexico and the Tulancingo Valley have a low mean annual precipitation ranging from 500 to 1,000 mm (Vivó Escoto 1964:fig. 10; see also Sanders 1971:3-4). Except in areas with the potential for permanent or floodwater irrigation, this environmental characteristic poses problems for consistently high agricultural production. This situation is particularly true for the city-state areas of Tulancingo, Tepeapulco, and Otumba (Charlton 1977a, 1991; Offner 1980). In the lower inhabited zones within the subregion Jorge Vivó Escoto (1964:fig. 7) notes mean annual temperatures of 15° C (cf. Sanders 1971:3).

The Tulancingo City-State

The Late Postclassic city-state center of Tulancingo was located in the upper Metztitlan Valley, immediately adjacent to and south of the Tulancingo obsidian source area. Tulancingo, at an elevation of 2,154 m, was situated at the junction of a hillslope and an alluvial plain, permanently irrigated in prehispanic times (Carrasco 1963:88; Charlton and Spence 1982; M. E. Snow and E. F. Snow 1969). The Pachuca obsidian source area is about 20 km to the west and the Tecocomulco obsidian source area about 25 km to the southeast (Charlton and Spence 1982). Although the hills around Tulancingo reach elevations between 2,800 and 3,000 m, numerous passes provide easy routes of communication out of the valley in all directions. This location—where several different routes come together—probably contributed to Tulancingo's access to and control over an ecologically varied region, ranging from the plateau surface to an elevation of about 200 m to the east (Gerhard 1972:335; Offner 1983:12). The complete and precise boundaries of the city-state are unknown. On the south Tulancingo appears to have shared a frontier with the Tepeapulco city-state (Offner 1983:4).

The limited survey and excavations carried out in the Tulancingo city-state have generally focused on the Epi-Teotihuacan settlement at Huapalcalco and the exploitation of obsidian at the Tulancingo-Pizarrín obsidian locality. Remnants of Tulancingo, along with other Late Postclassic communities, have been reported in the Tulancingo Valley. As yet only limited intensive surface survey has been carried out in this city-state.

The Tepeapulco City-State

The Late Postclassic city-state center of Tepeapulco was located between 35 and 40 km southwest of Tulancingo, as measured along either one of the two optimal routes for foot travel. Tepeapulco (elevation of ca. 2,500 m) was located on a hillslope above an alluvial plain that forms an attenuated section of the much larger and more famous Plains of Apan, situated to the south and east, north of the Tlaxcalan uplands. Numerous communication routes converge on Tepeapulco from the southwest, north, northeast, southeast, and southwest, creating a critical junction (Charlton 1978a; García Cook 1982).

Although some of this area is permanently irrigated today, the *Relación Geográfica* of Tepeapulco indicates that there was no permanent irrigation at the time of contact (Acuña 1984-1987:v.3:171-172, 177). Undoubtedly flood-water irrigation was feasible on terrace systems and on flat lands throughout the city-state area not inundated during the rainy season.

The city-state area consisted of a series of small internal drainage basins at elevations between 2,400 m and 2,600 m, some with permanent lakes, surrounded by mountains reaching between 2,800 m and 3,200 m in eleva-tion. Although the precise borders have not been determined, the city-state was situ-ated between Otumba to the west, Tulancingo to the northeast, Tliliuhquitepec to the east, and Tlaxcala (Tlaxcalla) to the south (Davies 1968:Mapa 3; Gerhard 1972:52-53; Jones 1977:23-25; Offner 1983:4, 13-14). The Malpais obsidian source area is about 10 km to the southwest and the Tecocomulco obsidian source area about 35 km to the northeast (Charlton 1978a; Charlton and Spence 1982).

Surveys and collections, at different levels of intensity, have been carried out in most sections of the Tepeapulco city-state. In addition excavations have focused on the Teotihuacan period site of Tepeapulco located north of the mod-ern and Aztec towns of the same name.

The Otumba City-State

The Late Postclassic city-state center of Otumba was located about 23 km south-west of Tepeapulco measured along the most direct route for foot traffic. The center (elevation 2,350 m), was situated at the edge of the middle Teotihuacan Valley alluvial plain to the west, the upper Teotihuacan Valley alluvial plain to the north, and a piedmont which gently rises to the east. The city-state as a whole falls primarily within the eastern or upper Teotihuacan Valley. The Otumba obsidian source area is about 10 km east of Otumba and the Malpais obsidian source area slightly more than 20 km to the east, behind the Sierra del Malpais. Numerous routes for foot travel to the west, northeast, southeast, south, and southwest converge on Otumba.

Although there are no permanent rivers or springs within the city-state area, floodwater irrigation was feasible on the alluvial plains and on terraces along drainages running from the surrounding hills. The southern and eastern bound-aries of the Otumba city-state are well marked by two mountain ranges reach-ing up to 3,000 m. There are no topographic barriers to the west, where the alluvial plain terminates at the ruins of Teotihuacan. To the north and northeast the boundaries are similarly poorly defined in an area of ridges connecting iso-lated extinct volcanic cones that reach elevations between 2,500 m and 3,000 m (Charlton 1991:223-227).

The Otumba city-state was bordered on the west by Teotihuacan, on the south by Texcoco, on the east by Tepeapulco, and on the north by Zempoala (Çempoalan) (Gerhard 1972:207-209; Jones 1977:23-25; Offner 1983:4). Ar-chaeological research in the Otumba city-state has involved intensive surveys and selected excavations since the late 1950s. Of the three city-states examined in this paper, Otumba's archaeology is the best known.

Summary

Although there were specific differences in the physical settings of the three city-states under discussion, the settings did share several features. Each city-state included at least one obsidian source area. All city-state centers were located near alluvial plains with permanent irrigation (Tulancingo) or floodwater irrigation (Tepeapulco and Otumba). Within the city-state areas terracing and floodwater irrigation would have enabled each to be agriculturally self-sufficient despite the relative harshness of the environment (Charlton 1991:223-227; Offner 1983:14). Of particular relevance is the crossing of each city-state by numerous communication routes running both within and between regions, and the location of each city-state center at points where these routes converged.

As I shall detail below, archaeological data from each city-state indicate the development of nonagricultural activities in the form of craft production. Such craft production was at a level of intensity greater than the nonspecialized or part-time activities Brumfiel describes at the city-state of Huexotla (1976, 1980) and the Late Postclassic community of Xico (1986) in the Basin of Mexico

RESEARCH BACKGROUND

The data on which this paper is based were developed through fieldwork and analyses carried out within the contexts of several research projects between 1960 and 1989. These projects include William T. Sanders's Teotihuacan Valley Project and my Post-Conquest Developments, Trade Route, and Otumba Projects, part of the latter conducted in collaboration with Deborah L. Nichols. As discussed below, other projects have also contributed to our knowledge of these three city-states; however, variability in field and laboratory methodologies and the extent to which the data have been reported preclude direct comparability of their results with those derived from the projects mentioned above.

Surface Survey Methodologies

The specific methodologies applied in surface survey varied according to the goals of the project and the years during which each project was conducted. Basic survey and collection methodologies were developed in Sanders's Teotihuacan Valley Project (TVP) and modified in the Post-Conquest Developments (PCDP) and Trade Route Projects (TRP). The main differences in survey methodologies involved a shift to the use of survey teams instead of individuals, a focus on initial, complete areal coverage instead of the intensive survey of sites previously located through reconnaissance or general survey, and the use of standardized forms on which to record survey data and collection data.

Teotihuacan Valley Project. The procedures and changes during the Teotihuacan Valley Project are discussed by William Sanders (1965:12-13) and William Mather (1968:12-14, 46-52). Sanders et al. (1979:20-23) detail the survey methodologies used for the Basin of Mexico surveys, which include the 1963, 1964, and 1966 field seasons of the Teotihuacan Valley Project conducted in part in the Otumba city-state. There most surveys were carried out by one experienced person, a faculty member or graduate student, accompanied at times by an undergraduate and one or two local Mexican workers. Although a standardized form was filled in for each site surveyed, no such form was completed for each field surveyed or each collection made. Occasionally fields, which served as survey units, were numbered. Collections were usually made during survey.

Post-Conquest Developments Project. Surveys of the Post-Conquest Developments Project in 1968 and 1969 were restricted to the Otumba city-state area. We used survey teams of two to five trained individuals, graduate students and faculty, as developed by Sanders in the fall of 1963 while surveying the area north of Cerro Gordo. Survey data for each numbered field (survey unit) were recorded in a notebook, but not on a standardized form. All occupation, preconquest and postconquest, was recorded. No collections were made during survey.

Trade Route Project. The Trade Route Project of 1975 continued the use of survey teams composed of graduate students, undergraduates, a skilled Mexican worker, and a faculty member, varying in size from two to five individuals. Again numbered fields served as survey units but the data from each was recorded on a standardized form. As before we recorded all occupations but took no collections while carrying out intensive survey.

Otumba Project. The survey methodology described for the Trade Route Project was routinely applied during the current Otumba Project in 1987-1989 (Charlton 1987, 1988; Nichols et al. 1990:12-14).

Collection Methodologies

The collection methodologies used in the several projects (TVP, PCDP, TRP) as part of Stage I research evolved through three variants of purposive selection strategies. Subsequently, during Stage II research, these purposive selection strategies were complemented by various sampling strategies (used during the Otumba Project) (Cowgill 1975:260-261).

Collections made within Sanders's TVP and my PCDP and TRP fall into the category of purposive selection as defined by George L. Cowgill (1975). There are important differences between them, however. Consequently neither the use of a single descriptive term "grab sample" nor the implied attendant restriction on the use of the data generated applies equally to all data from these collections. To be sure that these differences are understood, I shall briefly describe them here.

The main refinements in selection strategies were: increased standardization of collection unit size, collection duration, collection team composition, and an increasingly broader definition of the materials to be included within the surface collection. Another important change was to wait until after survey was completed and sites defined over a fairly extensive area before determining the areas to be collected. Once this decision was implemented all collections were made in fieldwork operations separate from the survey itself, effectively eliminating the "carrying capacity" problem (Sanders et al. 1979:27).

Teotihuacan Valley Project. Sanders (1965.12), Mather (1968:52-53) and Sanders et al. (1979:27-30) describe the general operating principles of what became a "fairly standardized system of surface collecting" (1979:28) with a chronological goal. This is the archetypical "grab sample" and characterizes the collections taken in the Otumba city-state during the Teotihuacan Valley Project (Mather 1968:52-53). These collections ranged in number from 60-120 sherds and emphasized rims, decorated body sherds, supports, handles, and basal angles. They came from areas of unequal sizes, from mounds or ceramic concentrations of varying densities, and were made by two or three people in 20-40 minutes. Some attempt was made to cover all areas within large sites but not on a random basis. The collections did not include obvious postconquest materials such as glazed wares but unintentionally included postconquest unglazed earthenwares. Neither obsidian nor groundstone artifacts were systematically collected although small clay artifacts such as spindle whorls and figurines were. Collection area size varied inversely with sherd density. Collections were made during survey and carried by survey teams throughout the day.

Post-Conquest Developments Project. The Post-Conquest Developments Project also used a purposive selection methodology to make surface collections (Charlton 1972a, 1972b). The main emphasis of the collections was on chronology but some attempt was made to evaluate site function. The collection units were defined after sites had been intensively surveyed, and the collection process was carried out independently of the survey. The size of the collection team was increased to six, usually consisting of four Mexican workers, one or two graduate students, and a faculty member, although occasionally consisting only of graduate students. The time devoted to each collection was restricted to 20-30 minutes.

Since the focus of the project was on the postconquest period, we chose mounds, ceramic concentrations, recent house ruins, and modern occupied structures for collections. Surface areas to be collected were standardized for each of these units. Notes describing collection units were kept but not systematically nor on a standardized form. We expanded the definition of materials to be collected in order to include data on postconquest occupations as well on some site functions. All glazed ceramics were collected as were all obvious nonaboriginal objects such as metal and glass. Unglazed materials were collected following the procedures used by Sanders. Collections included all rims, decorated body sherds, and those plain body sherds identifiable by function, chronology, or source. Groundstone artifacts, bricks, tiles, and clay artifacts (e.g. figurines, spindle whorls) were also collected. Only obsidian and Plain Orange bodies from jars, basins, and bowls were systematically excluded. The collections were made separately from the survey. Thus there were no conflicts in objectives, and larger collections were routinely made.

Trade Route Project. The collection methodology described above for the PCDP was followed and further refined during the Trade Route Project by collecting all cultural materials from within a spatially restricted area (20 m²) for a fixed period of time (20 minutes).

Otumba Project. Several changes characterized the collection methodology in the Otumba Project (Nichols et al. 1990:12-28). As part of Stage II research, we opted to use a stratified random sampling program within Otumba itself at a level of one percent over the entire site area with an additional four percent in areas where there were previously known heavy concentrations of artifacts indicating craft production. These samples were supplemented by nonrandomly chosen collection units within Otumba and within rural sites. All collection units were of the same size (25 m²), and all artifacts above the size of a thumbnail, preconquest and postconquest, were collected. No time limit was set for each collection. A standardized form, based on the field unit survey form, was used for each collection unit. The 1988 and 1989 collections in the Otumba city-state were designed to obtain representative and comparable artifact samples from occupation and production zones previously identified through earlier surveys and collections.

Implications of Survey and Collection Methodologies

As I shall detail below, only the TRP survey and collection methodologies have been applied in all three city-states—Tulancingo, Tepeapulco, and Otumba—

thus providing comparable data on occupation and economic complexity in each (figs. 9.2 and 9.3). The Otumba Project, the most recent in an evolving series of archaeological studies within the Otumba city-state, has clearly confirmed that such intensive surface survey, carried out by experienced persons in combination with purposive collections, can and does reveal archaeological evidence for economic complexity. Stage II research with randomly selected standardized collections certainly provides a statistically more secure basis on which to make comparisons and determinations of craft intensity. Nevertheless, sampling within Stage II research does not substitute for Stage I survey as a discovery mode, unless carried out with a very large sampling fraction. The survey and collection data from all three city-states form a solid basis for an evaluation of Basin-wide economic complexity.

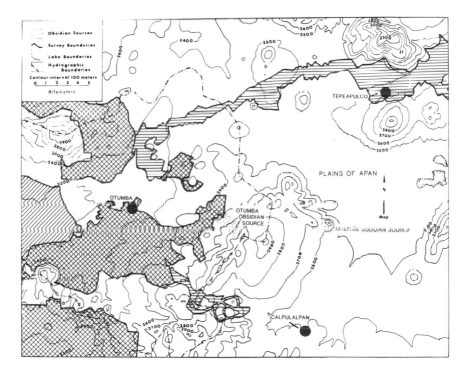

Fig. 9.2. The Eastern Teotihuacan Valley and the Northern Plains of Apan. Major archaeological sites and surveyed areas are shown. Diagonal hatching, city of Teotihuacan survey (Millon 1973); diagonal cross-hatching, Teotihuacan Valley and Texcoco area surveys (Charlton 1972a, 1972b; Sanders et al. 1979); horizontal hatching, Trade Route Project surveys (Charlton 1978a). Base map after Charlton 1978a:1234, fig. 6.

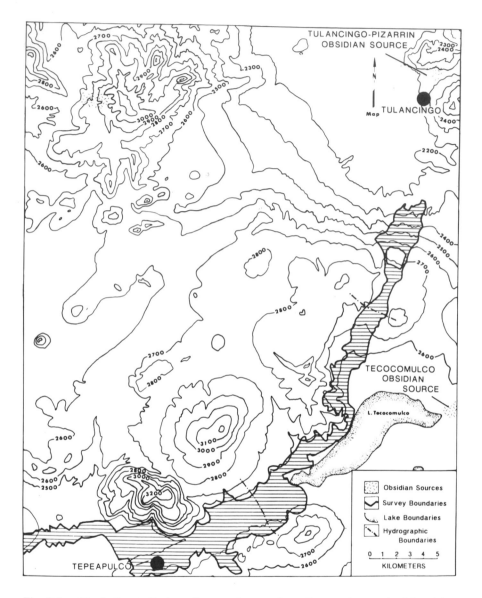

Fig. 9.3.   Trade Route Project. Surveyed areas from Tepeapulco to the Metztitlan
Valley are shown. Base map after Charlton 1978a:1230, fig. 3.

RESEARCH RESULTS

The Otumba City-State

Of the three city-states under discussion Otumba has the most complex sequence of research with the most complete and intensive areal coverage.Most of the data are derived from surface surveys of varying intensities and from surface collections. Some excavations of residences have been conducted along with test pits to help reconstruct the chronology.

Although Paul Tolstoy visited the southwest area of the city-state center of Otumba (TA-80), taking one collection there and another to the west of the site (1958:72), the seminal research directed by William T. Sanders in his Teotihuacan Valley Project was the first to include systematic surveys and collections both from Otumba (TA-80) and at numerous rural sites throughout the city-state area (Sanders 1965). As part of that project, William G. Mather surveyed Otumba (TA-80) in 1963 and was the first to report archaeological evidence of craft specialization at an Aztec city-state center (Sanders 1965; Mather 1968). He located and defined three obsidian workshops and one area of figurine molding during his mapping of the residential and civic-ceremonial areas of the site (1968.125,163). Evidence of obsidian working also was reported by Mather and Charles S. Fletcher for TA-90 and by Fletcher for TA-81 (Mather 1968), recently investigated by Susan T. Evans (1988). Jeffrey R. Parsons noted evidence for obsidian working in TA-36, TA-39, TA-56, TA-74, and TA-79 (fig. 9.4).

Following up on Sanders's research initiative between 1968 and 1978, I directed three projects which fell in part or entirely within the area of the Otumba city-state. Two, the Post-Conquest Developments Project, [fieldwork 1968-1969], and the Trade Route Project [fieldwork 1975], yielded substantial additional information on the locus, scale, variability, and extensiveness of craft production in the Otumba city-state (Brodkey 1978; Charlton 1971a, 1972a, 1972b, 1975a, 1975b, 1977a, 1980, 1981; Wiltfang 1975). The third project, the Otumba Irrigation Project, [fieldwork 1977 and 1978] dealt with agricultural intensification in Otumba (TA-80) and revealed a long sequence of floodwater irrigation (Charlton 1977b, 1978b, 1979a-d).

By 1981 the major outlines of craft production in the Otumba city-state were clear. Three major productive activities were restricted to the city-state capital: figurine manufacture, obsidian core-blade production, and lapidary production. Although the volume and extensiveness of production debris for each activity varied, all appeared to represent specialized workshops. Obsidian biface production occurred only in sites outside the city-state capital. There the production debris also indicated workshop activity. Fiber spinning, another major production activity, occurred in both urban and nonurban contexts. In the case of cotton spinning, a dispersed, generalized, household-based production sys-

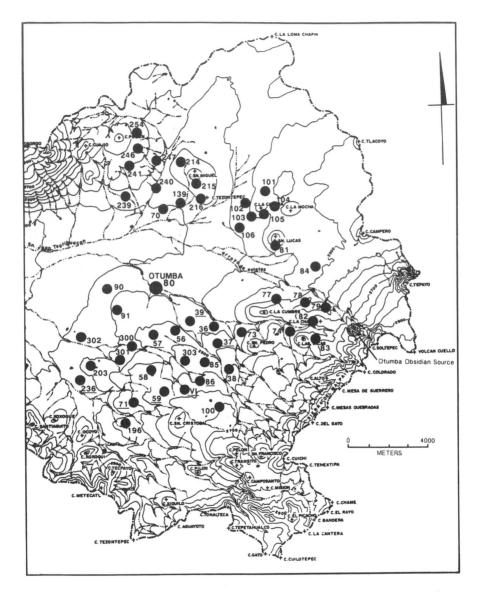

Fig. 9.4.   Late Aztec archaeological sites in the Otumba city-state (Charlton 1972a, 1972b; Sanders 1965). Base map after Lorenzo 1968:fig. 3.

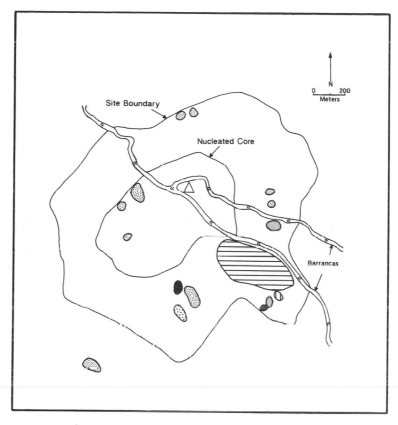

△ Central Pyramid

▦ Core-blade Workshop (Pachuca Obsidian-Green)

▦ Core-blade Workshop (Otumba Obsidian-Gray)

▨ Lapidary Workshops

■ Groundstone Workshops

▤ Figurine Workshops

Fig. 9.5.   Otumba (TA-80) Site Map, 1987. After Charlton 1988.

tem was present both in Otumba and in dependent outlying sites. Maguey fiber spinning occurred in a dispersed, household-based production system in rural areas and in a workshop context in the urban setting. These data from the Otumba city-state, gathered over the years by many individuals from separate projects, indicated substantial craft production throughout the Aztec occupation (Charlton 1971a, 1980, 1981)—production greater than the nonspecialized or part-time activities described at Huexotla and Xico (Brumfiel 1976, 1980, 1987:109).

In January, 1987, in collaboration with Cynthia Otis Charlton and Evaristo Tenorio C., I initiated the current Otumba Project. We carried out an intensive field by field resurvey of the site area (Charlton 1987, 1988) and confirmed the existence of two major residential zones within the site, along with extensive evidence of intensive craft production. This evidence included that noted previously along with some new information (fig. 9.5).

Evidence for maguey fiber spinning was confirmed and found to be associated with heavy concentrations of green obsidian prismatic blades and fragments of basalt *hachas,* possibly tools related to fiber extraction and to dyeing and weaving. The lapidary workshop was confirmed and additional evidence for such production noted in two other areas. The previously known core-blade workshops were confirmed, and an additional seven areas were mapped, plus a concentration originally located in 1968. All seem to represent debris from core-blade production. Figurine production was confirmed and the area expanded to cover almost 10 ha, suggesting a barrio of households specializing in figurine manufacture. Two previously unreported concentrations of chipped basalt flakes and fragments of groundstone tools were located, suggesting the possibility of a new craft activity, groundstone tool production.

Every Stage I survey and collection project at Otumba from 1963 to 1987 confirmed and expanded the evidence for an economic complexity greater than that proposed for Huexotla or Xico. In order to evaluate and detail these data, Deborah L. Nichols and I directed Stage II fieldwork at Otumba in 1988 and 1989 (Charlton and Nichols 1990; Charlton et al. 1991; Nichols, chap. 7; Otis Charlton, chap. 8). Currently I am directing the analyses of the new data from Otumba and the reanalysis of those from the Tepeapulco and Tulancingo city-states.

The Tepeapulco City-State

Several projects have been conducted within the boundaries of the Tepeapulco city-state. Angel García Cook excavated in a cave near the Teotihuacan period site of Tepeapulco (1982). Angel García Cook and Leonor Merino C. (1977) and Fernando Cortés de Brasdefer (1978), working from Tlaxcala to the south, have described Aztec period or Late Postclassic settlement patterns near Apan and Malpais, which would fall in the southern part of the city-state. Raziel Mora López (1980) directed a survey in southeastern Hidalgo which included the entire city-state of Tepeapulco. Unfortunately his maps do not break the sites down by period or phase although he does reference the kinds of ceramics found (1980:28). Eduardo Matos's project at the Teotihuacan period site of Tepeapulco (Matos M. et al. 1981) recorded the Aztec occupation at the site and complements the TRP, which did not include it. Subsequent research there included the excavation of one Aztec residential structure by Fernando López A. and Rosalba Nieto C. (López A. 1988). My main corpus of information on the economic complexity of the Tepeapulco city-state, however, is derived from the TRP.

In the TRP I traversed the city-state of Tepeapulco from southwest to northeast, from the Teotihuacan Valley to the Metztitlan Valley (figs. 9.2 and 9.3) (Charlton 1975b, 1976, 1977a, 1978a) (see also Sanders and Santley 1983:fig. 11.5). The survey crossed the northern Plains of Apan to the Teotihuacan period site of Tepeapulco, covered the area between there and the modern/Aztec town of Tepeapulco, continued through a broad flat valley leading northeast to Lake Tecocomulco, and from there turned north into the Metztitlan Valley.

Data from the survey indicate that most of the Tepeapulco city-state center lies under present-day Tepeapulco. Late Postclassic settlement density is greatest in the Tepeapulco Area, a zone with a radius of about 4 km around Tepeapulco, within the drainage of the northern Plains of Apan (fig. 9.6). Although there are three additional moderate-sized sites located to the east and northeast at a distance of 6 km, and another at 10 km to the northeast of Tepeapulco, most of the remaining sites within the Lake Tecocomulco drainage of the Tepeapulco city-state are quite small. With the exception of the aceramic carrying sites and the obsidian quarrying sites (Charlton 1978a) few of these small sites appear to demonstrate evidence of significant levels of craft production. When craft production is evident, it is usually restricted to biface manufacture. The level of craft production within this hinterland of the Tepeapulco city-state is currently under review by William J. Parry.

Within Tepeapulco and in the sites within a 4 km radius to the northwest, however, there is good evidence of numerous anomalous concentrations of obsidian debitage from core-blade and biface production. The raw materials were obtained primarily from the Pachuca, Otumba or Malpais, and Tecocomulco source areas, with some traces of Pizarrín-locality obsidian (Charlton 1976, 1977a; Charlton and Spence 1982). William J. Parry is currently studying these materials in order to compare them with the Otumba data. The analyses completed in 1978 (Charlton 1978b) coupled with Parry's (William J. Parry, personal communication, 1993) preliminary results provide an adequate basis for the current discussion.

Within the area of Aztec Tepeapulco (48) still open for survey in 1975 we encountered four areas with moderately heavy concentrations of obsidian, each covering about .25 ha. We took collections from three of the four concentrations. The densities (avg. 10/m^2), forms, and sources (ca. 90% Pachuca)

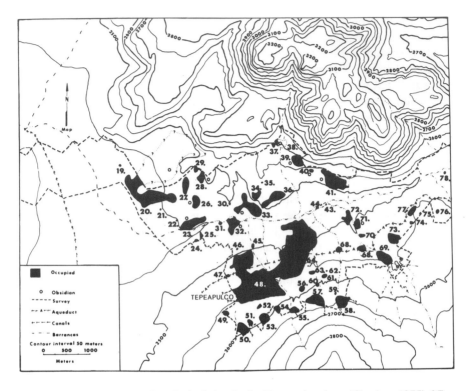

Fig. 9.6.   Late Aztec archaeological sites in the Tepeapulco Area (Charlton 1975b:25).

represented suggest that these concentrations represent household-based production of prismatic blades from already prepared Pachuca cores of Pachuca obsidian to be used for as yet undefined activities in the area of the households. Some obsidian from the Otumba and Tecocomulco source areas was also used.

North of Tepeapulco there is a large number of sites with anomalous concentrations of obsidian debris on the surface. Historically this area has been an important setting for obsidian working (Charlton 1978a). When, however, we selected only those sites with unequivocal Late Postclassic ceramic occupation associated with obsidian also characteristic of that period, one cluster of sites with workshops remains. This cluster, to the northwest of Tepeapulco, includes sites 20, 23, 26, 28, and 32. No collections were taken from most of site 20 in accordance with our agreement with Matos's Tepeapulco Project.

One site, 28, appears to have produced prismatic blades from prepared cores of Pachuca obsidian for use on the site. This collection is similar to those from Tepeapulco in densities (avg. 7/m^2), forms, and sources. The obsidian concentration covered about .25 ha. Approximately 70 percent of the obsidian by count was from Pachuca.

Two sites, 23 (center) and 32, present evidence of small-scale household-based production of cores and prismatic blades probably for use on the site. These sites have higher proportions of debitage to finished tools than the sites which produced only blades for household consumption. The obsidian at site 23 (center) ($21/m^2$) came primarily from Pachuca (75%) while that at site 32 ($16/m^2$) originated both at Pachuca (54%) and Tecocomulco (34%). The concentration of obsidian in site 32 covered about .25 ha while in site 23 the obsidian was found in moderate to heavy densities throughout the 14.5 ha site area. Site 23 (east end) ($20/m^2$) exhibits evidence for minor biface production from gray obsidian, either Otumba or Malpais in origin. Similar, but less abundant, biface production may have occurred in site 23 (center). Biface production could pre-date the Aztec occupation.

Site 26 was a large-scale core-blade workshop using obsidian from three source areas, Pachuca (35%), Tecocomulco (37%), and Otumba or Malpais (26%). The concentration of obsidian in the site covered about .25 ha ($162/m^2$).

The initial analyses suggest that the obsidian concentrations in the Tepeapulco Area reflect three different activities. The household-based production of prismatic blades from previously prepared cores of Pachuca obsidian for consumption within a household context occurred both in the urban context and within the more dispersed settlement to the north. This stage of prismatic blade production was not noted at Otumba. Another activity, prismatic blade core and blade production took place in two kinds of contexts within the northern area of dispersed settlement, with variable source area preference. One is small-scale household-based production; the other is large-scale workshop production. One of the household-based core-blade production sites north of Tepeapulco may also have produced bifaces of Otumba or Malpais obsidian.

Evidence for one other craft industry was found north of the barranca in site 32. This consisted of a large number of roughed-out but unfinished sherd discs. The function of these discs remains unknown. Other evidence for craft production within the Tepeapulco city-state is the presence of large and small spindle whorls in many households, suggesting dispersed, low intensity spinning, and possibly weaving, of maguey and cotton fibers. It should be noted, however, that spindle whorls drastically decline in frequency east of the Tepeapulco Area.

The Tulancingo City-State

Various research projects, both surveys and excavations, have focused on the upper Metztitlan Valley within the Tulancingo city-state. Although most of the excavations and many of the surveys have concentrated on the Epi-Teotihuacan occupation at Huapalcalco and the Tulancingo obsidian source area (Charlton and Spence 1982; Gaxiola G. and Guevara H. 1989; Lizardi Ramos 1957, 1958, 1960; Müller 1957, 1960, 1963; Müller and Lizardi Ramos 1959; Snow, M. E. and E. F. Snow 1968, 1969; Snow E. F. and M. E. Snow 1970), some studies have located and investigated sites within the area from Lake Zupitlan in the northwest to Hueyapan in the southeast (Charlton 1976, 1977a, 1978a; Mora López 1980; Noguera 1970; Snow, M. E. and E. F. Snow 1969; Snow E. F. and M. E. Snow 1970)

As a result of the limited survey and excavations around Tulancingo, we are confident that the Late Postclassic city-state center of Tulancingo is located below the modern community of the same name. Michael E. Snow and Elizabeth F. Snow noted a Late Postclassic occupation at Zapotlan, a modern and prehispanic pottery-making barrio in Tulancingo (1969:18), but they provide no further details on this possible remnant of the city-state center. Consequently, except for the equivocal evidence for Late Postclassic obsidian working at the Pizarrín locality of the Tulancingo obsidian source area (Charlton and Spence 1982:29-34), all other evidence for craft activities in the Tulancingo city-state derives from one area south of Santiago Tulantepec, between 5 km and 12 km south of the city-state center.

Although other Late Postclassic communities have been reported in the Tulancingo Valley, the only intensive systematic surface survey was the last section of Route 3 of the TRP (figs. 9.3, 9.7). This section runs from the watershed between the Lake Tecocomulco Basin and the upper Metztitlan Valley to the edge of the modern town of Santiago Tulantepec, which is located on the edge of the permanently irrigated plain about 5 km south of Tulancingo (Charlton 1976, 1977a, 1978a; Charlton and Spence 1982:33-34; Sanders and Santley 1983:fig. 11.5).

Data from the TRP survey and collections reveal numerous Late Postclassic sites and anomalous, dense, but small (generally less than .2 ha) concentrations of obsidian in this area. The identifiable Late Postclassic sites located here range in size from 2 ha to 14 ha with the larger sites being located close to the edge of modern Tulantepec. Obviously there was a very dispersed population from the edge of the alluvial plain, up the mountains, to the watershed between there and the Lake Tecocomulco drainage. Two of the obsidian concentrations occur in sites with both Terminal Formative and Late Postclassic ceramics (106 and 109). The others are either aceramic (the majority) or Late Postclassic in date.

The sheer number and extent of obsidian concentrations in this rural section of the Tulancingo city-state reflect a very complex situation which is more reminiscent of the area between Tepeapulco and the watershed than the areas close to either Tepeapulco or Otumba. This complexity is further compounded by the number of obsidian source areas used, along with the extreme variation in their frequencies from concentration to concentration (Charlton 1977a:48). On the basis of densities, forms, and sources, I have argued that many of the

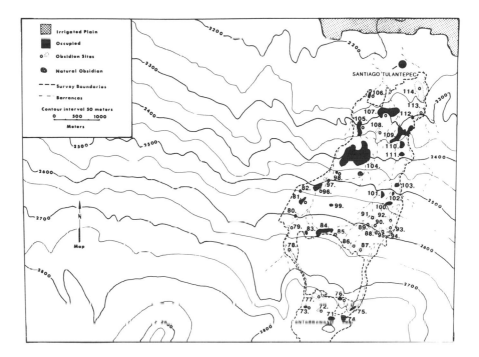

Fig. 9.7.   Late Aztec and aceramic archaeological sites in the Metztitlan Valley (Charlton 1976:19).

aceramic concentrations between Tepeapulco and Santiago Tulantepec are the remains of carrying sites (Charlton 1978a). A recent review of the materials by William J. Parry (personal communication 1993) suggests that some of these might be pre-Aztec camp sites with an emphasis on Tecocomulco obsidian. Most Late Postclassic sites have evidence for prismatic blade consumption, frequently emphasizing Pachuca obsidian.

Two sites, 91 (aceramic) and 108 (Late Postclassic), and one collection from site 104 (Late Postclassic), reflect early stages of the reduction of Tulancingo obsidian and lack finished tools (William J. Parry, personal communication, 1993). These are probably production or processing sites, also found between the Tecocomulco source area and Tepeapulco with an emphasis on Tecocomulco obsidian.

Only one type of craft activity seems to be associated with Late Postclassic sites in the Metztitlan Valley sites near Santiago Tulantepec. This is the initial reduction of Tulancingo obsidian, probably from the Pizarrín locality. So far the kind and destination(s) of the finished products are unknown. Obviously this pattern differs from those found at both Tepeapulco and Otumba. No other evidence for craft production was found in the rural Metztitlan Valley during the survey. Spindle whorls are conspicuous by their virtual absence suggesting limited involvement in spinning (but cf. Hicks, chap. 4).

COMPARISON AND DISCUSSION

Craft Production

Otumba, Tepeapulco, and Tulancingo were variably engaged in obsidian based craft activities. Precise comparisons are difficult, however, because of the extensive modern occupation covering the city-state center of Tepeapulco, the virtually complete destruction of that of Tulancingo, the existence of detailed surveys only in a small rural segment of the Tulancingo city-state, and the substantial number of aceramic, currently undatable, obsidian concentrations in both the Tepeapulco and Tulancingo city-states. Nevertheless, some comparisons are possible and potentially very useful.

Biface production appears to be a nonurban activity in two city-states. At Otumba the distances from the urban zone to the more distant biface workshops are greater than those at Tepeapulco, perhaps distorted by the proximity of the nearby Otumba obsidian source from which most Late Postclassic bifaces were made. Biface production in association with Late Postclassic occupation has not been identified in the Tulancingo city-state. However, taking into account the complex of sites located between Tepeapulco and Santiago Tulantepec, including the carrying sites—absent to the best of my knowledge from the Otumba city-state—it is quite possible that there was a much heavier exploitation of obsidian in these sections of the Tepeapulco and Tulancingo city-states, than in Otumba. In other words, there is evidence for a major focus on the exploitation of regional obsidian resources, materials from which circulated in local and regional trade and tribute networks. This is, of course, reflected in the greater number of obsidian source areas represented in the obsidian debris, both in the Tepeapulco Area and in the area near Santiago Tulantepec.

Prismatic core-blade production also occurred in two of the three city-states. At Otumba, core preparation and blade production appear to have been two aspects of a single operation, all occurrences of which were restricted to the city-state center. Other sites consumed blades but did not produce them (Parry 1990). Pachuca obsidian was preferred, but Otumba obsidian was also used. The pattern is different at Tepeapulco. There, obsidian from Pachuca, Otumba, and Tecocomulco was used in varying quantities for core-blade production in one large and several small workshops outside of the city-state center to the north, where cores were formed and blades removed. Other households, both north of Tepeapulco and within the city-state center, apparently produced prismatic blades from prepared cores of Pachuca obsidian, possibly for local consumption in as yet undefined activities. Such blades are present in quantities greater than those usually associated with domestic residences. In the Tulancingo city-state no core-blade workshops were defined although consumption was evident. More data from the Tulancingo city-state would be helpful, especially from near the city-state center where I suspect that core-blade workshops occurred if the Otumba, Tepeapulco, and Teotihuacan data (Spence 1984) reflect locational patterning for blade production. The few sites with evidence of obsidian craft activities reflect initial reduction of Pizarrín locality obsidians south of Santiago Tulantepec and may be related either to a ruralized and decentralized control of tool production for local consumption unlike that which occurs at Tepeapulco or Otumba or to the extensive trade in obsidian from various sources through this area.

Obviously all three city-states and the city-state of Teotihuacan (Spence 1984) share some general similarities in that obsidian-based lithic industries were well developed in each. Just as obviously there are some differences which suggest differential development and control over these craft industries. More impressive differences emerge, however, when other craft industries are examined. First, cotton and maguey fiber spinning occurred only within the Otumba and Tepeapulco city-states. At Tepeapulco, they were restricted to the city-state center and to sites within a 4-6 km radius of Tepeapulco itself, at a level of intensity equivalent to the rural area of the Otumba city-state. To the east, spindle whorls decline in frequency and rarely are found in the Tulancingo city-state. The only other potential craft industries occurred in the Tepeapulco city-state. These industries produced and consumed large quantities of prismatic blades or produced sherd discs. No additional craft industries have been identified in the Tulancingo city-state.

There are several questions to be examined. What was going on in the near and far northeastern Basin of Mexico during the Late Postclassic to result in such craft elaboration? Why were there both similarities and differences between city-states along this northeastern corridor? What were the roles of ecology, locational history, demography, and political and economic systems in their development? I shall address these four factors.

Ecology

The northeastern Basin of Mexico is generally of moderate to high risk for agricultural activities due to rainfall and temperature considerations (see also Sanders et al. 1979:81-84); at the same time the area is rich in obsidian deposits (Charlton 1978a; Charlton and Spence 1982). It is possible that this combination of agricultural unreliability and obsidian availability may have contributed to the elaborate development of nonagricultural craft production in this area during the Late Postclassic. Certainly this has been previously argued by Evans (1980, 1990) for Otumba, and by Nichols and Charlton (1988:9) for Otumba and Tepeapulco. It is reasonable to consider that such resources would not be ignored as part of economic diversification in a less than reliable environmental situation. It is unlikely, however, that ecological factors alone, although necessary, could be sufficient to account for such developments. They must be considered in combination with other factors.

Locational History

By looking at locational history I refer to the nature of pre-Aztec occupation in each of the three city-states. There had been a significant occupation in the Tepeapulco Area during the Teotihuacan period associated with obsidian exploitation, production, and trade (Matos M. et al. 1981; Charlton 1978a; Charlton and Spence 1982). The Epi-Teotihuacan period site of Huapalcalco, adjacent to Tulancingo, was heavily involved in obsidian exploitation, production, and trade (Charlton and Spence 1982; Gaxiola G. and Guevara H. 1989). Since their locations gave them access to trade routes and raw materials, these areas shared certain characteristics that had favored the prior development of political unit which emphasized nonagricultural production and trade.

   In contrast, the eastern Teotihuacan Valley, which shares these characteristics of routes and raw materials with Tulancingo and Tepeapulco, does not develop a regionally oriented, independent state based at least in part on nonagricultural production and trade until the emergence of the Otumba city-state during the Late Postclassic (Charlton 1981:7-8). Consequently, while ecological and historical-locational factors contribute to our understanding of these developments, they cannot explain them in all specific instances.

Demography

Demographic discussions are inextricably linked with ceramics, and ceramics in turn, with absolute dates of which few are available for the Postclassic period. If we were to plot the densities of Aztec II Black-on-Orange ceramics along a line from Xaltocan, through Teotihuacan, Otumba, Tepeapulco, and Santiago Tulantepec, the densities would decline from west to east until virtually none are found in the Tulancingo city-state. Most of the area with which I am concerned appears to have lacked a substantial population associated with Aztec II style ceramics. In Otumba and Tepeapulco this indicates a population loss after the fall of Tollan (ca. A.D. 1150) and a gradual reoccupation beginning with Aztec II ceramics.

There does not at the moment appear to be a local ceramic phase falling between Mazapan and Aztec II ceramics in either the Otumba or Tepeapulco city-states. In the Tulancingo city-state, the local ceramic sequence still needs to be defined for the period following Huapalcalco and before the appearance of Aztec II ceramics. I believe, however, that a local ceramic tradition did develop there after the Epi-Teotihuacan occupation at Huapalcalco, subsequently co-existing with Aztec II, III, and IV ceramics of the Late Postclassic and Early Colonial periods. Thus, there was population continuity within this city-state.

With the exception of the core-blade industry at Teotihuacan to the west of Otumba (Spence 1984) and possibly the core-blade industry at Otumba, there seems to be no evidence for incipient craft industries in any of the city-states at this time. The ceramics definitely associated with all of the industries are Late Aztec III and Early Colonial Aztec III and IV. The main population growth in all three city-states occurred in association with Aztec III ceramics.

Craft industries in Tulancingo, Tepeapulco, and Otumba are positively correlated with population growth. Certainly this correlation may have had a certain degree of causality, working in association with ecological and historical-locational factors to bring about an emphasis on nonagricultural productivity in areas with restricted agricultural productivity, available resources, and good routes to other areas. Local population growth may have prompted and absorbed some of the output. Nevertheless, from what we know of the extent of obsidian crafts in all three city-states—fiber crafts at Otumba and Tepeapulco, and lapidary, groundstone, and clay crafts at Otumba—much of the production must have been destined for consumers outside the city-states (Charlton 1978a; Nichols, chap. 7; Otis Charlton, chap. 8).

Population growth as a factor in the development of these craft industries, must be understood as population growth throughout the Basin of Mexico and not just within the local context.

Some of the differences in intensity and variety of craft activities present in the three city-states may also be understood in the context of the sequence of population growth and the relative proximity of each to areas of dense population. If, as I suspect, population growth occurred first in the Otumba city-state, and slightly later in the Tepeapulco city-state, the initial increase in local demand for craft products would have priority at Otumba. In addition Otumba was closer to the main population centers of the Basin, and growth there would also have increased demand for craft products. Tepeapulco, on the other hand, would have experienced the impact of local population growth later. This priority in increased demand might then be related to the obviously much greater intensification of a broad range of craft activities at Otumba. If correct I would expect to find a similar level of such activities in the city-state of Teotihuacan where Spence (1984) has described Early and Late Aztec core-blade production consistent with such expectations.

The development of craft industries in the Tulancingo city-state along quite different lines would have been affected by locational factors, including distance from the Basin of Mexico population centers, maintenance of a pre-existing system of obsidian exploitation, production, and trade, and stronger links to areas to the east and north. The obsidian craft industry at Tulancingo clearly differs from that at Tepeapulco and Otumba. In addition there is virtually no archaeological evidence for the integration of this area into the Basin of Mexico cloth economy. Jerome Offner (1983:15), however, lists *mantas* among Tulancingo's preconquest tribute.

Although ecological, locational-historical, and demographic factors contributed to Late Postclassic heterogeneity in the development of nonagricultural craft production in the northeastern Basin of Mexico, the expansion of political systems from the central Basin of Mexico provided a broader context and additional motivation for these developments.

Political Systems

Beginning in the middle of the fourteenth century, the Acolhua and the Tepaneca sought to consolidate power within the Basin and to extend it outside of that region. Although the details vary, historical records indicate competing Acolhua and Tepaneca interests in Otumba, Tepeapulco, and Tulancingo. It is possible that the limited amounts of Aztec II ceramics found in all three city-states reflect this early political expansion. If so, the expansion must have been directed more toward the acquisition of raw materials than finished products since developed craft activities are not associated with Aztec II ceramics in these city-states. As noted above, the city-state of Teotihuacan on the western edge of the area under consideration does have evidence for core-blade production associated with Aztec II ceramics (Spence 1984) indicative of production in an area near the major population build-up.

At the same time, if Aztec III ceramics began to replace Aztec II ceramics during the last half of the fourteenth century, their distribution could reflect some type of economic integration that might have preceded, accompanied, or even operated independently of the early attempts at political domination by the Acolhua and Tepaneca. An additional marker of such economic integration could be Texcoco Fabric-marked pottery used in salt making and transport and found widely throughout all three city-states. The presence of this type of pottery would indicate the movement of products from the central Basin of Mexico to the areas under discussion. At this time then, prior to the formation of the Triple Alliance, an economic integration of disparate regional economies, through local and regional markets, trade, and tribute systems, would have provided the framework for craft intensification in the northeast, building on the pre-existing systems. The political impact on the economy of each city-state would have been conditioned by the structure of the pre-existing economic system, which in turn would have been heavily influenced by ecological, historical-locational, and demographic factors.

The formation and expansion of the Triple Alliance continued, in a more stable form, the political context for craft intensification. Acolhua influence was paramount throughout the area under consideration (Offner 1983:10-18). Otumba's development of craft production was the most spectacular. Location near the main population centers in the Basin and a slight demographic priority gave Otumba a developmental edge once the political system stabilized. Otumba's industries were variably integrated into (1) local, regional, and inter-regional markets, (2) trade, and (3) tribute for raw material acquisition and product distribution (see Otis Charlton, chap. 8). Unlike the city-states in the central Basin of Mexico Otumba's nonagricultural economy flourished. Such development was similar to that which occurred in Teotihuacan's obsidian industry to the west, as described by Spence (1984).

Craft industry development at Tepeapulco took a different trajectory, due in part to a greater impact of historical-locational factors and the slight lag in population growth. Heir to a tradition of the manufacture and export of obsidian tools from the area, Tepeapulco functioned within the context of local, regional, and inter-regional markets, trade, and tribute outside of the central Basin of Mexico (Charlton and Spence 1982:73). At the same time craft production by the general population of the city-state was integrated into the Acolhua tribute system through the spinning and weaving of cotton and maguey fibers at a low level of intensity within a household context.

Craft industry development in the Tulancingo city-state was apparently the least affected by the political expansion of the Acolhua. Distance from the central Basin of Mexico meant that local factors of ecology, demography, and locational history remained more important. Also heir to a long tradition of obsidian exploitation, production, and trade (Hassig 1985:114), Tulancingo focused on three nearby source areas and was integrated into local, regional, and inter-regional market, trade, and tribute systems (Charlton and Spence 1982:73). Spindle whorls, markers of integration into the Acolhua politically-based tribute system, are absent from the area surveyed in the TRP (but cf. Hicks, chap. 4).

CONCLUSION

The three city-states of Otumba, Tepeapulco, and Tulancingo, located in the Acolhua hinterland of the northeastern Basin of Mexico and the adjacent Metztitlan Valley, demonstrate the existence of impressive, but regionally varied, nonagricultural craft production during the Late Postclassic. These include obsidian core-blade and biface production at Otumba and Tepeapulco, as well as at Teotihuacan, along with early stages of obsidian reduction at Tulancingo. Other craft activities include cotton and maguey fiber spinning (and presumably weaving) in Otumba and Tepeapulco, lapidary, groundstone, and ceramic production (figurines, spindle whorls, censers, and local pottery) at Otumba.

When taken in context with the other areas of the Basin of Mexico, it is readily apparent that there was economic heterogeneity, rather than homogeneity, in the Basin economic system at this time. This was evident both in the relative intensities of craft production in different areas of the Basin and in the varied systems—market, trade, and tribute—with their local regional, and inter-regional linkages, which integrated the Basin and regional economies. Although it is tempting to attribute the development of the Late Postclassic economic system to political decisions about conquest and economic administration (cf. Brumfiel 1991:191-193), political systems constitute only one set of relevant factors.

The political system provides the context for the economic system and, therefore, provided opportunities for and demands on craftsmen. It is not all-determinant. Rather it is best viewed as a shell within which opportunities are presented and exploited, but in which regional factors such as ecology, locational history, and demography continue to exert important influences on the state dimensions of the economy.

ACKNOWLEDGMENTS

My research within the three city-states discussed in this paper has been carried out since 1966 with the support of numerous agencies and the help of many individuals. The National Science Foundation has supported research in the Otumba city-state through three research grants (GS-2080, 1968-1972, [PCDP], and BNS-871-9665, 1988-1990, [OP], T. H. Charlton, Principal Investigator, and BNS-871-8140, 1988-1990, D. L. Nichols, Principal Investigator, [OP]). The National Endowment for the Humanities has supported research in the Otumba city-state through four research grants to Thomas H. Charlton as Principal Investigator (RO-21447-75-138, 1975-1977, [TRP], RO-20173-81-2231, 1982-1983, [PCDP], RO-21705-88, 1989, [OP], and RO-22268-91, 1992-1993, [OP]). The Trade Route Project [TRP], supported by the NEH, (1975-1977), included the city-states of Tepeapulco and Tulancingo. Other agencies supporting my research include the Canada Council (1966), the Associated Colleges of the Midwest (1967), and the University of Iowa through a Research Assignment (1975), three Developmental Assignments (1982, 1988, 1993), four Old Gold Summer Faculty Research Fellowships (1968, 1970, 1980, 1985), and many small but vital awards of research funds from the Graduate College under the leadership of D. C. Spriestersbach.

Deborah L. Nichols received support for the Otumba Project from the Claire Garber Goodman Fund, the Dartmouth Class of 1962, and the Dartmouth Faculty Research Committee.

William J. Parry reviewed an earlier draft of this paper and made some helpful suggestions; he also provided me with summary information from his reanalysis of the Trade Route obsidian. I, of course, am responsible for all interpretations presented here.

Of the many individuals who have participated in the projects upon which this paper is based I especially wish to thank two whose continuity has been essential to the success of the various projects, Evaristo Tenorio Coronel of San Salvador Cuahtlacingo, Estado de México, and Cynthia Otis Charlton. Their contributions in the field, during analyses, and while formulating this paper have been extremely insightful and valuable. I would also like to acknowledge the important collaborative contributions of Deborah L. Nichols during the on-going Otumba project.

Studies of materials from all three city-states continued during 1992 and 1993, supported by the National Endowment for the Humanities, the University of Iowa, Dartmouth College, and the Missouri University Research Reactor Facility. Those participating include Martin F. Biskowski, Emily McClung de Tapia, Cynthia Otis Charlton, and William J. Parry.

All field and laboratory research was carried out under the authorization of permits issued by the Instituto Nacional de Antropología e Historia and with the active support of members of the Departamento de Monumentos Prehispánicos, the Dirección de Arqueología, and the Consejo de Arqueología.

All figures were prepared by Cynthia Otis Charlton.

REFERENCES CITED

Acuña, René (editor)
   1984-1987 *Relaciones Geográficas del siglo XVI.* 9 vols. Universidad Nacional Autónoma de México, Instituto de Investigaciones Antropológicas, Mexico City.

Brasdefer, Fernando Cortés de
   1978 *Asentamientos humanos: un análisis del patrón en el area de Calpulalpan, Tlaxcala.* 2 vols. Unpublished thesis, Escuela Nacional de Antropología e Historia, Instituto Nacional de Antropología e Historia, Mexico City.

Brodkey, Dale D.
   1978 Postconquest Settlement Patterns of the Otumba Area, Mexico. Manuscript on file at the Department of Anthropology, University of Iowa, Iowa City.

Brumfiel, Elizabeth M.
   1976 *Specialization and Exchange at the Late Postclassic (Aztec) Community of Huexotla, Mexico.* Ph.D. dissertation, Department of Anthropology, University of Michigan. University Microfilms, Ann Arbor.

   1980 Specialization, Market Exchange, and the Aztec State: A View from Huexotla. *Current Anthropology* 21:459-478.

1983   Aztec State Making: Ecology, Structure, and the Origin of the State. *American Anthropologist* 85:261-284.

1986   The Division of Labor at Xico: The Chipped Stone Industry. In *Economic Aspects of Prehispanic Highland Mexico,* edited by Barry L. Isaac, pp. 245-279. Research in Economic Anthropology, Supplement 2. JAI Press, Greenwich.

1987   Elite and Utilitarian Crafts in the Aztec State. In *Specialization, Exchange and Complex Societies,* edited by Elizabeth M. Brumfiel and Timothy K. Earle, pp. 102-118. Cambridge University Press, New York.

1991   Tribute and Commerce in Imperial Cities: The Case of Xaltocan, Mexico. In *Early State Economics,* edited by Henri J. M. Claessen and Pieter van de Velde, pp. 177-198. Transaction Publishers, New Brunswick.

Carrasco, Pedro
1963   Los caciques chichimecas de Tulancingo. *Estudios de Cultura Náhuatl* 4:85-91.

Charlton, Thomas H.
1969   Texcoco Fabric-Marked Pottery, Tlateles, and Salt-Making. *American Antiquity* 34:73-76.

1971a Informe sobre trabajos del laboratorio, enero-mayo, 1971. Report submitted to the Departamento de Monumentos Prehispánicos, Instituto Nacional de Antropología e Historia, Mexico City. Multilithed.

1971b Texcoco Fabric-Marked Pottery and Salt-Making: A Further Note. *American Antiquity* 36:217-218.

1972a *Post-Conquest Development in the Teotihuacan Valley, Mexico. Part I: Excavations.* Report No. 5, Office of the State Archaeologist, University of Iowa, Iowa City.

1972b Population Trends in the Teotihuacan Valley, A.D. 1400-1969. *World Archaeology* 4:106-123.

1975a Reconocimientos superficiales de rutas de intercambio prehispánico, primera parte: introducción, metodología, ruta No. 1. Report submitted to the Departamento de Monumentos Prehispánicos, Instituto Nacional de Antropología e Historia, Mexico City. Multilithed.

1975b Reconocimientos superficiales de rutas de intercambio prehispánico, segunda parte: ruta No. 2. Report submitted to the Departamento de Monumentos Prehispánicos, Instituto Nacional de Antropología, Mexico City. Multilithed.

1976   Reconocimientos superficiales de rutas de intercambio prehispánico, tercera parte: ruta No. 3. Report submitted to the Departamento de Monumentos Prehispánicos, Instituto Nacional de Antropología e Historia, Mexico City. Multilithed.

1977a Final Report of a Surface Survey of Preconquest Trade Networks in Mesoamerica. Report submitted to the Instituto Nacional de Antropología e Historia, Mexico City, and the National Endowment for the Humanities. Multilithed.

1977b Report on a Prehispanic Canal System, Otumba, Edo. de Mexico. Archaeological Investigations, August 10-19, 1977. Report submitted to the Instituto Nacional de Antropología e Historia, Mexico City. Multilithed.

1978a Teotihuacan, Tepeapulco and Obsidian Exploitation. *Science* 200:1227-1236.

1978b Investigaciones arqueológicas en el municipio de Otumba, temporada de 1978. 1a parte: resultos preliminares de los trabajos de campo, 1978. Report submitted to the Instituto Nacional de Antropología e Historia, Mexico City.

1979a Investigaciones arqueológicas en el municipio de Otumba, temporada de 1978. 2a parte: la cerámica. Report submitted to the Instituto Nacional de Antropología e Historia, Mexico City.

1979b Investigaciones arqueológicas en el Municipio de Otumba, temporada de 1978. 3a parte: la cerámica de superficie. Report submitted to the Instituto Nacional de Antropología e Historia, Mexico City.

1979c Investigaciones arqueológicas en el municipio de Otumba, temporada de 1978. 4a parte: la obsidiana de superficie. Report submitted to the Instituto Nacional de Antropología e Historia, Mexico City.

1979d Investigaciones arqueológicas en el municipio de Otumba, temporada de 1978. 5a parte: el riego y el intercambio: la expansión de Tula. Report submitted to the Instituto Nacional de Antropología e Historia, Mexico City.

1980   Comment on "Specialization, Market Exchange and the Aztec State: A View from Huexotla", by E. M. Brumfiel. *Current Anthropology* 21:468-469.

1981   Otumba: Archaeology and Ethnohistory. Paper presented at the 46th Annual Meeting of the Society for American Archaeology, San Diego.

1984   Urban Growth and Cultural Evolution from a Oaxacan Perspective. Review of *Monte Albán,* by Richard E. Blanton, and *Ancient Mesoamerica,* by Richard E. Blanton et al. *Reviews in Anthropology* 11:197-207.

1987   Otumba, México, reconocimientos de superficie del sitio de TA-80, Otumba. Informe Técnico Parcial 1. Report submitted to the Dirección de Monumentos Prehispánicos and to the Consejo de Arqueología, Instituto Nacional de Antropología e Historia, Mexico City.

1988   Otumba, México: reconocimientos de superficie del sitio de TA-80, Otumba. Informe Técnico Final. Report submitted to the Instituto Nacional de Antropología e Historia, Mexico City.

1990   Economics and Politics: the Case of Aztec Otumba. Paper presented at the 55th Annual Meeting of the Society for American Archaeology, Las Vegas.

1991   Land Tenure and Agricultural Production in the Otumba Region 1785-1803: Lands of the Indigenous Communities. In *Land and Politics in the Valley of Mexico,* edited by H. R. Harvey, pp. 223-263. University of New Mexico Press, Albuquerque.

Charlton, Thomas H., David C. Grove, and Philip K. Hopke
1978   The Paredon, Mexico, Obsidian Source and Early Formative Exchange. *Science* 201:807-809.

Charlton, Thomas H., and Deborah L. Nichols (editors)
1990   *Early State Formation Processes: The Aztec City-State of Otumba, Mexico, Part 1, Preliminary Report on Recent Research in the Otumba City-State.* Report

No. 3. Mesoamerican Research Colloquium, Department of Anthropology, University of Iowa, Iowa City.

Charlton, Thomas H., Deborah L. Nichols, and Cynthia Otis Charlton
1991   Aztec Craft Production and Specialization: Archaeological Evidence from the City-State of Otumba, Mexico. *World Archaeology* 23:98-114.

Charlton, Thomas H., and Michael W. Spence
1982   Obsidian Exploitation and Civilization in the Basin of Mexico. In *Mining and Mining Techniques in Ancient Mesoamerica,* edited by Phil C. Weigand and Gretchen Gwynne, pp. 7-86. Anthropology 4(1-2), State University of New York, Stony Brook.

Cowgill, George L.
1975   A Selection of Samplers: Comments on Archaeo-Statistics. In *Sampling in Archaeology,* edited by James W. Mueller, pp. 258-274. University Arizona Press, Tucson.

Davies, Nigel
1968   *Los señoríos independientes del imperio azteca.* Instituto Nacional de Antropología e Historia, Mexico City.

Evans, Susan T.
1980   *A Settlement System Analysis of the Teotihuacan Region, Mexico:* A.D. *1350-1520.* Ph.D. dissertation, Department of Anthropology, Pennsylvania State University, University Park. University Microfilms, Ann Arbor.

1988   Excavations at Cihuatecpan: An Aztec Village in the Teotihuacan Valley. *Vanderbilt University Publications in Anthropology* No. 36. Vanderbilt University, Nashville.

1990   The Productivity of Maguey Terrace Agriculture in Central Mexico During the Aztec Period. *Latin American Antiquity* 1:117-132.

García, Enriqueta
1968   Clima actual en Teotihuacán. In *Materiales para la arqueología de Teotihuacán,* edited by José Luis Lorenzo, pp. 9-28. Instituto Nacional de Antropología e Historia, Mexico City.

García Cook, Angel
1982   Análisis tipológico de artefactos. Instituto Nacional de Antropología e Historia, Mexico City.

García Cook, Angel, and Leonor Merino C.
1977   Notas sobre caminos y rutas de intercambio al este de la cuenca de México. *Comunicaciones* 14:71-82.

Gaxiola G., Margarita, and Jorge Guevara H.
1989   Un conjunto habitacional en Huapalcalco, Hgo., especializado en la talla de obsidiana. In *La obsidiana en Mesoamérica,* edited by Margarita Gaxiola G. and John E. Clark, pp. 227-242. Instituto Nacional de Antropología e Historia, Mexico City.

Gerhard, Peter
1972   *A Guide to the Historical Geography of New Spain.* Cambridge University Press, Cambridge.

Gibson, Charles

1956 Llamamiento General, Repartimiento, and the Empire of Acolhuacan. *His panic American Historical Review* 36:1-27.

Gould, Stephen J.

1986 Glow, Big Glowworm. *Natural History* 95 (12): 10-16.

Hassig, Ross

1985 *Trade, Tribute, and Transportation: The Sixteenth Century Political Economy of the Valley of Mexico.* University of Oklahoma Press, Norman.

1988 *Aztec Warfare: Imperial Expansion and Political Control.* University of Oklahoma Press, Norman.

Jones, David M.

1977 *Nineteenth Century Haciendas and Ranchos of Otumba and Apan, Basin of Mexico.* Unpublished Ph.D. dissertation, University of London.

Lizardi Ramos, César

1957 Arquitectura de Huapalcalco, Tulancingo. *Revista Mexicana de Estudios Antropológicos* 14(2):111-115.

1958 Arqueología del valle de Tulancingo. *Cuadernos Americanos* 98:107-126.

1960 El patio más antiguo de Mesoamérica. In *Men and Cultures,* edited by Anthony F. C. Wallace, pp. 618-626. Selected Papers of the 5th International Congress of Anthropological and Ethnological Sciences. University of Pennsylvania Press, Philadelphia.

López Aguilar, Fernando

1988 Tepeapulco como "centro provincial" del clásico y del postclásico. *Arqueología* 4:77-97.

Lorenzo, José Luis

1968 Clima y agricultura en Teotihuacán. In *Materiales para la arqueología de Teotihuacán,* edited by José Luis Lorenzo, pp. 51-72. Instituto Nacional de Antropología e Historia, Mexico City.

Maldonado-Koerdell, Manuel

1964 Geohistory and Paleogeography of Middle America. In *Natural Environment and Early Cultures,* edited by Robert C. West, pp. 3-32. Handbook of Middle American Indians, vol. 1, Robert Wauchope, general editor. University of Texas Press, Austin.

Mather, William G.

1968 *The Aztec State of Otumba, Mexico: An Ethno-Historical Settlement Pattern Study.* Unpublished Master's thesis, Department of Anthropology, Pennsylvania State University, University Park.

Matos Moctezuma, Eduardo, María Teresa García García, Fernando López Aguilar, and Ignacio Rodríguez García

1981 Proyecto Tepeapulco: resumen preliminar de las actividades realizadas en la primera temporada de trabajo. In *Interacción cultural en México central,* edited by Evelyn Childs Rattray, Jaime Litvak King, and Clara Díaz Oyarzabal, pp. 113-148. Instituto de Investigaciones Antropológicas. Universidad Nacional Autónoma de México, Mexico City

Millon, René
1973 The Teotihuacan Map, Part 1, Text. In *Urbanization at Teotihuacan, Mexico, vol. 1: The Teotihuacan Map,* edited by René Millon. University of Texas Press, Austin.

Mora López, Raziel
1980 Proyecto: arqueología del sureste de Hidalgo, subproyecto: arqueología de area-recorrido arqueológico sistemático de superficie. Informe preliminar de trabajo al Consejo de Arqueología del Instituto Nacional de Antropología e Historia, Temporada 1978-1979. Manuscript on file at the Department of Anthropology, University of Iowa, Iowa City.

Müller, Florencia Jacobs
1957 El valle de Tulancingo. *Revista Mexicana de Estudios Antropológicos* 14(2):129-137.

1960 The Preclassic Ceramic Sequence of Huapalcalco, of Tulancingo, Hgo. In *Men and Cultures,* edited by Anthony F. C. Wallace, pp. 601-617. Selected Papers of the 5th International Congress of Anthropological and Ethnological Sciences. University of Pennsylvania Press, Philadelphia.

1963 Exploración arqueológica en Huapalcalco, Hgo. quinta Temporada, 1959. *Anales* (6a) 15:75-97. Instituto Nacional de Antropología e Historia, Mexico City.

Müller, Florencia Jacobs, and César Lizardi Ramos
1959 La pirámide 6 de Huapalcalco, Hidalgo, México. In *Proceedings of the 33rd International Congress of Americanists* (San José, Costa Rica) 2:146-157.

Nichols, Deborah L., and Thomas H. Charlton
1988 Processes of State Formation: Core versus Periphery in the Late Postclassic Basin of Mexico. Paper presented at the 53rd Annual Meeting of the Society for American Archaeology, Phoenix.

Nichols, Deborah L., Thomas H. Charlton, Cynthia Otis Charlton, and Evaristo Tenorio Coronel
1990 The Intensive Surveys and Surface Collections, 1988. In *Early State Formation Processes: The Aztec City-State of Otumba, Mexico, Part 1, Preliminary Report on Recent Research in the Otumba City-State,* edited by Thomas H. Charlton and Deborah L. Nichols, pp. 11-28. Report No. 3. Mesoamerican Research Colloquium, Department of Anthropology, University of Iowa, Iowa City.

Nicholson, Henry B.
1974 Tepepolco, the Locale of the First Stage of Fr. Bernardino de Sahagún's Great Ethnographic Project: Historical and Cultural Notes. In *Mesoamerican Archaeology: New Approaches,* edited by Norman Hammond, pp. 145-154. University of Texas Press, Austin.

Noguera, Eduardo
1970 Exploraciones estratigráficas en Xochimilco, Tulancingo y Cerro de la Estrella. *Anales de Antropología* 7:91-130.

Offner, Jerome A.
1980 Archival Reports of Poor Crop Yields in the Early Postconquest Texcocan

Heartland and their Implications for Studies of Aztec Period Population. *American Antiquity* 45:848-856.

1983 *Land and Politics in Aztec Texcoco.* Cambridge University Press, Cambridge.

Otis Charlton, Cynthia

1993 Obsidian as Jewelry: Lapidary Production in Aztec Otumba, Mexico. *Ancient Mesoamerica* 4:231-243.

Otis Charlton, Cynthia, Thomas H. Charlton, and Deborah L. Nichols

1993 Aztec Household-Based Craft Production: Archaeological Evidence from the City-State of Otumba, Mexico. In *Prehispanic Domestic Units in Western Mesoamerica: Studies of the Household, Compound, and Residence,* edited by Robert S. Santley and Kenneth G. Hirth, pp. 147-171. CRC Press, Boca Raton.

Parry, William J.

1990 Analysis of Chipped Stone Artifacts from Otumba (TA-80) and Neighboring Rural Sites in the Eastern Teotihuacan Valley of Mexico. In *Early State Formation Processes: The Aztec City-State of Otumba, Mexico, Part 1, Preliminary Report on Recent Research in the Otumba City-State,* edited by Thomas H. Charlton and Deborah L. Nichols, pp. 73-88. Report No. 3. Mesoamerican Research Colloquium, Department of Anthropology, University of Iowa, Iowa City.

Sanders, William T.

1956 The Central Mexican Symbiotic Region. In *Prehistoric Settlement Patterns in the New World,* edited by Gordon R. Willey, pp. 115-127. Viking Fund Publications in Anthropology No. 23. Wenner Gren Foundation for Anthropological Research, New York.

1965 *Cultural Ecology of the Teotihuacan Valley.* Unpublished report to the Wenner Gren Foundation for Anthropological Research, New York. Manuscript on file at the Department of Sociology and Anthropology, Pennsylvania State University, University Park.

1971 Settlement Patterns in Central Mexico. In *Archaeology of Northern Mesoamerica,* pt. 1, edited by Gordon F. Ekholm and Ignacio Bernal, pp. 3-44. Handbook of Middle American Indians, vol. 10, Robert Wauchope, general editor. University of Texas Press, Austin.

Sanders, William T., Jeffrey R. Parsons, and Robert S. Santley

1979 *The Basin of Mexico: Ecological Process in the Evolution of a Civilization.* Academic Press, New York.

Sanders, William T., and Robert S. Santley

1983 A Tale of Three Cities: Energetics and Urbanization in Pre-Hispanic Central Mexico. In *Prehistoric Settlement Patterns: Essays in Honor of Gordon R. Willey,* edited by Evon Z. Vogt and Richard M. Leventhal, pp. 243-291. University of New Mexico Press, Albuquerque.

Snow, Elizabeth F., and Michael E. Snow

1970 Report on the Second Season of Archaeological Investigations in the

Tulancingo Valley, Hidalgo, Mexico. Report submitted to the Instituto Nacional de Antropología e Historia, Mexico City.

Snow, Michael E., and Elizabeth F. Snow
1968   Archaeological Investigations at Huapalcalco, Hidalgo. Report submitted to the Instituto Nacional de Antropología e Historia, Mexico City.

1969   Report on the First Season of Archaeological Investigations in the Tulancingo Valley, Hidalgo, Mexico. Report submitted to the Instituto Nacional de Antropología e Historia, Mexico City.

Spence, Michael W.
1984   Specialized Production in Rural Aztec Society: Obsidian Workshops of the Teotihuacan Valley. In *Contributions to the Archaeology and Ethnohistory of Greater Mesoamerica,* edited by William J. Folan, pp. 76-125. Southern Illinois University Press, Carbondale.

Tamayo, Jorge L., in collaboration with Robert C. West
1964   The Hydrography of Middle America. In *Natural Environment and Early Cultures,* edited by Robert C. West, pp. 84-121. Handbook of Middle American Indians, vol. 1, Robert Wauchope, general editor. University of Texas Press, Austin.

Tolstoy, Paul
1958   *Surface Survey of the Northern Valley of Mexico: The Classic and Post-Classic Periods.* Transactions of the American Philosophical Society 48(5). Philadelphia.

Vivó Escoto, Jorge A.
1964   Weather and Climate of Mexico and Central America. In *Natural Environment and Early Cultures,* edited by Robert C. West, pp. 187-215. Handbook of Middle American Indians, vol. 1, Robert Wauchope, general editor. University of Texas Press, Austin.

West, Robert C.
1964a Surface Configuration and Associated Geology of Middle America. In *Natural Environments and Early Cultures,* edited by Robert C. West, pp. 33-83. Handbook of Middle American Indians, vol. 1, Robert Wauchope, general editor. University of Texas Press, Austin.

1964b The Natural Regions of Middle America. In *Natural Environments and Early Cultures,* edited by Robert C. West, pp. 363-383. Handbook of Middle American Indians, vol. 1, Robert Wauchope, general editor. University of Texas Press, Austin.

Wiltfang, Daniel A.
1975   *Aztec and Postconquest Spindle Whorls of the Teotihuacan Valley, Mexico: Markers of Technological Change.* Master's thesis, Department of Anthropology, University of Iowa, Iowa City.

10

Late Postclassic Salt Production and Consumption in the Basin of Mexico

Some Insights from Nexquipayac

Jeffrey R. Parsons

The production and distribution of salt has been of great economic and sociopolitical significance in preindustrial society (e.g., Bloch 1963; Multhauf 1978). In Europe, Africa, North America, and Asia, preindustrial saltmaking has long been the subject of intensive ethnographic, historical, and archaeological studies (e.g., Aggarwall 1976; Brown 1980; de Brisay and Evans 1975; Keslin 1964; Lovejoy 1986; Muller 1984; Nenquin 1961; Potts 1984; Riehm 1961; Sun Ying-Hsing 1966; Willeman 1889; Zwehtkoff 1888). Similarly, scholars working throughout Mesoamerica have documented the importance of salt production and exchange in prehispanic, colonial, and modern times (e.g., Andrews 1983; Berdan 1975; Besso-Oberto 1980; Ewald 1985; Hewitt et al. 1987; MacKinnon and Kepecs 1989; McVicker 1969; Mendizabal 1946; Moriarity 1968; Peterson 1976; Quijada 1984; Reina and Monaghan 1981; Seager 1867; Sisson 1973).

The Basin of Mexico, with its huge reservoir of salt in and around saline Lake Texcoco (fig. 10.1), has long been recognized as an especially important locus of salt production and consumption: several sixteenth-century documentary sources describe the highlights of salt production and distribution on the eve of the Spanish conquest and in the early post-conquest decades (Gibson 1964; Ivanhoe 1978; Martyr 1628; Sahagún 1969); several nineteenth and twen-

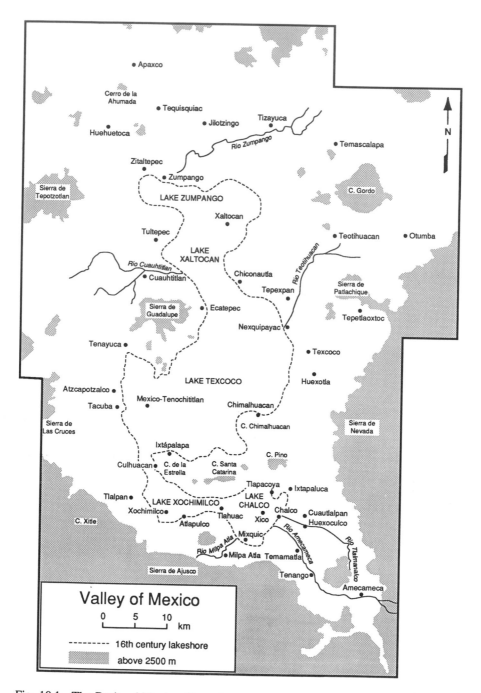

Fig. 10.1. The Basin of Mexico. Nexquipayac and important Postclassic communities are shown.

tieth century writers observed later manifestations of the traditional processes (Apenes 1944; Humboldt 1811; Orozco y Berra 1864); and archaeological studies have illuminated some aspects of prehispanic saltmaking (Baños 1980; Blanton 1972; Charlton 1969, 1971; Mayer-Oakes 1959; Noguera 1975; Parsons 1971; Sanchez 1987; Sanders et al. 1979; Talavera 1979; Tolstoy 1958; Vaillant 1930).

Archaeological surveys during the 1960s and 1970s have located a series of probable Postclassic saltmaking sites around the edges of former Lakes Texcoco and Zumpango (Blanton 1972; Parsons 1971; Sanders et al. 1979). These sites are usually recognized on the basis of irregular mounding (presumably produced in the course of saltmaking) and heavy concentrations of fabric-marked pottery (presumably used in the manufacture and packaging of salt). Two sixteenth-century sources provide important additional insights into what may have happened at these sites:

> They go from Ixtapalapa to Tenustitan [Tenochtitlan] ... upon a wall of stone. ... The cities adjoining to the bridge make salt, which all the nations of the country use. Of the salt water of the lake, they make it harde, conveying it by trenches into the earth to thicken it. And, being hardened and congealed they boil it, and after make it into round lumps or balls, to be conveyed to markets or fairs for exchange of foreign commodities. (Martyr 1628:188)

> The seller of salt is a salt producer or a salt retailer. The salt producer gathers [salty] earth, hills it up, wets it, distils, makes brine, makes ollas for salt, cooks it. The salt retailer displays salt. He sets out on the road, travels with it, goes from market to market, makes use of markets, sells salt. He sells salt balls, salt bars, salt ollas— thick, clean, full-bodied; like white chalk; of good taste, savory; tasting of lime, bitter ...; tasteless, insipid salt, salty, very salty, briny. He sells thin bars of salt. ... (Sahagún 1950-1982:bk.10:84)

In 1940 Ola Apenes (1944) described salt production at San Cristobal Nexquipayac, a village of some 900 inhabitants on the northeastern shore of Lake Texcoco (figs. 10.1 and 10.2). Even at that time Nexquipayac was the last locality in the Basin of Mexico with any significant involvement in saltmaking. Apenes described a process of filtering water through salty earth that had been placed inside a conical pit dug into the ground. The water then trickled slowly downward through the earth-filled pit and through a narrow cane tube leading out from the base of the pit into a ceramic jar. Apenes (1944:37) also described a simpler saltmaking process still in operation on the lakeshore near Nexquipayac in which the salt that formed naturally on the surface of shallow saline ponds

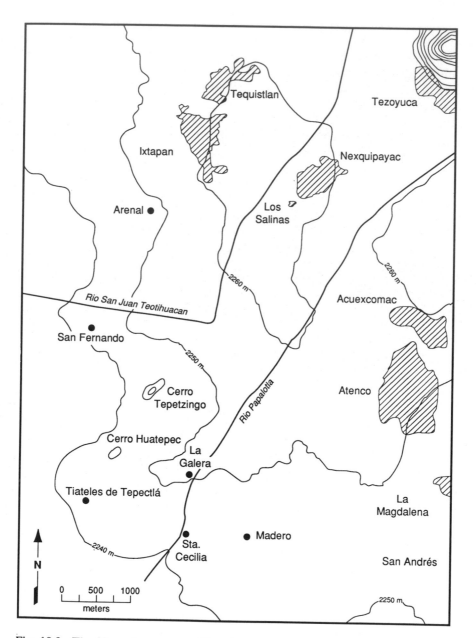

Fig. 10.2. The Nexquipayac area. The six sources of saline soil used by modern saltmakers are indicated with filled circles.

Fig. 10.3. Texcoco Fabric-Marked Pottery.

was collected: "Sometimes special ponds are dug, in which the agua salada is allowed to evaporate under the sun."

In 1967, during the course of archaeological surveys in the Texcoco Region, JoAnn Moran and I made some brief observations at Nexquipayac (Moran 1967; Parsons 1971). We found that saltmaking still continued there, apparently identical to that described earlier by Apenes. We were especially interested to note that the leached earth from the pits was discarded in the immediate vicinity of the workshops. It became clear to us that over the years this discarding of leached soil had produced the huge earth mounds that underlay the entire saltmaking area at Nexquipayac. We concluded that a comparable process had formed the prehispanic saltmaking sites around the edges of Lake Texcoco. It subsequently became known that the fabric-marked pottery so common at many of these lakeshore saltmaking sites (fig. 10.3) also occurred in very small quantities at Middle and Late Postclassic archaeological sites throughout the Basin of Mexico. This suggested that in later Postclassic times the salt produced on the lakeshore was packaged and widely distributed in containers made of this crude fabric-marked ceramic ware.

Despite the general knowledge about the importance of Postclassic saltmaking in the Basin of Mexico, there is still little specific information about this activity, especially for earlier periods of prehistory for which the ethnohistoric sources are much less helpful and for which there does not appear to have been a distinctive, specialized type of pottery (analogous to Texcoco Fabric Marked) associated with saltmaking. Although several recent studies have greatly clarified our understanding of late prehispanic saltmaking in the Basin of Mexico (e.g., Baños 1980; Sanchez 1987; Talavera 1979), we do not yet fully understand how fabric-marked pottery was actually used; or how salt was actually made (for example, were boiling techniques used, or was most production done by solar evaporation?); or how much human labor and fuel saltmaking consumed; or what levels of salt output may have been feasible; or whether saltmaking was a seasonal occupation; or how saltmaking was organized (i.e., was salt produced by generalists or by specialists, and to what extent did salt enter into market exchange and/or tribute?); or what changes may have occurred in all these parameters over time.

It was with these kinds of questions in mind that I decided to undertake in 1988 a detailed ethnographic study of the last remnants of traditional saltmaking at Nexquipayac. I felt that because most archaeologists had such a limited understanding of traditional saltmaking in the Basin of Mexico, it was difficult for them to develop a good understanding of either the technology or the sociology of salt production and distribution. Basically, I wanted to use new ethnographic data to help go beyond the limits of our present ability to understand prehispanic saltmaking. To this end, I spent five weeks at Nexquipayac during July and August 1988. My immediate objective was to record the details of a dying traditional craft in order to provide archaeologists working in the Basin of Mexico (and perhaps elsewhere as well) with a better base from which to make inferences about prehispanic salt production, distribution, and consumption.

However, my larger concern in this study is prehispanic political economy in the Basin of Mexico. My hope is that a better understanding of the changing technology and organization of salt production and distribution in this region will provide new insights into the larger dynamics of prehispanic polity and economy. It seems to me that a study of salt production offers an unusually good way for an archaeologist working in the Basin of Mexico to approach this larger problem: although the end product (salt) is itself archaeologically invisible, the locus of its production is often unusually predictable and visible to the archaeologist. Furthermore, because salt was apparently packaged for transport in distinctive ceramic containers (at least during later Postclassic times), there is an unusually good possibility that archaeologists can trace the outlines of its distribution and consumption.

I am under no illusion that what I saw at Nexquipayac in 1988, or that what Apenes had observed there in 1940, can be projected directly back to the prehispanic era. Many technological, environmental, and organizational changes have greatly obscured the linkages across more than 450 years. If this ethnographic study is to have any applicability to archaeological research on prehispanic saltmaking, it must be considered squarely within the context of these historical changes.

A SYNOPSIS OF SALTMAKING AT NEXQUIPAYAC

Saltmaking at Nexquipayac involves six basic sequential steps: (1) collecting the soils whose salts are to be leached; (2) mixing the soils in the correct manner so as to produce one of the four desired end products (*sal blanca, sal negra, sal amarilla,* or saltpeter); (3) filtering water through the soil mixture in order to leach out the salts and concentrate them in a brine solution; (4) boiling the brine to obtain crystalline salt; (5) drying the crystalline salt; and (6) selling the dried salt. Long-term salt production requires three main kinds of overhead costs: (a) maintaining the workshop facilities; (b) securing access to sources of the appropriate soils; and (c) acquiring fuel for boiling operations.

Selecting, Procuring, and Mixing the Soils

Each of the four different crystalline end products requires different kinds of soils and different preparation techniques. There are two basic kinds of soil used in saltmaking: (1) various types of natural deposits that occur at and around the edges of the former lakebed at few kilometers to the west and south of Nexquipayac (fig. 10.2); and (2) various kinds of previously-leached soil that have accumulated at saltmaking workshops in and around the village (ranging in age from prehispanic to recent). The latter soils serve to "dilute" the strength of the lakeshore soils and thereby facilitate the crystallization process. I was told that if the lakeshore soils were used alone, the boiling process would produce only foam, and no salt crystals would form.

There are several different categories of lakeshore soils, each of which is identified on the basis of its color and taste. Each soil type is appropriate for making one of the two principal end products *(sal blanca)* and *(sal negra)*. Similarly, for each desired end product there is an appropriate type of leached workshop soil that must be mixed with the requisite lakeshore soil. The different categories of lakeshore and workshop soils are located and distinguished and combined on the basis of a truly formidable knowledge accumulated through

Fig. 10.4. Skimming off soil for saltmaking, at the San Fernando source.

years of practical experience. This knowledge and experience are absolutely essential to the success of saltmaking because even minor errors in judgement or procedure can seriously affect both the quality and quantity of salt production. It is important to realize that the appropriate lakeshore soils are not widely or uniformly distributed, but must be carefully searched out and located on the basis of substantial expertise. At the time of our study, there were only six known localities where suitable lakeshore soil could be obtained (fig. 10.2).

Once a lakeshore source is located, a shallow layer of soil, seldom more than 5 cm thick, is skimmed off the ground surface with a flat-bladed shovel (fig. 10.4). This soil is either piled up on the spot, to await future transport back to the workshop, or is loaded onto a burro cart or flat-bed truck for immediate transport to the workshop. The sources of lakeshore soils are generally 2-5 km from the workshops. Soil collecting and transport is preferably done during the dry season, but it can be performed any time of year, particularly if burro carts are used. If a flat-bed truck is used, one or two large loads, sufficient for many months or even the whole year, are typically brought into the workshop over a

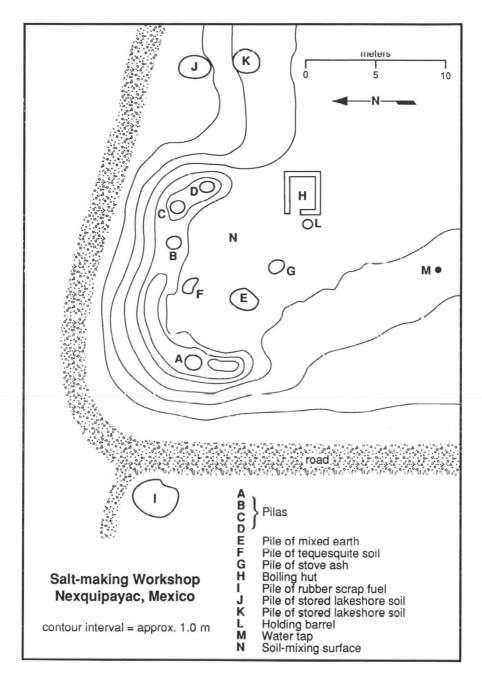

meters

0   5   10

N

road

**Salt-making Workshop
Nexquipayac, Mexico**

contour interval = approx. 1.0 m

A
B } Pilas
C
D
E Pile of mixed earth
F Pile of tequesquite soil
G Pile of stove ash
H Boiling hut
I Pile of rubber scrap fuel
J Pile of stored lakeshore soil
K Pile of stored lakeshore soil
L Holding barrel
M Water tap
N Soil-mixing surface

Fig. 10.5. Plan of saltmaking workshop, Nexquipayac.

Fig. 10.6. Mixing soil at saltmaking workshop, Nexquipayac.

short time span during the dry season. When carts are used, hauling must be done on a more piecemeal basis. We were told that prior to about 25-30 years ago no carts or trucks were used, and soil transport was done exclusively with burros carrying large bags of earth on their backs.

Most of the leached workshop soils needed for the soil mixtures are acquired from the immediate vicinity of the workshop itself, and so the transport and storage of these materials is logistically much simpler than for the lakeshore soils. In some cases, however, these leached workshop soils also must be acquired from more distant localities, and so their transport and storage are sometimes quite formidable.

Since the 1950s, with the rapid decline in the numbers of saltmakers at Nexquipayac and adjacent villages, there has been virtually no need to locate new lakeshore soil sources or to regulate the use of existing soil sources. At the present time the three surviving saltmakers are free to take whatever soil they need from sources located on the communal or *ejido* lands of several different local communities. However, until about 1950 these use-rights had to be secured and periodically renewed by means of an annual payment from each saltmaker to the appropriate local authorities.

Once the soils have been transported to the workshop, each soil type is physically segregated and covered with a plastic sheet to protect it from rainfall (in some cases the earth is simply bagged in large plastic sacks). We were told that in the pre-plastic era (i.e., prior to about 20 years ago) soil was stored at the workshops in small adobe huts. Appropriate quantities and proportions of the different soils are then mixed together, as required, on a hard-packed earth surface in the central part of the workshop area (figs. 10.5 and 10.6). The mixing operation is performed with a flat-bladed shovel and involves carefully turning over and intermixing all the component soils. Thorough mixing is critically important for consistent and dependable production.

Fig. 10.7. Loading mixed soil into a *pila,* Nexquipayac.

Leaching the Soil Mixture

The soil mixture is then loaded into one or more conical pits *(pilas)*, which measure about 40-50 cm deep and 90-100 cm in diameter at the ground surface (fig. 10.7), that have been dug into the banks of discarded previously-leached earth that surround the mixing surfaces at all workshops (fig. 10.8). A typical *pila* load contains between 120-140 kg of dry earth mixture. The earth is carefully packed down inside the *pila,* and after that between 108-126 liters of clean water are gradually poured into it. Packing the soil inside the *pila* is another important procedure which must be correctly performed for successful

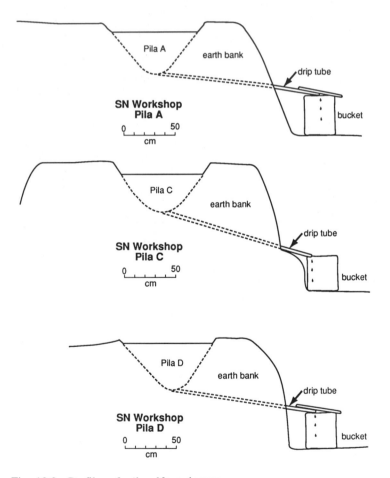

Fig. 10.8. Profiles of *pilas,* Nexquipayac.

Fig. 10.9. Loaded *pila* in operation, Nexquipayac.

salt production: If the soil mixture is too tightly packed in the *pila*, then filtration will be too slow, and the resulting brine will be too saline, and/or the crystalline salt will be too dark in color; if the packing is too loose, then the filtration will be too rapid, and the brine less saline than necessary.

The water slowly filters down through the packed soil in the *pila*, leaching out the salts, and finally drains downward through a long cane tube that exits from the bottom of the *pila* and empties into a container (plastic, metal, or ceramic) (fig. 10.9). This filtration takes about 20 hours to complete, and each *pila* load generally produces about 30-35 liters of concentrated brine.

Boiling, Drying, and Selling

The brine is then poured into a large metal pan *(paila)* that rests atop a brick oven (fig. 10.10) inside a small adobe hut. A fire of scrap rubber is kindled inside the oven and continues to be supplied with fuel over the course of the next 1.5-2.0 hours while the brine is boiled to produce crystalline salt. This

Fig. 10.10. Boiling leached brine, Nexquipayac.

boiling operation demands constant attention and mental concentration to keep the boiling moderate and even by means of carefully and continuously adding small quantities of fuel (too rapid boiling will cause the salt crystals to deposit as a hard layer on the bottom of the pan). When the crystallization is judged to be complete, the dripping-wet solid salt is then scooped out of the boiling pan and placed on a coarse piece of cloth. The cloth rests atop a specially prepared drying bed formed of earth and ash in one corner of the boiling hut, or just outside the hut's entrance. The salt dries there overnight, and the next day is removed and put into a large basket that is kept in the saltmaker's residence. On Saturday, the accumulated salt from the previous week's production is sold, most of it within the local community or at a nearby market.

Maintenance of Facilities

The primary maintenance connected with salt production involves the conical leaching pit *(pila)*, the metal boiling pan *(paila)*, and (at longer intervals)

Fig. 10.11. Removing leached soil from *pila,* Nexquipayac.

the boiling hut. I was told that each *pila* lasts for about five years. It must be dug, lined with salt-free clay about 3-4 cm thick, and the hole for its drip-tube punched through the earth bank with a long iron rod. After each 20-hour filtration sequence, the leached earth must be removed from the pit (taking care not to damage the clay liner). This leached earth is tossed to one side (fig. 10.11), and over the course of years, it is this discarded earth which builds up the large earth mounds that underlie and surround the saltmaking workshops. The clay liner must then be smoothed and resurfaced (using a soft scraper made of an old hard-rubber shoe sole) (fig. 10.12), and then covered with a thin layer of ash (taken from the boiling oven). This ash layer prevents the clay from sticking to the compacted soil mixture that will soon be loaded into the *pila.*

The sheet metal boiling pans usually last for about three years before they rust through. Some care must betaken to wash the pan thoroughly after each use so that accumulated salts do not corrode the sheet metal too quickly.

Fig. 10.12. Resurfacing *pila,* Nexquipayac.

The boiling hut is essential to protect the saltmaker during bad weather and to prevent wind-blown dust and other impurities from mixing with the boiling brine or the drying salt. These huts are always made from adobe bricks, with a flat roof formed of wooden posts, leafy thatch, and scraps of sheet metal. Under normal circumstances the main structure of a well-built hut will last for many years, but the flat roof and chimney are particularly vulnerable to weathering and collapse and so must be extensively repaired or replaced every few years.

Fuels

Prior to about 1970, almost all saltmaking was carried out using local organic fuels for boiling. The main fuels (in approximate order of importance) were (1) dried maize roots from harvested agricultural fields, (2) bushy and weedy vegetation from nearby stream banks, (3) the sharp-edged grass *(sacahuistle)* that grows thickly on the nearby lakeshore plain, (4) dried animal manure, (5) fallen leaves from a few relatively large stands of trees, and (6) an occasional (but rare) batch of firewood. The only exception to this pattern seems to have been a brief period of experimentation with gas-fired boilers in the 1960s, which proved unsuccessful because of prohibitive cost.

The collection, storage, and utilization of these organic fuels absorbed tremendous quantities of time and energy throughout the entire annual cycle: approximately half of all human energy expended in saltmaking. Since about 1970, saltmakers have relied for their fuel needs almost exclusively on industrial rubber scrap. Most of this scrap is purchased in large lots, a few times each year, from professional dealers who haul in large quantities of this material on flat-bed trucks from shoe factories at the edge of Mexico City. Quantities of old rubber tires are also acquired by the saltmakers, who periodically collect them from local tire repair shops and haul them into their workshops in burro carts. Thus, for the past two decades, saltmakers have wholly abandoned the highly labor-intensive procurement of organic fuel.

Water

The availability of clean water is an essential aspect of the saltmaking process. Water is used (1) to clean the numerous utensils and tools which have come into contact with saline solutions, (2) to pour into the loaded *pilas* to initiate the filtration process; (3) to sprinkle liberally onto the surface of the drying salt in order to further whiten it; (4) to clean the saltmaker's own hands as he shifts from one task where his hands get quite dirty (e.g., mixing soils) to another which demands clean hands (e.g., boiling and drying the salt); (5) to add in small quantities to the soils, as they are being mixed in the workshop, in order to change their consistency slightly and thereby facilitate the mixing operation; and (6) to sprinkle in small quantities over the surfaces of the *pilas'* clay linings as they are being smoothed and repaired after each filtration sequence.

Seasonality of Salt Production

Twentieth century saltmaking at Nexquipayac has apparently always been a year-round activity, with no significant seasonality of production. As we will try to make clear below, this may not necessarily have always been the case in prehispanic times.

SOME ARCHAEOLOGICAL IMPLICATIONS

Technological Systems

The sixteenth-century sources noted above suggest that there may have been two different saltmaking processes in operation around Lake Texcoco at the time of Spanish conquest: (1) a process comparable to that observed in modern Nexquipayac, which involved leaching salty earth and boiling the resulting brine; and (2) a simpler process which relied on solar evaporation from shallow pools of salty water. Both Martyr (1628:188) and Sahagún (1950-82:bk.10:84) distinctly mention boiling, but Martyr's indication that salty lake water was "conveyed" through trenches to a point where it was "thickened" might signify something analogous to the no-longer-used solar evaporation noted by Apenes (1944) at Nexquipayac in 1940.

The Workshops—Location, Facilities, and Tool Kits. There is every reason to suppose that prehispanically, like today, virtually all accessible saline soils in the Basin of Mexico were restricted to the lakeshore of Lake Texcoco and adjacent Lake Xaltocan-Zumpango. My observations at Nexquipayac indicate that some 23-26 kg of earth and 20-24 liters of water are required for the production of each kilogram of dried salt. With a waste product of over 95 percent by weight, soil-processing facilities must of necessity have been located close to sources of water and saline soil. Soil and water are both very heavy, and neither could have been transported very far in any quantity with a prehispanic technology—except possibly by canoe along the shoreline.

Today saltmaking workshops are located up to five kilometers from lakeshore soil deposits. Even with burro carts and motorized trucks, soil transport costs are high, and they were even higher 30-50 years ago when all soil was transported on the backs of burros. In prehispanic times, when only human carriers were available for overland transport, such transport costs would have been proportionately much higher. On the other hand, canoes would have been able to move large quantities of soil fairly easily along the immediate lakeshore itself. In prehispanic times the lakeshore zone would also have provided a virtually infinite supply of water for leaching the soil mixture. From a logistical perspective, the lakeshore zone that was accessible to canoe transport would have provided the ideal setting for saltmaking, for it was only within this narrow band that the appropriate parent materials (water and saline soil) would have been available, and it was only within this narrow band that large quantities of saline earth could have been effectively transported.

That known (or suspected) saltmaking sites conform closely to the narrow lakeshore zone makes perfect sense in this regard, and we should not expect to find prehispanic saltmaking workshops anywhere in the Basin of Mexico outside this narrowly-defined niche. It is even probable that in order to minimize transport costs, virtually all prehispanic saltmaking workshops would have been located right at the best soil sources, and that they would have been relocated if a particular soil source was exhausted.

Any significant link between lakeshore saltmaking and canoe transport would also imply that any seasonal, annual, or periodic fluctuations in lake level would have had an impact on the logistics and organization of saltmaking. It is well known, for example, that there have been significant seasonal fluctuations in lake level, in accordance with the markedly seasonal rainfall (e.g., Palerm 1973). During much of the dry season, canoe transport along the lakeshore margins would probably have been much more difficult than during the wet season. This might have imposed some degree of seasonal variability in saltmaking.

One possible impact might have been that soil could have been collected and transported to workshops only during the wet season, for storage at the workshops over the rest of the annual cycle. Or, perhaps wet-season workshops were situated at slightly higher elevations (which defined the lakeshore during the wet season), whereas dry-season workshops were located at slightly lower elevations, close to the more restricted navigable water of the dry months. Or, dry-season salt production may have relied more heavily on solar evaporation from isolated shallow pools of saline water stranded along the lake margins as the main body of water retreated from its rainy-season maximal level. Such wet-season versus dry-season workshops might have been quite different in character, especially if the dry-season workshops employed solar evaporation while the wet-season workshops used soil-leaching and brine-boiling techniques.

Although Sahagún's description of sixteenth-century saltmaking suggests that something quite similar to the modern leaching boiling process was involved, I have been puzzled by his assertion that the saltmaker "hills up" the earth before mixing it with water. This might suggest that the conical leaching pit *(pila)* technique was not used and that leaching was somehow done with the earth piled up on the ground surface rather than being packed into a pit. However, upon further reflection, I think what Sahagún may have been referring to was the hilling up of the soil involved in combining the components of the soil mixture. This process, of course, produces a sizable hill of soil on the mixing floor, a hill which is turned over and reformed several times during the course of the mixing operation (fig. 10.6).

If I am correct, then Sahagún appears to have omitted mention of the *pila* component of the saltmaking process. The omission of such a highly visible and distinctive aspect of saltmaking is puzzling. I confess that it makes me wonder whether soil leaching in prehispanic saltmaking might not have been accomplished in some other way. If *pilas* were missing from the prehispanic process, then prehispanic workshops (and their archaeological remains) would probably look quite different from the modern ones.

With all these considerations in mind, I am nonetheless still convinced that many prehispanic saltmaking workshops (at least in Postclassic times) probably performed the same basic functions and contained the same basic facilities and implements (with stone, wood, and ceramics replacing metal, plastic, rubber, etc.) as those observed at Nexquipayac over the past half century: mixing floor, leaching pits, brine receptacles, massive ridges of discarded leached soil, facilities for storing soil, boiling facilities, larger storage containers for water and brine, smaller containers for moving water and brine around within the workshop, scraping tools for preparing and repairing the *pila* surface, digging and pounding tools for excavating the *pila* pit and hardening its walls, and facilities for drying the dripping-wet, fresh salt.

The precise forms and characteristics of these facilities and implements are less easy to predict, particularly since so few extensive excavations of prehispanic saltmaking workshops in the Basin of Mexico have been carried out and reported. The amorphous mounds associated with many probable prehispanic saltmaking sites around the edges of Lake Texcoco certainly appear to have been formed by discarded leached soil. Aside from this, there are as yet very few archaeological features or artifacts that stand out as the unequivocal analogues of functions and processes at modern saltmaking workshops. Even the distinctive fabric-marked pottery, so abundant at many probable Postclassic saltmaking sites, remains problematical in terms of its precise role and function.

The studies of Elena Talavara (1979), Eneida Baños (1980), and María Sanchez (1987) have greatly clarified our understanding of late prehispanic saltmaking in the Basin of Mexico. They have indicated, for example, that brine was boiled on special stoves and that different kinds of vessels made of crude fabric-marked pottery probably functioned both to evaporate brine and to package crystalline salt for distribution to consumers. The indication that this fabric-marked pottery was apparently produced in standard forms and volumes (Baños 1980:65-69) is also suggestive of its role in the distribution of salt through market or tributary networks.

We still know virtually nothing about the production of fabric-marked pottery, but it is likely that it was manufactured locally at or very close to most saltmaking workshops; thus, we should probably expect to find archaeological remains of its manufacture at or near many Late Postclassic saltmaking sites. In fact, it is quite possible that some of the archaeological sites we have previously identified as saltmaking workshops are actually the places where fabric-marked pottery was manufactured. Furthermore, fabric-marked pottery related to saltmaking apparently dates exclusively to the Middle and Late Postclassic periods, which immediately raises the question of if and how salt production and distribution may have differed in earlier times.

Recycling Soil. I was much impressed by the degree to which soil is processed, discarded, and recycled in saltmaking at Nexquipayac. The two huge artificial mounds underlying and surrounding the modern workshops there are eloquent testimony to how much soil is consumed and discarded. Just as impressive is the degree to which any given mass of soil, once it enters the saltmaking process, continues to remain within that process and to actively move around ..nd change location over time. This is due, of course, to the use of previously-leached workshop soil as a major component of each new soil mixture that is packed into a *pila* pit. If we can assume that something comparable was part of the prehispanic saltmaking process, then there are significant archaeological implications.

Over time, soils at saltmaking workshops are continually being reworked, reexcavated, redigested, rediscarded, and repositioned. The contents of much older workshops can (and do) get combined with those of much younger workshops, and the combined contents, in their turn, may be recombined with other older and younger materials over the course of decades and even centuries. It is widely known, of course, that archaeological materials often get mixed and recombined and redeposited in virtually all kinds of sites. However, the potential for such archaeological mischief seems unusually great in saltmaking sites around the edges of Lake Texcoco. Such sites are potential archaeological nightmares, and their potential complexity should be recognized and appreciated when any serious effort is made to interpret their contents.

Expertise and Knowledge: Leaching and Boiling versus Solar Evaporation

Successful saltmaking at Nexquipayac requires careful attention to detail and a great deal of technical knowledge, especially in the contexts of finding and combining the different types of soils appropriate for saltmaking. Such knowledge and expertise can only be acquired over a long period of practical experience. In modern Nexquipayac such knowledge and expertise have been accumulated in the context of long-term household specialization, in which the saltmaking craft is handed down from one generation to the next as children work closely with parents and gradually acquire full expertise through long and continuous involvement. I expect that something similar would necessarily have happened in prehispanic times.

Saltmaking involving leaching lakeshore soils is not something that can be taken up casually. A saltmaker of this type must either already have the necessary expertise or must be in a position to acquire it. Furthermore, such a saltmaker would need direct access to a narrow band of lakeshore where there was a proper combination of saline soil, water, and (in prehispanic times) canoe transport. I would expect that prehispanic saltmakers of this type would have been part-time or full-time specialists, residing in households that were fully involved in long-term salt production.

As previously noted, Apenes (1944) tells us that until the 1940s there also co-existed at Nexquipayac a much simpler form of saltmaking based on solar evaporation in shallow pools around the Lake Texcoco shoreline. This was probably a very effective way to produce salt during the dry season. Solar evaporation requires little specialized knowledge, few facilities or implements, and is something that almost anyone with access to the proper lakeshore niche could have become involved in on an intermittent or casual basis. Such salt production could have been considerably expanded and developed through the construction of artificial evaporating ponds, but this would not have required much specialized knowledge or expertise.

Apenes (1944) has indicated that in the early 1940s both types of saltmaking (leaching-boiling and solar evaporation) were going on concurrently in Nexquipayac. I see no reason why both could not also have been concurrently practiced in prehispanic times. As I have already suggested, the workshops associated with these two different types of salt production would probably have been quite different in character, appearance, content, and perhaps even location. For example, a workshop based on solar evaporation would have lacked all the facilities, implements, and refuse associated with collecting soil, mixing soil, leaching soil, and boiling brine. Such workshops would probably have been very ephemeral, and archaeologically they might appear as nothing more than a modest sherd scatter.

In sum, an archaeologist must think about at least two basically different kinds of salt production loci: (1) well defined and probably long-established workshops, operated by full-time or part-time specialists who produce salt by means of boiling brine obtained by leaching salty earth; and (2) poorly defined, perhaps very ephemeral and short-lived workshops, probably operated mainly in the dry season by nonspecialists who obtained salt by solar evaporation. Various combinations of these polar workshop types are, of course, also possible. For example, we might expect to find workshops at which both solar evaporation and leaching-boiling were practiced. Or, specialized saltmakers may have shifted seasonally between wet-season leaching-boiling workshops and dry-season solar evaporation workshops, located at higher versus lower elevations, respectively, along the lakeshore.

Fuel Costs: Leaching and Boiling versus Solar Evaporation

The availability of fuel for boiling brine and the high labor intensity of fuel procurement and use are important factors in thinking about the operation and organization of prehispanic salt production. In Nexquipayac prior to about 20-25 years ago saltmakers needed to invest large amounts of time and labor in the procurement and use of organic fuel. Fuel would have been of comparable importance in prehispanic saltmaking, especially in view of the sixteenth-century statements about the importance of boiling. This issue, of course, pertains only to the leached-earth process; salt production by means of solar evaporation has virtually no fuel costs.

Prehispanic saltmakers would have lacked access to any significant quantities of animal manure for use as boiling fuel. In other respects, however, the problems associated with prehispanic fuel procurement and use were probably much the same as those confronting modern saltmakers prior to the introduction of industrial scrap rubber fuel in the late 1960s. I estimate that one modern Nexquipayac workshop annually uses about 7,500 kg of rubber scrap to produce about 2,150 kg of salt. Thus, about 1.0 kg of rubber scrap is needed to produce about 0.3 kg of salt. It should eventually be possible to convert this ratio of rubber scrap:salt into an equivalent ratio of organic fuel:salt. Whatever the precise figure may be, it seems clear that a large quantity of fuel is required to produce salt by means of boiling brine.

This high fuel cost makes me wonder whether solar evaporation may have been more important than boiling brine in prehispanic salt production in the Basin of Mexico. It is true that both Sahagún and Martyr specifically mention salt boiling for sixteenth-century saltmaking in this region. Furthermore, Sanchez (1987) has made a convincing case for late prehispanic salt boiling on the basis of recent archaeological evidence from the western shore of Lake Texcoco. However, I am also much impressed with the high costs associated with the procurement and use of organic fuels, and I am reluctant to abandon the idea that solar evaporation may have been at least as important as boiling in prehispanic saltmaking in the Basin of Mexico.

I am aware that the past 450 years have witnessed massive deforestation and environmental deterioration in highland Central Mexico as the result of the introduction and overgrazing of sheep and other domestic herbivores (e.g., Melville 1983). I also realize that in prehispanic times firewood and charcoal would have been significantly more available than they are at present for salt-boiling fuel, especially during periods prior to the substantial regional population buildups that occurred in the Basin of Mexico after ca. A.D. 1200 (Sanders et al. 1979).

Nonetheless, I am convinced that fuel costs (in terms of both availability and transport) would have been sufficiently great for prehispanic salt boiling in the Basin of Mexico such that solar evaporation would always have been the preferred technique *unless comparatively high levels of salt production were required and/or unless comparatively large numbers of people became involved as full-time or part-time specialists in saltmaking.* These conditions would have created a need (and opportunity) for year-round production of large quantities of salt that could not be supplied by seasonal solar evaporation.

There is nothing in either Martyr's or Sahagún's sixteenth-century accounts which precludes the use of solar evaporation to produce concentrated brine, which could subsequently be boiled—historically such procedures are documented for traditional saltmaking in Japan (Willeman 1889), China (Zwehtkoff 1888), and India (Choudhury 1979). Martyr's description (see above), in fact, strongly suggests that he was describing precisely this kind of operation. In this way Late Postclassic salt production might have directly combined solar and boiling techniques in a manner that would maximize annual output and minimize fuel consumption.

The Uses of Salt

Here I am concerned about the degree to which new or changing uses of salt in Postclassic times may have stimulated greater demand for the product and thus a shift away from generalized solar evaporation and toward more specialized leaching-boiling techniques. One factor, of course, would have been the rapid population growth that occurred throughout the Basin of Mexico after ca. A.D. 1200 (Sanders et al. 1979): more people would simply have consumed more salt. This might have been particularly true if population growth were accompanied by the adoption of new cooking techniques that included greater use of salt in food preparation. The notable increase of ceramic *comales* (tortilla griddles) and *molcajetes* (interior-striated bowls for grinding soft vegetables and fruits into sauces) throughout highland Central Mexico after the beginning of the Postclassic period, for example, might be manifestations of such new types of food preparation. I think it is also important to appreciate that in the preindustrial world salt has several important uses apart from its importance as a dietary condiment, particularly as a preservative of animal flesh, as a mordant for fixing textile dyes, as a medium of exchange, and as a principal component in the preparation of soaps and cleansing agents.

In this regard, it is also important to realize that only a part of the "salt" that has been, or can be, produced around the margins of Lake Texcoco is sodium chloride (NaCl). Chemical analyses (e.g., Flores 1918:8-9) have shown that the two dominant chemical compounds in the soil and water of Lake Texcoco are sodium sequiscarbonate and sodium chloride; however, there are also many significant secondary compounds, including carbonates, chlorides, and silicates of calcium, magnesium, and potassium. There also appears to be some variability in the chemical compounds which precipitate in different parts of Lake Texcoco (Flores 1918:12). Consequently, traditional "saltmaking" around Lake Texcoco has always involved a complex and variable series of potential end products—Sahagún (1969:bk.3:147), for example, speaks of the several different kinds of "salt" offered for sale in sixteenth-century markets. In the historic period this diversity came to include the production of saltpeter for gunpowder and other agents for tanning animal hides (Ewald 1985:24-25, 240-241).

Charles Gibson (1964:339-341) has noted the importance of lake fishing in the Basin of Mexico during the Early Colonial period. If increasing quantities of lake fish needed to be preserved with salt in order to facilitate their exchange in expanding market and tributary economies, could this not have stimulated increases in salt production around the margins of Lake Texcoco during the Postclassic period?

It is also interesting that Late Postclassic fabric-marked pottery seems to occur in two standard sizes (Baños 1980). This might indicate that standard quantities of salt, packaged in ceramic vessels of standard form and volume, were becoming increasingly involved in new types of market exchanges, which required specific equivalences to facilitate impersonal relationships (e.g., Durand-Forest 1971).

Even more important, perhaps, might be the new importance of textiles in facilitating market exchange and tribute payments (Hicks 1987, and see also Hicks, chap. 4), in validating socio-political relationships and alliances (Carrasco 1976, 1978; see also Murra 1962, 1989 for a similar theme in an Andean context), and in denoting status categories by means of differences in clothing (Anawalt 1980, 1981, 1990). Of special importance here are Patricia Anawalt's clear demonstrations of how differences in the form, style, decoration, and color of costumes functioned as material symbols of a complex social hierarchy in Aztec society.

The archaeologically observed great proliferation of spindle whorls throughout highland Central Mexico during Postclassic times suggests a great expansion in cloth production during this period (Parsons and Parsons 1990). An increased need for dyed textiles may have triggered a concomitant expansion of the production of "salt" for use as a mordant (color-fixing) agent in the dyeing process Such a use for "salt" (or, alkaline solutions in general) is historically and ethnographically well documented for Mesoamerica (Ewald 1985:13; Hernandez 1959:v.2:212-213; Johnson 1989, personal communication 1991), for South America (Ravines 1978; Triana 1922), for Africa (Barbour and Simmonds 1971; DeNegri 1966; Dodwell 1955; Harris 1950; Picton and Mack 1979; Wenger and Beier 1957), and for Asia (Fraser-Lu 1988; Gittinger 1982; Levey 1955; Shea 1975). Furthermore, some African and Asian sources describe a consistent spatial association between saltmaking and textile dyeing (Chiang 1976; Goody 1967:184; Shea 1975:178).

Many ethnographic and ethnohistoric descriptions of textile dyeing in Mesoamerica refer to the use of *tequesquite* (sodium sesquicarbonate) as a mordant agent (Ewald 1985:13; Gibson 1964:339; Johnson 1989, personal communication 1991). Although quantitative information is difficult to come by, the few available references (Johnson 1989, personal communication 1991) indicate that very substantial quantities of *tequesquite* are required for each individual dye bath. As noted earlier, sodium sesquicarbonate is one of several kinds of "salts" produced around Lake Texcoco during the recent past (Flores 1918). It is conceivable that some of what we now interpret archaeologically as Late Postclassic "saltmaking" around the margins of Lake Texcoco is, in fact, the remains of facilities for producing *tequesquite* for use as a mordant in textile-dyeing operations. I am even tempted to wonder whether some of the large concentrations of fabric-marked pottery so commonly found at such "saltmaking" sites might represent the remains of dye-pots. If so, then how many of the Late Postclassic archaeological sites we have long viewed as saltmaking workshops might actually be locations where textiles were dyed?

It is also interesting that *tequesquite* was important for making soap in early Colonial times in the Valley of Mexico (Ewald 1985:13; Gibson 1964:339; and Leevy 1954 offers an interesting perspective on the use of similar kinds of deposits in ancient Mesopotamian soapmaking). Although virtually nothing is known about the existence or manufacture of soap in prehispanic times, it is certainly conceivable that the large, Late Postclassic urban populations would have benefitted greatly, in terms of personal and household hygiene, by the availability of such a product. Do some of the archaeological "saltmaking" sites around the margins of Lake Texcoco actually represent soap-making operations?

This paper thus poses the following (still unanswerable) question: would the increased need in Postclassic times for "salt" from Lake Texcoco (for use in new cooking techniques, new kinds of market exchange, more extensive fish preservation, increased textile dyeing, and new forms of urban hygiene), plus the increased dietary needs of an expanding population, have been sufficient to produce a shift away from part-time salt production that had been based mainly, or exclusively, on generalized solar evaporation during Formative and Classic times to more intensive and more specialized forms of full-time saltmaking based on both solar evaporation and leaching-boiling techniques during the later Postclassic period?

I know of nothing in the archaeological record prior to the Middle Postclassic period (A.D. 1150-1350) to compare with what appears to be a great expansion of "saltmaking" around the margins of Lake Texcoco after ca. A.D. 1200 (although something similar, on a smaller scale, may have occurred around the northern shores of Lake Xaltocan-Zumpango in the northern Basin of Mexico during the antecedent Early Postclassic period, presumably in association with the expansion of nearby Tula as a regional center). Most of the earlier archaeological sites in the immediate shore zone of Lake Texcoco are relatively much fewer in number and smaller in size, and none show any clear-cut sign of high proportions of a single, highly-specialized pottery type, analogous to the Middle and Late Postclassic fabric-marked ware, that can be linked to "salt" production (although Mayer-Oakes' [1959] study of ceramics from the El Risco site, on the northwestern shore of Lake Texcoco, hints that such pottery may exist in both Early Postclassic and Classic archaeological lakeshore deposits).

Particularly interesting in this regard is the Terminal Formative (Patlachique phase, 250-100 B.C.) site of El Tepalcate (Tx-TF-46), located well within the lakebed in the southeastern corner of Lake Texcoco (Noguera 1943; Parsons 1971). This site is quite unusual for its combination of large size (ca 19 ha) and saline-lakebed location; it also shows a very high proportion of one or two types of undecorated pottery (Noguera 1943:43). Because of its location well within the borders of a saline lake, the El Tepalcate site makes little sense as an agricultural settlement. Does it represent a very early and unusually large focus of salt production during the era of initial state development in the Basin of Mexico? If so, why was saltmaking so concentrated and tightly focused in space during the Terminal Formative period, and so much more dispersed during the subsequent Classic and Postclassic periods?

Leaving aside for the moment the potential enigma of El Tepalcate during the Terminal Formative period, our present understanding of the archaeological record of the Basin of Mexico hints at a major expansion of "saltmaking" after about A.D. 1200 and a shift away from a predominant reliance on generalized solar evaporation techniques toward something comparable to the leaching boiling process still practiced at Nexquipayac.

GENERAL SUMMARY

Modern saltmaking at Nexquipayac seems to be a direct descendant of late prehispanic saltmaking that formerly was practiced around the entire perimeter of Lake Texcoco. Here salt is acquired by boiling brine obtained by leaching salty earth. This paper describes the highlights of the modern production processes and begins to consider their archaeological implications. There is good reason to believe that for centuries (and perhaps millennia) salt has also been produced in this same zone by means of solar evaporation during the dry season from shallow pools along the lake margins. The two production methods have been employed concurrently during historic times, and it is likely that they were both used in the prehispanic era as well.

I have argued that because of (1) high fuel costs, and (2) the need for great knowledge and technical expertise, which only specialized production could provide, it is unlikely that the leaching-boiling method was very significant prior to Middle Postclassic times in the Basin of Mexico. The stimulus for the shift from a more generalized form of production based upon solar evaporation to a more specialized form of production based on leaching-boiling may have been a combination of two basic factors that produced a need for significantly higher levels of salt production after ca. A.D. 1200: (1) substantial and sustained regional population growth, and (2) changes in the political economy such that much larger quantities of preserved fish, dyed textiles, cleansing agents, and uniformly-packaged salt were required for expanding and increasingly urbanized populations, for new kinds of market and tributary economies, and for the definition of a more complex socio-political hierarchy. Future archaeological studies of prehispanic saltmaking in the Basin of Mexico should provide us with important new perspectives on Aztec society.

ACKNOWLEDGMENTS

This paper is based upon fieldwork carried out at Nexquiapayc, Estado de México in 1988 with the support of the National Geographic Society and the University of Michigan. I am also grateful to Sr. Sebastian Nopaltictla and Sr. Ignacio Casareal, both of Nexquipayac, for their generous assistance in teaching me about traditional saltmaking. A shorter Spanish version of this paper was published in *Arqueología* n.s. 2:69-80, 1991.

REFERENCES CITED

Aggarwal, Shugan
   1976   *The Salt Industry in India.* Government of India Press, New Delhi.
Anawalt, Patricia Reiff
   1980   Costume and control: Aztec sumptuary laws. *Archaeology* 33:33-43.
   1981   *Indian Clothing before Cortes: Mesoamerican Costumes from the Codices.* University of Oklahoma Press, Norman.
   1990   The Emperors' Cloak: Aztec Pomp, Toltec Circumstances. *American Antiquity* 55:291-307.
Andrews, Anthony P.
   1983   *Maya Salt Production and Trade.* University of Arizona Press, Tucson.
Apenes, Ola
   1944   The Primitive Salt Production of Lake Texcoco. *Ethnos* 9:24-40.
Baños, Eneida
   1980   *La industria salinera en Xocotitlan, Cuenca de México.* Thesis, Escuela Nacional de Antropología e Historia, Mexico City.
Barbour, Jane, and David Simmonds (editors)
   1971   *Adire Cloth in Nigeria: The Preparation and Dyeing of Indigo Patterned*

Cloths among the Yoruba. Institute of African Studies, Ibadan University, Ibadan, Nigeria.

Berdan, Frances F.

1975 *Trade, Tribute, and Market in the Aztec Empire.* Ph.D. dissertation, Department of Anthropology, University of Texas, Austin. University Microfilms, Ann Arbor.

Besso-Oberto, Humberto

1980 Las salinas prehispánicas de Alahuiztlan, Guerrero. *Boletín, Instituto Nacional de Antropología e Historia* 29:23-40.

Blanton, Richard E.

1972 *Prehistoric Settlement Patterns of the Ixtapalapa Peninsula Region, Mexico.* Occasional Papers in Anthropology No. 6. The Pennsylvania State University, University Park.

Bloch, Michael

1963 The Social Influence of Salt. *Scientific American* 209:88-99.

Brown, Ian

1980 *Salt and the Eastern North American Indian: An Archaeological Study.* Lower Mississippian Survey, Bulletin No. 6. Harvard University, Cambridge.

Carrasco, Pedro

1976 La sociedad mexicana antes de la conquista. In *Historia general de México,* vol. 1, pp. 165-288. Daniel Cosío Villegas, general editor. El Colégio de Mexico, Mexico City.

1978 La economía del México prehispánico. In *Economía política e ideología en el México prehispánico,* edited by Pedro Carrasco and Johanna Broda, pp. 13-74. Instituto Nacional de Antropología e Historia, Mexico City.

Charlton, Thomas H.

1969 Texcoco Fabric-Marked Pottery, Tlateles, and Salt-Making. *American Antiquity* 34:73-76.

1971 Texcoco Fabric-Marked Pottery and Salt Making: A Further Note. *American Antiquity* 36:217-218.

Chiang, Tao-Chang

1976 The Production of Salt in China, 1644-1911. *Annals of the Society of American Geographers* 66:233-258.

Choudhury, Sudananda

1979 *Economic History of Colonialism: A Study of British Salt Policy in Orissa.* Inter-India Publications, New Delhi.

de Brisay, Kay, and K. Evans (editors)

1975 *Salt: The Study of an Ancient Industry.* Colchester Archaeological Group, Colchester, U.K.

DeNegri, Eve

1966 Nigerian Textile Industry before Independence. *Nigeria Magazine* 89:95-101.

Dodwell, C.

1955 The Town of Weavers. *Nigeria Magazine* 46:118-143.

Durand-Forest, Jacqueline de
  1971   Cambios económicos y moneda entre los Aztecas. *Estudios de Cultura Náhuatl* 9:105-124.
Ewald, Ursula
  1985   *The Mexican Salt Industry, 1560-1980: A Study in Change.* Gustav Fischer Verlag, Stuttgart and New York.
Flores, Teodoro
  1918   *El tequesquite del lago de Texcoco.* Anales No. 5. Instituto Geológico de México, Mexico City.
Fraser-Lu, Sylvia
  1988   *Handwoven Textiles of South-East Asia.* Oxford University Press, Oxford.
Gibson, Charles
  1964   *The Aztecs under Spanish Rule: A History of the Indians of the Valley of Mexico, 1519-1810.* Stanford University Press, Stanford.
Gittinger, Mattiebelle
  1982   *Master Dyers to the World: Techniques and Trade in Early Indian Dyed Cotton Textiles.* The Textile Museum, Washington, D.C.
Goody, Jack
  1967   The Kingdom of Gonja. In *West African Kingdoms,* edited by D. Forde and P. Kaberry, pp. 179-205. Cambridge University Press, Cambridge.
Harris, P. G.
  1950   Notes on Dyeing in Argungu. *Farm and Forest* 10:33-35.
Hernández, Francisco de
  1959 [1576] *Historia natural de Nueva España.* 2 vols. Universidad Nacional Autónoma de México, Mexico City.
Hewitt, William, Marcus Winter, and David Peterson
  1987   Salt Production at Hierve el Agua, Oaxaca. *American Antiquity* 52:799-816.
Hicks, Frederic
  1987   First Steps toward a Market-Integrated Economy in Aztec Mexico. In *Early State Dynamics,* edited by Henri Claessen and Pieter Van de Velde, pp. 91-107. E. J. Brill, Leiden.
Humboldt, Alexander von
  1811   *A Political History of the Kingdom of New Spain.* 4 vols. Longmans, Hurst, Rees, and Brown, London.
Ivanhoe, Francis
  1978   Diet and Demography in Texcoco on the Eve of the Spanish Conquest: A Semi-Quantitative Reconstruction from Selected Ethnohistorical Texts. *Revista Mexicana de Estudios Antropológicos* 24:137-144.
Johnson, Irmgard Weitlaner
  1989   The *huisho* and the *quechquemitl* in Santiago Temoaya, State of Mexico. In *Homenaje a Isabel Kelly,* edited by Yolotl González, pp. 149-168. Instituto Nacional de Antropología e Historia, Mexico City.

Keslin, Richard
  1964 Archaeological Implications on the Role of Salt as an Element of Cultural Diffusion. *The Missouri Archaeologist* 26:1-181.
Levey, Martin
  1954 The Early History of Detergent Substances. *The Journal of Chemical Education* 31:521-524.
  1955 Dyeing Auxiliaries and Assistants in Ancient Mesopotamia. *Centaurus* 4:126-131.
Lovejoy, Paul
  1986 *Salt of the Desert Sun: A History of Salt Production and Trade in the Central Sudan.* Cambridge University Press, Cambridge.
MacKinnon, J. Jefferson, and Susan Kepecs
  1989 Prehispanic Saltmaking in Belize: New Evidence. *American Antiquity* 54:522-533.
Martyr, Petrus
  1628 *The Decades of the Newe World or West India.* 2nd edition. London.
Mayer-Oakes, William
  1959 A Stratigraphic Excavation at El Risco, Mexico. *Proceedings of the American Philosophical Society* 103:332-373. Philadelphia.
McVicker, Donald
  1969 *The Place of Salt: Archaeological Survey and Excavations in the Valley of Ixtapa, Chiapas, Mexico.* Unpublished Ph.D. dissertation, Department of Anthropology, University of Chicago.
Melville, Elinor
  1983 *The Pastoral Economy and Environmental Degradation in Highland Central Mexico, 1530-1600.* Ph.D. dissertation, Department of Anthropology, University of Michigan. University Microfilms, Ann Arbor.
Mendizabal, Miguel Othon de
  1946 Influencia de la sal en la distribución geográfica de los grupos indígenas. *Obras Completas* 2:181-344. Mexico City.
Moran, JoAnn
  1967 Salt Making at Las Salinas in the Valley of Mexico. Manuscript on file at the Museum of Anthropology, University of Michigan, Ann Arbor.
Moriarity, James
  1968 The Socio-Political and Economic Influences Related to the Production and Distribution of Salt. *Anthropological Journal of Canada* 6:2-15.
Muller, Jon
  1984 Mississippian Specialization and Salt. *American Antiquity* 49:489-507.
Multhauf, Robert
  1978 *Neptune's Gift: A History of Common Salt.* Johns Hopkins University Press, Baltimore.

Murra, John
   1962   Cloth and its Functions in the Inca State. *American Anthropologist* 64:710-728.
   1989   Cloth and its Functions in the Inka State. In *Cloth and Human Experience,* edited by Annette B. Weiner and Jane Schneider, pp. 275-303. Smithsonian Institution Press, Washington, D.C.

Nenquin, Jacques
   1961   *Salt, A Study in Economic Prehistory.* De Tempel, Brugge.

Noguera, Eduardo
   1943   Excavaciones en El Tepalcate, Mexico. *American Antiquity* 9:33-43.
   1975   Identificación de una saladera. *Anales de Antropología* 12:118-151. Universidad Nacional Autónoma de México, Mexico City.

Orozco y Berra, Manuel
   1864   *Memória para la Carta Hidrográfica del Valle de México.* A. Boix, Mexico City.

Palerm, Angel
   1973   *Obras hidraúlicas prehispánicas en el sistema lacustre del Valle de México.* Instituto Nacional de Antropología e Historia, Mexico City.

Parsons, Jeffrey R.
   1971   *Prehistoric Settlement Patterns in the Texcoco Region, Mexico.* Memoirs No. 3. Museum of Anthropology, University of Michigan, Ann Arbor.

Parsons, Jeffrey R., and Mary H. Parsons
   1990   *Maguey Utilization in Highland Central Mexico: An Archaeological Ethnography.* Anthropological Papers No. 82. Museum of Anthropology, University of Michigan, Ann Arbor.

Peterson, David
   1976   *Ancient Commerce.* Ph.D. dissertation, Department of Anthropology, State University of New York at Binghamton. University Microfilms, Ann Arbor.

Picton, John, and John Mack
   1979   *African Textiles: Looms, Weaving and Design.* British Museum Publications, London.

Potts, Daniel
   1984   On Salt and Salt Gathering in Ancient Mesopotamia. *Journal of the Economic and Social History of the Orient* 27:225-271.

Quijada, Cesar
   1984   *El Salitre—una salina prehispánica en Tonatico, Edo. de México.* Thesis, Escuela Nacional de Antropología e Historia, Mexico City.

Ravines, Roger
   1978   Tintes y diseños textiles actuales de Cajamarca. In *Tecnología Andina,* edited by Roger Ravines, pp. 395-398. Instituto de Estudios Peruanos, Lima.

Reina, Ruben, and John Monaghan
   1981   The Ways of the Maya: Salt Production in Sacapulas, Guatemala. *Expedition* 23:13-33.

Riehm, Karl
1961   Prehistoric Salt Boiling. *Antiquity* 35:181-191.
Sahagún, Fray Bernardino de
1950-1982   *Florentine Codex: General History of the Things of New Spain.* Translated and edited by Arthur J. O. Anderson and Charles E. Dibble. 12 books. School of American Research and the University of Utah Press, Santa Fe and Salt Lake City.

1969   *Historia general de las cosas de Nueva España.* 4 vols. 2nd edition. Editorial Porrúa, Mexico City.

Sánchez, María
1987   Un sitio productor de sal en Zacatenco, D. F. *Cuaderno de Trabajo* No. 6, pp. 51-56. Departamento de Salvamento Arqueológico, Instituto Nacional de Antropología e Historia, Mexico City.

Sanders, William T., Jeffrey R. Parsons, and Robert S. Santley
1979   *The Basin of Mexico: Ecological Processes in the Evolution of a Civilization.* Academic Press, New York.

Seager, D.
1867   *The Resources of Mexico apart from the Precious Metals.* J. White, Mexico City.
Shea, Philip
1975   *The Development of an Export Oriented Dyed Cloth Industry in Kano Emirate of the 19th Century.* Ph.D. dissertation, Department of History, University of Wisconsin. University Microfilms, Ann Arbor.

Sisson, Edward B.
1973   *First Annual Report of the Coxcatlan Project.* Tehuacan Project Reports No. 3. R. S. Peabody Foundation for Archaeology, Andover, Massachusetts.

Sung, Ying-Hsing
1966   *Chinese Technology in the 17th Century.* Translated by E-Tu Zen Sun and Shiou-Chuan Sun. Pennsylvania State University Press, University Park.

Talavera, Elena
1979   *Las salinas de la Cuenca de México y la cerámica de impresión textil.* Thesis, Escuela Nacional de Antropología e Historia, Mexico City.

Tolstoy, Paul
1958   *Surface Survey of the Northern Valley of Mexico: The Classic and Postclassic Periods.* Transactions of the American Philosophical Society 48(5). Philadelphia.

Triana, Miguel
1922   *La civilización Chibcha.* Escuela Tipográfica Salesiana, Bogota.
Vaillant, George C.
1930   *Excavations at Zacatenco.* Anthropological Papers of the American Museum of Natural History, vol. 32, pt. 1. New York.

Wenger, S., and H. Beier
1957   Adire-Yoruba Pattern Dyeing. *Nigeria Magazine* 54:208-225.

Willeman, A.
   1889   Salt Manufacture in Japan. *Transactions of the Asiatic Society of Japan* 17:1-66. Tokyo.
Zwehtkoff, P.
   1888   Remarks on the Production of Salt in China. *Journal of the China Branch of the Royal Asiatic Society for the Year 1887* 22:81-89.

11

Economic Alternatives under Imperial Rule

The Eastern Aztec Empire

Frances F. Berdan

Much of eastern Mexico, from the highland valleys to the Gulf coastal low lands, fell under Aztec domination during the fifteenth and early sixteenth centuries. A wide diversity of peoples, especially Nahua, Totonac, Huaxtec, Tepehua, and Otomí, lived in this eastern realm and had long traditions of specialized production, regional trade, focal trading centers, and hierarchical systems of political control and economic redistribution (in the form of tribute). City-states formed the basic organizational principle, and notions of dominance-subordination were well established in the region. These traditions long predated the arrival of the imperial forces of the Aztec Triple Alliance. Aztec conquest did, however, leave its imprint in the region, altering and at times intensifying economic patterns of production, trade, and redistribution, and in some cases shifting about political relationships and military alliances.

It is generally understood that Aztec conquest resulted in relatively few internal changes in conquered city-states, and that this was particularly true in regions far from the imperial capitals. Existing dominant-subordinate relationships were normally retained; Aztec imperialism merely added another layer of political subjugation and economic obligation. Local rulers, as long as they accepted the terms of Aztec conquest, were allowed to continue in their positions of power. Yet a close inspection of the admittedly rather sparse documentary data for the eastern imperial realm suggests that, while the Aztecs clearly built on existing patterns and traditions, they also occasionally took an active hand in molding the region to their imperial goals.

THE REGION

As defined here, the eastern realm of the Aztec or Triple Alliance empire stretched from just beyond the volcanos east of the Basin of Mexico, through the high valleys of the Puebla-Tlaxcalla region, and spread out to the Gulf coast (table 11.1; fig. 11.1). It stretched from Oxitipan province in Huaxtec country in the north, to Tochtepec province in the south, an important jumping-off point for imperially-subsidized merchants traveling to trading entrepots beyond the bounds of the empire. The conquered provinces just to the south of enemy Tlaxcalla are included—Tepeacac, Acatlan, Ahuatlan—but the complex region farther south in Oaxaca is not; that area's involved history is best treated separately (see Barbosa-Cano, chap. 4).

The eastern imperial domain was one of considerable geographic and cultural diversity. High altitude valleys dropped into lush semitropical mountain-and-barranca settings, which in turn sloped down to verdant tropical

Table 11.1   Provinces of the eastern Aztec empire

No.	Province	Type
1.	Oxitipan	tributary
2.	Huexotla	strategic
3.	Tzicoac	tributary
4.	Tochpan	tributary
5.	Atlan	tributary
6.	Atotonilco (el Grande)	tributary
7.	Cuauhchinanco	strategic
8.	Tlapacoyan	tributary
9.	Tetela	strategic
10.	Tlatlauhquitepec	tributary
11.	Misantla	strategic
12.	Xalapa	strategic
13.	Cempoallan	strategic
14.	Quauhtochco	tributary
15.	Cuetlaxtlan	tributary
16.	Tochtepec	tributary
17.	Tepeacac	tributary
18.	Ahuatlan	strategic
19.	Acatlan	strategic

coastal lowlands. The highlands abounded with maguey, wood products and game; the semitropical mountains and coastal lowlands yielded prized luxuries and specialties such as greenstones, turquoise, precious feathers, gold, liquidambar, rubber, cacao and cotton.[1] Foodstuffs, from staples such as maize, beans, squash and chiles, to regional specialties of fish, fowl, and bee honey, were abundant and food production was quite reliable.[2] Competition over these resources was ancient and intense, and resulted in a history of regional warfare, conquest, and unstable political relations.

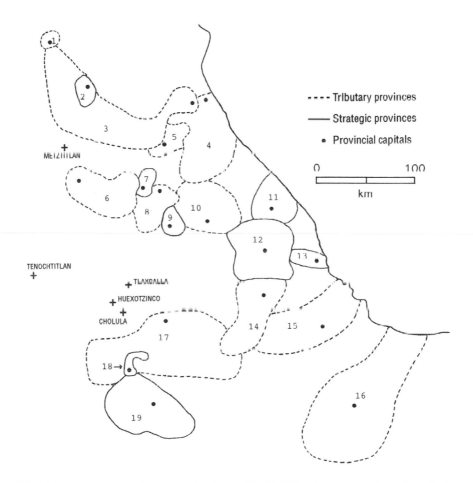

Fig 11.1. The eastern Aztec empire (see table 11.1 for the names of provinces). A more refined and detailed map of the Aztec empire's outer provinces, including this eastern realm, appears in *Aztec Imperial Strategies* (Berdan et al. 1994).

Linguistic Patterns

Culturally and linguistically, the region included peoples from three different language families—Uto-Aztecan, Mayan and Oto-Manguean. Speakers of very different languages often lived in close proximity, and in some communities bilingualism was present. The Codex Mendoza province of Atlan, for example, encompassed speakers of Nahuat(l), Otomí, Huaxtec and two versions of Totonac, each unintelligible to the other (*Papeles de Nueva España* 1905-1948:v.5:219-220). In Papantla (Tochpan province), some Totonac speakers also understood "mexicana" (García Payón 1965:62). Similarly, in Tochpan itself, some of the native Huaxtec speakers also spoke Nahuatl (Alvarado Tezozomoc 1975:315).

Sometimes language mosaics reflected complex histories of population movements and political dominance. This appears to have been the case in the important centers of Tecamachalco and Cachulac in Tepeacac province, where the majority of the population spoke Popoluca, except that all the nobles spoke at least some "mexicana" (Nahuatl) (*Papeles de Nueva España* 1905-1948:v.5:20). In the same province, the city-state of Tecalli had Popolucan and Otomí minorities, while the ruler and most of his subjects spoke Nahuatl (Gerhard 1972:255). In this province, the city-states of Tepeacac, Cachulac, Tecamachalco and Tecalli were the major seats of political power, dominated by Nahuatl-speaking rulerships. Similarly, in Atotonilco (el Grande) province, Otomí was the predominant language; Nahuatl was spoken only in the major centers of Atotonilco and Quauhquechaloyan, suggesting Nahuatl was an intrusive administrative or prestige language in the area (*Papeles de Nueva España* 1905-1948:v.3:90, 92).

Historical Perspective

Historically, the region prior to, as well as during and after the arrival of the Aztec forces was the scene of much political and military activity. It was an arena for population movements, shifting political alliances, and large and small wars. For example, Acazacatlan (ultimately part of Matrícula/Mendoza Tlapacoyan province) was included with Tlaxcalla, Cholula and other states as engaging in hostilities with the Mexica during the 1470s (Durán 1967:v.2:265). It was still considered an enemy polity at least until 1487, when the ruler of Acazacatlan along with several other enemy rulers was invited to secretly witness the dedication of the Tenochtitlan Templo Mayor (Durán 1967:v.2:339). Tlapacoyan, however, had by that time fallen to the Triple Alliance empire (under Motecuhzoma I, A.D. 1440-1468). After Acazacatlan's incorporation into the Aztec empire, it engaged in fighting its former ally Tlaxcalla. But, at that same time, one of Acazacatlan's subject towns also carried on intermittent warfare with a subject town of neighboring Tetela, also an Aztec imperial conquest. Indeed, the borderlands surrounding the major independent city-states of Metztitlan in the north, Tlaxcalla in the "center," and the Chinantecs and Mixtecs in the south were regions of fairly constant military skirmishes and political machinations—with conditions of alliances and hostilities shifting frequently (see also Isaac 1983). The presence of strong unconquered city-states not only at exterior borders of the empire, but also within the general imperial realm (Tlaxcalla), was an important factor in the history of Aztec empire building in the east.

Another significant factor in the region's imperial history was the involvement of the Acolhua in eastern conquests, to the extent that Barlow (1949) calls much of the region "The Old Acolhua Domain." While Alva Ixtlilxochitl (1965) presents an assuredly biased account glorifying the deeds of the Texcocan Acolhua, there is sufficient additional data to suggest at least some military, political and economic involvement in the eastern realm. For instance, Misantla, near the Gulf coast, was reportedly subjected to invasions from the ruler of Huexotla (an Acolhua city-state near Texcoco) in the late 1100s (*Relación de Misantla* 1962:13; García Payón 1947:74). Misantla was later conquered by the Mexica ruler Axayacatl in 1480 (Ramírez Lavoignet 1953:317) or by the Texcocan ruler Nezahualpilli in 1486, or both (*Relación de Misantla* 1962:149-150). Nearby Nautla fell under equally ambiguous conquest conditions (Berdan et al. 1994). Similarly conflicting accounts pertain all up and down the east coast: the conquest was made by a Mexica ruler, by a Texcocan king; tributes in goods and labor were due to Tenochtitlan alone, to Texcoco alone, to all three Triple Alliance partners. It is likely that the conquests themselves were Triple Alliance enterprises, involving not only the imperial heads but also other Basin of Mexico imperial subjects (such as Chalco and Xochimilco). Tribute and conquest honors, then, might indeed have been shared by the imperial partners, which would explain some of the documentary ambiguity.

Triple Alliance military incursions and conquests into the eastern region occurred primarily during the reigns of Motecuhzoma I (1440-1468), Axayacatl (1468-1481) and Ahuitzotl (1486-1502). These reigns also corresponded roughly to the powerful reigns of Nezahualcoyotl and Nezahualpilli of Texcoco. During the reigns of these Mexica rulers, all of the head towns of the Matrícula/Mendoza tributary provinces in the east were conquered, although some of the towns recorded in these provincial groups were in fact conquered at different times and by different rulers (see fig. 11.2). With only one exception, provincial head towns were conquered earlier than their component towns, or at least during the same military campaign.[3]

The considerable military efforts of the second Motecuhzoma (who reigned 1502-1520) were primarily directed, in the east, to reconquering recalcitrant subjects or to subduing city-states that existed as relatively small enclaves near already conquered polities. Some of these, like Papantla and Ahuilizapan, were tagged onto "pre-formed" tributary provinces (Tochpan and Quauhtochco respectively).[4] Others remained separate imperial entities, which have been dubbed "strategic provinces" (see Berdan et al. 1994).

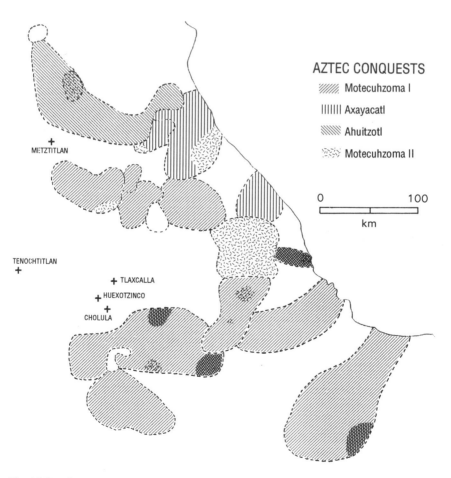

AZTEC CONQUESTS

- Motecuhzoma I
- Axayacatl
- Ahuitzotl
- Motecuhzoma II

0   100
km

+
METZTITLAN

TENOCHTITLAN
+

+ TLAXCALLA

+ HUEXOTZINCO
+
CHOLULA

Fig 11.2.   Aztec conquests of the eastern empire.

AZTEC IMPERIAL STRATEGIES IN THE EAST

For the eastern realm, as well as all outer Aztec provinces, it is useful to distinguish between those city-states arranged as "provinces" on the Matrícula/ Mendoza tribute rolls, and other city-states conquered by the powers of the Triple Alliance, but not included on those lists. The former have been designated "tributary provinces" and the latter "strategic provinces". The use of these types quite specifically reflects the history of conquests, imperial structures, the dynamics of imperial expansion, and the importance of regional conditions in Aztec empire building in the eastern domain (Berdan et al. 1994).

The Economic Strategy: Tributary Provinces

Imperial provinces resulted from two basic administrative strategies pursued by the Aztec or Triple Alliance powers in all parts of their outer realm. One may be called an economic strategy, represented by the empire's tributary provinces. These provinces are the 38 well-known entities depicted in part 2 of the *Codex Mendoza* (1992) with similar depictions in the *Matrícula de Tributos* (1980) and the *Información of 1554*.[5] These numerous city-states and their dependencies were arranged into provinces that paid tribute in goods[6] on a regularized schedule,[7] apparently in the context of an imperial administrative structure. This structure assured a rather stabilized and predictable flow of goods from conquered city-states to the seats of imperial power. In the east, these provinces were important sources of clothing, warriors' costumes, cotton, cacao, staple foodstuffs (maize, beans, chiles and perhaps chia and amaranth),[8] wood products, precious metals, prized feathers, and fine stones. The eastern tributary provinces especially provided significant quantities of high quality luxury goods—those expensive and exquisite objects and materials reserved for the imperial nobility and the burgeoning needs of state, palace, and temple.

Towns included in these provincial groupings were generally in close proximity to one another. Contrary, however, to the classic map of the Aztec empire drawn by Robert Barlow in 1949, these tributary provinces were not neatly contiguous administrative entities, nor were they as grand in geographical territory.[9] For example, the tributary province of Tlatlauhquitepec clung to the eastern sierra and did not extend on to the coastal lowlands (fig. 11.3). Likewise, Quauhtochco was a mountainous province that did not reach the sea. The tributary towns of Tochtepec province were oriented toward major inland-to-coast rivers, and only a few towns in that province were actually located at any distance from those major thoroughfares (fig. 11.4). A revised map of the empire, following the boundaries of Codex Mendoza city-states and their dependencies, has a discontinuous appearance to it (fig. 11.1). A detailed revised map of the Aztec empire is presented in Berdan et al. (1994).

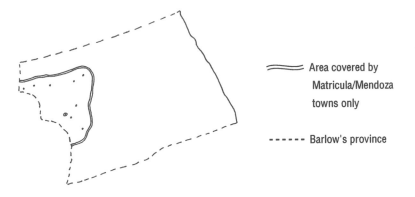

Fig 11.3.   The tributary province of Tlatlauhquitepec. The revised map, based primarily upon towns included in the *Matrícula de Tributos* and the *Codex Mendoza* (1992) covers much less area than Barlow's (1949) map of the province.

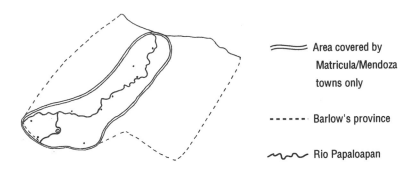

Fig. 11.4.   The tributary province of Tochtepec. The revised map, based primarily upon towns included in the *Matrícula de Tributos* and the *Codex Mendoza* (1992) covers much less area than Barlow's (1949) map of the province.

Historically, all of the eastern tributary provinces were conquered by fifteenth-century Triple Alliance rulers, although Motecuhzoma II made numerous conquests in the early sixteenth century that did not make the Codex Mendoza tributary lists. The relatively early dates of eastern conquests suggests that provinces on the regularized tribute rolls had some time depth in their association with the empire. In addition, the "tributary" conquests had not been "friendly capitulations"; available documentation suggests that conquests of these areas were hard-fought, not negotiated.

Upon conquest by the Mexica and their allies, a city-state was typically allowed to retain its traditional ruler(s), and noble-level integration into the imperial structure was solidified through marriage alliances, gift exchanges, and common participation in religious ceremonies and political events. In general, imperial interference in local affairs was minimal (see, for instance, Smith 1986; Berdan 1975). Alongside this locally-based traditional leadership system, a hierarchical tribute collection structure was imposed by the Aztecs in the conquered realms. Documentary support for such a structure comes primarily from the Spanish commentaries accompanying the *Codex Mendoza:* statements on some folios state that Mexica *calpixque* (tribute collectors) were placed in each town listed, and that a Mexica provincial governor presided over them.[10] The implication is that the various *calpixque* collected tributes from their respective localities, delivered them to the head tribute collector ("governor") at the provincial "capital," from whence they were delivered to the Mexica overlords. In the eastern empire, additional documentary information indicates that at least some of the towns in the tributary province of Tochtepec brought tribute to their local rulers, who took it to Tochtepec, from where it was forwarded to the imperial center(s) (*Papeles de Nueva España* 1905-1948:v.5:2, 5).[11] Also, Mexica *calpixque* were placed in Tepeacac and three of its associated towns (Tecalco, Cuauhtinchan and Acatzinco) after its conquest by Motecuhzoma I (Alvarado Tezozomoc 1975:309), and Acolhua rulers reportedly installed tribute collectors in Tochpan, Tzicoac, and Tulancinco (Alva Ixtlilxochitl 1965:v.2.196-199). Additional details on the workings of the tribute system are less precise; usually the specific destination and process of tribute collection are not mentioned at all. Most likely, local rulers and imperial tribute collectors carried out their duties in a parallel but separate fashion. Tribute destined for imperial coffers was collected by imperial *calpixque,* tribute produced for the local *tlatoani* was organized by that leader and his own cadre of officials, who also handled local administrative affairs.

The structure of tribute collection was somewhat complicated by the occasional shuffling of traditional head towns by the conquering Mexica. There are some cases where the most important city-state of a province—in terms of size, hereditary leadership, military strength, and political and economic importance—is not the head town designated by the Mexica for tribute collection and imperial administration. While this is more obvious in other areas of the empire (e.g., Coyolapan, Coayxtlahuacan), in the east the strategically important center of Tulancinco was subsumed in the tributary province of Atotonilco el Grande; Atotonilco was clearly the lesser center. In this and related cases, the imperial strategy may have been to channel imperial demands through a lesser center, thus muting the power held by a long-established rulership (Berdan et al. 1994).

The Frontier Strategy: Strategic Provinces

City-states in outlying strategic provinces were incorporated into the Aztec imperial realm, but on different bases than were the tributary provinces, establishing client-like relations with their conquerors. Instead of paying regular, periodic tribute, they offered "gifts" from time to time. Most strategic provinces were fairly late conquests under the banner of the second Motecuhzoma (1502-1520). They had relatively little time, therefore, to develop entrenched relations with their imperial overlords. Their geographic location is significant: for the most part they lay along hostile borderlands and had military value; or they dominated routes which served as major arteries for trade and/or extended military action; or they were situated handily for commerce and functioned as trading entrepots.

An important function of the strategic provinces was to insulate tributary provinces from powerful hostile city-states (e.g., Tlaxcalla and Metztitlan). As with the Tarascans in the west, the Aztecs faced a particularly tenacious military foe in the east: the Tlaxcallans. But rather than ringing those volatile borderlands with fortresses and garrisons to "hold the borders," the Aztecs tended to rely on establishing relations with borderland city-states that had historically fought with the Tlaxcallans and their allies. The documentation for this is especially clear for the northern and southern Tlaxcallan borders. Many strategic provinces lay near or along these borderlands and carried on low-level endemic warfare with the Aztec enemies.

On the northern border of Tlaxcalla, the city-state of Tetela provides a nice example of "client states." Edward Luttwak applies the concept of client state to the expansion of the Roman empire, arguing that some areas beyond direct Roman rule constituted an "inner zone of diplomatic control" (1976:22). Client states in this zone provided a perimeter of defense for the Romans against "low intensity" threats of petty infiltration, transborder incursion, or localized attack" (Luttwak 1976:19). Unlike static buffer zones, clients were "inherently dynamic and unstable," requiring "the constant management of a specialized diplomacy" (Luttwak 1976:30). Tetela was, by the early 1500s, strategically situated between the tributary province of Tlatlauhquitepec, the ambiguous city-state of Acazacatlan,[12] and the hostile city-state of Tlaxcalla (fig. 11.5). Tetela warred with Tlaxcalla and Acazacatlan; in these wars it was supported by the "king of Mexico" who gave the Tetela warriors shields and other offensive arms (*Papeles de Nueva España* 1905-1948:v.5:147). In return, Tetela sent Tlaxcallan and Acazacatlan war captives to the "king of Mexico" by way of friendship and kinship (*Papeles de Nueva España* 1905-1948:v.5:161). The Nahuatl-speaking Tetela claims to have never been conquered by the Aztecs (*Papeles de Nueva España* 1905-1948:v.5:144), and worshipped Huitzilopochtli, patron god of the Mexica, who they brought from Mexico (*Papeles de Nueva España* 1905-

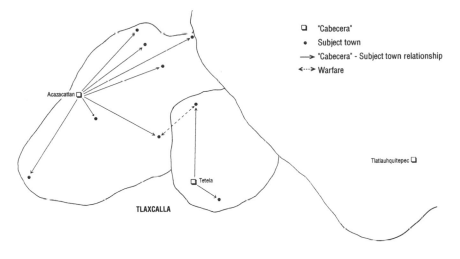

Fig. 11.5. Map of the Acazacatlan and strategic province of Tetla.

1948.v.5.147).[13] In all, this city-state seems to have had a special diplomatic relationship with the Mexica; the local leaders originally came from the "province of the Chichimecs" (*Papeles de Nueva España* 1905-1948:v.5:145) and shared some elements of language, kinship and religion with the Mexica. Most important to the Mexica, Tetela held a portion of the unstable Tlaxcallan border, in effect insulating the tributary provinces to the north and east from borderland hostilities. It all resembles a "low intensity" state of animosities characteristic of Luttwak's client states.

In the give-and-take of war materiel and battlefield captives, Tetela proper played an indirect role. Instead of Tetela warring directly with Tlaxcalla or Acazacatlan, one of Tetela's subject towns fought with subject towns of the enemy states. Captives won in these battles were given to the *sujeto's* "señor" who in turn presented them to the "señor" of Tetela, who then sent them on to Mexico (*Papeles de Nueva España* 1905-1948:v.5:145). Instead of major wars breaking out between the lead towns of these city-states, it appears that wars were fought and captives gained through smaller-scale battles between their subject towns; the object may have been to maintain a balance of power more than to effect a conquest.

A rather different set of arrangements prevailed along the southern Tlaxcalla border. There, the tributary province of Tepeacac ran along almost the entire hostile borderland. But instead of involving Tepeacac as a client state, the Mexica, under Axayacatl, conquered Tepeacac and its powerful, associated city-states (*Codex Mendoza* 1992:f.10v) and demanded considerable regular tribute payments[14] (see Rojas, chap. 15). Furthermore, instead of receiving war mate-

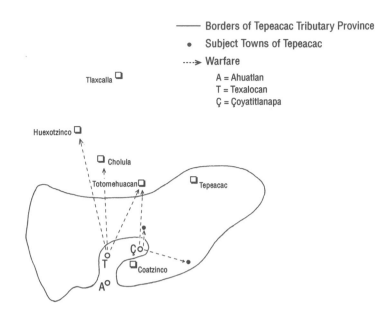

Fig. 11.6. The wars of Ahuatlan strategic province.

riel to aid them in their battles, the city-states of Tepeacac province were required to deliver such goods in tribute to the lords of Mexico, along with captives from Tlaxcalla, Cholula, and Huexotzinco. This was the only tributary
province to do so. Tepeacac provided 8000 canes for making arrows to its
Mexica overlords (*Codex Mendoza* 1992:f.42r); more specifically, the Tepeacac
provincial town of Coatzinco paid its tribute to Motecuhzoma in strong canes,
shields of stout canes, blades for lances, bows and arrows, and white lime
(*Papeles de Nueva España* 1905-1948:v.5:95). All but the lime could be considered military apparatus, and since much of this is not listed in the *Matrícula*
or *Mendoza*, it may have been delivered directly to Tenochtitlan rather than
passing through Tepeacac.[15]

The nearby city-states of Ahuatlan, Texalocan and Çoyatitlanapa had yet a
different relationship with their Mexica overlords (fig. 11.6). All three city-
states were subject to Motecuhzoma and his "pasados" (*Papeles de Nueva España*
1905-1948:v.5:82-83, 86, 90). The tribute they rendered included shields of stout
canes, large stout canes, blades to insert in lances, raw cotton for armor, and
Texalocan gave captives from its wars with enemy Totomehuacan, Cholula,
Huexotzinco and Coyxco (*Papeles de Nueva España* 1905-1948:v.5:86). Apparently this tribute did not pass through administrative structures of nearby
tributary provinces, but went directly to Tenochtitlan. Nonetheless, Motecuhzoma
had placed two high-ranking Mexica officials in Texalocan as judges (*Papeles*

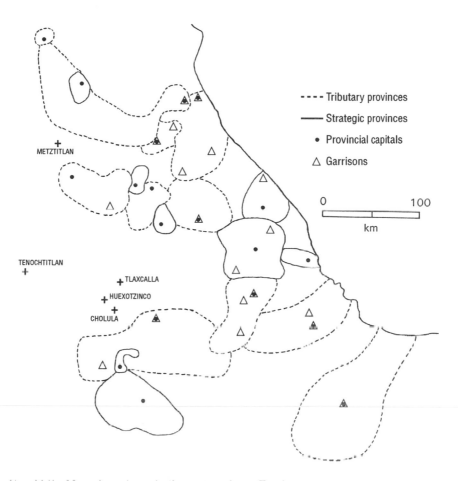

Fig. 11.7. Map of garrisons in the eastern Aztec Empire.

de Nueva España 1905-1948:v.5:87).[16] While not directly bordering on Tlaxcalla, towns in Ahuatlan strategic province nevertheless battled regularly with the Tlaxcallans and their allied neighbors, surely diverting their military attentions somewhat from the neighboring tributary province of Tepeacac. The presence of such strategic provinces, however, could not entirely thwart the military goals and political machinations of major enemy states. Tlaxcalla, for example, repeatedly encouraged rebellion in Cuetlaxtlan tributary province, only to desert the rebels and leave them to reconquest and the wrath of Aztec military might.

At the more distant eastern and southern reaches of this imperial realm, the Mexica and their allies established fortresses and garrisons.[17] Fortresses and garrisons are associated here with both strategic and tributary provinces (fig. 11.7). While the precise location of some of these sites is problematical, they were especially well-situated to guard frontier borders or to control critical points along major military and trade routes. Holt (1979) suggests several functions for these installations, such as guarding borders, assuring internal security, and protecting commercial activities. With the remapping of the empire, it is more apparent that garrisons and fortresses were situated and stationed largely near provincial borders with implied functions of guarding hostile borderlands. While troops stationed at these garrisons would have been available for problems of local unrest, in some cases the garrisons appear to have been situated in areas of relatively low local population density and may have been truly frontier outposts (e.g., Atlan, Teçapotitlan, garrisons in Misantla and Xalapa).

Mexican military presence was a prominent feature of some major trade and market centers, especially those contained within tributary provinces (such as Tochtepec, Tochpan, or Itzocan) or those external to the empire (such as Xicalanco); however, it was not necessarily required for the smooth or reliable operation of trading centers. A good example comes from the strategic province and trading center of Huexotla (in present-day Hidalgo). It is explicitly stated that no fortress was present in this northeastern town (*Papeles de Nueva España* 1905-1948:v.6:190), although the people of Huexotla carried on wars with several neighboring towns in the region (*Papeles de Nueva España* 1905-1948:v.6:188-189).[18]

This same Huexotla was conquered by the Aztecs[19] but is not included on the Matrícula/Mendoza tribute tallies. Huexotla's value as a strategic province certainly lay somewhat with its warlike relations with towns at the enemy Metztitlan border, but perhaps preeminently with its role as a trading entrepot. Huexotla was situated on major north-south/east-west land routes, at the base of mountains between the sierra and the lowlands. It served as a major trading center for salt and cotton (*Papeles de Nueva España* 1905-1948:v.6:186, 187, 190). This trading entrepot attracted merchants from considerable distances who may have established some permanency in the Huexotla area; these merchants may have included Tepehuas, Totonacs, Cholulans, and the famed *pochteca*.[20] Aztec commercial presence may have been significant: Roberto Williams García (1963:56) observes that *tiyankis* (*tianquiztli:* marketplace) is among the very few Nahuatl words that has worked its way into the local Tepehua.

Aside from direct military or commercial value, some city-states appear as strategic provinces because of their indirect military or commercial importance or both. For example, Cuauhchinanco and Xicotepec were situated along the most important trade and transport route from Tulancinco on the Mesa Central to the northeastern region of Veracruz. This route opened the way to Totonacapan and the land of the Huaxtecs, where active trading and rich tribute were the prizes (fig. 11.8). These city-states provided "en route" military supplies to troops on the march. Control of the strategic trade and transport route, through Cuauhchinanco and Xicotepec, was very much in Aztec interest.[21]

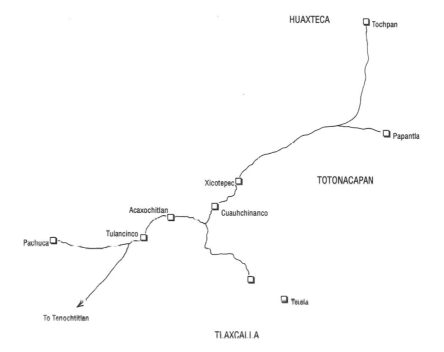

Fig. 11.8. Cuauhchinanco and routes to the northeast.

Overall, city-states which were conquered by the Mexica or Triple Alliance but not included on the Matrícula/Mendoza tribute rolls tended to exhibit particular strategic features. Most of these city-states were located along hostile borderlands. In some cases the Mexica developed client-like relationships with the city-states they conquered; in others they maintained the conquests as buffers, sometimes establishing fortresses or garrisons at their borders. The former strategy prevailed along the Tlaxcallan border, while the latter was more common in externally-facing city-states. In either case, these strategic provinces had military value in insulating tributary provinces from warlike activity along enemy borders. Other strategic provinces gained imperial value from their commercial role, or from their location along trade and transport routes; this latter was important to the Mexica both in facilitating trade and in allowing unimpeded movements of troops to distant wars of conquest. The conquests of the last Mexica ruler, Motecuhzoma II, almost exclusively resulted in provinces of the strategic variety. This may signify a change in earlier imperial policy, the particular conditions of provinces "left" in these later conquests (e.g., as borderlands or trading centers), or a general historical progression whereby strategic provinces may become transformed into tributary provinces over time.

THE ECONOMIC IMPACT OF EMPIRE

The city-states that fell to Aztec armies were generally well-accustomed to re-lations of dominance-subordination, and to tribute production and payment. Aztec conquest did not introduce any particularly novel political or economic notions or practices. This does not mean, however, that such conquest had no impact on the subjugated region.

The tributary provinces were, first and foremost, suppliers of tribute to their imperial overlords. When a city-state or group of city-states were conquered, a tribute was established. The types of goods to be paid were reportedly those which were locally available. In many cases this meant that the items were locally produced. In other cases—for example turquoise paid by Tochpan province and amber lip plugs from Tochtepec and Cuetlaxtlan provinces—the goods (and/or their raw materials) were produced elsewhere and entered the conquered region through trade and market exchange. Imperial tribute demands in a newly conquered area tended to intensify and even increase trade and market exchange across borders. Rather than form solid political boundaries, Aztec conquest at times demanded the borders remain open to long-standing trading traditions (Berdan 1975, 1980).

The incorporation of tributary regions into the empire also opened up large areas for fairly reliable trade and market networks, enhancing a sustained and quite predictable flow of goods to the markets, merchant guilds, and kings' coffers of the imperial cities. Professional merchants *(pochteca)* could travel relatively unmolested within the imperial domain; an expansion of that domain therefore extended trading networks. Indeed, some guild-organized pochteca were restricted from trading beyond the empire; as the empire expanded, so did the economic opportunities for these merchants.

Aside from staple foodstuffs and certain raw materials such as cotton, gold dust, feathers and live eagles, the bulk of imperial tribute from the east was paid in manufactured or partially manufactured goods. Cotton clothing and tex-tiles, feathered warrior costumes, beads of jadeite or gold, lip plugs of amber and crystal, turquoise mosaics and preformed planks and beams all attest to considerable economic specialization in the distant eastern provinces of the empire. Much of this tribute was of a "luxury" nature, but the production of cotton cloth was the domain of all women, and the fashioning of wooden beams and carrying frames was undoubtedly not in the luxury sphere. The general predominance of manufactured goods over raw materials in tribute demands suggests that these payments did much to support manufacturing in the prov-inces and contributed relatively little to the urban specialists (with the possible exception of feathers for the privileged featherworkers).

I have mentioned that some conquered city-states needed to import goods to meet their tribute payments. Conversely, many provinces had resources which were not demanded by the imperial powers. For instance, cacao, chicle, and honey were available in Tochpan, yet not demanded in their tribute duties. Such products were not disdained by the conquerors, indeed some of them were highly valued and paid by other provinces. These discrepancies between available resources and tribute demands may represent imperial priorities. The turquoise of Tochpan may have been a greater prize than its cacao and honey, which could easily be provided by other provinces. Many similar examples leave the impression that imperial tribute assessment was not entirely province-specific; even though a desirable product was locally available, it may not have been required in tribute. Tribute demanded of a province may well have been dependent on that gleaned from other tributary provinces, weighed against the changing needs of the imperial centers.

The empire's economic impact on strategic provinces had a different character. Instead of sending formalized tribute on a regular schedule, strategic provinces offered "gifts" when asked, or just from time to time. Tetela, for example, sent "gifts" of battlefield captives; in return the Mexica sent them arms to sustain those battles. Cuauhchinanco provisioned Aztec armies on the march; as willing allies of the Mexica in their campaign against the Huaxtecs (Durán 1967:v.2: 328), they undoubtedly gained economic rewards and political favor. The Aztec relations with strategic provinces contain an element of reciprocity absent in their relations with tributary provinces; strategic provinces, after all, did a great deal to maintain the empire's distant borderlands at a low cost to the empire itself.

* * *

Aztec military, political, and economic control in the eastern portion of its empire was a blend of imperially generated processes and responses to variable regional conditions. Regionally, both type and intensity of control exerted by the empire were influenced by resource availability, strength and proximity of hostile city-states, historic relations between neighboring polities, location and development of economic distribution points (such as trading entrepots or tribute collection centers), and established trading and market networks. Imperially generated goals stemmed from such processes in the context of a growing demand for status-linked luxury goods for an expanding urban nobility, competition over politically powerful positions, population growth necessitating increased requirements for a reliable food supply, pre-existing tribute patterns, and changing relations with powerful, traditional enemies. The blending of these imperial processes and regional responses resulted in two basic imperial strategies, economic and frontier, evident not only in the eastern realm, but in other areas of the outer Aztec empire. To implement these strategies, the imperial powers drew on well-established Mesoamerican political and economic processes, and fine-tuned those processes to meet their internal needs and external threats.

NOTES

1.   Information on resource availability is derived from tribute lists and six-teenth-century descriptions of production. For individual towns or provinces, the tribute lists may indicate local production, or availability of products through trade (see Berdan 1980).

2.   The Huaxtec region, at least, was notable for its food production. During the famous famine of 1450, some people from the Basin of Mexico sold themselves and their family members to Huaxtecs in exchange for subsistence maize. The Huaxtec area continued to produce maize in abundance, even during the famine years (Durán 1967:v.2:243-244).

3.   Small Tlachquiauhco—nestled between the southern tributary provinces of Yoaltepec and Coayxtlahuacan, and bordering on independent Mixtec domains—was conquered by Motecuhzoma II in 1511 or 1512 and is found on the Matrícula/Mendoza tribute rolls.

4.   For instance, Atotonilco (el Grande) was conquered by Motecuhzoma I; Hueyapan, a town in that same province, was apparently not subdued until the reign of Motecuhzoma II (*Codex Mendoza* 1992:f.8r, f.16r). Quauhtochco, head town of the province of the same name, was conquered by Motecuhzoma I; Ahuilizapan, in the same province, fell to the following ruler, Axayacatl (*Codex Mendoza* 1992:f.8r, f.10v). Similarly, Papantla, in Tochpan province, entered the empire under the second Motecuhzoma, while its head town was conquered much earlier. These provinces, there-fore, did not always enter the empire as complete "packages".

5.   There is some variation in the provincial information presented in these three documents, but they exhibit remarkable similarity (see Berdan et al. 1994). The provin-cial arrangements of the *Codex Mendoza* (1992) are followed here.

6.   An exception was the province of Tepeacac which was responsible for deliv-ering enemy war captives from neighboring Tlaxcalla, Huexotzinco, and Cholula as part of its regular tribute payments (*Codex Mendoza* 1992:f.42r).

7.   Tribute was due every 80 days (interpreted as four times a year), semi-annu-ally, or annually. The period of payment normally varied with the type of good paid: for instance, warriors' costumes and staple foodstuffs were paid annually; clothing was due every 80 days (in the *Matrícula de Tributos*) or semi-annually (in the *Codex Mendoza*). Most provinces paid their tribute on a mixed schedule, some goods due annually, others every 80 days or semi-annually.

8.   The *Matrícula de Tributos* specifies only maize and beans in its annotations; the *Codex Mendoza* adds chia and amaranth.

9.   Barlow's (1949) overly large provinces resulted from his inclusion of conquered towns not listed in the Matrícula or Mendoza tribute tallies, and his propensity for filling in all geographical space with imperial provinces. See discussion in Berdan et al. 1994.

10.   For example, the commentary accompanying the tribute account for the prov-ince of Acolhuacan reads as follows:

> The lords of Mexico, after having conquered the twenty-six towns
> drawn and named on the following two pages, placed in each town
> *calpixques,* and in the principal one, a governor to rule over them,

to maintain peace and justice, assure tribute payment, and prevent rebellion ... [*Codex Mendoza* 1992:f.21r. Translation by the author]

The "governor," according to an earlier folio, is one called *petlacalcatl.* This was an office associated directly with overseeing tribute, probably in the imperial capitals (Sahagún 1950-1982:bk.8:44). These statements in the *Mendoza* do not seem to refer to military or political governors such as the *tlacochcalcatl* or *tlilancalqui.*

11. According to Scholes and Warren (1965:781), "In the principal settlements of the province the Aztec rulers had placed officials who were responsible for the collection of tribute and exercised supervisory authority, subject to the superior jurisdiction of the military commander and the judges resident in Tuxtepec." Tochtepec was also a major center for *pochteca* who traveled long distances beyond the southern imperial frontier from various Basin of Mexico cities. Additional examples of provincial hierarchies are found in Hicks 1984:238-239.

12. Acazacatlan is listed in the Matrícula/Mendoza tributary province of Tlapacoyan. It sat at the southernmost edge of this province, adjacent to Tlaxcalla. The date of its conquest by the Aztecs is unknown, but at least during the mid to late fifteenth century, it was a persistent enemy and associated with Tlaxcalla. On the other hand, it also recorded wars against Tlaxcalla in which Motecuhzoma provided aid (García Payón 1965:38). Davies (1968:79) thinks it may have been semi-independent, although it is included in the Matrícula/Mendoza.

13. While the people of Tetela itself seem to have worshipped Huitzilopochtli, and one of its *sujetos* (Çuçumba) followed suit, other subject towns had different patron gods. The people of Tzanaquatla worshipped the god Haztacoatl ("Crane Serpent"), Capulapa revered Matlalcuhetl ("Blue Skirt"), and Tutula included Totonac and Nahua gods in its pantheon.

14. Tepeacac was clearly a tributary province, and the records of its conquest and tribute are considerable. Nevertheless, in the sixteenth-century *Relación Geográfica,* the claim was made that "... no reconocían superioridad a Motecuhcoma señor de México ... sino tan solamente le tenían por amigo y confederado para las guerras que los de México trayan con los de Tlaxcala y Vexotzingo. ... " (*Papeles de Nueva España* 1905-1948:v.5:14-15).

15. There is also the possibility that the tribute mentioned for Coatzinco represents a time period not reflected in the Matrícula/Mendoza pictorials.

16. Ahuatlan seems to have been the most important city-state among these three, with Texalocan as its subject town (*Papeles de Nueva España* 1905-1948:v.1:202). The titles of the Mexica officials stationed in Texalocan were *Tzipayn Tlacochcalcatl* and *Acolnahuacatl Tlacatecatl.* These titles suggest military duties as well as legal ones.

17. There is considerable debate about whether such locales were permanent installations with readily available troops (established in fortresses) or whether they were the temporary sites of troops who were needed at a particular place at a particular time (see Davies 1978; Zantwijk 1967; Holt 1979). In the latter case, the *guarnición* is defined literally as a body of troops. The location of movable *guarniciones,* then, would be strongly dependent on activities and relationships at specific points in time; some recorded by Cortés and Bernal Díaz del Castillo, for example, may well reflect military positioning vis-a-vis the inward march of the Spaniards. A *guarnición* at

Tepeacac, then, may have been a response to Spanish presence rather than a regular fixture in that city.

18. Two of these towns, Tlachinolticpac and Cuezalinco, have been located. They were south of Huexotla, close to (or perhaps part of) the domain of Metztitlan. Metztitlan retained its independence from the Mexica.

19. Torquemada (1969:v.1:193) says that Ahuitzotl *re*conquered Huexotla; the people of Huexotla had rebelled, assaulting the imposed majordomos and other officials, and failing to deliver tribute to Mexico and Texcoco. Kelly and Palerm (1952:297) show a Huexotla conquest by Axayacatl, but feel it is the Huexotla in the Valley of Mexico.

20. Names of some of the Huexotla *estancias* are suggestive: Chololan (Cholula), Totonacapan (Totonac), Puchtlan *(pochteca)* and Tepevacan (Tepehua) *(Papeles de Nueva España* 1905-1948:v.6:187).

21. Reportedly, both Cuauchinanco and Xicotepec came under Aztec rule through "peaceful capitulations," and Nezahualcoyotl left the local rulerships intact (Alva Ixtlilxochitl 1965:v.2:198; Torquemada 1969:v.1:167-168).

REFERENCES CITED

Alva Ixtlilxochitl, Fernando de
  1965   *Obras históricas.* Edited by Alfredo Chavero. 2 vols. Editorial Nacional, Mexico City.

Alvarado Tezozomoc, Fernando de
  1975   *Crónica mexicana.* Commentary by Manuel Orozco y Berra. Editorial Porrúa, Mexico City.

Barlow, Robert H.
  1949   *The Extent of the Empire of the Culhua Mexica.* Ibero-Americana No. 28. University of California Press, Berkeley.

Berdan, Frances F.
  1975   *Trade, Tribute and Market in the Aztec Empire.* Ph.D. dissertation, Department of Anthropology, University of Texas at Austin. University Microfilms, Ann Arbor.

  1980   Aztec Merchants and Markets: Local-Level Economic Activity in a Non-industrial Empire. *Mexicon* 2(3):37-41. Berlin.

Berdan, Frances F., Richard E. Blanton, Elizabeth H. Boone, Mary G. Hodge, Michael E. Smith, and Emily Umberger
  1994   *Aztec Imperial Strategies.* Dumbarton Oaks, Washington, D.C. In press.

Codex Mendoza
  1992   *The Codex Mendoza.* Edited by Frances F. Berdan and Patricia Reiff Anawalt. 4 vols. University of California Press, Berkeley.

Davies, Nigel

1968 *Los señoríos independientes del imperio azteca.* Instituto Nacional de Antropología e Historia, Mexico City.

1978 The Military Organization of the Aztec Empire. In *Mesoamerican Communication Routes and Cultural Contacts,* edited by Thomas A. Lee and Carlos Navarrete, pp. 223-230. Papers of the New World Archaeological Foundation No. 40. Brigham Young University, Provo, Utah.

Durán, Fray Diego

1967 *Historia de las indias de Nueva España e Islas de la Tierra Firme.* Edited by Angel María Garibay K. 2 vols. Editorial Porrúa, Mexico City.

García Payón, José

1947 Sinópsis de algunos problemas arqueológicos de Totonacapan. *El México Antiguo* 6:301-332.

1965 *Descripción del pueblo de Gueytlalpan (Zacatlan, Jujupango, Matlatlan y Chila, Papantla) por el alcalde major Juan de Carrion, 30 de mayo de 1581.* Cuadernos de la facultad de filosofía, letras, y ciencias 23. Universidad Veracruzana, Jalapa, Mexico.

Gerhard, Peter

1972 *A Guide to the Historical Geography of New Spain.* Cambridge University Press, Cambridge.

Hicks, Frederic

1984 La posición de Temascalapan en la Triple Alianza. *Estudios de Cultura Náhuatl* 17:235-260.

Holt, H. Barry

1979 *Mexica-Aztec Warfare: A Developmental and Cultural Analysis.* Ph.D. dissertation, Department of Anthropology, University of Texas at Austin. University Microfilms, Ann Arbor.

Isaac, Barry L.

1983 The Aztec 'Flowery War': A Geopolitical Explanation. *Journal of Anthropological Research* 39:415-432.

Kelly, Isabel, and Angel Palerm

1952 *The Tajín Totonac. Part I. History, Subsistence, Shelter, and Technology.* Institute of Social Anthropology Publication 13. Smithsonian Institution, Washington, D.C.

Luttwak, Edward

1976 *The Grand Strategy of the Roman Empire.* Johns Hopkins University Press, Baltimore.

Matrícula de Tributos

1980 *Matrícula de Tributos.* Commentary by Frances F. Berdan and Jacqueline de Durand-Forest. Akademische Druck-u. Verlagsanstalt, Graz, Austria.

Papeles de Nueva España
1905-1948 *Papeles de Nueva España.* Segunda serie, Geografía y Estadística. Edited by Francisco del Paso y Troncoso and Luis Vargas Rea. 9 vols. Tipográfico Sucesores de Rivadeneyra, Madrid.

Ramírez Laviognet, David
1953 Notas históricas de Misantla. In *Huastecos, totonacos, y sus vecinos,* edited by Ignacio Bernal and E. Dávalos Hurtados, pp. 315-331. Sociedad Mexicana de Antropología, Mexico City.

Sahagún, Fray Bernardino de
1950-1982 *Florentine Codex: General History of the Things of New Spain.* Translated and edited by Arthur J. O. Anderson and Charles E. Dibble. 12 books. School of American Research and the University of Utah Press, Santa Fe and Salt Lake City.

Scholes, France V., and Dave Warren
1965 The Olmec Region at Spanish Contact. In *Archaeology of Southern Mesoamerica,* pt. 2, edited by Gordon R. Willey, pp. 776-787. Handbook of Middle American Indians, vol. 3, Robert Wauchope, general editor. University of Texas Press, Austin.

Smith, Michael E.
1986 The Role of Social Stratification in the Aztec Empire: A View from the Provinces. *American Anthropologist* 88:70-91.

Torquemada, Fray Juan de
1969 *Monarquía Indiana.* 3 vols. Editorial Porrúa, Mexico City.

Williams García, Roberto
1963 *Los tepehuas.* Universidad Veracruzana, Jalapa, Mexico.

Zantwijk, Rudolph van
1967 La organización de once guarniciones aztecas: una nueva interpretación de los folios 17v y 18r del Códice Mendocino. *Journal de la société des Americanistes* 56:149-160.

12

Economies and Polities in Aztec-Period Morelos

Ethnohistoric Overview

Michael E. Smith

The core area of the Aztec realm, the Basin of Mexico, has been the focus of the vast majority of scholarly research on conquest-period Central Mexico. This is due partly to the interests of scholars in the political and cultural center of the Aztec empire and partly to the far greater abundance of documentary source material for the Basin of Mexico as compared with other areas. But if we are to understand fully the nature of the Aztec core zone, there are two compelling reasons to expand our perspective to include areas outside of the Basin of Mexico. First, detailed studies of economic and political organization in other areas are needed to evaluate the significance and uniqueness of the Basin of Mexico. Were well-known Aztec institutions such as city-states and market systems limited to the Aztec core, or were they more widely distributed? Second, more data from other regions of Central Mexico are needed in order to better understand the spatial context of Aztec imperial expansion and other processes of interregional interaction.

In this paper I review ethnohistoric information on economies and polities in Late Postclassic Morelos, the area immediately south of the Basin of Mexico. I argue that most of the major political and economic institutions in the two areas were quite similar. The city-state was the dominant political institution, population densities were high, intensive agriculture was common, and there was a high volume of exchange through both market systems and hierarchical tribute networks. The greatest difference between Morelos and the Basin of Mexico was their relative positions in the Aztec empire as conquered and conqueror, province and core. Morelos was the first area outside of the Basin of Mexico to be conquered by the expanding Aztec empire, a development explained by its proximity, its distinctive resources, a high level of political development, and a history of trade and interaction between the two areas.

Although the Aztec empire clearly was an important force in Central Mexico, it was but one institution among many with economic and political influence in Morelos. Several previous studies of Late Postclassic Central Mexico have begun with the Aztec empire and proceeded to discuss conquered areas as if their role as imperial provinces was their most salient characteristic (e.g., Barlow 1949; Davies 1973; Hassig 1988). When analysis is focused on local patterns in the Aztec provinces, however, it becomes clear that many of the key political and economic processes were only marginally influenced by the empire (see Berdan et al. 1994). Provincial areas need to be analyzed on their own terms, and this paper contributes to such a task for the region that today is the Mexican state of Morelos.

POLITICAL AND TERRITORIAL ORGANIZATION

At the time of the Spanish conquest in 1519, the territory of Morelos was divided into nearly 70 city-states. Although conquest-period documentation is scanty, existing sources indicate that the Morelos city-states were smaller than their better-known counterparts in the Basin of Mexico but similar in organization (for Morelos city-states, see Gerhard 1970a, 1970b, 1975, or Carrasco 1964b; Basin of Mexico city-states are discussed by Gibson 1964:32-57, Hodge 1984, Hodge, chap. 2, and Licate 1980). City-states were ruled by a *tlatoani* of the noble class who resided in the capital settlement, where the administrative, religious and (to a lesser extent) economic functions of the polity were concentrated. The hereditary noble class, more or less synonymous with the city-state government, was supported primarily by tribute in labor and goods from commoners, most of whom lived in rural villages and hamlets scattered throughout the polity. Of fundamental importance to the power and status of the Morelos nobility was their control over the irrigated farmland of the city-state (Carrasco 1968, 1972, 1976a).

Most of the Morelos city-states were organized into six larger conquest-states: Quauhnahuac, Yauhtepec, Huaxtepec, Totolapan, Yacapitztlan and Ocuituco. Tepoztlan was an independent city-state, as were several polities in the Zacualpan region. As discussed in Smith (1986), conquest-states were formed when one city-state managed to conquer adjacent polities and institute tribute payments. The subject city-states retained a relatively high degree of economic and political autonomy, however. Local political authority continued to be vested in the individual *tlatoque*, and there is no indication that the conquest-states were involved in the organization or direction of economic production at the local level (except within their own home territory). These conquest-states were actively involved in many external wars and conquests during the Late Postclassic period. For example, Quauhnahuac waged wars with Malinalco, Cohuixco, Tlachco (Taxco), and other nearby polities (Acuña 1984-1987:v.7:127; Alva Ixtlilxochitl 1975:v.1:473; Anales de Tlatelolco 1948:57); Yacapiztlan sacrificed victims captured in wars with Mixtec states (Acuña 1984-1987:v.6:218); and Huaxtepec, Tetela and Totolapan all fought battles with polities in the Puebla-Tlaxcala Valley (Acuña 1984-1987:v.6:203, v.7:267, v.8:162). The Morelos conquest-states also warred among themselves (Acuña 1984-1987:v.6:188; Torquemada 1969:v.1:149), and their territorial extent in 1519 was the result of several centuries of expansion and conquest (O'Mack 1985; Smith 1986).

My reconstruction of the Morelos city-states and conquest-states is portrayed in figure 12.1; the polities are listed in table 12.1. A discussion of the methods and data employed may be found in Smith (1983:120-128). Briefly, I follow Gerhard's (1970a) lead in territorial reconstruction, although my reliance upon a 1532 listing of Cortés's Morelos encomiendas (Cortés 1869: 560f) leads to the designation of more city-states than Gerhard finds. The polities of Morelos were incorporated into the Triple Alliance empire under the tributary provinces of Quauhnahuac and Huaxtepec (*Codex Mendoza* 1992:f.23r-25r). The former coincided with the Quauhnahuac conquest-state, while the latter included the independent states of Huaxtepec, Yauhtepec, Tepoztlan, Totolapan and Yacapitztlan. This situation was quite common, as a source from 1532 reveals:

> Mutizuma ponía un calpisque o mayordomo en una provincia, y muchas cabezeras y pueblos, que eran por sí, contribuían a do[nde] estaba el calpisque, y estos no se deben tener por subjectos. (Ramírez de Fuenleal 1870a:236)

> [Mutizuma [Motecuhzoma, or any Mexican emperor] would install a *calpixque* or tribute-collector in a province, and many independent capitals and towns would deliver tribute to the calpisque center. These capitals and towns should not be viewed as subjects [of the calpisque center].] (author's translation)

Fig. 12.1. Territorial organization in Late Postclassic Morelos. City-state boundaries are thin lines; city-state capitals are circles. Conquest-state boundaries are heavy lines; conquest-state capitals are triangles. See table 12.1 for the key to polity names.

In the case of Huaxtepec, we are explicitly told that although a Triple Alliance *calpixque* was stationed in the town, "asimismo ellos tenían otro señor natural [i.e., *tlatoani*] a quien obedecían y reconocían por señor" [these also had a separate local lord [i.e., *tlatoani*] whom they obeyed and recognized as lord] (Acuña 1984-1987:v.6:201). Thus the tributary provinces of the Triple Alliance empire were somewhat arbitrary units that did not necessarily correspond to local political units, and descriptions of these provinces (e.g., Barlow 1949) cannot be used to reconstruct local patterns of territorial organization (see Hicks [1984a] or Berdan et al. [1994] for discussion of this issue). Quauhnahuac and the Morelos polities in the

Table 12.1   Morelos polities in 1519   (see fig. 12.1 for locations)

No.	City-State	Modern Town	No.	City-State	Modern Town
Quauhnahuac Conquest-State			*Yauhtepec Conquest-State*		
1.	Quauhnahuac	Cuernavaca	38.	Yauhtepec	Yautepec
2.	Acatlipac	Acatlipa	39.	Atlhuelican	Atlihuayan
3.	Amacoztitlan	Amacuzac	40.	Coacalco	Oacalco
4	Amatitlan	Amatitlan,	41.	Huitzillan	Huitzililla
		Cuernavaca	42.	Tlaltizapan	(same)
5.	Atlicholoayan	Atlacholoaya	*Yacapitztlan Conquest-State*		
6.	Atlpoyecan	Alpuyeca			
7.	Coatlan	Coatlan del Río	43.	Yacapitztlan	Yecapixtla
8.	Cohuintepec	Cuentepec	44.	Amayucan	Amayuca
9.	Quauhchichinola	Cuachichnola	45.	Atotonilco	(same)
10.	Huitzillapan	Huitzilac	46.	Ayoxochapan	Axochiapan
11	Yztepec	Ahuacatitlan	47.	Tecpantzinco	Tepalcingo
12.	Yztlan	Puente de Ixtla	48.	Tetellan	Tetelilla
13.	Mazatepec	(same)	49.	Tlayacac	(same)
14.	Miacatlan	(same)	50.	Xantetelco	Jantetelco
15	Molotlan	(unidentified;	51.	Xaloztoc	(same)
		Tetelpa?)	52.	Xonacatepec	Jonacatepec
16.	Ocpayucan	(unidentified)	*Tepoztlan*		
17.	Panchimalco	(same)			
18.	Tehuixtlan	Tehuixtla	53.	Tepoztlan	(same)
19.	Temimiltzinco	(same)	*Totolapan Conquest-State*		
20.	Teocaltzinco	Teocalcingo, Gro.			
21.	Tequesquitenco	(same)	54.	Totolapan	(same)
22.	Tezoyucan	Tezoyuca	55.	Atlatlauhcan	(same)
23.	Tlaquiltenanco	(same)	56	Nepopoalco	(same)
24.	Xiuhtepec	Jiutepec	57.	Tehuizco	(unidentified)
25.	Xochitepec	(same)	58.	Tlayacapan	(same)
26.	Xoxotlan	Jojutla	*Ocuituco Conquest-State*		
27.	Zacatepec	(same)			
Huaxtepec Conquest-State			59.	Ocuituco	(same)
			60.	Acatzinco	Ecatzingo, Mex.
28.	Huaxtepec	Oaxtepec	61.	Hueyapan	(same)
29.	Ahuehuepan	(none)	62	Nepopoalco	(unidentified;
30.	Amiltzinco	(same)			Huejotengo?)
31.	Anenecuilco	(same)	63.	Tetellan	Tetela del Volcan
32.	Quauhtlan	Cuautla	64.	Xumiltepec	Jumiltepec
33.	Quauhtlixco	Cuautlixco	*(southern group)*		
34	Yzamatitlan	Itzamatitlan			
35.	Olintepec	Olintepec	65.	Quauhzolco	Huazulco
36.	Xochimilcatzinco	(unidentified)	66.	Temoac	(same)
37.	Zonpanco	(unidentified)	67.	Tlacotepec	(same)
			68.	Zacualpan	(same)

Aztec province of Huaxtepec were integrated into the Triple Alliance empire through both official channels (their status and responsibilities as tributary provinces) and more informal mechanisms like trade and elite interaction (Smith 1986).

The Ocuituco area in the northeast corner of Morelos stands apart from the other Morelos polities; its city-states were subject to Quauhquechulan (in modern Puebla) in 1487 (Durán 1967:v.2:334), and later to Xochimilco at the time of Spanish conquest (Acuña 1984-1987:v.7: 265, 267). Gerhard (1970b) discusses the territorial extent and political organization of the Ocuituco area, whose towns are not included in the *Codex Mendoza* (1992) or the 1532 encomienda list (Cortés 1869:556f). These polities served the Aztec empire as client states and they formed a "strategic province" of the empire (Berdan et al. 1994; Berdan, chap. 11). Although they paid only a modest tribute in goods (Acuña 1984-1987:v.7:267; Gerhard 1970b:110), these towns helped to maintain the frontier with Tlaxcala by fighting wars. The *Relación Geográfica* states, "era ... como frontera contra otras provincias" [this area was like a frontier against other polities] (Acuña 1984-1987:v.7:267).

DEMOGRAPHY AND SETTLEMENT PATTERNS

Early Colonial Spanish visitors to Morelos reported a dense population distributed in a relatively dispersed fashion, a pattern also found in the Basin of Mexico. For example, Fray Pedro Delgado, a Dominican priest writing in 1540, described the Huaxtepec areas as follows:

> En aquel tiempo estaban estas sierras, sus faldas y valles, pobladas de millares de almas que vivían, sugun su costumbre en varias rancherias divididas, a corta distancia las unas de las otras ... no había poblazon formada porque cada uno vivía donde tenía su maíz o le parecía. (Cruz y Moya 1954/55:v.2:133)

> [In those times these hills and valleys were populated with thousands of souls who lived, following their custom, in many scattered hamlets a short distance from one another ... there were not population centers [towns] because each person lived where he had his cornfields, or so it appeared.] (author's translation)

This description was part of an argument in favor of the *congregación* policy of gathering the rural population into nucleated towns (see Gerhard 1977) and thus may overemphasize the dispersed nature of settlement; other sources speak of "muchas y grandes pueblos de muy suntuoso edificios" [many and large towns with very sumptuous buildings] in Morelos (Códice Ramírez 1944:23). Nevertheless, the general picture of a dense, relatively dispersed population is supported by both Early Colonial census data and the archaeological record (see Williams, chap. 3, for a similar situation in the Basin of Mexico).

Methods and Models of Population Estimation

Population levels for Morelos in 1519 may be estimated from a number of published census documents from before 1575. For most entities, I provide two population estimates. The first set of estimates, labeled Model 1, rest upon the assumption that the post-1519 demographic decline was constant until 1568. I employ a rate of decline from Sanders's (1970) detailed and extensive analysis of Central Mexican historical demography. Sanders (1970: 427-430) suggests a 1519-1568 population loss of 77.3% for Morelos. Thus population declined by a factor of 4.405 in 49 years, or an average annual decline of 0.090. The assumption of a steady decline rate produces conversion factors of 1.62 for 1537 census data, 2.61 for 1548, and 2.88 for 1551. The population decline after 1568 was probably somewhat slower (Gerhard 1975), so I use a conversion factor of 5.0 for 1571 census figures in place of the constant-decline factor of 5.58 for 1571.

Model 2 uses the depopulation model derived for the Basin of Mexico by Whitmore's (1991, 1992) quantitative simulation study which employs information on the timing of the major epidemics. This is more realistic than the constant-decline model, but its applicability to Morelos needs to be confirmed. Conversion factors for the years of Morelos census data were obtained by measurements on Whitmore's most likely simulation graph (1991:478). These conversion factors are 1.90 for 1537, 3.33 for 1548, 3.64 for 1551, and 5.25 for both 1568 and 1571. This model produces slightly higher population estimates than the constant-decline model, but the two models are in general agreement for most estimates (see table 12.2 below). An alternative population decline model (Gerhard 1975:343) produces estimates for 1519 that are considerably higher than the two models presented here, but Gerhard does not provide sufficient detail to construct a third model.

In many cases the Colonial census figures include only the commoner population, since nobles were exempt from tribute payments. Where this appears to be the case, I add an additional two percent to the population to account for the Aztec-period nobility. While published sources are not very informative on the size of the Aztec nobility, we do know that in Yacapitztlan, nobles comprised just under one percent of all household heads (Carrasco 1976a:110), and noble households were larger than commoner households. For example, census data from 1537 show that the mean household size was 5.4 in Tepoztlan and 7.4 in five other Morelos communities at lower elevations (Carrasco 1964b:377), while noble households had as many as 15 to 23 members (Carrasco 1964a:190, 1972:232). Thus it is not unreasonable to use two percent as an estimate of the proportion of nobles in Late Postclassic Morelos.

A detailed census of Yacapitztlan from 1561 (*Visita, tasación y cuenta* 1946; see Sanders 1971:20) is not used here because of problems in separating the immediate estancias of Yacapitztlan from those in the more distant Tlalnahua area of southeast Morelos. It does appear, however, that the figures from this document yield population estimates for 1519 considerably lower than the other sources. Further research on the historical demography of Morelos is urgently needed to clarify such issues and provide more solid population figures than the provisional estimates presented here.

Population Estimates

My population estimates are listed in table 12.2, where all figures are rounded to the nearest hundred. The sources, assumptions, and calculations used to produce the population estimates listed in the notes to table 12.2. Sanders (1970:430) estimates the total population of Morelos in A.D. 1519 to have been 672,500 (table 12.2). This yields an areal density of 136 persons/km^2 (this is the midpoint of Sanders's range of 119-152 persons/km^2), somewhat lower than his estimate of 150-168 persons/km^2 for the Basin of Mexico at the same time. Gerhard (1975:343) furnishes a figure of 850,000 for Morelos in 1519 but does not explain how he arrives at this number. My application of Models 1 and 2 to the 1571 census data published by Gerhard (1975:344) yields total population estimates that more closely agree with Sanders's figures (table 12.2, calculation C).

The various estimates for the populations of the conquest-states in table 12.2 are in relative agreement. The population estimates for the capitals of conquest-states are in line with the sizes of the largest Aztec cities in the Basin of Mexico (apart from Tenochtitlan), which ranged from 10,000 to 30,000 inhabitants (Hodge, chap. 2; Sanders et al. 1979:154; Smith et al.

1994). Although the size of the city of Quauhnahuac impressed early Spanish visitors (e.g., de Solis 1924:v.2:230; Ponce 1873:v.1:197; *Títulos de Cuernavaca* 1947:222), the other Morelos capital cities did not excite much comment.

Figures for the populations of city-states are quite variable, with three clusters of values. The first four cases in table 12.2 fall between 7,500 and 6,000 persons; the next three estimates (from the same 1548 census data) range from 10,000 to 14,500 persons, and the estimates for the local city-state populations of the five capital polities range from 16,500 to 120,600. It is reasonable to expect that the densest populations in a conquest-state will occur near the capital city, but these later estimates appear to be out of line. Population estimates for city-state capitals all fall between 1,500 and 2,500 persons (table 12.2), somewhat smaller than the Basin of Mexico city-state capitals (estimated at 3-4,000 inhabitants [Sanders et al. 1979:54]); this size differential makes sense given the slightly lower population densities and lower level of economic complexity in Morelos. Comparison of these last two sets of figures reveals that the average city-state capital contained about 20-40% of the population of the total city-state territory, a figure comparable to Sanders's estimate that one-third of the population of the Basin of Mexico lived in towns and cities in 1519 (1970:449-450) and Hicks's (1982, 1984b) specific analysis of Texcoco. Similarly, ethnohistoric documents from nearby parts of Guerrero report that 30 to 50 percent of the population of city-states resided in the capital towns (Acuña 1984-1987:v.6:111-112; García Pimentel 1904:102-103). Documentary data assembled by Hodge (chap. 2), however, show a wider variation in the degree of population nucleation in Basin of Mexico polities.

The relatively small size of the Morelos city-state capitals, as estimated from sixteenth-century census data, is supported by recent archaeological research at Late Postclassic sites in western Morelos. As discussed in Smith (1989), most of the archaeologically-known city-state capitals are small sites (15 ha or less) with central civic and religious architecture but little evidence of craft specialization (see Mason [1980] for a study of one of these sites, Coatlan Viejo).

In sum, these population estimates paint a picture of a dense, widely-distributed population at the time of Spanish conquest. Although this is not the place to enter the debate over the total size of the native population of the New World when first encountered by Europeans (e.g., Dobyns 1993; Henige 1992), the above data are in closer accord with the lower central Mexican estimates of Sanders (1970) and Whitmore (1992) than with the unrealistically high estimates of Borah and Cook (1963).

Table 12.2 Population estimates for 1519

| Entity | Population | | Calculation | Census Year |
	Model 1	Model 2		
Entire Modern State				
	672,500	--	A	1568
	850,000	--	B	?
	677,600	711,500	C	1571
Conquest-States				
Quauhnahuac	253,100	302,000	D	1568
"	207,600	217,900	E	1571
"	220,500	278,700	F	1551
Tepoztlan	33,000	39,400	D	1568
"	45,100	47,300	E	1571
Yauhtepec	58,900	70,100	D	1568
"	79,800	83,800	E	1571
Totolapan	65,600	78,200	D	1568
"	79,600	83,500	E	1571
Huaxtepec	97,000	115,800	D	1568
"	62,800	65,900	E	1571
Yacapitztlan	62,700	74,800	D	1568
"	54,200	56,900	E	1571
Tlalnahua states[a]	47,800	61,600	D	1568
"	48,200	50,600	E	1571
Ocuituco	33,100	39,500	D	1568
"	47,800	50,200	E	1571
"	20,300	25,900	H	1548
Zacualpan states[a]	21,000	25,100	D	1568
"	27,000	28,400	E	1571
Capital Cities				
Quauhnahuac	31,800	40,200	G	1551
Tepoztlan	7,600	9,500	G	1551
"	6,500	7,600	K	1537
Yauhtepec	13,300	16,800	G	1551
Huaxtepec	5,500	7,000	G	1551
Yacapitztlan	15,800	20,000	G	1551

(continued)

Note: The various calculations used to estimate prehispanic population are derived as follows:

A. The midpoint of Sanders's (1970:430) range of estimates for the 1519 population of Morelos. This figure is based upon census data from 1568 presented by Sanders (1970).

B. Gerhard's (1975:345) figure for the 1519 population of Morelos. He does not discuss its origin or derviation.

C. The sum of the populations of the Late Postclassic conquest states as derived from the 1571 Ovando census; the data are presented in Gerhard (1975:344). The 1571 population is multiplied by the decline rate and the noble conversion factor (see text) to produce the total population in 1519.

D. The 1568 census data are published in Sanders (1970:415-416). I have aggregated the totals in terms of the 1519 political units and applied the 1568 conversion factors.

E. Census data from the Ovando reports of 1571(Gerhard 1975:344), with application of the conversion for a 2 percent noble population.

Table 12.2 (continued)

Entity	Population Model 1	Population Model 2	Calculation	Census Year
City-States				
Zacualpan	2,600	3,300	H	1548
Tlacotepec	2,700	3,500	H	1548
Quauhzolco	3,200	4,100	H	1548
Coatlan	4,900	6,200	H	1548
Tetellan	11,200	14,300	H	1548
Xumiltepec	11,400	14,500	H	1548
Temoac	10,100	12,800	H	1548
Quauhnahuac	95,400	120,600	I	1551
Tepoztlan	22,800	28,500	I	1551
Yauhtepec	39,900	50,400	I	1551
Huaxtepec	16,500	21,000	I	1551
Yacapitztlan	47,400	60,000	I	1551
Mean, Quauhnahuac area	5,100	5,600	J	--
Mean, Yauhtepec area	7,400	6,600	J	--
Mean, Huaxtepec area	7,000	7,700	J	--
Mean, Yacapitztlan area	1,200	700	J	--
City-State Capitals				
Quauhchichinola	1,600	1,900	K	1537
Molotlan	1,600	1,900	K	1537
Panchimalco	2,000	2,300	K	1537
Huitzillan	2,400	2,900	K	1537

F. Based upon Carrasco's (1976a:193) publication of a 1551 census figure of 13,899 commoner household heads for all of Curenavaca and its subjects (i.e., the Cuauhnahuac conquest-state).

G. Urban population figures are based on a separate 1551 encomienda census reported by Riley (1973:133), who gives total urban populations plus breakdowns by sex and age. Riley's figures appear to represent the total population of the city-state associated with each capital (including rural areas) and therefore must be reduced in order to reach estimates of strictly urban population levels. Based upon Hick's analysis of Texcoco (1982, 1984b), I assume that one-third of the total population of a city-state resided in the urban core; thus the estimates for 1519 are divided by three in order to reach the figures shown in the table. The total polity populations are included under calculation I below.

H. Population data from the *Suma de visitas* ... (1905) of ca. 1548. This document gives the number of houses for Ocuituco (p.167) and Coatlan (p. 80), and the number of *"hombres"* or *"tributarios"* for the other towns. The census figures are multiplied by a household size of 5.4 persons, and then the 2 percent noble conversion is applied. It is not certain if this Coatlan pertains to the Morelos city-state capital or to another town of the same name.

I. City-state populations from the 1551 encomienda census discussed under calculation G above.

J. Mean city-state populations derived by taking the mean of the different estimates for the population of the conquest-state capital and dividing it by the number of subject city-states in the conquest-state.

K. Population data from the 1537 town census lists analyzed by Carrasco (1964b:377). It is not clear whether these figures represent the populations of only the central towns or of whole polities (i.e., *cabecera* plus rural *estancias*); however, when the figures are compared to independent sources, the former seems more likely for all towns but Tepoztlan, where the large population must pertain to the entire city-state. Thus for Tepoztlan only, the 1519 figure is divided by three following the procedure outlined under calculation G above.

[a] The Tlalnahua states may have been part of the Yacapitztlan conquest-state, and, similarly, the Zacualpan states may have been part of the Ocuituco conquest-state, but these relationships remain unclear (see Gerhard 1970a for discussion). These states are represented as separate entities in the above population figures.

ENVIRONMENT AND AGRICULTURE

The dense populations of Late Postclassic Morelos were supported by intensive agricultural methods that took advantage of the nature of the rivers and slopes in the area. Morelos is surrounded on all sides by mountains and comprises a natural physiographic unit. It is separated from the Basin of Mexico to the north by the Sierra de Ajusco. Moving south, elevation drops off quickly at first, then more gradually, with most of the state less than 1,500 m above sea level. Climate below this elevation is subtropical, with annual rainfall averaging between 800 and 1,100 mm and mean temperatures between 20° to 24° C; winter frosts are virtually unknown below the northern slopes. Because of its warm climate, Morelos is referred to in native historical accounts from the Basin of Mexico as the "tierra caliente" [hot land] (Durán [1967], Torquemada [1969], and others use this term for the specific region of Morelos, not as a label for a general climatic zone as is common today).

In spite of the area's favorable climate, the extent of agriculture in Morelos is limited by topography and soils. Much of the state is mountainous, and apart from rich alluvial deposits along some of the major rivers (see below), soils are generally quite thin and poor for agriculture. Only 27 percent of the surface area of the state (1,355 out of 4,941 km²) supports rainfall agriculture *(temporal)* today (SARH 1977), and much of this represents recent clearing of poor mountainside milpas in response to demographic increase and other modern socioeconomic changes (Bolio 1976). Maize, often intercropped with beans, is by far the most common temporal crop, covering about 60 percent of the nonirrigated farmland (other major crops grown with temporal cultivation today are sorghum, peanuts, tomatoes, and onions—see Bolio [1976:67]).

Irrigation

Far more significant than rainfall agriculture is irrigation in both prehispanic and modern Morelos. A number of Morelos rivers, particularly the Chalma, Apatlaco (or Cuernavaca), Yautepec and Cuautla Rivers, are associated with significant areas of rich alluvium that are relatively easy to irrigate with simple technology. Early Spanish observers were struck by the high agricultural productivity of Morelos which suggests irrigation was important in the Late Postclassic period as well. The Códice Ramírez, for example, states that the area, "es muy fertil y abundante de todo lo necessario" [is very fertile and abundant in everything neccessary] (1944:22; see also Durán 1967:v.2:23, 393; Torquemada 1969:v.1:287). It is no coincidence that the areas of greatest population concentration in Late Postclassic and modern times are the valleys of the Cuernavaca and Cuautla Rivers, which support the largest areas of irrigated farmland in the state. Furthermore, the most powerful conquest-states in Late

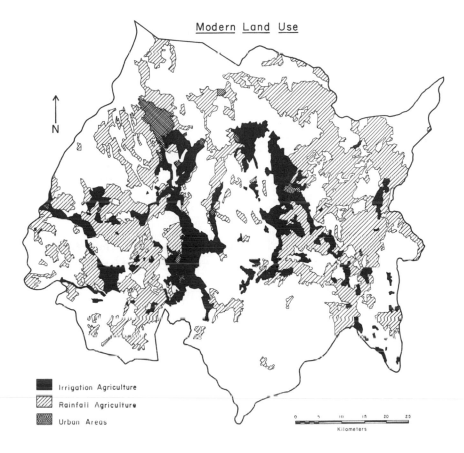

Fig. 12.2. Modern land use in Morelos. Map based upon SARH (1977).

Postclassic Morelos (Quauhnahuac, Yauhtepec, Huaxtepec and Yacapitztlan) all had general north-south orientations along major irrigated river valleys such that none were dependent upon other states for their water supply (see figure 12.1).

The extent of modern irrigation, which covers approximately 503 km² or 10.2 percent of the state (SARH 1977), is shown in figure 12.2. Based upon the assumption that nearly all areas under irrigation at the time of the Spanish conquest continued to be used for irrigation agriculture during the Colonial and modern periods (see below), figure 12.2 provides a maximum limit for the extent of prehispanic irrigation in Morelos. Since the mid-sixteenth century, the most important irrigated crop has been sugar cane, which occupies approximately half of the irrigated fields today (Bolio 1976:67). Other important, modern irrigated crops include cotton, rice, and beans (the extent of irrigated maize production is not reported in this source).

Table 12.3 Irrigation and cotton cultivation in Early Colonial Morelos

Polity	No.	Irrig.	Cotton	Year	Source
Quauhnahuac Conquest-State					
Quauhnahuac	1	A	--	1533	Declaración de los tributos (1970:145)
Quauhnahuac	1	A	--	1584-86	Ponce (1873:v.1:197)
Atlpoyecan	6	C	--	1743	Villaseñor y Sánchez (1952:169)
Tlaltenanco	11	A	--	1520s	document in Dubernard (1975:28)
Molotlan	15	A	--	1530s	Carrasco (1972:229ff; 1976b:46)
Tetelpan	15	--	X	1743	Villaseñor y Sánchez (1952:171)
Panchimalco	17	--	X	1743	Villaseñor y Sánchez (1952:171)
Xiuhtepec	24	A	--	1584-86	Ponce (1873:v.1:199)
Xoxotlan	26	--	X	1743	Villaseñor y Sánchez (1952:171)
Huaxtepec Conquest-State					
Huaxtepec	28	A	--	1580	Acuña (1984-1987:v.6:207)
Amiltzinco	28	B	--	1580	Acuña (1984-1987:v.6:35)
Ixcatepec	28	--	X	1580	Acuña (1984-1987:v.6:34)
Yzamatitlan	34	A	--	1584-86	Ponce (1873:v.1:201); see Palerm (1972:46) for location
Yauhtepec Conquest-State					
Yauhtepec	38	--	X	1580	Acuña (1984-1987:v.6:195)
Huitzillan	41	B	--	1592	Códices indígenas (1933: no. 30)
Ticoman	42	--	X	1743	Villaseñor y Sánchez (1952:174)
Yacapitztlan Conquest-State					
Yacapitztlan	43	A	X	1561	Visita (1946:219-247)
Suchitlan	43	A	X	1561	Visita (1946:219-247)
Amayucan	44	A	X	1561	Visita (1946:219-247)
Atotonilco	45	A	X	1561	Visita (1946:219-247)
Tecpantzinco	47	A	X	1561	Visita (1946:219-247)
Tetellan	48	A	X	1561	Visita (1946:219-247)
Xantetelco	50	A	X	1561	Visita (1946:219-247)
Xonacatepec	52	A	X	1561	Visita (1946:219-247)
Amacuitlapilco	52	A	X	1561	Visita (1946:219-247)
Chalcatzinco	52	A	X	1561	Visita (1946:219-247)
Tepoztlan					
Tepoztlan	53	--	X	1551	Proceso de Tepoztlan y Yautepec:7
Ocuituco Conquest-State					
Ocuituco	59	A	--	ca. 1548	Suma de visitas (1905:183)
Quauhzolco	65	C	X	ca. 1548	Suma de visitas (1905:66)
Temoac	66	A	--	ca. 1548	Suma de visitas (1905:184)
Tlacotepec	67	A	--	ca. 1548	Suma de visitas (1905:195)
Zacualpan	68	A	--	ca. 1548	Suma de visitas (1905:65)

Note: Source refers to the use of irrigation as follows: (A) for subsistence crops and/or cotton; (B) for crops, type not specified. (C) source states that irrigation is *not* present. (X) source specifically mentions cotton cultivation.

Early Colonial sources reported an abundance of irrigated land in Morelos. For example, Ponce wrote in 1584/86 that, "hay abundancia de agua para regarle todo" [there is an abundance of water to irrigate everything] (1873:v.1:198), and the ability of irrigated land to produce two crops per year was described in 1533: "se cogía dos veces fruto en un año, a causa que [las tierras] eran de regadío" [two crops of fruit were harvested yearly, because [the fields] were irrigated] (*Declaración de los tributos* 1870:145; see also *Visita, tasación y cuenta* 1946:219ff). Information on Colonial irrigation in Morelos must be treated carefully in the reconstruction of prehispanic practices because of the early introduction of irrigated cane cultivation during the sixteenth century. The soils and hydrology of the alluvial zones of Morelos are ideal for cane cultivation, and Cortés and other early encomenderos lost no time in planting the crop in irrigated zones throughout the state (Riley 1973:64-66). The replacement of irrigated maize, cotton, and other indigenous crops by cane during the sixteenth century proceeded so quickly that by 1600, Morelos had ceased to be self-sufficient in maize and had to import the grain from surrounding regions (Moreno Toscano 1965). Because cane must be irrigated, the simple mention of irrigation in Colonial documents may refer to newly-constructed canals for cane and not to irrigation systems in existence during prehispanic times.

Published data on sixteenth-century irrigation in Morelos are assembled in table 12.3 (see also Maldonado [1990:135-188] on conquest-period irrigation). This list, which indicates the presence of irrigation in 17 of the Morelos city-states, augments considerably the number of references to prehispanic irrigation published by Palerm (1972:46). In table 12.3, category A includes only those references to irrigation where subsistence crops or cotton are specifically mentioned; some of these citations note that both cane and subsistence plots were irrigated. Category B consists of two citations that mention irrigation without specifying the nature of the crops, and "no" indicates two citations that specifically declare an area as not irrigated. It should be noted that the references in category A range from statements of extensive irrigated land in an area (e.g., "todo es de regadío" [everything is irrigated] in Temoac, and "se riegan muchas y grandes sementeras de maíz" [many large fields of maize are irrigated] in Huaxtepec) to simple declarations that irrigation was practiced (e.g. "es tierra de regadío" [this is irrigated land] in Tlacotepec).

In figure 12.3, the data of table 12.3 are plotted by city-state (see table 12.1 for a key to the names of city-states). The whole area of a city-state is hatched if irrigation is mentioned as occurring anywhere within the polity; the map thus does not illustrate the actual extent of irrigation within polities (refer to figure 12.2 for a closer approximation of the maximum extent of irrigation). The lack of evidence for irrigation along the Chalma and Amacusac Rivers in western Morelos is almost certainly a function of the general lack of Early Colonial documentation for this area (Nicholson 1971; Riley 1973); the floodplains of

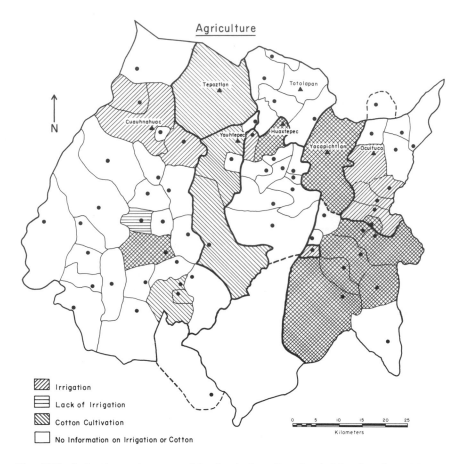

Agriculture

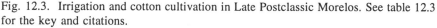

Fig. 12.3. Irrigation and cotton cultivation in Late Postclassic Morelos. See table 12.3 for the key and citations.

these rivers are irrigated today (SARH 1977) and were probably irrigated in prehispanic times as well. The presence of prehispanic irrigation probably can be inferred for areas with cotton cultivation in the sixteenth century because of the documented use of irrigation to grow that crop (see below); this inference increases the number of city-states with irrigation from 17 to 22 or 23 (table 12.3; figure 12.3).

Cotton

Cotton was the most important nonsubsistence crop grown in Morelos at the time of the Spanish conquest. Cotton textiles in the form of mantas were common media of exchange in Late Postclassic Central Mexico. They were among the most numerous items of tribute at all levels (see below) and were traded extensively in marketplaces (Berdan 1987; Hicks, chap. 4). Cotton does not grow in the Basin of Mexico, and woven textiles were imported by the hundreds of thousands each year through imperial tribute (*Codex Mendoza* 1992) and various trade mechanisms. The low weight of cotton textiles made them a significant means for the long-distance transfer of economic value in an economy based upon human transport (Berdan 1987; Drennan 1984). Morelos was the closest cotton-producing area to the Basin of Mexico, and its textiles played an important role in the inter-regional exchange networks of the Central Mexican highlands.

Early Colonial descriptions of Morelos usually comment on the quantity and quality of Morelos cotton. For example, Durán writes that Morelos was "riquisima de algodón, donde acude el trato de toda la tierra en el" [very rich in cotton, and traded it with the whole land] (1967:v.2:23; see also Torquemada 1969:v.1:104). Morelos polities annually provided tribute of 32,000 cotton mantas and garments to the Triple Alliance (see below), and these goods are also common in sixteenth-century local encomienda tribute lists. Archaeological studies have documented widespread cotton-spinning activities at Late Postclassic sites in the state (Smith and Heath Smith, chap. 13; Smith and Hirth 1988). In table 12.3 I list references to cotton cultivation in Early Colonial Morelos; mere mentions of cotton tribute are not included since tribute goods often were not produced locally.

References from the relatively late date of 1743 are appropriate for inferring prehispanic cotton cultivation because of the great decline in the Morelos cotton industry in the sixteenth and seventeenth centuries (it is unlikely that cotton cultivation spread to new areas between 1519 and 1743). Riley (1973:45-47, 70ff) documents a situation where local tribute payments progressively changed from cotton mantas to money as populations declined and intensive agricultural systems were converted to cane or abandoned. The cotton industry in Morelos did not expand again until the mid-twentieth century (Bataillon 1972:207), but by 1974, cotton had become the fifth most profitable cultigen in Morelos, covering at least 5,000 hectares (Bolio 1976:30). Some indication of continuity in the Morelos cotton industry from prehispanic to Colonial times comes from a Colonial period archaeological site, RCT-79. This site has no apparent prehispanic remains, but the cotton-spinning artifacts from the site are identical to prehispanic examples from other parts of the state (Kenneth G. Hirth, unpublished data).

Of the 17 towns cited as growing cotton in Early Colonial times, nine are listed as having irrigated cotton fields, one is said specifically not to have irrigation, and nothing is said of irrigation for the remaining seven. In his study of Late Postclassic irrigation in the Balsas River drainage (which includes Morelos),

Armillas (1949:112) found that the number of towns listing cotton as an irrigated crop was second only to the number of towns listing maize. Thus, it appears that cotton was almost always irrigated in Morelos and the general Balsas area, as it is today. There is little published information on specific techniques of cotton cultivation in Morelos, but one source states that cotton and maize were often grown together in the same field (*Visita, tasación y cuenta* 1946:180, 220ff). As in the case of the documentation of irrigation practices, cotton cultivation was almost certainly more extensive in Late Postclassic Morelos than the published sources indicate.

Other Crops

In addition to cotton, maize, beans, chia and amaranth, all of which were provided to the Triple Alliance in tribute (*Codex Mendoza* 1992:f.23r-25r), other indigenous agricultural crops cultivated in Early Colonial Morelos included tomato, chile, jicama and camote (*Visita, tasación y cuenta* 1946:219-231), several kinds of fruit (Ponce 1873:v.1:198), and maguey. The "pulque maguey" variety, used economically for sap and fibers, only grew in the northern part of the state where elevations were highest (Acuña 1984-87:v.6:192, 207-208, 218; v.7:267; v.8:163). The two Triple Alliance tributary provinces of Morelos, Quauhnahuac and Huaxtepec, are the only areas listed as suppliers of paper to the empire. Paper was among the gifts brought by Morelos nobles to Mexica state ceremonies (Durán 1967:v.2:297), and several documents emphasize the importance of amate bark paper production in Tepoztlan (Acuña 1984-1987:v.6:192; Proceso de Tepoztlan y Yauhtepec 1551:8) and the Ocuituco region (Gerhard 1970b:110ff). Ground stone bark-beaters, indicative of prehispanic paper production, are commonly found at Late Postclassic archaeological sites (Mason 1980:165; Smith and Heath-Smith, chap. 13). Morelos also provided flowers for use in state ceremonies in the Basin of Mexico (Torquemada 1969:v.2:477; see also Carrasco 1968:372).

Cacao is commonly found in Early Colonial encomienda tribute documents from Morelos (e.g. Carrasco 1964a:187, 1968:374, 1972:229ff; Riley 1973:37f). Although several sources explicitly state that cacao was not grown locally and had to be obtained through exchange (Acuña 1984-1987:v.6:222; *Declaración de los tributos* 1870:145), it is possible that some cacao was grown in the high rainfall zones of the northern part of the state. According to the Relación de Huaxtepec (Acuña 1984-1987:v.6:201), both cacao and rubber plants were transplanted from Veracruz to Motecuhzoma's Huaxtepec botanical garden (see also Armillas 1949:100f). The growing requirements of cacao are similar to those for coffee (Palerm 1967:40), which is cultivated in small amounts in Tepoztlan and Cuernavaca today. Furthermore, there was a sixteenth-century settlement named Cacahuamilpan (literally "cacao field") in the prehispanic state of Tlachco (ancient Taxco) along the Morelos border where cacao was reportedly grown in the sixteenth century (Acuña 1984-1987:v.7:123). However, the use of cacao was so extensive in Late Postclassic Morelos (e.g., the *Relación de Tepoztlan* noted an active trade in cacao through local markets; see Acuña 1984-1987:v.6:195) that the bulk of it must have been obtained through trade, probably with the Pacific coastal areas of modern-day Guerrero or Oaxaca (see Bergmann 1969).

Discussion

The dense population of Late Postclassic Morelos was supported by intensive agricultural methods. In addition to the ethnohistorically documented irrigation systems discussed above, archaeological fieldwork has revealed extensive areas of agricultural terracing throughout the state. Price and Smith (1992) and Smith and Heath-Smith (chap. 13) describe two types of stone terraces—contour terraces on hillsides and cross-channel terraces in ravines—that have been excavated at the sites of Cuexcomate and Capilco in western Morelos. It appears that all available land was probably under cultivation at the time of the Spanish conquest. Alluvial lowlands were irrigated and upland areas were terraced. Only the widespread use of intensive agricultural techniques could have produced the situation noted in the Códice Ramírez (1944:22) of a land: "muy fertil, abundante de todo lo necessario" (see above). This description would not accurately describe Morelos farming without the use of irrigation and terracing. Further discussion of Late Postclassic agriculture in Morelos may be found in Maldonado (1990), who reviews the relevant published and archival sources.

TRIBUTE

A primary mechanism for moving cotton and other agricultural products from producers to consumers was the tribute system. Tribute payments were of fundamental importance to the sociopolitical order of Postclassic Central Mexico. The nobility were distinguished from and supported by commoners on the basis of tribute, and tribute was the goal of military expansion by city-states, conquest-states, and empires. In Morelos there were four levels of tribute payments which may be mapped onto three levels of political organization. The two lowest levels of tribute comprised payments in goods and services that may be termed a form of tax ("a payment levied on individuals," [Mair 1977:98]). These levels (nos. 3 and 4 below) concerned relations between commoners and nobles and relations among nobles, and the payments took place within the context of

Table 12.4 Cotton textile tribute from Quauhnahuac and Huaxtepec

Category	Level	Quauh-nahuac	Huaxtepec			
			Tepoztlan	Yauhtepec	Huaxtepec	Yacapitztlan
A. Total population	--	245,200	41,200	73,200	83,400	114,200
B. Total commoner households	--	45,410	7,630	13,560	15,440	21,150
C. No. of subject city-states	--	27	--	5	10	10

MODEL 1

Conquest-State Tribute

D. Tribute to Aztec empire	1	16,000	3,200	3,200	3,200	3,200
E. Tribute taken in	2	25,353	7,850	7,850	10,502	4,986
F. Tribute rate	--	.631	.408	.408	.305	.642

City-State Tribute

G. Average tribute paid out	2	939	--	1,470	1,050	499
H. Tribute rate (assumed)	--	.40	--	.40	.40	.40
I. Average tribute taken in	3	2,348	--	3,925	2,625	1,248
J. Total tribute taken in	3	63,383	--	19,625	26,255	12,465

MODEL 2

Conquest-State Tribute

D. Tribute to Aztec empire	1	16,000	3,200	3,200	3,200	3,200
E. Tribute taken in	2	41,353	11,050	11,050	13,702	8,186
F. Tribute rate	--	.387	.290	.290	.234	.391

City-State Tribute

G. Average tribute paid out	2	1,532	--	2,210	1,370	819
H. Tribute rate (assumed)	--	.40	--	.40	.40	.40
I. Average tribute taken in	3	3,830	--	5,525	3,425	2,048
J. Total tribute taken in	3	103,383	--	27,625	34,255	20,465

Note: Tribute figures are expressed in numbers of mantas paid per year. The sources and calculations used are described below:

A. Total population of each conquest-state, calculated as the mean of estimates D and E in table 12.2. The Yacapitztlan conquest-state is assumed to include the Tlalnahua states of southeastern Morelos; this is reflected in the population figure, the number of city-states, and the encomienda tribute used to estimate category E.

B. A rough estimate that permits an assessment of the tribute burden on the household level. B is calculated by dividing the commoner population by 5.4, the mean household size in Tepoztlan (see notes to table 12.2).

C. The number of city-states subject to each conquest-state (see table 12.1; methods are described in Smith [1983]).

D. The number of cotton mantas paid to the Aztec empire by the provinces of Quauhnahuac and Huaxtepec (16,000 each) as reported in the *Codex Mendoza* (1992:23r-25r). These figures follow from Berdan's (1976:138) analysis of tribute levels in this source. Briefly, each manta glyph with a "400" glyph is assumed to represent 400 mantas, not 400 loads of mantas as suggested by Barlow (1949) and Drennan (1984). The imperial tribute of Huaxtepec province has been apportioned evenly among the five constituent states—Tepoztlan, Yauhtepec, Huaxtepec, Yacapitztlan, and Totolapan. Totolapan is not included in the table because of a lack of comparable data for encomienda tribute levels (category E).

city-states. The upper two levels of payment constituted tribute properly speaking ("a lump sum demanded from a subject area," [Mair 1977:98]). Level 1 tribute defined relationships between local polities (both city-states and conquest-states) and the Triple Alliance empire, and Level 2 defined relationships between city-states and their dominant conquest-state. The term *tequitl* was used to designate all four levels. A major uncertainty is the extent to which these levels were integrated into a single coherent system.

Level 1

The highest level of tribute, that paid to the Triple Alliance, is the best documented portion of the entire tribute hierarchy. In Morelos, this level was initiated within a year or two of Itzcoatl's conquest of Quauhnahuac in 1438 (Smith 1987). In 1519, the Quauhnahuac and Huaxtepec tributary provinces each supplied the Mexica with cotton textiles, warriors' costumes and shields, paper, grain (maize, beans, chia, huautli), and gourd bowls (*Codex Mendoza* 1992:f.23r-25r). The absolute quantities of goods paid to the Triple Alliance have been the subject of some dispute because of ambiguities in the sources and discrepancies among the major tribute lists (*Codex Mendoza* 1992; *Matrícula de Tributos* 1980; Scholes and Adams 1957). Berdan (1976) discusses these problems, and on the basis of her conclusions, the textile tribute of the Quauhnahuac and Huaxtepec provinces as stated in the *Codex Mendoza* may be put at 16,000 cotton items (mostly mantas) per province per year. These figures form the starting point of a quantitative reconstruction of cotton textile tribute in Morelos at the city-state and conquest-state levels. The numerical estimates are presented in table 12.4, and the necessary citations and explanations are discussed in the notes to the table. For the sake of simplification, all items of

E.   Projection of conquest-state tribute income in 1519. Calculations start with textile tribute levels from a *tasación* of 1534 (Riley 1973:45); these are standardized for the population at that time (1534 population estimates are interpolated using the Model 1 post-conquest population decline rate discussed in the text). The resulting rate of mantas per person per year is then applied to the estimated populations for 1519 from table 12.2. The unadjusted 1534 manta tribute levels for the five polities (in the order they are listed in the table above) are as follows: 9,120; 5,920; 5,920; 7,920; and 3,760. The estimates for 1519 tribute are listed as category E for Model 1, while these figures plus the category D imperial tribute constitute the category E estimates in Model 2.

F.   The proportion of conquest-state tribute income that was paid out to the Aztec empire (D ÷ E).

G.   Estimate of the average amount of textile tribute paid by subject polities to to their conquerors. Calculated by dividing the tribute income of the conquest-states by the number of constituent city-states. Tepoztlan had no subject city-states (E ÷ C).

H.   A tribute rate of 40% is assumed in order to estimate tribute income at the city-state level.

I.   Estimate of the textile tribute income of the average city-state, calculated according to the assumed 40% tribute rate (G ÷ H).

J.   The total textile tribute income for all of the city-states in a conquest-state, calculated using the 40% tribute rate (E ÷ H).

cotton cloth are counted as one manta in table 12.4. While this obscures differences in value among the types of items (e.g., mantas, naguales, huipiles) and among the types of mantas, it is unlikely that such distinctions would greatly modify the patterns evident in the table.

There is little explicit information in the ethnohistoric sources on the precise mechanisms by which imperial tribute was produced, collected, transported and generally administered. Imperial tribute collectors *(calpixque)* were sent to the provinces to oversee collection and shipment (Berdan 1982:38), but from their small numbers and the lack of additional imperial infractructure in provincial areas, I would infer that most of the activities of production, collection, and administration prior to final shipment were under local control (Rojas, chap. 15). I have argued elsewhere (Smith 1986) that one reason for the rapid expansion of the Triple Alliance empire was the ability of the imperial states to tap into pre-existing local tribute systems. Provincial polities could be relied upon to produce and collect their share of imperial tribute, circumventing the need to establish an entirely new, elaborate imperial bureaucracy in the provinces. A number of documentary sources substantiate this view, and suggest that Level 1 tribute was merely added to existing tribute networks, while the lower three levels continued to function as they had prior to incorporation into the empire (e.g., Zorita 1963:121; see discussion in Gibson [1971]).

Level 2

The second level of tribute consisted of payments made by dependent city-states to the conquest-state capitals. This tribute was presumably assessed by city-state rather than by household or *calpulli* so that the conquest-state did not have to involve itself in local tribute administration and collection (Zorita 1963:118). Two types of Early Colonial documents dating before 1550 provide data on this level of tribute in Morelos: lists of the total tribute receipts of the encomiendas, and lists of the encomienda payments of individual subject towns.

Encomienda tribute lists. Lists of tribute paid to encomenderos provide information on the total tribute received as income by the conquest-states, and thus give a picture of the upper end of Level 2 tribute (in Morelos encomiendas were assigned on the basis of native conquest-states, in contrast to the Basin of Mexico where they were assigned following city-state territories; see Smith 1983:121-122). Between 1522 and 1530, the peoples of Morelos provided varied and extensive goods and services to Hernán Cortés and the other encomenderos. Among goods found in these lists are cotton textiles, foodstuffs, cacao, firewood, fodder, building materials, gold jewelry, and tropical feathers, plus slaves and general labor service (Riley 1973:35-40, 143).

A list of tribute to the Cuernavaca encomienda in 1533 contains goods and services similar to those in the 1522-1530 period, but also includes labor in the encomendero's maize and cotton fields, laborers and food provisions for nearby mines in Guerrero, and tribute in pottery; the source also states that such Level 2 tribute was recorded in pictorial documents (*Declaración de los tributos* 1870), although none of these have survived for Morelos. In 1534, Morelos encomienda tribute was adjusted and standardized by royal decree in a series of *tasaciones;* after this time only cotton textiles and foodstuffs (primarily turkeys and tortillas) were included, and by 1550 most tribute was paid in money.

The 1534 *tasaciones* (Riley 1973:45) provide the opportunity to quantify cotton textile tribute at this level. Based on the fact that Morelos encomiendas were established in terms of conquest-states, and given the general continuity in tribute from 1519 to 1534 (Riley 1973:35-48), the quantities of textiles collected by the encomienda in 1534 may be projected back to 1519. As explained in the notes to table 12.4, I first standardized the tribute levels from 1534 for population size, then apply the resulting rate (mantas per person) to the 1519 populations of the conquest-states. The resulting tribute estimates for 1519 are included as category E in table 12.4. Two alternative reconstructions (Models 1 and 2) are presented in the table. Model 1 assumes that Spanish encomienda tribute levels included the imperial tribute collected by conquest-states and delivered to the Triple Alliance before 1519. Model 2 assumes that the encomienda tribute was a continuation of only the local portion of the pre-1519 conquest-state tribute. In this model, the imperial tribute has to be added to the estimated conquest-state income (category E) in order to establish the total amount of textiles collected by the conquest-states.

Tribute rates, defined as the proportion of tribute income paid out to higher-level polities, are calculated for both models in table 12.4 (category F). Such rates should be inversely correlated with the politico-economic power of the polity relative to its superior state (i.e., a weak subject state under strong control by a powerful state would control fewer independent resources and thus keep less tribute for itself than a strong state only loosely controlled by an external polity). Given the relative strength and power of the Quauhnahuac conquest-state and the looseness of imperial control in the provinces (see Smith 1986), a lower tribute rate is more appropriate (at least for this polity), and thus Model 2 with its lower rates provides a better fit to the available data. There is little comparative information on tribute rates, although a .50 level is reported by Roscoe (1911:245) for the Baganda of Africa (see Steponaitis [1984:147] for discussion).

Tribute paid to encomenderos by individual towns. The second type of documentation for Level 2 tribute consists of lists of tribute paid to encomenderos by individual subject towns. I assume that Early Colonial tribute by towns to encomiendas represents a continuation of prehispanic tribute by city-states to conquest-states. Examples of this Colonial tribute are listed for the towns Tetela, which in 1549 paid mantas, honey, turkeys, tortillas, maguey and fodder (*Libro de las tasaciones* 1952:436), and Zacualpa, which in 1548 paid mantas, honey, aji and salt (*Suma de visitas* 1905:65). The sources clearly indicate that considerable tribute at this level consisted of goods not native to Morelos (salt, cacao, gold jewelry, tropical feathers); these were almost certainly obtained by exchange through markets or specialized long-distance merchants.

Estimates of textile tribute amounts at this level are provided in category G of table 12.4. These figures result from dividing the tribute income of each conquest-state by its number of constituent city-states. The plausibility of these figures is shown by the actual textile tribute amounts paid by certain towns to their encomenderos in the sixteenth century. These amounts, adjusted for 1519 population levels as described in the notes to table 12.4, are 1,520 mantas annually from Tetela (based upon 1549 tribute [*Libro de las tasaciones* 1952:437]), and 589 from Zacualpan, 503 from Huazulco and 1,192 from Temoac (all based upon 1548 tribute [*Suma de visitas* 1905:65, 66, 195]). These city-states are not included in the *Codex Mendoza* tributary provinces, and therefore are not represented in table 12.4, but they do suggest that the estimates for average city-state textile tribute in Morelos are not unreasonable.

Table 12.4 also provides estimates for the average tribute income of the city-states as well as the total income per conquest-state at this level. These estimates are based upon an arbitrary .40 tribute rate since following the logic presented above, the rate at the city-state level should be somewhat higher than the rate at the conquest-state level. The amount of textile tribute taken in by city-states is relatively modest when calculated by household (category B in table 12.4); on average, each commoner household in Morelos would have paid only about 3 mantas total per year to support city-states, conquest-states, and the Triple Alliance. Actual household tribute production was much higher than this, however, because local tribute (levels 3 and 4) must be considered.

Level 3

At the third level of tribute, nobles supported their local *tlatoani,* thereby supporting the local city-state government. Although documentation for this level is scanty, the Nahuatl census documents do provide at least one example. The noble Molotecatl tecuhtli, head of the *calpulli* of Molotlan, paid an annual tribute of 20 "Cuernavaca mantas" *(cuauhnauacayotl),* 40 "tribute mantas" *(tequicuachtli),* 8 worked garments, 26 "toallas," 1800 cacao beans, 13 turkeys, several other food items, plus various service obligations, the latter presumably carried out by his dependent commoners (Carrasco 1972). This tribute probably represents a continuation of prehispanic payments to the local *tlatoani*. Molotecatl and his family did not have to produce the tribute goods or perform the service labor directly, but he did have responsibility for gathering, delivering, and organizing his share of city-state tribute. It is instructive that in the census documents, commoners dependent upon local nobles are referred to as both *ytech poui,* "those who pertain to him," and *tequinanamique,* "those who help pay tribute" (Carrasco 1972).

Level 4

At the lowest level of tribute, commoners supported their local nobles with goods and services. The goods included foodstuffs, raw cotton, and cotton mantas; the services included agricultural labor, household service (particularly corn grinding), and labor for the manufacture of textiles. Some of this tribute went to support the noble household, but much of it was destined to be passed along to the local *tlatoani* as Level 3 tribute (Carrasco 1968, 1972, 1976a, 1976b; Cortés 1865). In many cases, the commoners were provided with land by the local noble, and their tribute could be viewed as an exchange for use of the land. For example, Molotecatl tecuhtli distributed 228 *brazas* of his own 600 *brazas* of land to 10 dependent households, who provided him annually with a total of seven mantas plus food and labor services (Carrasco 1972:243). Carrasco's studies make it clear that tribute levels of individual households were fixed on the basis of land allotments (1964b:376, 1968:373ff, 1972:242, 1976a), a pattern also found in the Basin of Mexico (Gibson 1964:198, 518).

A comparison of the seven mantas received annually by Molotecatl with the 94 cotton items that he had to pay out in Level 3 tribute (see above) points to a discrepancy of 87 items per year. A major portion of these items probably were manufactured for Molotecatl by dependent commoner women. It was a routine practice for commoner women from households dependent upon local nobles to come to the nobles' houses for two major kinds of labor service: kitchen labor (primarily grinding maize and making tortillas) and spinning and weaving textiles (Carrasco 1968:374, 1972:233, 1976a:107; Cortés 1865:542). In the case of Molotecatl's immediate dependents, four of the commoner households contributed textile labor (Carrasco 1972:243). If this were the only source of additional cotton items, then each of the four households would have contributed the labor to make approximately 22 mantas annually (in addition to their other tribute obligations). This figure probably should be increased significantly because nobles like Molotecatl must have required mantas beyond their tribute quotas in order to exchange for luxury items and other goods in the markets. It is therefore likely that Molotecatl had additional textile income (either in finished pieces or in labor) beyond that provided by the commoners listed as his immediate dependents (see Hinz et al. [1983] for the text of the Molotla census).

In summary, the four levels of tribute in Late Postclassic Morelos constituted a single integrated hierarchical system. At least some of the goods paid at
the lowest level (Level 4) worked their way up the hierarchy to end up at
Tenochtitlan in the Basin of Mexico. The most problematic aspect of the above
reconstruction is Level 3 because there is little information from Morelos or
elsewhere on the precise obligations of nobles to their local *tlatoani* and city-
state government. Apart from the food supplied to nobles from their dependent
commoners, cotton textiles were by far the most numerous and important item
of tribute at all levels in Morelos. As the reconstruction shown in table 12.4
demonstrates, the total quantity of textiles moving through the tribute system
was quite large. Although documentation is not extensive, textiles and other
goods probably moved back and forth between the tribute system and the market system at all levels (see Berdan 1987). The comparison of population figures
with textile tribute requirements suggests that state-level cotton tribute (Levels
1 and 2) did not represent a very heavy burden on most commoners (table 12.4),
but the actual effects of tribute on the household level cannot be ascertained
until we have information on two key issues. First, we need to know more about
the intensity of tribute quotas at Levels 3 and 4, particularly the service or labor
requirements. Second, we need to know just how much labor was needed to
manufacture mantas and other cotton items. As pointed out by Berdan (1987),
the latter issue is more complex than it might seem, although some suggestions
are presented by Hicks (chap. 4).

TRADE AND MARKETS

Marketplaces are noted in early documentary sources at five conquest-state
capitals and four city-state capitals as well as at several smaller settlements
(table 12.5). As is the case for irrigation and cotton cultivation, the available
documentary evidence almost certainly underestimates the number of prehispanic
markets in Morelos, especially in the Quauhnahuac state. The *Relaciones
Geográficas* indicate a lively trade in a number of Morelos marketplaces
and mention the following as goods traded locally in the Morelos markets:
cotton, paper, cacao, fruit, honey, and lime plaster (Acuña 1984-1987:v.6:195,
211, 222; v.7:270; v.8:164). Other sources discuss the sale in the markets of
salt and various food items (*Visita, tasación y cuenta* 1946:236), and possibly
slaves (Carrasco 1968:375). The nonlocal products in Level 2 tribute lists
(e.g., tropical feathers and gold jewelry [see above]) were probably traded in
the Morelos markets as well. There are several additional lines of documentary
evidence for long-distance trade connections reaching outside of Morelos

Table 12.5   Marketplaces in Early Colonial Morelos

Town	City-State	Date	Source
Conquest-State Capital Cities			
Quauhnahuac	1	16th Cent.	Durán (1967:v.1:23)
Huaxtepec	28	1561	Visita (1946:244)
"		1580	Acuña (1984-1987:v.6:202)
Yacapitztlan	43	1561	Visita (1946:220-240)
Tepoztlan	53	1580	Acuña (1984-1987:v.6:195)
Totolapan	54	1580	Acuña (1984-1987:v.8:164)
City-State Capitals			
Xantetelco	50	1561	Visita (1946:220ff)
Tlayacapan	58	1743	Relación de Tlayacapan (1980:60)
Hueyapan	61	1580	Acuña (1984-1987:v.7:270)
Tetellan	63	1580	Acuña 1984-1987:v.7:270)
Subject Towns (estancias or barrios)			
Ocotepec	1	1552	Títulos de Cuernavaca (1947:218)
Tianguistenco	1	1552	Títulos de Cuernavaca (1947:219)
Suchitlan	43	1561	Visita (1946:243)
unnamed	43	1561	Visita (1946:230)

Note: The numbers under the category "City-State" indicate the states to which the market towns belong (see table 12.1 and fig. 12.1).

proper. For example, the Tlahuica of Morelos were one of a number of Central Mexican ethnic groups (including the Mexica) who used a common trade route to the Tehuantepec area during the time of Ahuitzotl (Durán 1967:v.2:357), and a document cited by Carrasco (1968:374) mentions *pochteca* trading in Morelos (see also O'Mack 1985).

These data on markets and merchants paint a picture of significant commercial activity throughout Morelos. The presence of markets at even very small settlements (table 12.5) suggests that all sectors of society, from the urban elite to rural commoners, were served by the market system. This interpretation is borne out by archaeological evidence for external trade contacts during the Late Postclassic period. There is evidence for the importation of obsidian, salt and ceramics from the Basin of Mexico; obsidian and bronze artifacts from western Mexico; and ceramics from several other areas of the Central Highlands (Smith 1987, 1990, 1994; Smith et al. 1984; Smith and Heath-Smith, chap. 13). Cotton was an item traded from Morelos throughout the Central Mexican area. Durán (1967:v.2:23) states that "toda la tierra" traded with Morelos to obtain cotton. Raw cotton was bought in Morelos by people from the Basin of Mexico to be spun and woven at their homes (Acuña 1984-1987:v.7:244), and we know that merchants from Yacapitztlan sold Morelos cotton in Basin of Mexico markets (*Visita, tasación y cuenta* 1946:222). Quauhnahuac mantas were regarded as the finest available in Central Mexico (Ramírez de Fuenleal 1870b:256) and must have been widely traded since they are listed as local tribute items in other parts of the Central Highlands (e.g., *Libro de las tasaciones* 1952:557).

Most of this external exchange was carried out through channels independent of Triple Alliance control. Spence (1985) and Isaac (1986) have argued that only a small portion of the Late Postclassic obsidian industry was controlled by the Mexica state, and there is no evidence that the Mexica administered the exchange of salt or ceramics. Many of the finished cotton textiles moving from Morelos to the Basin of Mexico were part of the state-controlled tribute system, but the sources suggest that most of the trade in raw cotton was carried out independently. In Late Postclassic archaeological sites in the Basin of Mexico, the prevalence of ceramic spindle whorls for spinning cotton indicates that this trade, from Morelos and other areas, must have been quite extensive (Parsons 1972; Hicks, chap. 4). In summary, it appears that a large part of Late Postclassic inter-regional exchange in Central Mexico was not under the control of the Triple Alliance empire.

CONCLUSIONS

For the last seven or eight decades prior to the Spanish conquest, the Triple Alliance empire covered nearly all of Central Mexico. This has led many authors to think that an adequate understanding of social and economic organization within the area can be gained by focusing on the empire (e.g., Barlow 1949; Davies 1973). The data presented in this paper, however, suggest that this is not the case. Incorporation into the empire had relatively modest direct effects upon social and economic patterns in provincial areas, and much of the interaction within and between regions took place through channels independent of the Triple Alliance states. This is not to say that the existence of the Triple Alliance empire was of little consequence to provincial areas of Central Mexico. Although direct effects of imperial conquest were relatively modest, incorporation into the empire brought about a number of very significant indirect effects in the provinces. Not only were local rulers left in power by the empire, but in some cases, their rule was supported and strengthened (Smith 1986). With Triple Alliance support, provincial conquest-states could increase their own nonimperial tribute demands, and when city-state and lower-level tribute is added in, the total tribute exacted from commoner households must have had a significant impact on their domestic economies (Hicks, chap. 4).

Morelos was the first area outside of the Basin of Mexico to be conquered by the Aztec empire, partly because of its proximity and partly because of its high level of political and economic development. It is easier for an empire to administer an area of established hierarchical political organization than an area without such a condition. Economically, the dense populations of Morelos provided labor for the empire (indirectly through the cultivation of cotton and he production of textiles), and the intensive agricultural systems provided grains, cotton, and other goods for imperial tribute and trade. These attractions for the Triple Alliance resulted from socioeconomic conditions in Late Postclassic Morelos. Economic and political patterns were quite similar to those in the better-documented Basin of Mexico. This situation is only revealed when detailed studies are carried out in areas beyond the Basin of Mexico. Such studies suggest that the economies and polities of Morelos and other provincial areas are better understood as local phenomena with wide interactions than as simple victims or recipients of Aztec imperialism.

ACKNOWLEDGMENTS

My knowledge of Morelos ethnohistory has benefitted greatly from conversations and correspondence with Druzo Maldonado, who not only provided bibliographic help but also made available some of his unpublished transcriptions of sixteenth-century documents. Mrs. Ruth Lewis kindly allowed me to study Oscar Lewis's transcriptions of documents concerning Tepoztlan. I have also benefitted from discussions with the following persons on the ethnohistory and archaeology of Late Postclassic Morelos: Jorge Angulo, Raul Arana, Carlos Barreto, Frances Berdan, Pedro Carrasco, Ann Cyphers Guillén, Hortensia de Vega Nova, Juan Dubernard, Silvia Garza de González, Norberto González Crespo, David Grove, Rafael Gutierrez, Cynthia Heath-Smith, Kenneth Hirth, Jaime Litvak King, Roger Mason, Scott O'Mack, William T. Sanders, Juan Antonio Siller, and Osvaldo Sterpone. The comments of Cynthia Heath-Smith and Robert Santley have been particularly helpful in the preparation of this article.

REFERENCES CITED

Acuña, René (editor)
  1984-1987 *Relaciones geográficas del siglo XVI.* 9 vols. Universidad Nacional Autónoma de México, Mexico City.
Alva Ixtlilxochitl, Fernando de
  1975-1977 *Obras históricas.* Translated by Edmundo O'Gorman. 2 vols. Universidad Nacional Autónoma de México, Mexico City.

Anales de Tlatelolco

1948 *Anales de Tlatelolco: Unos anales históricos de la nación Mexicana, y códice de Tlatelolco.* Edited by Heinrich Berlin. Antiguo Librería Robredo, Mexico City.

Armillas, Pedro

1949 Notas sobre sistemas de cultivo en mesoamérica: Cultivos de reigo y de humedad en la cuenca del Río del Balsas. *Anales del Instituto Nacional de Antropología e Historia,* Serie 6, vol. 3:85-113.

Barlow, Robert H.

1949 *The Extent of the Empire of the Culhua Mexica.* Ibero-Americana No. 28. University of California Press, Berkeley.

Bataillon, Claude

1972 *La ciudad y el campo en el México central.* Siglo Veintiuno, Mexico City.

Berdan, Frances F.

1976 A Comparative Analysis of Aztec Tribute Documents. In *Actas del XLI Congreso Internacional de Americanistas: México, 2 al 7 de septiembre de 1974* 2:131-142. Instituto Nacional de Antropología e Historia, Mexico City.

1982 *The Aztecs of Central Mexico: An Imperial Society.* Holt, Rinehart, and Winston, New York.

1987 Cotton in Aztec Mexico: Production, Distribution, and Uses. *Mexican Studies/ Estudios Mexicanos* 3:235-262.

Berdan, Frances F., Richard E. Blanton, Elizabeth H. Boone, Mary G. Hodge, Michael E. Smith, and Emily Umberger

1994 *Aztec Imperial Strategies.* Dumbarton Oaks, Washington, D.C. In press.

Bergmann, Richard E.

1969 The Distribution of Cacao Cultivation in Pre-Columbian America. *Annals of the Association of American Geographers* 59:85-96.

Bolio Villanueva, Eduardo

1976 *La economía del estado de Morelos.* 2nd ed. Sistema Bancos de Comercio, Mexico City.

Borah, Woodrow, and Sherburne F. Cook

1963 *The Aboriginal Population of Central Mexico on the Eve of the Spanish Conquest.* Ibero-Americana No. 54. University of California Press, Berkeley.

Carrasco, Pedro

1964a Family Structure of Sixteenth-century Tepoztlan. In *Process and Pattern in Culture: Essays in Honor of Julian H. Steward,* edited by Robert A. Manners, pp. 185-210. Aldine, Chicago.

1964b Tres libros de tributos del Museo Nacional de México y su importancia para los estudios demográficos. In *XXXV Congreso International de Americanistas, México, 1962: actas y memorias* 3:373-378. Editorial Libros de México, Mexico City.

1968 Las clases sociales en el México antiguo. *Verhandlungen des 38. Internationalen Amerikanistenkongresses, Stuttgart-Munchen, 12. bis 18. August, 1968* 2:371-376. K. Renner, Munich.

1972 La casa y hacienda de un señor Tlahuica. *Estudios de Cultura Náhuatl* 10:225-244.

1976a Estratificación social indígena en Morelos durante el siglo XVI. In *Estratificación social en la Mesoamérica prehispánica,* edited by Pedro Carrasco and Johanna Broda, pp. 102-117. Instituto Nacional de Antropología e Historia, Mexico City.

1976b The Joint Family in Ancient Mexico: The Case of Molotla. In *Essays on Mexican Kinship,* edited by Hugo Nutini, Pedro Carrasco, and James M. Taggert, pp. 45-64. University of Pittsburgh Press, Pittsburgh.

Cline, S. L. (editor)

1993 *The Book of Tributes: Early Sixteenth-Century Nahuatl Censuses From Morelos.* University of California at Los Angeles Latin American Center, Los Angeles.

Codex Mendoza

1992 *Codex Mendoza.* Edited by Frances F. Berdan and Patricia Reiff Anawalt. 4 vols. University of California Press, Berkeley.

Códice municipal de Cuernavaca

1973 Códice municipal de Cuernavaca. In *Fernando Cortés and the Marquesado in Morelos,* by G. Micheal Riley, pp. 100-109. University of New Mexico Press, Albuquerque.

Códice Ramírez

1944 *Códice Ramírez: Relación del origen de los indios que habitan esta Nueva España, según sus historias.* Editorial Leyenda, Mexico City.

Códices indígenas de algunos pueblos

1933 *Códices indígenas de algunos pueblos del Marquesado del Valle de Oaxaca.* Archivo General de la Nación, Mexico City.

Cortés, Hernán

1865 Carta de Hernán Cortés, al Consejo de Indias ... sobre la constitución de la propiedad de las tierras entre los indios (1538). *Colección de documentos inéditos ... de indias* 3:535-543. Real Academia de la Historia, Madrid.

1869 Testimonio de una petición, presentado por Hernán Cortés a la Audiencia de México, dando cuenta de los pueblos que ya tenía ... (1532). *Colección de documentos inéditos ... de indias* 12:554-563. Real Academia de la Historia, Madrid.

Cruz y Moya, Juan de la

1954-1955 *Historia de la santa y apostólica provincia de Santiago de Predicadores de México en la Nueva España.* 2 vols. Manuel Porrúa, Mexico City.

Davies, Nigel

1973 *The Aztecs: A History.* University of Oklahoma Press, Norman.

Declaración de los tributos

1870 Declaración de los tributos que los indios de la provincia de Guanavaquez ... hacían a su señor el Marqués del Valle (1533). *Colección de documentos inéditos ... de indias* 14:142-147. Real Academia de la Historia, Madrid.

Dobyns, Henry F.
1993 Building Stones and Paper: Evidence of Native American Historical Numbers. *Latin American Population History Bulletin* 24:11-19.

Drennan, Robert D.
1984 Long-distance Transport Costs in Pre-Hispanic Mesoamerica. *American Anthropologist* 86:105-112.

Dubernard, Juan
1975 *Santa Ana Amanalco (Cuernavaca, Morelos).* Private publication, Cuernavaca.

Durán, Fray Diego
1967 *Historia de Las Indias de Nueva España e Islas de la Tierra Firme.* Edited by Angel María Garibay K. 2 vols. Editorial Porrúa, Mexico City.

García Pimentel, Luis
1904 *Relación de los obispados de Tlaxcala, Michoacan, Oaxaca y otros lugares en el siglo XVI.* Private Publication, Mexico City.

Gerhard, Peter
1970a A Method of Reconstructing Pre-Columbian Political Boundaries in Central Mexico. *Journal de la Société des Américanistes de Paris* 59:27-41.

1970b El señorío de Ocuituco. *Tlalocan* 6(2):97-114.

1975 Continuity and Change in Morelos, Mexico. *Geographical Review* 65:335-352.

1977 Congregaciones de indios en la Nueva España ántes de 1570. *Historia Mexicana* 26:347-395.

Gibson, Charles
1964 *The Aztecs Under Spanish Rule: A History of the Indians of the Valley of Mexico, 1519-1810.* Stanford University Press, Stanford.

1971 Structure of the Aztec Empire. In *Archaeology of Northern Mesoamerica,* pt. 1, edited by Gordon F. Ekholm and Ignacio Bernal, pp. 276-394. Handbook of Middle American Indians, vol. 10, Robert Wauchope, general editor. University of Texas Press, Austin.

Hassig, Ross
1988 *Aztec Warfare: Imperial Expansion and Political Control.* University of Oklahoma Press, Norman.

Henige, David
1992 Native American Population at Contact: Discursive Strategies and Standards of Proof in the Debate. *Latin American Population History Bulletin* 22:2-23.

Hicks, Frederic
1982 Tetzcoco in the Early 16th Century: The State, the City and the Calpolli. *American Ethnologist* 9:230-249.

1984a La posición de Temazcalapan en la Triple Alianza. *Estudios de Cultura Náhuatl* 10:235-260.

1984b Rotational Labor and Urban Development in Prehispanic Texcoco. In *Explorations in Ethnohistory,* edited by Herbert R. Harvey and Hanns Prem, pp. 147-174. University of New Mexico Press, Albuquerque.

Hinz, Eike, Claudine Hartau, and Marie-Luise Heimann-Koenen (editors)
   1983   *Aztekischer Zensus: Zur Indianischen Wirtschaft und Gesellschaft im Marquesado um 1540.* 2 volumes. Verlag für Ethnologie, Hanover.

Hodge, Mary G.
   1984   *Aztec City-States.* Memoirs No. 18. Museum of Anthropology, University of Michigan, Ann Arbor.

Isaac, Barry L.
   1986   Notes on Obsidian, the Pochteca, and the Position of Tlatelolco in the Aztec Empire. In *Economic Aspects of Highland Central Mexico.* Research in Economic Anthropology, Supplement No. 2, edited by Barry L. Isaac, pp. 319-343. JAI Press, Greenwich.

Libro de las tasaciones
   1952   *El libro de las tasaciones de pueblos de la Nueva España: Siglo XVI.* Edited by Francisco González de Cossio. Archivo General de la Nación, Mexico City.

Licate, Jack A.
   1980   The Forms of Aztec Territorial Organization. In *Historical Geography of Latin America,* edited by William V. Davidson and James J. Parsons, pp. 27-45. Geoscience and Man Vol. 21. Louisiana State University, Baton Rouge.

Mair, Lucy
   1977   *African Kingdoms.* Oxford University Press, Oxford.

Maldonado Jiménez, Druzo
   1990   *Cuauhnahuac y Huaxtepec: Tlalhuicas y Xochimilcas en el Morelos prehispánico.* Centro Regional de Investigaciones Multidisciplinarias, Universidad Nacional Autónoma de México, Cuernavaca.

Mason, Roger D.
   1980   *Economic and Social Organization of an Aztec Provincial Center: Archaeological Research at Coatlan Viejo, Morelos, Mexico.* Ph.D. dissertation, Department of Anthropology, University of Texas. University Microfilms, Ann Arbor.

Matrícula de Tributos
   1980   *Matrícula de Tributos.* Commentary by Frances F. Berdan and Jacqueline de Durand-Forest. Akademische Druck-u. Verlagsanstalt, Graz, Austria.

Moreno Toscano, Alajandro
   1965   Tres problemas en la geografía del maíz, 1600-1624. *Historia Mexicana* 14:631-655.

Nicholson, H. B.
   1971   Pre-Hispanic Central Mexican Historiography. In *Investigaciones contemporáneas sobre historia de México,* pp. 38-81. El Colegio de México and University of Texas Press, Mexico City and Austin.

O'Mack, Scott H.
   1985   *Yacapitztlan: Ethnicity and Ethnohistory in Late Postclassic Central Mexico.* Unpublished Master's thesis, Department of Anthropology, University of Kentucky.

Palerm, Angel

1967   Agricultural Systems and Food Patterns. In *Social Anthropology,* edited by Manning Nash, pp. 26-52. Handbook of Middle American Indians, vol. 6, Robert Wauchope, general editor. University of Texas Press, Austin.

1972   Distribución geográfica de los regadíos prehispánicas en el área central de mesoamérica. In *Agricultura y civilización en mesoamérica,* edited by Angel Palerm and Eric R. Wolf, pp. 30-64. Secretaría de Educación Pública, Mexico City.

Parsons, Mary H.

1972   Spindle Whorls from the Teotihuacan Valley, Mexico. In *Miscellaneous Studies in Mexican Prehistory,* edited by Michael W. Spence, Jeffrey R. Parsons and Mary H. Parsons, pp. 45-80. Anthropological Papers No. 45. Museum of Anthropology, University of Michigan, Ann Arbor.

Ponce, Fray Alonso

1873   *Relación breve y verdadera de algunas cosas de las muchas que sucedieron al padre Fray Alonso Ponce en la provincia de Nueva España.* 2 vols. Imprenta de la Viuda de Calero, Madrid.

Price, T. Jeffrey, and Michael E. Smith

1992   Agricultural Terraces. In *Archaeological Research at Aztec-Period Rural Sites in Morelos, Mexico, Volume 1: Excavations and Architecture,* by Michael E. Smith, pp. 267-291. Monographs in Latin American Archaeology No. 4. University of Pittsburgh, Pittsburgh.

Proceso de Tepoztlan y Yautepec

1551   Proceso de Tepoztlan y Yautepeque (1551). Archivo Nacional de la Nación, Mexico City, Legajo 289, no. 100. Unpublished transcription by Oscar Lewis.

Ramírez de Fuenleal, Sebastián

1870a Carta a su magestad del obispo de Santo Domingo ... sobre licencias que se daban para que los españoles tuviesen indios ... (1532). *Colección de documentos inéditos ... de indias* 13:233-237. Real Academía de la Historia, Madrid.

1870b Carta a su magestad del obispo de Santo Domingo ... tratando de varias cosas pertenecientes al gobierno y real hacienda de aquel reino (1532). *Colección de documentos inéditos ... de indias* 13:250-261. Real Academía de la Historia, Madrid.

Relación de Tlayacapan

1980   Una relación inédita de Tlayacapan, Morelos, en el siglo XVIII (1743), edited by Teresa Rojas R. *Cuicuilco* 2:59-62.

Riley, G. Micheal

1973   *Fernando Cortés and the Marquesado in Morelos, 1522-1547.* University of New Mexico Press, Albuquerque.

Roscoe, John

1911   *The Baganda.* Macmillan, London.

SARH

1977   *Morelos: carta sinóptica (escala 1:250,000).* Secretaría de Agricultura y Recursos Hidraúlicos, Mexico City.

Sanders, William T.

1970 The Population of the Teotihuacan Valley, the Basin of Mexico, and the Central Mexican Symbiotic Region in the 16th Century. In *The Teotihuacan Valley Project, Final Report,* by William T. Sanders, Anton Kovar, Thomas Charlton and Richard A. Diehl, pp. 385-452. Occasional Papers in Anthropology No. 3. Department of Anthropology, Pennsylvania State University, University Park.

1971 Settlement Patterns in Central Mexico. In *Archaeology of Northern Mesoamerica,* pt. 1. edited by Gordon R. Ekholm and Ignacio Bernal, pp. 3-44. Handbook of Middle American Indians, vol. 10, Robert Wauchope, general editor. University of Texas Press, Austin.

Sanders, William T., Jeffrey R. Parsons, and Robert S. Santley

1979 *The Basin of Mexico: Ecological Processes in the Evolution of a Civilization.* Academic Press, New York.

Scholes, Frances, and Eleanor Adams

1957 *Información sobre los tributos que los indios pagaban a Moctezuma, año de 1554.* Editorial Porrúa, Mexico City.

Smith, Michael E.

1983 *Postclassic Culture Change in Western Morelos, Mexico: The Development and Correlation of Archaeological and Ethnohistorical Chronologies.* PhD dissertation, Department of Anthropology, University of Illinois. University Microfilms, Ann Arbor.

1986 The Role of Social Stratification in the Aztec Empire: A View from the Provinces. *American Anthropologist* 88:70-91.

1987 The Expansion of the Aztec Empire: A Case Study in the Correlation of Diachronic Archaeological and Ethnohistorical Data. *American Antiquity* 52:37-54.

1989 Cities, Towns, and Urbanism: Comment on Sanders and Webster. *American Anthropologist* 91:454-461.

1990 Long-Distance Trade Under the Aztec Empire: The Archaeological Evidence. *Ancient Mesoamerica* 1:153-169.

1994 Social Complexity in the Aztec Countryside. In *Archaeological Views from the Countryside: Village Communities in Early Complex Societies,* edited by Glenn Schwartz and Steven Falconer, pp. 143-159. Smithsonian Institution Press, Washington, D.C.

Smith, Michael E., Cynthia Heath-Smith, Ronald Kohler, Joan Odess, Sharon Spanogle, and Timothy Sullivan

1994 The Size of the Aztec City of Yautepec: Urban Survey in Central Mexico. *Ancient Mesoamerica* 5:1-12.

Smith, Michael E. and Kenneth G. Hirth

1988 The Development of Cotton Spinning Technology is Postclassic Morelos, Mexico. *Journal of Field Archaeology* 15:349-358.

Smith, Michael E., Jerrel H. Sorensen, and Philip K. Hopke
   1984   Obsidian Exchange in Postclassic Central Mexico: New Data from Morelos. Paper presented at the 1984 International Symposium on Archaeometry (Washington, D.C.).

Solis, Antonio de
   1924   *Historia de la conquista de Méjico.* 2 vols. Casa Editorial Garnier Hermanos, Paris.

Spence, Michael W.
   1985   Specialized Production in Rural Aztec Society: Obsidian Workshops of the Teotihuacan Valley. In *Contributions to the Archaeology and Ethnohistory of Greater Mesoamerica,* edited by William J. Folan, pp. 76-125. Southern Illinois University Press, Carbondale.

Steponaitis, Vincas P.
   1984   Some Further Remarks on Catchments, Nonproducers, and Tribute Flow in the Valley of Mexico. *American Anthropologist* 86:143-148.

Suma de visitas
   1905   *Suma de visitas de pueblos por orden alfabética.* Translated by Francisco del Paso y Troncoso. Papeles de Nueva España Vol. 1. Sucesores de Rivadeneyra, Madrid.

Títulos de Cuernavaca
   1947   Unos títulos de Cuernavaca (1552), translated by Arnulfo Velasco. *Tlalocan* 2(3):215-222.

Torquemada, Fray Juan de
   1969   *Monarquía Indiana.* 3 vols. Editorial Porrúa, Mexico City.

Visita, tasación y cuenta
   1946   Visita, tasación y cuenta de la villa de Yecapixtla, Morelos (1561). *Nuevos documentos relativos a los bienes de Hernán Cortés, 1547-1947,* pp. 169-260. Archivo General de la Nación, Mexico City.

Whitmore, Thomas M.
   1991   A Simulation of the Sixteenth-Century Population Collapse in the Basin of Mexico. *Annals of the Association of American Geographers* 81:461-487.
   1992   *Disease and Death in Early Colonial Mexico: Simulating Amerindian Depopulation.* Westview Press, Boulder.

Zorita, Alonso de
   1963   *Breve y sumaria relación de los señores de la Nueva España.* Universidad Nacional Autónoma de México, Mexico City.

13

Rural Economy in
Late Postclassic Morelos

An Archaeological Study

Michael E. Smith and Cynthia Heath-Smith

What was life like in the rural communities of Central Mexico in the Late Postclassic period? How were these communities affected by their conquest and incorporation into the Aztec empire? Our recent archaeological fieldwork in the modern Mexican state of Morelos, Mexico, provides new information on the nature of peasant households and communities in a provincial area of the Aztec empire. We recovered evidence for a densely settled, socially complex rural landscape. Elites lived at both rural and urban sites; craft production and intensive agriculture were prominent activities, and marketplace exchange with near and distant areas was commonplace. In this paper we explore these and other economic issues as documented by the Postclassic Morelos Archaeological Project, an excavation-based study of socioeconomic conditions among rural[1] households at the sites of Cuexcomate and Capilco in western Morelos. After presenting information on household economy, we explore the implications of these data for some of the important issues in the analysis of Aztec economics, including the role of population growth, the effects of imperial conquest, and the degree of centralized political control over economic activities.

EXCAVATIONS AT CAPILCO AND CUEXCOMATE

The Postclassic Morelos Archaeological Project excavations at Capilco and Cuexcomate were conducted in part to investigate the possibility of rural social complexity in this region. Ethnohistoric documents and prior archaeological research suggested that western Morelos had dense rural populations that were well integrated into Aztec-period exchange networks (see Smith, chap. 12). Capilco and Cuexcomate, located about 20 km southwest of the large urban center of Quauhnahuac (Cuauhnahuac; see chap. 1, fig. 1.2), were first investigated by Kenneth G. Hirth's (1994) Xochicalco Mapping Project. This preliminary research revealed a high surface visibility of Late Postclassic residential architecture and significant variability in structure-based artifact collections.

Capilco and Cuexcomate were excavated in 1986 with a research design intended to gather data on household social and economic conditions, residential architecture, and community organization (fig. 13.1). Among the specific topics of investigation were the presence and role of rural elites, the nature of socioeconomic variation among households, the nature of economic activities and conditions, and the impact of Aztec conquest on provincial society (Smith 1992). House foundations at these sites were visible on the surface, and random samples of houses were tested at each site to investigate site-wide patterns of

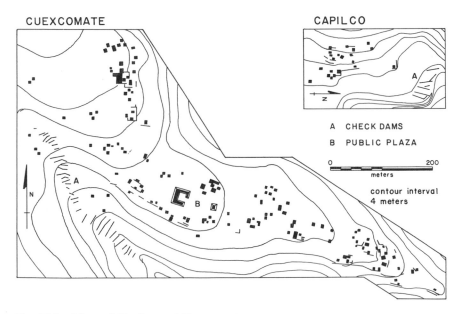

Fig. 13.1. Maps of Capilco and Cuexcomate.

variability. Selected houses were cleared completely, including large exterior areas, in order to address the issues of domestic conditions and activities in greater detail. Also, a number of nonresidential structures and features were excavated, among them a temple-platform, possible granaries, ritual deposits, and agricultural terraces. The excavations and architectural remains are described in detail in Smith (1992); preliminary discussions may also be found in Smith et al. (1989).

Three chronological periods are represented at Capilco and Cuexcomate. The Temazcalli phase (A.D. 1200-1350) is present in only two refuse deposits at Capilco. The Early Cuauhnahuac phase (abbreviated here as "EC") dates to A.D. 1350-1430, and the Late Cuauhnahuac phase ("LC") follows from A.D. 1430-1550 (see Smith and Hodge, chap. 1, fig. 1.3). Both sites were abandoned early in the Spanish Colonial period, probably in response to Spanish administrative decree. The chronology is based upon radiocarbon dates, stratigraphy, and quantitative ceramic seriation (see Smith and Doershuk 1991).

ENVIRONMENTAL AND SOCIAL CONTEXT

The Environmental Setting

Cuexcomate and Capilco are located 3 km apart near the ruins of the large Epiclassic city of Xochicalco. Today precipitation is adequate for *temporal* (nonirrigated) agriculture (900 mm per year), but the thin rocky soils around the sites limit agricultural productivity in the area. Hirth (1994) estimates the average yield of traditional nonmechanized farming in the immediate area (prior to the use of industrial fertilizers) to have been approximately 550 kg of maize per hectare. The sites are situated at the southern extreme of a large Plio-Pleistocene alluvial fan known as the Buenavista Lomas (part of the Cuernavaca Formation; see Fries 1960). Because the lomas are cut by numerous, deeply entrenched, seasonal streams, the amount of level land for cultivation is limited. Only a few very small tracts of land along the Tembembe and Cuentepec Rivers can be irrigated, in contrast to other parts of Morelos where Late Postclassic irrigation along the major rivers was extensive (Maldonado 1990; Smith, chap. 12).

During the Epiclassic period (A.D. 750-950), the agricultural heartland of Xochicalco was oriented to the south rather than north into the Buenavista Lomas (Hirth 1994). The lomas supported only a few scattered settlements throughout most of the Prehispanic epoch until the Cuauhnahuac phase, when a major colonization of this area took place. Settlement of this marginal zone became possible with the construction of extensive systems of agricultural terraces of both the contour and cross-channel varieties. Thus, Cuexcomate and Capilco are located in a marginal environment without great agricultural potential.

Apart from agricultural production, other significant local economic resources include a low-grade chert used for tools, which occurs in nodules in the limestone of the adjacent Xochicalco Formation (Fries 1960), and abundant wild fig trees *(amate)* from which bark could be removed for the manufacture of paper *(amate* pollen was recovered, as were tools for papermaking). The vertisol soils provide suitable clays for a ceramics industry (jars and *comals* are made in the nearby village of Cuentepec today), but there is no direct evidence for ceramic manufacture at any of the Cuauhnahuac phase sites in the area (see Goodfellow 1990). Vesicular basalt for the manufacture of metates and other groundstone tools could have been obtained from Real del Puente, about 5 km east of Cuexcomate.

Demography

A massive population growth between the Temazcalli and EC phases in western Morelos had important effects on economic organization. There are several types of evidence for this population explosion. On a regional scale, the number of occupied sites located by Hirth's Río Chalma survey southwest of the study area jumps markedly between Temazcalli and EC times (Hirth, unpublished notes). Surface survey and mapping in the Buenavista Lomas by Osvaldo Sterpone (1988), Scott O'Mack (1991), and Michael E. Smith confirm extensive Cuauhnahuac phase occupation with few earlier sites apparent.

At the level of individual sites, demographic reconstructions for Cuexcomate and Capilco show significant population growth at this time (table 13.1). The population estimates in table 13.1 are based upon occupation patterns extrapolated from the random sample of houses at the two sites; the estimates use household size constants of 5.5 persons per house for commoners (Kolb 1985) and 11 persons per house for elite residences (see Smith [1992:335-345] for a full discussion of the demographic data and methods). Capilco was first settled in the Temazcalli phase and continued to grow throughout the final three prehispanic phases. Cuexcomate, on the other hand, was occupied initially in EC times and rapidly grew into a minor town center of 800 persons. When the phased occupation patterns at the excavated sites are applied to unphased Middle/Late Postclassic sites located by Hirth in a 6 km² area around Xochicalco, the reconstructed population levels for the Temazcalli, EC, and LC phases are 460, 1,690, and 4,000 persons respectively. These data suggest very rapid rates of population growth in the immediate vicinity of Cuexcomate and Capilco: 1.6% annually between the Temazcalli and EC phases, and 1.0% annually between the EC and LC phases (Smith 1992).

Table 13.1 Demographic data for Capilco and Cuexcomate

Context	Phase		
	Temazcalli	Early Cuauhnahuac	Late Cuauhnahuac
Number of Houses			
Capilco (nonelite)	5	13	21
Cuexcomate: elite	--	4	7
Cuexcomate: nonelite	--	35	132
Number of Persons			
Capilco (nonelite)	28	72	116
Cuexcomate: elite	--	44	77
Cuexcomate: nonelite	--	193	726
Cuexcomate: total	--	237	803
Settlement Area (hectares)			
Capilco	0.14	0.60	1.15
Cuexcomate	--	9.94	14.58
Population Density (persons per hectare)			
Capilco	197	121	101
Cuexcomate	--	24	55

Rural Society

At the time of Spanish conquest, western Morelos was divided into a number of small city-states, all subject to the larger conquest-state of Quauhnahuac (Maldonado 1990; Smith, chap. 12). The city-state capitals nearest to Cuexcomate and Capilco were Cohuintepec (near modern Cuentepec) to the northwest, Miacatlan to the southwest, and Acatlipac to the east. We do not know, however, to which polities the excavated sites pertained. In spite of high population densities (over 600 persons per km^2 for the region in the LC phase) the immediate area around Cuexcomate and Capilco can be considered rural in the Cuauhnahuac phase because of a lack of cities (see note 1). In fact much of western Morelos outside of the city of Quauhnahuac (estimated population of 67,000) was rural in character since the major "urban" settlements, the city-state capitals, were quite small in size (Mason 1980; Smith, chap. 12).

Capilco was a small settlement (fig. 13.1) which grew from a tiny hamlet in the Temazcalli phase to a village of around 100 persons in LC times (table 13.1). Cuexcomate was first occupied in the EC phase and from the start was a much larger and more complex settlement containing an elite residential compound, a modest temple platform, and a central public plaza (fig. 13.1). Smith suggests elsewhere (Smith 1992) that its rapid growth was due to the presence of an elite group in EC times, which probably attracted further commoner settlement (although by what means is not clear). The elite resided in a large, distinctive compound (patio group 6) with a plan similar to the standard Aztec palace layout identified by Susan Evans (1991). The inhabitants of patio group 6 are classified as elite on several bases: the large size of their residence; the high energetic cost of its construction; the architectural distinctiveness of the compound relative to other houses and house groups (e.g., raised rooms, ample use of lime plaster); its resemblance to the Aztec palace plan; its location on the public plaza; and the distinctiveness of its artifactual inventories, which generally have higher frequencies of imported and decorated ceramics than other houses (see discussion in Smith [1992]). Patio group 6 and several other groups are illustrated in figure 13.2.

In the LC phase, population growth continued at a somewhat slower rate, and a general decline in the standard of living occurred. Patio group 6 was abandoned, and the more modest patio group 7 was built on an adjacent side of the public plaza, probably as an elite compound. Although far less imposing or distinctive than its predecessor, patio group 7 still stands out relative to contemporaneous houses in terms of its architecture and artifacts (fig. 13.2).

If we make the reasonable assumption that the Cuexcomate elite resembled the ethnohistorically documented rural nobility of Morelos (e.g., Carrasco 1976; Smith 1993a), then this class probably controlled most if not all of the land in the immediate vicinity of the sites. Commoners would have been under the control of these elite, paying them tribute in goods and services. Rural commoners were probably members of the residential units known as *calpulli*. In contrast to Zorita's (1963) well-known view of the *calpulli* as an egalitarian, land-holding kin group that was outside of noble control, the Morelos *calpulli* were controlled by nobles who owned the land and extracted tribute from the commoners (Carrasco 1976; Smith 1993a).

PRODUCTION

Agriculture

The bulk of the diet at Cuexcomate and Capilco was from agricultural crops. Faunal remains are scanty, suggesting that animal protein contributed little to the diet. The majority of the nonhuman bones are turkey, dog, and rabbit, with a minor contribution from deer and various small mammals and reptiles. Pollen studies show the presence of a number of wild economic species, but there are also traces of many domesticates in the household middens. Prominent domes-

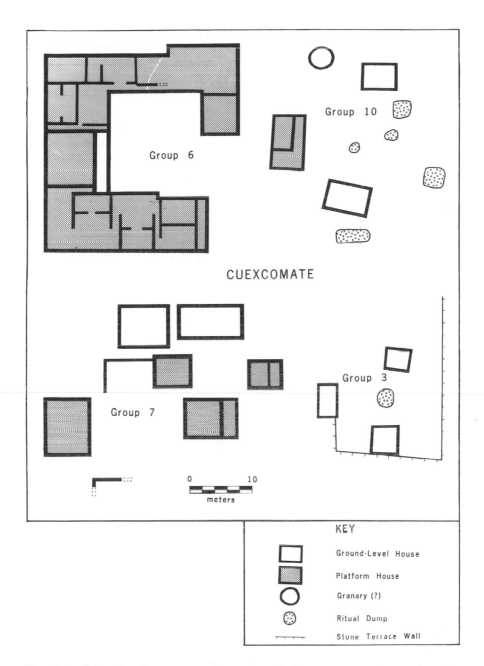

Fig. 13.2. Selected patio groups at Cuexcomate. Patio groups 6 and 7 were the elite compounds in the Early Cuauhnahuac and Late Cuauhnahuac phases respectively.

ticates include maize, tomato, squash, avocado, and several arboreal fruits (Amie Limón, personal communication). Although no cotton pollen was recovered, the cultivation of cotton can be inferred from the abundance of cotton spinning artifacts at the sites (see below). Extensive flotation of midden sediments yielded only a few beans and maize kernels due to poor conditions of preservation (Virginia Popper, personal communication).

Both excavated sites are associated with areas of stone agricultural terrace walls (Price 1988). There is a small area of alluvial fields created by cross-channel terraces (also known as check-dams) just north of Capilco, and a small drainage on the southwest side of Cuexcomate is crossed by over 30 of these terraces (fig. 13.1). Excavations and sediment analyses show that the stone walls were built up gradually over a long period of time. In one case, a short wall was built and the terrace filled in fairly rapidly by natural transport with turbulent stream flow. The wall was breached, causing a major erosion gully that was subsequently filled in again. After this, the terrace went through a long period of gradual enlargement, leading to the expansion of the cultivated field through continuous deposition by gentle stream flow. Soil analyses reveal the presence of at least two buried topsoils with elevated concentrations of organic matter and available phosphorus, coupled with a condition of general nutrient depletion in the terrace soils relative to surrounding soils; these findings provide strong evidence that these terraces were indeed farmed in the past. Artifactual remains date the terraces to the Cuauhnahuac phase in general, and one carbon date with a calibration curve intercept of A.D. 1476 (ETH-6309) dates the period of gradual expansion to the Late Cuauhnahuac phase (see Price and Smith [1992] for further discussion and Sandor et al. 1990 for discussion of terrace archaeology).

In addition to the cross-channel terraces, there are extensive zones of contour terracing in this area. The hillslopes that surround Cuexcomate on three sides are covered with abandoned terraces, which come up to the edge of the settled area. Both types of terraces were needed by the expanding Late Postclassic populations. A preliminary reconstruction of carrying capacity in the area around Xochicalco (Price and Smith 1992) suggests that dry farming on flat areas (without terraces) could support only about 1,200 persons in a 6 km^2 area, a population level passed by EC times (see above). The productivity of terrace agriculture has yet to be modelled for this area, but it seems likely that the extensive Cuauhnahuac phase terraces (coupled with dry farming) would have been capable of producing enough maize to support the local population as well as to fulfill regional- and perhaps imperial-level tribute requirements.

Craft Production

A number of different craft products were manufactured in domestic contexts at Cuexcomate and Capilco as evidenced by production tools (ce-

Table 13.2 Mean values of craft production measures

Category	Temazcalli (A)	Early Cuauhnahuac (A)	(B)	(C)	Late Cuauhnahuac (A)	(B)	(C)
No. of houses[a]	2	5	3	4	9	22	4
Ceramics (percentage of all vessels and artifacts)							
Spinning bowls	2.6	4.2	5.6	3.7	6.2	5.5	4.7
Spindle whorls	0.1	1.3	2.9	1.1	2.7	2.2	1.3
Worked sherds	0.2	0.2	0.4	0.1	0.1	0.4	0.5
Other (frequency per 1,000 sherds)							
Chert	7	3	14	9	5	13	7
Polishing stones	.22	.16	.31	.10	.22	.39	--
Bark beaters	.22	.10	--	--	.09	.08	--
Paint stones	--	.03	.10	.38	.13	.26	.53
Copper tools	.12	.10	.21	--	.03	.06	--

Note: Column headings represent types of social contexts as follows: (A) nonelite houses at Capilco, (B) nonelite houses at Cuexcomate, and (C) elite houses at Cuexcomate.

[a] Number of excavated residential middens for each social context.

ramic spindle whorls and spinning bowls, worked sherds, basalt polishing stones and bark beaters, and copper tools), production byproducts (chert debitage), and other materials (paint stones). Quantitative data on these artifacts are listed in table 13.2, which presents mean values for various social categories by phase.[2] These social categories are Capilco houses (column A), Cuexcomate nonelite houses (column B), and Cuexcomate elite houses (column C; these are patio groups 6 and 7 in the EC and LC phases respectively).

By far the most widespread and intensive craft activity was *cotton spinning*. Ceramic spindle whorls and spinning bowls were found in every excavated domestic context. Frequencies of spinning artifacts among individual houses are illustrated graphically in figure 13.3. These graphs (and table 13.2) show little difference between elite and nonelite contexts in cotton spinning, although the elite means are lower than the nonelite means at Cuexcomate. The major change through time was an increase in spinning artifacts at Capilco (table 13.2). Cotton textiles were important items of trade and tribute (Berdan 1987; Smith and Hirth 1988; see Hicks, chap. 4), and much of the textile production was probably destined for export. Similar patterns of abundant whorls and spinning bowls are reported for almost all known Late Postclassic sites in western Morelos (e.g., Smith and Hirth 1988).

Evidence for other types of craft production is far less visible when compared with that for cotton spinning. *Chert tools* were manufactured at

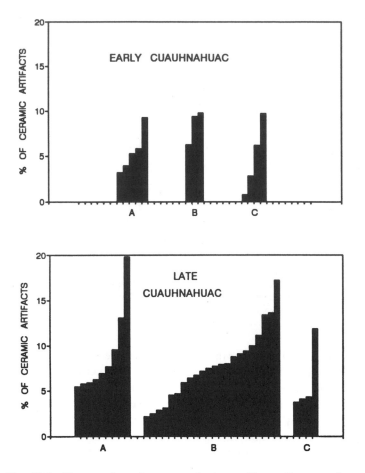

Fig. 13.3. Frequencies of cotton spinning artifacts. Data are from domestic middens for the EC and LC phases. Each bar represents a single house, and the bars are grouped in three categories: *(A)* nonelite houses at Capilco; *(B)* nonelite houses at Cuexcomate; *(C)* elite houses at Cuexcomate.

both sites from locally-available stone, but overall, frequencies of chert artifacts are low (table 13.2). The major material for lithic tools was imported obsidian (see below). Chert tool production debris is found in many deposits, which suggests scattered domestic manufacture. *Basalt polishing stones* are rare but widely distributed artifacts (table 13.2), recovered from 90% of the houses with large samples of excavated midden (over 4 m³).[3] We do not know what function they served, but these smoothed stones were probably a tool in some sort of craft activity. *Worked sherds* (round disks and other shapes) are rare, enigmatic artifacts that may have been used in some phase of craft production—smoothing ceramic vessels is a possibility although we have no other evidence for ceramic production (see below).

The manufacture of *paper* from the bark of the *amate* tree is indicated by the presence of grooved, rectangular, basalt tools commonly known as "bark beaters." Although these tools are quite rare (table 13.2), they do occur in 70% of the houses with large samples of excavated midden, suggesting that paper production was widespread among households. *Copper and bronze artifacts,* while not common, are broadly distributed among domestic middens (table 13.2). Most of these artifacts are tools, such as needles, chisels, and awls. Jewelry and other nonutilitarian objects are not included in calculations for table 13.2. The needles were probably used with textiles, and the chisels and awls may have been used in woodworking (Dorothy Hosler, personal communication).

Mineral paint pigments are another uncommon artifact found in midden deposits. Three colors are represented: red (hematite), yellow (limonite), and black (graphite). Of all types of evidence for craft manufacture, these items show the highest degree of spatial concentration and the strongest association with elite contexts (table 13.2). Paint stones have a minor positive association with elite contexts in both Cuauhnahuac phases. In the EC phase, four of the 12 examples of paint stones (33%) are from the elite patio group; in the LC phase, two of the 43 examples (5%) are from the elite compound and another 28 paint stones (67%) from one single house group, patio group 10. Patio group 10 is not an elite compound (based on a number of architectural and artifactual indicators), but its intensive use of paints could have been in the service of the LC elite who resided nearby. These pigments could have been used to paint manuscripts on bark paper (group 10 also has a large number of bark beaters), an activity associated with the nobility in Late Postclassic Central Mexico (Boone 1994).

Ceramic vessels and obsidian tools are the most abundant artifacts at both sites, but we have no evidence that these goods were produced at either one. Goodfellow's (1990) reconstruction of regional ceramic production and exchange suggests that multiple production centers served Cuexcomate and Capilco, but the locations of production centers have yet to be identified on the ground. Obsidian is quite abundant (we recovered over 12,000 pieces in total), but there is almost no evidence for the production of blades or other tools (Sorensen 1988). There is a production locale or workshop for prismatic blades at the nearby site of El Ciruelo from which the inhabitants of Capilco and Cuexcomate may have obtained their obsidian blades (Sorensen et al. 1989).

EXCHANGE

All three of the major Aztec-period Central Mexican exchange mechanisms—tribute, long-distance trade, and market trade—operated in Morelos. The multilevel tribute system involved payments to local lords, to *tlatoque* at one or more levels, and to the Aztec empire. Merchants from Quauhnahuac traded as far away as Xoconochco, and *pochteca* from the Basin of Mexico traded in the small towns of western Morelos. Markets were common at all levels of the political hierarchy: Quauhnahuac had a large market, many or all city-state capitals had markets, and even some smaller towns held periodic markets (see Smith, chap. 12, for the ethnohistoric evidence for this description). Given the existence of multiple exchange systems and the high rural population density, it is not surprising to find a high frequency of imported goods at the excavated houses.

Frequencies of the three major imports—ceramics, obsidian, and copper—are listed in table 13.3. Two patterns in these data stand out: the large number of imports and their extensive distribution among households. Averaged over all houses, imported ceramics constitute 11.7% of all domestic vessels in Temazcalli phase houses, 11.2% in EC phase houses and 8.3% in LC phase houses. Most of these imports come from the Basin of Mexico. Imports from other parts of Morelos, primarily from the Cuernavaca area, are also common, with some sherds from the Yauhtepec area and eastern Morelos. There are a few sherds from Cholula, the Mixteca, Guerrero, and the Toluca Valley, mainly in EC phase contexts. The decline in frequency of imported ceramics from EC to LC times

Table 13.3   Mean values of imported artifacts

Category	Temazcalli	Early Cuauhnahuac			Late Cuauhnahuac		
	(A)	(A)	(B)	(C)	(A)	(B)	(C)
Ceramics (percentage of all vessels and artifacts)							
Aztec salt vessels	2.4	2.6	3.5	3.8	2.7	4.4	4.4
Aztec III bowls	--	0.8	2.6	5.3	0.7	1.5	2.9
Aztec spinning bowls	0.5	1.7	1.9	1.3	1.6	1.6	2.7
Other Aztec types	0.1	0.3	1.1	0.3	1.2	0.2	--
Total Aztec imports	3.0	5.4	9.1	10.7	6.2	7.7	10.0
Morelos imports	8.6	3.1	0.3	3.0	1.7	0.4	0.9
Other imports	0.1	0.4	0.3	0.9	0.2	--	--
Other (frequency per 1000 sherds)							
Obsidian	15	20	32	38	21	45	24
Total copper	.22	.32	.21	.10	.20	.10	--

Note: Column headings represent types of social contexts as follows: (A) nonelite houses at Capilco, (B) nonelite houses at Cuexcomate, and (C) elite houses at Cuexcomate.

primarily occurs in types from the Cuernavaca area (table 13.3). During the LC phase, however, it is not possible to distinguish the polychromes of the Cuernavaca area from those of western Morelos (unlike the situation during earlier phases), and this "decline" in imports from other areas of Morelos (e.g., Cuernavaca) may be more apparent than real.

Nearly all of the obsidian recovered is of the green variety from the Pachuca source area. Domestic inventories average between 30 and 40 pieces per 1,000 sherds; the figures for ceramic vessels (not sherds) are closer to 20 pieces of obsidian per 100 vessels. Obsidian density in domestic middens averages between 25 and 50 pieces per m^3.

Not only were imports abundant, they were also widely distributed. Every excavated house had some Aztec (Basin of Mexico) ceramics, and all but one had obsidian. Copper artifacts (tools and ornaments), although rare, were also widely distributed—present in 80% of the houses with extensively excavated midden deposits (see note 3). Although the elite houses had higher frequencies of some imports (e.g., Morelos ceramic imports in the EC phase, and Aztec III bowls in both EC and LC phases), they did not by any means monopolize these goods.

In sum, rural households at Cuexcomate and Capilco were well integrated into regional and long-distance exchange networks. Exotic goods were normal components of domestic utilitarian inventories, and a number of goods produced by these households (textiles and bark paper at least and probably agricultural goods as well) were destined for export at either the local, regional, or long-distance levels. The lack of any apparent elite monopolies suggests that exchange was most likely independent of elite control, but this is difficult to establish securely with our data.

CONSUMPTION

Evidence for elite-commoner differences in consumption practices is surprisingly scarce. No artifact categories, apart from architecture, show an exclusively elite association. Perhaps the strongest a priori candidates for sumptuary goods are luxury items of personal adornment, but none of the 19 examples of jewelry (jade beads, obsidian lip plugs, and shell pendants) were recovered in elite contexts. A number of ceramic categories do show statistical associations with the elite residences in each phase, but these are far from exclusive associations.

Based upon the cross-cultural validity of household possessions as wealth indicators (Smith 1987a), two artifactual indices were constructed to study variability among houses in wealth levels. For the first index, the architectural distinctiveness

Table 13.4   Mean values of wealth indices and ceramic markers of wealth

Category	Temazcalli	Early Cuauhnahuac			Late Cuauhnahuac		
	(A)	(A)	(B)	(C)	(A)	(B)	(C)
Wealth indices							
Index 1	--	-1.26	-5.03	3.83	-.50	-.77	3.11
Index 2	51.4	43.3	43.0	62.5	37.2	34.5	48.3
Ceramic types (percentage of all vessels and artifacts)							
Morelos imports	8.6	**3.1**	**0.3**	**3.0**	1.7	0.4	0.9
Other decorated bowls	4.0	**2.9**	**0.3**	**3.5**	1.7	0.7	0.2
Total bowls	48.4	**46.7**	**38.4**	**50.1**	**41.1**	**39.3**	**42.5**
Aztec III bowls	--	**0.8**	**2.6**	**5.3**	**0.7**	**1.5**	**2.9**
Polished red bowls	10.8	**4.5**	**5.5**	**12.9**	**4.5**	**7.2**	**9.9**
Tlahuica polychrome	11.6	15.6	10.2	8.9	**12.5**	**6.2**	**8.7**
Incense burners	2.6	3.3	6.1	3.7	**3.1**	**3.2**	**4.7**

Notes: Column headings represent types of social contexts as follows: (A) nonelite houses at Capilco, (B) nonelite houses at Cuexcomate, and (C) elite houses at Cuexcomate.

Bold figures denote the five phase-specific wealth indicators for each phase that were used in the calculation of wealth index 1.

of patio groups 6 and 7 was inferred to signal the presence of elite groups in the EC and LC phases respectively. Five ceramic variables or types were chosen that best differentiated the elite from the nonelite houses at Cuexcomate in each phase; these are listed in table 13.4 (three types served in both phases). These five variables were used to construct wealth index 1,[4] a phase-specific index of wealth variation among households. Wealth index 2 was calculated to examine change over time since values of the first index are not directly comparable between phases. Index 2 is the simple sum of the frequency of local decorated ceramics and two times the frequency of imported ceramics, calculated for each house. This index ranges from 19.7 to 68.2; table 13.4 shows the mean values.

The wealth indices suggest a number of conclusions on consumption patterns at Cuexcomate and Capilco. First, all three social categories (Capilco, Cuexcomate nonelite, and Cuexcomate elite) manifest an overall decline in standard of living through time. Second, the elite households show distinctive patterns of ceramic usage in both phases. Third, elite-commoner differences were much reduced in the LC phase as measured by both wealth indices. The decline in the fortunes of the elite as measured by portable artifacts is matched by the architecture: the LC elite compound is far less imposing and distinctive than the EC compound, although it is still the largest residential group at the sites in LC times. Furthermore, the lack of conformity of this compound to the Aztec palace plan suggests a lower level of involvement in long-distance elite interactions at this time.

SUMMARY OF SOCIAL AND ECONOMIC CHANGES

The excavations at Cuexcomate and Capilco have allowed us to document a number of social and economic changes in the three phases of occupation—population growth, agricultural intensification, increasing textile production, changing configurations of long-distance trade partners, decline of the standard of living, and modifications of elite/commoner distinctions. We summarize these changes here for each of the phase transitions.

Temazcalli to Early Cuauhnahuac Transition

Reconstruction of the socioeconomic system during the Temazcalli phase (1200-1350) is limited by the small number of excavated deposits from this phase (two refuse deposits at Capilco). Nevertheless, the artifacts from these deposits can be compared with the more abundant Early Cuauhnahuac (1350-1430) materials to suggest patterns of change. There was clearly a major growth in population as Capilco expanded and Cuexcomate was founded; this pattern is repeated in Smith's (1992) demographic reconstruction for the area around the two sites, where the annual population growth rate was an estimated 1.6%. This population surge was accompanied by the construction of agricultural terraces in the study area. No pre-Cuauhnahuac agricultural terraces have been documented (Hirth 1994; Price and Smith 1992), and although only one of the check-dams at Cuexcomate can be unequivocally assigned to a phase on the basis of a chronometric date (LC), strong indirect evidence points to an EC origin for the terracing (Price and Smith 1992).

The frequencies of cotton spinning artifacts increase dramatically from Temazcalli to EC times (table 13.2), conforming to a pattern previously documented at nearby Xochicalco and Coatetelco (Smith and Hirth 1988). This apparent growth in the textile industry was not equalled by other craft activity, most of which continued at low levels. Trade with the Basin of Mexico (as measured by imported ceramics and obsidian) increased greatly, while exchange within Morelos declined (table 13.3). Wealth index 2 declines (except for the EC elite compound), but we do not see this as indicating a drop in standards of living since the numerical decline is due almost entirely to the decline in Morelos ceramic imports (table 13.3; see note 4). Other evidence, reviewed below, points to the EC phase as a time of prosperity and expansion.

Early Cuauhnahuac to Late Cuauhnahuac Transition

The rate of population growth decreased from the Early Cuauhnahuac phase (1350-1430) to the Late Cuauhnahuac phase (1430-1550), from 1.6% to 1.0%, but it was still quite high, and the magnitude of the population increase was impressive (table 13.1; see Smith 1992:335-345). Agricultural intensification in the form of terracing continued until nearly all available land in the Buenavista Lomas was under cultivation (O'Mack 1991; Price and Smith 1992). Although productivity studies have not been carried out, it appears that the population had exceeded the carrying capacity of the land; Smith (1992:335-345) estimates the LC population density in this area at over 600 persons per km.[2]

The frequency of cotton spinning artifacts in individual household deposits increases by 50 percent at Capilco, with little change at Cuexcomate. When increased population at these settlements is considered, however, the overall level of textile production increased dramatically. Several lines of evidence point to lowered standards of living in LC times. Wealth index 2 shows a decline in all social categories (table 13.4). There is less variability in artifactual wealth indicators, including a lower level of elite/commoner differences. This pattern is exhibited even more strongly in residential architecture, with elite abandonment of the imposing patio group 6 and construction of the more modest group 7 (fig. 13.2). The abandonment of patio group 6 between EC and LC probably signals a major social change, but we do not know its cause or significance (see discussion below).

These changes from the Temazcalli through Late Cuauhnahuac phases are all clearly documented in the archaeological record at Capilco and Cuexcomate. Their causes and consequences are discussed below under three headings: the role of the elite, Aztec conquest, and economic growth cycles.

PROCESSES OF CHANGE

The Role of the Elite

The degree of centralized political control over the economy is an important issue in Aztec economics (Smith and Hodge, chap. 1), although with archaeological data it is difficult to distinguish state control from control by elites acting independently of the state. Brumfiel and Earle (1987) describe three models of economic organization and social complexity that help frame the issue of elite control. In their *commercial development model,* production and exchange are relatively independent of elite interference. On the other hand, elites may take an active role in the organization of economic activity. In the *adaptationist model,* elites serve a managerial function, producing social benefits for everyone. In the *political model,* however, elites act in a controlling and monopolizing capacity, benefitting themselves primarily. In our view, the data from Cuexcomate and Capilco are most consistent with the *commercial development model,* with "bottom-up" forces primary in the generation of Postclassic economic change in this area (see Blanton 1983a; Maclachlan 1987).

The expansion of terraced farming is the most visible aspect of Postclassic agricultural change in the Cuexcomate/Capilco area. Although terracing is a more intensive practice than level-field rainwater cultivation, it is not nearly as intensive as the irrigation or raised field techniques used elsewhere in Late Postclassic Central Mexico. Following Turner and Doolittle (1978), we define intensification as agricultural change that involves increased labor investment to produce higher yields per unit of land. Terracing is generally carried out on the household level (Netting 1968, 1990; Wilken 1987), and unlike the methods of irrigation or raised field cultivation, terracing does not require or stimulate collective or centralized organization (Sanders et al. 1979; Wilken 1987). Our stratigraphic evidence for an extended period of check-dam enlargement conforms with this pattern. Netting's (1990) model of intensification (as a household-level adaptation to population pressure that does not necessarily lead to political centralization or control) seems applicable to this case. It is not necessary to invoke a model of elite control of production to account for the expansion of terracing. On the other hand, attempts by elites to increase production within their territory are a common incentive to intensification cross-culturally (e.g., Brumfiel and Earle 1987; Polgar 1975), and this possibility cannot be ruled out.

With the possible exception of the use of paint stones, there was little elite control over craft production. Textiles, paper, and other goods were manufactured at the elite compounds, but not at higher levels than at nonelite houses (table 13.2; fig. 13.3). This finding surprised us, since regional ethnohistorical sources indicate that commoners went to noble compounds to spin and weave, (e.g., Cortés 1865:542; Smith, chap. 12); we had expected therefore to find evidence of more intensive textile manufacture in such contexts.

No imported artifacts have an exclusively elite association although some imported ceramic types show statistical associations with elite contexts (e.g., Morelos imports in the EC phase; Aztec III in both EC and LC phases; see table 13.4). All excavated houses had access to imported ceramics and obsidian tools, and many had copper artifacts. Moreover, exotic items of rare, valuable jewelry (jade beads, obsidian earspools, shell pendants) were found almost exclusively in nonelite contexts. Apart from architecture, our analyses found no examples of sumptuary goods to distinguish elite from commoner contexts. On this basis, we see no evidence for elite control over exchange. Imports were probably obtained through the market system where noble and commoner had equal access.

In sum, there is little evidence for elite control over production or exchange activities, and a "bottom-up" economic model appears to be most appropriate for agricultural production, craft industries, and exchange. The diminished elite/ commoner distinctions in the LC phase indicate that the decline in standards of living was not due to greater exploitation at the hands of the local Cuexcomate elite. Nevertheless, this and other changes from EC to LC could have resulted from exploitation by external elites centered in either Quauhnahuac and/or the Basin of Mexico. In other words, the actions of elites may have had important repercussions on rural conditions, but if so, the relevant elite groups were not those resident at Cuexcomate.

Aztec Conquest

The EC and LC phases correspond to the periods before and after western Morelos was conquered and incorporated into the Aztec empire (Smith 1987b; Smith and Doershuk 1991). We distinguish three types of effects that Aztec imperialism may have had on rural sites: the direct effects of conquest, the impact of Aztec tribute, and the indirect effects that derived from regional changes brought about by Aztec imperialism. Although all three may have played a role, we believe the indirect effects had the most significant influence on rural socio-economic patterns.

The evaluation of the effects of Aztec conquest at Cuexcomate and Capilco is complicated by the earlier conquest of western Morelos by the Quauhnahuac polity in the 1420s (Smith 1986). The only likely direct effect of foreign conquest that we can identify is the abandonment of the patio group 6 elite compound at Cuexcomate. This could have been caused by the killing or destruction of the EC phase elite household by either the Quauhnahuac polity in the 1420s or by the Aztec empire in the late 1430s.

The direct tributary demands of the Aztec empire probably had little impact on settlements like Capilco and Cuexcomate. This area was within the territory of the Quauhnahuac conquest-state, which corresponded to the Aztec tributary province of the same name. The major tribute items paid to the Aztecs by Quauhnahuac were cotton textiles, grains, bark paper, and warrior costumes (see Smith, chap. 12). At least three of the observed archaeological changes—increased agricultural production, increased textile manufacture, and lowered standards of living—could be direct results of Aztec tributary exploitation. Smith's quantitative reconstruction of Morelos demography and tribute (chap. 12), however, suggests that on the household level, imperial tribute was quite modest (the rate for cotton textiles was under one manta or piece per household per year).

Imperial tribute alone would not cause the EC to LC archaeological changes; nevertheless, the indirect effects of Aztec imperialism could have had a greater impact. In an earlier article, Smith (1986) presents a model that shows the importance of interaction between the ruling dynasties of Quauhnahuac and Tenochtitlan as a mechanism of integration within the empire. This interaction, begun before the formation of the Aztec empire, increased in intensity after the conquest of Quauhnahuac in 1438. Smith hypothesizes that the Quauhnahuac nobility used their enhanced position within the Aztec empire to increase their own tributary exploitation of provincial commoners, augmenting tribute exactions beyond the relatively modest imperial quota for their own gain.

This model does not fit Cuexcomate elite, however, whose interaction with the Basin of Mexico declined in the LC phase (as judged by architectural styles and imports) while their economic position worsened. In fact, the EC phase elite may have been wiped out during the Aztec conquest (see above). Unlike the nobility in the capital city of Quauhnahuac, the LC Cuexcomate elite did not receive the benefits of Aztec imperial elite interaction networks. Rural populations like the inhabitants of Capilco and Cuexcomate were at the bottom of the Quauhnahuac tributary hierarchy (see Smith, chap. 12), and commoners and elite alike at these sites were probably exploited by regional elites at both city-state capitals and Quauhnahuac. The combined effects of increased tribute at the imperial and regional state levels probably contributed to the observed changes in agricultural production, textile manufacture, standard of living, and elite conditions. These indirect effects of Aztec conquest were not autonomous causes of the archaeological changes, however. Rather, they were but one component of a complex system of forces that generated economic change in Postclassic western Morelos.

An Economic Growth Cycle

The various processes of change outlined above began in Temazcalli and EC times well before the formation of the Aztec empire in 1430, a strong argument against Aztec conquest as their primary direct or indirect cause. We interpret these changes as components of a dynamic system of economic growth characterized by complex feedback relationships. This system fueled a regional agrarian cycle of boom and bust, where initial growth, expansion, and prosperity lead to contraction, decline, and crisis.

The population increase between the Middle and Late Postclassic periods was one of the more dramatic developments of the Postclassic epoch throughout Central Mexico. This demographic process has been discussed in terms of both causal population pressure models (Sanders et al. 1979) and systemic feedback models (Blanton 1983b). The rough chronological framework in the Basin of Mexico has prevented detailed analysis, however, and much of the population pressure debate proceeds more from theoretical first principles than from empirical evidence (Smith 1993b). The greater chronological control in western Morelos permits the process of population growth to be examined more closely. Based upon our admittedly limited data, it appears that the greatest regional surge occurred in the fourteenth century (Temazcalli - EC transition), with slower but still significant growth continuing through the fifteenth century

(EC - LC transition); annual regional growth rates at these two transition periods averaged 1.6% and 1.0% respectively (Smith 1992:335-345).

The fourteenth-century surge led to large-scale colonization of the Buenavista Lomas, probably by peoples from the more productive, irrigated, alluvial areas of Central Morelos. Capilco already existed at this time, but Cuexcomate was initially settled as a relatively large center of 10 hectares with over 200 inhabitants. Agricultural terracing was required by the large number of new settlers, and population pressure was a major force leading to agricultural intensification. On the other hand, the economic success of the EC phase (see below) probably served as a feedback loop that further stimulated population growth. Once a successful terracing program was established, the economy initially would have faced labor shortages rather than land shortages, a condition favorable to demographic growth (Polgar 1975). Later, local and regional tribute demands may have contributed to the forces stimulating population growth. Eventually, by LC times, economic growth slowed down as the lomas area filled up. Continued population growth became a major contributor to lowered standards of living.

The network of interactions among demography, economic forces, and household level craft production is an important component of this model. Many of the documented craft activities—chert tool manufacture and production activities that involved polishing stones, worked sherds and/or copper tools— were apparently performed at all or most houses for domestic purposes. These activities fit Peacock's (1982) category of "household production," or low-level domestic production for immediate household use. Two products—cotton textiles and bark paper—were also manufactured in domestic contexts but with some production for exchange beyond the immediate family. In the case of textiles, production was quite intensive (inferred from the high frequencies of spindle whorls and spinning bowls), and fits Peacock's "household industry" category (see Hicks, chap. 4) in which production is carried out in domestic contexts for both use and exchange, usually by part-time producers (see Nichols, chap. 7, and Otis, chap. 8, for discussions of the scale of craft production at the city of Otumba).

Part-time, rural textile manufacture conforms to Brumfiel's (1987) model of Aztec craft production in which utilitarian items were made by part-time, independent rural artisans and luxury items by full-time urban specialists attached to noble courts. We believe, however, that the economic context of rural production differs somewhat from Brumfiel's account. She proposes (Brumfiel 1987; Brumfiel and Earle 1987:5) that rural craft producers do not have sufficient, steady, aggregate demand to specialize full time, so they adopt farming as a buffer against fluctuations in supply and demand. On the other hand, ethnographic and historical accounts suggest that the opposite process may in fact be more common: rural farmers take up part-time craft production to supplement their income. This pattern commonly occurs under conditions of growing rural population, land shortages, and poverty that lead peasant households to try to augment their declining agricultural income with cottage industries (Arnold 1985:171-196; Miller and Hatcher 1978; Thirsk 1961).

Data from Cuexcomate and Capilco suggest this latter process occurred in the Late Cuauhnahuac phase. The progressive decline in wealth index 2 (table 13.4) over the three phases is accompanied by increases in the frequency of cotton spinning artifacts (table 13.2), particularly at the site of Capilco. More telling is the situation in the LC phase. In EC times, no single house stands out with excessive amounts of textile artifacts, but in LC times one nonelite house at each site exceeds the phase mean by more than two standard deviations. These houses with greatly intensified cotton spinning (houses 102 and 261) are also among the lowest in values for wealth index 1, as shown in figure 13.4. Admittedly, there is little overall statistical association between cotton spinning and wealth, but it may be important that the two houses with the most intensive spinning are among the poorest houses at these sites. At Capilco in the EC phase, house 102 was involved in craft production using copper tools and had the highest wealth index at that site. In the LC phase, however, both of its

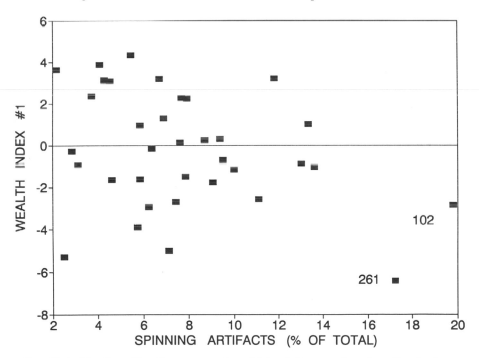

Fig. 13.4. Textile artifact frequency and wealth level. Data are from Late Cuauhnahuac households at Cuexcomate and Capilco.

wealth indices plummeted and the inhabitants of house 102 intensified both textile production and the use of copper tools.

The above observations may be summarized as follows. The EC phase was a time of economic growth and general prosperity at Cuexcomate and Capilco. Population was growing and new lands were put into production with terracing. Population levels were well within the carrying capacity of terraced agriculture. Compared to Temazcalli times, trade increased with all areas except perhaps Quauhnahuac, and textile production was carried out at higher levels. A prosperous and powerful elite group was linked architecturally and stylistically with the Central Mexican elite class, and the commoners appear to have had relatively high standards of living (to judge by the wealth indices and access to imported goods). By contrast, the LC phase showed a decline in living conditions. The extremely high population density probably taxed the limits of terrace agriculture (a study of terrace chronology and productivity is badly needed). All social sectors experienced decreases in standards of living and the relative and absolute position of the LC elite was greatly reduced. The two major forces leading to this socioeconomic downturn were the demographic/agricultural crisis and the increased tribute demands of Quauhnahuac and the Aztec empire. Aztec conquest did not create the problems, but the indirect effects of Aztec imperialism must have exacerbated local troubles, adding further to the economic difficulties of rural households.

This overall pattern of development from Temazcalli through Late Cuauhnahuac times is an example of an economic cycle common in pre-industrial states with dense peasant populations. In the first half of the cycle, population grows, new lands are colonized, trade and manufacturing expand, and towns prosper. As growth continues beyond some threshold, however, the economy is transformed from a condition of excess land and a shortage of labor to one with surplus labor and a shortage of land. In this second half of the cycle, cultivable land is filled in, productivity declines, prices rise, the countryside becomes impoverished, and many peasant households take up cottage industries to supplement falling agricultural income. Two well-documented historical examples of this agrarian cycle are England in the twelfth and thirteenth centuries (Miller and Hatcher 1978) and southern France in the fifteenth and sixteenth centuries (Le Roy Ladurie 1972). In another case, Blanton et al. (1993:50-105) present archaeological evidence for similar prehispanic growth cycles in the Valley of Oaxaca. We believe that these examples are comparable to the changes observed from the excavations at Capilco and Cuexcomate.

CONCLUSIONS

The rural economy of Late Postclassic western Morelos was more complex and dynamic than ethnohistoric accounts of Aztec society would suggest. The inhabitants of Capilco and Cuexcomate were not simple peasants toiling away to support nobles and states. Instead, these people, elites and commoners, were well connected to Central Mexican exchange networks. They carried out a variety of productive activities in addition to agriculture, and their towns and villages exhibited a high level of social heterogeneity. These patterns cannot be recovered from generalized ethnohistoric accounts of sixteenth-century Central Mexico, nor are they clear from local administrative documents from Morelos. Local social and economic conditions and the ways in which they changed through time can only be understood when detailed archaeological data are gathered and analyzed within a comparative social framework that integrates local, regional, and macroregional data into a comprehensive model.

The model of change that we propose above provides a good fit to the observed archaeological changes at Capilco and Cuexcomate. This model should be viewed as an exploratory account, however, until comparable data from other areas become available. The processes we single out as important—population growth, agricultural intensification, craft production, social stratification, and external conquest—operated at regional and macroregional scales, and this description of change at two small sites can only provide a partial view of Late Postclassic rural conditions in Central Mexico. Nevertheless, this study demonstrates the value of the household archaeology approach as a method for generating useful social and economic data. As more such studies are carried out, our models will continue to improve, and earlier normative and static accounts of Aztec rural society will be replaced by a more accurate appreciation of the dynamic and diverse nature of Aztec economies and societies.

ACKNOWLEDGMENTS

The Postclassic Morelos Archaeological Project was supported by funds from the National Science Foundation, the National Endowment for the Humanities, and Loyola University of Chicago. Permission for the fieldwork and analyses was granted by the Instituto Nacional de Antropología e Historia. We would like to thank Arqueólogos Norberto González Crespo, Joaquín García-Bárcena, Angel García Cook and Lorena Mirambel of the Instituto for helping the project in many ways. Elizabeth Brumfiel, Frederic Hicks and Mary Hodge provided helpful comments on an earlier draft of this paper.

NOTES

1.   In this paper we use the concept "rural" as an attribute of regions (rather than as an attribute of individual settlements). A rural region is an area with a low level of urbanization in the sense that it contains few cities or else has a low proportion of the population living in cities.

2.   All quantitative data on artifact distributions in this article describe materials from well-phased, domestic midden deposits associated with individual houses. Ceramic artifacts are quantified in terms of minimum numbers of vessels per type per context (based upon rim sherds), which are expressed as percentages for each context. Other artifacts are quantified in terms of abundance relative to ceramics; the measure used is frequency per 1,000 sherds. These measures are discussed in Smith (1992).

3.   Out of a total of 56 well-phased, residential midden deposits at Capilco and Cuexcomate, 10 have excavated volumes greater than 4 m³ (for a single phase). These 10 deposits cover all three phases and both sites. Because of the statistical problem of underrepresentation of rare categories in small collections, these 10 deposits are used to monitor the ubiquity of rare artifact types on a general level.

4.   Two methods were used to select the five ceramic types for calculation of wealth index #1. Analysis of variance established the variables that most consistently differed between elite and nonelite houses, and comparisons of means revealed the magnitudes of the group differences. Combining the results of the two methods, the five most sensitive variables were selected for each phase. Percents were transformed to standardized Z-scores (within each phase separately), and the five scores summed, giving each house a value that ranged from -7.9 to +7.0; a score of 0 would be the "average" wealth level. The figures in table 13.4 are means by social category.

REFERENCES CITED

Arnold, Dean
   1985   *Ceramic Theory and Cultural Processes.* Cambridge University Press, New York.
Berdan, Frances F.
   1987   Cotton in Aztec Mexico: Production, Distribution, and Uses. *Mexican Studies/Estudios Mexicanos* 3:235-262.
Blanton, Richard E.
   1983a Factors Underlying the Origin and Evolution of Market Systems. In *Economic Anthropology: Topics and Theories,* edited by Sutti Ortiz, pp. 51-66. University Press of America, Lanham, Maryland.
   1983b Advances in the Study of Cultural Evolution in Prehispanic Highland Mesoamerica. *Advances in World Archaeology* 2:245-288. Academic Press, New York.
Blanton, Richard E., Stephen A. Kowalewski, Gary M. Feinman, and Laura M. Finsten
   1993   *Ancient Mesoamerica: A Comparison of Change in Three Regions.* 2nd ed. Cambridge University Press, New York.

Boone, Elizabeth H.

1994 Manuscript Painting in Service of Imperial Ideology. In *Aztec Imperial Strategies,* by Frances F. Berdan, Richard E. Blanton, Elizabeth H. Boone, Mary G. Hodge, Michael E. Smith and Emily Umberger. Dumbarton Oaks, Washington, D.C. In press.

Brumfiel, Elizabeth M.

1980 Specialization, Market Exchange, and the Aztec State: A View from Huexotla. *Current Anthropology* 21:459-478.

1987 Elite and Utilitarian Crafts in the Aztec State. In *Specialization, Exchange, and Complex Societies,* edited by Elizabeth M. Brumfiel and Timothy K. Earle, pp. 102-118. Cambridge University Press, New York.

Brumfiel, Elizabeth M., and Timothy K. Earle

1987 Specialization, Exchange, and Complex Societies: An Introduction. In *Specialization, Exchange, and Complex Societies,* edited by Elizabeth M. Brumfiel and Timothy K. Earle, pp. 1-9. Cambridge University Press, New York.

Carrasco, Pedro

1976 Estratificación social indígena en Morelos durante el siglo XVI. In *Estratificación social en la Mesoamérica prehispánica,* edited by Pedro Carrasco and Johanna Broda, pp. 102-117. Instituto Nacional de Antropología e Historia, Mexico City.

Cortés, Hernán

1865 Carta de Hernán Cortés, al Consejo de Indias ... sobre la constitución de la propiedad de las tierras entre los indios (1538). In *Colección de documentos inéditos ... de Indias,* vol. 3, pp. 535-543. Real Academia de la Historia, Madrid.

Evans, Susan T.

1988 *Excavations at Cihuatecpan, an Aztec Village in the Teotihuacan Valley.* Vanderbilt University Publications in Anthropology No. 36. Vanderbilt University, Nashville.

1991 Architecture and Authority in an Aztec Village: Form and Function of the Tecpan. In *Land and Politics in the Valley of Mexico,* edited by Herbert R. Harvey, pp. 63-92. University of New Mexico Press, Albuquerque.

Fries, Carl, Jr.

1960 *Geología del estado de Morelos y de partes adyacentes de México y Guerrero.* Boletín No. 60. Instituto de Geología, Universidad Nacional Autónoma de México, Mexico City.

Goodfellow, Susan T.

1990 *Late Postclassic Period Economic Systems in Western Morelos, Mexico: A Study of Ceramic Production, Distribution and Exchange.* PhD dissertation, Department of Anthropology, University of Pittsburgh. University Microfilms, Ann Arbor.

Hirth, Kenneth G.

1994 *Ancient Urbanism at Xochicalco.* Manuscript on file at the Department of Anthropology, Pennsylvania State University.

Kolb, Charles C.
1985 Demographic Estimates in Archaeology: Contributions from Ethnoarchaeology on Mesoamerican Peasants. *Current Anthropology* 26:581-600.

Le Roy Ladurie, Emmanuel
1972 *The Peasants of Languedoc.* University of Illinois Press, Urbana.

Maclachlan, Morgan D.
1987 From Intensification to Proletarianization. In *Household Economies and Their Transformations,* edited by Morgan D. Maclachlan, pp. 1-27. University Press of America, Lanham, Maryland.

Maldonado Jiménez, Druzo
1990 *Cuauhnahuac y Huaxtepec: Tlalhuicas y Xochimilcas en el Morelos prehispánico.* Centro Regional de Investigaciones Multidisciplinarias, Universidad Nacional Autónoma de México, Cuernavaca.

Mason, Roger D.
1980 *Economic and Social Organization of an Aztec Provincial Center: Archaeological Research at Coatlan Viejo, Morelos, Mexico.* PhD dissertation, Department of Anthropology, University of Texas. University Microfilms, Ann Arbor.

Miller, Edward, and John Hatcher
1978 *Medieval England: Rural Society and Economic Change, 1086-1348.* Longman, New York.

Netting, Robert McC.
1968 *Hill Farmers of Nigeria: Cultural Ecology of the Jos Plateau.* University of Washington Press, Seattle.

1990 Population, Permanent Agriculture, and Polities: Unpacking the Evolutionary Portmanteau. In *The Evolution of Political Systems: Sociopolitics in Small-Scale Societies,* edited by Steadman Upham, pp. 21-61. Cambridge University Press, New York.

O'Mack, Scott H.
1991 *Final Report of the Tetlama Lienzo Project.* Report submitted to the National Geographic Society.

Peacock, D. P. S.
1982 *Pottery in the Roman World: An Ethnoarchaeological Approach.* Longman, New York.

Polgar, Steven
1975 Population, Evolution, and Theoretical Paradigms. In *Population, Ecology, and Social Evolution,* edited by Steven Polgar, pp. 1-26. Mouton, The Hague.

Price, T. Jeffrey
1988 *Investigation of Agricultural Features at Two Rural Late Postclassic Sites in Western Morelos, Mexico.* Unpublished Master's thesis, Department of Anthropology, University of Georgia.

Price, T. Jeffrey, and Michael E. Smith
1992 Agricultural Terraces. In *Archaeological Research at Aztec-Period Rural Sites in Morelos, Mexico, Volume 1: Excavations and Architecture,* by

Michael E. Smith, pp. 267-292. Memoirs in Latin American Archaeology No. 4. University of Pittsburgh, Pittsburgh.

Sanders, William T., Jeffrey R. Parsons, and Robert S. Santley
1979   *The Basin of Mexico: Ecological Processes in the Evolution of a Civilization.* Academic Press, New York.

Sandor, Jon A., P. L. Gersper, and J. W. Hawley
1990   Prehistoric Agricultural Terraces and Soils in the Mimbres Area, New Mexico. *World Archaeology* 22:70-86.

Smith, Michael E.
1986   The Role of Social Stratification in the Aztec Empire: A View from the Provinces. *American Anthropologist* 88:70-91.

1987a Household Possessions and Wealth in Agrarian States: Implications for Archaeology. *Journal of Anthropological Archaeology* 6:297-335.

1987b The Expansion of the Aztec Empire: A Case Study in the Correlation of Diachronic Archaeological and Ethnohistorical Data. *American Antiquity* 52:37-54.

1992   *Archaeological Research at Aztec-Period Rural Sites in Morelos, Mexico, Volume 1: Excavations and Architecture.* Memoirs in Latin American Archaeology No. 4. University of Pittsburgh, Pittsburgh.

1993a Houses and the Settlement Hierarchy in Late Postclassic Morelos: A Comparison of Archaeology and Ethnohistory. In *Prehispanic Domestic Units in Western Mesoamerica: Studies of the Household, Compound, and Residence,* edited by Robert S. Santley and Kenneth G. Hirth, pp. 191-206. CRC Press, Boca Raton.

1993b New World Complex Societies: Recent Economic, Social, and Political Studies. *Journal of Archaeological Research* 1:5-41

Smith, Michael E., Patricia Aguirre, Cynthia Heath-Smith, Kathryn Hirst, Scott O'Mack, and T. Jeffrey Price
1989   Architectural Patterns at Three Aztec-period Sites in Morelos, Mexico *Journal of Field Archaeology* 16:185-203.

Smith, Michael E., and John F. Doershuk
1991   Late Postclassic Chronology in Western Morelos, Mexico. *Latin American Antiquity* 2:291-310.

Smith, Michael E., and Kenneth G. Hirth
1988   The Development of Prehispanic Cotton-Spinning Technology in Western Morelos, Mexico. *Journal of Field Archaeology* 15:349-358.

Sorensen, Jerrell H.
1988   Rural Chipped Stone Technology in Late Postclassic Morelos, Mexico. Paper presented at the 1988 Annual Meeting, American Anthropological Association, Phoenix.

Sorensen, Jerrell H., Kenneth G. Hirth, and Stephen M. Ferguson
1989   The Contents of Seven Obsidian Workshops Around Xochicalco, Morelos. In *La obsidiana en Mesoamérica,* edited by Margarita Gaxiola and John E. Clark, pp. 269-276. Instituto Nacional de Antropología e Historia, Mexico City.

Sterpone, Osvaldo
   1988   Late Postclassic Settlement Patterns in Northwestern Morelos. Paper presented at the 1988 Annual Meeting of the American Anthropological Association, Phoenix.

Thirsk, Joan
   1961   Industries in the Countryside. In *Essays in the Economic and Social History of Tudor and Stuart England, in Honor of R. H. Tawney,* edited by F. J. Fisher, pp. 70-88. Cambridge University Press, Cambridge.

Turner, B. L., II, and William E. Doolittle
   1978   The Concept and Measure of Agricultural Intensity. *Professional Geographer* 30:297-301.

Wilken, Gene C.
   1987   *Good Farmers: Traditional Agricultural Resource Management in Mexico and Central America.* University of California Press, Berkeley.

Zorita, Alonso de
   1963   *Breve y sumaria relación de los señores de la Nueva España.* Universidad Nacional Autónoma de México, Mexico City.

14

Huaxyacac

Aztec Military Base on the Imperial Frontier

Manlio Barbosa-Cano

The great majority of scholars who write about the city of Oaxaca are skeptical that a prehispanic city once existed at the site of the modern one. This skepticism continues despite the abundance of references to and descriptions of such a settlement that are made in indigenous codices, colonial documents, colonial and modern writings, as well as various descriptions and studies of an historical nature. Still lacking is the definitive proof for a settlement: the archaeological evidence.

The work presented here is part of a larger study that demonstrates the existence and location of the prehispanic city of Huaxyacac and discusses its urban, political, and military characteristics. This study involves a reevaluation of the sources in relation to the treatment they have been given in previous studies as well as an effort to integrate them with each other. The integration of the sources is important since each one, while providing valuable information, also contains errors, omissions, contradictions, or interpretations that are deceptive or incomplete.

This methodology reveals the existence of a city that was a center for tribute collection and a seat of the civil and military hierarchies, and of political, military, and commercial control. It also shows the city's transformation into a military base for the subjugation of the region and for the conquest of or commercial trading with the wealthy Maya states. The study also finds areas of agreement and congruity among the sources (duly integrated) as well as with the logic of the historical process. I wait with interest the critical evaluation of my work and the pointing out of errors by my peers, just as I have considered the work of some authors and sources cited here.

WHEN DID HUAXYACAC BECOME A MEXICA SEAT OF POWER?

The precise date of the founding of the first human settlement at what today is the city of Oaxaca has not been determined. It is feasable to suppose that it took place during the prehistory of the Oaxacan valleys, even though for the moment there are no data to document this assertion. For the Preclassic and Classic periods, given the extraordinary importance of Monte Alban, it would be very odd if a human settlement with economic, political, and even military functions had not developed at the base of the hills of that city. Such characteristics are amply documented for the Postclassic period with respect to the city called Huaxyacac (Huaxacac), which the Aztecs converted into one of their most important enclaves on the southeast periphery of the domain they came to govern. The dates of the Aztec arrival at and conquest of Huaxyacac are under debate. Durán (1967:v.2:205) contends that this event took place during the reign of Motecuhzoma I (Motecuhzoma Ilhuicamina), and Antonio Herrera y Tordesillas (1729) agrees with him:

> En la Era del primero Moteçuma, deseando acabar de conquistar este Reino Misteco, viendo que no lo podia hacer por fuerza de Armas, tuvo forma, para que por traición fuese muerto el Cacique de Ianguitlan, hombre valeroso, que le hacia gran resisencia, que se llamaba el Señor Tres Micos, i con su muerte todos se le sujetaron, i le tributaron Plumas verdes, Chalchuites, que son sus quentas preciadas, Ropa, grana, Cochinilla: beneficiabanle algunas sementeras: con todo lo cual acudian a las Guarniciones del Rei. (Herrera y Tordesillas 1729:Década 3a, bk 3, chap. 8:99)

> [In the reign of the first Moteçuma, desiring to complete the conquest of this Mistec Kingdom, seeing that he could not do it by force of arms, so by treason the Cacique of Ianguitlan [Yancuitlan] was killed, a valliant man who had put up a strong resistance, whom they called the lord Three Monkey, and with his death everyone was subjugated [by Motecuhzoma], and they paid him tribute in green feathers, chalchuites, which are their precious beads, clothing, grain, cochineal: they cultivated some sown fields for him: with all that applied to the Garrison of the King.]

Among modern scholars, only Iturribarría (1955:41) agrees with those cited above; without mentioning his sources, he dates the conquest of Huaxyacac to 1458, under the power of Motecuhzoma I. In contrast, the majority of authors who allude to this historical event place it in the reign of Ahuitzotl, in 1486 (see, for example, Chance [1978:18]; Gay [1982:101]; Jiménez Moreno [1970:27]; Seler [1904]). The work of these authors, even though they may not always explicitly say so, is grounded in the indigenous codices. The codices are direct sources that can serve not only to clarify the time of the event but also some of its characteristics that have not yet received the attention of historians and chroniclers, as well as to correct certain errors that the colonial chroniclers committed in copying or annotating them. The *Códice Vaticano-Ríos* (1964:268, lámina 124) describes a series of conquests and their dates (fig. 14.1), which Corona Núñez (1964a) translates as follows:

> EL año *Ome Tochtli,* dos conejo, 1493, sujetaron los mexicanos un pueblo de *Oaxaca,* ... El individuo vestido con las ropas del sacrificio lleva en la cabeza el jeroglífico de *Oaxaca,* ... En el siguiente año, *Yei Acatl,* tres caña, 1494, conquistaron los mexicanos al pueblo de *Teutzapotlan,* lugar de zapote divino; por este nombre, el guerrero vestido para el sacrificio, que está bajo el cuadrete de esta fecha, tiene sobre la cabeza una rama de zapote. (Corona Núñez 1964a:268)

> [The year *Ome Tochtli,* 2 Rabbit, 1493, the Mexicans subjugated a town of *Oaxaca,* ... The individual dressed in sacrificial clothing carries on this head the hieroglyph for *Oaxaca,* ... In the following year, *Yei Acatl,* 3 Reed, the Mexicans conquered the town of *Teutzapotlan,* place of the divine zapote; for this name, the warrior dressed for sacrifice who is beneath the square containing this date has a branch of zapote over his head.]

The *Códice Telleriano-Remensis,* on lámina 22 of the third part (fig. 14.2), shows the same ideograms with minor variations. The main difference between the two codices is that the latter includes an "explanation" by the scribe, in the Spanish of the sixteenth century: "Año de ... 1494 sujeptaron los mexicanos al pueblo de Mictla que es en la provincia de Huaxaca. Año de ... 1495, sujeptaron los mexicanos al pueblo de Teutzapotlan, que era la cabeçera de la provincia de Huaxaca" (*Códice Telleriano-Remensis* 1964:302, lámina 22) [Year of ... 1494 the Mexicans subjugated the town of Mictla which is in the province of Huaxaca. Year of ... 1495, the Mexicans subjugated the town of Teutzapotlan, which was the capital of the province of Huaxaca]. Corona Núñez interprets this plate and text as follows:

Fig. 14.1. Conquest of Huaxtlan. The conquest of Huaxtlan by Ahuitzotl in the year 2 Rabbit (1493) is depicted in the *Códice Vaticano-Ríos* (1964:268, lámina 124).

Fig. 14.2. Conquest of Huaxtlan. The conquest of Huaxtlan by Ahuitzotl in the year 2 Rabbit (1494) is depicted in the *Códice Telleriano-Remensis* (1964:302, lámina 22).

El año ... 1494, conquistaron los mexicanos Mictla, ... de la provincia de Oaxaca. El personaje vestido de Huitzilopochtli significa que los prisioneros obtenidos en la guerra de Oaxaca fueron sacrificados, pues el jeroglífico que tiene en la cabeza pertenece a este lugar, antes llamado Huaxyácac. En el año siguente, ... 1495, hicieron la conquista de la antigua cabecera de la provincia de Oaxaca, llamada en zapoteco Zaachila-yoo, *la fortaleza de Zaachila,* y en náhuatl se llamaba Teutzapotlan, *Zapote divino,* y tal es el jeroglífico que trae el guerrero que va a ser sacrificado disfrazado de Huitzilopochtli. (Corona Núñez 1964b:302)

[The year ... 1494, the Mexicans conquered Mictla, ... of the province of Oaxaca. The personage dressed in the manner of Huitzilopochtli signifies that the prisoners taken in the war with Oaxaca were sacrificed, since the hieroglyph on the head of the character pertains to that city, previously called Huaxyácac. In the following year, ... 1495, they conquered the ancient capital of the province of Oaxaca, called in Zapotec Zaachila-yoo, *the fortress of Zaachila,* that in Nahuatl was called Teutzapotlan, *Divine Zapote,* and which is the hieroglyph worn by the warrior who is going to be sacrificed costumed as Huitzilopochtli.]

The interpretation of the place name in the Spanish text of the codex, where it appears written as Mictla, as well as Corona Núñez's acceptance of this translation (an error of the *Códice Telleriano-Remensis* which he passes on in his interpretation of the *Códice Vaticano-Ríos*) constitute the same confusion as that incurred by Gay and Paddock, which I discuss later in this chapter. In fact, the glyph drawn in both codices corresponds to *huajes,* which has no association with either Mictlan or Huaxyacac. In the *Codex Mendoza* (1992:f.16v) one finds a description of the conquest of Mictlan (fig. 14.3). Its ideogram shows the symbols that represent its name—a dark background with black dots, framed in a square that is defined on three sides by human bones. On the other hand, the ideogram corresponding to Huaxyacac includes a *huaje* tree that grows out of the end of the nose of a human face, because the toponym expresses precisely *huajes* (Huaxin) and nose (yacatl) (fig. 14.4; *Codex Mendoza* 1992:f.17v). The same error may be seen in the *Códice Chimalpopoca:*

7 *tochtli.* En este año murió Tiçoçicatzin; luego se entronizó Ahuitzotzin, que reinó en Tenochtitlan.

En este año se destruyeron los cozcaquauhtenancas, lo mismo que los tlappanecas, los tziuhcohuacas y los mictlanquauhtlatlaca. (*Códice Chimalpopoca* 1945:57)

Fig. 14.3.   Conquest of Mictlan. The conquest of Mictlan (lower left) by Motecuhzoma II is depicted in the *Codex Mendoza* (1992:f.16v).

204) 8 *acatl*. En este año se dedicó en Tenochtitlan la casa de Huitzilopochtli ... Se dedicó con los cautivos que había. Aquí se cuentan los muertos de todos los pueblos: tzapotecas muertos, 16,000; ... tziuhcohuacas muertos, 24,400, porque se suman los que eran cozcaquauhtenancas y mictlanquauhtlatlaca. (p. 58)

Se fué [Ahuitzotzin] apoderando de los pueblos que aquí se mencionan y los aplicó a su reino: el primero, del lugar llamado Tlappan; y ... Tzapotlan, ... Coyolapan, ... Tequantépec, ... (p. 67)

[7 *tochtli* ... In this year Ticocicatzin died; later succeeded Ahuitzotzin, who reigned in Tenochtitlan.

In this year the Cozcaquauhtenancas were destroyed, the same as the Tlappanecas, the Tziuhcohuacas, and the Mictlanquauhtlatlaca.

204) 8 *acatl*. In this year the house of Huitzilopochtli was dedicated in Tenochtitlan ... It was dedicated with the captives that were there. Here is the count of the dead of all of the peoples: Tzapotecas dead 16,000; ... Tziuhcohuacas dead, 24,400, because those who were Cozcaquauhtenancas and those who were Mictlanquauhtlatlaca are combined.

He [Ahuitzotzin] went forth taking possession of the towns that are mentioned here and making them his subjects: the first, of the place called Tlappan; and ... Tzapotlan, ... Coyolapan, ... Tequantépec, ...]

Fig. 14.4. Huaxyacac Glyph. The glyph for Huaxyacac (center) appears in the *Codex Mendoza* (1992:f.17v).

I contend that the above allusions to Mictlan and Zapotlan (Teozapotlan) imply—or include—the original site of Oaxaca. Evidently this confusion of place names originated in the colonial translations or interpretations of the prehispanic codices. This error must be pointed out where it appears in the *Códice Chimalpopoca* and in the Spanish annotation in the *Códice Telleriano-Remensis*. Those who have accepted and repeated the error in the *Códice Vaticano-Ríos* need to be corrected, and scholars must recognize the correct reading of the ideogram, which denotes the original name of the site. These two codices *(Telleriano-Remensis* and *Vaticano-Ríos)* show drawings of two personages dressed in the attire of Huitzilopochtli, which as Corona Núñez notes, signifies that individuals from the conquered sites were sacrificed. The glyph just above each figure indicates the place name of the site from which the victims came. Therefore, the ideogram above these personages, erroneously associated with Mitla and Oaxaca, must be translated as *Huaxtlan* since the element that denotes the toponym is simply a tree with *huajes.* This is the procedure Corona Núñez (1964a:262) follows when, for example, with regard to lámina 121 of the *Códice Vaticano-Ríos,* he translates as Tzapotlan (toponym) a place "que tiene por jeroglífico una rama de este árbol con sus frutos" [that has as its hieroglyph the branch of this tree [the zapote] with its fruits]. In the case of Teozapotlan, the scribe noted in correct form the Nahua name that the site had in the sixteenth century, the same name by which it is referred to in other sources such as the *Relaciones Geográficas* (Acuña 1984-1987). Moreover, the written name and the ideogram coincide.

It is significant that the name of the site drawn with the *huaje* glyph that is noted in the codices *Vaticano-Ríos* and *Telleriano-Remensis,* even though it does not correspond to the name of Huaxyacac, evidently has an association with the Postclassic city of that name. *Huajes* are abundant in the area and surely have identified the settlement since its beginnings. Their inclusion in both codices cannot allude to any place but Huaxyacac. Nevertheless, the differences in the form of the glyph as drawn in the codices *Vaticano-Ríos* and *Telleriano-Remensis* compared with a similar glyph in the *Matrícula de Tributos* (1968:f.17v) and the *Codex Mendoza* (1992:f.17v, f.44r) clearly reflect that the same site had first one name and later another because the originals of the first two codices chronologically predate those of the second two. I believe that correctly reading the site name, based on the codices mentioned above as well as on the consultation and interpretation of other sources cited below, will help us to explain certain aspects of the history of the city of Oaxaca.

The site that the codices *Vaticano-Ríos* and *Telleriano-Remensis* indicate was conquered by the Mexica is Huaxtlan—the original name of the city of Oaxaca in 1494. The conquest of Huaxtlan must have provided the Mexica with important support during their subsequent conquest of Teozapotlan; hence its conquest is noted in both codices. Given the extraordinary strategic importance of Huaxtlan and because of the larger rebellion that the city-state instigated and led some years later (see discussion of Durán [1967] below), upon its reconquest by the Mexica, Huaxtlan was repopulated, transformed, and renamed: Huaxtlan became Huaxyacac, and the armies under the direction of the Mexica *tlatoani* converted the city into a Mexica military base. This is why the city-state later appears as a seat of high civil and military rank in the *Matrícula de*

Tributos (1968:f.17v) and the *Codex Mendoza* (1992:f.17v, f.44r), but with a new ideogram that expresses the strategic character of the place (see fig. 14.4). The *huajes*, which had appeared alone in the earlier documents, are now shown anchored to the nose of a face. Durán, among others, relates that when the leaders of the city saw that they were defeated, they asked for pardon from the Mexica military, but the Mexica responded that their "sentencia" [sentence] was final: "no ha de haber ciudad que se llame Guaxaca, ni memoria ha de quedar de ella" (Durán 1967:v.2:230) [there is to be no city that is called Guaxaca, nor is a memory to remain of it].

Manuel Martínez Gracida makes an extraordinary contribution, which supports my hypothesis, in his "Colección de cuadros sinópticos ..." notes the names, and their roots, of the city of Oaxaca in different languages of the region:

> Los zapotecos le llaman Luhulaa, que quiere decir lugar de huajes. Etimología: Luhuo ó luho, lugar de; laa, guaje. Los mixtecas le dan el nombre de nuhundúa, que también quiere decir tierra de los huajes. Etimología: nuhu, pueblo o tierra; ndúa, guaje. En mixe se llama Huac Huin, que quiere decir a la vista de los guajes. Etimología: Huac, guaje; huin, ojo, vista. Los chinantecos le llaman Nicuhui, que significa en la punta de los guajes. (1888, Anexo 50)

> [The Zapotecs call it Luhulaa, which means the place of the huajes. Etymology: luhuo or luho, place of; laa, guaje. The Mixtecs give it the name of nuhundúa, which also means land of the huajes. Etymology: nuhu, town or land; ndúa, guaje. In Mixe it is called Huac Huin, which means the view of the guajes. Etymology: Huac, guaje; huin, eye, view. The chinantecos call it Nicuhui, which means at the point of the guajes.]

All of the translated meanings of the terms described above are in accordance with my interpretation as Huaxtlan of the ideogram that appears in the codices *Vaticano-Ríos* and *Telleriano-Remensis*. On the other hand, the meaning of the components of the name of the city imposed by the Aztecs, "en la nariz de los guajes. Etimología: Huaxin, huaje; yacatl, nariz, punta o extremidad; y c de ca, en" (Martínez Gracida 1888, Anexo 50) [on the nose of the guajes. Etymology: Huaxin, huaje; yacatl, nose, point, or extremity; and c of ca, on] corresponds to the ideogram in use after the city's transformation and name change to Huaxyacac. In the same vein, and in accordance with the *Matrícula de Tributos* and *Codex Mendoza*, the meaning that Martínez Gracida gives with respect to the name of the city of Huaxyacac in the Chocho language is very revealing: "le nombran Cunchaa, que significa cabeza de autoridad (mas propiamente 'capital donde residen los poderes públicos'). Etimología : cun, cabeza; chaa, autoridad" (Martínez Gracida 1888, Anexo 50) [they name it Cunchaa, which means head of authority (or more properly 'capital where the public powers reside'). Etymology: cun, head; chaa, authority].

The rebellions extinguished by the last Mexica sovereigns are described in various sources, and some of those closest to Huaxyacac are alluded to here. Dahlgren (1966:60) notes that "Moctezuma II [Motecuhzoma Xocoyotzin] tuvo que enfrentarse a una serie de sublevaciones mixtecas en territorios no mencionados entre las conquistas de sus predecesores" [Moctezuma II had to confront a series of Mixtec uprisings in territories that are not mentioned among the conquests of his predecessors]. Certainly the reason that the *Codex Mendoza* does not refer to the conquest of Huaxtlan is because, at the time it was written, the city already was being converted into a Mexica settlement of great importance. Moreover, given that the document was written years after the initial conquest of Huaxtlan, the facts were not recorded accurately, and the reconquest of the place remained encompassed in that of other places described in the codex, as is the case of Zapotlan (fig. 14.5; *Codex Mendoza* 1992:f.13r) Coyolapan (fig. 14.6; *Codex Mendoza* 1992:f.13v) or Mictlan (see fig. 14.3; *Codex Mendoza* 1992:f.16v). Even so it is possible that the author of the *Codex Mendoza* believed—years after the events and the deaths of the principal protagonists—that the conquest of Mictlan was that of Huaxtlan, perpetuating the confusion in the "tradition" of the codices *Telleriano-Remensis* and *Chimalpopoca.*

What has led to the confusion that identifies Huaxtlan with Mictlan? The attack suffered by the Mexicas unleashed a general rebellion and culminated with the reconquest of the area. That this attack took place in Mitla contributed to the association of this site with Huaxtlan. Although Durán (1967) describes the event clearly, the editors of both the *Vaticano-Ríos* and the *Códice Chimalpopoca* were confused and wrote down Mictlan in place of Huaxtlan. Perhaps the translators and their respective informants had already forgotten the name Huaxtlan and did not mention Huaxyacac because this name was the result of the reconquest of the site, not the site originally conquered. On the other hand, Mictlan, the city, was taken and conquered by Motecuhzoma II in 1501. Neither the Spanish chroniclers nor the indigenous writers of the mid-sixteenth century had any notion of these different events; they confused incidents and identified some with others. Durán contributes his share of confusion by associating the reconquest of the site and its transformation into Huaxyacac with Motecuhzoma I; the event actually occurred in the reign of Motecuhzoma II, as established on the basis of the codices cited above. Durán's mention of the sacrifice of prisoners at the inauguration of the Templo Mayor reveals that this chronicler confused events that occurred under Ahuitzotl with others associated with Motecuhzoma II, errors that he never realized he had made.

We can reconstruct the sequence of events of this part of the history of Oaxaca on the basis of what is found recorded in the most ancient codices. The

Fig. 14.5. Conquest of Zapotlan. The conquest of Zapotlan (middle row, left) by Ahuitzotl is depicted in the *Codex Mendoza* (1992:f.13r).

Fig. 14.6. Conquest of Coyolapan. The conquest of Coyolapan (second from left) by Ahuitzotl is depicted in the *Codex Mendoza* (1992:f. 13v).

clarity and congruity of the codices *Vaticano-Ríos* and *Telleriano-Remensis* contrast with the errors of the Spanish copyists who produced the codices *Mendoza* and *Chimalpopoca* several years after the Spanish conquest. The sources from the colonial chroniclers complement this information if we correct for their errors in chronological placement. It is the colonial chroniclers—Durán and Herrera y Tordesillas—who link the conquest of the original site of Oaxaca with Motecuhzoma I. The events described by Durán agree with the rest of the information that is authentically documented, if not with the dates.

Fig. 14.7. Conquest of Tehuantepec. The conquest of Tehuantepec by Motecuhzoma II is depicted in the *Códice Vaticano-Ríos* (1964:274, lámina 127).

  The work of Herrera y Tordesillas is not only very late in relation to the events but also poorly supported. The imperial expansion of the Mexica was a gradual consolidation of territories linked together geographically. It would have been very difficult, or nearly impossible, for the Mexica to have conquered Oaxaca, as Durán says, or Yancuitlan, as Herrera y Tordesillas states, without previously building logistical outposts between these sites and the capital of the empire, Tenochtitlan. In this respect, the *Códice Chimalpopoca* (1945:67) relates that Motecuhzoma I killed the ruler of Cohuayxtlahuacan "porque no quiso servir a la monarquía mexicana" [because he did not want to serve the Mexican monarchy]. It is possible that the incorrect reading of this and other sources led Herrera y Tordesillas to interpret the event as a conquest of the Mixtec "kingdom," when it seems to have been a very localized conflict, more political than military in character.

  It was Ahuitzotl who conquered the original site of Oaxaca, called Huaxtlan, in 1494, as stated in the codices *Vaticano-Ríos* and *Telleriano-Remensis*. I have shown that the first fixes the date of the conquest in 1493, one year earlier than the latter. I have accepted the later date following Corona Núñez (1964a), who writes that, "este códice [*Códice Vaticano-Ríos*] tiene una correlación en años cristianos atrasada en un año" (1964a:286, note to lámina 133) [this codex has a correlation in Christian years that is one year behind].

Fig. 14.8. Conquest of Tehuantepec. The conquest of Tehuantepec by Motecuhzoma II is depicted in the *Códice Telleriano-Remensis* (1964:304, lámina 23).

The *Codex Mendoza* (1992:f.13r, f.13v) and the *Códice Chimalpopoca* (1945:67) attribute the conquests of both Coyolapan (later called Cuilapan) and Zapotlan (later called Teozapotlan) to Ahuitzotl. Both sites are located near Oaxaca; in fact, whoever conquered Coyolapan and Zapotlan did the same to Oaxaca (i.e., Huaxtlan). As explained above, neither codex mentions Huaxtlan because by the time these documents were written, Huaxtlan had been transformed into an important Mexica enclave with a new name. Nevertheless, the *Codex Mendoza*, whose objective was the description of the provinces and their tribute requirements, fundamentally indicates the conquest of the region, noting the name of Coyolapan. Coyolapan was the capital of the tributary province at that time, as indicated by its appearance at the top of the list of towns that paid tribute to Tenochtitlan (*Codex Mendoza* 1992:f.44r). The same sort of reference occurs in the *Matrícula de Tributos* (1968:54).

Somewhat after 1502, Motecuhzoma II retook Huaxtlan, quashing the regional Mixtec-Zapotec rebellion and leveling the city. He converted it into a Mexica military base and changed its name to Huaxyacac. Durán (see below) reconstructs the sequence of events, although he places them incorrectly from a chronological viewpoint. The *Códice Vaticano-Ríos* (1964:274, lámina 127) as well as the *Códice Telleriano-Remensis* (1964:304, lámina 23) describe the conquest of Tehuantepec by Motecuhzoma II (figs. 14.7, 14.8), when Huaxyacac and other military bases were strengthened. In the same manner, the *Codex Mendoza* (1992:f.16v) attributes

Table 14.1   Mexica conquests in Oaxaca

Year	Event	Source
1440-1469	Conquest of Coayxtalhuacan, Cuetlaxtlan, and Quauhtochco by Motecuhzoma I	Codex Mendoza (1992:f.7v, f.8r)
1481-1486	Conquest of Yancuitlan by Tizoc	Codex Mendoza (1992:f.12r)
1486-1502	Conquest of Tehuantepec, Zapotlan, and Coyolapan by Ahuitzotl	Codex Mendoza (1992:f.1r, f.13v)
1493	Conquest of Huaxtlan by Ahuitzotl	Codex Vaticano-Ríos (1964:268)
1494	Conquest of Huaxtlan by Ahuitzotl	Codex Telleriano-Remensis (1964:302)
4 Acatl 1483?	Conquest of Mictlan by Ahuitzotl	Codex Chimalpopoca (1945:57)
8 Acatl 1487?	Conquest of Teozapotlan, Cuilapan, and Tehuantepec by Ahuitzotl	Codex Chimalpopoca (1945:58, 67)
1502-1520	Conquest of Nochiztlan, Tlachquiyauhco, and Mictlan by Motecuhzoma II	Codex Mendoza (1992:f.15v-f.16v)
1502	Rebellion and reconquest of Huaxtlan; conversion of Huaxtlan to Huaxyacac by Motecuhzoma II	Durán (1967:v.2:225-231); Alva Ixtlilxochitl (1975:v.2:183); Codex Vaticano-Ríos (1964:268); Codex Telleriano-Remensis (1964:302)

the conquest of Mictlan and other nearby towns to Motecuhzoma II. As can be seen, the indigenous documents agree one way or another in ascribing the conquest of the region of Oaxaca (Huaxtlan, Coyolapan, Teozapotlan) to Ahuitzotl. Durán's chronicle, which links regional religious and military events with the dedication of the Templo Mayor in Tenochtitlan, supports these assertions, even though its author believes they are associated with another Mexica *tlatoani*.

Summary

In summary, following the codices *Vaticano-Ríos* and *Telleriano-Remensis,* Ahuitzotl conquered Huaxtlan in 1494. As Durán describes in detail, Motecuhzoma II reconquered Huaxtlan and changed its name to Huaxyacac, converting the city into a military base and regional administrative capital; hence, its appearance in the *Codex Mendoza* with a new ideogram to relect its new status as a seat of high civil and military rank. The codices cited above describe Mexica conquests of territories to the east of Huaxyacac (Tehuantepec and Mictlan among others), but only after Huaxyacac had been reenforced as a military base. In the *Codex Mendoza* the chronological sequence of the Mexica imperial expansion is coherent from a logistical point of view (table 14.1): Motecuhzoma I conquered Coayxtlahuacan, Cuetlaxtlan, and Quauhtochco (1992:f.7v, f.8r); Tizoc subdued Yancuitlan (1992:f.12r); Ahuitzotl conquered Tequantepec (Tehuantepec), Zapotlan, and Coyolapan (1992:f.13r, f.13v); and Motecuhzoma II took Nochiztlan, Tlachquiyauhco and Mictlan (1992:f.15v, f.16r, f.16v). The only inconguruency is Tequantepec although there is documentary evidence that the Mexica penetration of that area was mediated through diplomatic agreements and political alliances supported by marriage ties at the level of the Mexica and Zapotec elites. It is also possible that the Tequantepec mentioned in the *Codex Mendoza* is not the Zapotec Tehuantepec of the isthmus.

THE MEXICA MIGRATION TO OAXACA

José Antonio Gay (1982:103) corrects Durán on the basis of the *Códice Telleriano-Remensis,* but he interprets the events described by Durán incorrectly. He confuses the conquest of Mictlan with the attack on the Aztec merchants that took place there, alluding to both events as the "war of Mitla." Similarly, Paddock (1975:7) interprets Durán's description to mean that Mictlan received the punitive Aztec attack, intending to refute Durán with evidence from archaeological excavations at Mitla: the excavations do not reveal any indications that the city was destroyed and later rebuilt, and the radiocarbon dates show that the buildings there date to the time of the founding of Tenochtitlan. But, as we have seen, the content of Durán's chronicle only alludes to Mictlan as the place where the *pochteca* were assaulted; the reprisals were not directed at Mictlan because this city was not responsible, rather they were made against Huaxtlan (the ancient city later named Huaxyacac). The very title of Durán's chapter leaves no room for doubt: "De cómo los de la ciudad de Guaxaca mataron los mensajeros reales que iban a Guazacualco y de cómo los mexicanos les dieron guerra y asolaron la ciudad y la poblaron de mexicanos y tezcucanos y xuchimilcas" (Durán 1967:v.2:225) [On how those of the city of Guaxaca killed the royal messengers who were going to Guazacualco and on how the Mexicans made war on them and laid waste that city and populated it with Mexicans and Tezcucans and Xuchimilcas].

After describing the incident with the merchants and the subsequent Mexica victory, Durán describes the destruction of Huaxtlan:

> 34. Viendo los señores de Guaxaca la destruición de su ciudad, vinieron llorando y las manos cruzadas, a pedir misericordia y perdón … Pero, en lugar de oírlos, les respondieron: … "ya está dada la

sentencia que no ha de haber ciudad que se llame Guaxaca, ni memoria ha de quedar de ella." (Durán 1967:v.2:230)

... quedó la ciudad toda destruida, ... toda llena de cuerpos muertos y todo robado y destruido ...

36. Lo cual concluido, enviaron a sus mensajeros a Cuilapan y a los demás pueblos comarcanos: ... si se inquietaban y hacían alguna traición, que lo mismo se haría con ellos que de los de Guaxaca habían hecho.

37. Los mixtecas y zapotecas humillándose, dijeron ... que ellos estaban prestos y aparejados a los servir y obedecer como a señores. (p. 231)

[34. The lords of Guaxaca seeing the destruction of their city, came crying and with hands crossed, to ask for mercy and forgiveness ... But, instead of hearing them, they [the Mexica] reponded: ... "the sentence already is given that there is to be no city called Guaxaca, nor is a memory to remain of it."

the city was left totally destroyed ... all full of dead bodies and all looted and destroyed ...

36. At which conclusion, they [the Mexica] sent their messengers to Cuilapan and to the the rest of the towns of the region: ... if they should cause a disturbance or commit some act of treason, the same would happen to them as had been done to those of Guaxaca.

37. The Mixtecs and Zapotecs humbling themselves, said ... that they were disposed and ready to serve and to obey them [the Mexica] as rulers.]

Durán's description is quite clear; it deals not only with the assasination of the emissaries of the Mexica *tlatoani* at a place near Mictlan but also with a genuine, popular rebellion of the Mixtec and Zapotec peoples who had been conquered previously. The leadership of this rebellion was based in the city whose name at that time was Huaxtlan but which later was renamed Huaxyacac; this is why Durán refers to the city as Guaxaca. The punitive expedition sent by Motecuhzoma II was intended to punish the city and to teach a lesson to the surrounding towns, which is why the Mexica did not grant pardon to the defeated nobles who were entreating them for mercy; the order was to destroy the city and a portion of its inhabitants and to remit the rest for sacrifice in the great capital of Tenochtitatlan. If the Mixtecs and Zapotecs acquiesced to submission, it was because they had participated in the rebellion. On this point Durán's narrative is in accordance with that of Alva Ixtlilxochitl (1975), who states that in the reign of Nezahualpilli various provinces rebelled and among them figured,

Coixtlahuaca, Zozolan, Tototépec, Tequantépec y Yopitzinco, y los
otros fueron los de las provincias de hacia Huaxaca, Tlachquiauhco,
... el rey de Tetzcuco ... fue compelido a juntar sus gentes y formar
sus ejércitos, enviándolos con los de los reyes Motecuhzoma y
Totoquihuatzin ... y así fueron sobre estas provincias, y las sujetaron
y redujeron al imperio. (Alva Ixtlilxochitl 1975:v.2:183)

[Coixtlahuaca, Zozolan, Tototépec, Tequantépec and Yopitzinco, and
the others were those of the provinces near Huaxaca, Tlachquiauhco,
... the king of Tetzcuco ... was compelled to gather his people and
to form his armies, sending them with those of the kings
Motecuhzoma and Totoquihuatzin ... and so they went out to these
provinces, and they subdued them and subjugated them to the empire.]

To eliminate the threat that Huaxyacac might once again become the center
of another rebellion and to ensure the loyalty of its inhabitants to the Aztec
empire, Motecuhzoma II ordered that the city's land be divided among colonists coming from Texcoco and Tlacopan, with 60 families a piece, and from
Tenochtitlan, Xochimilco, Chalco, Tierra Caliente (Morelos), and Mazahuas in
undetermined numbers, making a total of 600 heads of families with their spouses
and children, some 3,000 people in all. The colonists, freed from tribute obligations, securely established themselves in *calpullis* (Durán mentions "barrios"),
according to their town of origin.

19. Motecuhzoma llamó a su primo Atlazol y le hizo virrey
de toda aquella gente y mandó que ordenase la ciudad de tal arte
que los mexicanos estuviesen por sí y los tezcucanos por sí y los
tepanecos por sí, xuchimilcas por sí, y todos por sí en sus barrios.
(Durán 1967:v2:238)

21. Llegados a Guaxaca, asentaron su ciudad y pobláronla
conforme a la instrucción que le dio el rey, poniendo a cada nación
en su barrio. (p. 239)

[19. Motecuhzoma called his cousin Atlazol and made him viceroy of all that people and commanded that he order the city in such
a way that the Mexicans should be to themselves and the Tezcucans
to themselves and the Tepanecs to themselves, Xuchimilcas to themselves and everyone to themselves in their barrios.

21. On arriving in Guaxaca they established their city and populated it consistent with the instructions that the king had given,
putting each people in their barrio.]

Durán notes that Motecuhzoma ordered the towns of the region to provide the newcomers with, "todo lo que tuviesen necesidad y les proveysen de ollas, platos, escudillas, vasos y piedras de moler, y les ayudasen a edificar sus casas" (Durán 1967:v.2:238) [all that they might need and they were to provide them with pots, plates, bowls, drinking vessels and grinding stones and they were to help them to build their houses]. The new viceroy of Huaxyacac would be, "padre y madre" [father and mother] of the Nahua immigrants, who served him with contentment (Durán 1967:v2:239).

Durán's chronicle provides the key to the Aztec reoccupation and rebuilding of Huaxyacac. We can only suppose that the founding of the first settlement in the area of modern Oaxaca dated to the Preclassic or Classic periods, but Durán's account of the rebuilding of Huaxyacac coincides with the logistic location, the imperial interests of the Aztecs, and the spatial organization and system of land tenency that existed in the native communities that surrounded colonial Antequera, of which even today vestiges remain in the modern city of Oaxaca. John Chance's (1978, 1986) research on colonial Antequera and the surrounding indigenous communities at the beginning of the colony reveal that this segregation of the distinct Nahua groups who had come from the Basin of Mexico had deep roots.

COLONIAL EVIDENCE FOR NAHUATL IMMIGRANTS

John Chance notes evidence for ethnic divisions of Nahuatl peoples in Oaxaca in several places in his book, *Race and Class in Colonial Oaxaca* (1978:19), "About the social organization of Huaxyacac we know very little ... Ethnic subdivisions among the Náhuatl-speaking population were retained, with the different groups living in separate barrios, a practice that continued well into the sixteenth century." And,

> The numerous Aztecs and Tlaxcalans of the Orozco expedition established themselves in Huaxyacac (henceforth to be known as the Villa de Oaxaca) and the two adjoining towns of San Martín Mexicapan and Santo Tomás Xochimilco. San Martín, founded on land ceded by the Mixtec cacique of neighboring San Juan Chapultepec, grew to be quite large in the 1520's. (Chance 1978:32)

Further on, Chance (1978:88) again asserts the same, "The policy of ethnic segregation practiced by the Aztecs in the settling of Huaxyacac in prehispanic times and later by the Spanish colonial administration encouraged ethnic diversity." He persists in this viewpoint in a more recent publication:

Los indígenas que vivían en y alrededor de Antequera en el siglo
XVI eran predominantemente de habla náhuatl, descendientes de
los habitantes de Huaxyácac antes de la conquistsa, o de los nahuas ...
que llegaron ... en 1521. (Chance 1986:163)

[The indigenous people who were living in and around Antequera in
the sixteenth century were predominantly Nahuatl speakers, descendants of the inhabitants of Huaxyacac prior to the conquest, or of
the Nahuas ... who arrived ... in 1521.]

Nevertheless, Chance contradicts his own assertions and the important evidence revealed by his research when he writes concerning the communities
alluded to previously, "the Nahua towns of Santo Tomás Xochimilco, San Martín
Mexicapan, Jalatlaco, and the Villa de Oaxaca were established at the time of
the [Spanish] conquest or soon thereafter" (Chance 1978:82). Beyond this small
error, Chance's work is the first analysis and publication of the documentation
concerning the differential settlement of diverse Nahua peoples of the Basin of
Mexico in and around Huaxyacac before the Spanish occupation. The colonial
documents that Chance consults objectively reflect this phenomenon: for example, the names of the barrios of some of these towns (Chiautla, Tula,
Mexicapan, Ixtapalapa, Tepoztlan, Tlacopan); or that "the Aztec goddess
Tonantzin (the predecessor of Mexico's patron saint, the Virgin of Guadalupe,
who began to supplant her in the early sixteenth century) was worshiped in
Jalatlaco, the only known instance of this practice in the Valley of Oaxaca"
(Chance 1978:89).

It would be absurd to suppose that those Nahua groups could have come
with the Spanish who arrived at Huaxyacac in 1521 or 1522, or with those who
were brought by Peláez de Berrio in 1529, and then go on to distribute themselves in such an organized manner, differentiated according to the Aztec model,
and to transplant the Aztec religion and precolonial Nahua dieties such as the
cult of Tonantzin, among other traits, in their new settlements. These manifestations could only have arisen from an organized, directed transfer of people
that took place without the cultural influences later imposed by the Spanish
colonial system; in other words, this situation could only have occurred under
the circumstances related by Durán, and there are sufficient elements to support
the veracity of his acccount.

William Taylor (1986:159) describes documents concerning San Juan
Chapultepec, one of the "barrios" or *calpullis* of Huaxyacac, which in 1521
received titles to property for persons of the town and for the town itself. In this
way, the interests of the cacique and his descendants, as well as those of the
town, were legitimized in accordance with Spanish law. This case demonstrates
that San Juan Chapultepec already existed in 1521.

The *Crónica mexicayotl* corroborates Durán's statement that Atlazotl was appointed to rule in Huaxyacac:

> 202.   Huehue Moteuhctzoma Ilhuicaminantzin, y Tlacayeleltzin aún ellos le asentaron como señor al de nombre Atlazol, él quien allá primeramente fué a reinar Huaxacac, éste su nietecito de Ocelopan, en Tenochtitlan posee morada, y cuando allá fué a reinar a Huaxac su mensajero se hizo de los mencionados reyes. (Alvarado Tezozomoc 1975:113)

> [202.   The emperor Moteuhctzoma Ilhuicaminantzin, and Tlacayeleltzin even they themselves appointed as ruler the one named Atlazol, he who went there first to rule Huaxacac, this one the grandson of Ocelopan, possessed a house in Tenochtitlan, and when he went there to rule over Huaxac he became the messenger of the kings mentioned.]

The city of Huaxyacac served as a civic-ceremonial center—alongside of which, surely, resided the elites—just as did the aforementioned settlements. Some of these settlements later were renamed, putting the name of some Christian saint before their original appelations. This practice resulted in designations like San Martín Mexicapan, Santo Tomás Xochimilco, San Juan Chapultepec, and Jalatlaco, and thus preserved the names of these settlements up to the present. Many factors contributed to the transformation of the garrison at Huaxyacac into an Aztec military base like others in that and various subject provinces: the succesive, constant conquests of the Aztec military expansion; the rebellions that had to be checked and suppressed; the necessity to protect imperial traders along the important commercial route to the southeast; and so that Huaxyacac might serve not only as a center for tribute collection but also as a way station for supplies, food, and military effects for the empire's campaigns in that province and in others farther away.

FROM GARRISON TO MILITARY BASE

The frontier of the entire empire required the placement of logistical outposts such as Huaxyacac. Huaxyacac not only found itself on the frontiers of the conquered Aztec territories but also very near the powerful kingdom of Tututepec, which had not been conquered by the Mexica. All of these factors led to the conception of a city populated by Nahuas from the center of the empire, who were freed from the payment of tribute and also received part of the tribute of the towns of the province in order to secure their loyalty to the empire (see below).

Durán states that the people of Tehuantepec rebelled against the rule of the Aztecs during the reign of Ahuitzotl, who enroute with his army to subjugate them, arrived at the city of Oaxaca (Durán 1967:v.2:359). Durán describes the use of Huaxyacac as an Aztec military base in which the army was resupplied with resources furnished by the inhabitants of the city. Further on, he describes Huaxyacac serving the same function when the Mexica extended their conquests in battles against Xoconochco and other provinces of the southeast; in order to achieve this, the Mexica *tlatoani* "con todo su ejército, llegó a la ciudad de Oaxaca, donde halló al señor de Tecuantepec con todos los señores y caballeros de aquella comarca que le estaban esperando" (Durán 1967:v.2:385) [with his whole army, he arrived at the city of Oaxaca, where he found the ruler of Tecuantepec with all the rulers and nobles of that region who were waiting for him]. Because of its location—at the foot of Monte Alban, on the eastern limits of the Aztec empire, and at the midpoint of the route between Tenochtitlan and the rich Maya states—Huaxtlan acquired a rare importance in the function of Mexica imperial logistics and interests; hence, its conquest in 1494 has been noted in both the *Códice Vaticano-Ríos* and *Códice Telleriano-Remensis*.

The existence of Huaxtlan, transformed into Huaxyacac, is clearly documented in the *Matrícula de Tributos* and the *Codex Mendoza*, coinciding with Durán's account. In his interpretation of folio 17v of the *Codex Mendoza* (1992), for example, Corona Núñez notes the following:

> En esta lámina comienzan los pueblos que fueron regidos por los caciques o gobernadores nombrados por los señores de México, ... son el Tlacatectli (Tlacatecuhtli): *Principal o Jefe de las Gentes,* y Tlacochtectli (Tlacochtecuhtli): *Jefe de las Flechas o de la Guerra.* Oaxaca y Zozolan tuvieron las dos clases de gobernadores, según se muestra aquí, y Tetenanco: ... solamente tuvo el Jefe de las Gentes... (Corona Núñez 1964c:v.1:38)

> [On this lamina begin the towns that were governed by caciques or governors appointed by the rulers of Mexico, ... they are the Tlacatectli (Tlacatecuhtli): *Principal or Chief of the Peoples,* and Tlacochtectli (Tlacochtecuhtli): *Chief of the Arrows or of the War.* Oaxaca and Zozolan had both classes of governors, according to what is shown here, and Tenanco: ... only had a Chief of the Peoples.]

Based on the ideograms of the text, Corona Núñez describes Aztec Huaxyacac as an important military base (though he does not use that term), which was led by civil and military officials of high rank. The politico-military characteristics of the site are even clearer in his description of the contents of folio 18r of the *Codex Mendoza* where he alludes to other, similar bases, for example, "... Tlacochcalli: casa de las flechas, cuartel, y ahí se muestran un gobernador militar y otro civil; el lugar donde se encuentra este cuartel es Oztuma" (1964c:38,40) [... Tlacochcalli: house of the arrows, barracks, and there are shown a military governor and another civil one, the place where this barracks is found is Oztuma]. Other towns listed on the same page of the document include Aztacan, Atlan, Xoconochco, and Teozapotitlan.

Corona Núñez in his interpretation of the *Matrícula de Tributos* describes the characteristics of Oztuma (Oztoma), which are surely the same as those of Huaxyacac:

> Oztuma ... Este lugar aparece en el folio 18, recto, del Códice Mendoza, como un pueblo o fortaleza puesta por los mexicanos en el actual Estado de Guerrero, en la frontera de los tarascos para defensa de su imperio. Por lo tanto, pertenecía directamente a Tenochtitlan. (Corona Núñez 1968:11, 12)

> [Oztoma ... This place appears on folio 18, recto, of the *Codex Mendoza,* as a town or fortress placed by the Mexicans in what to-day is the state of Guerrero, at the frontier with the Tarascans for the defense of their empire. Therefore, it belongs directly to Tenochtitlan.]

Corona Núñez later mentions Oztuma (Oztoma) as "el fuerte de Oztuma, para contener a los tarascos ... cuyas ruinas han sido localizadas por los arqueólogos" (Corona Núñez 1958:40) [the fort of Oztuma, (built) to contain the Tarascans ... whose ruins have been located by archaeologists]. The *Codex Mendoza* contains a very clear explanation concerning the above; folios 17v and 18r describe neither tribute, nor tributary provinces, but places that were surely seats of the military and of the Mexica imperial administration. Of a total of 22 place names, only seven appear with ideograms corresponding to functionaries; of these only five reveal the presence of Tlacatecuhtli and Tlacochtecuhtli, among them Huaxyacac. On folio 18r, a sixteenth-century text in Spanish explains as follows:

> The towns drawn and numbered on this page and on the preceding page were governed by the *caciques* and *principales* of Mexico, placed [there] by the the lords of Mexico for the protection and good government of the *naturales.* And they had complete charge of collecting and ordering the collection of the rents and tributes

which [the towns] were obligated to give to the state of Mexico, and
[they were in charge of] preventing the towns from rebelling. (*Codex
Mendoza* 1992:v.4:41)

From the above, Barlow writes the following: "Guaxacac ... is one of the
Garrison towns mentioned in folio 17 of the Mendocino ..." (Barlow 1949:120).
On the basis of various sources he alludes to other garrisons and centers of
tribute collection. The *Relaciones Geográficas* of the sixteenth century confirm
this phenomenon. The *Relación de Amatlán* states that "Solían tener guerras
con la gente de guarnición que MONTEZUMA tenía en el pu[ebl]o de los indios de
Guaxaca, porque allí tenía capitanes y soldados" (Acuña 1984-1987:v.2:70)
[They used to have wars with the people of the garrison that MONTEZUMA had in
the town of the indians of *Guaxaca,* because there he had captains and sol-
diers]. The *Relación de Teozapotlan* is clearer:

> ... había aquí, cuando vinieron [los] españoles, una guarnición junto
> a donde es ahora la *ciudad de Antequera,* la cual guarnición era de
> MONTECZUMA. Ésta, dicen los indios que había puesto allí por vía de
> buena amistad y sin guerra, para pasar por allí adelante a *Tecoantepec*
> y *Guatemala.* (Acuña 1984-1987:v.3:162)

> [... there was here, when the Spanish came, a garrison near to where
> the *city of Antequera* is now, which garrison was MONTECZUMA'S:
> this, say the indians, that was placed there for a route of good friend
> ship and without war, in order to pass by there on the way to
> *Tecoantepec* and *Guatemala.*]

In the *Relación de Guaxilotitlan* one finds explicit that which was implicit
in the *Relación de Teozapotlan:*

> Y, tenía, para recoger este tributo, tres principales, que los llamaban
> CALPIZQUES: el uno estaba en *Guaxaca* y, el otro, en este pu[ebl]o, y
> otro, en *Cuextlahuaca* (que es en la provi[nci]a de *la Mixteca*).
> (Acuña 1984-1987:v.2:214)

> [And, it had, for collecting this tribute, three principales, who were
> called CALPIZQUES: one was in *Guaxaca* and, the other, in this town,
> and another, in *Cuextlahuaca* (that is in the province of the *Mixteca*).]

Furthermore, the first viceroy of New Spain recorded in his *Instrucciones*
in regard to the location of Guaxaca:

me habian informado que estaba en mal sitio; y hame parecido lo
contrario, porque es el mejor que hay en la comarca, y así por tal
tenia Motezuma la guarnicion de mexicanos en él con que aseguraba
la tierra. (Mendoza 1873:44)

[they had informed me that it was in a bad location; and it seems to
me to be the contrary, because it is the best [site] that there is in the
region, and for this Motezuma had the garrison of Mexicans in it
with which he secured the land.]

Herrera y Tordesillas, referring to the "Provincias Mistecas Çapotecas,"
asserts that Motecuhzoma,

para tenerlos en obediencia ... tenia de ordinario grandes
Guarniciones en aquellas Provincias, especialmente en la Tierra de
Guaxaca. (Herrera y Tordesillas 1729:Decada 3a, Cap. 11:95, 97)

[in order to keep them in obediance ... he commonly had large Garrisons in those Provinces, especially in the Land of Guaxaca.]

Further, Cervantes de Salazar states that,

Hallo el capitán Orozco en Guaxaca una muy gran guarnición de
indios mexicanos. (Cervantes de Salazar 1914:354)

[Captain Orozco found in Guaxaca a very large garrison of Mexican
indians.]

Martínez Gracida, for his part, describes in a hypothetical dialogue between
the "King" Cocijoeza of Zaachila and his "Minister" the precise date of the
founding of Huaxyacac and those of its tranformation into a military base:

En mala hora del 30 de junio de 1486 ... mi padre Zaachila III fue a
permitir la fundación de Huaxyácac ... en 1497 la vemos repoblado por
Ahuízotl. Acaba Moctezuma II de robustecerla en 1505, con el pretexto
del paso de sus tropas a Guatemala. (Martínez Gracida 1888:31)

[In a bad hour of the thirtieth of June, 1486 ... my father Zaachila III
went to allow the founding of Huaxyácac ... in 1497 we saw it repopulated by Ahuízotl. Moctezuma II finished reenforcing it in 1505, on
the pretext of the passage of his troops enroute to Guatemala.]

In summary, we can extract from the aforementioned texts the following: Huaxyacac was converted first into a garrison; later it was transformed into a military base in which tribute was amassed, subject provinces of the region were watched, and new military campaigns were launched towards the southeast. The establishment of Huaxyacac was not exclusively for military purposes; it also served political, administrative, commercial, and religious functions, and as the seat of the Nahua population that arrived from the center of the empire. Durán's description coincides with the accounts of the codices *Vaticano-Ríos* and *Telleriano-Remensis,* with the *Codex Mendoza* and the *Relaciones Geográficas,* as well as with the texts of Antonio de Mendoza, Cervantes de Salazar, and Antonio de Herrera y Tordesillas.

CONCLUSIONS

The contents of the *Matrícula de Tributos* and the *Codex Mendoza* have been analyzed and interpreted on occasion in terms of economic geography, which is only correct for the purpose of framing them in a much wider context. On the other hand, this approach has led some authors to underestimate the level of production and tribute obligations alluded to in the above codices. The politico military characteristics of Huaxyacac that I have put forth here explain the channeling of tribute towards the ranks of this submetropolis; at the same time, they help us to understand that, for the great city of Tenochtitlan, it was more convenient to sacrifice part of their tribute in exchange for maintaining regional politico-commercial control in this region as well as in areas farther away. On this basis, we can assert that production of goods (for tribute and circulation) was much greater than that listed in the codices mentioned above.

For the prehispanic city of Huaxyacac to be reliably documented—its beginnings in the Colonial period with the characteristics that the ruling Mexicas imposed on it, which in part it preserved and still preserves—archaeological research in the area must reorient itself in order to contribute material evidence of the settlement of Huaxyacac. That such evidence exists already has been demonstrated in open plazas or ditches dug for modern urban projects, but the areas where there are indications that the principal civic-ceremonial center was located have not been systematically sampled: the Mercado 20 de Noviembre, the Templo de San Juan de Dios, the Asiento de la Alhondiga, and other open spaces.

Huaxyacac came to be the most important city on the eastern front of the Aztec empire, and the economic system, the political system, and military strategy were inseparable aspects of the city's development. I feel therefore that future research must be directed towards these issues—in Oaxaca and in other key places—not only in the study of written documents but also in the orientation of archaeological work, which as yet has given little attention to relations between the Aztec empire and the southeastern states.

ACKNOWLEDGMENTS

This article was translated from the original Spanish by Cynthia Heath-Smith. Funds for the translation of the article were provided through a grant from the University of Houston-Clear Lake.

REFERENCES CITED

Acuña, René (editor)
  1984-1987 *Relaciones Geográficas del siglo XVI.* 9 vols. Universidad Nacional Autónoma de México, Instituto de Investigaciones Antropológicas, Mexico City.
Alva Ixtlilxochitl, Fernando de
  1975 *Obras históricas.* Edited by Edmundo O'Gorman. 2 vols. Universidad Nacional Autónoma de México, Mexico City.
Alvarado Tezozomoc, Fernando de
  1975 *Crónica mexicayotl.* Translated by Adrián León. Universidad Nacional Autónoma de México, Mexico City.
Barlow, Robert
  1949 *The Extent of the Empire of the Culhua Mexica.* Iberoamericana Vol. 28. University of California Press, Berkeley.
Cervantes de Salazar, Francisco
  1914 Crónica de la Nueva España. 3 vols. Edited by Francisco del Paso y Troncoso. In *Papeles de la Nueva España.* Sucesores de Rivadeneyra, Madrid.
Chance, John
  1978 *Race and Class in Colonial Oaxaca.* Stanford University Press, Stanford.
  1986 La dinámica étnica en Oaxaca colonial. In *Etnicidad y pluralismo cultural: La dinámica étnica en Oaxaca,* edited by Alicia Barabas and Miguel Alberto Bartolomé, pp. 145-172. Instituto Nacional de Antropología e Historia, Mexico City.
Codex Chimalpopoca
  1945 *Códice Chimalpopoca.* Translated by Primo Feliciano Velázquez. Universidad Nacional Autónoma de México, Mexico City.

Codex Mendoza

1992 *The Codex Mendoza.* Edited by Frances F. Berdan and Patricia R. Anawalt. 4 vols. University of California Press, Berkeley.

Codex Telleriano-Remensis

1964 Explicación del Códice Telleriano-Remensis. In *Antigüedades de México basadas en la recopilación de Lord Kingsborough,* vol. 1, edited by José Corona Núñez, pp. 151-337. Secretaría de Hacienda y Crédito Público, Mexico City.

Codex Vaticano-Ríos

1964 Explicación del Códice Vaticano Latino 3738. In *Antigüedades de México basadas en la recopilación de Lord Kingsborough,* vol. 3, edited by José Corona Núñez, pp. 7-313. Secretaría de Hacienda y Crédito Público, Mexico City.

Corona Núñez, José

1964a Commentary on the Codex Vaticano-Ríos. In *Antigüedades de México basadas en la recopilación de Lord Kingsborough,* vol. 3, edited by José Corona Núñez, pp. 7-313. Secretaría de Hacienda y Crédito Público, Mexico City.

1964b Commentary on the Codex Telleriano-Remensis. In *Antigüedades de México basadas en la recopilación de Lord Kingsborough,* vol. 1, edited by José Corona Núñez, pp. 151-337. Secretaría de Hacienda y Crédito Público, Mexico City.

1964c Commentary on the Codex Mendoza. In *Antigüedades de México basadas en la recopilación de Lord Kingsborough,* vol. 1, edited by José Corona Núñez, pp. 1-149. Secretaría de Hacienda y Crédito Público, Mexico City.

1968 Commentary on the *Matrícula de tributos,* edited by José Corona Núñez. Secretaría de Hacienda y Crédito Público, Mexico City.

Dahlgren de Jordán, Barbro

1966 *La Mixteca: Su cultura e historia Prehispánicas.* Universidad Nacional Autónoma de México, Mexico City.

Durán, Fray Diego

1967 *Historia de las Indias de Nueva España e Islas de la Tierra Firme.* Edited by Ángel María Garibay K. 2 vols. Editorial Porrúa, Mexico City.

Gay, José Antonio

1982 *Historia de Oaxaca.* Porrúa, Mexico City.

Herrera y Tordesillas, Antonio de

1729 *Historia general de los hechos de los Castellanos en las Islas y Tierra Firme del Mar Océano.* Academía de la Historia, Madrid.

Iturribarría, Jorge Fernando

1955 *Oaxaca en la historia.* Editorial Stylo, Mexico City.

Jiménez Moreno, Wigberto

1970 *Historia de México.* Editorial Porrúa, Mexico City.

Martínez Gracida, Manuel

1888 *El rey Cocijoeza y su familia.* Oficina Tipográfica de la Secretaría de Fomento, Mexico City.

Matrícula de Tributos
1968   *Matrícula de tributos.* Edited by José Corona Núñez. Secretaría de Hacienda y Crédito Público, Mexico City.

Mendoza, Antonio de
1873   *Instrucciones que los Virreyes de Nueva España dejaron a sus sucesores,* vol. 1. Imprenta de Ignacio Escalante, Mexico City.

Paddock, John
1975   Comunicación Escrita. *Boletín* 4:5-10. Centro Regional Oaxaca, Instituto Nacional de Antropología e Historia.

Seler, Eduard
1904   The Wall Paintings of Mitla, a Mexican Picture Writing in Fresco. In *Mexican and Central American Antiquities, Calendar Systems, and History,* edited by Charles P. Powditch, pp. 247-324. Bureau of American Ethnology Bulletin 28. Smithsonian Institution, Washington, D.C.

Taylor, William
1986   Cacicazgos coloniales en el Valle de Oaxaca. In *Lecturas históricas de Oaxaca,* pp. 149-191. Instituto Nacional de Antropología e Historia, Mexico City.

15

After The Conquest

Quauhtinchan and the Mexica Province of Tepeacac

José Luis de Rojas

The chapters in this volume demonstrate an increasing level of interaction among archaeologists and ethnohistorians who study Central Mexico. This cooperation is helping to bridge the gulf between the disciplines of archaeology and ethnohistory that was noted nearly 40 years ago by H. B. Nicholson (1955, 1979). Both archaeology and ethnohistory have much to contribute to the study of the Mexica "empire," relying as they do on different sources of information. Recent studies of specific, local areas—a specialty of archaeology—have increased our understanding of the nature of the different regions within Central Mexico and are improving our ability to learn through the correlation of information from documents with the results of excavations.

Among scholars a common concern has arisen: What is meant by the term "Aztec Empire"? The traditional image is centralist, based on studies of Tenochtitlan and using sources from diverse places to describe a "single" culture. This view relies on topics dealt with in the ethnohistorical documents without attempting to fill in the gaps or to consider the data within a theoretical framework. Fortunately, the situation has improved, which a review of recent research will confirm.

My own interest currently is centered on the structure of the empire; not solely on either the political structure or the economic structure, but on both, since the two together are an expression of relations of domination. Because they are aspects of the same thing, artificially separating them may lead to misinterpretation. For example, the second part of the *Codex Mendoza* (1992) has been interpreted with great frequency as merely a list of tribute when it in fact is something more complex: appearing together with the tribute list is the administrative hierarchy of both the economic and the political systems; apparently, both functions were linked in ancient Mesoamerica. In many places, the tribute collectors were captains sent by Motecuhzoma (Rojas 1991). The study of tribute, local as well as imperial, reveals relations of power and helps to explain the manner in which prehispanic society was organized and conquered areas were assimilated. This field of study is not simply an economic subject but also a political and a social one (see Rojas 1993a and 1993b).

Some recent books have analyzed the Mexica empire from fresh viewpoints (Hassig 1988; Lameiras 1985; Zantwijk 1985), contributing interesting, new ideas. Lameiras and Hassig place a major emphasis on wars and conquests and stress the complexity of the creation of the empire. They stop, however, with conquest itself, and it is necessary to explore what happened in an area after it was conquered. Some lines of investigation have been suggested already (Rojas 1991), but there are others that should be considered, such as the eventual process of "aztecization" of the empire in the manner of the "romanization" of the empire of ancient Rome. This is a field for archaeological research, but in many cases, regional archaeological studies have paralleled traditional ethnohistorical studies by failing to take into account that the area under examination was at some point subject to a foreign power. There have not been enough regional investigations that address the consequences of imperial incorporation and that compare findings with other regions. This criticism applies to studies of many phenomena—ceramics, architecture, sculpture, social organization, settlement patterns, etc. The Templo Mayor excavations are demonstrating provincial influences in the capital, and now is the time to consider the inverse relationship (see chaps. 11, 13, 14, and 16).

THE IMPERIAL IMPACT

In these pages, I would like to look at the impact of Mexica conquest on the subject provinces. We know that in some cases the leaders of a province were replaced; but regardless of whether a new dynasty was installed or the existing one respected, among other changes, the Mexica imposed tribute and established garrisons. Sometimes the people of an area were moved. We do not know, however, if these changes were accompanied by the foundation of new cities and towns, the repopulation of abandoned areas, the introduction of stylistic changes in manufacturing or construction, or the modification of customs. For example, did the Mexica-imposed obligation to worship Huitzilopochtli, which did not mean the abandonment of other gods, require the construction of temples? If so, in what style? Did incorporation into the imperial market system change local markets? In what ways—their frequency, their personnel, the products sold? Did tribute payment require modification of economic patterns?

Some answers may be found once we accept that we are not dealing with undeveloped areas that were suddenly invaded by a foreign culture, but rather areas that were already civilized with their own ancient heritages. Conquest was nothing new to these regions, and perhaps the most dramatic economic and political changes were caused by other factors. It is possible that the Mexica conquerors were limited in their exercise of a privileged position. Most likely, as more regional studies are made, we will find a wide range of solutions to these questions.

THE QUAUHTINCHAN-TEPEACAC REGION

My decision to use the Quauhtinchan-Tepeacac region as a case study arises from the abundance of documents from that area, its inclusion in the major economic codices, and the preferential treatment it has received on the part of ethnohistorians. We have therefore a considerable body of information that allows us to trace the results of imperial incorporation in the second half of the fifteenth century.

Contemporary studies of the area share one feature: they are regional analyses with great time depth, largely due to the sources they are able to employ. The *Historia Tolteca-Chichimeca* (1976), for example, begins with the twelfth century and reaches to the end of the sixteenth and beginning of the seventeenth centuries. These sources primarily focus on the Spanish conquest, and little attention is given to the Mexica conquest of the area or its incorporation into the Aztec empire. They fail to consider that these provinces were already integrated into the larger political, economic, and social entity of the Aztec empire at the time of their invasion by the Spanish. Nevertheless, their existence makes it possible for us to undertake such a study. The three books of the *Historia Tolteca-Chichimeca* tell of a region in conflict--one in which various towns of differing status struggled among themselves for supremacy with varied results.

Accounts of such events from areas that bordered on the empire began to attract my attention even more on reading Ross Hassig's book, *Aztec Warfare* (1988). This study raised questions for me because it is based upon a premise with which I disagree: Hassig states that the struggles among the tributary provinces did not affect their relations with the Aztecs, but he does not demonstrate this (Rojas 1992). I believe this region provides enough information to look at the behavior of the conquerors and the conquered and to open avenues of investigation into the structure of the empire.

Historical Chronology of the Quauhtinchan Region

The authors mentioned above give a complete overview of historical events in the Quauhtinchan region. Here, I highlight only those incidents most relevant to this study.

The first event was the arrival of the Tolteca-Chichimeca and their settlement in the region with the permission of the rulers of Cholula, whose subjects they became. The nature of Cholula's control over the Tolteca-Chichimeca is not clearly explained, but the Cholulans were the acting rulers of that region. The various towns were multiethnic, each with its own ruler, and their relations of domination changed through the years. The settlement of the migrants and the resultant reorganization of space constitute a fascinating theme in themselves that could teach us much about the organization of prehispanic Mesoamerica. The causes and consequences of peoples' movements have not been sufficiently explained, and here we find ourselves with a well-documented case that could lead to a better understanding of the customs of the area.

The emphasis on the role of Cholula as the primary center of influence in the region is interesting, although the sources do not specifically refer to either political or economic subjugation. The vague nature of this reference could be a consequence of the origin of the documentation since the subject towns had a marked tendency, following the Spanish conquest, to deny their subordination. No less a city-state than Tepeacac (fig. 15.1), whose conquest by the Mexica is well known, denied its subject status in the *Relaciones Geográficas:*

> Y estos señores no reconocían superioridad a MOTECUHZOMA, señor de *México* (que el nombre de MOTECUHZOMA quiere decir "señor sañudo"), sino tan solamente le tenían por amigo y confederado para las guerras que los de *México* traían con los de *Tlaxcala* y *Huexotzingo.* (Acuña 1984-1987:v.5:226)

> [And those rulers did not recognize the supremacy of MOTECUHZOMA, the ruler of *Mexico* (whose name MOTECUHZOMA means "angry lord") except as a friend and ally during the wars that those of *Mexico* brought against those of *Tlaxcala* and *Huexotzingo.*]

Chronologically, the three conquests of the Quauhtinchan area that we must analyze are those that were carried out by Tlatelolco, Tenochtitlan, and Spain, respectively. The aforementioned works give each conquest a growing impor-

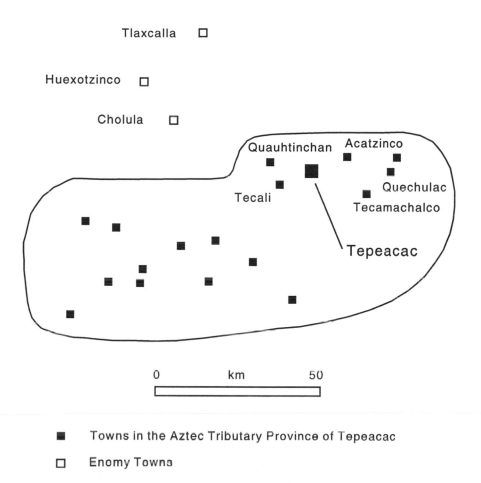

Tlaxcalla □

Huexotzinco □

Cholula □

Quauhtinchan   Acatzinco

Tecali   Quechulac
Tecamachalco

Tepeacac

0   km   50

■   Towns in the Aztec Tributary Province of Tepeacac

□   Enemy Towns

Fig. 15.1. The Aztec tributary province of Tepeacac. Map by Michael E. Smith.

tance, attributing the most significant changes to the last. Mercedes Olivera (1976, 1978) considers that despotism did not begin in the region until peoples from the Basin of Mexico began to make conquests there—as if the distribution of land at the time of the arrival of the Chichimeca would not have affected those peoples that were already established in the area:

> La conquista de los mexicanos liquidó el señorío de los chichimecas; pues muy al contrario de lo que éstos esperaban, los mexicanos implantaron su propio poderío en la región e hicieron cambios radicales. Desde el punto de vista político-administrativo dividieron el territorio de Cuauhtinchan en cinco provincias, cuyas

cabeceras fueron Cuauhtinchan, Tepeaca, Tecali, Tecamachalco y Quecholac, asignando a cada una un *tlahtoani* de origen pinome y marcando entre ellas límites geográficos bien precisos, sin importar la filiación étnica de los habitantes ni los límites de las antiguas propiedades de los cuauhtinchantlacas.

La nueva estructura político-administrativa sirvió para organizar un sistema tributario rígido, generalizado y perfectamente definido en cada una de las provincias. Los tlatoanis pinomes locales reconocidos como jefes de las provincias ya no se consagraron más en Cholula, sino que, reconociéndose tributarios de los mexicas, tomaron sus cargos y dieron servicios en Tenochtitlan. Los antiguos dueños chichimecas empequeñecidos no cesaron de reclamar sus antiguas posesiones en Acacingo, Tecali, Ocelocintlan, Techimalco y Tochtepetl y otros lugares que posteriormente les fueron restituidos parcialmente por los españoles. Pero los cambios impuestos por los mexicanos fueron definitivos; los terrenos y los macehuales tuvieron nuevos dueños, representantes del sistema tributario mexica, que fortalecieron localmente el régimen señorial. (Olivera 1976:193-194)

[The conquest by the Mexica destroyed the supremacy of the Chichimecs; very much in contrast to what the Chichimecs had expected, the Mexica imposed their own control over the region and made radical changes. From the politico-administrative viewpoint, they divided the territory of Cuauhtinchan into five provinces, whose capitals were Cuauhtinchan, Tepeaca, Tecali, Tecamachalco, and Quecholac, assigning to each one a *tlahtoani* of Pinome [Mixtec] origin and marking well-defined geographical boundaries between them without regard to the ethnic affiliation of the inhabitants nor to the borders of the ancient properties of the people of Cuauhtinchan.

The new politico-administrative structure served to organize a rigid tribute system, generalized and perfectly defined in each one of the provinces. The local Pinome tlatoanis, recognized as chiefs of the provinces, no longer gave allegiance to Cholula, instead they acknowledged themselves as tributary subjects of the Mexica, and they received their duties from and gave their service to Tenochtitlan. The ancient Chichimec rulers, diminished in power, did not cease attempts to reclaim their ancient possessions in Acacingo, Tecali, Ocelocintlan, Techimalco, Tochtepetl, and other places, some of which later were partially restored to them by the Spanish. But the changes imposed by the Mexica were definitive: the lands and the macehuales had new masters, representatives of the Mexica tribute system, which locally strengthened the ruling regime.]

Following this interpretation, the Mexica conquest imposed great change in the region, and we might presume that it created animosity between the Mexica and their subjects. But the opposite could be argued—that the subject provinces had reason to be grateful to their new rulers. The repeated claims of the dispossessed are interesting although it would be valuable to be able to state exactly to whom they were making them—to the Mexica, perhaps? Later, they made them to the Spanish in the hope of better luck. More important to us, however, is that things were not as clear cut as Olivera might lead us to believe.

In another work, Olivera explains the tribute system that existed in Tecali following the Spanish conquest:

> La familia de macehuales constituía en esta época la unidad para producción y para el pago de la renta de la tierra a los pillis que las poseían; así ocurría también en la época prehispánica, con la diferencia de que entonces sobre la misma base se establecía el tributo para el estado, que de hecho se confundía con la renta formando una misma unidad. Renta y tributo para el estado se entregaban al teuhctli *conjuntamente,* sin diferenciar con claridad el pago que se hacía al cacique del que correspondía a los mexicanos en señal de vasallaje; se incluía en todo el beneficio para la clase dominante y los pagos para la administración política y religiosa, funciones todas que se concentraban en la élite.
>
> La situación prehispánica se transformó con la conquista, pues se separó definitivamente la renta para el cacique del tributo para la Corona o para el encomendero, que también era renta de la tierra. (Olivera 1978:171-172)

> [At this time, the macehual family was the unit for production and for payment of land rent to the pillis (nobles) who controlled them [the *macehuales*]; this was the situation in the prehispanic epoch as well, with the difference that state tribute also was taken from this same base and in fact was confused with the rent, the two lumped into the same unit. Rent and state tribute were delivered to the teuhctli *together* [by the *macehuales*], without clearly distinguishing the payment being made to the cacique from that pertaining to the Mexica in token of the peoples' vassalage; included in the total were both their obligations to the dominant class and the tribute to the politico-religious administration, whose functions were concentrated entirely in the hands of the elite.
>
> The prehispanic situation was transformed with the conquest; rent to the cacique was definitively separated from tribute for the [Spanish] Crown or payment to the encomendero, which also was a form of land rent.]

Since this passage was published, the analysis of tribute and of prehispanic and colonial social organization has progressed sufficiently such that now we may take a dissenting position. In the above, Olivera contrasts the prehispanic situation with that of the Colonial period without considering the changes produced by the Mexica conquest and with the assumption that the *macehuales* were those responsible for imperial tribute payment. I believe that the *macehuales* were paying their immediate rulers and that it was these rulers who kept up with tribute obligations to their superiors because they were interested in achieving the highest possible position (see Smith, chap. 12). This idea of the primacy of personal relations is favored by the evidence for political alliances, whether through marriage or of another sort, between the governors of different areas. The change following the Spanish conquest was gradual, and we can date it from the establishment of tribute through taxation. Up until that time, the form in which tribute payments were made in the Colonial period seems to have been very similar to that of prehispanic times (Rojas 1993a).

The Conquest by Tlatelolco

Scholars have given insufficient attention to the conquests made by Tlatelolco in the Quauhtinchan region. The sources are unclear on this subject, but they permit us to go a bit further if we adopt another point of view. One problem of interpretation is that we do not generally attribute to Tlatelolco an "empire" or sphere of influence and therefore do not treat its conquests with the same importance we give to those of the Mexica. Olivera (1978:76) mentions that Cuauhtlatoa of Tlatelolco conquered Tepeacac and Tecali, and adds the following:

> También es necesario aclarar que la conquista de los tlatelolca no implicó la reestructuración del señorío, ni la imposición de gobernantes de fuera de la región. Ninguna fuente deja clara la posición de los tlatelolca en Cuauhtinchan después de esas luchas. (Olivera 1978:78)

> [Also, it is necessary to make clear that the conquest by the Tlatelolca did not imply the restructuring of the polity, nor the imposition of governors from outside the region. No source leaves clear the position of the Tlatelolca in Cuauhtinchan following those battles.]

Why then did Tlatelolco carry out the conquest? Perhaps the Tlatelolca had an important role in the reorganization of the polity. Not only did they not hinder it, but it is possible that they directed it to their own benefit.

In an earlier work, Olivera notes that the Tlatelolca were called on to assist a faction that had arisen in arms:

> Para obtener el triunfo, los rebeldes pidieron ayuda a los tlatelolcas, los señores más poderosos del valle de México en ese momento; por eso, con el pretexto de hacer la paz en Cuauhtinchan, Cuautlatoa, señor de Tlatelolco, tomó las tierras del señorío y entregó el poder local en forma vicaria a los rebeldes pinome (de origen mixteco) tanto en Cuauhtinchan como en Tepeaca y otros lugares del antiguo señorío. (Olivera 1976:192)

> [In order to triumph, the rebels asked for help from the Tlatelolca, the most powerful rulers in the Valley of Mexico at that time; therefore, under the pretext of making peace in Cuauhtinchan, Cuautlatoa, the ruler of Tlatelolco, took over the lands of that polity and handed over local power to the rebel Pinomes (of Mixtec origin) not only in Cuauhtinchan but also in Tepeaca and other places of the ancient dominion.]

We do not know the conditions under which Tlatelolco lent its help. It is clear, however, that its intervention had lasting repercussions.

For his part, Hildeberto Martínez (1984a:35) points out one consequence of the 1398 conquest of Quauhtinchan by Tlatelolco—the divestment of the power and lands of the lineage of Teuhctlecozauhqui—adding that this situation was made more acute following Quauhtinchan's conquest by the Mexica in 1466. Reyes García also refers to this incident:

> En Cuauhtinchan en particular después de la conquista tlatelolca de 1398 ocurre que los chimalpaneca imponen, como se ha dicho, a un nuevo señor llamado Coxanateuhctli que probablemente era de origen mixteca popoloca pues a sus descendientes en el siglo XVI se les llama pinome. (Reyes García 1977:86)

> [In Cuauhtinchan, in particular following the conquest by Tlatelolco in 1398, it happened that the Chimalpaneca imposed, as has been said, a new ruler called Coxanateuhctli who probably was of Mixteca-Popoloca origin since his descendants in the sixteenth century were called Pinome.]

Perhaps the use of the term "conquest" gives rise to ambiguity, and we should speak of "victory" instead since the beneficiaries seem to have been one part of the community to the detriment of another. In this case, Tlatelolco would have been a decisive ally within an internal conflict, but the victors would have been the *Pinome*.

A fines del siglo XIV, la parcialidad de los pinome solicitaron a los tlatelolco de México que conquistaran a la parcialidad de los naua.

e).—Con el apoyo de los conquistadores tlatelolca los pinome se apoderan del gobierno en Cuauhtinchan, Tepeyacac, Tecalco, Tecamachalco y Quecholac; esta situación se mantiene hasta la llegada de los españoles. (Reyes García 1977:121)

[At the end of the fourteenth century, the partisans of the Pinome solicited the Tlatelolca of Mexico for assistance to conquer the partisans of the Naua.

e).—With the support of the Tlatelolca conquerors, the Pinome seized power of the government of Cuauhtinchan, Tepeyacac, Tecalco, Tecamachalco and Quecholac; this situation was maintained until the arrival of the Spanish.]

This does not mean to say that there were not already struggles for power, as we shall see below.

Teuhctlecozauhqui was vanquished and lost his rulership, but if we believe the sources, his descendants soon after obtained lands in the region:

98.　　Teuhctlecozauhqui y su esposa murieron en el camino y su hija Tepexochtzin fue llevada a México Tlatelolco.

99.　　Y cuando allá la hicieron llegar luego la tomó por esposa el *tlahtoani* Cuauhtlatoatzin.

100.　　De allí luego nació Moquiuixtzin quien fungió como *tlahtoani* y en su tiempo fue destruída la tierra allá en Tlatelolco, en el año siete *calli,* hace ya ochenta y un años [1472 dC]. Esto es lo que señalamos.

101.　　Y de Tepexochtzin el primer hijo se llamó Moquiuix, el segundo Cuauhtomicicuil y el tercero Ayapan, todos hijos de Cuauhtlatoatzin.

102.　　Moquiuixtzin fungió como *tlahtoani* allá en Tlatelolco. Y Tepexochtzin vivió veinte años en Tlatelolco y luego vino aquí a Cuauhtinchan; trajo consigo a sus dos hijos: Cuauhtomicicuil y Ayapan.

103.　　Allí llegaron a establecerse Zacauillotlan. Se vinieron en el año tres *calli,* hace ya ciento treinta y seis años [1417 dC].

104.　　Y fue entonces cuando llegaron a tomar su tierra, su cerro, allí en Teuhctlecozauhcan, en Chiyatzinco y en otras [partes]. (*Manuscrito de 1553* 1978:88-89)

[98.　　Teuhctlecozauhqui and his wife died on the road and their daughter Tepexochtzin was taken to Mexico Tlatelolco.

99. And when they brought her there later she was taken as a wife by the *tlahtoani* Cuauhtlatoatzin.

100. From there later was born Moquiuixtzin who acted as *tlahtoani* and in his time the land there in Tlatelolco was destroyed, in the year seven *calli,* now eighty-one years ago [A.D. 1472]. This is what we determined.

101. And from Tepexochtzin the first son was called Moquiuix, the second Cuauhtomicicuil and the third Ayapan, all sons of Cuauhtlatoatzin.

102. Moquiuixtzin served as *tlahtoani* there in Tlatelolco. And Tepexochtzin lived twenty years in Tlatelolco and later came here to Cuauhtinchan; she brought her two sons with her: Cuauhtomicicuil and Ayapan.

103. There they arrived to found Zacauillotlan. They came in the year three *calli,* now 136 years ago [A.D. 1417].

104. And it was then when they arrived to take their land, their hill, there in Teuhctlecozauhcan, in Chiyatzinco and in other [parts].]

There is a problem with the dates in this document: if the conquest took place in 1398, Cuauhtlatoa could not have led it; Cuacuauhpitzahuac must have been the Tlatelolca leader. Robert H. Barlow (1989a:26) comments on this problem and suggests that two cycles of Tlatelolca conquests in the region are being confused. Indeed, in another work Barlow (1989b:39-40) describes the participation of the Tlatelolca of Cuauhtlatoa in the conquest of Tepeacac in 1466. In appendix 2 of that work, Barlow (1989b:54-56) analyzes the "false death" of Cuauhtlatoa, which could have occurred in 1427. Perhaps the previous reference was to a different personage of the same name who might have had a role in the conquest of Quauhtinchan in 1398.

Regardless, there remains the problem of Moquiuix, the son of Cuauhtlatoa (reign 1427 to 1467). It would be difficult for him to be the son of Tepexoch and the Tlatelolca *tlatoani* if we follow the dates given in the 1553 manuscript. Barlow (1989b:31) says that Cuauhtlatoa must have been very young when he took power because he died after governing for 40 years. We lack data concerning the birth date of Moquiuix, but by the 1460s he was already heading the army. He could have been the son of Cuauhtlatoa and Tepexochtzin, but the timeframe seems a little forced. Nor is there a clear explanation of the abandonment of Tlatelolco by the wife of the future *tlatoani,* leaving behind one of their sons who would inherit the title 50 years later. None of these problems are dealt with in the studies of the region. Nevertheless, let us return to these studies and their sources in order to see what happened between the establishment of the *Pinome* government and the arrival of the Mexica.

The distinct polities that made up the Tepeacac province had conflicts among themselves. Reyes García sums up much of the problem:

> Tepeyacac se convirtió en un serio problema para Cuauhtinchan pues desde mediados del siglo XV trataron de reivindicar el territorio de la población nativa y apoyados por los mexica de Tenochtitlan, despojaron a Cuauhtinchan del enorme territorio que originalmente Cholula había adjudicado a los cuauhtinchantlaca. (Reyes García 1977:56)

> [Tepeyacac became a serious problem for Cuauhtinchan because from the middle of the fifteenth century it tried to reclaim the territory from the native population and, supported by the Mexica of Tenochtitlan, dispossessed Cuauhtinchan of a large territory that Cholula originally had adjudicated to the Cuauhtinchantlaca.]

Seen from the perspective of the conquerors from Tepeacac, the situation was quite different:

> La conquista de Tepeyacac sobre Cuauhtinchan en 1458, por ejemplo, trajo como consecuencia que Acatzinco, Oztoticpac y parte de las tierras y terrazgueros de algunos señores de Cuauhtinchan pasaran a pertenecerle, hecho que fue confirmado después por los mexica al incluirlos dentro de sus linderos en 1467. Con la dependencia, Acatzinco y Oztoticpac perdieron todo derecho a poseer un territorio propio, con mojoneras precisas e independientes: los linderos de uno y otro quedaron incluidos dentro de los límites del territorio señorial asignado a Tepeyacac. La posesión de un territorio y la inclusión de Oztoticpac y Acatzinco dentro de sus fronteras fue el argumento principal que los *tlahtoque* de Tepeyacac utilizarían a menudo para reclamar su autonomía y para exigir la sujeción de ambos pueblos a su cabecera. La sujeción, no obstante, muestra grados y características distintos: Oztoticpac conservó su tradición *tlahtoani,* es decir, el derecho a "elegir" a su señor y a regirse sin la intervención directa de los tepeyacactlaca, pero fue despojado de sus barrios y estancias sujetos, y con ello de su calidad de cabecera. Acatzinco, en cambio, conservó su jurisdicción territorial y, en cierto modo, su categoría de cabecera, pero sus *tlahtoque* estuvieron directamente bajo el control de un gobernante impuesto por los tepeyacactlaca. Acatzinco, por lo tanto, adquirió una categoría política ambivalente: la de cabecera por su dominio sobre un conjunto de poblaciones sujetas, y la de pueblo sujeto por su posición subordinada a Tepeyacac. (Martínez 1984a:126-127)

[The conquest of Cuauhtinchan by Tepeyacac in 1458, for example, had as a consequence that Acatzinco, Oztoticpac, and part of the lands and the peasants of some of the nobility of Cuauhtinchan came under the control of Tepeyacac, a fact confirmed later by the Mexica who included them within their boundaries in 1467. With this dependency, Acatzinco and Oztoticpac lost all rights to possess their own territories with precise, independent boundaries: the boundaries of one and another remained included within the limits of the city-state territory assigned to Tepeyacac. The possession of a territory and the inclusion of Oztoticpac and Acatzinco within its frontiers was the principal argument used often by the *tlahtoque* of Tepeyacac in order to reclaim Tepeyacac's autonomy and to demand the subjection of both towns to it. The subjection, even so, shows grades and distinct characteristics: Oztoticpac retained its *tlahtoani* tradition, that is the right to "elect" its own ruler and to govern itself without the direct intervention of the Tepeyacactlaca, but was dispossessed of its barrios and subject hamlets and therefore its status as a cabecera (capital town). Acatzinco, on the other hand, retained its territorial jurisdiction and to a certain extent its cabecera status, but its *tlahtoque* were directly under the control of a governor imposed by the Tepeyacactlaca. Acatzinco, therefore, acquired an ambivalent political status: that of cabecera because of its dominion over a group of subject towns, and that of subject town for its subordinate position to Tepeyacac.]

This subordinate position included the obligation to pay tribute on the part of the *tlahtoque* of Acatzinco (Martínez 1984a:46); therefore, it is not strange that they were not happy with the new situation:

Las luchas de Acatzinco por liberarse de la sujeción se remontan a la época prehispánica: la primera mención data de 1493, cuando su *tlacochcalcatl* (gobernante militar impuesto por los tepeyacactlaca) pretende aliarse con Tlaxcala y Cholula en la guerra que sostenían contra Tepeaca, Cuauhtinchan y los otros señoríos comarcanos. La rebeldía, entonces, es castigada con el asesinato:

"... 1 *calli* [=1493]. En él fueron muertas las gentes del *tlacochcalcatl* Queceuatl de Acatzinco, a causa de que sus informes entraban en Cholollan y Tlaxcallan. Además, en su casa entraban en secreto los chololteca y tlaxcalteca. Por eso fueron muertos, a causa de que había guerra y

> eran nuestros enemigos el chololtecatl y el tlaxcaltecatl [*Historia Tolteca-Chichimeca,* 1976:226, par. 398]." (Martínez 1984a:171-172)

[The struggles of Acatzinco to free itself from subjection arise in the prehispanic epoch: the first mention dates to 1493, when its *tlacochcalcatl* (the military governor imposed by the Tepeyacactlaca) tried to ally himself with Tlaxcala and Cholula in their war against Tepeaca, Cuauhtinchan and the other bordering city-states. This rebellious leader was punished by assassination:

> "... 1 *calli* [=1493]. In this year were killed the people of the *tlacochcalcatl* Queceuatl of Acatzinco, because their reports were entering Cholollan and Tlaxcallan. Moreover, the Chololteca and Tlaxcalteca were entering their house in secret. For this reason they were killed, because there was a war going on and the Chololteca and Tlaxcalteca were our enemies."]

It is interesting to see how Tepeacac modified the boundaries and the conditions of its conquests to suit its interests. The sources mention the year 1458, and although that may have been the beginning of the conquests, the process terminated with the Mexica intervention in 1466. That is the only way in which to understand the following statement of the *Historia Tolteca-Chichimeca* (1976:224 [par. 382]): "Antes todo se decía era Quauhtinchan, el quauhtinchantlacatl tenía todo el gobierno." [It is said that before all else was Quauhtinchan, the Quauhtinchantlacatl [ruler] had all the ruling power.]

The Mexica Conquest

Depending on the sources one consults, the Mexica conquest was carried out by the Mexica, the Tlatelolca, or the Texcocans (Barlow 1989b). We already know the biased nature of the majority of the sources; therefore, this case should not surprise us. As we have seen, the people of Tepeacac declared that they were allies of the Mexica and that they had not been conquered.

The Mexica attack was made as a reprisal for the massacre of some merchants (Durán 1967:v.2:156). It was carried out simultaneously against four city states: Tepeacac, Acatzinco, Quauhtinchan, and Tecali (Durán 1967:v.2:157), and those of Tepeacac did not put up any resistance:

31. Lo que dijeron los de Tepeaca a los mexicanos fue rogarles cesasen de matarlos y destruirlos, prometiéndoles serles perfectos tributarios y darles tributos de maíz, chile, sal, pepitas, mantas, cotaras, esteras de palma, cueros de venado; obligándose a irles sirviendo en los caminos de acémilas, y llevarles sus cargas, comidas y matalotajes, y de irles sirviendo en las guerras, haciéndoles chozas y armándoles tiendas, y que desde aquel día tomaban a los mexicanos por señores y por padre y madre para su defensa, y que desde aquel día se les sujetaban para todo lo que quisiesen y mandasen. (Durán 1967:v.2:158)

[31. What those of Tepeaca said to the Mexica was to beseech them to stop killing them and destroying them, promising to be perpetual subjects and to give to them tribute in maize, chile, salt, squash seeds, mantas, sandals, palm mats, deerskins; obligating themselves to follow them serving as burden-bearers on the roads and to carry their loads, food and stores for them, and to follow them serving in the wars, making their shelters and pitching their tents for them, and from that day they would take the Mexica as their rulers and as father and mother for their defense, and from that day they would subject themselves for all that the Mexica might want or command.]

Tecali, Quauhtinchan, and Acatzinco also gave servitude to the Mexica (Durán 1967:v.2:159).

The Consequences

According to Mesoamerican rules of conduct, by not putting up resistance, Tepeacac should have obtained more favorable treatment, and that is what happened. Tepeacac became the head of the reorganized province as depicted in the *Codex Mendoza* (1992) and the *Matrícula de Tributos* (1980); Durán (1967:v.2:334) says of it, "Y a la primera ciudad y provincia a que llegaron fue a Tepeaca; la cual tenía de jurisdicción cuatro pueblos muy principales sujetos a sí, que eran Cuauhtinchan, Tecalli, Acatzinco y Oztoticpac. Los cuales tenía bajo su sujeción el señor de Tepeaca." [And the first city and province that they arrived at was Tepeaca; that which used to have in its jurisdiction four very important towns, which were Quauhtinchan, Tecalli, Acatzinco and Oztoticpac. The ruler of Tepeaca used to have these towns under his control.]

The reorganization entailed the establishment of new rulers and imperial functionaries in order to govern and collect tribute: "luego por estos pueblos comenzaron á tener *calpixques* los reyes de México, para el tributo de cada pueblo un mexicano *calpixque,* y que á este tal lo tuviesen por padre y señor despues del rey Moctezuma." (Alvarado Tezozomoc 1980:309) [later for these towns the kings of Mexico began to have *calpixques,* for the tribute of each town a Mexican *calpixque,* and that for this he was taken as father and ruler after the king Moctezuma].

The final phrase speaks for the character of the governing of the *calpixque,* whose function went beyond the collection of tribute goods (see Rojas 1991). The *calpixque* of Tepeacac, who was called "governor," had the greatest authority. In his speech to the Tepeacac nobles, the Mexica official Tlacaelel stated:

> "Mirad que en ello no haya falta ni quiebra, y para que esto mejor se cumpla, quiere os poner un gobernador de los señores mexicanos al cual habéis de obedecer y tener en lugar de la real persona, el cual se llama Coacuech." (Durán 1967:v.2:162)

> ["Seeing that in it [an agreement between Tepeacac and the Mexica ruler] there would be no default nor failure, and so that it might be better fulfilled, he [Motecuhzoma] wants to place over you a governor of the Mexican nobility, whom you are to obey and to have as representative of the royal person, the one who is named Coacuech."]

Durán goes on to note that the nobles honored this governor, giving him houses in which to live and lands on which to dwell:

> 53. Le obedecían y reverenciaban ni más ni menos que al mismo rey de México. El cual (gobernador) tenía gran cuidado de recoger los tributos reales, de ochenta a ochenta días, y enviarlos a su rey. (Durán 1967:v.2:162)

> [53. They obeyed him and revered him neither more nor less that the king of Mexico. He took great care to collect the royal tribute, every eighty days, and to send it to his king.]

The changes in rulers were made in other towns as well:

> 185.   Y he aquí lo que declaramos, lo que sucedió en año seis *tecpatl,* hace ya ochenta y dos años [1471 dC] que los mexica vinieron a establecer *teuhctli* aquí en Cuauhtinchan. Vinieron a colocar como *teuhctli* a Totomochtzin y a Cuitlauatzin que fungió como *chichimecateuhctli,* a Couatecatl y al *tezcacoacatl* Cuaytztzin. (*Manuscrito de 1553* 1978:98)

[185.   And here is what we declare, that which took place in the year six *tecpatl*, now eighty-two years ago [A.D. 1471] that the Mexica came to establish *teuhctli* (lords) here in Cuauhtinchan. They came to place as *teuhctli* Totomochtzin and Cuitlauatzin who acted as *chichimecateuhctli*, Couatecatl and as *tezcacoacatl* Cuaytztzin.]

The reforms were not limited to the imposition of these rulers, but also affected the composition of the polities. We have already discussed the case of Acatzinco and Oztoticpac. The Mexica intervention affected, above all, Quauhtinchan, which seems to have been the dominant center before the confrontation with Tepeacac. We return to the *Historia Tolteca-Chichimeca* for a narration of the events:

En ese entonces no había linderos, todo se decía Quauhtinchan. No había linderos hacia el tepeyacactlacatl; no había linderos hacia en tecalcatl; no había linderos hacia el tecamachalcatl; no había linderos hacia el quechollactlaca; todos estábamos juntos, sólo se citaba un solo pueblo: Quauhtinchan.

[373]   Y cuando fueron conquistados los de Tepeyacac, terminó la guerra; luego ya les da trabajo el mexicatl para que le sirvan, a causa de que se convirtieron en su escudo-flecha, en la conquista de Axayacatzin, *tlatouani* de Mexico.

[374]   Y cuando al tepeyacactlaca le fue dado trabajo, luego ya conversan los *tlatoque* tepeyacactlaca, dijeron:

—¿Dónde iremos a tomar con qué servir al *tlatouani* Axayacatzin si no es nuestra tierra, no es nuestra propiedad sobre la que estamos, si todo es tierra del quauhtinchantlacatl? Que nos escuche nuestra madre y nuestro padre el mexicatl, que nos dé límites, que nos dé linderos para que en ella sirvamos a Axayacatzin, *tlatouani* mexicatl.

[375]   Y luego se trasladaron a Mexico los tepeyacactlaca … fueron a rogarle al *tlatouani* Axayacatzin. Y cuando llegaron a Mexico le dijeron:

[376]   ¡Oh *pilli* mío! ¡Oh señor! ¡Oh *tlatouani*! hemos venido a rogarte nosotros, tus *maceualli* los tepeyacactlaca; no estamos en propiedad nuestra, no estamos a solas, sino que todo es tierra propiedad de los *tlatoque* quauhtinchantlaca. En su tierra tomamos agua, nos alimentamos. ¿Sobre qué te serviremos, dónde tomaremos y sacaremos lo que te hemos de dar? Tal vez en alguna parte delimítamos una propiedad, un regalo. Ustedes pongan nuestros linderos, que estemos separados; sea aparte para nosotros lo que tú desees.

[377]   Y les respondió:

—Está bien, he escuchado su palabra, se hará lo que deseen.

[378]   Luego va Axayacatzin envía a cinco mexica que vienen a poner linderos hacia los tepeyacactlaca, tecamachalca, quechollactlaca y tecalca; vinieron a dividir en cinco partes el pueblo de Quauhtinchan. (*Historia Tolteca-Chichimeca* 1976:222)

[In that time there were no boundaries, all was called Quauhtinchan. There were no boundaries with the Tepeyacactlacatl; there were no boundaries with the Tecalcatl; there were no boundaries with the Tecamachalcatl; there were no boundaries with the Quechollactlaca; we were all together, there was only one polity: Quauhtinchan.

[373]   And when those of Tepeyacac were conquered, the war ended; then right away the Mexicatl gives [*sic*]them work so that they should serve him, because they had become his shield and arrows [military conquest] in the conquest by Axayacatzin, *tlatouani* of Mexico.

[374]   And when work was given to the Tepeyacactlaca, then right away the Tepeyacactlaca *tlatoque* conversed, they said:

—Where will we go to get what is needed to serve the *tlatouani* Axayacatzin if it is not our land, if the land that we are on is not our property, if it is all land of the Quauhtinchantlacatl? Our mother and our father the Mexicatl should listen to us, he should give us borders, he should give us boundaries so that on [the land] we might serve Axayacatzin, *tlatouani* Mexicatl.

[375]   And next the Tepeyacactlaca went to Mexico ... they went to petition the *tlatouani* Axayacatzin. And when they arrived in Mexico they said to him:

[376]   Oh my *pilli*! Oh Lord! Oh *tlatouani*! we have come to petition you, your *maceualli* the Tepeyacactlaca; we are not on our own land, we are not alone here, since all the land is property of the *tlatoque* Quauhtinchantlaca. On their land we drink water, we feed ourselves. On what will we serve you, where will we get and where will we take that which we are to give to you? Maybe in some place we may delimit a property, a gift. You are the one who sets our boundaries, that we might be separated; let it be set aside for us that which you desire.

[377]   And he responded to them:

—That is fine, I have listened to your speech, what you wish will be done.

[378]   Then Axayacatzin sent five Mexica who came to set boundaries between the Tepeyacactlaca, Tecamachalca, Quechollactlaca and Tecalca; they came to divide the land of Quauhtinchan into five parts.]

The establishment of these boundaries gave rise to a lawsuit in the sixteenth century which appears in various documents (see Reyes García 1978). Martínez blames the Mexica for the suit:

> [Con la conquista mexica en 1466] el extenso territorio del señorío chichimeca es dividido en cinco señoríos independientes entre sí: Tecali, Tecamachalco, Tepeaca, Quecholac y Cuauhtinchan, sujetos en adelante al yugo mexica que impone *teuhctli* deshonestos en Cuauhtinchan, "que tomaron la tierra ajena y convirtieron a la gente en *maceualli* [*Manuscrito de 1553:* par. 187]." (Martínez 1984a:35)

> [[With the Mexica conquest in 1466] the large territory of the Chichimec state is divided into five independent states: Tecali, Tecamachalco, Tepeaca, Quecholac and Quauhtinchan, subjects from that time forth to the Mexica yoke that imposes dishonest *teuhctli* in Quauhtinchan, "who took another's land and turned the people into *maceualli.*"]

Olivera gives a different interpretation:

> Así, podemos decir que la provincia de Tepeaca t[e]nía cinco partes (cabeceras en la época colonial) perfectamente delimitadas desde el punto de vista geográfico, debido a la imposición mexica. Cada parte estaba dividida en tres o cuatro parcialidades (a veces también se las llama cabeceras), cada una con un *tlahtoani* del que dependían los otros dos o tres señores *teuhctli* de parcialidad. Cada parte (cabecera) era una unidad política tributaria en la época mexica, y probablemente tenía que entregar su tributo al *calpixque* de Tepeaca. (Olivera 1978.105)

> [Thus, we can say that the Tepeaca province used to have five parts (cabeceras in the colonial epoch), perfectly delimited from the geographic point of view, due to the imposition of the Mexica. Each part was divided into three or four parcels (also at times called cabeceras), each with a *tlahtoani* on whom the other two or three *teuhctli* nobles of the parcel depended. Each part *(cabecera)* was a tributary political unit in the Mexica epoch, and probably had to deliver its tribute to the *calpixque* of Tepeaca.]

Only a few pages before this passage, Olivera describes the composition of the tribute system as having a different form:

Todos los campesinos eran macehuales de un pilli que podía tener o
no el cargo de *teuhctli* o *tlahtoani;* todos los pillis y *teuhctli*
dependían a su vez de los *tlahtoani* que reconocieron o impusieron
los señores mexica en la región y éstos, naturalmente, reconocieron
como señor al de Tenochtitlan. Para cada uno de estos niveles había
una forma especial de tributar, pero todas tenían su correspondiente
justificación ideológica en el pago de servicios administrativos y
religiosos que recibían del gobierno. (Olivera 1978:102)

[All of the peasants were macehuales of a pilli who might or might
not have had the office of *teuhctli* or *tlahtoani;* all of the pillis and
teuhctli depended in their turn on the *tlahtoani* that the Mexica rulers recognized or imposed on the region and these, naturally,
recognized the ruler of Tenochtitlan as their lord. For each one of
these levels there was a special manner for rendering tribute, but all
of them had a corresponding ideological justification in the payment of administrative and religious services that they received from
the government.]

The provincial level has disappeared in the above description, along with
the role of the governor of Tepeacac as a link between the provincial rulers
and the Mexica ruler. This would have been an important role if Tepeacac
were responsible for payment of the province's tribute. Perhaps these doubts
do not conflict with the interpretation that Olivera gives for the installation of
the boundaries:

Los señores de Tepeaca tenían que entregar el tributo de toda
la provincia a los mexica, ya que "se convirtieron en su escudo[-
]flecha" durante la conquista; pero los tepeyacactlaca no tenían
suficiente poder para cobrarlo, pues su situación de dependencia en
relación con los *tlahtoani* cuauhtinchantlaca no se había resuelto y,
sobre todo, las tierras y los macehuales que las trabajaban seguían
perteneciendo a los señores de Cuauhtinchan; entonces fue preciso
destruir de hecho la situación privilegiada de los pillis cuauhtinchantlacas para establecer las nuevas formas tributarias adecuadas al
sistema tenochca. (Olivera 1978:89)

[The rulers of Tepeaca had to deliver the tribute of the whole
province to the Mexica, since the province "had become the shield
and arrows [military conquest]" of the Mexica during the conquest;
however, the Tepeyacactlaca did not have enough power to collect
it, as their situation of dependency in relation with the Cuauhtinchantlaca *tlahtoani* had not been resolved, and above all, the lands and

the macehuales that were working for them continued to belong to the lords of Cuauhtinchan; hence it was necessary to destroy in fact the privileged situation of the Cuauhtinchantlaca pillis in order to establish new tributary forms suitable to the Tenochca system.]

I think that the destruction of Quauhtinchan had as its objective the benefit of Tepeacac, whose petition for assistance to Axayacatl seems to be in accord with the lack of resistance it offered during the conquest. This event appears to have been a territorial reorganization carried out by Tenochtitlan with the collaboration of Tepeacac, which would obtain primacy over the region. The division into *cabeceras* seems to correspond with the type of organization that appears in the *Codex Mendoza* (1992), which lists the glyphs of towns in which there were *calpixque;* even though I have argued many times that it was the towns that were responsible for payment. The analysis of the tribute system seems to indicate, moreover, that it was the nobles who had to pay and not the town as a corporate body since in many cases they were not so organized. In this region, some towns had various *tlahtoque* without an expression of subordination among them (Acuña 1984-1987:v.5:240).

The problem is complex. Twenty-two towns appear on the page of the *Codex Mendoza* (1992:f.42r) that corresponds to the province of Tepeacac (see fig. 15.1); but if one turns to other sources, there used to be many more towns, with different ranks. The *Relación de Tepeaca* (Acuña 1984-1987:v.5:239) cites 73 *aldeas* or hamlets. The dates of the conquests are also unclear. Durán (1967:v.2:155-158) puts the conquest of the region in the time of Motecuhzoma I, which agrees with the date of 1466 in the other sources. The *Codex Mendoza* (1992:f.10v), however, lists Tepeacac and Tecalco as conquests of Axayacatl, and the *Historia Tolteca-Chichimeca* (1976:221-222) also states that Axayacatl conquered Tepeacac. Atezcahuacan was subjugated by Tizoc (*Codex Mendoza* 1992:f.12r). Quauhtlatlauca was declared to have been a vassal of one Ocelotzin (Acuña 1984-1987:v.5:203), and in the part corresponding to Huehuetlan (Acuña 1984-1987:v.5:209), one reads that "Eran vasallos, en t[iem]po de su gentilidad, de un principal que se decía MEXICATECUHTLI." [they were vassals, in the time of their heathendom, of one chief who was called MEXICATECUHTLI.] This agrees with the narrated events discussed above. Of others we have no information.

The jurisdiction of the towns was at times complex as revealed in the *Relación de Tepeaca:*

[Todo esto], con declaración que las d[ic]has aldeas destos dos pueblos, *Tecamachalco* y *Quecholac,* muchas dellas son de ambos los d[ic]hos dos pueblos por mitad, y más y menos, porque el término destos dos pueblos está PRO INDIVISO, si no común entre ambos pueblos; y, ansí, algunas de las d[ic]has aldeas que son de ambos pueblos

> tienen dos iglesias, y cada pueblo reconoce sus v[ecin]os, para cobrar
> dellos los tributos que deben y hacerles acudir a las demás obras
> públicas a que son obligados. Y esta división es entre ellos con mucha
> claridad, que jamás tienen ninguna diferencia. Y la causa desta junta
> ha sido que, en tiempo de la infidelidad, estos dos pueblos fueron de
> un señor llamado AQUECALECA, y después se dividieron, venidos los
> españoles. (Acuña 1984-1987:v.2:240)

> [[All of this], with the declaration that the said hamlets of these
> two towns, *Tecamachalco* and *Quecholac,* many of them [were
> divided more or less equally between the two towns]; and, thus,
> some of the said hamlets of both towns had two churches, and each
> town recognizes its citizens, in order to collect from them the trib-
> ute that they owe and make them comply with the rest of the public
> tasks to which they are obligated. And this division between them is
> so clear, that they never have any disputes. And the cause of this
> union has been that, in the time of infidelity, these two towns be-
> longed to one ruler called AQUECALECA, and later they were divided,
> when the Spanish came.]

Nevertheless, the sources cited previously state that boundaries were established between the two towns.

A comparison of the tribute that appears in the codices with what is listed in the *Relación de Tepeaca* (Acuña 1984-1987:v.5:242-243) is interesting. Obviously, the quantities do not coincide, but neither do the products. This clearly indicates a transformation of tribute. What Motecuhzoma was receiving was not merely an accumulation of that which was paid by the towns or the rulers to the provincial authorities. It was something more complex that required extra economic activities.

The economic consequences of the Mexica conquest have been analyzed by Berdan (1975, 1978, 1980; see also chap. 11). In her work of 1980, she alludes to Tepeacac, after making reference to the existence of complex economic systems prior to the arrival of the Mexica in several regions: "Since many goods were demanded in tribute that were *not* actually produced within the province, it is likely that the mechanisms by which those goods worked their way into the province were more ancient than the imposition of tribute" (Berdan 1980:38).

She insists that the imposition of tribute did not imply a reduction of the local markets:

> With Triple Alliance conquest, the provincial markets were not
> reduced in importance. Rather, the tribute system to a great ex-
> tent depended on the existence of viable market networks, as did
> *pochteca* activity. When a region was conquered, tribute did not

replace marketplace and merchant activities, but intensified them. The imposition or increase in tribute demands required more goods, and/or different kinds of goods, to flow through the market network, in cases where tribute goods were obtained in this manner. (Berdan 1980:39)

In the case of Tepeacac, the market suffered some modifications:

> This city [Tepeacac], upon its conquest by the Aztecs, was required to hold a market on a designated day. A wide variety of goods, including rich mantas, stones, jewels, feathers of different colors, gold, silver (and other metals), skins of jaguars and ocelots, cacao, rich loin clothes and sandals were to be sold in that market (Durán 1967, II:162). Given the types of goods to be available, it is likely that the Valley of Mexico *pochteca* frequented this provincial marketplace. It may well have been regulated in this manner for purposes of making these localized and often tropical goods more readily available to the *pochteca*. (Berdan 1980:40)

Moreover, the law of the establishment of the market demands that all outsiders who would want to establish themselves in the city be accepted and given lands where they might settle (Durán 1967:v.2:162).

All of these arrangements appear just after the conquest. Afterward, the designated functionaries were put in charge of imperial affairs, but when necessary, the Mexica presence made itself felt. In the case of Queceuatl of Acatzinco, discussed above, the intervention of the Mexica is not expressly mentioned, but the *Historia Tolteca-Chichimeca* gives two cases in which such intervention did take place:

> [403] ... Año XI *acatl*. En él fue conquistado Tlachquiyauitl que fungía como *tlatouani* de Tepexic; el mexicatl vino a destruirlo. Fue conquistado a causa de que Tlachquiyauitl tramó destruir a Ocellotzin, que era *tlatouani* de Quauhtlatlauhcan; cuando se enteró el mexicatl de que había sido destruido Ocellotzin, *tlatouani* de Quauhtlatlauhcan luego el mexicatl vino a destruir al tepexictlacatl. (*Historia Tolteca-Chichimeca* 1976:227)

> [[403] ... Year 11 *acatl*. In this year Tlachquiyauitl, who acted as *tlatouani* of Tepexic, was conquered; the Mexicatl [Mexica ruler] came to destroy him. He was conquered because Tlachquiyauitl plotted to destroy Ocellotzin, who was *tlatouani* of Quauhtlatlauhcan; when the Mexicatl was informed that Ocellotzin, the *tlatouani* of Quauhtlatlauhcan, had been destroyed later the Mexicatl came to destroy the Tepexictlacatl [Tepexic ruler].]

This Ocellotzin must be the same individual who is noted in the *Relación de Quauhtlatlauca,* as mentioned above.

> [410] ... Año I *tochtli.* En él murió Totec de Tecalco; lo mataron los mexica por autorización de Moteuhczomatzin. Fue conquistado porque tramaba destruir al quauhtinchantlacatl. Cuando se enteraron los quauhtinchantlaca luego se lo comunicaron a Moteuhczomatzin, y cuando lo supo se enojó mucho, por eso fue muerto Totec. (*Historia Tolteca Chichimeca* 1976:228)

> [[410] ... Year 1 *tochtli.* In this year Totec of Tecalco died; the Mexica killed him by authorization of Moteuhczomatzin. He was conquered because he was plotting to destroy the Quauhtinchan-tlacatl [ruler of Quauhtinchan]. When the Quauhtinchantlaca were informed of this, they communicated it to Moteuhczomatzin, and when he knew of it, he became very angry, for this reason Totec was killed.]

CONCLUSIONS

The data of the documents seem to indicate that Tepeacac played a decisive role in the incorporation of the region into the Mexica empire, which gave Tepeacac a preeminent place in the new order of things. We could assert that Tepeacac benefited from the conquest since it obtained a power that previously it lacked. This means that the Mexica were not conquering regions just because they were able to; rather, they had a preconquest strategy that included the possibility of aiding unfavored sectors or peoples. This strategy could be called "intrigue," and its existence in Mesoamerican societies was well manifested in the alliances that were produced with the arrival of Hernán Cortés—with the stellar example in Texcoco of Cacamatzin and Ixtlilxochitl. We must then expand our studies of the empire to the periods both before and after the Mexica imperial conquest.

The region of Quauhtinchan-Tepeacac permits us to show that Mexica conquest was not limited to the "burning of the temple" and the establishment of new rulers over those on whom tribute was imposed; it also could imply, as in this instance, a political reorganization of the region with lasting consequences. Among these consequences were changes in the relations of power in the region, the establishment of new boundaries between the city-states, and the dispossession of some city-states in order to benefit others—conduct that generated enemies for the Mexica but, at the same time, ensured the loyalty of those who benefited. Furthermore, there was a form of vigilance, with the direct intervention of the Mexica when necessary. In disputes among subjects of the empire, the Mexica took whichever side suited their imperial objectives. They monitored these disputes with a view toward maintaining the security of their realm. Even Quauhtinchan, which had been harmed by the conquest, turned to the Mexica when it considered itself in danger.

In the economic sector, the imposition of tribute was not the only change brought about by the empire. The Tepeacac market provides an example. It is likely that a market previously existed, and that the empire modified its frequency and "quality." That is, it was converted into the principal market of the region, which must necessarily have been to the detriment of the previous center. Such acts imply deliberate economic change tied to a geopolitical strategy. Tepeacac seems to have received all the benefits, including becoming capital of the province. We do not know if the change in Tepeacac's status carried with it an alleviation in its tribute payments since we do not know the amount that each town was required to contribute to the provincial tribute; but what *is* clear is that, with these reforms, the possibility that Tepeacac could pay its tribute with less effort was increased. Following Berdan's (1980; see also chap. 11) analysis of Durán (1967), this market favored the interests of the *pochteca*, providing a relatively close and secure place where they could obtain lowland products. At the regional level, there were probably major modifications not only in the system of trade but also in the place that each town occupied in the economic network.

Everything seems to indicate that the empire had a logic. The annexation of provinces was not unplanned nor were they incorporated haphazardly into the empire. There was an imperial structure in charge of the administration and control of the provinces, and perhaps we find little integration because of the short duration of the empire. Only 50 years passed between the conquest of Tepeacac to the arrival of the Spanish in Anahuac. This is a short time in which to have achieved an "aztecization" of the provinces, and it is up to the archaeologists to determine if an "Aztec horizon" can be delimited. In fact, they are already laying the foundation for this work, as the articles in this volume testify.

ACKNOWLEDGMENTS

This article was translated from the original Spanish by Cynthia Heath-Smith. Funds for the translation of the article were provided through a grant from the University of Houston-Clear Lake.

REFERENCES CITED

Acuña, René (editor)
1984-1987 *Relaciones Geográficas del siglo XVI.* 9 vols. Universidad Nacional Autónoma de México, Instituto de Investigaciones Antropológicas, Mexico City.

Alvarado Tezozomoc, Hernando
1980 *Crónica mexicana.* Commentary by Manuel Orozco y Berra. 3rd ed. Editorial Porrúa, Mexico City.

Barlow, Robert H.
1989a Un problema cronológico: la conquista de Cuauhtinchan por Tlatelolco. In *Obras completas de Robert Barlow.* Vol. 2; Tlatelolco rival de Tenochtitlan, edited by Jesús Monjarás Ruiz, Elena Limón and María de la Cruz Paillés, pp. 25-30. Instituto Nacional de Antropología e Historia, Mexico City.

1989b Cuauhtlatoa: el apogeo de Tlatelolco. In *Obras completas de Robert Barlow.* Vol. 2: Tlatelolco rival de Tenochtitlan, edited by Jesús Monjarás Ruiz, Elena Limón y María de la Cruz Paillés, pp. 31-57. Instituto Nacional de Antropología e Historia, Mexico City.

Berdan, Frances F.
1975 *Trade, Tribute and Market in the Aztec Empire.* Ph.D. dissertation, Department of Anthropology, University of Texas at Austin. University Microfilms, Ann Arbor.

1978 Replicación de principios de intercambio en la sociedad mexica: de la economía a la religión. In *Economía política e ideología en el México prehispánico,* edited by Pedro Carrasco and Johanna Broda, pp. 175-193. Nueva Imagen, Mexico City.

1980 Aztec Merchants and Markets: Local-level Economic Activity in the Non-industrial Empire. *Mexicon* 2(3):37-41.

Codex Mendoza
1992 *The Codex Mendoza.* Edited by Frances F. Berdan and Patricia Reiff Anawalt. 4 vols. University of California Press, Berkeley.

Durán, Fray Diego
1967 *Historia de las Indias de Nueva España e Islas de la Tierra Firme.* Edited by Angel María Garibay K. 2 vols. Editorial Porrúa, México City.

Hassig, Ross
1988 *Aztec Warfare: Imperial Expansion and Political Control.* University of Oklahoma Press, Norman.

Historia Tolteca-Chichimeca
1976 *Historia Tolteca-Chichimeca.* Edited by Paul Kirchhoff, Linda Odena Güemes, and Luis Reyes García. Instituto Nacional de Antropología e Historia, Mexico City.

Lameiras, José
1985 *Los déspotas armados.* El Colegio de Michoacán, Zamora, Michoacan.

Manuscrito de 1553
  1978 Manuscrito de 1553. Archivo Municipal de Cuauhtinchan, paquete II, exp. 9. In *Documentos sobre tierras y señoríos de Cuauhtinchan,* edited by Luis Reyes García, pp. 80-100. Instituto Nacional de Antropología e Historia, Mexico City.

Martínez, Hildeberto
  1984a *Tepeaca en el siglo XVI: tenencia de la tierra y organización de un señorio.* Centro de Investigaciones y Estudios Superiores en Antropología Social, Mexico City.
  1984b *Colección de documentos coloniales de Tepeaca.* Instituto Nacional de Antropología e Historia, Mexico City.

Matrícula de Tributos
  1980 *Matrícula de Tributos.* Jacqueline Durand Forest and Frances F. Berdan, editors. Akademische Druck und Verlaganstalt, Graz.

Nicholson, H. B.
  1955 Native Historical Traditions of Nuclear America and the Problem of their Archaeological Correlation. *American Anthropologist* 57:594-613.
  1979 Correlating Mesoamerican Historical Traditions with Archaeological Sequence. In *Actes du XLII Congrès International des Américanistes, Paris, 1-9 Septembre 1976* 9B:187-198. Société des Américanistes, Paris.

Olivera, Mercedes
  1976 El despotismo tributario en la región de Cuauhtinchan-Tepeaca. In *Estratificación social en la Mesoamérica prehispánica,* edited by Pedro Carrasco and Johanna Broda, pp. 181-206. Instituto Nacional de Antropología e Historia, Mexico City
  1978 *Pillis y macehuales: las formaciones sociales y los modos de producción de Tecali del siglo XII al XVI.* Centro de Investigaciones y Estudios Superiores en Antropología Social, Mexico City.

Reyes García, Luis
  1977 *Cuauhtinchan del siglo XII al XVI.* Franz Steiner Verlag, Wiesbaden.
  1978 *Documentos sobre tierras y señoríos de Cuauhtinchan.* Instituto Nacional de Antropología e Historia, Mexico City.

Rojas, José Luis de
  1991 La organización del imperio mexica. *Revista Española de Antropología Americana* 21:145-169.
  1992 Review of Aztec Warfare by Ross Hassig. *Revista Española de Antropología Americana* 22:216-221.
  1993a *A cada uno lo suyo: el tributo indígena en la Nueva España en el siglo XVI.* El Colegio de Michoacán, Zamora, Michoacan.
  1993b La sociedad indígena novohispana en el siglo XVI a través del tributo. *Revista Española de Antropología Americana* 23:153-164. Universidad Complutense de Madrid.

Zantwijk, Rudolph van
  1985 *The Aztec Arrangement.* University of Oklahoma Press, Norman.

16

The Impact of the Xochiyaoyotl in Southwestern Puebla

Patricia Plunket and Gabriela Uruñuela

If there is any information in the ethnohistorical literature regarding the Postclassic period in the Valley of Atlixco, it is information about war. The sources do not inform us about the accomplishments of the local leaders nor do they refer to the kinds of tribute exacted from them and their subjects by the major powers of Central Mexico during the last decades before the Spanish Conquest. If any of the towns of the region, such as Atlixco, Atzizihuacan, Tochimilco or Quauhquechulan, are mentioned, they almost certainly appear in the context of a formal military engagement known as the *xochiyaoyotl,* or Flowery Wars (see, for example, Chimalpahin [1965]; Durán [1967:v.2]; Muñoz Camargo [1978]; and the *Historia Tolteca-Chichimeca* [1976]). It would seem that, at least in the eyes of the chroniclers, the Valley of Atlixco symbolized war and was important mainly as a battlefield, a place where tens of thousands of warriors (Durán 1967:v.2:433-434) fought in confrontations between the Triple Alliance and the independent kingdoms of Puebla-Tlaxcala, the two most powerful political confederations of the fifteenth and sixteenth centuries.

For the archaeologist, the specific components of these wars can be difficult to identify. If asked what the archaeological manifestation of a battlefield might be, many of us would probably reply that such features would be represented by high concentrations of projectile points or other armaments in large, open fields. However, our survey work in the Valley of Atlixco (fig. 16.1), a region famous for the large and apparently spectacular battles fought there during the Late Postclassic period, has shown this not to be the case. The number

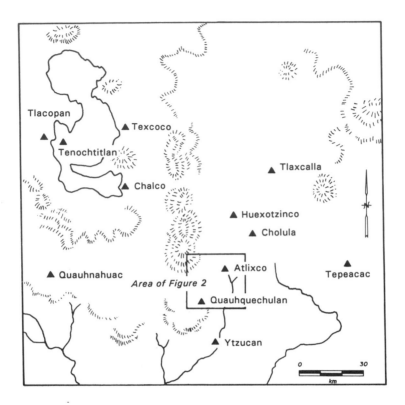

Fig. 16.1. Map of Late Postclassic Central Mexico. The location of the
Valley of Atlixco is shown in relation to the major sites in the region.

of projectile points and other artifacts which might have been used as weaponry
is surprisingly low, and there do not appear to be any areas with significant
concentrations of these items. We must conclude then, that, at least in the case
of the Valley of Atlixco, weapons found in surface surveys do not seem to be
very reliable indicators of warfare.

One of the keys as to what war looks like archaeologically can be found in
the ethnohistorical literature. Writing about the hostilities that developed between Tlaxcalla and Huexotzinco early in the sixteenth century, and basing his
reconstruction on information from Muñoz Camargo, Barlow (1990:163) notes
that the Mexica sent their armies to help the Huexotzinca and crossed into their
territory by way of Tetella, Tochimilco and Quauhquechulan, an area controlled
by the Triple Alliance. Apparently, anticipating Motecuhzoma's intentions, the
Tlaxcallans decided to meet the Mexica armies and their allies well before they
reached Tlaxcalla, and they advanced easily into the Valley of Atlixco from the

north—through Texcaltitlan, Acapetlahuacan and Atlixco—because these settlements, and others on the valley floor, had been abandoned temporarily due to the hostilities. This passage suggests that one of the main indicators of a war zone would be the desertion of towns and villages as the population flees from danger. For this phenomenon to be visible in the archaeological record, however, the abandonment must be for a fairly long period of time.

In the northern part of the Atlixco Valley, the people probably stayed away from their homes only for the duration of the conflicts between Huexotzinco and Tlaxcalla, a period of about ten years just prior to the arrival of the Spaniards, and consequently the incident Barlow records is not archaeologically recognizable. However, for the settlements in the southern valley, where the frontier between the Triple Alliance and the kingdoms of Puebla-Tlaxcala seems to have been located (Plunket and Uruñuela 1991-1992), this phenomenon is easier to detect: the abandonment lasted much longer, perhaps for several generations, as the people fled their communities and eventually even left their agricultural fields untended. That this situation lasted well into the Colonial period is supported by the fact that as Spanish settlers from Puebla began to acquire land grants in the valley during the 1530s, the documentation of these transactions specifically states that these were sparsely inhabited and uncultivated lands (Prem 1984:213-215, 224-225); at the same time, there is the mention of an old irrigation canal, which would seem to indicate that the lands had been under cultivation in the not-too-distant past (Dyckerhoff 1988:26, n.54).

One reason why the southern part of the valley was so susceptible to warfare during the Late Postclassic period has to do in large part with its strategic geographical position as a major communication route between the Basin of Mexico and the Puebla-Tlaxcala Valley. As the Triple Alliance tried again and again to surround and conquer the Tlaxcalans and their allies (Hassig 1988:219-235), the open plains of the southern Valley of Atlixco developed into a frontier, a no-man's-land between the Aztecs and the independent kingdoms (see Berdan, chap. 11). Most, but not all (see, for example, Chimalpahin 1965:216), of the wars fought on the battlegrounds of Atlixco are described as *xochiyaoyotl,* or Flowery Wars, and it is likely, as Isaac (1983:425) suggests, that this ceremonial warfare was a convenient label for a conflict which the Triple Alliance could not entirely be sure of winning. Incidentally, one might suspect that this is the reason that the confrontations between the Chalca and the Mexica were also classified as *xochiyaoyotl:* they consisted of years and years of military engagements where the outcome was by no means certain.

In addition to geography, the history of the preceding centuries also played a significant role in determining the fate of the southern section of the Valley of Atlixco (fig. 16.2), and it is illustrative to outline the sequence of events recorded in the literature that led up to the peculiar situation extant in this area during the latter years of preconquest times.

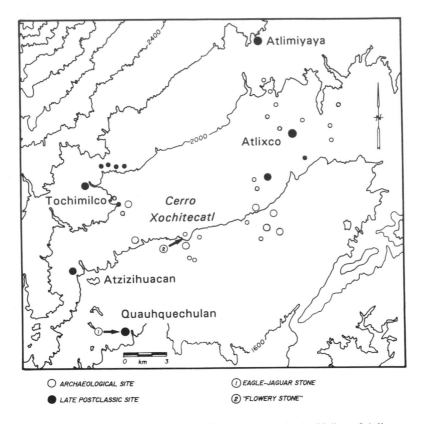

Fig. 16.2.   Late Postclassic period settlement patterns in the Valley of Atlixco.

The Middle and Late Postclassic periods are characterized in the ethnohistorical record as times of increasing conflict in southwestern Puebla. During the thirteenth and fourteenth centuries the *Historia Tolteca-Chichimeca* and the *Anales de Cuauhtitlan* both mention a number of battles involving the kingdoms of the region, in particular Huexotzinco, Cholula, Totomihuacan, Tepeacac, Quauhtinchan, Quauhquechulan and Huehuetlan (see Rojas, chap. 15); in two instances, the wars were fought between the Puebla kingdoms and Chalco on the other side of the Sierra Nevada (Martínez 1984:26). It is likely that these conflicts were the initial attempts at alliance formation and empire building in the area, developments which appear to parallel the situation unfolding among the city-states in the Basin of Mexico.

Beginning in the second half of the fifteenth century, a series of wars broke out between the Quauhquechultecas, who inhabited the Valley of Atlixco, and several of the Puebla kingdoms, in particular the Huexotzinca. In collaboration with its neighbor Calpan, Huexotzinco conquered the Quauhquechultecas, whose *cabecera* was located near the present-day city of Atlixco (an event which took place in either 1391 or 1443), and forced them to resettle in the southern extreme of the valley in what is now the town of Huaquechula. The winners of the conflict then divided the rest of the valley between themselves and populated their newly-gained lands with colonists. Calpan annexed the area around the Pedregal de Nealtican, which bordered its own territory, and Huexotzinco took the center of the valley—including the *cabecera* of the Quauhquechultecas, Huehuequauhquechulan (Dyckerhoff 1988:20-21).

The new settlement of the Quauhquechultecas, referred to as Quauhquechulan, was subsequently conquered by the members of the Triple Alliance although the date of that conquest remains unclear. If the Quauhquechultecas were expelled from their original *cabecera* Huehuequauhquechulan in 1391, then it would be possible that Quauhquechulan was indeed taken by Iztcoatl in 1432, as Chimalpahin states (1965:194); but if the rout of the Quauhquechultecas did not occur until 1443, then it is more likely that it was defeated by Motecuhzoma Ilhuicamina, either during his campaign into Morelos (Hassig 1988:321) or in 1466, as part of the conquest of Tepeacac (Dyckerhoff 1988:20-21). Whatever the date for this event, it is clear that during the second half of the fifteenth century the Valley of Atlixco was divided into two antagonistic areas: the southern part, controlled by the Triple Alliance through its garrison stationed at Quauhquechulan (Dyckerhoff 1988:26), and the northern part, subjugated and colonized by Huexotzinco and Calpan. The stage was set for the region to become a buffer zone between the two most powerful political alliances in the Central Highlands during the Late Postclassic period: Tenochtitlan-Texcoco-Tlacopan and Tlaxcalla-Huexotzinco-Cholula. Once the Triple Alliance had defeated Chalco in 1465 (Chimalpahin 1965:204) the door was opened for the beginning of major military engagements with their most dangerous competitors from the Valley of Puebla-Tlaxcala.

The division of the Valley of Atlixco into north and south during the Late Postclassic period, as documented in the ethnohistorical sources, is also visible in both settlement pattern data and ceramic distributions from the area, and represents an important departure from what we know about either the Early or Middle Postclassic periods in the region. During the Early Postclassic period, settlements are located on the valley floor and in the lower piedmont, as they had been during both the Preclassic and Classic periods; there is a marked change, however, in the ceramic inventory, as Teotihuacan affiliated ceramics disappear and are replaced with different varieties of black-on-orange wares (Plunket 1990:6-7), which according to Noguera (1954:101) are typical of Early Postclassic Cholula (Cholulteca I or Aquiahuac Phase [Lind et al. 1990]). It is probable that these black-on-orange wares are components of both the Early and Middle Postclassic periods in the Valley of Atlixco although we do not yet have stratigraphic excavations which can securely establish this. In addition, those sites that have early black-on-orange wares usually also contain *guinda* ceramics which may be more typical of the Middle and Late Postclassic periods (see Smith 1990:154). Taken as a whole, these data seem to indicate little change in the settlement patterns between the Early and Middle Postclassic periods.

The distribution of Late Postclassic settlements and ceramics appears to be quite different from that of the preceding periods. Sites on the valley floor in the southern part of the region, whose collections include Early and Middle Postclassic ceramics, do not contain any of the ceramic groups we have considered diagnostic of the Late Postclassic period: Aztec III Black-on-Orange, Black-on-Cream (Plunket 1990) and the Nila and Catalina groups of Cholula Polychrome (Lind 1990). These ceramic markers *do* occur, however, at Quauhquechulan, which according to tradition was founded during this period, and also at piedmont sites around Tochimilco, which are located within the area controlled by the Aztecs. This distributional pattern leads us to believe that the valley floor in the area between Quauhquechulan in the south and Atlixco in the north was uninhabited during the Late Postclassic period, thus confirming the information we have outlined above from the ethnohistorical literature.

It is instructive to look at the distribution of the Late Postclassic diagnostic ceramics throughout the Valley of Atlixco since here too we can see the impact of the intrusion of the Triple Alliance from the south and the independent kingdoms of Puebla-Tlaxcala from the north. Aztec III Black-on-Orange pottery is not abundant anywhere in the area, but it is found most commonly at Quauhquechulan which was not only under Aztec control but also was home to a military garrison of the Triple Alliance. In addition, the *guinda* ceramic group is much more common in the southern part of the valley than in the north, a fact which probably reflects more fluid trade relationships with the Basin of Mexico, Morelos and other parts of southern Puebla (see Smith 1990:154). *Guinda* ceramics do occur in Cholula and Huexotzinco, but the forms and decorative attributes differ somewhat from those of the *guinda* wares from the southern part of the Valley of Atlixco. A third ceramic group, common at Quauhquechulan and in the southern area but virtually non-existent in the north, is a Black-on-Cream ware similar to ceramics found in Morelos at Las Pilas (Smith, personal communication). Again, the southern region's ties with areas dominated by the Triple Alliance are emphasized, rather than its ties with areas affiliated with the independent kingdoms of Puebla-Tlaxcala. In contrast, the ceramic collections from the northern part of the Valley of Atlixco include important percentages of the Nila and Catalina groups of the Cholula Polychromes (Noguera's *Decoración Sencilla* and *Laca* groups; see Lind 1990) and domestic wares, such as San Andres Red and Momoxpan Orange, which dominate Late Postclassic ceramic inventories in and around Cholula.

The settlement patterns and the ceramic data, however, are not the only archaeological evidence left by the battles fought on the plains of Atlixco during the Late Postclassic period. Two monumental zoomorphic stone sculptures, carved to symbolically embody the military and religious ideology of the *xochiyaoyotl,* have been found in this area (Plunket and Uruñuela 1991-1992). Today, one is located in the plaza of Huaquechula and the other is situated on the southern slope of a hill known locally as the Xochitecatl ("flowery or decorated stone") which rises 12 km south of Atlixco in the middle of the valley.

The monument in Huaquechula (fig. 16.3) is a representation of an eagle perched on the shoulder of a jaguar. On the jaguar's back is a shield, decorated with 19 down balls, which is set on top of four atlatl darts; to one side is an atlatl surrounded by *aztaxelli,* feather decorations used by certain warriors and gods but most particularly by Tezcatlipoca (Aguilera 1987:72), a god of great importance to Aztec warriors. The darts and the shield form one of the classic metaphors for warfare or conquest: *mitl-chimalli* (Dibble 1971:324; Molina 1970:v.2:54). The stone probably represents the eagle and jaguar warriors who were stationed at the garrison in Quauquechulan. It also makes a reference, however, to the *xochiyaoyotl,* whose purpose was publicly defined as a means to obtain sacrificial victims for Huitzilopochtli. A "smoking" heart (that is, a heart freshly removed from a sacrificial victim, and pierced by an atlatl dart) is sculpted on the left shoulder of the jaguar. The original location of this monument is not known, but when Guillermo Dupaix (1969:v.2:lámina 13) first reported it at the beginning of the nineteenth century, it was in a field on the outskirts of town. We suspect that it was situated north of the modern town in an area where we have documented the archaeological remains of the Postclassic settlement.

The second monument (fig. 16.4), on the southern slope of the Xochitecatl, represents a feathered rattlesnake from whose body flow streams of "precious liquid" (references to either water or blood) and volutes of smoke or mist. This is Mixcoatl, the Cloud Serpent, who is also Camaxtli, the tutelary god of the Huexotzinca. Like Huitzilopochtli, Camaxtli required the blood of sacrificial victims. There are two kinds of references to sacred warfare on the Xochitecatl monument. The first is a shield decorated with nine down balls which encircle a "smoking" heart; the shield is placed on top of what might be a set of atlatl darts to form the phrase *mitl-chimalli.* The second is two *atl-tlachinolli* ("burning-water") symbols, a specific and well-known metaphor for sacred warfare (Dibble 1971:324; Molina 1970:v.2:54).

We have suggested elsewhere (Plunket and Uruñuela 1991-1992) that these two monuments are territorial markers created to define the battlefield where the *xochiyaoyotl,* and perhaps other confrontations, took place.

It is clear then that both the ethnohistorical sources and the archaeological evidence strongly support the Valley of Atlixco's war zone status during the Late Postclassic period, and as we mentioned above, the main reason for this

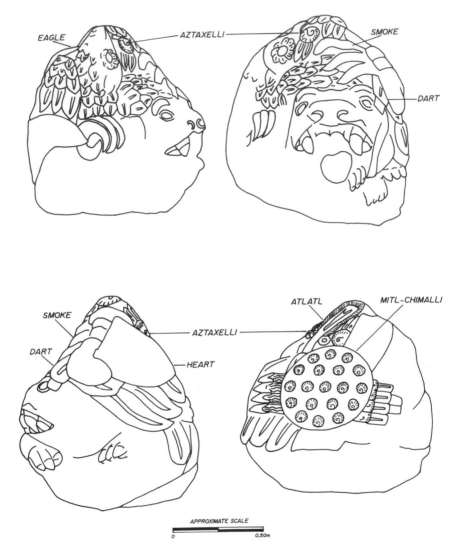

Fig. 16.3. The Eagle-Jaguar Stone of Huaquechula. Drawing by Gabriela Uruñuela.

situation appears to be the growth of a major political and military alliance with expansionist tendencies in each of the large valleys on either side of the Sierra Nevada. The small kingdom of Quauquechulan was not able to defend itself from the imperial designs of these states, and its territory was eventually invaded to be used as a frontier where the Triple Alliance and the independent kingdoms of Puebla-Tlaxcala battled to defend or further their interests.

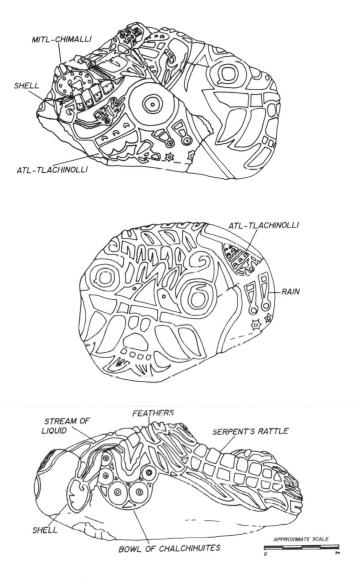

Fig. 16.4. The "Flowery Stone" of Cerro Xochitecatl. Drawing by Gabriela Uruñuela.

There is no question that the Valley of Atlixco was used by the Triple Alliance and the kingdoms of the Puebla-Tlaxcala Valley as a frontier zone in which they fought their battles; both the ethnohistorical record and iconography sculpted on stone monuments by both factions make it clear that the wars fought on the plains of Atlixco were the *xochiyaoyotl*, the Flowery Wars. For the local population, these military engagements disrupted everyday life forcing whole communities to relocate, causing the unintentional fallowing of farmland, and interfering with both internal and external trade networks. How does this information reflect on the nature of these conflicts and the relations between the Aztecs and the Tlaxcallans and their allies?

The situation we have outlined for the Late Postclassic period in the Valley of Atlixco does not seem to have existed at any other time in the region's prehistory. During the Preclassic period, when most areas of Mesoamerica developed chiefdom societies or even in some cases incipient states, the political and economic structure of the Valley of Atlixco resembled those of the Basin of Mexico or the Valley of Puebla at that time, even though these regions were much larger with decidedly greater productive potential. There is one major Preclassic site, Colotzingo, with 30 ha of monumental architecture; several smaller sites with minor architectural remains; and a number of settlements that are represented simply by sherd scatters. This pattern suggests that during the Middle to Late Preclassic periods the valley saw the emergence of a large chiefdom and the development of a three-tiered administrative hierarchy that encompassed the entire region. Ceramics from Colotzingo provide evidence of ties not only to the Basin of Mexico and Puebla-Tlaxcala but also to eastern Morelos, West Mexico and the Gulf Coast (Uruñuela 1989), indicating that this regional center actively participated in the social and economic exchange networks of its time. We have no reason to believe that Colotzingo was unable to defend its sovereignty or compete effectively with its neighbors in the Central Highlands.

It was during the Classic period, with the development of powerful states in the adjoining valleys, that the Atlixco region became unable to sustain a viable independent polity. Its size and carrying capacity were not sufficient to support a political and economic apparatus that could retain autonomy from Teotihuacan or Cholula. Consequently, Atlixco, and other regions like it, were forced into subordinate, and perhaps colonial, relationships. Settlements were dispersed throughout the valley floor and the lower piedmont, but none of them appear to have been more than small towns, or perhaps in the case of Huehuequauhquechulan, small city-states. The interest of the major centers seems to have focused on the geographical importance of the valley as a trade route to the southeast for the procurement of commodities from the towns of Puebla, Oaxaca, and Guerrero, items which included Thin Orange vessels or their contents. Perhaps of equal significance was the potential for the cultivation of agricultural produce, such as avocado, guayaba, *guajes,* flowers, or cotton, which do not grow well above 2000 m. With the rise of urban centers in the adjoining highland valleys during the Classic period, Atlixco seems to have become a province of Teotihuacan's "outer hinterland" (Hirth 1978:331-332). It is premature to assume, however, that what appear to be Teotihuacan artifacts in the Valley of Atlixco could not have come from nearby Cholula (Noyola 1991; Plunket and Blanco 1989; Sánchez de la Barquera 1991).

It could be argued that the presence of two major powers bordering the Valley of Atlixco during the Classic period, Teotihuacan in the Basin of Mexico and Cholula in the Valley of Puebla, should have generated a situation similar to the one we have described for the Late Postclassic period when the area was the subject of competitive intervention. The archaeological record, however, does not provide any evidence for a confrontational situation in the region during this time period. The abundance and even distribution of Teotihuacan-style ceramics throughout the valley and the non-defensive locations of sites in addition to their lack defensive features suggest that the relationship between Teotihuacan and Cholula was not competitive and that perhaps Cholula was, as has often been claimed, allied to Teotihuacan.

During the Early and Middle Postclassic periods, a time of balkanization and the formation of small independent kingdoms in the Central Highlands, Atlixco was once again able to maintain a political and economic structure capable of competing with its neighbors. Its documented participation in the wars and power struggles of southwestern Puebla at this time suggests that Atlixco (Huehuequauhquechulan) was one of a series of petty kingdoms which vied with each other for the control of local resources. During the Late Postclassic period, however, both the archaeological evidence and the ethnohistorical data point to a situation in which Atlixco as a political entity was again reduced to a provincial status. Huge expansionist polities developed in the Basin of Mexico and the Valley of Puebla-Tlaxcala, and took over the region, not for its productive potential, but rather for its strategic military value. As a small Postclassic city-state bordering the two most powerful regions of highland Mesoamerica, Quauhquechulan was not able to compete with or effectively protect itself from those complex and aggressive political structures, and consequently, its territory was converted into a frontier zone where the great battles of the *xochiyaoyotl* were fought.

The creation of a *xochiyaoyotl* battlefield on the plains of Atlixco was an important element in the overall Aztec strategy concerning the Valley of Puebla-Tlaxcala, but whether this strategy was geared to conquest or containment is difficult to say (see, for example, Hicks 1979 and Isaac 1983). Hassig (1988:255) suggests that the Flowery Wars were "an efficient means of continuing a conflict that was too costly to conclude immediately" and that two tactics were employed in the slow weakening of their opponents: encirclement and undercutting by chipping away at enemy territories, and cutting off allied support. The data we have presented here agree with this interpretation in so far as the frontier which was established between Atlixco and Quauhquechulan resulted in the severing of effective relations between the independent kingdoms and their potential allies in southwestern Puebla; at the same time, the frontier formed one of the essential elements of the noose that the Aztecs were tightening around Tlaxcalla and it allies.

REFERENCES CITED

Aguilera, Carmen
  1987 Iztac Mixcóatl en vasija del Templo Mayor. In *Historia de la religión en Mesoamérica y áreas afines: primer coloquio,* edited by Barbro Dahlgren de Jordan, pp. 69-82. Instituto de Investigaciones Antropológicas, Universidad Nacional Autónoma de México, Mexico City.

Barlow, Robert H.
  1990 *Los mexicas y la triple alianza.* Edited by Jesús Monjarás, Elena Limón and María de la Cruz Paillés, pp. 155-172. Instituto Nacional de Antropología e Historia and Universidad de las Américas-Puebla, Mexico City.

Chimalpahin Quauhtlehuanitzin, Don Francisco de San Antón Muñón
  1965 *Relaciones originales de Chalco Amequemecan escritas por Don Francisco de San Antón Muñón Chimalpahin Cuauhtlehuanitzin.* Edited and translated by Sylvia Rendón. Fondo de Cultura Económica, Mexico City.

Dibble, Charles
  1971 Writing in Central Mexico. In *Archaeology of Northern Mexico,* pt. 1, edited by Gordon Ekholm and Ignacio Bernal, pp. 322-332. Handbook of Middle American Indians, vol. 10, Robert Wauchope, general editor. University of Texas Press, Austin.

Dupaix, Guillermo
  1969 *Expediciones acerca de los antiguos monumentos de la Nueva España: 1805-1808.* Edited with introduction and notes by José Alcina Franch. Ediciones José Porrúa Turanzas, Madrid.

Durán, Fray Diego
  1967 *Historia de las Indias de Nueva España e Islas de la Tierra Firme.* Edited by Angel María Garibay K. 2 vols. Editorial Porrúa, Mexico City.

Dyckerhoff, Ursula
  1988 La época prehispánica. In *Milpa y hacienda: tenencia de la tierra indígena y española en la cuenca del Alto Atoyac, Puebla, México (1520-1650),* edited by Hanns J. Prem, pp. 18-34. Centro de Investigaciones Superiores del Instituto Nacional de Antropología e Historia, Instituto Nacional de Antropología e Historia, and Secretaría de Educación Pública, Mexico City.

Hassig, Ross
  1988 *Aztec Warfare: Imperial Expansion and Political Control.* University of Oklahoma Press, Norman.

Hicks, Frederic
  1979 "Flowery War" in Aztec History. *American Ethnologist* 6:87-92.

Hirth, Kenneth G.
  1978 Teotihuacan Regional Population Administration in Eastern Morelos. *World Archaeology* 9:320-333.

Historia Tolteca-Chichimeca
  1976 *Historia Tolteca-Chichimeca*. Edited by Paul Kirchhoff, Lina Odena
  Güemes and Luis Reyes García. Instituto Nacional de Antropología e Historia,
  Mexico City.

Isaac, Barry
  1983 The Aztec "Flowery War": A Geopolitical Explanation. *Journal of Anthropological Research* 39:415-432.

Lind, Michael, Catalina Barrientos, Chris Turner, Charles Caskey, Geoffrey McCafferty,
Carmen Martínez, and Martha Orea
  1990 Cholula Polychrome. Manuscript on file at the Archaeology Laboratory of
  the Universidad de las Américas, Cholula, Puebla.

Martínez, Hildeberto
  1984 *Tepeaca en el siglo XVI: tenencia de la tierra y organización de un señorío.*
  Centro de Investigaciones y Estudios Superiores en Antropología Social,
  Mexico City.

Molina, Fray Alonso de
  1970 *Vocabulario en lengua castellana y mexicana y mexicana y castellana.*
  Facsimile edition of the 1571 original with a preliminary study by Miguel León-
  Portilla. Editorial Porrúa, Mexico City.

Muñoz Camargo, Diego
  1978 *Historia de Tlaxcala.* Edited by Alfredo Chavero. Editorial Inovación,
  Mexico City.

Noguera, Eduardo
  1954 *La cerámica de Cholula.* Editorial Guaranía, Mexico City.

Noyola, Andrés
  1991 *La excavación de una unidad habitacional del clásico en San Juan Tejupa,
  Atzizihuacan, Puebla.* Unpublished licenciatura thesis, Universidad de las
  Américas, Cholula, Puebla.

Plunket, Patricia
  1990 Arqueología y etnohistoria en el Valle de Atlixco. *Notas Mesoamericanas*
  12:3-18.

Plunket, Patricia, and Mónica Blanco
  1989 Teotihuacan y el Valle de Atlixco. *Notas Mesoamericanas* 11:120-132.

Plunket, Patricia, and Gabriela Uruñuela
  1991-1992 La escultura postclásica del Valle de Atlixco. *Notas Mesoamericanas*
  13:35-49.

Prem, Hanns J.
  1984 Early Spanish Colonization and Indians in the Valley of Atlixco, Puebla.
  In *Explorations in Ethnohistory: Indians of Central Mexico in the Sixteenth
  Century*, edited by H. R. Harvey and Hanns J. Prem, pp. 205-228. University
  of New Mexico Press, Albuquerque.

Sánchez de la Barquera, Elvia
  1991   *Figurillas prehispánicas del Valle de Atlixco, Puebla.* Unpublished *licenciatura* thesis, Universidad de las Américas, Cholula, Puebla.
Smith, Michael E.
  1990   Long-Distance Trade Under the Aztec Empire: The Archaeological Evidence. *Ancient Mesoamerica* 1:153-169.
Uruñuela y Ladrón de Guevara, Gabriela
  1989   Investigaciones arqueológicas en Colotzingo, Puebla. *Notas Mesoamericanas* 11:110-119.

17

Late Postclassic Imperial Expansion and Economic Exchange within the Tarascan Domain

Helen Perlstein Pollard and Thomas A. Vogel

In prehistoric Mesoamerica obsidian was both a basic and a luxury resource; it was traded in local and regional markets as well as in long-distance networks and was exchanged in both raw and manufactured form. For these reasons, the study of obsidian has occupied a prominent position in formulating and testing models of the emergence, structure, and collapse of Mexican states and empires. Three central questions have been addressed by a recent study of obsidian artifacts from the Late Postclassic Tarascan state (A.D. 1350-1520): (1) What was the relationship between political borders and economic networks in prehispanic Mesoamerica? In the Tarascan case, what was the relationship between economic networks maintained by tributary relations and those maintained by market relations? (2) What role did basic resources play in the emergence or maintenance of stratified societies? Did control of obsidian mines or obsidian exchange routes serve as a source of political power for the Tarascan elite? (3) What types of realignments in macro-regional and local exchange networks take place when new political/economic cores emerged? How did the growth of the Tarascan state affect obsidian supply networks in central and western Mexico? In this chapter we will discuss the results of the obsidian study to date and their significance in understanding both internal and external interactions of the Tarascan state within Late Postclassic Mesoamerica.

At the time of European contact in the early sixteenth century more than 75,000 km^2 of western Mexico were under the political power of the Tarascan

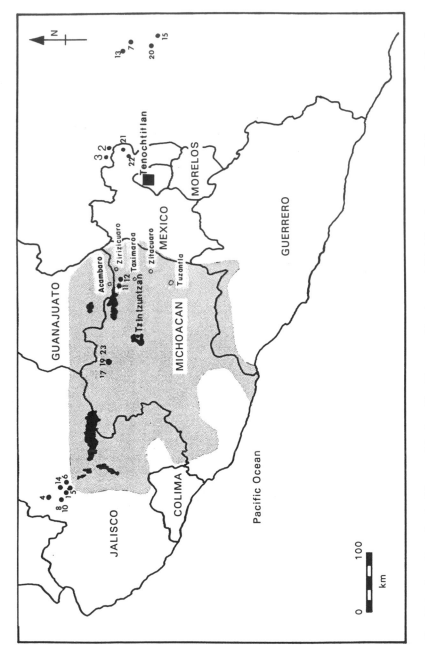

Fig. 17.1. Late Postclassic Western Mexico, The Tarascan Empire, and Obsidian Sources. Obsidian sources: 1. La Joya, 2. Tulancingo-Pizarrin, 3. Pachuca, 4. Llano Grande (Magdelena), 5. La Mora-Teuchitlan, 6. Amatitan, 7. Altotongo, 8. Sta. Teresa, 9. Los Saaverda (not located), 10. Balvandeda, 11. Zinapecuaro, 12. Ucareo and Zinapecuaro 3, 13. Zaragoza, 14. Tequila, 15. Tozongo, 16. C. de Minas (not located), 17. C. Varal, 18. Los Sandovales (not located), 19. C. Zinaparo-La Guamina, 20. Guadalupe Victoria, 21. Tecocomulco-Paredon, 22. Otumba, 23. C. Prieto.

state (fig. 17.1). It was the second largest empire in Mesoamerica in 1519 and is known to us through both documentary and archaeological information (Pollard 1993). Control of the state was in the hands of a royal dynasty, resident at the capital city Tzintzuntzan in the Lake Patzcuaro Basin. Previous studies have indicated that the Tarascan economy was dominated by two largely independent flows of goods and services--state-controlled tribute and regional markets (Pollard 1982; Gorenstein and Pollard 1983). The tributary network and other state controlled economic resources (including state lands, mineral resources, and long-distance merchants) were congruent with the territorial borders of the state. They included both basic and luxury (or status) goods, both of which were destined primarily for use by the elite. These economic flows are relatively well documented in the ethnohistoric records of the sixteenth century (see Gorenstein and Pollard 1983:app.3). The market networks were local and regional, and are believed to have included basic goods and services primarily destined for commoners. Unfortunately, relatively little was written about native markets, and the primary source of information about the Tarascans, the *Relación de Michoacán,* documents market activity only when marketplaces were settings for legends about the royal dynasty (1956 [1541]: 39, 83, 91, 144, 213).

THE ANALYSIS OF TARASCAN OBSIDIAN

Obsidian is a basic resource for which there is scant documentary evidence. Apart from the mention of "precious stones" obtained for the king by long-distance merchants (*Relación de Michoacán* 1956:178), obsidian is absent from any list of tributary goods or state gift exchange. Nevertheless, more than 90 percent of the lithic artifacts recovered in a survey of the capital Tzintzuntzan are of obsidian (Pollard 1972). Clearly Tarascan settlements were obtaining obsidian, and the logical conclusion is that this occurred through the regional marketing networks. As a nonperishable basic resource, obsidian is an excellent material with which to "trace" the Late Postclassic market system. Furthermore, because obsidian was a resource used by both elites and commoners, the study of its distribution within the Tarascan capital offers an opportunity to observe the interaction between tributary and market-based consumption.

The Obsidian Sample

A collection of 853 obsidian artifacts from Tarascan sites was available for study (table 17.1). The sample includes 707 artifacts obtained by H. Pollard at the

Table 17.1 Obsidian collection available for analysis

Category	Total Collection		XRF Sample	
	No.	%	No.	% of Total
Tzintzuntzan (Late Postclassic)				
Flakes	79	11.2	41	51.8
Cores	42	5.9	16	38.1
Blades	485	68.6	275	56.7
Scrapers	55	7.8	18	32.7
Other Tools	24	3.4	9	37.5
Projectile Points	11	1.6	10	90.9
Adornment	11	1.6	10	90.9
Total	707	100.0	379[a]	53.6
Tarascan Border Sites (Late Postclassic)				
Tuzantla	50	37.9	14	28.0
Taximoroa	34	25.8	7	20.6
Zitacuaro	9	6.8	2	22.2
Ziriricuaro	25	18.9	6	24.0
Acambaro	14	10.6	8	57.1
Total	132	100.0	37	28.0
Other Sites				
Patzcuaro Basin[b]	7	53.8	3	42.9
Zacapu	3	23.1	0	--
Zinapecuaro	1	7.7	0	--
Teotihuacan	2	15.4	2	100.0
Total	13	100.0	5	38.5
Source Samples				
Zinapecuaro	10	90.9	5[c]	50.0
Ucareo	1	9.1	1	100.0
Total	11	100.0	6	54.5

[a] Six artifacts were processed as both pellets and disks, bringing the total number of readings for the Tzintzuntzan collection to 385.

[b] Erongaricuaro and Ihuatzio.

[c] Source samples were processed as both pellets and disks.

Tarascan capital of Tzintzuntzan during a surface survey of the city (1970-1972) and 132 artifacts obtained by S. Gorenstein during her study of the Tarascan-Aztec military border (1971-1975) (Gorenstein 1985). The artifacts from Tzintzuntzan are located by collection unit (site) and include material from three types of workshops, public ceremonial zones, and both elite and commoner residential zones (Pollard 1977). The artifacts from Tarascan fortified sites along the Tarascan-Aztec military border include material from Acambaro (Cerro Chivo), Taximaroa, Tuzantla, Zirizicuaro and Zitacuaro (see figure 17.1). In addition, source samples have been collected from two of the quarries believed to be likely Tarascan sources: Zinapecuaro (by Pollard in 1976) and Ucareo (by Gorenstein in 1971).

In 1987, 29 artifacts from Tzintzuntzan and six source samples from Zinapecuaro were prepared and analyzed for trace elements using X-ray fluorescence spectrometry under the supervision of John Wilband, Department of Geological Sciences, Michigan State University. All samples were cleaned with acetone to remove surface contamination; source samples were sawn to remove the outer surface. The samples were then crushed to clay size. X-ray fluorescence analyses were done for 11 trace elements (Cr, Ni, Cu, Zn, Rb, Sr, Y, Zr, Nb, La, Ba) on pressed powders using standard techniques (Bower and Valentini 1986). Based upon the results obtained from this small sample, the study was expanded in 1989-1990, under the supervision of Thomas Vogel.

The expanded study included 379 artifacts from Tzintzuntzan and 37 artifacts from the border sites. In the interests of time, cost of analysis, and the scientific and cultural value of the objects, rather than grinding them to produce pellets, artifacts were X-rayed whole, and only the five elements that clearly differentiated samples were measured (Sr, Zr, Rb, Y, Nb). In order to analyze whole artifacts, standards had to be developed. First, the portions of the Zinapecuaro obsidian nodules which had been used to produce the pellets were cut into disks and analyzed. The results of these analyses were used as calibrations for the whole artifact samples. As a check, the remaining portions of three large flakes which had been broken in order to produce the powder for the pellets in the first phase of analysis, were reanalyzed as whole objects (table 17.2). In this way it was possible to measure the error created by using whole objects with non-planar surfaces. Finally, in their role as standards in the measurement process, two of the source samples were reanalyzed (one 17 and the other 18 times) and one artifact was reanalyzed once.

Based upon these procedures it has been possible to establish a range of variation in readings due to (1) technique of analysis (pellet vs. whole artifact) and (2) machine variance in concentrations. Given the constraints of study and the need to compare results with published concentrations for other Mesoamerican sources, the most accurate source identifications are believed to be based upon comparison of ratios of the three most reported elements (Sr, Zr, Rb) and the absolute concentrations of two others (Y, Nb). Ratios of Y and Nb are not used because many of the comparative samples lacked analyses of these elements.

Table 17.2 Trace element composition of Mesoamerican obsidian source samples

Source Samples	Ref.	Trace Element Quantity (ppm)					Rel. Frequency			Total
		Sr	Zr	Rb	Y	Nb	Sr	Zr	Rb	
Tecocomulco-Paredon	1	90	70	130	--	--	.31	.24	.45	290
Tecocomulco-Paredon	1	150	120	160	--	--	.35	.28	.37	430
Tulancingo-Pizarrin	2	bd[b]	584	125	--	--	--	.82	.18	709
Tulancingo-Pizarrin	2	bd	696	151	--	--	--	.82	.18	847
Pachuca	3	bd	700	200	55	80	--	.78	.22	900
Pachuca	3	bd	970	220	55	85	--	.82	.18	1,190
Otumba	4	100	56	114	--	--	.37	.21	.42	270
Otumba	4	125	105	133	--	--	.34	.29	.37	363
La Joya	3	5	865	145	50	85	--	.85	.14	1,015
La Joya	3	10	1,000	165	55	100	.01	.85	.14	1,175
Llano Grande-Mag.	5	bd	704	171	74	47	--	.80	.20	875
Llano Grande-Etz.	5	bd	619	163	--	--	--	.79	.21	782
La Mora-Teuchitlan	5	bd	549	178	79	44	--	.76	.24	727
La Mora-Teuchitlan	6	bd	472	174	--	--	--	.73	.27	646
La Mora-Teuchitlan	6	bd	478	182	--	--	--	.72	.28	660
Sta. Teresa	5	8	242	155	49	36	.02	.60	.38	405
C. Prieto	7	200	167	108	bd	33	.42	.35	.23	477
C. Varal-Zinaparo	7	74	129	122	bd	16	.23	.40	.38	325
C. Varal-Zinaparo	7	87	141	126	bd	28	.25	.40	.36	354
C. Zinaparo	7	127	185	127	bd	19	.29	.42	.29	439
C. Zinaparo	7	135	189	137	bd	29	.29	.41	.30	461
Zinapecuaro 1	8	4	101	196	47	20	.01	.34	.65	302
Zinapecuaro 1	8	4.4	100	189	46	20	.01	.34	.64	293
Zinapecuaro 2	8	5.2	101	192	46	20	.02	.34	.64	298
Zinapecuaro 3	8	9	103	168	42	18	.03	.37	.60	281
Zinapecuaro 3	8	7.9	101	175	42	18	.03	.36	.62	283
Ucareo	8	9.7	108	166	38	18	.03	.38	.59	282
Guadalupe Victoria	3	80	70	110	10	15	.31	.27	.42	260
Zaragoza	9	32	163	123	32	18	.10	.51	.39	318
Zaragoza	9	36	215	141	34	20	.09	.55	.36	392
Altotonga	2	bd	170	132	--	--	--	.56	.44	302
Altotonga	2	bd	226	151	--	--	--	.60	.40	377
Amatitlan	5	bd	333	196	93	64	--	.63	.37	529
Balvandeda	5	6	118	163	35	28	.02	.41	.57	287
Tequila	5	51	225	110	27	22	.13	.58	.28	386
Los Sandovales	5	114	204	118	21	20	.26	.47	.27	436
Los Saavedra	5	19	259	137	42	31	.05	.62	.33	415
Tozongo	3	bd	30	90	35	--	--	.25	.75	120
Cerro de Minas	3	35	55	120	10	15	.17	.26	.57	210

[a] Key to references: (1) Charlton et al. (1978), (2) Boksenbaum et al. (1987), (3) Stross et al. (1976), (4) Nelson et al. (1977), (5) Trombold et al. (1993), (6) Ericson and Kimberlin (1977), (7) Darras and Nelson (1987), (8) Pollard and Vogel (present study), (9) Ferriz (1985).

[b] "bd" signifies quantities are below the detection limits of the instrument.

Source Identification

The absolute concentrations of the five measured elements and the ratios of three elements (Sr, Zr, Rb) were graphically compared with the published values of 21 obsidian sources in central Mexico and the determined values for the Zinapecuaro and Ucareo sources (table 17.2 and figs. 17.2 and 17.3). Where published values indicated a range of variation for an element, two entries were made, reflecting the upper and lower values, respectively. The concentrations for samples collected from the three separate flows at Zinapecuaro were listed individually. Once a source was assigned to an artifact, the information was added to the artifact catalog. This catalog includes the artifact type, color, location by site (for the border sites) or unit and zone (for Tzintzuntzan), source, and the presence of cortex material. (The elemental concentrations, the multiple analyses of source samples, and the artifact catalog have not been included here due to space limitations. They can be obtained from H. Pollard upon request.)

The bulk of the grey-black and all of the red-black and striated clear obsidians were relatively simple to discriminate. The Zinapecuaro and Ucareo obsidians are markedly different in elemental composition from all other Central Mexican sources, if not by relative concentrations of Sr, Zr, and Rb, then by abundances of Y and Nb. Zinapecuaro flows 1 and 2 are also easily distinguished from Ucareo obsidian, even though they are located only 20 km apart. Zinapecuaro flow 3 overlaps with the values for Ucareo obsidian. There is no evidence, however, that flow 3 was used prehispanically as a quarry. Therefore, artifacts with concentrations in the range of the Ucareo-Zinapecuaro flow 3 have been interpreted as coming from Ucareo obsidian alone (see table 17.3). The vast majority of artifacts studied were assigned to the Ucareo source, including 76% of those from Tzintzuntzan and 89% of those from the border sites. When the artifacts assigned to the Zinapecuaro source are added to these, the combined totals for the Zinapecuaro-Ucareo source area are 83% of the artifacts from Tzintzuntzan and 89% of the artifacts from the border sites.

Before the XRF analysis began, all grey-black artifacts were assigned a number based upon their perceived color. The color classes distinguished light and dark grey, opaque and translucent, streaked and unstreaked. Once artifacts had been assigned to sources based on the XRF concentrations, the source classifications were compared to the color classes. Among the artifacts and sources represented in this analysis no consistent association was found between color and source (see table 17.4). The Ucareo source assignment is associated with light and dark grey, opaque and translucent, streaked and unstreaked, and even clear striated obsidian. Sixty-five percent of the Ucareo-assigned artifacts are opaque, dark grey in color, but 15% are light grey, and 14% are a combination of light and dark grey, often with clear bands. For the other grey obsidian sources represented by this collection, the samples are too

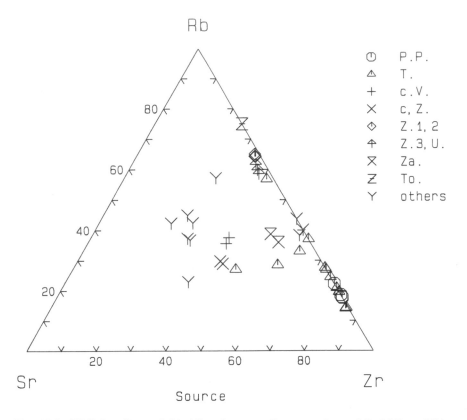

Fig. 17.2. XRF Readings of Obsidian Sources. Concentrations of Rubidium (Rb), Strontium (Sr) and Zirconium (Zr) in sources listed in table 17.2 converted to relative proportions of the three elements. P.P.=Pizarrin-Pachuca (Central Mexican green), T.=Tequila (West Mexican green), C.V.=C. Varal, C.Z.=C. Zinaparo, Z.1,2=Zinapecuaro flows 1 & 2, Z.3,U=Zinapecuaro flow 3 & Ucareo, Za.=Zaragoza, To.=Tozongo, Others=Tecomulco-Paredon, Otumba, Sta. Teresa, C. Prieto, Guadalupe Victoria, Altotonga, C. de Minas.

small to describe a full range of color assignments. Nevertheless, each source includes more than one color category.

Artifacts with predominantly red color clearly can be assigned to the Cerro Zinaparo obsidian source. Those with large clear bands or artifacts that are completely clear come from the Cerro Varal source. Both quarries are in the Zinaparo source zone in northwest Michoacan and are markedly different in chemical composition from each other and all other central Mexican sources (Darras and Nelson 1987). Both quarries also contain fine quality, grey-black obsidian that was utilized in other parts of the Protohistoric Tarascan territory, including Zacapu (Darras, personal communication 1987; Michelet et al. 1989).

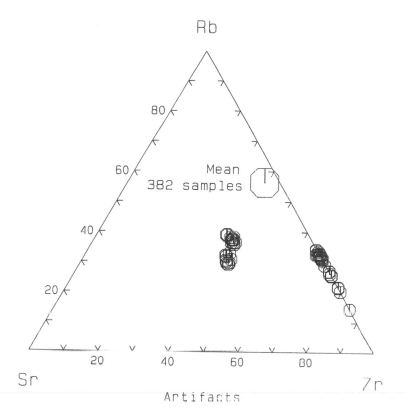

Fig. 17.3. XRF Readings of Obsidian Artifacts. Concentrations of Rubidium (Rb), Strontium (Sr), and Zirconium (Zr) in artifacts tested converted to relative proportions of the three elements. The 382 artifacts that fell within the area depicted on the graph labeled "mean 382 samples" include the following readings: Rb: $\bar{x}$=56.3 s.d. 3.3; Sr: $\bar{x}$=4.6 s.d.=1.3; Zr: $\bar{x}$=39.1 s.d.=2.6.

The remaining artifacts represent grey-black obsidian from three known and two unknown sources and green obsidian from several known and unknown sources. The 21 grey-black artifacts probably include obsidian from Zaragoza and Tozongo and may also include seven pieces from Balvandeda, Jalisco. The Balvandeda obsidian is extremely close to, or even within the range of, the Ucareo obsidians; hence, this identification is tentative. At least two unknown sources are represented, one in the Tzintzuntzan collection and the other in the Acambaro collection. The green obsidians are the hardest to associate with specific sources. Although they are clearly distinguishable from non-green sources, they are difficult to distinguish from each other. Of particular concern is the

Table 17.3 Assignment of artifacts to obsidian sources by XRF

Obsidian Source	Source No.	Artifacts	
		No.	%
Tzintzuntzan			
Ucareo and Zinapecuaro 3	12	290	76.1
Zinapecuaro 1 and 2	11	24	6.3
C. Varal, Michoacan (clear)	17	13	3.4
Unknown 4 (green)	106	10	2.6
Unknown 1	201	9	2.4
C. Zinaparo, Michoacan (red)	19	8	2.1
Balvandeda, Jalisco	10	7	1.8
La Mora-Teuchitlan, Jal. (green)	5, 104	5	1.3
Amatitlan, Jal. (green)	6, 101, 103	4	1.0
Zaragoza, Puebla	13	3	.8
Llano Grande, Jal. (green)	4, 105	3	.8
Tozongo, Puebla	15	2	.5
Tulancingo-Pizarrin (green)	2, 107	1	.3
La Joya, Jal. or Pachuca (green)	1, 3, 108	1	.3
Unknown 3 (green)	102	1	.3
Tarascan Border Sites			
Ucareo and Zinapecuaro 3	12	33	89.2
Unknown 2	202	2	5.4
C. Zinaparo, Michoacan (red)	19	1	2.7
Amatitlan, Jalisco (green)	101	1	2.7
Other Patzcuaro Basin Sites			
Ucareo	12	2	66.7
Zinapecuaro 1 and 2	11	1	33.3

apparent overlap in chemistry of the green obsidians from the Guadalajara, Jalisco vicinity and those from Pachuca, Hidalgo. In addition there may be at least two unknown sources of green obsidians. We suspect that some of this problem is due to inadequate attention to the establishment of ranges of variation for these sources and to the need to consider more trace elements.

The source identification has revealed a number of significant patterns in the utilization of obsidian at Tzintzuntzan and the border sites. First, the primary source for both sets was Ucareo specifically, and the Ucareo-Zinapecuaro zone in general. More than 94% of the tested grey-black obsidian artifacts from the Tzintzuntzan collection were assigned to this source zone. More than 94% of the grey-black obsidian artifacts tested from the border sites came from Ucareo.

Table 17.4   Comparison of sources and color of obsidian artifacts

Source	Light grey				Dark grey				Mixed grey		Red	Clear	Green
	1	1.5	2	2.5	3	3.5	4	4.5	5	5.5	20	30	10
Ucareo	10	2	16	19	104	98	5	12	2	32	1	9[a]	--
Zinapecuaro	4	--	7	5	2	2	1	--	--	2	1	--	--
Balvandeda	1	--	--	--	4	1	--	--	--	1	--	--	--
Unknown 1	--	--	--	1	4	4	--	--	--	--	--	--	--
Unknown 2	1	--	--	--	--	1	--	--	--	--	--	--	--
Zaragoza	--	--	--	--	1	--	--	--	--	--	--	2	--
Tozongo	1	--	--	1	--	--	--	1	--	--	--	--	--
C.Varal	--	--	--	--	3	1	--	--	--	1	--	8	--
C.Zinaparo	--	--	--	--	--	1	--	--	--	--	7	1	--
La Mora-T.	--	--	--	--	1	--	--	--	--	--	--	--	4
Others, #101-108	--	--	--	--	--	--	--	--	--	--	--	--	20

Note: Key to color numbers:

1	light grey opaque	4	dark grey translucent
1.5	light grey streaked	4.5	dark grey translucent streaked
2	light grey translucent	5	light and dark grey
2.5	light grey translucent streaked	5.5	light and dark grey streaked
3	dark grey opaque		
3.5	dark grey opaque streaked		

[a] Predominantly clear with 3.5 and 4.5 grey.

Although Ucareo is the closest source of high quality obsidian to the sites along the Tarascan frontier, and might therefore have been expected to be the source for the border sites, no such claim can be made for its predominance in the Tzintzuntzan collection. Tzintzuntzan is approximately 90 km from Ucareo and 60 km from Zinaparo, both source zones of high quality grey-black obsidian. The XRF analysis reveals, however, that the Zinaparo sources were used selectively for their red and clear obsidians. The single red artifact from a border site is also assigned to the Zinaparo source, suggesting that this pattern of selective use extended beyond the Tarascan capital to the northeast zone of the state.

More than 88% of the obsidian at Tzintzuntzan, and 92% of the obsidian at the border sites, can be assigned to sources that were located within the political boundaries of the Tarascan state. Most of the obsidian that must have been imported into the Tarascan territory is green in color. Given the problems of assigning sources to the green artifacts, any statements about them are tentative. Nevertheless, it seems likely that most of the green obsidian came from the Volcán de Tequila, Jalisco sources to the west of the Tarascan state. Small quantities were probably also imported from the eastern sources (Pachuca and Tulancingo).

THE POLITICAL ECONOMY OF TARASCAN OBSIDIAN

Obsidian at the Capital

The 707 artifacts comprising the obsidian collection from Tzintzuntzan were acquired during a surface survey of the Late Postclassic capital (Pollard 1972, 1977). The collection was exported with the permission of the Instituto Nacional de Antropología e Historia (1970). The collection, while small, was designed to be representative of the range of obsidian artifacts in the Late Postclassic assemblage. Nevertheless, the method of collection, "grab samples", biased the sampling toward larger, more diagnostic artifacts. During the survey, debitage was noted, but small flakes and blade fragments were rarely collected. An additional source of bias was the state of the main ceremonial platform at Tzintzuntzan itself. As the locus of the official tourist site and many seasons of INAH excavations, the main platform was essentially swept bare.

Of the 707 artifacts available for analysis, 379 were analyzed by XRF (see table 17.1). Not all artifact classes were equally well represented in the analysis. Larger flakes and scrapers were too large for XRF analysis and would have required breakage. Because the non-grey artifacts, especially the greens, pose particular questions about prehispanic trade networks, these obsidians were preferentially chosen for study, which explains the high proportion of projectile points and objects of adornment that were analyzed (table 17.1).

Lithic Workshops

Within Tzintzuntzan three types of individual workshops have been isolated, based upon high concentrations of lithic remains (see Smith and Hodge, chap. 1, for discussion of recent archaeological approaches to the study of workshops).

Type 1 workshops. Workshops characterized by unretouched prismatic blades, blade cores, and macroflakes (also referred to as macroblades or crude blades) are called Type 1. The absence of large quantities of debitage and a high proportion of prismatic blades (65%) and macroflakes/flakes (20%) suggests these are areas where macrocores were reduced to blades and other obsidian tools by specialists such as the "navajeros" depicted in the *Relación de Michoacán* (1956:172). Five sites are considered Type 1 workshops, and 64 artifacts from them have been analyzed by XRF (table 17.5). Each site contains obsidian from three to five different sources, and a total of eight sources are represented by these sites. Ucareo obsidian is the most abundant, accounting for 78% of the artifacts, although Zinaparo clear and red obsidians are found, along with three different green obsidians.

Table 17.5   Obsidian sources in urban zones at Tzintzuntzan

Zone	No. Sites	Total Obsid.	No. XRF	No. Sources	Sources per Site	Comments
Lithic Workshops						
Type 1	5	132	64	8	3-5	78% Ucareo
Type 2	4	74	41	9	4-5	49% Ucareo; 27% green
Type 3	2	19	4	1	1	100% Ucareo
Public / Ritual Zones						
Public 1	7	55	23	3	1-2	91% Ucareo
Public 2	5	26	18	5	1-3	78% Ucareo
Residential Zones						
Type 1	31	199	96	8	1-5	90% Ucareo- Zin; 26 sites only Ucareo
Type 2	11	126	80	8	1-6	6 sites only Ucareo
Type 3	15	115	59	11	1-4	6 sites only Ucareo

Type 2 workshops. Workshops characterized by large quantities of debitage, microflakes (24%) and flakes (38%) are called Type 2. More than 50% of the red and green obsidian found in the survey come from these workshops. A number of unfinished objects, including ear plugs, disks and cylinders, are included in the assemblages from the four Type 2 workshops, which support the conclusion that these were manufacturing zones for the production of nonutilitarian goods associated with high-status residential sites. The artisans associated with these individual workshops are believed to have been attached to elite patrons, if not the royal palace itself. The XRF analysis of 41 artifacts from these sites reveals that each site received obsidian from four or five sources, including at least one source of green obsidian (table 17.5). Three of the four sites have also yielded artifacts of both the clear and red obsidians from Zinaparo and at one site three different sources of green obsidian are represented.

Type 3 workshops. Two sites with very high proportions of obsidian scrapers comprise the Type 3 workshops. Seventy-four percent (74%) of the artifacts from these sites are scrapers, and they include 50% of the end and bilateral scrapers collected in the surface survey. A lack of debitage suggests these were loci of activities that use scrapers, such as woodworking or leatherworking, rather than places of scraper manufacture. The *Relación de Michoacán* (1956:172) depicts a number of types of artisans, each working under the supervision of a steward. Many were probably attached to the royal palace although the ethnohistorical documents leave the status of these artisans unclear. The four artifacts analyzed by XRF all came from Ucareo obsidian (table 17.5).

Public/Ceremonial Zones

Two types of public\ceremonial zones were isolated in the Tzintzuntzan survey: (1) the primary ceremonial zone, which includes the main platform or central plaza with five pyramids *(yácatas),* and related residential and storage buildings, and two adjacent platforms with four additional pyramids; and (2) secondary ceremonial zones, which functioned as religious centers for the wards of the city. Within each type of zone the artifact collections are relatively small due to the extremely disturbed nature of the sites.

The seven sites comprising the primary ceremonial zone are part of the modern tourist site and the locale for extensive excavations by the Instituto Nacional de Antropología e Historia. None of the lithic material from these excavations has been analyzed and published. Several artifacts are on display in the Museo Michoacano (Morelia) and the National Museum of Anthropology (Mexico City) which are from burials excavated on the main platform, and they include large prismatic blade cores, large bifacially pressure flaked knives, and a variety of objects of adornment of grey, red, and green obsidians. The 23 artifacts analyzed by XRF from the survey collection are from Ucareo (21), Zinapecuaro (1) and one green artifact (table 17.5).

Four of the five sites designated as secondary religious centers contain the remains of sixteenth century chapels. While this later use supports the sacred association of the sites, it also limits the value of surface material for behavioral analysis. Only 18 artifacts were analyzed by XRF. Material from three of the sites comes only from Ucareo, but two other sites, located adjacent to two of the former, contain artifacts of Zinaparo and green obsidians as well (table 17.5).

Residential Zones

Three types of residential zones were isolated in the Tzintzuntzan survey: (1) Type 1, the commoner residential districts; (2) Type 2, the upper elite residential district; and (3) Type 3, the lower elite residential districts.

Type 1: the commoner districts. XRF analysis was done on 96 artifacts from 31 of the 53 sites associated with commoner habitation (Type 1). Although eight distinct sources are represented by these artifacts, 26 of the sites (84%) contain only Ucareo-Zinapecuaro obsidian and of these 22 have only Ucareo obsidian (table 17.5). All but three of the 96 artifacts tested are grey obsidians; the exceptions include two green artifacts and one clear artifact. More than 51% of the obsidian artifacts from commoner habitation sites are prismatic blade fragments (n=102), with additional tools including drills, burins, scrapers, notched tools and projectile points. The presence of crude blades (12% of the Type 1 artifacts) suggests that some tool manufacture took place within residences despite the existence of specialized workshops. This is believed to represent primarily domestic use and falls within the category of household production (Smith and Hodge, chap. 1). Indeed the ethnohistoric record of Tarascan conquests states that during war bows and arrows were made by the people of Tzintzuntzan each day (*Relación de Michoacán* 1956:177).

Type 2: the upper elite district. The elite residential zone, called Type 2, includes the royal compound and adjacent households of the upper class. The two clusters of sites associated with the elite were identified using ethnohistoric documents and by their unusually high proportions of polychrome ceramics, plates, and imported vessels. The collection consists of 126 obsidian artifacts from the 11 sites of this zone and includes one of the three ear/lip plugs found in the survey. Eighty artifacts were subjected to XRF analysis (table 17.5). As at the Type 1-commoner sites, the bulk of the obsidian is derived from Ucareo (78%), and the number of sources represented at each site varies from one to six. However, seven sites have obsidian from only one source, one site has obsidian from two sources (Ucareo and Zinapecuaro), two sites have obsidian from three sources (including the grey source referred to as Unknown 1) and only one site has material from six sources. This one site is also unusual in its location adjacent to the main ceremonial platform and the presence of high quantities of pipe fragments associated with ritual use. In general the high proportion of prismatic blades (69%) and the small number of crude blades and flakes suggests little, if any, manufacture of lithic tools.

Type 3: the lower elite residential districts. The 15 sites included in the Type 3 zone are believed to represent the habitation areas of the lower levels of the elite class and possibly some of the higher status artisans. Of the 115 obsidian artifacts available for study, 59 were examined by XRF (table 17.5). Between one and four obsidian sources are represented at each site, and 11 different sources are represented overall. Five of the sites contain some green obsidian, from four different sources. Nevertheless more than 81% of the obsidian comes from the Ucareo-Zinapecuaro source area. The proportion of crude blades and unmodified flakes (24%) in the total collection suggests than some obsidian tool manufacture took place in this zone, probably within the category of household production (Smith and Hodge, chap. 1).

Ethnic or Temporal Variation in the City

Either a small group of non-Tarascans resided within the capital in the area now known as the Ojo de Agua barrio, or an earlier Middle Postclassic occupation was located there (Pollard 1972, 1977). The isolation of this unit is based upon the ceramic analysis of survey material and comparison with contemporary ceramics from the Tarascan-Aztec border region. Current research at Urichu, in the Patzcuaro basin, should clarify the spatial-temporal range of Querenda ware ceramics, the marker for this unit at Tzintzuntzan. Six sites are associated with the greatest concentrations of Querenda ware ceramics, and 19 obsidian artifacts from these sites were analyzed by XRF. All but one of these are from the Ucareo-Zinapecuaro source, and that single piece is from Zinaparo. Thus the raw materials for all of the obsidian artifacts came from sources within the borders of the Tarascan state.

Market and Tributary Networks

When the study of source identification is combined with information about artifact type and site location it is possible to ask where, how, and for whom obsidian was acquired by Tarascan communities. Two complexes of obsidian quarries were operating within the borders of the state: Ucareo-Zinapecuaro in the northeast and Zinaparo-Varal in the northwest. Together they supplied more than 88% of the tested obsidian at the Tarascan capital and 92% of the tested obsidian from eastern border sites. Their association with the Tarascan word *thzinapu* (knife) and the definition of *Tzinapupiquaro* [sic] in the sixteenth century as a "mina de navajas de pedernal" (mine of stone knives) (Warren 1990:822) suggests that they had a long history of providing obsidian for Tarascan-speaking populations.

The use of these quarries appears to reflect both regionalization of markets and specialization in obsidian distribution. Although either zone could have provided grey-black obsidian, both the capital and the eastern border were supplied from Ucareo-Zinapecuaro. Reports from the CEMCA study of the Zacapu region, just south of Zinaparo, indicate that other regions within Tarascan territory acquired grey-black obsidian from Zinaparo-Varal. These data suggest that for most obsidian there were regional marketing districts. The presence of two unknown grey obsidians, one at the capital and another at Acambaro, may indicate that such districts crossed the political boundaries of the state. If this was the case, it occurred through marketing patterns, not tribute or long-distance merchant activity. Thus, the distribution of grey-black obsidians indicates that market and tribute units were not congruent.

The study also indicates that marketing networks cross-cut each other when specialized resources were desired. The capital and eastern border obtained both red and clear obsidian from the Zinaparo-Varal zone, while avoiding the grey-black obsidian from these same quarries. This pattern points to a high degree of specialization at the quarry and a targeting of production for consumer demand. Most of the Zinaparo-Varal obsidian was processed in lithic workshops at Tzintzuntzan, especially in those where elite-associated objects were produced. Its presence in small quantities in upper and lower elite residential zones as well as in the elite burials excavated on the main platform indicates that the primary consumers were members of the Tarascan upper class. Scattered artifacts of red or clear Zinaparo obsidian in the commoner residential zone of the capital and at one of the border sites, however, suggest that although the material was acquired primarily by the elite, it flowed through the market networks rather than tributary or patronage networks.

A small proportion of the Ucareo-Zinapecuaro assigned artifacts contain cortex material (table 17.6), which suggests that at least some of the grey-black obsidian was imported into the Tarascan capital in the form of macrocores. Further reduction of the cores to produce prismatic blades or other tools would have taken place at lithic workshops (Type 1) or within commoner residential zones. The high level of reuse of cores and the relatively few concentrations of surface debitage, however, may indicate that the bulk of Ucareo obsidian was imported into the capital in the form of prismatic blades. Current research at the Ucareo quarries should clarify this situation (D. Healan, personal communication 1990, 1993).

Table 17.6 Source and color of obsidian artifacts with cortex

Site	Source	XRF Sample		Color
		Total	w/ Cortex	
Tzintzuntzan	Ucareo	290	11	grey
Tzintzuntzan	Zinapecuaro	25	2	grey
Tzintzuntzan	C. Zinaparo	8	3	red
Tzintzuntzan	C. Varal	13	1	clear
Tzintzuntzan	La Mora-Teuch	5	2	green
Tzintzuntzan	Unknown 4	10	6	green
Tuzantla	Ucareo	14	2	grey
Zirizicuaro	C. Zinaparo	1	1	red
Acambaro	Ucareo	12	1	grey
Acambaro	Unknown 2	2	1	grey

Although the number of artifacts made of red or clear Zinaparo obsidian is rather small (n=21), the high proportion of these with cortex material suggests they were routinely imported into the capital in the form of macrocores. Indeed, there are no red colored prismatic blades in the collection (table 17.7), and the red obsidian may have been imported in the form of raw nodules and then processed at the Type 2 lithic workshops.

The remaining obsidians are green and were probably acquired by the state-sponsored long-distance merchants. They account for most of the obsidian coming across the political borders of the state and represent up to eight differ-

Table 17.4 Comparison of sources and color of obsidian artifacts

Source	Light grey				Dark grey				Mixed grey		Red	Clear	Green
	1	1.5	2	2.5	3	3.5	4	4.5	5	5.5	20	30	10
Ucareo	10	2	16	19	104	98	5	12	2	32	1	9[a]	--
Zinapecuaro	4	--	7	5	2	2	1	--	--	2	1	--	--
Balvandeda	1	--	--	--	4	1	--	--	--	1	--	--	--
Unknown 1	--	--	--	1	4	4	--	--	--	--	--	--	--
Unknown 2	1	--	--	--	--	1	--	--	--	--	--	--	--
Zaragoza	--	--	--	--	1	--	--	--	--	--	--	2	--
Tozongo	1	--	--	1	--	--	--	1	--	--	--	--	--
C.Varal	--	--	--	--	3	1	--	--	--	1	--	8	--
C.Zinaparo	--	--	--	--	--	1	--	--	--	--	7	1	--
La Mora-T.	--	--	--	--	1	--	--	--	--	--	--	--	4
Others, #101-108	--	--	--	--	--	--	--	--	--	--	--	--	20

Note: Key to color numbers:

1	light grey opaque	4	dark grey translucent
1.5	light grey streaked	4.5	dark grey translucent streaked
2	light grey translucent	5	light and dark grey
2.5	light grey translucent streaked	5.5	light and dark grey streaked
3	dark grey opaque		
3.5	dark grey opaque streaked		

[a] Predominantly clear with 3.5 and 4.5 grey.

ent sources. They are found highly concentrated at Type 2 lithic workshops and at elite burials in the main platform, confirming ethnohistoric indications that the consumption of green obsidian was limited to the upper class and under the control of the Tarascan king. The range of green obsidians found at any one site (three different sources at one site, for example), and the total range of green obsidians from both the west (Jalisco) and the east (Hidalgo), suggest that long-distance merchants acquired them from intermediaries or other merchants who pooled quality stones from a variety of sources. The small scale of use and the distances involved make it highly unlikely that Tarascan merchants went further than Taximaroa, Zacatula, and Lake Chapala (to mention locations supported by ethnohistoric references) in order to acquire these rare raw materials. The relatively high proportion of green artifacts that retain some cortex or are crude blades and flakes suggests that merchants were acquiring raw obsidian nodules or macrocores, which were later worked at selected locations in the capital city.

Political Power

The relationship among basic resources, social class, and political power is a far more difficult set of interactions to document without recourse to ethnohistoric evidence. Technically, all land titles within the Tarascan domain were justified on the basis that they came from the King. These titles included agricultural land, fishing rights, mineral resources (such as copper mines), and hunting territories (*Relación de Michoacán* 1956; *Relaciónes Geográficas* 1985: Tiripitio; García Alcaraz 1976:228-229; Pollard 1987). Just as there is no mention of obsidian in the context of the tributary requirements of communities, there is no mention of obsidian quarries as state-owned resources. Of course, this does not mean that quarries were locally or privately controlled, only that they were of no interest to the Spanish colonists. Nevertheless, according to the *Relación de Michoacán* (1956:151-155) both the Zinapecuaro and Zinaparo zones were included in the sequence of conquests that formed the Tarascan domain and were apparently incorporated into the state by A.D. 1440. The legendary history recounted in this document indicates that marketplaces were flourishing well before the unification of the state, and recent archaeological research in the Patzcuaro and Zacapu basins documents the use of Ucareo and Zinaparo obsidian prior to the emergence of the Late Postclassic state (Michelet et al. 1989; Pollard, research in progress). Moreover, at the thermal springs in Zinapecuaro there was a major cult center for the Tarascan creator-rain goddess Cuerauáperi. Pending contradictory evidence from the quarries themselves, the logical conclusion is that obsidian mines were not controlled by the royal dynasty. Although they may have been a source of local political power, there is no evidence that either the mines or the trade was a source of power for the Tarascan elite. Tarascan long-distance merchants acquired various rare resources from outside state territory, acting under direct requests from the royal dynasty (Pollard 1982). Although access to these resources was controlled by the King, and the goods themselves were a mark of high social status, there is no evidence that the Tarascan political elite directly controlled the trade routes, or that they had established their political power based upon their access to these routes.

Emergence of the Tarascan Core Region

With the emergence of the Tarascan state in the last two centuries before European contact, the Lake Patzcuaro Basin became a demographic, political and economic core region in western Mexico (Blanton and Feinman 1984). Large quantities of food, cloth, metals, tropical goods and manufactured products were sent into central Michoacan through the tribute system (Pollard 1982). In addition, the labor of large numbers of people was under the direct control of the royal dynasty resident at Tzintzuntzan and included those in military service, household servants, corvee labor, and agricultural workers on state lands. The effect of these political and economic realignments on the marketing networks is difficult to discern, since it requires information on a macroregional scale.

The flow of Zinapecuaro-Ucareo obsidian within Mesoamerica appears to have been highly responsive to political changes. During the Early and Middle Formative periods this obsidian was widely traded in central and southern Mexico, appearing archaeologically in the Basin of Mexico (Boksenbaum et al. 1987) and Oaxaca (Winter and Pires-Ferreira 1976). It has been found in Late Formative contexts in Morelos and Oaxaca (Winter and Pires-Ferreira 1976; Hirth 1984a). In the Early and Middle Classic periods, during the height of Teotihuacan's power, Ucareo obsidian apparently was not used in the Basin of Mexico, but it does appear at sites in the Maya lowlands (Nelson 1985; Moholy-Nagy and Nelson 1990) and in the Soconusco region (Clark et al. 1989) at this time. Following the demise of Teotihuacan, Ucareo obsidian again flowed into central Mexico. Ucareo was the primary source for grey-black obsidian at Tula (Healan 1989:224-234) and Xochicalco (Hirth 1984b, 1989), and replaced Pachuca obsidian at Azcapotzalco in the Basin of Mexico (García Chávez et al. 1990); at the same time, it continued to be traded into the Maya Lowlands (Nelson 1985) and the Soconusco region (Clark et al. 1989). During the Early Postclassic period Ucareo obsidian continued to be used at Tula, although in reduced amounts, and continued to be traded into Morelos (Smith 1984), the Maya Lowlands (Nelson 1985) and Soconusco (Clark et al. 1989). Unfortunately at the present time there is no comparable evidence of Ucareo obsidian use within western Mexico.

By the Late Postclassic period, however, more than 90 percent of the grey-black obsidian used at Tzintzuntzan and the eastern frontier settlements came from Ucareo, while it is absent in the Basin of Mexico. The effect of the formation of the Tarascan state on trading networks is difficult to discern in the literature. For example, although Ucareo obsidian was used in Morelos, Soconusco, and the Maya Lowlands during the Late Postclassic period, it is not clear whether Aztec conquests/dominance of Morelos, Soconusco, and the coastal trading ports had any effect on local obsidian supplies. Given the increased needs of the Tarascan state for obsidian, both for its expanding population and for armaments, and the high level of hostility maintained between the Tarascan and Aztec polities, it would be surprising if obsidian routes had not been affected. On the other hand, unlike the case of Teotihuacan, at the present time there is no evidence of Tarascan state intervention in obsidian production and distribution. Therefore there is no reason to assume that a total redirection of obsidian trade took place. Current research by Dan Healan at the Ucareo-Zinapecuaro quarries should provide evidence of the way in which quarry activity was affected by the new political economy of the Tarascan state.

An unresolved question of Tarascan obsidian procurement is why the Ucareo-Zinapecuaro source dominated the Tzintzuntzan market when high quality grey obsidian was available from the closer mines at Zinaparo. The use of red and clear obsidian from the Zinaparo sources demonstrates that access to market networks was not a problem. Among various possibilities, the Late Postclassic pattern may reflect (1) the continuation of earlier distribution networks, (2) a higher value placed on obsidian coming from a major religious center, and (3) the ability of local producers at Ucareo to respond to changes in market demands.

As this and other questions raised by the study of Tarascan obsidian make apparent, the economic and political relationships of communities in hierarchically organized complex societies are neither congruent, nor easily untangled. Each group of obsidians studied here was acquired through different mechanisms, distributed in different forms, processed in different workshops or habitation zones, used to produce different sets of artifacts, and used by different social classes in highly varied contexts. The results of this study remind us of the important role archaeologically-derived data serve in understanding Contact-period societies and that dynamic political and economic realities were often omitted or grossly simplified in the ethnohistoric record.

ACKNOWLEDGMENTS

The XRF analysis has been funded by an All-University Research Grant from Michigan State University (1988-1990). I wish to thank Shirley Gorenstein for the loan of the border sites collection and Thomas Vogel for taking over the laboratory analysis after the unexpected death of his colleague John Wilband. The following students participated in the research project: Timothy Higgins (1987), Amy Hirshman (1988), Christine Stephanson Brantsner (1989-1990), Julie Yakes (1989-1990) and Christopher Fisher (1989-1990). Both obsidian collections were obtained under research permits granted by the Consejo de Arqueología, Departamento de Monumentos Prehispánicos, Instituto Nacional de Antropología e Historia, Mexico.

REFERENCES CITED

Blanton, Richard E., and Gary M. Feinman
  1984 The Mesoamerican World System. *American Anthropologist* 86:673-682.
Boksenbaum, Martin W., Paul Tolstoy, G. Harbottle, J. Kimberlin, and Mary Neivens
  1987 Obsidian Industries and Cultural Evolution in the Basin of Mexico before 500 B.C. *Journal of Field Archaeology* 14:65-75.
Bower, W. C., and G. Valentini
  1986 Critical Comparison of Sample Preparation Methods for Major and Trace Element Determinations Using X-ray Fluorescence. *X-Ray Spectrometry* 15:73-78.
Charlton, Thomas H., David C. Grove, and Philip K. Hopke
  1978 The Paredon, Mexico, Obsidian Source and Early Formative Exchange. *Science* 201:807-809.

Clark, John E., Thomas A. Lee, Jr., and Tamara Salcedo
1989 The Distribution of Obsidian. In *Ancient Trade and Tribute: Economies of the Soconusco Region of Mesoamerica,* edited by Barbara Voorhies, pp. 268-284. University of Utah Press, Salt Lake City.

Darras, Véronique, and Fred W. Nelson
1987 Nota informativa: primeros resultados de la caracterización química por medio de los elementos traza de los yacimientos de obsidiana en la región de Zináparo-Purépero, Michoacán. *Trace* 12:76-79.

Ericson, J. E., and J. Kimberlin
1977 Obsidian Sources, Chemical Characterization and Hydration Rates in West Mexico. *Archaeometry* 19:157-166.

Ferriz, Horacio
1985 Caltonac, a Prehispanic Obsidian-mining Center in Eastern Mexico?: A Preliminary Report. *Journal of Field Archaeology* 12:363-370.

García Alcaraz, Agustín
1976 Estratificación social entre los Tarascos prehispánicos. In *Estratificación social en la Mesoamérica prehispánica,* edited by Pedro Carrasco and Johanna Broda, pp. 221-244. Instituto Nacional de Antropología e Historia, Mexico City.

García Chávez, Raúl, Michael D. Glascock, J. Michael Elam, and Harry B. Iceland
1990 The INAH [Instituto Nacional de Antropología e Historia] Salvage Archaeology Excavations at Azcapotzalco, Mexico. *Ancient Mesoamerica* 1:225-232.

Gorenstein, Shirley
1985 *Acambaro on the Tarascan-Aztec Frontier.* Vanderbilt University Publications in Anthropology No. 32. Department of Anthropology, Vanderbilt University, Nashville.

Gorenstein, Shirley, and Helen Perlstein Pollard
1983 *The Tarascan Civilization: A Late Prehispanic Cultural System.* Vanderbilt University Publications in Anthropology No. 28. Department of Anthropology, Vanderbilt University, Nashville.

Healan, Dan M. (editor)
1989 *Tula of the Toltecs: Excavations and Survey.* University of Iowa Press, Iowa City.

Hirth, Kenneth G.
1984a Trade and Society in Late Formative Morelos. In *Trade and Exchange in Early Mesoamerica,* edited by Kenneth G. Hirth, pp. 125-146. University of New Mexico Press, Albuquerque.

1984b Xochicalco: Urban Growth and State Formation in Central Mexico. *Science* 225:579-586.

1989 Militarism and Social Organization at Xochicalco, Morelos. In *Mesoamerica After the Decline of Teotihuacan,* A.D. *700-900,* edited by Richard Diehl and Janet C. Berlo, pp. 69-81. Dumbarton Oaks, Washington, D.C.

Michelet, Dominique, Marie Charlotte Arnauld, and Marie-France Fauvet-Berthelot
1989 El proyecto del CEMCA en Michoacán, etapa I: un balance. *Trace* 16:70-87.

Moholy-Nagy, Hattula, and Fred W. Nelson
1990 New Data on Sources of Obsidian Artifacts from Tikal, Guatemala. *Ancient Mesoamerica* 1:71-80.

Nelson, Fred W.
1985 Summary of the Results of Analysis of Obsidian Artifacts from the Maya Lowlands. *Scanning Electron Microscopy* 2:631-649.

Nelson, Fred W., K. Nielson, N. Mangelson, M. Hill, and Ray T. Matheny
1977 Preliminary Studies of the Trace Element Composition of Obsidian Artifacts from Northern Campeche, Mexico. *American Antiquity* 42:209-226.

Pollard, Helen Perlstein
1972 *Prehispanic Urbanism at Tzintzuntzan, Michoacan.* Ph.D. dissertation, Department of Anthropology, Columbia University. University Microfilms, Ann Arbor.
1977 An Analysis of Urban Zoning and Planning in Prehispanic Tzintzuntzan. *Proceedings of the American Philosophical Society* 121(1):46-69. Philadelphia.
1982 Ecological Variation and Economic Exchange in the Tarascan State. *American Ethnologist* 9:250-268.
1987 The Political Economy of Prehispanic Tarascan Metallurgy. *American Antiquity* 52:741-752.
1993 *Tariacuri's Legacy, The Prehispanic Tarascan State.* University of Oklahoma Press, Norman.

Relación de Michoacán
1956 *Relación de las ceremonias y ritos y población y gobierno de Michoacán.* Reproducción Facsimilar del Ms. IV de El Escorial, Madrid. Aguilar Publicistas, Madrid.

Relaciones Geográficas
1985 *Relaciones y memorias de la provincia de Michoacán 1579-1581.* Edited by Alvaro Ochoa S. and Gerardo Sánchez D. Universidad Michoacana, Ayuntamiento de Morelia, Morelia, Michoacan, Mexico.

Smith, Michael E.
1984 *Fuentes geológicas de artifactos de obsidiana procedentes de sitios postclásicos en Morelos.* Report submitted to the Instituto Nacional de Antropología e Historia, Mexico.

Stross, Fred H., Thomas R. Hester, Robert F. Heizer, and Robert N. Jack
1976 Chemical and Archaeological Studies of Mesoamerican and Californian Obsidians. In *Advances in Obsidian Glass Studies: Archaeological and Geochemical Perspectives,* edited by R. E. Taylor, pp. 240-258. Noyes Press, Park Ridge, New Jersey.

Trombold, Charles D., James F. Luhr, Toshiaki Hasenaka, and Michael D. Glascock
1993 Chemical Characteristics of Obsidians from Archaeological Sites in Western Mexico and the Tequila Source Area: Implications for Regional and Pan-Regional Interaction within the Northern Mesoamerican Periphery. *Ancient Mesoamerica* 4:255-270.

Warren, J. Benedict (editor)
  1990   *Diccionario grande de la lengua de Michoacan.* Author or authors unknown. Edited with an introduction by J. Benedict Warren. Fimax Publicistas, Morelia, Michoacan, Mexico. (Original manuscript dates to the sixteenth century.)

Winter, Marcus C., and Jane Wheeler Pires-Ferreira
  1976   Distribution of Obsidian among Households in Two Oaxacan Villages. In *The Early Mesoamerican Village,* edited by Kent Flannery, pp. 306-311. Academic Press, New York.

Contributors

MANLIO BARBOSA-CANO is an anthropologist interested in the dynamics of interaction between Postclassic Mesoamerica and the Spanish state and in the resultant cultural changes. Centro INAH-Puebla, Unidad Cívica 5 de Mayo, Fuertes de Loreto y Guadalupe, C.P. 72270, Puebla, Puebla, Mexico.

FRANCES F. BERDAN is an anthropologist/ethnohistorian specializing in Aztec economic organization and pre- and post-conquest Nahua language and culture. Department of Anthropology, California State University, San Bernardino, California, 92407-2397.

M. JAMES BLACKMAN is a geochemist working on chemical characterization of lithics and ceramics. Senior Research Chemist, Conservation Analytical Laboratory, Smithsonian Institution, Washington, D.C., 20560

ELIZABETH M. BRUMFIEL is an archaeologist whose research focuses on the political economy of the Aztec state. Department of Anthropology & Sociology, Albion College, Albion, Michigan, 49224.

THOMAS H. CHARLTON is an anthropologist whose research focuses on the dynamics of preconquest and postconquest cultural evolution in Central Mexico. Department of Anthropology, University of Iowa, Iowa City, Iowa, 52242.

FREDERIC HICKS is a cultural anthropologist whose current research interests are in the economic and political organization of late prehispanic Central Mexico. Department of Anthropology, University of Louisville, Louisville, Kentucky, 40292.

CYNTHIA HEATH-SMITH is an archaeologist interested in the interaction of complex societies with their natural environments, particularly in highland Central Mexico. Institute for Mesoamerican Studies, University at Albany (SUNY), Albany, New York, 12222.

MARY G. HODGE is an anthropologist who has conducted archaeological and ethnohistorical investigatations of political and economic systems in Postclassic Mesoamerica. School of Human Sciences and Humanities, University of Houston Clear Lake, 2700 Bay Area Blvd., Houston, Texas, 77058.

LEAH D. MINC is an archaeologist whose research interests center on the organization of craft production and distribution systems in the Late Postclassic Basin of Mexico. Museum of Anthropology, University of Michigan, Michigan, Ann Arbor, Michigan, 48109.

DEBORAH L. NICHOLS is an archaeologist whose research deals with the development of prehispanic agricultural systems and economic and political organization in the Basin of Mexico. Department of Anthropology, Dartmouth College, Hanover, New Hampshire, 03755.

CYNTHIA OTIS CHARLTON is an independent scholar whose research interests include Mesoamerican ceramics and obsidian. 821 South Seventh Avenue, Iowa City, Iowa, 51140.

JEFFREY R. PARSONS is an archaeologist interested in the development of precolumbian complex societies in Mesoamerica and Andean South America. Museum of Anthropology, University of Michigan, Ann Arbor, Michigan, 48109.

PATRICIA PLUNKET is an archaeologist whose research deals primarily with the cultural development of Puebla and the Mixteca Alta. Departamento de Antropología, Universidad de las Américas, 72820 Cholula, Puebla, Mexico.

HELEN PERLSTEIN POLLARD is an archaeologist whose research focuses on the nature and evolution of the Tarascan State of Michoacan. Department of Anthropology, Michigan State University, East Lansing, Michigan, 48824

JOSÉ LUIS DE ROJAS is an anthropologist/ethnohistorian interested in the economic and political organization of Central Mexico before and after the arrival of the Spaniards. Departamento de Historia de América II, Facultad de Geografía e Historia, Universidad Complutense, 28040 Madrid, Spain.

TAMARA SALCEDO studied at the Escuela Nacional de Antropología e Historia, Mexico City, and has carried out fieldwork in Michoacan, Chiapas, and the Basin of Mexico. 424B Elm St., Lowell, Michigan, 49331.

DAVID K. SCHAFER has analyzed obsidian assemblages in the Naco Valley, Honduras, and the Basin of Mexico. Department of Anthropology, University of Massachusetts, Amherst, Massachusetts, 01003.

MICHAEL E. SMITH is an archaeologist whose research focuses on social and economic organization in Late Postclassic Central Mexico. Department of Anthropology, University at Albany (SUNY), Albany, New York, 12222.

GABRIELA URUÑUELA is an archaeologist whose research interests include culture change in the Puebla region and bioarchaeology. Departamento de Antropología, Universidad de las Américas, 72820 Cholula, Puebla, Mexico.

THOMAS A. VOGEL is Professor and Chair of the Department of Geological Sciences, Michigan State University, East Lansing, Michigan, 48824. His main research is in volcanology.

BARBARA J. WILLIAMS is a geographer whose research focuses on Contact period cultural ecology. Department of Geography and Geology, University of Wisconsin Center, 2909 Kellogg Ave., Janesville, Wisconsin, 53546.

Index

Acambaro, 451, 462
Acapetlahuacan, 435
Acatlipac, 353
Acatzinco, 416–419
Acazacatlan, 294, 300, 309
Acolhua, 6, 12, 139, 159, 164, 246
Acolhuacan, 73, 74, 195, 295
administrators, 53, 60
agricultural intensification, 17, 19,
    21, 25, 365
agriculture
    crops, 18
    intensive, 11, 18, 19–20, 85, 331
    methods, 18, 19–20, 80–84, 224
    (*see also* chinampas, irrigation,
    terracing)
Ahuatlan, 302, 309
Ahuilizapan, 295, 308
Ahuitzotl, 295, 310, 339, 379, 381,
    386, 388, 389, 390, 397
altepetl (city-state), 11–12, 62, 84
Amecameca, 139
Antequera, 394–396
archaeological survey, 45–46, 59, 223,
    227–231. *See also* Basin of Mexico
    Archaeological Survey Project
architecture. *See under specific types
    of buildings*
Atlan, 294, 304, 398
Atlixco, 433, 435, 442, 443
Atlixco Valley, 433–444
Atotonilco el Grande, 294, 299
Atzizihuacan, 433
Axayacatl, 14, 295, 301, 308, 310,

Axayacatl *(continued)*
    421, 425
ayates, 92
Azcapotzalco, 180, 466
Aztacan, 398
Aztec, definition, 2–3
Aztec empire, 13–14, 61–62, 297–305,
    406–407, 435
    effects on provinces, 126, 247, 299,
    306–307, 340, 366–367, 419–431,
    436–444
    organization of provinces, 13–14,
    62, 297–307, 334, 397–401,
    425–426
Aztec I ceramics, 140–165
Aztec II ceramics, 140–165, 195, 246
Aztec III ceramics, 22, 24, 208, 246,
    361, 365, 438

Baganda, 335
Balvanena, 455
bark beaters, 330, 359
Basin of Mexico Archaeological Survey
    Project, 10, 16, 74, 137, 140
battlefields, 433–435
beads, 200–203
bronze, 22, 359

cacao, 99, 293, 297, 307, 330, 338
Calixtlahuaca, 119
calmil (house garden), 80–84
Calpan, 437
calpixque (tribute collectors), 299, 308,
    316, 334, 406, 419, 425

calpulli, 20, 117–118, 176–177, 184, 196, 197, 202, 204, 205, 354, 393, 395
Camaxtli, 439
Capilco, 207–209, 331, 350–371
Central Mexican Symbiotic Region, 224
central place theory, 134
ceramics, 23–24, 133–168, 339, 437–438. *See also under Aztec ceramics*

production, 197, 204, 359
Cerro Varal, 454
Cerro Zinaparo, 454
Chalca, 139, 159
Chalco, 55, 139, 155, 186, 393, 436
check-dams, 356
chert, 201, 357
Chichimecs, 409–410
chicle, 307
Chimalhuacan, 58, 59, 64
chinampas (raised fields), 8, 19
Chinantecs, 295
Cholula, 14, 294, 308, 360, 408, 416, 417–418, 436, 437, 438, 442
chronology, Aztec period, 5–7, 63, 351
cities and towns, 8–11, 28, 45, 59–66, 176–178, 197. *See also under individual settlements*

size, 54–59, 320, 352
city-states, 9, 11–12, 13, 17, 27, 43–66, 137–140, 196, 227, 314–318, 321, 336. *See also under individual polities*

boundaries and territories, 43–66, 315–318
population, 54–59
client states, 14, 300
cloth, 22, 89–106, 197, 212, 281, 306
clothing, 97, 297
Coatepec, 47–52, 64
Coatlan Viejo, 9, 21, 178, 321
Coatlinchan, 64, 164

Coatzinco, 309
Cohuayxtlahuacan, 388
Cohuintepec, 353
Cohuixco, 315
Colotzingo, 442
confederations, 12–13, 64, 137–140, 159–160
congregación policy, 45, 319
consumption, 15, 22, 113, 239, 241, 243, 361–362, 465
copper tools, 339, 359, 361
Cortés, Hernán, 98, 327, 334
cotton, 90, 183, 243, 293, 297, 304, 328–330, 339, 356, 357
Çoyatitlanapa, 302
Coyolapan, 382, 386, 389
craft production, 21–23, 175–187, 195–214, 356–359, 364, 368
models, 22, 368–370
specialization, 10, 21–23, 95, 96–100, 184–186, 196–211, 227, 242–243

workshops, 22, 176–186, 196–211, 233, 242–243, 458–459
Cuauhchinanco, 304, 307, 310
Cuauhnahuac. *See* Quauhnahuac
Cuauhtepuztitla, 77
Cuauhtinchan. *See* Quauhtinchan
Cuauhtlatoa, 412–418
Cuerauáperi, 465
Cuernavaca, 335
Cuetlaxtlan, 306
Cuexcomate, 207–209, 331, 350–371
Cuitlahuac, 58, 155
Cuitlahuaca, 12, 159
Culhua, 12, 137, 139, 159
Culhuacan, 137, 159, 163, 164

demography, 16–18, 65, 244–246, 319–321, 352. *See also* population
diet, 18–19, 354
direct historical approach, 44

earspools, 183, 200–203
ecological diversity, 25
economic growth, 367
economic models, 21–23, 25–28, 176–178, 184–186, 212–213, 222–223, 364
El Ciruelo, 359
elites, 24, 61, 103, 126, 184–185, 198, 212, 364–367, 396, 461
encomienda, 78, 334–336
environmental degradation, 21
epidemics, 319
ethnic groups, 12, 26, 461–462
ethnicity, 114–120, 123–128, 202
exchange, 13, 23–24, 186, 202, 205, 210–211, 360–361. *See also* market exchange; tribute
exchange values, 99

fabric-marked pottery, 259, 261, 276, 281, 282
feathers, 293, 297
figurines, 183, 203–211, 233
fortresses and garrisons, 303–304, 309, 384, 396–401

gift exchange, 13, 89, 94, 102, 126, 300, 307, 449
gold, 293
ground-stone tools, 23, 182, 196, 236, 245, 248, 358
Guatemala, 399
Guerrero, 360

honey, 307
households, 94–96, 196–211, 461
houses, 8, 78–79, 80, 350
Huapalcalco, 225, 240, 244
Huasteca, 124
Huaxtecs, 294, 307, 308
Huaxtepec, 314, 315, 330, 333
Huaxtlan, 384–391, 391, 397

Huaxyacac, 377–402
Huazulco, 336
Huehuequauhquechulan, 437, 442
Huehuetlan, 436
Huexotla, Basin of Mexico, 9, 21, 58, 64, 95, 178–179, 185, 186, 223, 236, 295
Huexotla, eastern province, 304, 310
Huexotzinco, 14, 177, 308, 434, 436, 438
Hueyapan, 308
Huitzilopochtli, 95, 300, 309, 382, 439
hunting, 18

imperialism, 3, 13–14, 366–367, 428–429
irrigation, 19, 225, 226, 324–328, 329, 351, 435
Itzcoatl, 333, 437
Itzocan, 304
Ixtapalucan, 64

labor, 17, 20–21, 58, 368
Lake Chapala, 464
Lake Patzcuaro Basin, 14, 449, 465
Lake Texcoco, 257–263
land tenure, 20–21, 80–84, 101
lapidary production, 183–186, 197, 198–203, 233
Las Pilas, 438
lip plugs, 26, 28, 114–128, 183, 200–203, 306, 361
luxury goods, 200–203, 293, 297, 306, 361

macehualli (commoner), 15, 20, 73, 76, 411
maguey, 19, 22, 80, 82, 90, 182, 183, 243, 293, 330
Malinalco, 315
Malpais, 226

markets
  market exchange, 8, 23, 89, 101,
    247, 306, 331, 338–340, 462–464
  market systems, 12, 133, 154–160,
    161–168, 210, 426–427, 466
  marketplaces, 8, 12, 101, 175,
    196, 212, 304, 338, 360, 427
marriage alliances, 13
Matlatzinca, 124
Mayan languages, 294
mayeque (commoner), 20, 84
Mazahuas, 393
merchants, 339, 391, 418, 463–464,
  465. *See also pochteca*
metals, 297
Metztitlan, 96, 225, 239, 241, 295,
  300, 310
Mexica, 6, 13, 124, 126
Miacatlan, 353
Mictlan, 379, 381, 383, 386, 390, 391
migration, 17, 391–394
milcocoli, 74, 80
Misantla, 295, 304
Mixcoatl, 439
Mixquic, 155
Mixquica, 12, 159
Mixteca, 360
Mixtecs, 295, 392
Molotlan, 98, 336
money, 98, 100–102
Monte Alban, 378
Morelos, 17, 19, 207–209, 313–341,
  349–371, 393
Motecuhzoma I, 295, 299, 308, 378,
  386, 425, 437
Motecuhzoma II, 95, 295, 298, 300,
  305, 308, 386, 389, 393, 434

Nautla, 295
Nexquipayac, 259–284
Nezahualcoyotl, 310
Nezahualpilli, 295

nobles, 9, 13, 15–16, 20, 314, 320,
  337, 354, 392. *See also* elites

Oaxaca, 377–402
obsidian, 339, 340, 358, 447–467
  exchange, 200, 361, 447–467
  sources, 179, 221, 225, 226, 451–
    457
  tool production, 182–186, 197, 201,
    233, 237–243, 359, 458–459
Ocuituco, 314, 318, 330
Oto-Manguean languages, 294
Otomi, 118–128, 180, 294
Otonteuctli, 119
Otumba, 10, 21, 22, 95, 119, 175–
  187, 195–214, 222, 226–227,
  233–236, 242–247
Oztoticpac, 416–418
Oztuma, 398

Pachuca, 225, 456, 466
paint pigments, 359
palaces, 9, 15, 59, 354
Papantla, 295, 308
paper, 23, 330, 338, 359
pilli (noble), 15
pochteca (merchants), 2, 8, 23, 27,
  183, 186, 196, 206, 212, 304,
  306, 310, 339, 360, 391, 427
political centralization, 18, 28
political hierarchies, 11–16
polities
  boundaries, 44–52, 137–140, 159–
    160, 297, 421–431
population, 319–321
  Aztec, 16–17, 45, 321
  density, 11, 16–18, 318–319, 320
  growth, 17–18, 18, 21, 245–246,
    352, 367
  postconquest decline, 78, 319
  pressure, 18, 19, 356, 364
pottery. *See* ceramics

Quauhnahuac, 314, 321, 330, 333, 335, 338, 350, 353, 360, 366

Quauhquechulan, 318, 433, 436, 437, 438, 439, 443

Quauhtinchan, 13, 405–430, 436

Quauhtochco, 296, 297, 308

Quechulac, 410

regal-ritual center, 9

ritual, 119, 205–206, 460

rock crystal, 202

rubber, 293

rulers
imposition of, 420–421

rural areas, 58, 73–86, 349–371

sacrifice, human, 382, 392

salt, 257–284, 304

saltmaking, 263–273

settlement hierarchy, 53, 63

settlement patterns, 10–11, 74, 80–86, 318–319, 437–438

slaves, 95

social stratification, 15–16, 26, 202, 353–354, 361–362, 364–366, 411

spinning and spinning tools, 90 91, 95, 183, 184, 197, 233, 239, 243, 340, 357

Tarascan empire, 3, 14–15, 398, 447–467

Taximaroa, 451, 464

Tecali, 294, 410, 411, 412, 418–419

tecali (noble house). *See* palaces

Tecamachalco, 410, 425–426

Teçapotitlan, 304

Tecocomulco, 225, 226

tecpan. See palaces

Tehuantepec, 382, 389, 397

Temoac, 336

temple-pyramids, 9, 204, 353, 460

Templo Mayor, 9, 203, 294, 382, 390, 406

Tenanco, 58, 139

Tenochca, 12

Tenochtitlan, 8–9, 21, 45, 53, 100, 176, 186, 198, 338, 382, 389, 392, 401

Teotihuacan, Aztec site, 23, 178, 243, 246

Teotihuacan, Classic site, 22, 26, 177, 437, 442, 466

Teozapotitlan, 398

Teozapotlan, 379, 389

Tepaneca, 6, 12, 246

Tepeacac, 13, 294, 299, 301, 308, 405–430, 436

Tepeapulco, 10, 21, 179, 207, 222, 225–226, 236–239, 242–247

tepetate, 79

Tepetenchic, 98

Tepetlaoztoc, 58, 64, 73–86

Tepoztlan, 320, 330

tequesquite, 281–282

terracing, 82, 226, 331, 352, 356, 365

Tetela, 294, 300, 307, 309, 315, 336

Tetella, 434

teuctli (lord), 15

Texalocan, 302

Texcaltitlan, 435

Texcoco, 9, 45, 53, 58, 64, 177, 180, 186, 198, 321

textiles, 328, 333–338

Tezcatlipoca, 439

Tikal, 177

Tizoc, 381, 425

Tlacaelel, 420

Tlacatecuhtli, 398

Tlachco, 315, 331

Tlachquiauhco, 308

Tlacochcalli, 398

Tlacochtecuhtli, 398

Tlacotepec, 119, 210
Tlahuica, 124, 339
Tlalmanalco, 58
Tlapacoyan, 294
Tlappan, 382
Tlatelolco, 8, 101, 175, 412–418
Tlatlauhquitepec, 297, 300
tlatoani (ruler), 11, 53, 59, 62, 316, 336, 337
Tlaxcalla, 3, 14–15, 294, 295, 300–305, 308, 417–418, 434
tlaxillacalli (residential ward), 8, 75–77
Tochimilco, 433, 434, 438
Tochpan, 294, 296, 299, 304, 306, 307
Tochtepec, 297, 299, 304, 309
Toltecs, 163
Toluca Valley, 210, 360
Tonantzin, 395
Totolapan, 314, 315
Totomihuacan, 436
Totonac, 294
Tozongo, 455
trace element analysis, 148–154, 451–457
trade. *See* exchange
transport, 275
tribute, 8, 13, 16, 19, 89, 97–99, 185, 202, 297, 331–338, 360, 378, 394, 401, 411, 419, 426, 449, 465
    imperial, 13–14, 27, 62, 299, 306, 308, 333–334, 366, 389, 419–431
Triple Alliance. *See* Aztec empire
Tula, 6, 282, 304, 466
Tulancingo (Tulancinco), 222, 225, 239–247, 299
turquoise, 293, 306, 307
Tututepec, 396
Tuzantla, 451
Tzapotlan, 382
Tzicoac, 299

Tzintzuntzan, 449, 450, 453, 457, 458–467

Ucareo, 451, 453–457, 466
Urichu, 462
Uto-Aztecan languages, 294

Volcán de Tequila, 457

warfare, 14–15, 125, 294–295, 315, 433–437
wealth levels, 361–362, 367–370
weaving, 91–92

Xalapa, 304
Xaltocan, 114–128, 178–179, 180, 186, 223
Xicalanco, 304
Xico, 21, 178–179, 186, 223, 236
Xicotepec, 304, 310
Xochicalco, 350, 351
Xochimilca, 12, 139
Xochimilco, 58, 137, 139, 318, 393
Xochitecatl, 439
xochiyaoyotl ("flowery war"), 433–444
Xoconochco, 360, 397, 398

Yacapitztlan, 314, 315, 320, 340
Yancuitlan, 378, 388
Yauhtepec, 10, 98, 314, 360

Zaachila, 381, 400
Zacapu, 454, 462
Zacatula, 464
Zacualpan, 315, 336
Zapotecs, 392–394
Zapotlan, 383, 386, 389
Zaragoza, 455
Zinapecuaro, 451, 453–457, 466
Zirizicuaro, 451
Zitacuaro, 451